IFIP Advances in Information and Communication Technology 675

IFIP Advances in Information and Communication Technology

The IFIP AICT series publishes state-of-the-art results in the sciences and technologies of information and communication. The scope of the series includes: foundations of computer science; software theory and practice; education; computer applications in technology; communication systems; systems modeling and optimization; information systems; ICT and society; computer systems technology; security and protection in information processing systems; artificial intelligence; and human-computer interaction.

Edited volumes and proceedings of refereed international conferences in computer science and interdisciplinary fields are featured. These results often precede journal publication and represent the most current research.

The principal aim of the IFIP AICT series is to encourage education and the dissemination and exchange of information about all aspects of computing.

More information about this series at https://link.springer.com/bookseries/6102

Ilias Maglogiannis · Lazaros Iliadis ·
John MacIntyre · Manuel Dominguez
Editors

Artificial Intelligence Applications and Innovations

19th IFIP WG 12.5 International Conference, AIAI 2023
León, Spain, June 14–17, 2023
Proceedings, Part I

 Springer

Editors
Ilias Maglogiannis ⓘ
University of Piraeus
Piraeus, Greece

John MacIntyre ⓘ
University of Sunderland
Sunderland, UK

Lazaros Iliadis ⓘ
Democritus University of Thrace
Xanthi, Greece

Manuel Dominguez ⓘ
University of Leon
León, Spain

ISSN 1868-4238   ISSN 1868-422X (electronic)
IFIP Advances in Information and Communication Technology
ISBN 978-3-031-34113-7   ISBN 978-3-031-34111-3 (eBook)
https://doi.org/10.1007/978-3-031-34111-3

This Springer imprint is published by the registered company Springer Nature Switzerland AG
The registered company address is: Gewerbestrasse 11, 6330 Cham, Switzerland

Preface

The 19th *Artificial Intelligence Applications and Innovations* (AIAI) conference offered a deep insight into all recent scientific advances and timely challenges of AI. From a technical point of view, novel algorithms and potential prototypes suitable to offer solutions in a multidisciplinary spectrum of applications (e.g., industry, finance, healthcare, cybersecurity, education) were introduced.

Moreover, it discussed ethical aspects and moral questions arising from the ability of AI to act autonomously, something that calls for the development of new legislative frameworks.

AIAI is a long-standing, well-established, mature international scientific conference, that has been held all over the world continuously for 19 years in the row. Its history is long and very successful, following and spreading the evolution of intelligent systems.

The first event was organized in Toulouse, France in 2004. Since then, it has had a continuous and dynamic presence as a major global, but mainly European scientific event. More specifically, it has been organized in China, Greece, Cyprus, Australia, and France. It has always been technically supported by the International Federation for Information Processing (IFIP) and more specifically by the Working Group 12.5, which is interested in AI applications.

Following a long-standing tradition, this Springer volume belongs to the IFIP AICT Springer Series, and it contains the papers that were accepted to be presented orally at the AIAI 2023 conference. An additional volume comprises the papers that were accepted and presented at the workshops that were held as parallel events. The event was held during June 14–17, 2023, at the University of León, Spain. The diverse nature of papers presented demonstrates the vitality of AI algorithms and approaches. It certainly proves the very wide range of AI applications as well.

The response of the international scientific community to the AIAI 2023 main event call for papers was more than satisfactory, with 185 papers initially submitted. All papers were peer reviewed (single blind) by at least two independent academic referees. Where needed, a third referee was consulted to resolve any potential conflicts. A total of 75 papers (40.5% of the submitted manuscripts) were accepted to be published in the proceedings as full papers (12+ pages long) while at the same time 17 short papers (9 to 11 pages) were accepted due to their significant academic strength.

Workshops

In total, the following five (5) scientific workshops on timely AI subjects were organized under the framework of AIAI 2023.

- The **12th** *Mining Humanistic Data Workshop* **(MHDW 2023)**

Coordinators: Spyros Sioutas, University of Patras, Greece, Ioannis Karydis and Katia Lida Kermanidis, Ionian University, Greece. It aimed to bring together interdisciplinary approaches that focus on the application of innovative as well as existing artificial intelligence, data matching, fusion and mining, and knowledge discovery and management techniques to data derived from all areas of Humanistic Sciences. The abundance of available data, which is retrieved from or is related to the areas of Humanities and the human condition, challenges the research community in processing and analyzing it. The aim was two-fold: on the one hand, to understand human behavior, creativity, way of thinking, reasoning, learning, decision making, socializing and respective biological processes; on the other hand, to exploit the extracted knowledge by incorporating it into intelligent systems that will support humans in their everyday activities.

- The **8th Workshop on** *5G-Putting Intelligence to the Network Edge (5G-PINE 2023)*

Coordinator: Ioannis Chochliouros, Hellenic Organization of Telecommunications, Greece (OTE). The 8th 5G-PINE workshop was organized by the research team of the *Hellenic Telecommunications Organization* (OTE) in cooperation with many major partner companies. The 8th 5G-PINE Workshop was established to disseminate knowledge obtained from ongoing EU projects as well as from other actions of EU-funded research in the wider thematic area of "*5G Innovative Activities – Putting Intelligence to the Network Edge*", and had the aim of focusing on Artificial Intelligence in modern 5G telecommunications infrastructures. It emphasized associated results, methodologies, trials, concepts and/or findings originating from technical reports/deliverables, from related pilot actions and/or any other relevant 5G-based applications intending to enhance intelligence to the network edges.

- The **3rd Workshop on** *AI and Ethics* **(AIETH 2023)**

Coordinator: John Macintyre, University of Sunderland, UK.
    The 3rd AIETH workshop included short presentations from the panel members and an open Q&A session where the audience members were able to ask, and answer, important questions about the current and future development of *Generative AI* models. It aimed to emphasize the need for responsible global AI. The respective scientific community must be preparing to act preemptively and ensure that our societies will avoid negative effects of AI and of the 4th Industrial Revolution in general.

- **The 1st Workshop on** *Visual Analytics Approaches for Complex Problems in Engineering and Biomedicine* **(VAA-CP-EB)**

Coordinators: Ignacio Díaz Blanco, Jose María Enguita Gonzalez, University of Oviedo, Spain.
    Many problems in the fields of Biomedicine and Engineering involve huge volumes of data, and an extended spectrum of variables under highly complex underlying processes. Numerous factors influence their behavior, resulting in common challenges

in diagnosis, prognosis, estimation, anomaly detection, explainability, image analysis or knowledge discovery.

Machine learning (ML) algorithms allow modeling of complex processes from massive data, as they are able to surpass humans in well-defined tasks. However, they are prone to error under changes in the context or in the problem's definition. Also, they are often "black box" models, which makes their integration with an expert's domain knowledge difficult. Humans, in turn, although less precise, can work with poorly posed problems, perform well on a wide range of tasks, and are able to find connections and improve responses through an iterative, exploratory process. Aiming to embrace both approaches, Visual Analytics (VA) has emerged in recent years as a powerful paradigm based on the integration of ML and human reasoning by means of data visualization and interaction for complex problem solving.

• **The 2nd Workshop on *AI in Energy, Buildings and Micro-Grids* (AIBMG 2023)**

Coordinators: Iakovos Michailidis (CERTH Greece), Stelios Krinidis (IHU, CERTH, Greece), Elias Kosmatopoulos (DUTh, CERTH, Greece) and Dimosthenis Ioannidis (CERTH, Greece). Sustainable energy is hands down one of the biggest challenges of our times. As the EU sets its focus to reach its 2030 and 2050 goals, the role of artificial intelligence in the energy domain at building, district and micro-grid level becomes prevalent. The EU and member states are increasingly highlighting the need to complement IoT capacity (e.g., appliances and meters) with artificial intelligence capabilities (e.g., building management systems, proactive optimization, prescriptive maintenance). Moreover, moving away from the centralized production schema of the grid, novel approaches are needed for the optimal management/balancing of local (or remote aggregated net metering) generation and consumption rather than only reducing energy consumption for communities.

The aim of the AIBMG Workshop was to bring together interdisciplinary approaches that focus on the application of AI-driven solutions for increasing and improving energy efficiency of residential and tertiary buildings without compromising the occupants' well-being. Applied directly on either the device, building or district management system, the proposed solutions should enable more energy efficient and sustainable operation of devices, buildings, districts and micro-grids. The workshop also welcomed cross-domain approaches that investigate how to support energy efficiency by exploiting decentralized, proactive, plug-n-play solutions.

The accepted papers of the AIAI 2023 conference are related to the following AI algorithms, thematic topics and application areas:

Algorithms and Areas of Research:

Active Learning	Augmented Reality
Adversarial attacks	Autoencoders
Adversarial Neural Networks	Biomedical
Agents	Boosting
Anomaly Detection	Case-Based Reasoning
Artificial Neural Networks	Classification

Constraint Programming
Convolutional Neural Networks
  (YOLO)
Cyber Security
Deep Learning
Deep Neural Networks
Explainable AI
Federated Learning
Fuzzy Modeling
Generative Adversarial Neural
  Networks
Genetic – Evolution
Gradient Boosting
Graph Neural Networks

Image Analysis
IoT
Long-Short Term Memory
Machine Learning
Natural Language
Optimization
Recurrent Neural Networks
Reinforcement Learning
Robotics
Sentiment Analysis
Social Impact of AI
Spiking Neural Networks
Text Mining
Transfer Learning

The authors of the AIAI 2023 accepted papers came from the following **32** different countries from **5** continents.

Algeria
Austria
Brazil
People's Republic of China
Croatia
Cyprus
Czech Republic
France
Germany
Greece
Hungary
India
Israel
Italy
Lebanon
Malaysia

Malta
Montenegro
The Netherlands
New Zealand
Norway
Oman
Poland
Portugal
Romania
Saudi Arabia
Spain
Sweden
Turkey
UK
United Arab Emirates
USA

June 2023

Ilias Maglogiannis
Lazaros Iliadis
John MacIntyre
Paulo Cortez

Organization

Executive Committee

General Co-chairs

Ilias Maglogiannis   University of Piraeus, Greece
John Macintyre   University of Sunderland, UK
Manuel Domínguez   University of León, Spain

Program Co-chairs

Lazaros Iliadis   Democritus University of Thrace, Greece
Serafin Alonso   University of León, Spain

Steering Committee

Ilias Maglogiannis   University of Piraeus, Greece
Lazaros Iliadis   Democritus University of Thrace, Greece
Eunika Mercier-Laurent   University of Reims Champagne-Ardenne, France

Honorary Co-chairs

Nikola Kasabov   Auckland University of Technology, New Zealand
Vera Kurkova   Czech Academy of Sciences, Czech Republic

Organizing Co-chairs

Antonios Papaleonidas   Democritus University of Thrace, Greece
Antonio Moran   University of León, Spain

Advisory Co-chairs

George Magoulas   Birkbeck, University of London, UK
Paulo Cortez   University of Minho, Portugal
Plamen Angelov   Lancaster University, UK

Doctoral Consortium Co-chairs

Valerio Bellandi   Università degli Studi di Milano, Italy
Ioannis Anagnostopoulos   University of Thessaly, Greece

Publication and Publicity Co-chairs

Antonios Papaleonidas	Democritus University of Thrace, Greece
Anastasios Panagiotis Psathas	Democritus University of Thrace, Greece
Athanasios Kallipolitis	Hellenic Air Force (HAF)/University of Piraeus, Greece
Dionysios Koulouris	University of Piraeus, Greece

Liaison Chair

Ioannis Chochliouros	Hellenic Telecommunication Organization (OTE), Greece

Workshops Co-chairs

Spyros Sioutas	University of Patras, Greece
Peter Hajek	University of Pardubice, Czech Republic

Special Sessions and Tutorials Chair

Luca Magri	Politecnico di Milano, Italy

Program Committee

Alexander Ryjov	Lomonosov Moscow State University, Russia
Alexander Zender	Hochschule Darmstadt, Germany
Aliki Stefanopoulou	CERTH, Greece
Anastasios Panagiotis Psathas	Democritus University of Thrace, Greece
Andreas Kanavos	University of Patras, Greece
Andreas Menychtas	University of Piraeus, Greece
Ángel Lareo	Universidad Autónoma de Madrid, Spain
Antonino Staiano	University of Naples Parthenope, Italy
Antonio José Serrano-López	University of Valencia, Spain
Antonio Morán	University of León, Spain
Antonios Kalampakas	AUM, Kuwait
Antonios Papaleonidas	DUTh, Greece
Aristidis Likas	University of Ioannina, Greece
Asimina Dimara	CERTH, Greece
Athanasios Alexiou	NGCEF, Australia
Athanasios Kallipolitis	University of Piraeus, Greece
Athanasios Koutras	University of the Peloponnese, Greece
Athanasios Tsadiras	Aristotle University of Thessaloniki, Greece
Bernhard Humm	Darmstadt University of Applied Sciences, Germany
Boudjelal Meftah	University of Mustapha Stambouli, Mascara, Algeria
Catalin Stoean	University of Craiova, Romania
Cen Wan	Birkbeck, University of London, UK

Christos Diou	Harokopio University of Athens, Greece
Christos Makris	University of Patras, Greece
Christos Timplalexis	CERTH/ITI, Greece
Daniel Pérez	University of León, Spain
Daniel Stamate	Goldsmiths, University of London, UK
Davide Zambrano	CWI, The Netherlands
Denise Gorse	University College London, UK
Doina Logofatu	Frankfurt University of Applied Sciences, Germany
Duc-Hong Pham	Vietnam National University, Hanoi, Vietnam
Efstratios Georgopoulos	University of the Peloponnese, Greece
Elias Pimenidis	University of the West of England, UK
Emilio Soria Olivas	University of Valencia, Spain
Fabio Pereira	Universidade Nove de Julho, Brazil
Florin Leon	Technical University of Iasi, Romania
Francesco Marcelloni	University of Pisa, Italy
Francisco Carvalho	Universidade Federal de Pernambuco, Brazil
Francisco Zamora-Martinez	VERIDAS SL, Spain
George Anastassopoulos	Democritus University of Thrace, Greece
George Caridakis	National Technical University of Athens, Greece
George Magoulas	Birkbeck, University of London, UK
Georgios Alexandridis	University of the Aegean, Greece
Georgios Drakopoulos	Ionian University, Greece
Gerasimos Vonitsanos	University of Patras, Greece
Gul Muhammad Khan	UET Peshawar, Pakistan
Hakan Haberdar	University of Houston, USA
Harris Papadopoulos	Frederick University, Cyprus
Ignacio Díaz	University of Oviedo, Spain
Ilias Maglogiannis	University of Piraeus, Greece
Ioannis Chamodrakas	National and Kapodistrian University of Athens, Greece
Ioannis Chochliouros	Hellenic Telecommunications Organization S.A. (OTE), Greece
Ioannis Hatzilygeroudis	University of Patras, Greece
Ioannis Karydis	Ionian University, Greece
Ioannis Livieris	University of Patras, Greece
Isidoros Perikos	University of Patras, Greece
Ivo Bukovsky	University of South Bohemia, Czech Republic
Jielin Qiu	Shanghai Jiao Tong University, China
Joan Vila-Francés	University of Valencia, Spain
Jose Maria Enguita	University of Oviedo, Spain
Juan Jose Fuertes	University of León, Spain
Katia Lida Kermanidis	Ionian University, Greece
Kazuhiko Takahashi	Doshisha University, Japan
Kazuyuki Hara	Nihon University, Japan
Kleanthis Malialis	University of Cyprus, Cyprus
Konstantinos Delibasis	University of Thessaly, Greece

Konstantinos Demertzis	Democritus University of Thrace, Greece
Konstantinos Moutselos	University of Piraeus, Greece
Kostas Karatzas	Aristotle University of Thessaloniki, Greece
Kostas Karpouzis	ICCS-NTUA, Greece
Lazaros Iliadis	Democritus University of Thrace, Greece
Lei Shi	Durham University, UK
Leon Bobrowski	Bialystok University of Technology, Poland
Luca Oneto	University of Genoa, Italy
Manuel Domínguez Gonzalez	Universidad de León, Spain
Mario Malcangi	Università degli Studi di Milano, Italy
Michel Aldanondo	IMT Mines Albi, France
Miguel Ángel Prada	Universidad de León, Spain
Mihaela Oprea	Petroleum-Gas University of Ploiesti, Romania
Mikko Kolehmainen	University of Eastern Finland, Finland
Mirjana Ivanovic	University of Novi Sad, Serbia
Napoleon Bezas	Centre for Research & Technology Hellas (CERTH), Greece
Neslihan Serap Sengor	Istanbul Technical University, Turkey
Nikolaos Mitianoudis	Democritus University of Thrace, Greece
Nikolaos Passalis	Aristotle University of Thessaloniki, Greece
Nikolaos Polatidis	University of Brighton, UK
Nikolaos Stylianou	Aristotle University of Thessaloniki, Greece
Nikos Kanakaris	University of Patras, Greece
Nikos Karacapilidis	University of Patras, Greece
Panagiotis Pintelas	University of Patras, Greece
Paraskevas Koukaras	Centre for Research and Technology Hellas, Greece
Paulo Cortez	University of Minho, Portugal
Paulo Vitor Campos Souza	CEFET-MG, Brazil
Petia Koprinkova-Hristova	Bulgarian Academy of Sciences, Bulgaria
Petr Hajek	University of Pardubice, Czech Republic
Petra Vidnerová	Czech Academy of Sciences, Czech Republic
Petros Kefalas	University of Sheffield International Faculty, Greece
Phivos Mylonas	National Technical University of Athens, Greece
Hassan Kazemian	London Metropolitan University, UK
Raffaele Giancarlo	University of Palermo, Italy
Riccardo Rizzo	National Research Council of Italy, Italy
Salvatore Aiello	Politecnico di Torino, Italy
Samira Maghool	University of Milan, Italy
Sebastian Otte	University of Tübingen, Germany
Serafin Alonso	University of León, Spain
Sergey Dolenko	D.V. Skobeltsyn Institute of Nuclear Physics, M.V. Lomonosov Moscow State University, Russia
Shareeful Islam	Anglia Ruskin University, UK
Simone Bonechi	University of Siena, Italy
Sotiris Kotsiantis	University of Patras, Greece

Sotiris Koussouris	Suite5 Data Intelligence Solutions ltd, Cyprus
Spiros Likothanassis	University of Patras, Greece
Stefan Reitmann	TU Bergakademie Freiberg, Germany
Stefanos Kollias	University of Lincoln, UK
Stefanos Nikiforos	Ionian University, Greece
Stelios Krinidis	International Hellenic University (IHU), Greece
Vaios Papaioannou	University of Patras, Greece
Vasileios Mezaris	CERTH, Greece
Vilson Luiz Dalle Mole	UTFPR, Brazil
Vincenzo Piuri	University of Milan, Italy
Will Serrano	University College London, UK
Yiannis Kontos	Aristotle University of Thessaloniki, Greece
Ziad Doughan	Beirut Arab University, Lebanon

Local Organizing/Hybrid Facilitation Committee

Anastasios Panagiotis Psathas	Democritus University of Thrace, Greece
Athanasios Kallipolitis	University of Piraeus, Greece
Dionysios Koulouris	University of Piraeus, Greece
Guzmán González Mateos	Universidad de León, Spain
Héctor Alaiz Moretón	Universidad de León, Spain
Ioanna-Maria Erentzi	Democritus University of Thrace, Greece
Ioannis Skopelitis	Democritus University of Thrace, Greece
José Ramón Rodriguez Ossorio	Universidad de León, Spain
Lambros Kazelis	Democritus University of Thrace, Greece
Leandros Tsatsaronis	Democritus University of Thrace, Greece
María del Carmen Benavides Cuéllar	Universidad de León, Spain
Maria Teresa García Ordás	Universidad de León, Spain
Natalia Prieto Fernández	Universidad de León, Spain
Nikiforos Mpotzoris	Democritus University of Thrace, Greece
Nikos Zervis	Democritus University of Thrace, Greece
Panagiotis Restos	Democritus University of Thrace, Greece
Raúl González Herbón	Universidad de León, Spain
Tassos Giannakopoulos	Democritus University of Thrace, Greece

AIAI 2023 Doctoral Track

For the first time, the 19th International Conference on Artificial Intelligence Applications and Innovations (AIAI 2023) set up a Doctoral Track which was a special meeting place for all PhD Students on all conference subjects and topics.

The AIAI 2023 Doctoral Track was not configured just as a mentoring track. It was an open forum in which all PhD students could present their ideas and their "up to now" work, and exchange ideas and thoughts about their research and their ideas.

All PhD student authors of accepted AIAI 2023 papers together with PhD students who separately submitted for the doctoral track participated in this session.

In total there were 5 extra submissions for the doctoral track (apart from the student submissions at the main event). All those submissions were reviewed by the Program Co-Chairs of AIAI 2023 and based on their score the following one was selected for full oral presentation in the main event.

Keynote Lectures

Five keynote speakers gave state-of-the-art lectures (after invitation) on timely aspects and applications of Artificial Intelligence.

Evolutionary Neural Architecture Search: Computational Efficiency, Privacy Preservation and Robustness Enhancement

Yaochu Jin

Bielefeld University, Germany and University of Surrey, UK

Abstract. Evolutionary neural architecture search has received considerable attention in deep learning. This talk begins with a presentation of computationally efficient evolutionary neural architecture search algorithms by means of sampled training and partial weight sharing. Then, we introduce communication-efficient deep neural architecture search in a federated learning environment. Finally, a surrogate-assisted evolutionary search algorithm for neural architectures that are robust to adversarial attacks is described. The talk is concluded with a brief discussion of open questions for future research.

Interpretable-By-Design Prototype-Based Deep Learning

Plamen Angelov ·

Lancaster University, UK

Abstract. Deep Learning has justifiably attracted the attention and interest of the scientific community and industry as well as of the wider society and even policy makers. However, the predominant architectures (from Convolutional Neural Networks to Transformers) are hyper-parametric models with weights/parameters that are detached from the physical meaning of the object of modelling. They are, essentially, embedded functions of functions which do provide the power of deep learning; however, they are also the main reason for diminished transparency and difficulties in explaining and interpreting the decisions made by deep neural network classifiers. Some dub this the "black box" approach. This makes problematic the use of such algorithms in high-stakes complex problems such as aviation, health, bailing from jail, etc. where the clear rationale for a particular decision is very important and errors are very costly. This motivated researchers and regulators to focus efforts on the quest for "explainable" yet highly efficient models. Most of the solutions proposed in this direction so far are, however, post hoc and only partially address the problem. At the same time, it is remarkable that humans learn in a principally different manner (by examples, using similarities) and not by fitting (hyper-) parametric models, and can easily perform so-called "zero-shot learning". Current deep learning is focused primarily on accuracy and overlooks explainability, the semantic meaning of the internal model representation, reasoning and decision making, and its link with the specific problem domain. Once trained, such models are inflexible to new knowledge. They cannot dynamically evolve their internal structure to start recognising new classes. They are good only for what they were originally trained for. The empirical results achieved by these types of methods according to Terry Sejnowski "should not be possible according to sample complexity in statistics and nonconvex optimization theory". The challenge is to bring together the high levels of accuracy with the semantically meaningful and theoretically sound and provable solutions.

All these challenges and identified gaps require a dramatic paradigm shift and a radical new approach. In this talk, we present such a new approach towards the next generation of explainable-by-design deep learning. It is based on prototypes and uses kernel-like functions, making it interpretable-by-design. It is dramatically easier to train and adapt without the need for complete re-training, can start learning from few training data samples, explore the data space, detect and learn from unseen data patterns. Indeed, the ability to detect the unseen and unexpected and start learning this new class/es in real time with no or very little supervision is critically important and is something that no currently existing classifier can offer. This method was applied to a range of applications including but not limited to remote sensing, autonomous driving, health and others.

Intelligent Mobile Sensing For Understanding Human Behaviour

Oresti Baños Legrán

University of Granada, Spain

Abstract. Understanding people's behaviour is essential to characterise patient progress, make treatment decisions and elicit effective and relevant coaching actions. Hence, a great deal of research has been devoted in recent years to the automatic sensing and intelligent analysis of human behaviour. Among all sensing options, smartphones stand out as they enable the unobtrusive observation and detection of a wide variety of behaviours as we go about our physical and virtual interactions with the world. This talk aims to give the audience a taste of the unparalleled potential that mobile sensing in combination with artificial intelligence offers for the study of human individual and collective behaviour.

Intelligent Mobile Sensing For Understanding Human Behaviour

Abstract.

Secure, Efficient and High Performance Computing: A Computer Architecture Perspective

Tamara Silbergleit Lehman

University of Colorado Boulder, USA

Abstract. Distributed systems and new architectures introduce new sets of security risks. Microarchitectural attacks have presented many challenges in the computer architecture community and this talk will present a few of the methods that the Boulder Computer Architecture Lab (BCAL) has been studying in order to address these vulnerabilities. The talk will first introduce physical and microarchitectural attacks and why they are hard to mitigate. Then, the talk will introduce an efficient implementation of speculative integrity verification, Poisonivy, to construct an efficient and high-performance secure memory system. Finally, the talk will show how we can leverage emerging memory technologies such as near memory processing to defend and identify microarchitectural side-channel attacks. The talk will end by briefly introducing a new research direction that is investigating the Rowhammer attack impact on neural network accuracy running on GPUs and how we can leverage secure memory to protect the accuracy of the models.

How AI/Machine Learning Has the Power of Revolutionizing (for Good?) Cybersecurity?

Javier Alonso Lopez

Amazon, USA

Abstract. As we already know, Machine Learning is already used in various cybersecurity tasks such as malware identification/classification, intrusion detection, botnet identification, phishing detection, predicting cyberattacks like denial of service, fraud detection, etc. However, during recent years there has been a revolution in machine learning, specifically deep learning, that creates not only an unbelievable opportunity to develop more effective solutions but also represents a new threat and a new tool to be used to attack and gain control over systems, organizations and even countries.

In this talk, we will overview the major applications of Machine Learning in the field of cybersecurity both to prevent attacks but also to pose a threat. We will review the main advances of Deep Learning in the last 5 years and their applications in Cybersecurity. Finally, we will discuss the possible future trends we can expect (I do not expect high accuracy, but high recall :D) at the intersection of Deep Learning and Cybersecurity.

How AI/Machine Learning Has the Power of Revolution(ising) (for Good?) Cybersecurity?

Contents – Part I

Agents/Case Based Reasoning/Sentiment Analysis

CNN - Convolutional Neural Networks YOLO CNN

Doctoral Track

Contents – Part II

Graph Neural Networks/Constraint Programming

IoT/Fuzzy Modeling/Augmented Reality

Learning (Active-AutoEncoders-Federated)

Natural Language

Optimization-Genetic Programming

Robotics

Spiking NN

Text Mining/Transfer Learning

Deep Learning
(Reinforcement/Recurrent Gradient Boosting/Adversarial)

A Deep Learning-Based Methodology for Detecting and Visualizing Continuous Gravitational Waves

Emmanuel Pintelas[(✉)] [ID], Ioannis E. Livieris[ID], and Panagiotis Pintelas[ID]

Department of Mathematics, University of Patras, Patras, Greece
{e.pintelas,livieris}@upatras.gr

Abstract. Since the Gravitational Waves' initial direct detection, a veil of mystery from the Universe has been lifted, ushering a new era of intriguing physics, as-tronomy, and astrophysics research. Unfortunately, since then, not much progress has been reported, because so far all of the detected Gravitational Waves fell only into the Binary bursting wave type (B-GWs), which are cre-ated via spinning binary compact objects such as black holes. Nowadays, as-tronomy scientists seek to detect a new type of gravitational waves called: Continuous Gravitational Waves (C-GWs). Unlike the complicated burst na-ture of B-GWs, C-GWs have elegant and much simpler form, being able to provide higher quality of information for the Universe exploration. Never-theless, C-GWs are much weaker comparing to the B-GWs, which makes them considerably harder to be detected. For this task, we propose a novel Deep-Learning-based methodology, being sensitive enough for detecting and visualizing C-GWs, based on Short-Time-Fourier data provided by LIGO. Based on extensive experimental simulations, our approach significantly outper-formed the state-of-the-art approaches, for every applied experimental configuration, revealing the efficiency of the proposed methodology. Our expectation is that this work can potentially assist scientists to improve their detection sensitivity, leading to new Astrophysical discoveries, via the incor-poration of Data-Mining and Deep-Learning sciences.

Keywords: Deep learning · 2D image processing · SFT signal processing · remote sensing applications · ML methods for sensing systems

1 Introduction

Accelerated masses produce Gravitational Waves (GWs), which are disturbances or ripples in the curvature of spacetime that move as waves away from their source at the speed of light [6]. These cosmic ripples would move through space and time, bringing with them clues to the nature of gravity and information about their origins [26].

© IFIP International Federation for Information Processing 2023
Published by Springer Nature Switzerland AG 2023
I. Maglogiannis et al. (Eds.): AIAI 2023, IFIP AICT 675, pp. 3–14, 2023.
https://doi.org/10.1007/978-3-031-34111-3_1

In 2015, a signal produced by the merger of two black holes, was detected by the Laser-Interferometer-Gravitational-wave-Observatory (LIGO) gravitational wave detectors in Livingston Louisiana, and Hanford Washington, which was the GWs' initial direct observation [13]. This type of detected GWs are produced by orbiting pairs of massive and dense/compact objects such as white dwarf stars, black holes, and neutron stars. Neutron stars are extremely dense objects created by collapsed stars, which run out all of their energy [1,2]. Due to the compact-binary-spinning source mechanism of this type of waves, they took the name: *"compact Binary inspiral Gravitational Waves (B-GWs)"*. Furthermore, it is worth mentioning that, depending on the spinning pair's object type, the B-GWs are separated into the following three sub-categories: binary neutron star, binary black hole, neutron star-black hole binary [4,8].

However, scientists have predicted the existence of a new type of GWs called: *Continuous Gravitational Waves (C-GWs)*, which are created by the rotation of single non-perfect neutron stars spheres [3]. Unlike the complicated burst of B-GW, C-GWs are elegant, well-defined, and almost constant being able to provide much more information about universe wonders, like neutron stars. Via the detection of C-GWs we will get a better knowledge of stellar evolution and populations as well as the internal structure and evolutionary history of these exceptional and yet intriguing objects, which will offer insights into the invisible huge population of neutron stars that inhabits our Galaxy [3,24].

Unfortunately, despite all of this progress, since 2015 all of the objects LIGO has detected so far, fall only into the B-GWs category, while the direct detection of real C-GWs still remains an open problem. In contrast to the common detected B-GWs, C-GWs are much weaker, which makes them much harder to be detected. Therefore, we aim to propose a novel Deep-Learning-based methodology, being sensitive enough for detecting C-GWs.

Deep learning (DL) [22] is a subset of machine learning that utilizes neural networks with multiple layers to learn patterns and features from data. It has been particularly effective in tasks such as image and speech recognition, natural language processing, and decision making. Convolutional Neural Networks (CNNs) [10,30] are a type of DL algorithm, which are particularly well-suited for image and video processing, which were applied in a wide range of applications [14,15,18]. This type of models work by repeatedly applying a set of filters to the input data, which allows them to learn spatial hierarchies of features.

In this work, we propose a Deep-Learning methodology for detecting and visualizing C-GWs utilizing a dataset based on the LIGO laboratory. This dataset has a time-frequency form constituted of a set of Short-time Fourier Transforms (SFTs) with respect to the GPS time stamps for each interferometer (LIGO Hanford and LIGO Livingston). Each data sample contains either real or simulated noise and possibly a simulated C-GW signal, while the task is to identify when a C-GW signal is present in the data. More specifically, the main objective of our proposed methodology is to create a more robust and clear representation form removing noise, by incorporating SFT pre-processing techniques, comparing to the state-of-the-art end-to-end deep-learning baseline approach (initial representation form of LIGO laboratory which is fed into a CNN model). The proposed transformation methodology considerably outperformed the baseline approach, for every applied experimental configuration (e.g., CNN model, input-shape, and augmentation choices) revealing the efficiency of the proposed approach.

The main contributions of this work are summarized as follows: We propose a novel pre-processing and deep-learning-based methodology for detecting and visualizing C-GWs (C-GWs are much harder to detect comparing to B-GWs), managing to achieve high accuracy comparing to the baseline approaches. The proposed method, managed to achieve a high overall performance proving to be a promising supporting tool to Astronomy and Physics Scientists for detecting possible C-GWs signals. Also, the incorporation of SpecAugm [19] methodology, drastically improved the results for every utilized model in every configuration. Finally, this work can potentially help scientists detect the new type of GWs called C-GWs, while further studies of these waves may enable scientists to learn about the structure of the most extreme stars in our universe.

To the best of our knowledge there are not any noticeable Machine-Learning-based approaches for automatic detection of Continuous-Gravitational-Waves (C-GWs), although there are plenty of research works on detection of compact Binary inspiral Gravitational Waves (B-GWs) [27,31]. Due to the complicated SFT spectrogram form of LIGO provided data, the high difficulty detection level of C-GWs, and the totally different nature and shape-form between the B-GWs and the C-GWs [3,24], it is not possible and reasonable to utilize as baseline state-of-the-art approaches the ones proposed for B-GWs detection problem.

Thus, specifically for the C-GW problem, it is reasonable to consider as state-of-the-art baseline approach, an end-to-end deep-learning-based approach utilizing the initial SFT representation form of the data provided by LIGO. In this baseline approach, the multi-channel spectrogram-based data of LIGO are fed into a multi-channel pre-trained CNN model, in order to perform the final classification. Instead, in our proposed approach, we apply SFT pre-processing and transformation techniques in order to reduce the initial high dimension, remove noise, and create a more robust representation for feeding a pre-trained CNN model in order to perform the final classification task.

2 Methodology

In this section, we describe in detail the data acquisition procedure and our proposed DL methodology for detecting possible signals of C-GW.

2.1 LIGO Interferometers

LIGO [5] is a marvel of meticulous engineering and the biggest gravitational wave observatory in the world. LIGO, consists of two enormous laser interferometers separated by 3000 km km, uses the physical characteristics of light and space itself to detect and comprehend the origins of gravitational waves. In brief,

LIGO has two gravitational-wave interferometers: LIGO Hanford (H) and LIGO Livingston (L). Each of them has two 4 km long arms arranged in the shape of an "L", acting as antennae to detect gravitational waves.

The basic operation principle in which LIGO detects GWs is briefly described as follows: Space itself is stretched by gravitational waves in one direction, while it is also compressed in the opposite direction [5]. As long as a wave is passing, the one arm of the LIGO interferometer is getting longer while the other gets shorter. In this way, LIGO is able to detect a possible GW signal. Similarly, to a human ear, which is able to detect vibrations in a medium like air or water, LIGO acts as an antenna able to detect vibrations in the "medium" of space-time.

2.2   Description of Case-Study Dataset Used for Detecting C-GWs

The frequency and amplitude of a C-GW signal from a rotating neutron star will be almost precisely constant [3]. However, over a long period of time, since the neutron star loses energy as it emits gravitational and electromagnetic waves, which causes it to rotate more slowly, the frequency of the signal gradually changes. With regard to the neutron star, the detector on Earth is moving. This alters the gravitational wave frequency that the detector picks up. Monitoring all potential frequency changes can be very computationally challenging. For this reason, Short-time Fourier Transforms (SFTs) [7] are used for quantifying the change of a non-stationary signal's frequency and phase content over time.

The utilized dataset in this research is based on the LIGO laboratory, which contains time-frequency data from two gravitational-wave interferometers: LIGO Hanford (H) and LIGO Livingston (L). Each data sample contains either real or simulated noise and possibly a simulated C-GW signal. The task is to identify when a signal is present in the data.

More specifically, each sample is comprised of a set of Short-time Fourier Transforms (SFTs) and corresponding GPS time stamps for each interferometer H and L. The SFTs are not always contiguous in time since the interferometers are not continuously online. Each sample can be represented as a spectrogram of the Real and Imaginary part of the complex form of the furrier transform corresponding to each interferometer H and L. Therefore, each sample/instance has the following initial spectrogram representation input-shape format:

$$N_{\text{inter}} \times N_{\text{complex}} \times Freq \times Time \tag{1}$$

where $N_{\text{inter}} = 2$ represents the number of interferometers, $N_{\text{complex}} = 2$ represents the number of complex parts (real and imaginary), $Freq = 360$ represents the signal's frequency and $Time$ is time in GPS timestamp.

2.3   State-of-the-Art Baseline Approach

Figure 1 presents a high-level presentation of the *"baseline approach"* (a 4 channel-CNN based on the Initial SFT spectrogram representation form of LIGO laboratory).

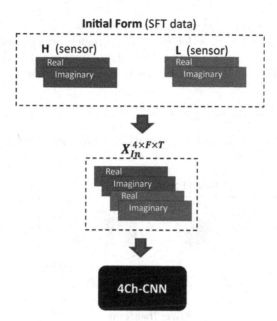

Fig. 1. Schematic presentation of the state-of-the-art end-to-end deep-learning baseline approach (a 4ch-CNN fed with the initial SFT form of LIGO laboratory)

Let assume the initial input matrices $\mathbf{H}_{\mathbb{C}}^{F \times T}$ and $\mathbf{L}_{\mathbb{C}}^{F \times T}$ corresponding to the SFT amplitudes $h_{f,t} \in \mathbb{C}$ and $l_{f,t} \in \mathbb{C}$ of the signals detected via the interferometers of LIGO Hanford (H) & LIGO Livingston (L) which are respectively defined by

$$
\mathbf{H}_{\mathbb{C}}^{F \times T} = \begin{bmatrix} h_{1,1} & \cdots & h_{1,t} & \cdots & h_{1,T} \\ \vdots & \ddots & \vdots & \ddots & \vdots \\ h_{f,1} & \cdots & h_{f,t} & \cdots & h_{f,T} \\ \vdots & \ddots & \vdots & \ddots & \vdots \\ h_{F,1} & \cdots & h_{F,t} & \cdots & h_{F,T} \end{bmatrix} \quad \text{and} \quad \mathbf{L}_{\mathbb{C}}^{F \times T} = \begin{bmatrix} l_{1,1} & \cdots & l_{1,t} & \cdots & l_{1,T} \\ \vdots & \ddots & \vdots & \ddots & \vdots \\ l_{f,1} & \cdots & l_{f,t} & \cdots & l_{f,T} \\ \vdots & \ddots & \vdots & \ddots & \vdots \\ l_{F,1} & \cdots & l_{F,t} & \cdots & l_{F,T} \end{bmatrix} \quad (2)
$$

where $f = 1, 2, \ldots, F$ corresponds to the frequency index, $t = 1, 2, \ldots, T$ to the timestamps-samples number and $\mathbb{C}$ to the complex numbers set. Each complex number is represented by a real and imaginary part; therefore, for the matrices defined in Eq. (2), we have

$$
\mathbf{H}_{\mathbb{C}} = \mathbf{H}_{\mathbb{R}}^{F \times T} + i\mathbf{H}_{\mathbb{I}}^{F \times T} \quad \text{and} \quad \mathbf{L}_{\mathbb{C}} = \mathbf{L}_{\mathbb{R}}^{F \times T} + i\mathbf{L}_{\mathbb{I}}^{F \times T} \quad (3)
$$

where i is the imaginary unit and $\mathbf{H}_{\mathbb{R}}, \mathbf{H}_{\mathbb{I}}, \mathbf{L}_{\mathbb{R}}, \mathbf{L}_{\mathbb{I}}$ correspond to the Real and Imaginary part of the $\mathbf{H}_{\mathbb{C}}$ and $\mathbf{L}_{\mathbb{C}}$ matrices, respectively. Thus, the input $\mathbf{X}_{In}^{4 \times F \times T}$ as defined in Eq. (4), is fed into a 4-channel CNN, corresponds to the state-of-the-art end-to-end deep-learning-based baseline approach.

$$
\mathbf{X}_{In}^{4 \times F \times T} = (\mathbf{H}_{\mathbb{R}}, \mathbf{H}_{\mathbb{I}}, \mathbf{L}_{\mathbb{R}}, \mathbf{L}_{\mathbb{I}}) \times 1e^{22} \quad (4)
$$

It is worth mentioning that the amplitude values $h_{f,t}$, $l_{f,t}$ range in $1e^{-22}$ order, since the initial signals detected are extremely weak. Feeding them in a CNN model would result in losing the numbers precision. For this reason, it is essential to multiply the input matrices with the term $1e^{22}$, as defined in Eq. (4).

2.4   Proposed Methodology

Figure 2 illustrates a schematic presentation of the *"proposed deep learning C-GW detection approach"*.

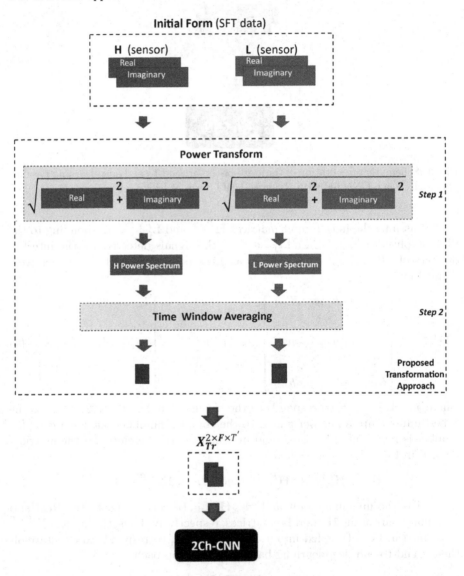

Fig. 2. Schematic presentation of the proposed DL C-GW detection approach

In order to create a robust representation and remove noise from the $\mathbf{H_C}$ and $\mathbf{L_C}$ spectrograms, we are able to compute their power spectrums $\mathbf{H}_P$ and $\mathbf{L}_P$ respectively (Step 1, Fig. 3), which are defined as follows:

$$\mathbf{H}_P = \begin{bmatrix} h_{1,1}^{(P)} & \cdots & h_{1,t}^{(P)} & \cdots & h_{1,T}^{(P)} \\ \vdots & \ddots & \vdots & \ddots & \vdots \\ h_{f,1}^{(P)} & \cdots & h_{f,t}^{(P)} & \cdots & h_{f,T}^{(P)} \\ \vdots & \ddots & \vdots & \ddots & \vdots \\ h_{F,1}^{(P)} & \cdots & h_{F,t}^{(P)} & \cdots & h_{F,T}^{(P)} \end{bmatrix} \quad \text{and} \quad \mathbf{L}_P = \begin{bmatrix} l_{1,1}^{(P)} & \cdots & l_{1,t}^{(P)} & \cdots & l_{1,T}^{(P)} \\ \vdots & \ddots & \vdots & \ddots & \vdots \\ l_{f,1}^{(P)} & \cdots & l_{f,t}^{(P)} & \cdots & l_{f,T}^{(P)} \\ \vdots & \ddots & \vdots & \ddots & \vdots \\ l_{F,1}^{(P)} & \cdots & l_{F,t}^{(P)} & \cdots & l_{F,T}^{(P)} \end{bmatrix} \quad (5)$$

where $h_{f,t}^{(P)} = \sqrt{(h_{f,t}^{(\mathbb{R})})^2 + (h_{f,t}^{(\mathbb{I})})^2}$ and $l_{f,t}^{(P)} = \sqrt{(l_{f,t}^{(\mathbb{R})})^2 + (l_{f,t}^{(\mathbb{I})})^2}$, while $h_{f,t}^{(\mathbb{R})}$, $h_{f,t}^{(\mathbb{I})}$, $l_{f,t}^{(\mathbb{R})}$, and $l_{f,t}^{(\mathbb{I})}$ are the amplitudes values of $\mathbf{H}_{\mathbb{R}}$, $\mathbf{H}_{\mathbb{I}}$, $\mathbf{L}_{\mathbb{R}}$ and $\mathbf{L}_{\mathbb{I}}$, respectively.

Since the data is time correlated with respect to the timestamps t, we further transform the data via a time-window-averaging approach (see Step 2 in Fig. 3), in order to further remove noise and create a compressed and even more robust final representation form, aiming to reveal possible signs of C-GWs (Fig. 4), defined as follows

$$\mathbf{H}_{PAv}^{F \times T'} = \begin{bmatrix} E\left(h_{1,1}^{(P)},\ldots,h_{1,k}^{(P)}\right) & \cdots & E\left(h_{1,k(j-1)}^{(P)},\ldots,h_{1,kj}^{(P)}\right) & \cdots & E\left(h_{1,k(T'-1)}^{(P)},\ldots,h_{1,kT'}^{(P)}\right) \\ \vdots & \ddots & \vdots & \ddots & \vdots \\ E\left(h_{f,1}^{(P)},\ldots,h_{f,k}^{(P)}\right) & \cdots & E\left(h_{f,k(j-1)}^{(P)},\ldots,h_{f,kj}^{(P)}\right) & \cdots & E\left(h_{f,k(T'-1)}^{(P)},\ldots,h_{f,kT'}^{(P)}\right) \\ \vdots & \ddots & \vdots & \ddots & \vdots \\ E\left(h_{F,1}^{(P)},\ldots,h_{F,k}^{(P)}\right) & \cdots & E\left(h_{F,k(j-1)}^{(P)},\ldots,h_{F,kj}^{(P)}\right) & \cdots & E\left(h_{F,k(T'-1)}^{(P)},\ldots,h_{F,kT'}^{(P)}\right) \end{bmatrix}$$

and

$$\mathbf{L}_{PAv}^{F \times T'} = \begin{bmatrix} E\left(l_{1,1}^{(P)},\ldots,l_{1,k}^{(P)}\right) & \cdots & E\left(l_{1,k(j-1)}^{(P)},\ldots,l_{1,kj}^{(P)}\right) & \cdots & E\left(l_{1,k(T'-1)}^{(P)},\ldots,l_{1,kT'}^{(P)}\right) \\ \vdots & \ddots & \vdots & \ddots & \vdots \\ E\left(l_{f,1}^{(P)},\ldots,l_{f,k}^{(P)}\right) & \cdots & E\left(l_{f,k(j-1)}^{(P)},\ldots,l_{f,kj}^{(P)}\right) & \cdots & E\left(l_{f,k(T'-1)}^{(P)},\ldots,l_{f,kT'}^{(P)}\right) \\ \vdots & \ddots & \vdots & \ddots & \vdots \\ E\left(l_{F,1}^{(P)},\ldots,l_{F,k}^{(P)}\right) & \cdots & E\left(l_{F,k(j-1)}^{(P)},\ldots,l_{F,kj}^{(P)}\right) & \cdots & E\left(l_{F,k(T'-1)}^{(P)},\ldots,l_{F,kT'}^{(P)}\right) \end{bmatrix}$$

where $k = \frac{T}{T'}$ is the averaging window size, $T' < T$, $k \in \mathbb{N}$ the new total timestamps of the compressed power spectrograms, and $E(\cdot)$ is the Expected value function (also called Average or Mean).

Thus, the input $\mathbf{X}_{Tr}^{2 \times F \times T'}$ of the 2Ch-CNN which corresponds to the Proposed Approach is defined as:

$$\mathbf{X}_{Tr}^{2 \times F \times T'} = (\mathbf{H}_{PAv}^{F \times T'}, \mathbf{L}_{PAv}^{F \times T'}) \times 1e^{22}.$$

Figure 3(a) presents an instance labeled as "C-GW" based on its initial SFT spectrogram representation form of LIGO laboratory. However, due to noise is almost impossible to identify signs of waves in this form making it appear as pure noise signal. Instead, based on the proposed transformed representation form (Fig. 3(b)), clearly signs of a C-GW are visualized[1].

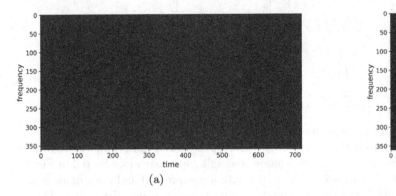

(a)   (b)

Fig. 3. Presentation of a "C-GW" instance based on (a) its initial SFT form of LIGO laboratory (a), compared to (b) its proposed transformed representation form

3   Experimental Results

In this section, we analyze and present our experimental setup, comparing the Proposed Approach, with the state-of-the-art end-to-end deep-learning approach (initial representation form of LIGO laboratory which feds a 4-channel CNN model), utilizing various CNN baselines, for different input shapes, using also sophisticated augmentation approach[2].

It is worth mentioning that the selection of the utilized CNN baselines in our experiments was based on those which managed to bring the best overall results.

Inception-v4 [28] is a deep convolutional neural network architecture for object recognition and image classification tasks being an extension of the Inception architecture. The key innovation in Inception-v4 is the use of residual connections, which have been shown to improve the performance of deep neural networks. ResNeSt [32] is a deep convolutional neural network architecture for image classification and object recognition tasks. The key innovation in ResNeSt is the use of split attention mechanism, which allows the network to attend to both global and local features simultaneously. DenseNet [11] is a deep convolutional neural network architecture for image classification and object recognition tasks. The key innovation in DenseNet is the use of dense connections, which

---

[1] For visualization purposes, we averaged the multi channels spectrograms to 1-channel.

[2] The datasets used in our research, can be found in https://www.kaggle.com/datasets/emmanuelpintelas/gw-datasets.

connect each layer to every other layer in a feed-forward fashion. Efficientnet-b8 [12] is a deep convolutional neural network architecture for image classification and object recognition tasks. The key innovation in EfficientNet is the use of compound scaling, which adjusts the depth, width, and resolution of the network to improve its performance.

In order to guarantee the reliability of the final experimental performance results, we performed a 5-fold-cross-validation averaging strategy for every utilized experimental configuration (CNN model, input-shape and augm. selection). The evaluation procedure was performed based on the following performance metrics: Accuracy (Acc), F_1-score (F_1), Sensitivity (Sen), Specificity (Spe), and the Area Under the Curve (AUC) [16,23].

It is worth mentioning that the initial frequency and time dimensions of every spectrogram instance 360 Hz and 4320 timestamps, respectively, which implies that for the baseline approach the input's data shape was $4 \times 360 \times 4320$. However, each utilized pre-trained model reported unsatisfactory performance. Therefore, we resized the input data to $4 \times 360 \times 720$ using bilinear interpolation, which reported the best performance. Additionally, for the proposed approach, we investigated its performance using various values for the parameter k, i.e. $2, 4, 6, 8, 12$ and 24). In our experiments, we selected $k = 6$ and $k = 24$, which implies that the input's data shapes for the proposed CNN model were $2 \times 360 \times 720$ and $2 \times 360 \times 180$, respectively.

We have also utilized the SpecAugmen [19] data augmentation method (this augmentation method was initially proposed and applied on automatic Speech Recognition), in order to prevent overfitting and increase the diversity of our training data, which managed to considerably improve the performance results.

Tables 1 and 2 summarize our experimental results. The proposed transformation methodology considerably outperformed the baseline end-to-end CNN approach (initial representation form of LIGO laboratory feeding a 4-channel CNN model), for every applied experimental configuration (e.g., CNN model, input-shape and augm. choices). The proposed method, managed to achieve a high overall performance proving to be a promising supporting tool to Astronomy and Physics Scientists for detecting possible C-GWs signals.

The incorporation of SpecAugm methodology, drastically improved the results for every utilized model in all input-shape configurations. The best results in overall were achieved for the lowest time compression size applied, while as the compression size was increased, the results significantly decreased.

Furthermore, regarding our experimental findings, it is worth mentioning that the best results in overall were achieved for the lowest time compression size applied, while as the compression size was increased, the results significantly decreased. This was probably due to the fact that on high dimensions, the input has more noise leading to model overfitting, while the C-GWs signal appear much weaker and unclear. In contrast on low sizes, the input becomes more robust enabling the C-GW signal to be much stronger and apparent assisting the CNN model to easily identify and reveal it.

Table 1. Experimental results based on the initial representation form of LIGO laboratory (baseline approach)

Augm.	CNN baseline	Input size	Acc	F_1	Sen	Spe	AUC
None	Inception-v4	$4 \times 360 \times 720$	66.5%	0.795	0.034	0.979	0.567
	ResNeSt		66.7%	0.778	0.0	1.0	0.573
	DenseNet		65.9%	0.799	0.011	0.995	0.543
	Efficientnet-b8		61.5%	0.732	0.208	0.827	0.556
SpecAugm	Inception-v4	$4 \times 360 \times 720$	66.2%	0.680	0.0	1.0	0.563
	ResNeSt		54.0%	0.551	0.534	0.533	0.547
	DenseNet		66.7%	0.789	0.0	1.0	0.564
	Efficientnet-b8		57.7%	0.659	0.335	0.697	0.571

Table 2. Experimental results based on the initial representation form of LIGO laboratory (proposed approach)

Augm.	CNN baseline	Input size	Acc	F_1	Sen	Spe	AUC
None	Inception-v4	$2 \times 360 \times 720$	66.7%	0.800	0.0	1.0	0.599
		$2 \times 360 \times 180$	65.5%	0.712	0.426	0.752	0.724
	ResNeSt	$2 \times 360 \times 720$	66.3%	0.792	0.005	0.992	0.612
		$2 \times 360 \times 180$	67.0%	0.750	0.394	0.791	0.697
	DenseNet	$2 \times 360 \times 720$	66.2%	0.791	0.070	0.958	0.622
		$2 \times 360 \times 180$	68.7%	0.757	0.553	0.753	0.762
	Efficientnet-b8	$2 \times 360 \times 720$	64.5%	0.758	0.254	0.851	0.624
		$2 \times 360 \times 180$	66.5%	0.763	0.381	0.823	0.750
SpecAugm	Inception-v4	$2 \times 360 \times 720$	62.2%	0.694	0.487	0.700	0.684
		$2 \times 360 \times 180$	66.5%	0.757	0.378	0.818	0.751
	ResNeSt	$2 \times 360 \times 720$	60.8%	0.640	0.757	0.545	0.709
		$2 \times 360 \times 180$	66.8%	0.754	0.458	0.777	0.752
	DenseNet	$2 \times 360 \times 720$	64.0%	0.744	0.319	0.815	0.671
		$2 \times 360 \times 180$	69.6%	0.775	0.511	0.793	0.774
	Efficientnet-b8	$2 \times 360 \times 720$	66.5%	0.798	0.0	0.997	0.661
		$2 \times 360 \times 180$	70.3%	0.748	0.782	0.667	0.796

4   Conclusions

In this work, we proposed a novel pre-processing and deep-learning-based methodology for detecting and visualizing C-GWs utilizing a dataset based on the LIGO laboratory as case-study scenario. This dataset has time-frequency form based on two gravitational-wave interferometers: LIGO Hanford and LIGO

Livingston. Each data sample contained either real or simulated noise and possibly a simulated C-GW signal. In brief, the task was to identify when a C-GW signal is present in the data.

Our proposed methodology aimed to create a more robust and clear representation form in order to feed a CNN model. Based on extensive experimental simulations, our approach significantly outperformed the state-of-the-art end-to-end deep-learning approach, for every applied experimental configuration, revealing the efficiency of the proposed methodology and proving to be a promising supporting tool to Astrophysical scientists for detecting possible C-GWs signals.

The con of this works lies on the fact that no time-series-based approached were investigated, since the initial type of data are time-correlated. Thus, in our future research, we intent to further improve our model's detection sensitivity by incorporating statistical analysis and time-series enhancing approaches [14,17]. Finally, we also intend to improve our work by adding the Explainability/Interpretability property [20,21,25] to our detection approach, which is obviously of crucial significance in Astrophysical sciences for unveiling and explaining the mysteries of Universe.

References

1. Abbott, B.P., et al.: GW170817: observation of gravitational waves from a binary neutron star inspiral. Phys. Rev. Letters **119**(16), 161101 (2017)
2. Abbott, B.P., et al.: Observation of gravitational waves from a binary black hole merger. Phys. Rev. Lett. **116**(6), 061102 (2016)
3. Abbott, B.P., Abbott, R., Abbott, T., Abraham, S., Acernese, F., Ackley, K., et al.: All-sky search for continuous gravitational waves from isolated neutron stars using advanced LIGO O2 data. Phys. Rev. D **100**(2), 102008 (2019)
4. Abbott, B.P., et al.: Exploring the sensitivity of next generation gravitational wave detectors. Classical and Quantum Gravity **34**(4), 044001 (2017)
5. Abbott, B., et al.: LIGO: the laser interferometer gravitational-wave observatory. Reports Progress Phys. **72**(7), 076901 (2009)
6. Abbott, R., et al.: Searches for gravitational waves from known pulsars at two harmonics in the second and third LIGO-Virgo observing runs. Astrophys J **935**(1), 1 (2022)
7. Byrne, C.L.: Signal Processing: a mathematical approach. CRC Press (2014)
8. Caprini, C., Figueroa, D.G.: Cosmological backgrounds of gravitational waves. Classical Quant. Gravity **35**(16), 163001 (2018)
9. George, D., Huerta, E.A.: Deep learning for real-time gravitational wave detection and parameter estimation: results with advanced LIGO data. Phys. Lett. B **778**, 64–70 (2018)
10. He, K., Zhang, X., Ren, S., Sun, J.: Deep residual learning for image recognition. In: Proceedings of the IEEE Conference on Computer Vision and Pattern Recognition, pp. 770–778 (2016)
11. Huang, G., Liu, Z., Van Der Maaten, L., Weinberger, K.Q.: Densely connected convolutional networks. In: Proceedings of the IEEE Conference on Computer Vision and Pattern Recognition, pp. 4700–4708 (2017)
12. Koonce, B., Koonce, B.: Efficientnet. Convolutional Neural Networks with Swift for Tensorflow: Image Recognition and Dataset Categorization, pp. 109–123 (2021)

13. Królak, A., Patil, M.: The first detection of gravitational waves. Universe **3**(3), 59 (2017)
14. Livieris, I.E., Pintelas, E., Kiriakidou, N., Stavroyiannis, S.: An advanced deep learning model for short-term forecasting us natural gas price and movement. In: Artificial Intelligence Applications and Innovations, pp. 165–176. Springer (2020)
15. Livieris, I.E., Pintelas, E., Pintelas, P.: A CNN-LSTM model for gold price time-series forecasting. Neural Comput. Appl. **32**, 17351–17360 (2020)
16. Livieris, I.E., Pintelas, P.: An adaptive nonmonotone active set-weight constrained-neural network training algorithm. Neurocomputing **360**, 294–303 (2019)
17. Livieris, I.E., Stavroyiannis, S., Pintelas, E., Pintelas, P.: A novel validation framework to enhance deep learning models in time-series forecasting. Neural Comput. Appl. **32**(23), 17149–17167 (2020). https://doi.org/10.1007/s00521-020-05169-y
18. Lu, L., Zheng, Y., Carneiro, G., Yang, L.: Deep learning and convolutional neural networks for medical image computing. Adv. Comput. Vis. Pattern Recognit. **10**, 978–3 (2017)
19. Park, D.S., et al.: Specaugment: A simple data augmentation method for automatic speech recognition. arXiv preprint arXiv:1904.08779 (2019)
20. Pintelas, E., Liaskos, M., Livieris, I.E., Kotsiantis, S., Pintelas, P.: A novel explainable image classification framework: Case study on skin cancer and plant disease prediction. Neural Comput. Appl. **33**(22), 15171–15189 (2021)
21. Pintelas, E., Livieris, I.E., Pintelas, P.: A grey-box ensemble model exploiting black-box accuracy and white-box intrinsic interpretability. Algorithms **13**(1), 17 (2020)
22. Purwins, H., Li, B., Virtanen, T., Schlüter, J., Chang, S.Y., Sainath, T.: Deep learning for audio signal processing. IEEE J. Selected Topics Signal Process. **13**(2), 206–219 (2019)
23. Raschka, S.: An overview of general performance metrics of binary classifier systems. arXiv preprint arXiv:1410.5330 (2014)
24. Riles, K.: Recent searches for continuous gravitational waves. Mod. Phys. Lett. A **32**(39), 1730035 (2017)
25. Roscher, R., Bohn, B., Duarte, M.F., Garcke, J.: Explainable machine learning for scientific insights and discoveries. IEEE Access **8**, 42200–42216 (2020)
26. Rothman, T.: The secret history of gravitational waves: contrary to popular belief, einstein was not the first to conceive of gravitational waves-but he was, eventually, the first to get the concept right. Am. Sci. **106**(2), 96–104 (2018)
27. Schäfer, M.B., Ohme, F., Nitz, A.H.: Detection of gravitational-wave signals from binary neutron star mergers using machine learning. Physical Review D **102**(6), 063015 (2020)
28. Szegedy, C., Ioffe, S., Vanhoucke, V., Alemi, A.: Inception-v4, inception-resnet and the impact of residual connections on learning. In: Proceedings of the AAAI Conference on Artificial Intelligence, vol. 31 (2017)
29. Szegedy, C., Liu, W., Jia, Y., Sermanet, P., Reed, S., Anguelov, D., Erhan, D., Vanhoucke, V., Rabinovich, A.: Going deeper with convolutions. In: Proceedings of the IEEE Conference on Computer Vision and Pattern Recognition, pp. 1–9 (2015)
30. Véstias, M.P.: Convolutional neural network. In: Encyclopedia of Information Science and Technology, Fifth Edition, pp. 12–26. IGI Global (2021)
31. Wei, W., Huerta, E.: Deep learning for gravitational wave forecasting of neutron star mergers. Phys. Lett. B **816**, 136185 (2021)
32. Zhang, H., et al.: Resnest: Split-attention networks. In: IEEE/CVF Conference on Computer Vision and Pattern Recognition, pp. 2736–2746 (2022)

A Sharpe Ratio Based Reward Scheme in Deep Reinforcement Learning for Financial Trading

Georgios Rodinos[✉], Paraskevi Nousi, Nikolaos Passalis, and Anastasios Tefas

Computational Intelligence and Deep Learning Research Group, Artificial Intelligence and Information Analysis Lab, Department of Informatics, Aristotle University of Thessaloniki, Thessaloniki, Greece
{grodinos,paranous,passalis,tefas}@csd.auth.gr

Abstract. Deep Reinforcement Learning (DRL) is increasingly becoming popular for developing financial trading agents. Nevertheless, the nature of financial markets to be extremely volatile, in addition to the difficulty of optimizing DRL agents, lead the agents to make more risky trades. As a result, while agents can earn higher profits, they are also vulnerable to significant losses. To evaluate the performance of the financial trading agent, the Profit and Loss (PnL) is usually calculated, which is also used as the agent's reward. However, in addition to PnL, traders often take into account other aspects of the agent's behavior, such as the risk associated with the positions opened by the agent. A widely used metric that captures the risk-related component of an agent's performance is the Sharpe ratio, which is used to evaluate a portfolio's risk-adjusted performance. In this paper, we propose a Sharpe ratio-based reward shaping approach that enables optimizing DRL agents by taking into account both PnL and the Sharpe ratio, with the objective to improve the overall performance of the portfolio, by mitigating the risk that occurs in the agent's decisions. The effectiveness of the proposed method to increase different performance metrics is illustrated using a dataset provided by Speedlab AG, which contains 14 instruments .

Keywords: Financial Trading · Reward Shaping · Deep Learning · Deep Reinforcement Learning

1 Introduction

Using traditional machine learning methods for automated financial trading can be very challenging. Most of the time, the creation of supervised labels is needed. In works, such as [14–17], Deep Learning (DL) models were used to predict the price movement and depending on the direction, a trader is able to make a decision to either go long or short. However, this task might be challenging because of the uncertainty of the financial markets. The use of Deep Reinforcement Learning (DRL) is an efficient way to follow, yet tough, to avoid the limitations of supervised learning. In works such as [1,3,13,18,19], a DRL framework was used to overcome possible restrictions occurring on supervised problems.

© IFIP International Federation for Information Processing 2023
Published by Springer Nature Switzerland AG 2023
I. Maglogiannis et al. (Eds.): AIAI 2023, IFIP AICT 675, pp. 15–23, 2023.
https://doi.org/10.1007/978-3-031-34111-3_2

DRL agents for automated financial trading are difficult to be developed since a carefully designed reward scheme is required [8]. As tasks get more complicated, reward shaping becomes more challenging, while recent applications have demonstrated that adapting it to the specific domain of its usage may considerably increase the agents' performance [10,11].

There are works that use the Profit and Loss (PnL) as a reward but the agent doesn't take into account the risk that often arises in the trades. In addition, some works also use the Sharpe ratio as a reward, however, sometimes seems not to work effectively, such as in [21]. In this work, instead of using rewards that are based only on the agent's PnL or the Sharpe ratio, we force the agent to take into account both PnL and the Sharpe ratio in the reward function.

Sharpe ratio was originally mentioned in the 1960s s by William F. Sharpe [5]. It is a measure of the risk-adjusted return of an investment or portfolio and constitutes one of the most widely used metrics in finance. The Sharpe ratio is calculated as the average return of an investment minus the risk-free rate of return, divided by the standard deviation of the investment's returns. In our case, the risk-free rate is assumed to be zero as a practical simplification. Keep in mind that in practice, the risk-free rate is never truly zero. The standard deviation measures the volatility of the investment's returns and captures the idea that higher returns should be associated with higher risk. A higher Sharpe ratio indicates that an investment has provided a better return for the amount of risk taken. The Sharpe ratio is used to evaluate the performance of individual investments as well as portfolios and is a useful metric for comparing different investment options and helping make investment decisions.

Even though the Sharpe ratio is widely used, currently there is no such work that takes advantage of it combined with a PnL-based reward, when training DRL agents. Sharpe ratio is usually calculated as an annualized metric, which means that in order to be calculated, takes into account the returns over a long period of time. In practice, the volatility of monthly returns is typically considered when using the Sharpe ratio, which is generally lower than that of daily returns, which are in turn less volatile than hourly returns. However, when training a trading agent, the returns that are available, are hourly sampled, and normally equal to the number of steps an agent makes in an RL episode. As a consequence, the existing volatility in an RL episode may be significant.

Our contribution can be summarized as follows. We propose a method to incorporate the Sharpe ratio into the training regime of a DRL agent, to mitigate the risk of the taken action by the agent. Specifically, to overcome the aforementioned limitations regarding the calculation of the Sharpe ratio, we introduce a window that dynamically changes its size, by taking into account the returns we have available inside an RL episode. Thus, we are able to have an approximation of the Sharpe ratio that can be included in the reward function.

The structure of this paper is as follows. In Sect. 2 the background is mentioned along with the proposed method which is introduced and analytically described. Then the dataset as well as the experimental evaluation are presented in Sect. 3. Finally, Sect. 4 concludes this paper.

2   Proposed Method

This Section introduces the background related to DRL. The baseline PnL reward is presented, followed by the PnL and Sharpe ratio reward scheme and the proposed one. All of them are determined and thoroughly explained.

2.1   Background

The DRL setup is briefly described in the next paragraphs. We follow a similar approach for financial trading that was used in [3,13].

In financial trading via DRL, the environment provides the agent with an observation, which consists of features generated from market data as presented in Sect. 3.2. Along with the observation, the current market position is provided, which is denoted as e_t, where $e_t \in \{1, 0, -1\} = \{long, neutral, short\}$. The combination of these two, forms the state of the environment, s_t, at time t, where time t, specifies the simulation moment in time. The dimensions of the state are equal to $d \times T$, where d is the number of features and T specifies the time steps that occurred prior to time t.

Every time t, the agent has the choice to either buy, sell or stay out of the market, depending on the state, s_t, that receives from the environment. For every action, at time t receives a reward, r_t. The proposed reward is received by the position currently held and is compared to two other methods. When the agent changes the current position held, a commission is paid to make the change. To make the simulation process easier, we chose a reasonable commission for all the transactions.

2.2   PnL Reward

Rewarding an agent based on the profit of the positions taken is a common methodology for financial trading with Reinforcement Learning, e.g., [1–3]. This approach is our base and is also separately tested in this study. The profit-based reward is defined as:

$$r_t^{(PnL)} = \begin{cases} z_t, & \text{if agent going long} \\ -z_t, & \text{if agent going short} \\ 0, & \text{if agent has a neutral position} \end{cases} \tag{1}$$

where z_t is the return change and is defined as:

$$z_t = \frac{p_c(t) - p_c(t-1)}{p_c(t-1)} \tag{2}$$

which is also referred to as the change of the close price p_c. With the return definition, the reward of Eq. 1 can be written as:

$$r_t^{(PnL)} = e_t \cdot z_t \tag{3}$$

When the agent changes position is obligated to pay an extra *fee*. That is called the *commission*, in which case an additional reward is formulated as:

$$r_t^{(fee)} = -c \cdot |e_t - e_{t-1}| \tag{4}$$

where c denotes the commission. The total PnL reward can be defined as:

$$r_t^{(total)} = r_t^{(PnL)} + r_t^{(fee)} \tag{5}$$

2.3 PnL and Sharpe Ratio Reward

As discussed previously, the Sharpe ratio is a metric that is usually calculated annually. However, in our study, we propose to include it in the reward as an approximation, in every RL episode. That means that we calculate it over a short period of time.

Let m be the number of time steps that an episode consists of. We introduce a window, let w be the window, over the period of m steps, which increases its size dynamically. The agent, in order to calculate the approximation of the Sharpe ratio, will take into consideration the trades that took place in the last $m/2$ steps, and in each step, its size grows, up to m. Reward, based on the approximated Sharpe ratio is defined as:

$$r_t^{(sr)} = \frac{E[\mathbf{z}]}{\sqrt{Var[\mathbf{z}]}} \cdot \alpha \quad t \in \{w, ..., m\}, \quad \mathbf{z} = (z_0, ..., z_t) \tag{6}$$

where $w = m/2$, $\mathbf{z}$ is a vector with the returns as defined in Eq. 2, and α is a constant value, typically less than 1, that can be adjusted and influence the agent's behavior. PnL rewards are normally in a very small range. Multiplying the approximated Sharpe ratio reward in Eq. 6, with a scale factor less than 1, we avoid overpowering the PnL reward. The total PnL and Sharpe ratio reward is defined as:

$$r_t^{(total)} = \begin{cases} r_t^{(PnL)} + r_t^{(fee)}, & t < w \\ r_t^{(PnL)} + r_t^{(fee)} + r_t^{(sr)}, & for \quad t \geq w \end{cases} \tag{7}$$

2.4 Proposed Reward

The proposed Sharpe ratio-based reward shaping scheme allows for training agents that handle the risk taken in every transaction, significantly improving their risk-adjusted performance and the total profits, as it is experimentally illustrated in Sect. 3. The total reward of the proposed scheme is defined as:

$$r_t^{(total)} = \begin{cases} r_t^{(PnL)} + r_t^{(fee)}, & t < w \\ r_t^{(PnL)} + r_t^{(fee)} + r_t^{(sr)}, & for \quad t = w \\ r_t^{(PnL)} + r_t^{(fee)} + r_t^{(sr)}, & if \quad r_t^{(sr)} > r_{t-1}^{(sr)} \quad for \quad t > w \\ r_t^{(PnL)} + r_t^{(fee)} - r_t^{(sr)}, & if \quad r_t^{(sr)} < r_{t-1}^{(sr)} \quad for \quad t > w \end{cases} \tag{8}$$

The objective in Eq. 8 is to achieve a higher Sharpe ratio in each step. For this reason, we compare the approximated Sharpe ratio from two consecutive steps. If we achieve a higher Sharpe ratio in the current step compared to the prior one, we enhance the agent by adding this value to the PnL reward, otherwise, we penalize the agent by subtracting the approximated Sharpe ratio.

3   Experimental Evaluation

The DRL setup is briefly described in this Section. In addition, the dataset used to run the simulation that interacts with the RL agents is presented. The impact of the proposed reward shaping is then evaluated and compared to the two reward schemes from Sects. 2.2 and 2.3. The number of steps that an RL episode consists of is equal to 100. Since we have hourly candles, as is analytically described in Sect. 3.2, the agent is trained for approximately 4 days in each episode. The constant value α in Eq. 6 is set to 0.01. Each experiment is executed 10 times, with each instance using a different random seed. The PnLs presented, were averaged throughout the 10 experiments as well as the annualized Sharpe ratios.

3.1   DRL Setup

The RL agent is trained using the Policy Gradient (PG) approach. More specifically, Proximal Policy Optimization (PPO) [4]. In addition, the neural network architecture is Long-Short Term Memory (LSTM)-based [6]. Finally, the loss was proposed in [7] for estimating the advantage from the temporal difference residual, and the optimizer used is Rectified Adam (RAdam) and was introduced in [9]. It is worth noting that the proposed method is not restricted to the aforementioned architecture.

3.2   Dataset

The proposed method was tested on a financial dataset that included Crypto trading data of 14 currency pairs such as the BTC/BUSD, BTC/USDT, and ETH/USDT among others. The Open-High-Low-Close (OHLC) price level technique was used to subsample the market data [20], which reduces the raw data into 4 values. The dataset consists of minute price candles gathered by SpeedLab AG from 2017-08-17 up to 2022-02-12.

To utilize the dataset, the minute-price candles are resampled to hour candles. More specifically, these values are the open price or the first traded price of the set interval, the highest and lowest traded prices within the interval, and finally, the last price that a trade did occur during the interval, also referred to as the close price. The following features are inspired by [12] and were created using the OHLC values:

1. $x_{t,1} = \dfrac{p_c(t) - p_c(t-1)}{p_c(t-1)}$ 4. $x_{t,4} = \dfrac{p_h(t) - p_c(t)}{p_c(t)}$

2. $x_{t,2} = \dfrac{p_h(t) - p_h(t-1)}{p_h(t-1)}$ 5. $x_{t,5} = \dfrac{p_c(t) - p_l(t)}{p_c(t)}$

3. $x_{t,3} = \dfrac{p_l(t) - p_l(t-1)}{p_l(t-1)}$

where $p_c(t)$ is the close price that occurred during an interval at time t and $p_h(t)$, $p_l(t)$ are the high and low prices within the same interval, respectively. Additionally, time-related features are created, including day, month, week, and year features. Note that $x_{t,1}$ denotes the return as specified in Sect. 2.2 in Eq. 2. The described features are concatenated into a feature vector $\mathbf{x}_t$ for each time t.

The dataset was divided into two parts, a training set, and a test set, with the training set spanning from the start of each instrument's period to 2021-03-15, and the test set ranging from there to 2022-02-12. In total, the dataset contains 439.737 candles, where the train/test candles are 327.596 and 112.141 candles, respectively.

3.3   Annualized Sharpe Ratio

The Sharpe ratio is used to compare the return of an investment with its risk and provides an insight that returns over a period of time may indicate volatility and risk. Let $\mathbf{z}$ be a vector with the hourly returns over the test period, since our dataset consists of hour candles as described in Sect. 3.2. When calculating the annualized Sharpe ratio using monthly returns, $\mathbf{z}$ is resampled to the frequency of 1 month and it is defined as:

$$sr^m_{ann} = \frac{E[\mathbf{z}_m]}{\sqrt{Var[\mathbf{z}_m]}} \times \sqrt{12} \tag{9}$$

where $E[\mathbf{z}_m]$, $\sqrt{Var[\mathbf{z}_m]}$ are the mean and the standard deviation of the resampled monthly returns, respectively. We multiply by the square root of 12 to annualize the Sharpe ratio. In the same manner, we calculate the annualized Sharpe ratio from the hourly returns. This time, there is no need for resampling since the returns are in the frequency of hours. It can be formulated as:

$$sr^h_{ann} = \frac{E[\mathbf{z}_h]}{\sqrt{Var[\mathbf{z}_h]}} \times \sqrt{8640} \tag{10}$$

where $E[\mathbf{z}_h]$ is the mean of the hourly returns and $\sqrt{Var[\mathbf{z}_h]}$ the standard deviation. In order to annualize the Sharpe ratio, we multiply by $\sqrt{8640}$ since there are approximately 8640 trading hours in a year for Crypto currencies.

3.4   Proposed Reward Evaluation

In Table 1, it is clearly shown from the annualized Sharpe ratio, that agents trained with the proposed reward scheme, outperform the baseline PnL-based reward and the PnL with the added Sharpe ratio since the greater a portfolio's Sharpe ratio, the better its risk-adjusted performance.

In addition, in Table 1, the annualized Sharpe ratio from hourly returns is presented. In practice, it is not a usual phenomenon since the volatility of the hourly returns is typically greater than the monthly returns. However, we consider that it is worth to be also calculated since in the proposed reward, we calculate the approximated Sharpe ratio from the hourly returns.

Table 1. Backtesting Annualized Sharpe Ratio.

Reward type	sr^m_{ann}	sr^h_{ann}
PnL	1.462 ± 0.055	2.374 ± 0.079
PnL + Sharpe ratio	1.499 ± 0.060	2.484 ± 0.090
Proposed	$\mathbf{1.617 \pm 0.056}$	$\mathbf{2.641 \pm 0.083}$

In Fig. 1, the cumulative PnL is depicted, comparing the profits achieved from the three different reward schemes that were described in Sects. 2.2, 2.3, and 2.4 respectively. The standard deviation of the PnL is also demonstrated for the three agents, to illustrate the statistical significance of the obtained results.

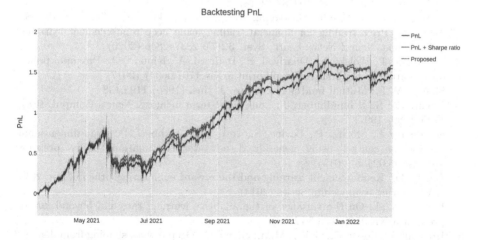

Fig. 1. Mean performance across 14 Cryptocurrency pairs of an agent trained with proposed reward vs. PnL vs. PnL + Sharpe ratio. The y-axis represents the cumulative Profit and Loss (PnL), while the x-axis represents the date.

4 Conclusion

In this work, a sharpe ratio-based reward shaping scheme was presented that was utilized in a Deep Reinforcement Learning (DRL) approach for training agents that are capable of trading profitably by boosting the risk-adjusted returns. The most notable contribution of this work is the introduction of a reward shaping scheme for decreasing the risk that often occurs in agents' trading decisions. The suggested scheme utilizes an approximation of the Sharpe ratio as an additional term to the Profit and Loss (PnL)-based reward, which motivates the agent to avoid trades that could incur losses. It was demonstrated through extensive experiments that using the proposed scheme can increase the profit and the overall portfolio performance with increased both PnL and the Sharpe ratio. To the best of our knowledge, this is the first attempt to use PnL and the Sharpe ratio as a reward function in financial trading with DRL.

Acknowledgement. This work has been co-financed by the European Union and Greek national funds through the Operational Program Competitiveness, Entrepreneurship and Innovation, under the call RESEARCH - CREATE - INNO-VATE (project code: T2EDK-02094).

References

1. Deng, Y., Bao, F., Kong, Y., Ren, Z., Dai, Q.: Deep direct reinforcement learning for financial signal representation and trading. IEEE Trans. Neural Netw. Lear. Syst. **28**(3), 653–664 (2017)
2. Huang, C.Y.: Financial trading as a game: A deep reinforcement learning approach, arXiv preprint arXiv:1807.02787 (2018)
3. Tsantekidis, A., Passalis, N., Toufa, A.S., Saitas-Zarkias, K., Chairistanidis, S., Tefas, A.: Price trailing for financial trading using deep reinforcement learning. IEEE Trans. Neural Netw. Learn. Syst. **32**(7), 2837–2846 (2020)
4. Schulman, J., Wolski, F., Dhariwal, P., Radford, A., Klimov, O.: Proximal policy optimization algorithms, arXiv preprint arXiv:1707.06347 (2017)
5. Sharpe, W.F.: Mutual fund performance. J. Bus. (1966) 119±138
6. Hochreiter, S., Schmidhuber, J.: Long short-term memory. Neural Comput. **9**(8), 1735–1780 (1997)
7. Schulman, J., Moritz, P., Levine, S., Jordan, M., Abbeel, P.: High-dimensional continuous control using generalized advantage estimation. arXiv preprint arXiv:1506.02438 (2015)
8. Dewey, D.: Reinforcement learning and the reward engineering principle. In: 2014 AAAI Spring Symposium Series (2014)
9. Liu, L., et al.: On the variance of the adaptive learning rate and beyond. arXiv preprint arXiv:1908.03265 (2019)
10. Hussein, A., Elyan, E., Gaber, M.M., Jayne, C.: Deep reward shaping from demon-strations. In: 2017 International Joint Conference on Neural Networks (IJCNN), 2017, pp. 510–517. https://academic.microsoft.com/paper/2596874484
11. Grzes, M.: Reward shaping in episodic reinforcement learning, 'adaptive agents and multi agents systems, pp. 565–573, 2017. https://academic.microsoft.com/paper/2620974420

12. Murphy, Technical analysis of the financial markets: A comprehensive guide to trading methods and applications. Penguin (1999)
13. Tsantekidis, A., Passalis, N., Tefas, A.: Diversity-driven knowledge distillation for financial trading using deep reinforcement learning. Neural Netw. **140**, 193–202 (2021)
14. santekidis, A., Passalis, N., Tefas, A., Kanniainen, J., Gabbouj, M., Iosifidis, A.: In: Proceedings of the IEEE Conference on Business Informatics (CBI), pp. 7–12 (2017)
15. Tsantekidis, A., Passalis, N., Tefas, A., Kanniainen, J., Gabbouj, M., Iosifidis, A.: Using deep learning to detect price change indications in financial markets. In: Proceedings of the European Signal Processing Conference (EUSIPCO), pp. 2511–2515 (2017)
16. Ntakaris, A., Kanniainen, J., Gabbouj, M., Iosifidis, A.: Mid-price prediction based on machine learning methods with technical and quantitative indicators. In: SSRN (2018)
17. Tran, D.T., Iosifidis, A., Kanniainen, J., Gabbouj, M.: Temporal attention-augmented bilinear network for financial time-series data analysis. In: IEEE Transactions on Neural Networks and Learning Systems (2018)
18. Moody, J., Saffell, M.: Learning to trade via direct reinforcement. IEEE Trans. Neural Netw. **12**(4), 875–889 (2001)
19. Moody, J.E., Saffell, M.: Reinforcement learning for trading. In: Proceedings of the Advances in Neural Information Processing Systems, pp. 917–923 (1999)
20. Nison, S.: Japanese candlestick charting techniques: a contemporary guide to the ancient investment techniques of the Far East. Penguin, (2001)
21. Liang, Z., Chen, H., Zhu, J., Jiang, K., and Li, Y.: Adversarial Deep Reinforcement Learning in Portfolio Management. (2018) https://doi.org/10.48550/arXiv.1808.09940

Algorithmic Forex Trading Using Q-learning

Hasna Haifa Zahrah[✉] and Jimmy Tirtawangsa

Telkom University, Bandung, Indonesia

hanazahrah30@gmail.com, jimmytirtawangsa@telkomuniversity.ac.id

Abstract. The forex market is a difficult market for traders to succeed. The high noise and volatility of the forex market make the traders very hard to open and close position accurately. Many approaches have been proposed to overcome these difficulties, including algorithmic trading. This research proposed a framework for algorithmic trading using Q-learning with the help of LSTM. The proposed framework uses a finite state space in reinforcement learning to use holding time and higher timeframe market data. The state space is designed so that the agent can open and close positions flexibly, without being restricted by a fixed time window. This allows the agent to take profits and avoid losses. The proposed framework was trained and tested using 15 years' worth of historical data of the EUR/USD currency pair in 5-min timeframe data. The system was evaluated based on various metrics such as profit, drawdown, Sharpe ratio, holding time, and delta time. The results show that with its designed finite state space and flexible time window, the proposed framework achieved consistent profits, reduced losses, and increased overall profits. This suggests that the proposed framework may be a suitable solution for forex market trading.

Keywords: Q-learning · LSTM · Forex

1 Background

The foreign exchange (forex) market is a financial market where currency trading takes place. Participants in this market range from large commercial banks to small retail traders who require a broker to access the trading platform. As a result, the forex market has become popular among retail speculators or day traders. Despite its numerous participants, Hayley and Marsh [1] reported a high rate of Forex traders losing money. This failure rate is largely due to various market characteristics [2], such as the influence of economics, politics, society, and traders' psychology.

These factors often cause traders to act impulsively, leading to noise in price data and distorted genuine market trends. The noise can also come from broker manipulation of market prices and volatility, which makes it difficult to determine when to open or close a position. These actions can significantly impact a trader's losses and profits in forex trading. The forex market has various time frame markets with its own level of volatility. The higher time frame market provides a larger picture of the price movement, while the

© IFIP International Federation for Information Processing 2023
Published by Springer Nature Switzerland AG 2023
I. Maglogiannis et al. (Eds.): AIAI 2023, IFIP AICT 675, pp. 24–35, 2023.
https://doi.org/10.1007/978-3-031-34111-3_3

lower time frame market provides detailed information. There are correlations between each time frame market that can be useful to forecast price trend of forex market.

Shavandi et al. [3] proposed a multi-agent deep reinforcement learning framework to trade in the forex market by utilizing multiple time frame markets, resulting in a 22.7% higher average cumulative return compared to a single time frame method. The research uses a fixed time window to open and close positions, aiming for consistent profits as reflected in the Sharpe ratio evaluation of 0.63. However, this fixed time window may miss potential profits if the position is closed before desired profit is achieved. Furthermore, the position could not close the position flexibly resulting in avoidable losses that may not occur if the position close before the loss.

Therefore, Removing the fixed time window can be a challenging task as it could result in inconsistent profits with potentially high loss values. However, the fixed time window may also lead to missed profits and unnecessary losses that could have been avoided. The question arises: Will removing the time window lead to increased profits and decreased loss because the time window does not restrict it?

This research aims to create a framework that facilitates the flexible opening and closing of positions in the forex market to achieve more profitable results. The framework employs reinforcement learning with LSTM to predict buying, selling, or holding actions based on price trends as the starting prediction rather than relying on random numbers. The use of Reinforcement Learning in the framework seeks to regulate losses and achieve profitable results by re-designing the state and Q-function. Prior studies on the finite state were conducted on the stock market [4], not the forex market, as most research [5–7] on the forex market utilized deep reinforcement learning. However, the previous research [4] only considered the historical price, whereas this study also considers other variables such as holding time to determine the optimal length of holding a trade position in addressing the research question.

The hypothesis for the research question is removing the fixed time window might lead to increased profit and decreased loss because there is no set time limit to open and close the position. Therefore, the independent variable is the time window of holding position and not opening a position in the forex market, while the dependent variables are profit and drawdown.

2 Related Studies

2.1 Fundamental Analysis

There are two main methods for trading in the forex market: fundamental analysis and technical analysis. Fundamental analysis considers economic, political, and social events and news that could have an impact on the forex market. An example of trading using fundamental analysis would be taking advantage of the release of non-farm payrolls news. This news reports the number of workers in the US, excluding those in agriculture and non-profit organizations. If the actual number is different from the expected number, it can cause a change in the price trend and provide an opportunity for a trader to open a position.

2.2 Technical Analysis

The other method is technical analysis, which is based solely on historical market data that reflect market participants' behavior towards economic, political, and social events [8]. Technical analysis employs several techniques, including technical indicators that are extracted to summarize market conditions, which can then be manually implemented by humans. These indicators may be based on mathematical calculations to predict price trends, such as moving average and relative strength indicator. Others may be based on market chart patterns, such as head shoulder or Elliot wave.

2.3 Algorithmic Trading

Another growing technique, particularly in the research field, is algorithmic trading. This is a method of trading that uses algorithms to automatically place and execute orders in the market [9]. These algorithms may contain simple rules, such as taking profit and stopping loss orders based on the current price and a certain length of time, or more complex methods, such as machine learning.

An example of using fundamental analysis for algorithmic trading can be found in [10]. This study utilized fundamental analysis to validate decisions made by other system strategies. Another research [11] proposed an expert advisor that leverages macroeconomic events to detect patterns and offer trading signals to day traders in the forex market. Another study [12] applied algorithmic trading using technical indicators such as RSI and MACD and achieved good results with returns up to 12%.

Reinforcement learning (RL), which is a type of machine learning, is a method in which a system learns in a certain environment by taking actions based on the given state and receiving rewards as feedback to determine if the action is good or bad. This method can replicate trading in the forex market, where the environment is the market with certain trading strategy rules. The method has also been implemented in the financial field, specifically in the forex market. In 2018 [5], deep RL was applied to forex trading algorithms with action augmentation techniques and produced positive returns in 12 different currency pairs. The same year, a forex trading system was proposed using RL with Q-networks [6], which produced an average total profit of $114.0 \pm 19.6\%$. In 2019 [7] proposed a RL method with the addition of trailing rewards for forex trading and obtained a profit of 28.6%.

3   Data

3.1   Data Description

The proposed system takes as input historical EUR/USD 5-min timeframe data similar to the baseline research [3], which was downloaded from Alpari Securities through the MetaTrader5 platform. Additionally, higher timeframe data such as 1-h and 4-h is also utilized to implement multiple time frame markets. However, this research trades in 5-min timeframe data. The data consists of date, timestamp, high price, open price, close price, low price, and volume. However, the volume feature is not utilized in this research. The data were collected from 2008 to 2016 and were used for training, which resulted in a total of 668, 752 rows. Meanwhile, 446, 458 rows of data from 2017 to 2022 were used as testing data. It's worth noting that the baseline research[3] used different historical data, specifically from 06/29/2012 to 05/25/2021, but still comparable results can be obtained as this research and baseline research used multiple years of historical data.

3.2 Data Preprocessing

This study had three possible bar trends to occur: an uptrend, a downtrend, and a flat trend which was also referred to as a no trend. To determine the trend, the close price and open price of each row data were compared. If the close price was higher than the open price, the trend was considered an uptrend. On the other hand, if the close price was lower than the open price, the trend was considered a downtrend.

In situations where the difference between the closing price and opening price was less than 3 pips, the trend was considered a flat trend. A pip is a unit of measurement used in trading and refers to the fourth decimal place in a currency pair's price. The threshold for determining the bar data as a flat varies for each time frame. 3 pips for 5-min, 5 pips for 1-h, and 10 pips for 4-h.

The action, profit, and loss values were calculated within a window data consisting of 48 rows of 5-min data, which were equivalent to 4-h. The range of window data was determined by the 4-h duration of the overlapping London and New York market sessions, which had the highest trading volume for EUR/USD and resulted in significant price movements. The window data shifted every one row; hence the current row data were the 48th data of the current window data and the next row data would be the 48th data of the next window data.

There are three values of action: buy, sell, and hold. The action value is determined by comparing the first close price and the last close price within the window data. If the last close price is higher than the first close price, the action is assigned as 'buy' to indicate opening a long position. Conversely, if the last close price is lower than the first close price, the action is assigned as 'sell' to indicate opening a short position. Long position is when a trader expects the price to move upward, while a short position is when they expect it to move downward. If the first and last close prices are the same, the action is assigned as 'hold'.

The profit was a positive number calculated as the earnings from opening and closing a position. The position was opened at the first data and closed at the last data within the window data. Therefore, the difference price between the last and the first data within the window data were calculated to get profit. The loss within the range of opening and closing a position was also calculated. Furthermore, if the value of loss was bigger than the profit value then the action was changed to 'hold' indicating a decision not to participate in the market as the chosen action results in a loss. The label for each row data was based on the action value in the next row data.

4 LSTM Training

The LSTM input was a window data consisting of 48 data with three features: bar trend 5-min, action, and profit loss. The training of LSTM model uses training data as described in Sect. 3.1 with 20 epochs. At each time step t the window data contained data from row $t - 47$ to t, hence the time step value started at 48. The label for the window data is the label value from row data t as described in Sect. 3.2. The window data is shifting by one step at each time step. The use of window data enables the LSTM model to identify patterns in the data and predict the next data trend.

The architecture of the LSTM model consists of a single layer of 64 units with a tanh activation function. In the output layer, a SoftMax activation is employed to generate the probability for each of the labels: buy, hold, and sell. The predicted action is chosen by selecting the label with the highest probability. Adam optimization algorithm is used to train the LSTM model with default hyperparameters. The output of the LSTM training is LSTM model with the best weight utilized in Reinforcement Learning training process.

5 Reinforcement Learning

The main model utilized in this research is the Reinforcement Learning model, which is composed of an Environment and an Agent as illustrated in Fig. 1. During training, the Environment received a predicted action from a previously trained LSTM. On the other hand, during testing, the Environment received a chosen action by the Agent using the Q-table trained with Q-learning algorithm.

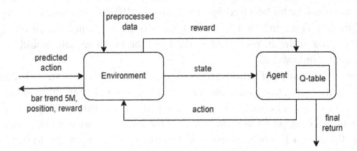

Fig. 1. Proposed Reinforcement Learning model

5.1 Reward Calculation in Environment

The environment outputs a reward to indicate whether the action taken by the agent was good or bad. The profit (P) was calculated as the difference between the close price at the current time step and the close price at the time the position was opened, as shown in Eq. 1.

$$P_t = (cp_t - cp_o) \times 10000 \tag{1}$$

where t is a time step, cp_t is a close price of time step t and cp_o is a close price of open position. The result was multiplied by 10, 000 to express it in pips, which is a tradeable unit as described in Sect. 3.2. Positive rewards were expressed as profit, while negative rewards were expressed as drawdown. The drawdown (d) as shown in Eq. 2

was calculated as the difference between the lowest close price before the agent closes the position and the close price at the open position.

$$d = (cp_{lowest\_price} - cp_o) \times 10000 \qquad (2)$$

Afterwards, the reward was calculated using profit, drawdown, and holding time as shown in Eq. 3. The holding time was the total number of bar data which the open position has been held.

$$R_t = \frac{\left(\frac{P_t}{holding\_time}\right) - (d \times holding\_time)}{(cp_o \times 10000)} \qquad (3)$$

The purpose of dividing the profit by holding time is to reduce the profit as the length of time a position is held increases. On the other hand, multiplying the drawdown by holding time maximizes the loss, meaning that holding a position for too long results in a small positive reward and a large negative reward. This calculation was used to teach the agent to not keep a position open for an excessive amount of time.

5.2 State Construction in Environment

This process generates a state that represents the information available when selecting an action. The state comprises various components as provided in Table 1.

Table 1. State components

Component	Value	Purpose
Position	*long, no, shortposition*	To define the position of agent based on action
Bar trend 5-min	*uptrend, flat, downtrend*	To know what the current trend of 5-min price is
Reward	+, 0, −	To Indicate whether the selected action is good or bad
Holding time or Delta time	30 min, 1 h, 4 h, one day	To Calculate the number of bar data that the open position has been held or the number of bar data that the agent does not open a position
Target pips	3, 10, 17, 27	To learn the closing position based on the obtained profit
Bar trend of higher timeframe	bar trend of 5-min = bar trend of 1-h or 4-h timeframe	To know whether the current 5-min trend matches the current higher time frame trend

5.3 Agent

The Agent was expected to select action from the Q-table. This was achieved by identifying the action with the highest Q-value for the current state provided by the Environment. The Q-table was a $n \times 3$ matrix where n represented the total number of determined states, and 3 represented the total number of actions, 'buy', 'sell', and 'hold'. At the beginning, the Q-table was empty, containing only zeros. Subsequently, during each iteration, the Q-function was used to update the values of each state-action pair in the Q-table. Temporal difference formula as shown in Eq. 4 was used to update the Q-value of the current state and action at time step t using the obtained reward and Q-value of the next state.

$$Q^\pi(s_t, a_t) = (1 - \alpha)Q^\pi(s_t, a_t) + \frac{\alpha(R_t + \gamma Max(Q^\pi(s_{t+1})))}{2} \qquad (4)$$

where s, a, t, R, α, and γ are state, action, time step, reward, learning rate, and discounted factor, respectively. α was set with values of 0.85 to give a fair amount of update to current Q-value. Meanwhile, a discount factor of 0.99 was set as γ to indicate that the total expected future reward was discounted by a small amount, but still considered in the calculation.

The division by 2 is the modification of temporal difference formula proposed in this research. It serves to update the Q-value with the total reward of the current state, rather than the expected future reward, so that the Q-value does not continue to increase indefinitely. Equation 4 aims to give a higher Q-value by selecting the maximum value of the next Q-value. It indicates that selected action a for state s obtained a positive reward.

On the other hand, for negative rewards, which are present in this research, the selection of maximum next Q-value is changed to the minimum as shown in Eq. 5. This modification is made to assign a lower Q-value to the selected action a for the state s that results in negative reward, thus preventing the agent from selecting action a when receiving state s from the environment.

$$Q^\pi(s_t, a_t) = (1 - \alpha)Q^\pi(s_t, a_t) + \frac{\alpha(R_t + \gamma Min(Q^\pi(s_{t+1})))}{2} \qquad (5)$$

5.4 Reinforcement Learning Training

The aim of the Reinforcement Learning training process is to update the Q-table, which is utilized by the Agent to select the best action when receiving a state from the Environment. In this training process, a random action is selected based on the state given by the Environment. The reward and next state obtained from this action are then used to update the Q-value for the current action and state using the Q-function as described in Sect. 5.3.

However, in this research, rather than selecting a random action when receiving a state from the Environment, a predicted action from a trained LSTM is used, as shown in Fig. 1. In each iteration, the Environment provides the LSTM model with a bar trend of 5-min data, position, and reward. The LSTM model then predicts the action. Additionally, a state that includes the bar trend of 5-min data, position, and reward is output from the Environment, along with the reward, and is given to the Agent to update the Q-value of the predicted action and state in the Q-table. After all the iterations, the updated Q-table is then utilized in the testing process.

5.5 Reinforcement Learning Testing and Evaluation

The Q-table generated from the training process is utilized by the agent to make decisions based on the state input received from the environment. It is expected that the Q-table contains optimized information from the LSTM, thus eliminating the need for the LSTM model to determine actions. At every time step, the environment gives the agent a state, and the agent selects the best action based on the received state by using the Q-table, as depicted in Fig. 1. After a predetermined number of timesteps, the agent will have the final profit calculated from the testing simulation.

The evaluation metrics for this research consists of several measures. The first one is the calculation of annual profit that indicates whether the system is making a profit or incurring a loss in a year. The profit calculation is described in Eq. 1. The lowest profit or the maximum drawdown indicates how much the agent loses when opening a position. It is calculated by finding the minimum value of Eq. 1 or the maximum value of Eq. 2. Furthermore, the Sharpe ratio is utilized to indicate whether the obtained profit is consistent.

The second metric is the average holding time which is the duration of time that the agent holds a position. This calculation measures the length of time the agent holds a position, whether it results in a profit or a loss. Additionally, the average delta time which is the interval between the end of the previous trade position and the beginning of the next one is also calculated. The percentage of profitable positions indicates the number of profitable positions out of all opened positions. The standard deviation of holding time is also calculated to know if the agent closes the position flexibly, hence the holding time value should vary.

6 Experiment

6.1 Experiment Scenarios

The aim of the experiment was to address the research question. The independent variable, which referred to the time window of holding a position and not opening a position (delta time), was manipulated to observe its impact on the dependent variables which were profit and drawdown. The first experiment used a fixed time window of 4 h, which was similar to the window data described in Sect. 3.2, as a baseline to compare with other experiments. The second experiment completely removed the time window from the system to see the effect without any time window involved. In the third experiment, a threshold value of one day was introduced to ensure that the holding position did not exceed one day despite the flexible position and to force the agent to open a new position at least once per day. In the fourth experiment, the threshold values of delta time were gradually increased from 30 min, 1 h to 4 h to allow the agent to open a position after a longer range from the previous closed position. It was expected to open the profitable position once the agent decided to open the position. Furthermore, target pips were added to make the agent close the position based on how much profit or loss the agent had obtained within a day.

These experiments as listed in Table 2 aimed to determine whether the system was able to achieve more profitable while reducing loss results. In each experiment, the values of the other components of the state used were constant as defined in Table 1, in addition to the values of holding time, delta time, and target pips. The starting balance for this experiment was set at $1, 000 USD. If the calculated balance reached 0 during testing, the system terminated. Furthermore, if the testing simulation reached one year, any opened position closed.

Table 2. Experiment scenarios

Scenario	Method	Parameter	
		Holding and Delta time	Target pips
1	Reinforcement Learning with fixed time window	4 h	–
2	Reinforcement learning without time window	–	–
3	Reinforcement Learning with one-daye threshold value	oneday	–
4	Reinforcement Learning with target delta time and target pips	30 min, 1 h, 4 h, one day	3, 10, 17, 27

6.2 Experiment Results

The data used in this study includes 446, 458 records spanning from 2017 to 2022. The testing simulation was performed on a yearly basis and the average result is calculated by taking the average of the results for each year. Experiment results are displayed in Table 3 and include metric information as outlined in Sect. 5.5.

The First Experiment. It involved the introduction of a time window to see if it had any effect on the results. This experiment achieved the lowest annual return, with a two-year simulation resulting in a loss in the total balance. The average profit was higher than the average loss, but the average highest profit was lower than the average maximum drawdown. This experiment had the highest Sharpe ratio value, due to the fixed time window leading to consistent profit. The average holding and delta time were 48 bar data or 4 h, as the fixed time window was set, leading to a low standard deviation of holding time since the agent did not close positions in a flexible manner. However, this experiment had the highest percentage of profitable positions among all the experiments.

The Second Experiment. It aimed to assess the impact of completely removing the time window. The results showed that this experiment achieved the highest annual return,

Table 3. Experiment results

Scenario	Annual return	Avg profit	Avg loss	Avg Highest profit	Avg Max. Drawdown	Avg Sharpe Ratio	Avg delta time	Avg holding time	Avg Std	Avg profitable position
1	36.2%	$14.2	−$13.95	$96.68	$124.845	1	48	48	0.6	50, 6%
2	654.8%	$4.5	−$3	$140.68	$74.34	0, 62	2	6	9.4	46%
3	440.4%	$2.7	−$2	$156.5	$89	0, 48	1	3	3.4	47.25%
4	42.1%	$2.8	−$2.4	$185.38	$43	0, 46	9	5	15.17	47.45%

likely because the average profit was higher than the average loss and there was a large gap between the highest profit and maximum drawdown. Additionally, the Sharpe ratio value was high enough to indicate that the profit was consistent. Although the average holding time and delta time were short (30 min and 10 min respectively), the longest holding time was 472 bar data which exceeded one day. The standard deviation of holding time was also high, indicating that the agent closed positions in a flexible manner. However, this experiment had the lowest percentage of profitable positions among the experiments.

The Third Experiment. It involved adding a threshold value of one day to the holding and delta time, making it a non-fixed time window that was part of the state component. This experiment resulted in the second highest annual return. The difference between average profit and average loss was small, with the average highest profit higher than the maximum drawdown. The average Sharpe ratio was lower than the first experiment, indicating that the profit was not as consistent. The average delta time was short, with the agent waiting only 5 min to open the next position, and the average holding time was 15 min (3 bar data). The standard deviation of holding time was lower than the first experiment but higher than the second experiment, meaning the holding time value varied but still in a flexible manner. The highest holding and delta time were 127 and 73 respectively, indicating success in restricting the agent to close positions within a day and open at least one position a day. The percentage of profitable positions was higher than the first experiment.

The Fourth Experiment. It was designed to increase the delta time with a gradient of threshold values and added the target pips alongside the one-day threshold value for holding time. This was motivated by the short delta times seen in the first and third experiments. The addition of the gradient threshold value for delta time was successful in increasing the delta time, but the target pips did not result in longer holding times, as the holding time was similar to the other experiments without fixed time window. The standard deviation value was the highest among all the experiments, indicating a high level of variation in the holding time value. The highest holding time was 475 bar data, likely due to the target pips allowing the agent to hold positions despite the one-day threshold for holding time. The highest delta time was 158 bar data. The difference between the average profit and average loss was small, resulting in a lower annual return than other experiments without fixed time window but still profitable due to the large gap between the highest profit and maximum drawdown.

6.3 Analysis Data

The second experiment, which removed the time window, resulted in a significant increase in profit, with an annual return of 654.8% compared to the baseline's 5.1% annual return [3]. The loss was also reduced, as the first experiment recorded a $74.34 loss or 7.4% average maximum drawdown, which was lower than the baseline's 11.89%. This might be due to the flexible close position, as shown in the standard deviation of holding time value, allowing the agent to close the position at a flexible time rather than a fixed time window.

Moreover, the implementation of threshold values and target pips also led to an increase in profit and a decrease in loss. The lowest maximum drawdown was obtained by implementing target pips. The threshold value and target pips did not restrict the closing position as the agent could open and close the position flexibly, as shown by the high standard deviation values in the third and fourth experiments. Contrary to the assumption, the removal of the fixed time window did not result in inconsistent profits. The first experiment, without a time window, achieved a Sharpe ratio of 0.62, which was slightly lower than the baseline's 0.63. However, Sharpe ratios in the third and fourth experiments were low, indicating that the profits were not as consistent.

The use of higher timeframes, such as 1-h and 4-h, was also beneficial. The profitable positions came from states where the bar trend of 5-min was the same as the bar trend of 1-h and 4-h timeframes. This indicates that the trend was occurring in both lower and higher timeframes and not just the volatility of the 5-min timeframe, leading to potential profits.

7 Conclusion and Recommendations

7.1 Conclusion

Removing the fixed time window for opening and closing positions in the forex market is a challenging task because it may result in inconsistent profits. However, removing this window may also lead to increased profits and reduced losses. This study proposes a reinforcement learning system with LSTM that enables flexible opening and closing of positions, eliminating the need for a fixed time window. The higher timeframe is also incorporated into the state design.

The results indicate that the proposed system without a time window improves profits by 654.8% and reduced losses by 7.4% compared to the system with a fixed time window of 4 h and the baseline paper. This is due to the flexibility of the proposed system in opening and closing positions, leading to increased profits. Furthermore, the fear of inconsistent profits due to the removal of the time window is disproven, as the proposed system still achieved consistent profits, reflected in the Sharpe ratio value of 0.62, which was only a 0.01 difference from the baseline paper.

Applying a fixed time window is found to be useful in obtaining consistent profits, as reflected in the Sharpe ratio value of 1. However, this is not suitable if the trader wants to obtain bigger profits instead of consistent profits, as it gives less profit compared to other experiments without a fixed time window.

7.2 Recommendations

This research has the possibility of being applied to different currency pairs, although it requires training on other pairs. It can also be improved by adding fundamental factors to determine forex market actions, due to their strong correlation.

References

1. Hayley, S., Marsh, I.W.: What do retail FX traders learn? J. Int. Money Financ. **64**, 16–38 (2016). https://doi.org/10.1016/J.JIMONFIN.2016.02.001
2. Moeeni, S.: Is It Necessary to Restrict Forex Financial Trading ? A Modified Model 1 Introduction, vol. 13(1), pp. 63–80 (2019)
3. Shavandi, A., Khedmati, M.: A multi-agent deep reinforcement learning framework for algorithmic trading in financial markets. Expert Syst. Appl. **208**, 118124 (2022): https://doi.org/10.1016/j.eswa.2022.118124
4. Chakole, J.B., Kolhe, M.S., Mahapurush, G.D., Yadav, A., Kurhekar, M.P.: A Q-learning agent for automated trading in equity stock markets. Expert Syst. Appl. **163**, 113761 (2021). https://doi.org/10.1016/j.eswa.2020.113761
5. Huang, C.Y.: Financial Trading as a Game: A Deep Reinforcement Learning Approach, pp. 1–15 (2018). http://arxiv.org/abs/1807.02787
6. Carapuço, J., Neves, R., Horta, N.: Reinforcement learning applied to Forex trading. Appl. Soft Comput. J. **73**, 783–794 (2018). https://doi.org/10.1016/j.asoc.2018.09.017
7. Zarkias, K.S., Passalis, N., Tsantekidis, A., Tefas, A.: Deep reinforcement learning for financial trading using price trailing. In: ICASSP, International Conference on Acoustics, Speech, and Signal Processing Proceedings, vol. 2019, pp. 3067–3071 (May 2019). https://doi.org/10.1109/ICASSP.2019.8683161
8. Pring, M.J.: Technical analysis explained : the successful investor's guide to spotting investment trends and turning points, p. 797
9. Treleaven, P., Galas, M., Lalchand, V.: Algorithmic trading review. Commun. ACM **56**(11), 76–85 (2013). https://doi.org/10.1145/2500117
10. Fundamental analysis in the multi-agent trading system I IEEE Conference Publication I IEEE Xplore. https://ieeexplore.ieee.org/abstract/document/7733396 (Accessed 02 Feb 2023)
11. Wanniarachchi, H.J., Rathnayake, R.M.S.J.K., Thilina, S.G.I., Ganegoda, G.U., Manawadu, I.: Macroeconomic event base expert advisor for forex trades: through algo trading. In: 21st International Conference on Advances in ICT for Emerging Regions, ICter 2021 - Proceedings, pp. 189–194 (2021). https://doi.org/10.1109/ICTER53630.2021.9774804
12. Salkar, T., Shinde, A., Tamhankar, N., Bhagat, N.: Algorithmic trading using technical indicators. In: Proceedings of International Conference on Communication, Information and Computing Technology, ICCICT 2021 (2021). https://doi.org/10.1109/ICCICT50803.2021.9510135

Control of a Water Tank System with Value Function Approximation

Shamal Lalvani[(✉)] [iD] and Aggelos Katsaggelos [iD]

Northwestern University, Evanston, IL 60208, USA
{shamal.lalvani,a-katsaggelos}@northwestern.edu

Abstract. We consider a system of two identical rectangular shaped water tanks. A source of constant water inflow is available, which may only be directed to one tank at a time. The objective is to find a control policy to maximize the final sum of the water levels at some terminal time T, subject to minimum water level constraints on each tank. Water exits each tank corresponding to Toricelli's law (i.e., the velocity depends on the current water level). We derive a closed form dynamic programming solution in discrete time to this problem without the water-level threshold constraints. Subsequently, we implement the value iteration algorithm on a set of support points to find a control policy with the threshold constraints, where a random forest regressor is iteratively used to update the value function. Our results show consistency between the dynamic programming solution and the value iteration solution.

Keywords: Reinforcement Learning · Optimal Control · Water Tank System

1 Introduction

Optimal control problems in which system feedback is observed between successive decisions are commonly solved using techniques that incorporate the Bellman equation (sometimes also referred to as the Hamilton-Jacobi equation) [1,2]. These techniques aim to solve a recursively defined function (sometimes called the 'cost-to-go function' or 'value function'), which defines the optimality of the different states of the system under the optimal policy. The value function may then be used to generate an optimal control policy [3]. A common approach to solve the Bellman equation is through dynamic programming, where the solution is obtained via backwards induction. However, it is generally not possible to solve all control problems through dynamic programming, and there is no guarantee that all control problems will have closed-form solutions [4].

In the machine learning literature, rather than explicitly solving for the value function, techniques that approximate the value function are commonly used [5]. One commonly used approach is the value iteration algorithm, where the value function is arbitrarily initialized at each point in the state space, and updated

© IFIP International Federation for Information Processing 2023
Published by Springer Nature Switzerland AG 2023
I. Maglogiannis et al. (Eds.): AIAI 2023, IFIP AICT 675, pp. 36–44, 2023.
https://doi.org/10.1007/978-3-031-34111-3_4

through experience with the dynamics of the system. If the state space itself is large (or even infinite), however, this approach may be computationally infeasible for every point in the state space. For large state spaces, one approach is to use the value iteration algorithm on a set of support points and use a function approximator (such as a neural network, gaussian mixture model or a set of basis functions) to generalize the value function to the entire state space (see [4–7]).

In this paper, inspired by [8], we consider a system of two identical rectangular water tanks subject to minimum water level constraints, with a constant source of inflow that may be directed to only one tank at a time. Our system is identical to [8], except we assume that water exits the tanks according to Toricelli's Law (see [9]), rather than at a constant outflow rate. We consider the objective of maximizing the sum of the water levels at a terminal time. First, we derive a solution to this problem through dynamic programming in discrete time without the water level constraints. Subsequently, we solve the problem using the value iteration algorithm with random forest regression to approximate the value function at all points of the state space. There exists a literature of control of water tank systems, such as with the use of PID controllers [10], control of water tanks in tandem [11] and control of water tanks with devices such as arduino [12]. To the best of our knowledge, however, this is the very first paper that addresses optimal control of the aforementioned model and objective.

2   The Model

Consider a system of two identical water-tanks, where the water levels at time t of each tank are denoted $X_1(t)$ and $X_2(t)$ respectively (Fig. 1). We assume that a water source with constant inflow w is available to fill either tank, and in particular may be directed at only one tank at a time. We assume the water source may be switched instantaneously between both tanks at any desired time. We let $c(t)$ denote the control variable, where

$$c(t) = \begin{cases} 1, \text{ if the hose is above tank 1 at time } t \\ 2, \text{ if the hose is above tank 2 at time } t \end{cases} \tag{1}$$

The objective is to find a control policy that maximizes the sum of the water-levels of the two tanks at some terminal time $T > 0$, which is denoted by the objective function $m(T)$, i.e.,

$$m(T) = X_1(T) + X_2(T) \tag{2}$$

We further impose the constraints that the water-levels of the two tanks must be above thresholds r_1 and r_2 respectively, i.e.,

$$X_i(t) \geq r_i, \text{ for all } t \in [0, T] \tag{3}$$

Assuming satisfaction of the constraints, the dynamics of the system may be described as

$$\frac{dX_i(t)}{dt} = w\mathcal{I}(c(t) = i) - v(X_i(t)) \tag{4}$$

where $\mathcal{I}$ denotes the indicator function, and $v(X_i(t))$ denotes the outflow rate, which is a function of the current water level of tank i at time t. Additionally, we assume water exits the tanks according to Toricelli's law, so that,

$$v(X_i(t)) = r\sqrt{2gX_i(t)} \tag{5}$$

for some constant r that depends on the dimensions of the water-tanks, where g denotes the magnitude of acceleration due to gravity. We apply an approximation to model the water level of the tanks. Note that for a rectangular tank (more generally, parallelepiped tank) with inflow w and an outflow rate given by Toricelli's Law, an equation exists to describe how the water levels change in a time period dt ([9]),

$$t = \frac{2}{z}[\sqrt{X(T-dt)} - \sqrt{X(T)} + w[ln(\frac{w - \sqrt{X(T-dt)}}{w - \sqrt{X(T)}})] \tag{6}$$

for some constant z that depends on the dimensions of the water tank. We now derive an approximation for the equation above. Note that a first degree taylor series approximation for $ln(x)$, centered around any constant $a > 0$ yields,

$$ln(x) = ln(a) + \frac{x - a}{a} \tag{7}$$

Choosing $x = w - \sqrt{X(T-dt)}$ and $x = w - \sqrt{X(T)}$, and substitution into Eq. 7, and further substituting into Eq. 6 gives,

$$t = \frac{2}{z}[\sqrt{X(T-dt)} - \sqrt{X(T)} + w\frac{\sqrt{X(T)} - \sqrt{X(T-dt)}}{a}] \tag{8}$$

Rearranging terms, and putting $k = \frac{z}{2}$ and $\beta = 1 - \frac{w}{a}$, (where we mandate that a is chosen so that $w \neq a$), it follows that,

$$\sqrt{X(T)} = \sqrt{X(T-dt)} - \frac{kdt}{\beta} \tag{9}$$

Note that if there is no inflow (i.e., $w = 0$), then $\beta = 1$, so that,

$$\sqrt{X(T)} = \sqrt{X(T-dt)} - kdt \tag{10}$$

An illustration of Eq. 9 and Eq. 10 is displayed in Fig. 2.

3   Dynamic Programming Solution

We provide a dynamic programming solution in discrete time to maximize the objective function $m(T)$. Let $dt > 0$ be small, and $N = \frac{T}{dt}$ denote the number of time-steps. For simplicity of notation, because dt is a constant, we absorb it into the coefficient k in Eq. 9 and Eq. 10. Further, we assume that $\beta < 0$ (i.e., $w > a$) if there is no source of inflow to a tank (this assumption is justified by centering a around $w - \sqrt{X(T)}$ and $w - \sqrt{X(T-dt)}$ to obtain Eq. 8). The solution below involves backwards induction on time, where Sect. 3.3 corresponds to the inductive step.

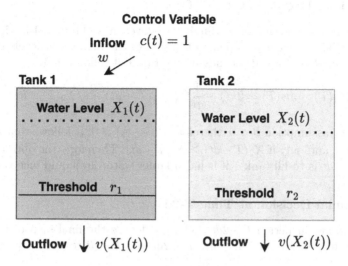

Fig. 1. Illustration of the Water Tank system. The water levels of tank 1 and tank 2 at time t are denoted by $X_1(t)$ and $X_2(t)$ respectively. The system constraints impose that water levels of tank 1 and tank 2 must be kept above the thresholds r_1 and r_2 respectively. When the control variable $c(t)$ is equal to 1, the constant inflow w enters tank 1, as illustrated above. When $c(t) = 2$, w enters tank 2. The outflow of tank i ($i = 1, 2$) at time t is given by $v(X_i(t))$.

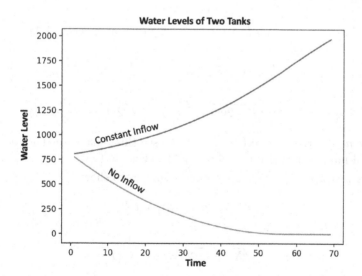

Fig. 2. Illustration of the dynamics of the tanks with a constant inflow (blue) and with no inflow (orange) for 70 s. Both tanks initially start at a water level of 800, an inflow $w = 34$ is used, and a spacing of $dt = 0.01$ is used. (Color figure online)

3.1 Optimal Decision at Time T-dt

Let $m_1(T)$ denote the sum of the final water levels if we fill tank 1 at time $t - dt$ for dt seconds, and let $m_2(T)$ denote the sum of the final water levels if we will tank 2 at time $t - dt$ for dt seconds. Using Eq. 9, it follows that,

$$m_1(T) - m_2(T) = 2k(1 - \frac{1}{\beta})(\sqrt{X_1(T - dt)} - \sqrt{X_2(T - dt)}) \tag{11}$$

Note that by assumption $\beta < 0$, therefore $2k(1 - \frac{1}{\beta}) > 0$. It follows that $m_1(T) - m_2(T) \geq 0$ if and only if $X_2(T - dt) \geq X_1(T - dt)$. Therefore, the optimal policy at time $T - dt$ is to fill tank 1 if it has a larger water level, and vice versa.

3.2 Optimal Decision at Time T-2dt

Suppose we are in period $t - 2dt$. Let $m_{i,j}$ denote the final sum of the water levels if we fill tanks i and j at times $T - 2dt$ and $T - dt$ respectively. We define $n_{i,j}$ as follows,

$$n_{i,j} = \frac{m_{i,j} - X_1(T - 2dt) - X_2(T - 2dt) - 2k^2 - 2\frac{k^2}{\beta^2}}{2k} \tag{12}$$

Note that since $2k > 0$, and because at time $T - 2dt$, we have that $-X_1(T - 2dt) - X_2(T - 2dt) - 2k^2 - 2\frac{k^2}{\beta^2}$ is a constant, maximizing $m_{i,j}$ is equivalent to maximizing $n_{i,j}$. It can be shown with substitution of Eq. 9 and Eq. 10 into Eq. 12 that,

$$n_{1,1} = -\frac{2}{\beta}\sqrt{X_1(T - 2dt)} - 2\sqrt{X_2(T - 2dt)} + k(\frac{1}{\beta^2} + 1) \tag{13}$$

$$n_{1,2} = n_{2,1} = -(1 + \frac{1}{\beta})\sqrt{X_1(T - 2dt)} - (1 + \frac{1}{\beta})\sqrt{X_2(T - 2dt)} + \frac{2k}{\beta} \tag{14}$$

$$n_{2,2} = -2\sqrt{X_1(T - 2dt)} - \frac{2}{\beta}\sqrt{X_2(T - 2dt)} + k(\frac{1}{\beta^2} + 1) \tag{15}$$

Note that $n_{1,2} = n_{2,1} \leq \max\{n_{1,1}, n_{2,2}\}$. To see this, first note that the square of any real number is greater than or equal to zero so that $(1 - \frac{1}{\beta})^2 \geq 0$, which expanding gives, $1 + \frac{1}{\beta^2} \geq \frac{2}{\beta}$. Therefore, it suffices to show,

$$b(t) \leq \{max\{a(t), c(t)\} \tag{16}$$

where,

$$a(t) = \frac{2}{\beta}\sqrt{X_1(T - 2dt)} - 2\sqrt{X_2(T - 2dt)} \tag{17}$$

$$b(t) = -(1 + \frac{1}{\beta})\sqrt{X_1(T - 2dt)} - (1 + \frac{1}{\beta})\sqrt{X_2(T - 2dt)} \tag{18}$$

$$c(t) = -2\sqrt{X_1(T - 2dt)} - \frac{2}{\beta}\sqrt{X_2(T - 2dt)} \tag{19}$$

Assume, for a contradiction, that $b(t) > a(t)$ and that $b(t) > c(t)$. It follows that $b(t) - a(t) = (1 - \frac{1}{\beta})(\sqrt{X_1(T - 2dt)} - \sqrt{X_2(T - 2dt)}) > 0$ and that $b(t) - c(t) = -(1 - \frac{1}{\beta})(\sqrt{X_1(T - 2dt)} - \sqrt{X_2(T - 2dt)}) > 0$. Without loss of generality, we assume $\sqrt{X_1(T - 2dt)} \neq \sqrt{X_2(T - 2dt)}$ (otherwise the choice of which tank to fill doesn't matter by symmetry of the system and objective function), and therefore $(1 - \frac{1}{\beta}) > 0$ and $(1 - \frac{1}{\beta}) < 0$, a contradiction. Therefore, the monotonic transformation of the objective function is given by $\max\{n_{1,1}, n_{2,2}\}$. Note that,

$$n_{1,1}(T) - n_{2,2}(T) = 2(1 - \frac{1}{\beta})(\sqrt{X_1(T - 2dt)} - \sqrt{X_2(T - 2dt)}) \quad (20)$$

It follows that $n_{1,1} \geq n_{2,2}$ if and only if $X_1(T - 2dt) \geq X_2(T - 2dt)$. Hence, the optimal policy at time $T - 2dt$ is to fill the tank with the larger water level. In the next section, we derive an inductive step to generalize the solution for backwards induction on time.

3.3   Lemma 1

Suppose that at time t_1, $1 \leq t_1 < T$, the objective function (i.e., the final sum of the water levels), under the optimal policy is given by, $O(t_1) = \max\{m_1(t_1), m_2(t_1)\}$ where,

$$m_1(t_1) = X_1(t_1) + X_2(t_1) - \frac{k_1}{\beta}\sqrt{X_1(t_1)} - k_1\sqrt{X_2(t_1)} + c$$

$$m_2(t_1) = X_1(t_1) + X_2(t_1) - k_1\sqrt{X_1(t_1)} - \frac{k_1}{\beta}\sqrt{X_2(t_1)} + c$$

For some constants $k_1 > 0$, $\beta < 0$ and real-valued c. Also assume that the optimal policy is to fill tank 1 if and only if $m_1(t_1) \geq m_2(t_1)$ (i.e., $X_1(t_1) > X_2(t_1)$). It follows that at time $t = t_1 - dt$, the optimal value of the objective function and optimal policy inherit the same form.

Proof. Suppose at time t, we fill tank 1 and act optimally thereafter. Then, by assumption, the final sum of the water levels is $\max\{f(t), g(t)\}$, where,

$$f(t) = X_1(t) + X_2(t) - (\frac{k + k_1}{\beta})\sqrt{X_1(t)} - (k + k_1)\sqrt{X_2(t)} + c + \frac{k}{\beta^2} + k^2 + \frac{kk_1}{\beta} + kk_1 \quad (21)$$

$$g(t) = X_1(t) + X_2(t) - (\frac{k}{\beta} + k_1)\sqrt{X_1(t)} - (k + \frac{k_1}{\beta})\sqrt{X_2(t)} + c + \frac{k}{\beta^2} + k^2 + \frac{2kk_1}{\beta} \quad (22)$$

On the other hand, suppose we fill tank 2 at time t and act optimally thereafter. Then, by assumption, the final sum of the water levels is given by $\max\{u(t), v(t)\}$, where,

$$u(t) = X_1(t) + X_2(t) - (k + \frac{k_1}{\beta})\sqrt{X_1(t)} - (\frac{k}{\beta} + k_1)\sqrt{X_2(t)} + c + \frac{k}{\beta^2} + k^2 + \frac{2kk_1}{\beta} \quad (23)$$

$$v(t) = X_1(t) + X_2(t) - (\frac{k+k_1}{\beta})\sqrt{X_1(t)} - (k+k_1)\sqrt{X_2(t)} + c + \frac{k}{\beta^2} + k^2 + \frac{kk_1}{\beta} + kk_1$$
$$(24)$$

Using proof by contradiction, a similar argument to the optimal policy at time $T - 2dt$ (see Sect. 3.2) may be used to show that $g(t) \leq \max\{f(t), v(t)\}$ and that $u(t) \leq \max\{f(t), v(t)\}$. It follows that, under the optimal policy, the final sum of the water levels is given by $\max\{f(t), v(t)\}$, and that at time t, the optimal decision is to fill tank 1 if and only if $f(t) \geq v(t)$.

3.4   Summary of the Optimal Policy

Note that at time $t - 2dt$, the assumption of Sect. 3.3 holds by solving Eq. 12 for $m_{i,j}$, where $n_{\{i,j\}}$ is defined in Eq. 13 to Eq. 15. Therefore, at time t-3dt, the Lemma may be iteratively be applied. Therefore, the optimal policy is that is always optimal to fill the tank with the higher water level.

4   Reinforcement Learning Solution with Function Approximation

We implement the value iteration desribed in Barton and Sutto (see [5]), with a set of support points (see Algorithm 1). A convergence bound z is used as a tolerance – when updates to the value function are less than z, the algorithm is assumed to have converged or be near convergence. In the algorithm, $V(s)$ denotes the value function, which is first updated at the support points, and then generalized to the entire state space in each iteration. We note that updates to the value function (i.e., $V(s) \leftarrow \max\{r_1 + V(s_1), r_2 + V(s_2)\}$) represent the maximum value from filling tank 1 and tank 2 respectively for dt seconds. In particular, note that R_1 and R_2 are the rewards for filling tanks 1 and 2 for

---

Algorithm 1. Value Iteration for Water Tank Control

Require: A convergence bound z
Require: A set of N support points $S = \{(x_{1i}(t_i), x_{2i}(t_i), t_i)\}_{i=1}^{N}$, where $0 \leq t_i \leq T$
   Initialize the value function $V(s) = 0$ for all s
   while $\theta < z$ **do**
   $\theta \leftarrow 0$
      for s in S **do**
         $v \leftarrow V(s)$
         $V(s) \leftarrow \max\{R_1 + V(s_1), R_2 + V(s_2)\}$
         $\theta \leftarrow \max\{\theta, |v - V_1(s)|\}$
      end for
   Update V to the entire state space based off of support points $\{s, V(s)\}_{s \in S}$
   end while
   Output the function V

---

dt seconds respectively, while s_1 and s_2 are the subsequent respective states. The rewards are use to optimize the objective function (i.e., the reward is zero unless the terminal time is reached, for which the reward is the sum of the water levels for both tanks). However, if the next state is less than the tank threshold (i.e., either $X_1 < r_1$ or $X_2 < r_2$), the reward is set to a negative value with large magnitude (i.e., -10^6) to discourage the algorithm from exploring these regions of the state space. After obtaining the value function, the optimal policy is implemented by choosing the action that achieves the larger value for the subsequent state. Note that this is computationally feasible because there are only two available actions at any time.

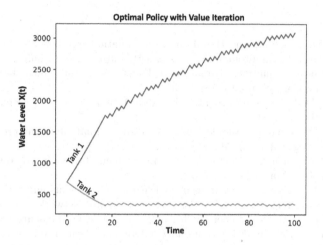

Fig. 3. Illustration of the optimal policy through value iteration.

The value function algorithm is implemented (see Fig 3) with initial values $X_1(0) = X_2(0) = 700$, thresholds $r_1 = 200$, $r_2 = 300$, time step $dt = 0.01$ and terminal time $T = 100$. The value function is updated in each iteration of Algorithm 1 using a random forest regressor with a depth of 10^6 trees in *Python* using the package *Sklearn*. The tolerance is chosen to be $z = 1$.

5   Conclusion

In Fig. 3, we observe the similarity of the solution from Algorithm 1 to the dynamic programming solution (which, however, did not account for the water level constraints). In particular, we note that the tank with the higher level (tank 1) is always filled, except when needed to prevent violation of the constraints (i.e., to keep the water level of tank 2 above 300). This results in frequent switching between the two tanks after time $t = 20$ onwards. Note that, except for satisfaction of constraints, the policy is exactly the same as the dynamic programming solution, which didn't take into account the constraints. In conclusion, the consistency of results from the dynamic programming approach and reinforcement learning approach illustrate that reinforcement learning with function approximation may be used to derive similar solutions to dynamic programming, without the explicit need for mathematical modeling of system dynamics. The computational cost of implementing reinforcement learning algorithms, however, may still be large with function approximation when the state space contains a variety of unique dynamics or is very large. Suggested future work involves optimizing the objective function with more than two tanks, and considering the case of when the tanks are not independent with each other (i.e., connected tanks).

References

1. Aliyu, M.D.S.: Solving the Hamilton-jacobi equation, pp. 333–357. Nonlinear H infinity -Control, Hamiltonian Systems and Hamilton-Jacobi Equations (2017)
2. Hamilton-Jacobi equations. Semiconcave Functions, Hamilton-Jacobi Equations, and Optimal Control, pp. 97–139 (2004)
3. Bertsekas, D.P.: Dynamic programming and Optimal Control. Athena Scientific, Belmont, Mass (2018)
4. Powell, W.B.: What you should know about approximate dynamic programming. Naval Res. Logist. (NRL). **56**, 239–249 (2009)
5. Sutton, R.S., Bach, F., Barto, A.G.: Reinforcement Learning: An Introduction. MIT Press Ltd, Massachusetts (2018)
6. Agostini, A., Celaya, E.: Reinforcement learning with a gaussian mixture model. In: The 2010 International Joint Conference on Neural Networks (IJCNN) (2010)
7. Ho, F., Kamel, M.: Reinforcement learning using a recurrent neural network. In: Proceedings of 1994 IEEE International Conference on Neural Networks (ICNN'94) (1994)
8. Lecture notes on hybrid systems - university of California, Berkeley, https://people.eecs.berkeley.edu/sastry/ee291e/lygeros.pdf
9. Atesmen, M.K.: Understanding the world around through simple mathematics: From credit card interest, basal metabolic rate to earthquake magnitude. Infinity Publishing, West Conshohocken, PA (2011)
10. Vojtesek, J., Dostal, P.: Adaptive control of water level in real model of water tank. 2015 20th International Conference on Process Control (PC). (2015)
11. Xiao, G., Liu, F.: PID- explicit predictive dual mode control for double-water tank. In: 2018 Chinese Control And Decision Conference (CCDC) (2018)
12. Godwin Premi, M.S., Malakar, J.: Automatic water tank level and Pump Control System. In: 2019 International Conference on Intelligent Computing and Control Systems (ICCS) (2019)

Decentralized Multi Agent Deep Reinforcement Q-Learning for Intelligent Traffic Controller

B. Thamilselvam$^{(\boxtimes)}$, Subrahmanyam Kalyanasundaram, and M.V. Panduranga Rao

Department of Computer Science and Engineering,
IIT Hyderabad, Kandi 502285, India
{cs17resch11005,subruk,mvp}@iith.ac.in

Abstract. Recent development of deep reinforcement learning models has impacted many fields, especially decision based control systems. Urban traffic signal control minimizes traffic congestion as well as overall traffic delay. In this work, we use a decentralized multi-agent reinforcement learning model represented by a novel state and reward function. In comparison to other single agent models reported in literature, this approach uses minimal data collection to control the traffic lights. Our model is assessed using traffic data that has been synthetically generated. Additionally, we compare the outcomes to those of existing models and employ the Monaco SUMO Traffic (MoST) Scenario to examine real-time traffic data.

Finally, we use statistical model checking (specifically, the Multi-VeStA) to check performance properties. Our model works well in all synthetic generated data and real time data.

Keywords: Multi agent systems · Deep Reinforcement learning · Statistical Model checking · Traffic controller

1 Introduction

Traffic management is one of the most important and challenging tasks in urban areas. Efficient operation of traffic lights is crucial in reducing congestion, improving road safety, and enhancing the overall mobility of the city. Conventional traffic light control methods, such as fixed-time [8,14] and actuated control [5,7,13], have been widely used for many years. However, these methods

B. Thamilselvam—Thamilselvam is supported by the DST NM-ICPS, Technology Innovation Hub on Autonomous Navigation and Data Acquisition Systems: TiHAN Foundation at Indian Institute of Technology IIT Hyderabad.
S. Kalyanasundaram—Subrahmanyam is supported by DST-SERB through the projects MTR/2020/000497 and CRG/2022/009400.

© IFIP International Federation for Information Processing 2023
Published by Springer Nature Switzerland AG 2023
I. Maglogiannis et al. (Eds.): AIAI 2023, IFIP AICT 675, pp. 45–56, 2023.
https://doi.org/10.1007/978-3-031-34111-3_5

suffer from several limitations, including suboptimal performance, inflexibility, and sensitivity to unexpected events. Traditional centralized approaches to traffic light control have several limitations. For example, large grid sizes hamper the effectiveness of the centralized control strategy they often result in sub-optimal solutions due to the difficulty of modeling complex traffic dynamics.

To address these limitations, decentralized multi-agent reinforcement learning (RL) has emerged as a promising approach for traffic light control [20]. The RL framework consists of multiple traffic signals acting as independent agents based on the information shared by its neighbours, each of which is responsible for controlling the timing of its own traffic lights. Moreover, multi-agent RL enables the traffic lights to learn to coordinate their actions, taking into account the impact of their decisions on the flow of vehicles in their vicinity and the network as a whole. These decentralized approaches allow for local decision-making and adaptation to changing traffic conditions, leading to improved traffic flow and reduced congestion.

Despite its potential, the application of decentralized multi-agent RL to traffic light control is still in its infancy, with limited work on the subject to date. For example, the linear weighted function [18] used to optimize an agent's reward may not fully capture the nonlinear throughput relationship between neighboring intersections. This limitation could potentially lead to biased optimal solutions. Moreover, the properties of the trained agent may not be satisfied. For instance, it is challenging to ensure that the maximum waiting time of vehicles does not exceed a certain threshold value.

In this paper, we propose employing Statistical Model Checking (SMC) [9] techniques in conjunction with RL for better traffic policies. The gap that RL leaves in terms of checking properties (like fairness) of a traffic policy is filled by SMC. These properties are established through SMC and the output is fed to the RL reward function. We present a comprehensive and decentralized multi-agent RL framework integrated with MultiVeStA [12] for traffic light control tested in both with synthetic and real world traffic scenario. The other problem we address in this paper is of large state representation in the RL model. Not only are such models computationally expensive, they require a lot of data as well. We develop models that use smaller state representation and reward functions that use only traffic delays only as in input. We experiment with our models and show that they compare favorably against the traditional single agent RL, actuated and fixed traffic light controllers. The idea of using RL coupled with SMC can be generalized to other domains through checking properties of models and including the results in the feedback.

The remainder of this paper is organized as follows: Sect. 2 briefly discusses some prerequisites for the paper. Section 3 reviews related work in the field of decentralized multi-agent RL for traffic light control. Section 4 presents the proposed decentralized multi-agent RL framework with MultiVeStA. Section 5 describes the simulation environment and experimental setup and Results and analysis. Section 6 concludes the paper with a discussion of future directions.

2 Preliminaries

In this section, we provide an overview of the preliminary concepts and mathematical frameworks required to understand the proposed decentralized multi-agent Reinforcement Learning (RL) framework for traffic light control.

2.1 Machine Learning Background

Reinforcement Learning: RL is a machine learning framework for learning from interaction with an environment [15] over
a sequence of time steps, where at each time step t, the agent observes the state s_t of the environment and selects an action a_t based on its policy π. The policy π is a function mapping the state to action. The action a_t then influences the state of the environment, resulting in a new state s_{t+1} and a reward r_{t+1}. The goal of the agent is to learn a policy π that maximizes the expected cumulative reward, defined as:

$$J(\pi) = \mathbb{E}_\pi \left[\sum_{t=0}^{\infty} \gamma^t r_{t+1} \right] = \mathbb{E}_\pi \left[r_1 + \gamma r_2 + \gamma^2 r_3 + \ldots \right] \tag{1}$$

where $\gamma \in [0, 1]$ is the discount factor, which determines the importance of future rewards. The expectation is taken over the distribution of states and actions induced by the policy π. Markov Decision Processes (MDPs) provide a mathematical framework for modeling [1].

Q-Learning: Q-learning [19] is a popular reinforcement learning (RL) algorithm that is used for solving problems in which an agent must learn to make decisions in an environment. In Q-learning, the agent learns a Q-function, which calculates the expected reward for taking an action in a given state.
The Q-function is typically represented as a table or a function that takes the current state and action as inputs and outputs a predicted reward. During training, the agent interacts with the environment, observing the current state, taking an action, receiving a reward, and transitioning to a new state.

$$Q(s, a) \leftarrow Q(s, a) + \alpha \left[r + \gamma \max_{a'} Q(s', a') - Q(s, a) \right] \tag{2}$$

Here, $Q(s, a)$ is the estimated value after taking an action a in state s, α is the learning rate, r is the reward received by taking action a in state s, γ is the discount factor, s' is the next state, and a' is the next action. The $\max_{a'} Q(s', a')$ term represents the maximum expected future reward from that next state s'.

Multi-Agent Reinforcement Learning: Multi-Agent RL [16] refers to a scenario where multiple agents interact with each other and with the environment to achieve their goals. In such scenarios, the actions of one agent can affect the state of the environment and the rewards received by other agents.

Decentralized Control: Decentralized control refers to a control system where multiple agents make decisions independently and locally, without relying on a central controller. Decentralized control can improve the scalability and robustness of control systems, as well as reduce the computational burden of centralized controllers.

With these concepts in mind, we now proceed to present the proposed decentralized multi-agent reinforcement learning framework for traffic light control.

2.2 Statistical Model Checking:

Statistical Model Checking (SMC) is a formal methods paradigm that provides a tool for a rapid analysis of properties expected out of (stochastic) systems [9]. The systems can be modeled as some appropriate variant of a transition system, or even a Discrete Event Simulator and the expected properties are expressed as queries written in an appropriate formal logic.

2.3 Tools

SUMO: Simulation of Urban MObility [11] is a microscopic traffic simulator widely used in the field of traffic engineering and transportation research. In addition to its standalone simulator, SUMO also offers a TraCI (Traffic Control Interface) interface, which allows external programs to interact with SUMO simulations in real-time. This is particularly useful for reinforcement learning (RL) applications, where agents need to observe the state of the simulation and take actions in response. The simulation then updates its state based on the agent's action, and the process repeats for the next step.

MultiVeStA: MultiVeStA [12] is a powerful statistical analysis tool that simplifies the integration of automated statistical analysis techniques from the Statistical Model Checking family with existing discrete-event simulators and agent-based models. It supports the use of temporal logic queries, including Probabilistic Computation Tree Logic (PCTL) and Continuous Stochastic Logic (CSL), as well as quantitative temporal expression queries such as Multiquatex. It also supports various analyses, including transient analysis, Counterfactual analysis etc. Integration of SUMO and MultiVeStA is done in [17], which we use in this work.

3   Previous Work

Li et al. [10] proposes a decentralized deep reinforcement learning (RL) approach for optimizing traffic signal timing. The authors present a novel method for using deep neural networks to approximate the Q-values of each traffic light in a decentralized RL framework, where each traffic light is treated as an independent agent that makes decisions based on local observations. This allows the system to operate in a distributed manner, making it suitable for large-scale networks with multiple traffic lights. But deep reinforcement learning algorithms can be sensitive to changes in the environment, and may not perform well in uncertain or dynamic traffic conditions. This can make it difficult to achieve robust and reliable performance in real-world traffic management systems.

Chen et al. [3] demonstrates the scalability and efficiency of the proposed algorithm in handling the complexity and heterogeneity of large-scale urban traffic systems. Although the authors evaluate the performance of the proposed algorithm using a large-scale simulation environment and real-world traffic data, its implementation in real-world traffic systems remains a challenge due to the complexity and heterogeneity of urban traffic systems. But this paper uses a relatively simple state representation that only considers the current traffic flow and the waiting time of vehicles at each intersection. This may not be sufficient to capture the complex interactions and dependencies between traffic signals in large-scale traffic systems and uses a simple reward function that only considers the average waiting time of vehicles at each intersection. This may not be sufficient to capture the complex objectives and trade-offs of traffic signal control, such as balancing the smooth flow of vehicles and reducing congestion and emissions.

Chen et al. [2] proposes a decentralized deep RL approach for traffic signal control, where each traffic signal is treated as an independent agent that learns its optimal control policy through deep RL. The approach is based on deep Q-network (DQN) algorithms. The authors evaluate the performance of the proposed algorithm using a large-scale simulation environment with real-world traffic data and compare the results with conventional methods such as fixed-time and actuated control. The proposed algorithm was evaluated using a large-scale simulation environment with real-world traffic data, but there is no real-world implementation of the algorithm reported in the paper. This limits the ability to assess the scalability and robustness of the algorithm in real-world scenarios and the traffic patterns can change over time, and the proposed algorithm does not take into account the potential for non-stationary traffic patterns.

A deep reinforcement Q-learning model [6] is suggested for enhancing traffic flow at an isolated intersection. The model takes into account partial observation of the environment and its outcomes are compared with those of full detection. However, the experiment's results are derived from a simulated traffic scenario from single intersection and do not reflect real-time traffic conditions.

An existing approaches try to maximize the reward of the agent without checking the properties of the agent. Since agent learns through experiences it is important to check the reliability of the decision. Our approach provides a solution for verifying the properties of an agent while it learns by interacting with statistical model checking (SMC). Subsequently, we evaluate the performance of our model by comparing an agent trained through SMC with an agent trained using the standard approach.

4   RL and SMC Based Approach

This section provides an overview of our approach. We use MultiVeStA for training and evaluating the RL agent model. In the training phase an RL agent collects data from SUMO and maximizes its expected reward. Additionally, it collects the output of a MultiQuatex query from MultiVeStA. The query typically would concern an important property of the RL agent's current state. In this work, we illustrate this using two queries. For a reward structure that is based on the change in cumulative waiting time between steps (minimal green time or action), the final reward is calculated as a weighted sum of SUMO data and MultiVeStA.

Reward without considering MultiVeStA output is given by:

$$\sum_{i=T-minGT}^{T} \sum_{j=1}^{N} WT_{i,j} - \sum_{i=T}^{T+minGT} \sum_{j=1}^{N} WT_{i,j}$$

where T is the current step, $minGT$ is the minimal Green Time, N is the number of incoming lanes and WT is the waiting time.

We modify the reward function as follows:

$$\sum_{i=T-minGT}^{T} \sum_{j=1}^{N} WT_{i,j} - \sum_{i=T}^{T+minGT} \sum_{j=1}^{N} WT_{i,j} - x \times (\text{output from MultiVesTA})$$

where x is a multiplicative factor that decides the importance of the query.

Finally, the MultiVeStA is again employed in the testing phase to evaluate the solution. Figure 1 illustrates this approach.

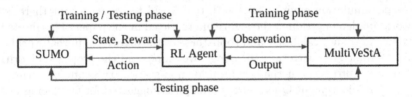

Fig. 1. Interconnection among SUMO, RL Agent and MultiVeStA

4.1   Multi Agent DQN Model for Traffic Signal Controller

Agent Actions and Action Space: The agent's actions in this context would involve deciding which traffic light phases to activate, based on the current state of the intersection, namely, the number of vehicles and pedestrians waiting at each approach. A phase is defined as a green signal to allow to move vehicles in some directions. For a pictorial illustration of phases, refer to Fig. 2. For example, in a four-legged intersection, P1 (phase 1) decides to allow vehicle movement from the north to all other directions (east, south, and west). P5 (phase 5) controls pedestrian movement. When P5 is green, all pedestrians at the intersection are allowed to move in any direction, while all other phases are red.

In this study, we focus on intersection scenarios with three and four legs. Specifically, for three-legged intersections, we analyze four distinct phases, while for four-legged intersections, we consider five phases. The agent responsible for selecting the subsequent phases uses a minimum green interval (also called a *step*). If the agent selects the ongoing phase, the current green interval is extended by the minimum green interval. On the other hand, if a different phase is chosen, the agent switches to the next phase with an intermediate yellow phase that has a minimal yellow interval. Consequently, the agent not only determines the next phase but also controls the duration of the ongoing phase by repeatedly selecting the same phase.

The action space is defined as the set of possible phases in a traffic program. As mentioned earlier in Fig. 2, a three-legged intersection has four possible actions, while a four-legged intersection has five possible actions. A phase is controlled by an action.

For a three-legged intersection, the action space is
$$A = [(W \rightarrow EN), (E \rightarrow WN), (N \rightarrow EW), (\text{all pedestrian crossing})].$$ Note that $|A| = 4$.

For a four-legged intersection, the action space is
$$A =$$
$$[(N \rightarrow SEW), (E \rightarrow WNS), (S \rightarrow NWE), (W \rightarrow ENS), (\text{all pedestrian crossing})],$$
with $|A| = 5$.

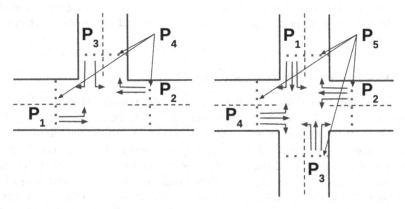

Fig. 2. An intersection with three/four legs with corresponding phases (Color figure online)

State Representation: We encode the state representation of an intersection's traffic light controller as an array of numbers, which encompasses various variables. These variables consist of the number of waiting vehicles and pedestrians approaching the intersection, the number of vehicles and pedestrians arriving at the intersection. Two observable categories exist, one within a 100-meter radius and the other within a 400-meter radius of the intersection. The state is array of size 20 representing waiting and arriving vehicle's list at an intersection.

Reward Function: We use the reward function as described in the beginning of the section, taking SUMO data and MultiVeStA output as input parameters.

Neural Network Architecture: In this approach, the neural network is trained on a dataset of traffic flow information, as per the state representation discussed previously. The neural network is designed to learn patterns in this data and predict the optimal timing of traffic lights for each intersection. By using a neural network to optimize the timing of traffic lights, it is possible to reduce delays and congestion at intersections, as well as improve the flow of traffic. However, it is important to note that the effectiveness of this approach depends on the quality of the data used to train the neural network, as well as the architecture and parameters of the neural network itself. We use the following parameters for our architecture. In the simplest setting, we train a single agent on a single intersection and test the model on multiple intersections. We call this setting the Single-RL. For such a scenario, the neural network architecture comprises an input size of 20 (state representation), and an output size of 4 (actions) for three-legged intersections and 5 (actions) for four-legged intersections.

The network comprises 4 hidden layers, each containing 400 neurons, with ReLU activation function. The optimizer used is Adam, with a learning rate of 0.001, and a batch size of 100. The discount factor used for future rewards is 0.75. The replay buffer size is set to 50000, allowing the network to learn from previous experiences. These hyperparameters are crucial in determining the performance of the neural network in the reinforcement learning task, and they can be fine-tuned to improve the learning efficiency and the overall performance of the network.

4.2 Decentralized Multi Agent Model

In decentralized Multi Agent systems agents can transfer their local data to neighboring agents. These agents then make decisions based on all the available data. We classify the agents into two categories: bordered and non-bordered. Bordered agents can receive data from only one neighbor, while non-bordered agents can obtain data from two neighbors located on the major or arterial road.

In our approach, we include additional data in the reward function of the model, as well as in the state representation. The state of the model consists of information on the current phase of neighboring agents, its geographical location, and the time elapsed during that phase. This state representation is adequate for independent model training and decision-making without requiring a centralized system. The reward includes delays from other intersections as well (Fig. 3).

4.3 MultiVeStA with Reinforcement Learning

Simple Query: What is the probability that the green time of a particular phase has crossed the threshold when there are vehicles waiting in the other direction at an intersection? This query is useful to check the fairness/liveness property of the RL agent. Since the RL agent tries to maximize the reward, if there are very less number of vehicles waiting in one direction and more number of vehicles waiting in another direction, the RL agent chooses to extend the current phase for heavy traffic side. This makes the side with less traffic to wait

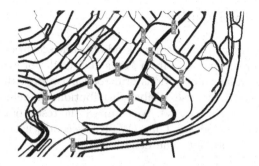

Fig. 3. Monaco SUMO Traffic (MoST) Scenario

more, which is undesirable. Result of the query is shown in Table 2, from the table we can see that the model trained with MultiVeStA yields less probability than the one without MultiVeStA, in both Low and High traffic scenarios. But at the same time it compromises the average waiting time. The ratio of the query satisfied between model trained with and model not trained with MultiVeStA is more in High than Low traffic scenario because normal RL agent tries to reduce the delay:

```
EMG(st) = if ( s.rval("step") <= st ) then
              ( if (s.rval("gtExceed") == 1 then (1)
                 else (0) fi)
           else #EMG((st)) fi ;
eval E[ EMG(st) ] ;
```

Listing 1.1. Probability of $MAX - GREEN$ crossed in particular phase.

```
t1Ut2(st,th,cp) = if( s.rval("step") <= st) then
         if ( s.rval("diff") > th ) then (1)
         else if ( s.rval("curPhase") == cp ) then
                   #t1Ut2((st),(th),(cp))
              else  (0) fi fi else (0) fi ;
eval E[t1Ut2(st,th,cp)];
```

Listing 1.2. Probability query using the Until Operator

Complex Query
What is the probability that the current phase will be prolonged, provided that the absolute difference between the number of vehicles waiting in the current phase and the other phases is a specified threshold (say 5)? This query assesses the potential for grouping vehicles in a single direction, enabling drivers approaching the traffic signal to make informed decisions about whether to slow down or speed up.

5   Experimental Results

In our experiments, we consider the two kind of traffic scenarios, one is synthetic and another one is real time data from Monaco city [4]. For synthetic generated traffic data, we use a six intersections grid road network with length of 550m. For training the model, we use Weibul distribution for vehicle generation of 1000 (500) per hour for High (Low). We compare the result of all the algorithms in terms of cumulative Waiting Time (WT) in seconds, averaged over the six intersections and cumulative Queue Length (QL).

5.1   Decentralized Multi-agent Model

In this experiment, we evaluate our reward function structure for the decentralized RL formulation. Table 1 shows the results.

Decentralized RL performs well, because it learns relationships among neighbours and takes action which leads to overall minimisation of delay and queue length.

The results for Monaco city are shown in Fig. 4. The cumulative delay at intersection level varies because the decentralized RL controller aims to reduce overall waiting time of all intersections. This can be seen through the mean waiting time (the dashed line of the controller).

Table 1. Waiting time and Queue length of all controllers in Grid Road Network

	Fixed-Time		Actuated		Single-RL		Decentralized-RL	
	WT(s)	QL	WT(s)	QL	WT(s)	QL	WT(s)	QL
Low	8498	48314	6375	34343	4206	23810	3728	19678
High	20887	134988	14404	91790	10273	64878	8340	58965

5.2   Reinforcement Learning with MultiVeStA

We use only one intersection in this case, to focus on the effect of employing inputs from MultiVeStA to the RL agent. Table 2 shows the results. *Prob* indicates the probability that the corresponding MultiQuatex query is satisfied. The multiplicative factor x used is -1 for the first query and +1 for the second query. Considering the queries, the signs are a natural choice; we choose the magnitude after some trials. The results indicate an advantage of incorporating Statistical Model Checking tools into RL systems.

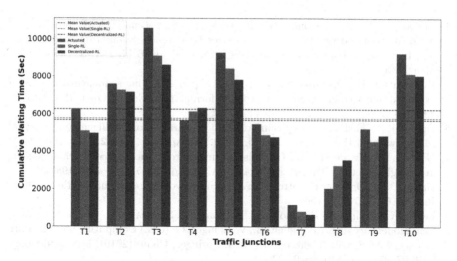

Fig. 4. Average Waiting Time at Intersections in the MOST (Monaco city) Scenario

Table 2. Result of Evaluation of Queries

	Model Trained Without MultiVeStA				Model Trained With MultiVeStA			
	Query-1		Query-2		Query-1		Query-2	
	Prob	WT(s)	Prob	WT(s)	Prob	WT(s)	Prob	WT(s)
Low	0.06	1.042	0.68	1.054	0.03	1.398	0.72	1.042
High	0.025	2.258	0.76	1.364	0.008	2.481	0.88	1.174

6 Future Directions

Our results indicate an encouraging new direction for using decentralized multi agent systems in conjunction with statistical model checking tools for traffic analysis. We believe that the following questions are interesting directions to pursue. What properties (MultiQuatex queries in our case) of the RL agent are best for fast convergence? We arrived at the multiplicative factor for the MultiVeStA input through trial and error. Is there a systematic approach to converge to the best value? How does our technique scale to large cities?

References

1. Bellman, R.: A Markovian decision process. J. Math. Mech. **6**, 679–684 (1957)
2. Chen, C., et al.: Toward a thousand lights: decentralized deep reinforcement learning for large-scale traffic signal control. In: Proceedings of the AAAI Conference on Artificial Intelligence, vol. 34, pp. 3414–3421 (2020)
3. Chen, Y., Li, C., Yue, W., Zhang, H., Mao, G.: Engineering a large-scale traffic signal control: a multi-agent reinforcement learning approach. In: IEEE Conference on Computer Communications Workshops (INFOCOM WKSHPS), IEEE INFOCOM 2021, pp. 1–6 (2021)

4. Codeca, L., Härri, J.: Monaco SUMO Traffic (MoST) scenario: a 3D mobility scenario for cooperative ITS. In: SUMO User Conference, Simulating Autonomous and Intermodal Transport Systems, SUMO 2018, 14–16 May 2018, Berlin, Germany, May 2018

5. De Schutter, B.: Optimizing acyclic traffic signal switching sequences through an extended linear complementarity problem formulation. Eur. J. Oper. Res. **139**(2), 400–415 (2002)

6. Ducrocq, R., Farhi, N.: Deep reinforcement Q-learning for intelligent traffic signal control with partial detection. Int. J. Intell. Transp. Syst. Res. **21**, 192–206 (2023)

7. Gallivan, S., Heydecker, B.: Optimising the control performance of traffic signals at a single junction. Transp. Res. Part B Methodol. **22**(5), 357–370 (1988)

8. Gazis, D.C.: Optimum control of a system of oversaturated intersections. Oper. Res. **12**(6), 815–831 (1964)

9. Legay, A., Lukina, A., Traonouez, L.M., Yang, J., Smolka, S.A., Grosu, R.: Statistical model checking. In: Steffen, B., Woeginger, G. (eds.) Computing and Software Science. LNCS, vol. 10000, pp. 478–504. Springer, Cham (2019). https://doi.org/10.1007/978-3-319-91908-9_23

10. Li, Z., Xu, C., Zhang, G.: A deep reinforcement learning approach for traffic signal control optimization. arXiv preprint arXiv:2107.06115 (2021)

11. Lopez, P.A., et al.: Microscopic traffic simulation using SUMO. In: The 21st IEEE International Conference on Intelligent Transportation Systems. IEEE, November 2018

12. Sebastio, S., Vandin, A.: MultiVeStA: statistical model checking for discrete event simulators. In: Horváth, A., Buchholz, P., Cortellessa, V., Muscariello, L., Squillante, M.S. (eds.) 7th International Conference on Performance Evaluation Methodologies and Tools, ValueTools 2013, pp. 310–315. ICST/ACM (2013)

13. Sen, S., Head, K.L.: Controlled optimization of phases at an intersection. Transp. Sci. **31**(1), 5–17 (1997)

14. Smith, M.: Traffic control and route-choice; a simple example. Transp. Res. Part B Methodol. **13**(4), 289–294 (1979)

15. Sutton, R., Barto, A.: Reinforcement learning: an introduction. IEEE Trans. Neural Netw. **9**(5), 1054–1054 (1998)

16. Tan, M.: Multi-agent reinforcement learning: independent vs. cooperative agents. In: Proceedings of the Tenth International Conference on Machine Learning, pp. 330–337 (1993)

17. Thamilselvam, B., Kalyanasundaram, S., Parmar, S., Panduranga Rao, M.V.: Statistical model checking for traffic models. In: Campos, S., Minea, M. (eds.) SBMF 2021. LNCS, vol. 13130, pp. 17–33. Springer, Cham (2021). https://doi.org/10.1007/978-3-030-92137-8_2

18. Wang, X., Ke, L., Qiao, Z., Chai, X.: Large-scale traffic signal control using a novel multiagent reinforcement learning. IEEE Trans. Cybern. **51**(1), 174–187 (2020)

19. Watkins, C.J., Dayan, P.: Q-learning. Mach. Learn. **8**, 279–292 (1992)

20. Zhou, P., Chen, X., Liu, Z., Braud, T., Hui, P., Kangasharju, J.: DRLE: decentralized reinforcement learning at the edge for traffic light control in the IoV. IEEE Trans. Intell. Transp. Syst. **22**(4), 2262–2273 (2020)

Deep Learning Based Employee Attrition Prediction

Kerem Gurler[1]([✉]), Burcu Kuleli Pak[1], and Vehbi Cagri Gungor[2]

[1] adesso Turkey, Istanbul, Turkey
{kerem.gurler,burcu.kuleli}@adesso.com.tr
[2] Abdullah Gul University, Kayseri, Turkey
cagri.gungor@agu.edu.tr

Abstract. Employee attrition is a critical issue for the business sectors as leaving employees cause various types of difficulties for the company. Some studies exist on examining the reasons for this phenomenon and predicting it with Machine Learning algorithms. In this paper, the causes for employee attrition is explored in three datasets, one of them being our own novel dataset and others obtained from Kaggle. Employee attrition was predicted with multiple Machine Learning and Deep Learning algorithms with feature selection and hyperparameter optimization and their performances are evaluated with multiple metrics. Deep Learning methods showed superior performances in all of the datasets we explored. SMOTE Tomek Links were utilized to oversample minority classes and effectively tackle the problem of class imbalance. Best performing methods were Deep Random Forest on HR Dataset from Kaggle and Neural Network for IBM and Adesso datasets with F1 scores of 0.972, 0.642 and 0.853, respectively.

Keywords: Machine learning · Deep learning · Employee attrition · Data imbalance

1 Introduction

Employees unexpectedly leaving their company is a crucial problem in many business sectors today. There may be various reasons affecting people's decision to leave their company such as working overtime for long periods of time, finding another job that pays higher wage, etc. This poses a major problem for companies because employees leaving can cause projects to be interrupted or slowed down, therefore harming the company. Even if companies can quickly replace the workers, adaptation time for new employees will potentially decrease the overall work efficiency. Recently, companies have started to use statistical methods to prevent employee attrition. They also use predictive machine learning models to determine which employees might leave.

© IFIP International Federation for Information Processing 2023
Published by Springer Nature Switzerland AG 2023
I. Maglogiannis et al. (Eds.): AIAI 2023, IFIP AICT 675, pp. 57–68, 2023.
https://doi.org/10.1007/978-3-031-34111-3_6

In this paper, we worked on three different datasets to analyze the reasons of employee attrition. These datasets are IBM Human Resources (HR) Dataset, another anonymous HR dataset from Kaggle and finally our own dataset collected in Adesso Turkey HR department. Data is obtained in an anonymized way not to violate employee privacy. We also built a predictive model with machine learning (ML) methods. Evaluated ML methods are Support Vector Machines (SVM), Linear Discriminant Analysis (LDA), Logistic Regression (LR), Random Forest (RF), K Nearest Neighbours (KNN), Naive Bayes (NB), AdaBoost (AB), XG Boost (XGB), Deep Random Forest [1] (DRF) and Artificial Neural Networks (ANN). In addition, feature importance scores were calculated with permutation importances using a random forest classifier. Features with negative or near zero scores were dropped for training. Hyperparameter optimization with Bayesian Search and cross validation was done to optimize classification performance.

It is important to note that the Kaggle and IBM HR datasets were very imbalanced. Attrition data in general is very likely to be imbalanced as people that left the company will increase over time or in the case of a fast growing company, active workers may increase rapidly thus, resulting in large number of negative attrition values. In order to handle imbalance SMOTE and Tomek Links were utilized [2,3]. Novel contributions that we provide are as follows:

- A novel dataset is obtained at Adesso company and employee attrition analysis and prediction are conducted on this dataset.
- Three different datasets are used for employee attrition analysis and Deep Learning methods showed the best performance for all of them. Therefore, deep learning approach can be utilized by other companies to effectively deal with problem of employee attrition prediction.
- Comparative performance results showed that Neural Network method performed better compared to existing studies conducted based on IBM dataset.

This paper is organized as follows. Related work on employee attrition studies are analyzed in Sect. 2. Datasets that are used are explained in Sect. 3. In Sect. 4, algorithms used in the paper and their results on all datasets are discussed. Finally in Sect. 5, the paper is concluded.

2   Related Work

Yadav et al. [4] worked on the Kaggle HR Dataset listed above. They used Recursive Feature Elimination with Cross Validation for feature selection. This approach uses various subsets of features to determine the best set of features. They applied LR, SVM, RF, Decision Tree (DT) and AdaBoost (AB). Best performing method was Random Forest with feature selection for both accuracy and F1 score metrics.

Another study was conducted on IBM HR dataset and a dataset from a bank by Zhao et al. [5] They achieved highest accuracy with LR, precision with

LDA, Recall and F1 score with a Neural Network (NN) and AUC with Gradient Boosting on IBM data with 1500 samples. On 1000 sample bank dataset, RF showed the best precision while XGB was best in the rest of the metrics. Some of the top feature importance scores for the bank data obtained with XGB are shown in Table 1.

Table 1. Feature Importances of Bank Data [5]

Feature	Importance Score
Last Pay Raise	214
Job Tenure	77
Age	63
Compensation	40
Specialized Area	36
Department	31
Education Background	31

Qutub et al. [6] applied DTs, RF, LR, GB, AB and Stochastic Gradient Descent (SGD) and also pairwise ensembles of some of these methods and found that Logistic Regression alone performed best. Another study conducted by Ozdemir. et al. [11] also identified Logistic Regression as the best method with accuracy of 0.871. In Table 2, some previous studies conducted on IBM data were listed.

Table 2. Comparison of best method of studies on IBM Dataset

Authors	Year	Method	Accuracy	Precision	Recall	F1 Score	AUC
Yiğit et al. [7]	2017	Support Vector Machines	0.897	0.98	0.37	0.53	
Boomhower et al. [8]	2018	Logistic Regression	74.59	-	-	-	-
Qutub et al. [6]	2021	Logistic Regression	0.88	0.74	0.46	0.57	0.8593
Fallucchi et al. [9]	2020	Logistic Regression	0.875	0.663	0.337	0.445	-
Proposed Method	2023	**ANN**	**0.885**	**0.66**	**0.625**	**0.642**	**0.831**

Existing studies give insights on causes of employee attrition and predict employee attrition with various models. However, deep learning methods are usually not used or were not very effective. In this study, we utilize two deep learning methods DRF and ANN and show that they outperformed other machine learning models.

3 Dataset

HR Analytics dataset obtained from Kaggle has 15000 samples with 3571 of them leaving the company. IBM HR Analytics is a synthetic dataset which has 35 features, 1470 samples and 237 of them have positive attrition value. Lastly, our own dataset collected in Adesso Turkey has 1087 samples and 18 features with 569 positive attrition. Permutation importances were used with base classifiers on three different datasets and results can be seen in Figs. 1, 2 and 3.

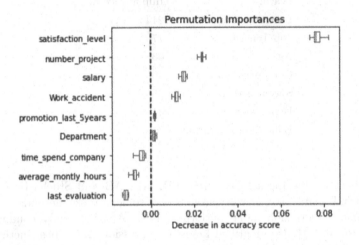

Fig. 1. Feature Importances on Kaggle HR Analytics Dataset

Overall, satisfaction level of employees, number of projects assigned, salary and whether they had a work accident is observed as a most important attrition factor for the first dataset. On IBM dataset, working overtime was the most important followed by income, distance from home, age, years at company and so on. City of residence in Adesso data had the highest score. This is caused by the fact that most of the employees working outside İstanbul left the company. We also see total experience, Adesso experience, graduated university, age and marital status have considerable impacts on employee attrition.

We can see that similar features are important across the datasets. For instance, income and satisfaction levels in first two datasets have high scores. We also observe evaluation scores of employees, gender and department had little to no effect on attrition across our datasets. Both IBM and Adesso datasets show that attrition is highly dependent on how long the employee was working in the company and also in their overall career. Employees with lower experience and age tended to leave more than the others in Adesso, however the opposite case was seen in IBM. Distance from home in IBM and city of residence in Adesso are similar features and they are both important.

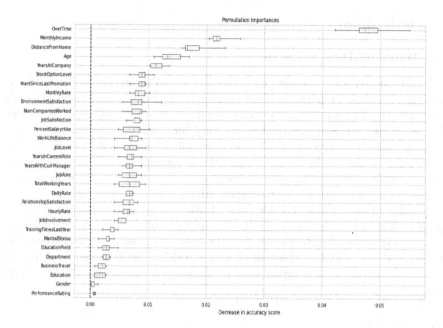

Fig. 2. Feature Importances on IBM HR Dataset

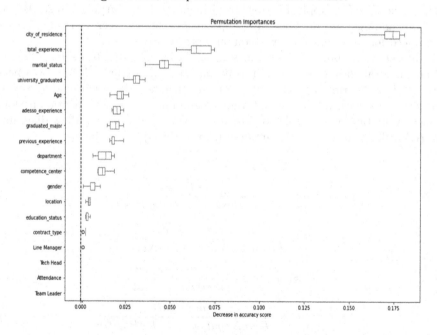

Fig. 3. Feature Importances on Adesso HR Dataset

4 Methodology

4.1 Handling Data Imbalance

In both IBM and other Kaggle HR datasets, there is a considerable data imbalance that needs to be handled. Oversampling and undersampling are two main approaches to data imbalance and for these datasets, oversampling is more compatible because the sample count is not very high. There are multiple ways of oversampling a minority class. Chawla et al. [3] proposed SMOTE method for this problem which works by creating synthetic samples instead of repeating the same examples multiple times. For every minority class sample, k amount of neighbours are selected and new samples are created in their direction.

Another method SMOTE with Tomek Links is proposed by Batista et al. [10] which utilizes smote for oversampling the minority class, but also uses Tomek links on over sampled data for cleaning the data and preventing overfitting. We applied SMOTE, Random Oversampling and SMOTE with Tomek Link on our data and observed great improvements to the performance with SMOTE Tomek Links.

4.2 Methods

In this study, we also applied various traditional machine learning and statistical methods and also two deep learning approaches, namely Deep Random Forests and a feed forward neural network on our three datasets.

Datasets were split as 70% train, 15% validation and 15% test sets. Different balancing strategies were tested on train dataset and feature selection was performed after determining the best balancing strategy. Hyperparamater tuning was performed with validation and train set and final model classification performance evaluation was completed. Figure 4 shows the overall workflow diagram. Metrics utilized for evaluation are described in the equations below.

$$Precision = \frac{TruePositive}{TruePositive + FalsePositive} \tag{1}$$

$$Recall = \frac{TruePositive}{TruePositive + FalseNegative} \tag{2}$$

$$F1Score = 2 * \frac{precision * recall}{precision + recall} \tag{3}$$

$$Specificity = \frac{TrueNegative}{TrueNegative + FalsePositive} \tag{4}$$

$$AUC = \int_0^1 sensitivity(Specificity^{-1}(x))\, d(x) \tag{5}$$

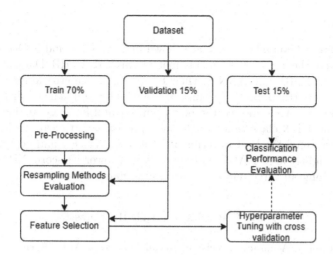

Fig. 4. Proposed Method Diagram

4.3 Hyperparameter Optimization

Hyperparameter optimization was applied with Bayesian search on ML models with search spaces that are commonly used for each algorithm. Optimization process was applied manually on Deep Random Forest and Neural Network models. For Neural Networks; various layer sizes, number of layers, activation functions, loss functions, optimizers, learning rates, weight initializations and regularizations were tested.

The final architecture used for the first dataset is 3 hidden layers with 64 neurons with relu activation, output layer with sigmoid, l2 regularization on layers with alpha 1e−3, node dropout of 5e−2 and uniform weight initialization in hidden layers, Xavier on output layer. Training was done with Adam optimizer with learning rate of 1e−2, batch size of 1024 and early stopping patience of 30.

For IBM, network of 4 layers of 128 neurons with l2 regularization with alpha 1e−3, dropout of 1e−1 with tanh activation in hidden layers and sigmoid at output and Xavier uniform initialization for weights was trained with Adam optimizer, mini batches of 256, learning rate of 1e−2 and early stopping patience of 30.

For Adesso data, 3 layers of 256 neurons with tanh activation and output neuron with sigmoid were used with Xavier uniform initialization, l2 regularization with alpha of 1e−1 and dropout of 1e−1. Adam optimizer with full batch, learning rate of 1e−3 and early stopping patience of 50 was used at training.

Binary cross entropy was used as a loss function for all datasets. For imbalanced datasets, binary cross entropy with weights based on class ratios was tested and although showing improvement when oversampling is not used, SMOTE Tomek link oversampling with normal binary cross entropy loss performed better.

4.4 Results

Experiment results on all datasets are shown in Tables 3, 4 and 5. Deep Random Forest showed the best scores in all metrics in Kaggle HR Dataset which is followed by XGB, RF and ANN by their F1 score. F1 is a critical metric in both IBM and Kaggle HR datasets because of their highly imbalanced distribution.

On IBM data, ANN showed the best accuracy and F1 score among all methods. SVM and KNN classifiers had the best precision and recall, respectively.

ANN performed the best in terms of F1 score, precision and accuracy. Deep RF showed slightly higher AUC score and slightly lower F1 score. NB performed the worst among all three datasets with a high margin.

Table 3. Results on Kaggle HR Dataset

Method	Accuracy	Precision	Recall	F1 Score	AUC	Specificity
RF	0.984	0.984	0.947	0.965	0.99	0.995
SVC	0.935	0.88	0.84	0.862	0.953	0.964
LDA	0.763	0.502	0.804	0.619	0.827	0.75
KNN	0.92	0.88	0.834	0.834	0.959	0.948
Bagging	0.935	0.875	0.843	0.862	0.92	0.964
AdaBoost	0.956	0.929	0.882	0.905	0.98	0.978
XGBoost	0.986	0.988	0.953	0.97	0.991	0.996
LR	0.771	0.514	0.81	0.629	0.828	0.759
NB	0.49	0.3	0.85	0.445	0.795	0.375
DRF	**0.987**	**0.99**	**0.955**	**0.972**	**0.99**	**0.997**
ANN	0.965	0.961	0.892	0.925	0.983	0.988

Table 4. Results on IBM HR Dataset

Method	Accuracy	Precision	Recall	F1 Score	AUC	Specificity
RF	0.864	0.647	0.392	0.488	0.783	0.957
SVC	0.894	0.812	0.464	0.59	0.849	0.978
LDA	0.882	0.9	0.321	0.473	0.824	0.992
KNN	0.62	0.284	0.857	0.426	0.738	0.573
Bagging	0.882	0.807	0.375	0.512	0.757	0.982
AdaBoost	0.858	0.571	0.571	0.571	0.813	0.915
XGBoost	0.852	0.55	0.589	0.568	0.801	0.904
LR	0.876	0.652	0.535	0.588	0.833	0.943
NB	0.676	0.275	0.589	0.375	0.696	0.693
DRF	0.87	0.636	0.5	0.56	0.8	0.943
ANN	**0.885**	**0.66**	**0.625**	**0.642**	**0.831**	**0.936**

Table 5. Results on Adesso HR Dataset

Method	Accuracy	Precision	Recall	F1 Score	AUC	Specificity
RF	0.802	0.802	0.821	0.811	0.87	0.782
SVC	0.697	0.676	0.797	0.732	0.84	0.589
LDA	0.771	0.783	0.773	0.778	0.833	0.769
KNN	0.802	0.77	0.88	0.822	0.862	0.717
Bagging	0.641	0.603	0.904	0.723	0.801	0.358
AdaBoost	0.777	0.76	0.833	0.795	0.837	0.717
XGBoost	0.796	0.793	0.821	0.807	0.864	0.769
LR	0.746	0.752	0.642	0.734	0.819	0.884
NB	0.759	0.857	0.589	0.375	0.696	0.693
DRF	0.839	0.822	0.88	0.85	0.928	0.794
ANN	**0.845**	**0.839**	**0.869**	**0.853**	**0.912**	**0.82**

Random oversampling, SMOTE and SMOTE with Tomek Links are applied for oversampling and balancing the class distributions on datasets except Adesso, which is already balanced. The results are compared with Logistic Regression as a base method in Tables 6 and 7. On IBM dataset, SMOTE with Tomek Links showed the best performance. Pure SMOTE was the worst performing one in terms of F1 score. On Kaggle HR dataset, three oversampling methods showed similar performance, but SMOTE methods were slightly better than Random Oversampling. Accuracy metric tends to be inflated in imbalanced datasets, because model can learn to mostly predict majority class. This is the reason Specificity and therefore, accuracy is higher with no oversampling in IBM dataset.

Table 6. Tests of Resampling Methods on IBM

Method	Accuracy	Precision	Recall	F1 Score	AUC	Specificity
No Oversampling	0.873	0.600	0.375	0.462	0.758	0.957
Random	0.745	0.300	0.562	0.391	0.747	0.777
SMOTE	0.841	0.444	0.375	0.407	0.723	0.920
SMOTE + Tomek Link	0.873	0.577	0.469	0.517	0.804	0.941

Table 7. Tests of Resampling Methods on Kaggle HR

Method	Accuracy	Precision	Recall	F1 Score	AUC	Specificity
No Oversampling	0.779	0.560	0.313	0.401	0.813	0.924
Random	0.759	0.495	0.798	0.611	0.822	0.747
SMOTE	0.761	0.498	0.807	0.616	0.823	0.747
SMOTE + Tomek Link	0.761	0.498	0.807	0.616	0.822	0.747

In addition, feature importances were calculated with permutation importance scores. Effect of feature selection was measured on a logistic regression base model and features were dropped iteratively from lowest to highest score until performance drops. For IBM, Performance Rating and Gender, for Kaggle data last evaluation and for Adesso data team leader, attendance, tech head, line manager and contract type features were dropped.

On IBM dataset, feature selection resulted in slight improvement for all five metrics with considerable around 6% increase in F1, recall and precision. For other datasets a notable improvement is not observed. Results are shown in Tables 8, 9 and 10.

Table 8. Feature Selection on IBM

Method	Accuracy	Precision	Recall	F1 Score	AUC	Specificity
Without Feature Selection	0.873	0.577	0.469	0.517	0.804	0.941
With Feature Selection	0.886	0.630	0.531	0.576	0.811	0.947

Table 9. Feature Selection on Kaggle HR

Method	Accuracy	Precision	Recall	F1 Score	AUC	Specificity
Without Feature Selection	0.761	0.498	0.807	0.616	0.822	0.747
With Feature Selection	0.763	0.501	0.792	0.613	0.822	0.754

Table 10. Feature Selection on Adesso

Method	Accuracy	Precision	Recall	F1 Score	AUC	Specificity
Without Feature Selection	0.778	0.736	0.848	0.788	0.827	0.711
With Feature Selection	0.778	0.736	0.848	0.788	0.831	0.711

5   Conclusion

In this paper, employee attrition was predicted with multiple Machine Learning and Deep Learning algorithms with feature selection and hyperparameter optimization and their performances are evaluated with multiple metrics. ANN in IBM dataset and Adesso HR dataset, and Deep RF in Kaggle HR dataset showed the best overall performance considering all metrics. In the first two datasets, positive attrition samples are minority, therefore specificity and accuracy values tend to be high. Precision and recall are more important for our use case and F1 score which gives as harmonic average of the two metric evaluates the overall performance of our models.

Multiple other studies on IBM dataset were also analyzed and the proposed method performed better than existing methods the literature. Our experiments suggest that deep learning methods are promising for the problem of predicting employee attrition.

Balancing the data with first oversampling the minority class with SMOTE and undersampling it with Tomek Links was very effective for our datasets and improved training performance considerably. SMOTE with Tomek Links performed better than no oversampling, random oversampling and SMOTE in IBM dataset. SMOTE Tomek Links and SMOTE only showed the best performance on Kaggle HR followed by random oversampling and no oversampling.

We also observed that similar features across different datasets showed similar permutation importance ranks. This shows us which factors should or should not be considered for employee attrition problem. Features, such as income, working overtime, experience and age, are observed to be important factors for employee attrition, whereas performance evaluation and gender were not critical features in multiple datasets.

In the future, Adesso HR dataset can be expanded with salary level or employee satisfaction values, since they proved to be a strong predictor for employee attrition in other two datasets. Experiments also demonstrate that Deep Learning approaches show very promising results for predicting employee attrition and can be studied further in the future with new models, architectures and approaches.

References

1. Zhou, Z.-H., Feng, J.: Deep Forest: towards an alternative to deep neural networks. In: Proceedings of the Twenty-Sixth International Joint Conference on Artificial Intelligence 2017, pp. 3553–3559. https://doi.org/10.24963/ijcai.2017/497
2. Tomek, I.: Two modifications of CNN. IEEE Trans. Syst. Man Cybern. **6**, 769–772 (1976)
3. Chawla, N.V., Bowyer, K.W., Hall, L.O., Kegelmeyer, W.P.: SMOTE: synthetic minority over-sampling technique. J. Artif. Intell. Res. **16**, 321–357 (2002)
4. Yadav, S., Jain, A., Singh, D.: Early prediction of employee attrition using data mining techniques. In: 2018 IEEE 8th International Advance Computing Conference (IACC) (2018). https://doi.org/10.1109/iadcc.2018.8692137
5. Zhao, Y., Hryniewicki, M.K., Cheng, F., Fu, B., Zhu, X.: Employee turnover prediction with machine learning: a reliable approach. In: Intelligent Systems and Applications, pp. 737–758 (2018). https://doi.org/10.1007/978-3-030-01057-7_56
6. Qutub, A., Al-Mehmadi, A., Al-Hssan, M., Aljohani, R., Alghamdi, H.: Prediction of employee attrition using machine learning and ensemble methods. Int. J. Mach. Learn. Comput. **11**, 110–114 (2021). https://doi.org/10.18178/ijmlc.2021.11.2.1022
7. Yiğit, I.O., Shourabizadeh, H.: An approach for predicting employee churn by using data mining. In: International Artificial Intelligence and Data Processing Symposium (IDAP), Malatya, Turkey, 16–17 September 2017. IEEE (2017). https://doi.org/10.1109/IDAP.2017.8090324
8. Frye, A., Boomhower, C., Smith, M., Vitovsky, L., Fabricant, S.: Employee attrition: what makes an employee quit? SMU Data Sci. Rev. **1** (2018). Article 9. https://scholar.smu.edu/cgi/viewcontent.cgi?article=1010&context=datasciencereview

9. Fallucchi, F., Coladangelo, M., Giuliano, R., William De Luca, E.: Predicting employee attrition using machine learning techniques. Computers **9**(4), 86 (2020). https://doi.org/10.3390/computers9040086

10. Batista, G., Prati, R., Monard, M.-C.: A study of the behavior of several methods for balancing machine learning training data. SIGKDD Exp. **6**, 20–29 (2004). https://doi.org/10.1145/1007730.1007735

11. Ozdemir, F., Coskun, M., Gezer, C., Gungor, V.: Assessing employee attrition using classifications algorithms, pp. 118–122 (2020). https://doi.org/10.1145/3404663.3404681

Deep Reinforcement Learning for Robust Goal-Based Wealth Management

Tessa Bauman$^{(\boxtimes)}$ ⓘ, Bruno Gašperov ⓘ, Stjepan Begušić ⓘ,
and Zvonko Kostanjčar ⓘ

University of Zagreb, Faculty of Electrical Engineering and Computing, Laboratory
for Financial and Risk Analytics, Unska 3, 10000 Zagreb, Croatia
`tessa.bauman@fer.hr`

Abstract. Goal-based investing is an approach to wealth management
that prioritizes achieving specific financial goals. It is naturally formulated as a sequential decision-making problem as it requires choosing
the appropriate investment until a goal is achieved. Consequently, reinforcement learning, a machine learning technique appropriate for sequential decision-making, offers a promising path for optimizing these investment strategies. In this paper, a novel approach for robust goal-based
wealth management based on deep reinforcement learning is proposed.
The experimental results indicate its superiority over several goal-based
wealth management benchmarks on both simulated and historical market data.

Keywords: Deep reinforcement learning · Goal-based wealth
management · Robustness · Portfolio optimization

1 Introduction

Goal-based wealth management (GBWM), also known as goal-based investing
[1], is a relatively new class of approaches to wealth management that focus on
attaining specific financial objectives (goals). As opposed to more traditional
approaches to wealth management, in which the notion of expected profit and
loss (PnL) plays a central role, GBWM revolves around maximizing the probability of goal attainment. Common investment goals include saving for college
tuition, retirement, or purchasing a home. Recent years have seen an uptick in
the popularity of GBWM [2], particularly through the use of target date funds
(TDFs). TDFs, also known as life-cycle funds [3] or target-retirement funds,
are mutual funds or exchange-traded funds that provide investors with an asset
allocation aimed at fulfilling a target (goal) by a specified target date (e.g. a
retirement date). Typically, as the target date approaches, the asset allocation
shifts towards a more conservative, i.e., less risky strategy. During earlier time
periods, there is a greater emphasis on investments in equities, while later time
periods are characterized by a higher concentration of investments in bonds.

© IFIP International Federation for Information Processing 2023
Published by Springer Nature Switzerland AG 2023
I. Maglogiannis et al. (Eds.): AIAI 2023, IFIP AICT 675, pp. 69–80, 2023.
https://doi.org/10.1007/978-3-031-34111-3_7

This pattern is typically illustrated by glide paths [4] - functions that show the percentage of wealth invested in a certain type of asset over time. However, using fixed glide paths can be suboptimal; for example, in situations when the target date draws close and the goal is not yet accomplished, it is clear that more risk should be taken on through larger positions in equity. This begets a new risk paradigm [5] according to which risk is not directly associated with the volatility of underlying assets, as is the case in traditional portfolio optimization, but rather with the prospect of not achieving the investment goal. Since GBWM involves making a series of investment decisions over time in fluctuating market conditions, each affecting the future position of the investor, it is naturally framed as a problem in sequential decision-making under uncertainty. Reinforcement learning (RL), due to its capacity to tackle sequential decision-making tasks in a data-driven fashion, offers a particularly promising path to GBWM, especially through its model-free and deep (DRL) algorithms. Multiple applications of (D)RL in quantitative finance exist, ranging from standard portfolio optimization [6,7], to market making[1] [9–11] and optimal trade execution [12]. On the other hand, applications of (D)RL to GBWM are still very scarce, despite its vast potential for the field. In this paper, a novel approach for GBWM based on DRL, with a focus on the robustness of the resulting strategies, is proposed. We demonstrate its superior performance over several standard GBWM benchmarks on both simulated and historical market data.

2   Related Work

2.1   Deterministic Glide Path

A deterministic glide path is a simple approach for GBWM. While essentially a heuristic, it has been adopted by many investors due to its simplicity and intuitive appeal. Note that rules of thumb, such as *100-age*, which suggests that an individual's stock allocation should be equal to 100 minus their age, are frequently used in retirement asset allocation [13,14]. However, this strategy has been criticized for its sole reliance on the time remaining to the target date [15,16]. Despite this, deterministic glide paths are frequently used for target date fund allocation as they provide a straightforward and systematic approach to managing risk as the target date approaches[2]. We focus on the form:

$$\alpha_t = 1 - \frac{t}{T},$$

where α_t is the portfolio weight of the stock at time t and T is the target time.

---

[1] Unlike in GBWM, in market making, increasing levels of risk are typically incurred as the terminal time is approached [8], resulting in weaker inventory penalization.

[2] An example is given by the asset allocation of Fidelity Freedom Funds (https://www.fidelity.com/mutual-funds/fidelity-fund-portfolios/freedom-funds).

2.2   Merton's Constant

In Merton's seminal work on lifetime portfolio selection [17], it is assumed that the riskless asset has a constant rate of return r, while the price of the risky asset $(S_t)_t$ follows the dynamics $dS_t = \mu S_t dt + \sigma S_t dZ_t$. Here, $Z(t)$ is a standard Brownian motion, μ is the expected rate of return and σ is the volatility of the underlying asset. Under this framework, it is demonstrated that, for an investor with a Constant Relative Risk Aversion (CRRA) utility[3], it is optimal to maintain constant portfolio weights of each asset. The optimal weight of the risky asset equals:

$$\alpha_t = \frac{\mu - r}{(1 - \gamma)\sigma^2}.$$

2.3   Variance Budgeting

Bruder *et al.* [18] describe an individual's risk aversion by specifying the maximum cumulative portfolio variance they are willing to take on over the investment period, called the variance budget. The authors consider this approach (restricted to the universe of two assets) and model their objective as maximizing the expected wealth at maturity $\alpha_t = \arg\max \mathbb{E}[X_T]$ subject to a predefined amount of risk $\int_0^T \alpha_t^2 \sigma_t^2 X_t^2 dt \leq V^2$, where V^2 is the total variance budget of the strategy from the start date to the target date. The optimal allocation strategy is given by:

$$\alpha_t = \frac{V}{\sigma_t \sqrt{T} X_t}.$$

2.4   Dynamic Programming

Das et. al [16] developed a discrete-time dynamic programming algorithm to create a portfolio trading strategy that maximizes the probability of an investor reaching its target wealth within a predetermined time frame. The approach utilizes portfolios from the efficient frontier, selecting one efficient portfolio at time step t to hold until the next period $t+1$. A state space consisting of time and wealth is divided into individual states by a grid. States are evaluated based on how likely they are to lead to states in which the goal is reached. This evaluation is used to determine, at each time step, the portfolio that is most likely to lead to states with larger values. Figure 1 is presented for a better understanding of the method. At time $T-1$, the investor's wealth is W_{T-1}. The investor then chooses the portfolio pair (μ, σ) from the efficient frontier that maximizes the probability of achieving the goal wealth at time T. The value of the state W_{T-1} is obtained and is then used to evaluate earlier states using backward recursion. In order to compute these probabilities, the evolution of the portfolio wealth needs to be modeled. The authors choose the Geometric Brownian motion, remarking that the method is also applicable to other models.

---

[3] The CRRA utility $\mathcal{U}$ is given by: $\mathcal{U}(x) = x^\gamma/\gamma$, $\gamma < 1$, where $1 - \gamma$ is the coefficient of relative risk aversion.

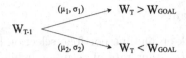

Fig. 1. Simplified diagram of the dynamic programming approach

2.5 Reinforcement Learning-Based Approaches

Pendharkar and Cusatis [19] use RL to construct a two-asset personal retirement portfolio optimized for long-term performance (i.e., a period of a decade or more). Yet the proposed approach uses neither goal-based reward criteria nor time as a state variable, making it difficult to classify it under GBWM. Dixon and Halperin [20] propose two practical algorithms - G-Learner, a generative framework, and GIRL, an extension of G-Learning to the setting of inverse RL. The focus is on their use for GBWM (optimization of retirement plans) in the context of robo-advising services. Another RL-based approach is provided by Das and Varma [21], where Q-learning is used to obtain the same strategy as in their previous work using dynamic programming [16]. The comparative advantages of the RL approach, particularly its superior handling of larger state and action spaces, are accentuated by the authors.

3   Methodology

We consider the GBWM framework as introduced in [16,21] and significantly expand it, primarily by a) putting forth a non-tabular approach based on deep neural networks (NNs) and b) introducing more rigorous training and testing procedures with an emphasis on robustness and generalization.

3.1   Markov Decision Process for Goal-Based Wealth Management

The underlying problem is modeled as a discrete-time Markov Decision Process (MDP) and then approached as an episodic RL task. An MDP is defined as a quintuple (S, A, P, R, γ), where S is the state space, A the action space, $P : S \times A \times S \mapsto [0,1]$ a transition probability function, $R : S \times A \mapsto R$ a reward function and $\gamma \in [0,1]$ a discount factor.

State Space. The state at time t is defined as $s_t = (\frac{t}{T}, \frac{W_t}{W_G})$, where W_t is the current total wealth, T the target date, and W_G the goal wealth. $W_t = w_B B_t + w_S S_t$, where B_t (S_t) is the price of the riskless (risky) asset at time t, which fluctuates in time, and w_B (w_S) the corresponding amounts held by the investor. We assume $w_B, w_S \geq 0$, i.e., short (negative) positions are not allowed. Clearly, $0 \leq \frac{t}{T} \leq 1$ and $0 \leq \frac{W_t}{W_G} < \infty$ (since $B_t \geq 0, S_t \geq 0$). The inclusion of $\frac{W_t}{W_G}$, a simple measure of how close the investor is (in relative terms) to achieving their goals, induces position-dependent behavior in policies, which is in line with the GBWM risk paradigm. The state space variables are normalized with respect to the reference (target) values.

Action Space. The action at time t is given by: $a_t = w_S$, where $w_S \in [0,1]$ represents the proportion of funds invested in the risky asset S_t at time t. Since $w_S + w_B = 1$, the weight corresponding to the riskless asset is uniquely defined.

Reward Function. GBWM objectives are naturally framed as binary goals. Consequently, the RL reward is only received at the end of the episode, provided the goal is reached ($r_T = \mathbb{1}_{\{W_T \geq W_G\}}$). Otherwise, the rewards equal zero. This is a case of sparse rewards, which generally tend to be more difficult to learn from.

3.2 Dataset

Our study uses a two asset model, which is a common approach in goal-based investing to balance capital preservation and growth. While this approach some-what limits the diversity of the portfolio, this paper focuses on a simple model which allows a direct comparison with other common approaches in the litera-ture. We employ a dataset of monthly returns of the S&P 500 index as the risky asset and bonds as the risk-free asset, made available by R. Shiller[4]. The dataset was split into a training set covering returns from 1901 to 1991 and a testing set covering returns from 1992 to 2022.

3.3 Training Procedure

First, each episode, representing 10 trading years, is split into 120 time steps of equal length, each corresponding to a single trading month. At the beginning of each time step, the investor decides what percentage to invest in the (non-)risky asset and allocates the wealth accordingly. This procedure is iterated until the target date is reached and the episode terminates. Considering that historical data only provides a single trajectory, while simulating data from a multivariate normal distribution with fixed parameters may detract from realism, we propose an alternative data simulation mechanism, presented below. The goal here is to both extract as much as possible from the historical market data and provide the DRL agent with a sufficiently large training set. For simplicity, it is assumed that the investor begins at state $s_0 = (0, 0.6)$, i.e., with the initial investment equal to 60% of the goal.

Data Generation Procedure. The training dataset is represented by $\{R_1, \ldots, R_{N_{train}}\}$, where $R_t = (R_t^{bond}, R_t^{stock})$ contains bond and stock returns at time t. The trajectories used for training the DRL agent are generated by the following procedure:

---

[4] http://www.econ.yale.edu/~shiller/data.htm.

1. choose an index $k \in \{n+1, ..., N_{train}\}$ randomly,
2. use the series of returns $\{R_{k-n}, ..., R_k\}$ to estimate the mean vector $\boldsymbol{\mu} = (\mu^{bond}, \mu^{stock})$ and the covariance matrix $\boldsymbol{\Sigma}$, where n denotes the window size of returns used for estimation $(n < k)$,
3. sample the multivariate normal distribution $\mathcal{N}(\boldsymbol{\mu}, \boldsymbol{\Sigma})$ to obtain a trajectory.

The parameter n was set to 120 months, the same as the trajectory (and episode) length. The main idea behind this type of procedure is to generate a variety of trajectories emanating from different distributions, with the goal of enhancing the robustness of the DRL agent by exposing it to varying conditions during training.

Algorithm and Network Architecture. Tabular RL methods (as seen in [21]) have difficulties in evaluating the values of rarely encountered states. This makes it challenging for the RL agent to determine the optimal policy. DRL approaches, employing function approximation, hence offer a more promising path. We use a state-of-the-art, actor-critic-based algorithm Proximal Policy Optimization (PPO) [22]. The objective function used by PPO is given by:

$$J(\boldsymbol{\theta}) = \mathbb{E}\left[\min\left(r_\theta A(s,a), \ \text{clip}(r_\theta, 1 - \epsilon, 1 + \epsilon)A(s,a)\right)\right],$$

where $\boldsymbol{\theta}$ denotes the policy parameters, $\mathbb{E}$ the empirical expectation, r_θ the ratio of probabilities under the new and old policies, ϵ a hyperparameter, and A the advantage function. The clipping factor (clip) is used to prevent large policy changes. A feed-forward NN with 2 hidden layers, 6 neurons each, is employed, with the ReLU activation function. The discount factor γ is set to 1, and the choice of the very small learning rate of 0.0001 was guided by the stochasticity of the environment. The Stable Baselines3 [23] library and PyTorch were used for the implementation.

4 Results

4.1 Reinforcement Learning Policy

The resulting DRL policy is shown[5] in Fig. 2. It depicts the state space and the actions selected by the agent in each state. If the agent is in a certain state, the color displayed on the heatmap presents the agent's action. The policy's dependence on both wealth and time is evident. The obtained policy is intuitive, easily interpretable, and satisfies properties associated with a glide path investment strategy, specifically taking on greater risk earlier on in the investment period. The agent uses a less risky portfolio when the current amount of wealth is sufficient or when there is still enough time to achieve the target. In contrast, a riskier portfolio is favored when the goal has not yet been reached despite the end of the episode drawing near.

---

[5] Since the original policy found by PPO is stochastic, its determinism is enforced by returning the mode of the distribution over the action space instead of sampling from it.

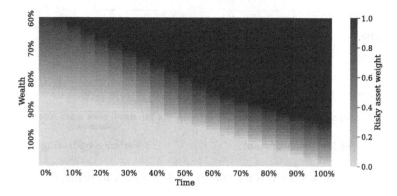

Fig. 2. Policy learned by the DRL agent. The agent was trained for 200000 episodes, 120 steps each, and the training wall-clock time was around 1 hour with the available computational resources.

4.2 Performance Results

The analytical and numerical approaches presented in Sect. 2 were used as benchmarks to evaluate the performance of the RL agent fairly. This ensures rigorous testing with as many as four benchmarks, surpassing the number of benchmarks used in previous literature. The risk parameters required for determining Merton's constant (risk aversion parameter γ) and the variance budgeting approach were chosen based on their performance on the training set. Figure 3 displays the percentage of successful episodes per value for each method, i.e., those that reached the goal for a certain fixed parameter. Subfigure 3a shows the selection of the risk aversion parameter for Merton's constant, which was searched for in the interval $[0.004, 0.05]$ to include all possible options for the constant strategy. This interval was selected because $\gamma \leq 0.004$ produces a stock-only portfolio, i.e., $\alpha = 1$, while values of $\gamma \geq 0.05$ result in a bond-only portfolio, i.e., $\alpha = 0$. The intermediate values of γ yield mixed portfolios. The best result on the training set was achieved with $\gamma = 0.004$. For the variance budgeting approach, the optimal risk budget on the training set was $v = 1.3\%$, as depicted in Subfigure 3b. The parameter was searched within the range of $[0.001, 0.02]$ for the same reason as in the case of Merton's constant.

To demonstrate the robustness of the trained RL agent, three distinct methods of testing were employed, based on the use of a) real historical trajectories, b) simulated data, and c) bootstrapped data. The aggregated results are shown in Table 1, with the following abbreviations: DG – Deterministic glide path, MC – Merton's constant, VB – Variance budgeting, DP – Dynamic programming, RL – Reinforcement learning.

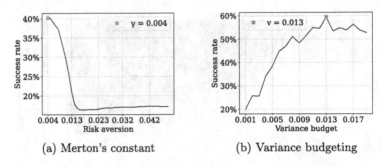

(a) Merton's constant   (b) Variance budgeting

Fig. 3. Choice of parameters for benchmark methods

Table 1. Comparison of results - DRL vs benchmarks

	Historical data	Simulated data (window size)			Bootstrapped data (block size)		
		36	{24, 36, 48}	60	1	{1,2,3}	{4,5,6}
DG	54.3%	70.5%	70.3%	69.7%	79.2%	76.9%	75.1%
MC	67.0%	71.8%	72.3%	67.0%	80.7%	77.4%	74.6%
VB	68.6%	74.1%	74.1%	70.6%	87.2%	83.5%	80.1%
DP	74.4%	73.7%	73.8%	74.7%	88.9%	84.4%	80.7%
RL	**77.5%**	**76.7%**	**76.4%**	**75.3%**	**90.8%**	**86.3%**	**82.3%**

Historical Market Data. The testing on historical market data was performed by using overlapping historical trajectories of monthly returns from January 1991 to June 2022. The testing dataset includes 378 data points. Considering that series of lengths 120 are needed (the number of months in 10 years), it is possible to generate 258 different (but overlapping) trajectories from the dataset. Table 1 shows the percentages of achieved targets for those time series. It is clear that the DRL agent outperforms all other benchmarks on historical market data. However, considering both the dependence between individual paths and the limited amount of historical data, it is essential to have another approach to test the robustness and efficacy of the obtained DRL agent.

Simulated Data. The data was acquired using the training procedure outlined in Subsect. 3.3, with the only difference being the use of historical market data from 1991 to 2022 as the underlying dataset. To construct a testing set that encompasses a wider range of potential scenarios, simulations were performed with different window sizes for parameter estimation in Step 2 of the procedure. Figure 4 shows the distributions of mean return estimates for different window sizes. We note that the use of shorter estimation windows results in an increase in the mean return variance. Consequently, returns generated from distributions calibrated on smaller window sizes are more versatile, leading to more diverse trajectories and, in turn, the enhanced robustness of the RL agent. Two fixed window sizes, 36 and 60, were considered, and an additional experiment was conducted in which a window size was randomly chosen from the set $\{24, 36, 48\}$ for every trajectory anew. For testing purposes, 10000 trajectories were simulated for each setting. The Table shows the percentage of successful portfolio allocations, i.e., ones that led to achieving the goal. Again, the DRL model outperforms the benchmark methods. Figure 5 displays the average proportion of the portfolio invested in the risky asset in the case of the window length equal to 36. Each point on the graph represents the average allocation of a given method at a specific time step. All of the obtained glide paths with the sole exception of MC indicate risk reduction over time, as is typical for GBWM.

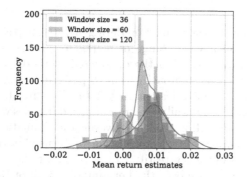

Fig. 4. Distribution of mean return estimates for each window size, together with Gaussian kernel density estimates.

Bootstrapped Data. The bootstrap, originally presented by Efron [24], is a statistical method that involves generating new data by simulating from an existing data set. It is a resampling approach in which multiple new samples are generated from the original dataset with replacement, thereby creating a new dataset that captures the variability and uncertainty of the original data. This technique was used to generate 10000 test trajectories from historical returns. Additionally, a variation of the bootstrap method known as block bootstrapping was employed. Block bootstrapping is specifically designed for time series data and involves sampling blocks of consecutive observations, preserving the correlations within each block while still generating synthetic data. It was used to generate 10000 trajectories, each one generated by first choosing a block size b from a given set of values, and then sampling from the testing set to acquire a 120-month-long series. If $b = 1$ the method deteriorates to regular bootstrapping. For $b = 2$ a trajectory is obtained by sampling 60 blocks of consecutive returns of two months. Three variations of block sizes were used for testing, and the corresponding success rates are presented in Table 1.

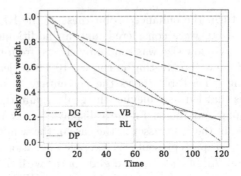

Fig. 5. Glide paths of different strategies

Given that the agent was trained on data generated by the simulator, it has been exposed to a much wider range of market conditions than those in the historical test set. However, all of the considered methods (all the benchmark methods and the proposed approach) seem to perform better on out-of-sample simulated data than on historical market data. This points to the fact that historical market data likely exhibits more complex dynamics which cannot easily be replicated by the simulation model - however, the simulation model allows us to generate a large number of trajectories, which is crucial in training the agent. Moreover, the results evidently testify to the fact that the proposed approach yields improved performance over the benchmarks in all of the considered test cases, including historical data.

5   Conclusion and Future Work

In this paper, a novel approach for goal-based wealth management based on deep reinforcement learning is presented. The results demonstrate that the proposed method outperforms multiple established benchmarks on both historical and simulated market data, using multiple testing procedures. Our study provides evidence that the proposed approach can be a valuable addition to existing wealth management strategies, as it offers improved performance and potential for practical applications in various financial settings. Despite the challenges posed by the complexity of decision-making processes in deep reinforcement learning, this paper presents a highly explainable policy for the agent, indicating that progress is being made in improving the interpretability of these systems. Future work should consider the following possibilities: First, the present work could be used in the context of regime-based asset allocation [25], for example by expanding the state space to include market regime-based features. This would require the development of a more complex financial market simulator capable of modeling non-stationary effects. Second, the approach might be recast from the perspective of more sophisticated GBWM frameworks that take into account multiple future goals [16,26]. Third, different risk preferences might be considered to pave the way toward more personalized wealth management. Using a non-binary reward function, as opposed to solely aiming to attain the predetermined target wealth, is expected to lead to more precise catering to investors' preferences. Additionally, cash infusion during the investment period could also be incorporated into the framework, as is typical in retirement and goal-based investing [16]. Lastly, generalizations to multi-asset scenarios present a potentially fruitful further step, as multi-asset allocation provides a more diversified investment portfolio, reducing overall risk and increasing the likelihood of achieving financial goals.

Acknowledgements. This work was supported in part by the Croatian Science Foundation under Project 5241, and in part by the European Regional Development Fund under Grant KK.01.1.1.01.0009 (DATACROSS).

References

1. Nevins, D.: Goals-based investing: integrating traditional and behavioral finance. J. Wealth Manage. **6**(4), 8–23 (2004). https://doi.org/10.3905/jwm.2004.391053
2. Iyer, A.K., Hoelscher, S.A., Mbanga, C.L.: Target date funds, drawdown risk, and central bank intervention: evidence during the COVID-19 pandemic. J. Risk Financ. Manage. **15**(9), 408 (2022). https://doi.org/10.3390/jrfm15090408
3. Gomes, F.: Portfolio choice over the life cycle: a survey. Ann. Rev. Financ. Econ. **12**, 277–304 (2020). https://doi.org/10.1146/annurev-financial-012820-113815
4. Blanchett, D.: Dynamic allocation strategies for distribution portfolios: determining the optimal distribution glide path. J. Financ. Plann. **20**(12), 68–81 (2007)
5. Capponi, A.: Robo-advising: personalization and goals-based investing. University of California Berkeley, Berkeley (2022). https://cdar.berkeley.edu/sites/default/files/slides_capponi.pdf
6. Zhang, Z., Zohren, S., Roberts, J.: Deep reinforcement learning for trading. J. Financ. Data Sci. **2**(2), 25–40 (2019). https://doi.org/10.48550/arXiv.1911.10107
7. Théate, T., Ernst, D.: An application of deep reinforcement learning to algorithmic trading. Expert Syst. Appl. **173**, 114632 (2021). https://doi.org/10.1016/j.eswa.2021.114632
8. Avellaneda, M., Stoikov, S.: High-frequency trading in a limit order book. Quant. Financ. **8**(3), 217–224 (2008). https://doi.org/10.1080/14697680701381228
9. Spooner, T., Savani, R.: Robust market making via adversarial reinforcement learning. In: Proceedings of the Twenty-Ninth International Joint Conference on Artificial Intelligence (IJCAI-20), (2020). https://doi.org/10.48550/arXiv.2003.01820
10. Gašperov, B., Kostanjčar, Z.: Market making with signals through deep reinforcement learning. IEEE Access **9**, 61611–61622 (2021). https://doi.org/10.1109/ACCESS.2021.3074782
11. Gašperov, B., Kostanjčar, Z.: Deep reinforcement learning for market making under a hawkes process-based limit order book model. IEEE Control Syst. Lett. **6**, 2485–2490 (2022). https://doi.org/10.1109/LCSYS.2022.3166446
12. Lin, S., Beling, P.A.: A deep reinforcement learning framework for optimal trade execution. In: Dong, Y., Ifrim, G., Mladenić, D., Saunders, C., Van Hoecke, S. (eds.) ECML PKDD 2020. LNCS (LNAI), vol. 12461, pp. 223–240. Springer, Cham (2021). https://doi.org/10.1007/978-3-030-67670-4_14

13. Hickman, K., Hunter, H., Byrd, J., Beck, J., Terpening, W.: Life cycle investing, holding periods, and risk. J. Portfolio Manage. **27**(2), 101–111 (2001). https://doi.org/10.3905/jpm.2001.319796
14. Bodie, Z., Crane, D.B.: Personal investing: advice, theory, and evidence. Financ. Anal. J. **53**(6), 13–23 (1997). https://doi.org/10.2139/ssrn.36158
15. Forsyth, P., Li, Y., Vetzal, K.: Are target date funds dinosaurs? Failure to adapt can lead to extinction. arXiv preprint arXiv:1705.00543 (2017). https://doi.org/10.48550/arXiv.1705.00543
16. Das, S.R., Ostrov, D., Radhakrishnan, A., Srivastav, D.: Dynamic portfolio allocation in goals-based wealth management. Comput. Manage. Sci. **17**(4), 613–640 (2019). https://doi.org/10.1007/s10287-019-00351-7
17. Merton, R.C.: Lifetime portfolio selection under uncertainty: the continuous-time case. Rev. Econ. Stat. **51**, 247–257 (1969). https://doi.org/10.2307/1926560
18. Bruder, B., Culerier, L., Roncalli, T.: How to design target-date funds? Available at SSRN 2289099 (2012). https://doi.org/10.2139/ssrn.2289099
19. Pendharkar, P.C., Cusatis, P.: Trading financial indices with reinforcement learning agents. Expert Syst. Appl. **103**, 1–13 (2018). https://doi.org/10.1016/j.eswa.2018.02.032
20. Dixon, M., Halperin, I.: G-learner and girl: goal based wealth management with reinforcement learning. arXiv preprint arXiv:2002.10990 (2020). https://doi.org/10.48550/arXiv.2002.10990
21. Das, S.R., Varma, S.: Dynamic goals-based wealth management using reinforcement learning. J. Investment Manage. **18**(2), 1–20 (2020)
22. Schulman, J., Wolski, F., Dhariwal, P., Radford, A., Klimov, O.: Proximal policy optimization algorithms. arXiv preprint arXiv:1707.06347 (2017). https://doi.org/10.48550/arXiv.1707.06347
23. Raffin, A., Hill, A., Gleave, A., Kanervisto, A., Ernestus, M., Dormann, N.: Stable-Baselines3: reliable reinforcement learning implementations. J. Mach. Learn. Res. **22**(1), 12348–12355 (2021)
24. Efron, B.: Bootstrap methods: another look at the jackknife. Annuals Stat. **7**(1), 1–26 (1979). https://doi.org/10.1214/aos/1176344552
25. Nystrup, P., Hansen, B.W., Madsen, H., Lindström, E.: ž: Regime-based versus static asset allocation: letting the data speak. J. Portfolio Manage. **42**(1), 103–109 (2015). https://doi.org/10.3905/jpm.2015.42.1.103
26. Capponi, A., Zhang, Y.: Goal Based Investment Management. Available at SSRN. https://ssrn.com/abstract=4121931 or https://doi.org/10.2139/ssrn.4121931 (2022). https://doi.org/10.2139/ssrn.4121931

DeNISE: Deep Networks for Improved Segmentation Edges

Sander Jyhne[✉], Jørgen Åsbu Jacobsen, Morten Goodwin,
and Per-Arne Andersen

Department of ICT, University of Agder, Grimstad, Norway
sander.jyhne@uia.no

Abstract. This paper presents Deep Networks for Improved Segmentation Edges (DeNISE), a novel data enhancement technique using edge detection and segmentation models to improve the boundary quality of segmentation masks. DeNISE utilizes the inherent differences in two sequential deep neural architectures to improve the accuracy of the predicted segmentation edge. DeNISE applies to all types of neural networks and is not trained end-to-end, allowing rapid experiments to discover which models complement each other. We test and apply DeNISE for building segmentation in aerial images. Aerial images are known for difficult conditions as they have a low resolution with optical noise, such as reflections, shadows, and visual obstructions. Overall the paper demonstrates the potential for DeNISE. Using the technique, we improve the baseline results with a building IoU of 78.9%.

Keywords: Remote Sensing · Deep Learning · Image Segmentation

1 Introduction

Building segmentation is a prominent area of research in computer vision. A common problem for building segmentation is the quality and edge sharpness of the segmentation masks. Therefore, using predicted segmentation masks is limited to applications that do not rely on precise delineations of buildings. The precision of the current methods allows the detection of new or demolished buildings, thereby being valuable for change detection and disaster impact assessment applications. However, improved precision is necessary for applications with strict data quality requirements, such as map creation.

Public authorities, like the Norwegian Mapping Authority (NMA) [15], use building data for map creation, policy-making, and city management [5]. NMA maintains a national building object database with essential information about each building. Furthermore, they update the database by manually measuring and annotating buildings in aerial imagery. Hence, using deep learning to annotate buildings reduces the cost and effort required to maintain an up-to-date database. With precise building masks, it is possible to incorporate building

I. Maglogiannis et al. (Eds.): AIAI 2023, IFIP AICT 675, pp. 81–89, 2023.
https://doi.org/10.1007/978-3-031-34111-3_8

annotations into the building objects with significantly less human intervention than currently possible. Additionally, precise mask boundaries provide the basis for determining the building footprint, detecting ridgelines, and even creating 3D models of buildings.

Producing accurate segmentation masks is challenging because the training data derives from real-world data with varying quality. Optical factors, such as shadows, reflections, and perspectives, are present in aerial imagery and negatively influence the model's predictions. In addition, visibility is a challenge, as trees, powerlines, and other structures can block the view [13]. Despite many advancements in semantic segmentation, none of the models produce a segmentation boundary that satisfies map production standards.

However, many applications can successfully leverage building segmentation, including urban planning, disaster damage estimation, and change detection. The main reason is that the aforementioned applications do not require the same precision as map production. As a result, there is a research gap in the accuracy of the segmentation masks. Additionally, the models must generalize to various building types, shapes, and surrounding nature, ranging from urban cities to remote settlements.

To improve the precision of the predicted edges, we propose DeNISE, a technique highlighting buildings using an edge detection or segmentation network known as Edge-DeNISE and Seg-DeNISE, respectively. DeNISE combines the output prediction probabilities with the original images, directly modifying them or adding the predictions as a fourth image channel. A second network receives the modified images as input for training and prediction.

The rest of the paper is structured as follows. Section 2 discusses related work to the proposed technique. Section 3 introduces the DeNISE method. Section 4, presents the results and ablation studies. Finally, Sect. 5 concludes the work and proposes paths for future work in enhanced segmentation boundaries.

2   Related Work

2.1   Semantic Segmentation

Semantic segmentation is finding and assigning the correct class to each pixel in an image, resulting in annotations of each class. Deep learning-based image segmentation research advances rapidly, with several new and novel architectures each year. One such architecture is the encoder-decoder architecture, which is proven successful for image segmentation tasks. U-Net [12] is a well-known segmentation model using the encoder-decoder architecture with skip connections to retain the resolution through encoding and decoding. However, the skip connections are not able to retain all details. The HRNet [16] is an architecture mitigating this issue, a slightly different approach where three parallel and interconnected convolution streams maintain the high-resolution representations. However, the retained resolution comes at the cost of being more computationally expensive. Another popular approach for segmentation is dilated convolutions, which are used in other state-of-the-art segmentation models. Dilated convolutions are convolutions with holes between the convolution points, which allows for a larger convolution filter with reduced computational cost. DeeplabV3+ [1] acquires state-of-the-art results on several tasks using this technique.

In recent years, the Transformer architecture has become popular for computer vision tasks. The authors of [3] propose the vision transformer leveraging attention mechanisms instead of convolutions. However, the attention mechanism of the transformer models is computationally expensive, limiting the resolution of the input image. The authors of [10] introduce a shifted windows (SwinT) approach, reducing computation. The shifted windows lower the scale of self-attention by limiting it to non-overlapping local windows while still allowing cross-window attention, enabling global pixel context. Furthermore, in [9], the authors propose a new transformer model building on SwinT to perform detection and segmentation in the same model, achieving state-of-the-art results.

2.2   Edge Detection

Edge detection is the task of precisely delineating objects in an image. Deep-learning-based techniques are currently dominating the field, with several different methods available. One of the most famous is HED [17], which uses a trimmed VGG16 backbone to generate multi-level features. Each layer produces a side output that is evaluated and backpropagated during training. A recent technique is the Bi-Directional Cascade Network (BDCN) [6]. The authors argue that using the same supervision for all network layers is not optimal due to the different scales in each layer. They solve it by focusing shallow layers on details, while deep layers focus on object-level boundaries. However, BDCN struggles to detect crisp edge maps free of localization ambiguity due to the mixing phenomenon of CNNs. In 2021, [7] introduces two novel modules; a tracing loss for feature unmixing and a fusion block for side mixing and aggregation of side edges. The modules can be paired with other edge detection models, such as BDCN, increasing the performance.

2.3   Aerial Image Segmentation

A common approach for aerial image segmentation is applying state-of-the-art segmentation models and training them to segment buildings, roads, or other objects. Among them, [11,18], and [19] have all used a U-Net architecture with relatively good results. Other approaches modify existing architectures to extract specific object features. [4] propose a technique to improve the segmentation masks of roads by utilizing edge detection. The model segments the images and passes them to an edge detection network with the encoded image. As a result, the edge detection module relies on the performance of the segmentation network. Additionally, the model is complex, and changing the edge detection part is not easy. Similarly, [8] also approaches the problem using two stages in the model. However, they utilize two segmentation networks in a two-scheme method using a novel boundary loss and a USIM module. The predictions of the first network are combined with the original image in the USIM module and passed through the second network. The method improves upon using one segmentation network. The complexity of the model makes it difficult to swap the existing models and causes the training to be resource-intensive. Lastly, they display the improvements of their method using older models that are not state-of-the-art.

3 Deep Networks for Improved Segmentation Edges (DeNISE)

The primary objective of DeNISE is to improve the boundary quality of segmentation masks for buildings compared to standalone segmentation models. Figure 1 depicts a high-level overview of DeNISE.

Both DeNISE approaches use the same structure, combining the strengths of two different neural networks to improve the precision of predicted edges. Because the architecture decouples both models, the user can easily swap the first and second neural networks with other models. The ability to quickly try different models allows rapid testing to find complementary models.

We propose two DeNISE approaches: (1) Seg-DeNISE, which uses two segmentation networks, and (2) Edge-DeNISE, using an edge detection network in conjunction with a segmentation network. In both approaches, the first model performs inference on the original training data, then combines the predictions with the data and uses the combination for training and inference in the second model.

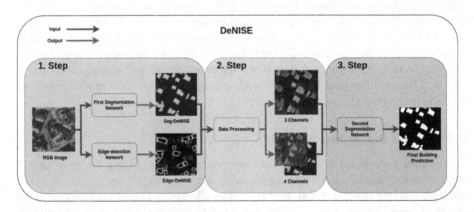

Fig. 1. A visual representation of DeNISE illustrating the process of combining the predictions of a neural network with the original image data in three steps. (1) A segmentation or edge detection model trains on the unenhanced dataset. (2) DeNISE generates training data by enhancing the original data with the predictions from the first network. (3) The second network uses the enhanced dataset for training and inference. The branches in the figure represent a choice between available methods at the current step.

3.1   Seg-DeNISE

The first segmentation network in Seg-DeNISE receives an input image and outputs the class probabilities. Seg-DeNISE can use the probabilities in two ways: they can be concatenated with the original input or merged into the image while retaining the original three channels. The merging consists of four steps to create the enhanced data. (1) Threshold the probabilities from the first neural network. We set all gradients equal to or greater than 0.5 to 1 and the rest to 0. (2) The thresholded predictions are dilated 15 pixels in each direction to ensure the mask covers the entire building. (3) All predictions are clipped values between 0.5 and 1.0. This step is crucial to include the background information when multiplying the prediction gradients with the original image. Additionally, clipping the gradients allow the second segmentation to find buildings that the first model missed. (4) The dilated and clipped predictions are multiplied by the original input image. The result shown in Fig. 2 is an image where all dilated building masks keep the original brightness while the rest is set to 50% brightness.

Fig. 2. An example of the enhanced data from 3-channel Seg-DeNISE, showing the dilated region surrounding the buildings.

3.2   Edge-DeNISE

The edge detection network in Edge-DeNISE receives an input image and predicts the corresponding building edge gradients. We use the predicted gradients in two ways. The gradients can be concatenated with the original input or merged into the image while retaining the three channels. The merging process for Edge-DeNISE is similar to Seg-DeNISE, using two steps. (1) The predicted gradients are thresholded and clipped between 0.5 and 1.0, preserving the background information. (2) The clipped gradients are multiplied with the original input image, keeping the original brightness on the predicted building edges while setting the rest of the image to 50% brightness.

3.3 NMA Dataset

We use a private dataset named NMA dataset for the experiments. The dataset consists of orthophotos and ground truth masks for buildings in Norway. The orthophotos are created using a Digital Terrain Model (DTM), which depicts the height of the terrain in a given area. All points in orthophotos created using a DTM are slightly skewed. As a result, the ground truth masks and buildings depicted in the orthophotos do not perfectly align. The dataset is divided into training, validation, and test splits with 22 892, 2861, and 2862 images, respectively.

4 Results

We evaluate Seg-DeNISE and Egde-DeNISE on the NMA dataset. For all experiments, we use three different segmentation models, and an edge detection model, namely Hierarchical Multi-Scale Attention (HMSA) [14], DeeplabV3+ (DL3) [1], U-Net [12], and CATS-BDCN (CATS) [7], respectively. For all experiments, the models train for 20 epochs with a batch size of 8 and a learning rate of 1e-4.

Furthermore, Seg-DeNISE always uses DL3 as the first segmentation network in Seg-DeNISE and evaluates using all models as the second segmentation network. Edge-DeNISE uses CATS as the first network and, similarly to Seg-DeNISE, evaluates using all segmentation models as the second network. None of the experiments utilize pre-trained encoders, mainly due to the lack of pre-trained encoders for 4-channel data, making a fair comparison difficult. For the evaluation of experiments, we use Intersection-over-Union (IoU) and Boundary IoU (BIoU) [2], an IoU measure focusing on the predicted segmentation edges.

4.1 Baseline

We run experiments with all segmentation models as a standalone network, creating a baseline for comparison. Table 1 display the baseline evaluation results, establishing the superiority of the HMSA model, followed by DL3 and U-Net.

4.2 Seg-DeNISE

Table 1 presents the results for Seg-DeNISE, revealing subpar evaluation scores where U-Net is the only model that improves upon the baseline. The evaluation results suggest that a relatively large gap in performance between the first and second segmentation models may negatively influence the accuracy of the predictions. Additionally, the evaluation scores indicate that the second segmentation network cannot correct the mistakes of the first network. Lastly, comparing the results for 3 and 4 channels, a slight trend in performance is present, where 3 channels have the best evaluation scores by a small margin.

Table 1. Evaluation results on the NMA dataset for all experiments. The results show DeNISE increasing the IoU and BIoU measures for the U-Net and DL3 models. However, it does not outperform the HMSA baseline.

Model	Dataset	Loss	Method	IoU	BIoU	Source
U-Net (Baseline)	NMA	RMI	Standalone	0.7657	0.6279	[12]
U-Net	NMA	RMI	Seg-DeNISE (3-channels)	0.7685	0.6343	Ours
U-Net	NMA	RMI	Seg-DeNISE (4-channels)	0.7730	0.6416	Ours
U-Net	**NMA**	**RMI**	**Edge-DeNISE (3-channels)**	**0.7742**	**0.6445**	**Ours**
U-Net	NMA	RMI	Edge-DeNISE (4-channels)	0.7739	0.6480	Ours
DL3 (Baseline)	NMA	RMI	Standalone	0.7850	0.6586	[1]
DL3	NMA	RMI	Seg-DeNISE (3-channels)	0.7802	0.6535	Ours
DL3	NMA	RMI	Seg-DeNISE (4-channels)	0.7778	0.6492	Ours
DL3	NMA	RMI	Edge-DeNISE (3-channels)	0.7882	0.6658	Ours
DL3	**NMA**	**RMI**	**Edge-DeNISE (4-channels)**	**0.7890**	**0.6691**	**Ours**
HMSA (Baseline)	**NMA**	**RMI**	**Standalone**	**0.8291**	**0.7284**	[14]
HMSA	NMA	RMI	Seg-DeNISE (3-channels)	0.8103	0.7003	Ours
HMSA	NMA	RMI	Seg-DeNISE (4-channels)	0.7997	0.6860	Ours
HMSA	NMA	RMI	Edge-DeNISE (3-channels)	0.8076	0.6968	Ours
HMSA	NMA	RMI	Edge-DeNISE (4-channels)	0.8057	0.6975	Ours

4.3 Edge-DeNISE

Table 1 reveals promising evaluation scores for Edge-DeNISE, as U-Net and DL3 improve upon the baselines. The results indicate that the edge detection network's performance relative to the segmentation network's is crucial for improving the results. Furthermore, the results suggest that the predictions from CATS for HMSA introduce noise instead of enhancing the data, negatively impacting the results. Dissimilar to Seg-DeNISE, the Boundary IoU scores for Edge-DeNISE slightly favor 4 channels compared to 3.

5 Conclusion

This paper proposes DeNISE, a data enhancement technique that uses either a segmentation (Seg-DeNISE) or an edge detection (Edge-DeNISE) network to enhance the original data using their predictions. Subsequently, a secondary segmentation network uses the enhanced data for training and inference, improving the precision of predicted segmentation masks. Our results for Seg-DeNISE show inconsistent performance, indicating that the first segmentation network can negatively or positively impact Seg-DeNISE results. However, Edge-DeNISE yields promising results and improves upon the baseline results for two out of three models. The results suggest that further advancement of edge detection literature will greatly benefit Edge-DeNISE.

5.1 Future Work

This paper proposes a new approach for improving the edges of the predicted segmentation masks. The results advocate further investigation into using neural networks to enhance the training data for a second neural network. Several new but potential directions for DeNISE need further research.

– Using an object detection model as the first network.
– Explore other combinations of segmentation and edge detection models for DeNISE.
– Improving the edge detection literature to further improve Edge-DeNISE.
– Training two segmentation models end-to-end, where the latent space from the first model is merged with the latent space of the second model.
– Reversing Edge-DeNISE by having the segmentation network first and edge detection last.

References

1. Chen, L.-C., Zhu, Y., Papandreou, G., Schroff, F., Adam, H.: Encoder-decoder with atrous separable convolution for semantic image segmentation. In: Ferrari, V., Hebert, M., Sminchisescu, C., Weiss, Y. (eds.) ECCV 2018. LNCS, vol. 11211, pp. 833–851. Springer, Cham (2018). https://doi.org/10.1007/978-3-030-01234-2_49
2. Cheng, B., Girshick, R., Dollar, P., Berg, A.C., Kirillov, A.: Boundary IoU: improving Object-Centric Image Segmentation Evaluation (2021). https://bowenc0221.github.io/boundary-iou
3. Dosovitskiy, A., et al.: An image is worth 16×16 words: transformers for image recognition at scale. In: Proceedings of the 9th International Conference on Learning Representations (ICLR), pp. 1–21 (10 2021). https://doi.org/10.48550/arxiv.2010.11929, https://arxiv.org/abs/2010.11929v2
4. Ghandorh, H., Boulila, W., Masood, S., Koubaa, A., Ahmed, F., Ahmad, J.: Semantic segmentation and edge detection—approach to road detection in very high resolution satellite images. Remote Sens. **14**(3), 613 (2022). https://doi.org/10.3390/RS14030613
5. Grecea, C., Bălă, A., Herban, S.: Cadastral requirements for urban administration, key component for an efficient town planning. J. Environ. Prot. Ecol. **14**, 363–371 (2013)
6. He, J., Zhang, S., Yang, M., Shan, Y., Huang, T.: Bi-Directional Cascade Network for Perceptual Edge Detection (2019). https://www.pkuvmc.com/dataset.html
7. Huan, L., Xue, N., Zheng, X., He, W., Gong, J., Xia, G.S.: Unmixing convolutional features for crisp edge detection. IEEE Trans. Pattern Anal. Mach. Intell. (2021). https://doi.org/10.1109/TPAMI.2021.3084197
8. Lee, K., Kim, J.H., Lee, H., Park, J., Choi, J.P., Hwang, J.Y.: Boundary-oriented binary building segmentation model with two scheme learning for aerial images. IEEE Trans. Geosci. Remote Sens. **60**, 1–17 (2022). https://doi.org/10.1109/TGRS.2021.3089623
9. Li, F., et al.: Mask DINO: Towards A Unified Transformer-based Framework for Object Detection and Segmentation (6 2022). https://doi.org/10.48550/arxiv.2206.02777, https://arxiv.org/abs/2206.02777v1

10. Liu, Z., et al.: Swin Transformer V2: Scaling Up Capacity and Resolution (2022). https://github.com/microsoft/Swin-
11. Pan, Z., Xu, J., Guo, Y., Hu, Y., Wang, G.: Deep learning segmentation and classification for urban village using a worldview satellite image based on U-Net. Remote Sens. **12**(10), 1574 (2020). https://doi.org/10.3390/RS12101574
12. Ronneberger, O., Fischer, P., Brox, T.: U-Net: convolutional networks for biomedical image segmentation. In: Navab, N., Hornegger, J., Wells, W.M., Frangi, A.F. (eds.) MICCAI 2015. LNCS, vol. 9351, pp. 234–241. Springer, Cham (2015). https://doi.org/10.1007/978-3-319-24574-4_28
13. Schlosser, A.D., Szabó, G., Bertalan, L., Varga, Z., Enyedi, P., Szabó, S.: Building extraction using orthophotos and dense point cloud derived from visual band aerial imagery based on machine learning and segmentation. Remote Sens. **12**(15), 2397 (2020). https://doi.org/10.3390/RS12152397
14. Tao, A., Sapra, K., Catanzaro, B.: Hierarchical Multi-Scale Attention for Semantic Segmentation. CoRR abs/2005.10821 (2020), https://arxiv.org/abs/2005.10821
15. The Norwegian Mapping Authority: The Norwegian Mapping Authority (9 2022)
16. Wang, J., et al.: Deep high-resolution representation learning for visual recognition. IEEE Trans. Pattern Anal. Mach. Intell. **43**(10), 3349–3364 (2021). https://doi.org/10.1109/TPAMI.2020.2983686
17. Xie, S., Tu, Z.: Holistically-Nested Edge Detection (2015)
18. Zhang, Z., Liu, Q., Wang, Y.: Road extraction by deep residual U-Net. IEEE Geosci. Remote Sens. Lett. **15**(5), 749–753 (2018). https://doi.org/10.1109/LGRS.2018.2802944
19. Zhao, X., et al.: Use of unmanned aerial vehicle imagery and deep learning UNet to extract rice lodging. Sensors **19**(18), 3859 (2019). https://doi.org/10.3390/S19183859

Detecting P300-ERPs Building a Post-validation Neural Ensemble with Informative Neurons from a Recurrent Neural Network

Christian Oliva[1]([⊠])(iD), Vinicio Changoluisa[2](iD), Francisco B. Rodríguez[1](iD), and Luis F. Lago-Fernández[1](iD)

[1] Grupo de Neurocomputación Biológica, Departamento de Ingeniería Informática, Escuela Politécnica Superior, Universidad Autónoma de Madrid, Madrid, Spain
`{christian.oliva,f.rodriguez,luis.lago}@uam.es`
[2] Grupo de Investigación en Electrónica y Telemática, Universidad Politécnica Salesiana, Quito, Ecuador
`fchangoluisa@ups.edu.ec`

Abstract. We introduce a novel approach for detecting the sample-level temporal structure of P300 event-related potentials. It consists of extracting the most informative neurons from a Recurrent Neural Network and building a post-validation neural ensemble (PVNE). The weights connecting the recurrent and the output layers are used to rank the recurrent neurons according to their relevance when generating the network's output. A set of neurons is selected according to their positions in this ranking, and their individual predictions are then combined to obtain the final model's output. This procedure discards neurons whose role could be more related to maintaining the network's hidden state than to detecting the P300 events, with an overall performance increase. The use of L1 regularization notably emphasizes this effect. We compare the performance of this approach with both Elman and LSTM RNNs and show that the PVNE is able to detect the sample-level temporal structure of P300 event-related potentials, outperforming the standard models. Sample-level prediction also allows for real-time monitoring of the EEG signal generation related to ERPs.

Keywords: LSTM · Elman RNN · Bayesian Linear Discriminant Analysis · Output Neurons Ensemble · Neurons relevance · Neurons interpretability · Brain-machine interface · Inter- and intra-subject variability

1 Introduction

Event-related potentials (ERPs) are commonly used for exploring the human mind and brain [19]. Electroencephalography (EEG) is one of the most widely

Published by Springer Nature Switzerland AG 2023
I. Maglogiannis et al. (Eds.): AIAI 2023, IFIP AICT 675, pp. 90–101, 2023.
https://doi.org/10.1007/978-3-031-34111-3_9

used ways to monitor brain activity related to ERPs, due to its good temporal resolution and relatively low cost. ERPs appear in EEG as positive and negative voltage deflections, maintaining a specific temporal structure according to the brain activity under study. When a set of frequent and infrequent stimuli is presented, a positive deflection is generated at 300 ms. This voltage deflection is known as P300, and it is one of the most widely used ERPs. From the seminal article presented by Sutton et al. [28] to date, many research works have been searching to understand its structure and functionality. Currently, the P300 ERP is known to be related to several cognitive processes, such as memory, learning, or attention [19].

One of the most widespread uses of P300 is its application in Brain-Computer Interfaces (BCIs) as a control signal [2]. In this context, a P300 is evocated when the subject detects one infrequent stimulus (called target stimulus) within a set of other (non-target) stimuli, and can be used to control an external device without any usual peripheral pathways. Despite the wide acceptance of P300-based BCIs, there are still some problems to be solved. One is the inter- and intra-subject variability, present due to different factors, such as age or stress [2,10]. Several methodologies have recently been proposed to deal with these variability problems [5–7]. Another problem is the low information transfer rate (ITR), due to the standard approaches that require processing entire one-second windows, increasing the target detection time [27].

There exist different techniques to detect P300s trial by trial. The most common is the use of machine learning models, such as discriminant analysis, support vector machines, or artificial neural networks (see [26] for a complete review of the different methods to detect visual P300-ERPs, and [18] for classification algorithms in general EEG-based BCIs). Currently, there are few pieces of evidence for the use of recurrent neural network (RNN) models in the P300-based BCI prediction [9,29,30], and some works that exist on LSTM perform a combination with convolutional neural networks (CNNs) to retrieve spatial information [1,3,12,16]. P300 ERP detection has much redundant information since the many EEG recording electrodes process different but related events [14,18]. It is also known that, due to the inter-variability between users, the P300 event does not always appear in the same waveform (latency and amplitude) [5,7,17,24]. Our work presents a continuous training mode from the input signals with P300-ERPs using recurrent neural networks (RNNs), based on previous research [21]. We extend this idea by selecting the most informative neurons according to their weights and combining their individual predictions in order to obtain the final output. The introduction of L1 regularization in the output layer appears to be decisive in this process. It allows for the creation of a post-validation neural ensemble (PVNE) which uses the output layer's weights as a metric for defining the neuron's voting, increasing the models' performance in ERP-based BCIs.

The remaining of the article is organized as follows. First, in Sect. 2, we describe the dataset used in our experiments, the preprocessing we apply to the data, and the models that we use. In Sect. 3 we present and analyze our results. Finally, in Sect. 4 we present the conclusions and further lines of research.

2   Materials and Methods

2.1   Data Description and Preprocessing

We use the dataset created by Hoffman et al. [14], whose paradigm is based on a six-choice P300. The dataset contains eight users, which have reacted to random sequences of six images (classes) with an Inter-Stimulus Interval (ISI) of 400 ms. Each image is flashed for 100 ms and, during the remaining 300 ms, nothing is displayed. The EEG signals were recorded at a 2048 Hz sampling rate from the standard 32 electrodes of the 10–20 international system [15]. The dataset is filtered with a sixth-order forward-backward Butterworth bandpass filter, cut-off frequencies are set to 1.0 Hz and 12.0 Hz, and its signals are downsampled from 2048 Hz to 32 Hz.

Standard Preprocessing. The standard preprocessing consists of extracting single windows of duration 1000 ms starting at the stimulus onset. In these conditions, the classification problem consists of using the 1000 ms windows to predict the corresponding class: *Target stimulus*, when the target image appears, versus *Non-Target stimulus*, when it does not [14]. This approach is followed by most research works, and we apply it to prepare the data for the Bayesian Linear Discriminant Analysis (BLDA) model introduced in Sect. 2.2, which we use as benchmark. In the context of a P300-based BCI, however, this procedure can result in a low ITR, since full one second signals must be processed prior to making a decision.

Sample-Level Preprocessing. Sample-level preprocessing, first implemented in [21], offers a methodology for training a Recurrent Neural Network to provide a continuous output, instead of classifying 1000 ms windows. Given that the exact window of the P300 event is not a priori known, two hyperparameters are used to appropriately define the network's expected output (Y_{True}) for each time step. The two hyperparameters are an *offset*, which represents the starting time of the P300 event, and a *window size*, which represents its duration. The *offset* and the *window size* define an *interest interval* where the P300 event is assumed to occur. The networks are thus trained to output 1 in this interval and 0 elsewhere. Figure 1 shows an example 1000 ms window, with the average signal recorded by the $Fp1$ electrode when target stimuli are presented to user 7 (top), and the expected output, Y_{True}, considering an *offset* of 437,5 ms and a *window size* of 250 ms.

2.2   Models

Bayesian Linear Discriminant Analysis (BLDA). BLDA is the method originally used by Hoffman et al. [14] for the P300-ERP recognition problem. It is an extension of Fisher's Linear Discriminant Analysis (FLDA) [4] that runs the regression in a Bayesian framework. It automatically estimates the

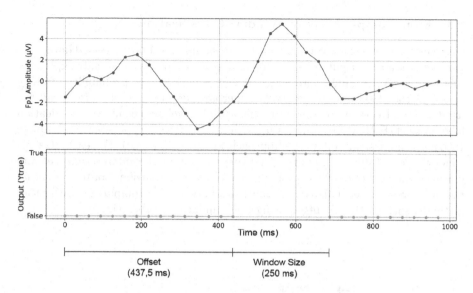

Fig. 1. Example of a 1000 ms window when a target stimulus is presented at time $t = 0$ ms. The top figure shows the average $Fp1$ electrode signal from user 7, sampled 32 Hz. The bottom figure is an example of the expected output, Y_{True}, using an *offset* of 437,5 ms and a *window size* of 250 ms.

degree of regularization, which prevents overfitting in noisy and high-dimensional environments. In our experiments we combine BLDA with the standard data preprocessing. We use the scikit-learn implementation [25].

Elman Recurrent Neural Network (Elman RNN). The Elman RNN [11] is one of the simplest neural models that introduces recurrent connections. Here we use the standard Keras SimpleRNN implementation [8], adding one output fully connected layer with a single sigmoid neuron. This output represents the probability of Y_{True} being 1, according to the sample-level preprocessing described in Sect. 2.1.

Long-Short Term Memory Networks (LSTM). LSTM networks [13] are one of the most commonly used RNN models, and they are a usual benchmark in many sequence modeling applications. The LSTM architecture introduces memory cells and gate units to mitigate the effects of the vanishing and the exploding gradients problems. We use the Keras implementation [8] and, as before, the final model includes a fully connected output layer with sigmoid activation, which is used to predict the value of Y_{True} using the sample-level preprocessing.

2.3   From Sample-Level to Window Classification

The recurrent neural networks, trained with sample-level preprocessed data, provide a continuous output signal with a frequency 32 Hz. As we already explained, this sample-level output represents, for each time step, the probability of being in one of the P300 interest intervals hyperparameterized by the *offset* and the *window size*. In order to transform this sample-level signal into a classification label (target/ERP-P300 vs non-target/non-ERP-P300) applicable to complete 1000 ms windows, we follow the approach in [21] (see Fig. 2). For each 1000 ms window, we obtain the maximum network output in the *interest interval* and use it as the predicted P300 probability. We apply a threshold of 0.5 to obtain the final predictions. This transformation allows for the comparison with other methods, such as BLDA, fitted using the standard preprocessing.

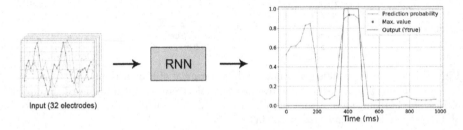

Fig. 2. Diagram of the sample-level rebuilt to window classification. A 1000 ms window with 32 electrodes is the input to the recurrent model, either an Elman or an LSTM network in our experiments. It returns one output for each time step, corresponding to the 32 samples of the 1000 ms input signal. Then, we get the *interest interval* with the *offset* (375 ms) and the *window size* (125 ms), colored in blue, and finally, we get the maximum value in this bounded window as the prediction probability.

2.4   Post-validation Neural Ensemble

As an alternative to the previous approach, we propose a novel strategy to transform the continuous network output so that it can be used to classify the 1000 ms windows. It consists of building an ensemble with the top-K most informative neurons from the recurrent layer, which act as single voters. The network output, for either the Elman or the LSTM models, is given by:

$$y_t = \sigma(\mathbf{w}^T \mathbf{h}_t + b), \tag{1}$$

where $\mathbf{h}_t$ is the activation vector of the recurrent layer at time t. The weight vector $\mathbf{w}$ determines how the neurons in the recurrent layer contribute to the network's output. These weights adjust the output of individual neurons from $\mathbf{h}_t$ in Eq. 1, so we can interpret the output layer as a weighted voting of individual neurons (plus a bias b). Hence, we can use the absolute value of each weight, $|w_i|$, as a measure of the relative importance of its corresponding neuron i. Then, the recurrent neurons are ranked according to this relevance, and the activations of the K most relevant neurons are combined to build the final decision. We have named this procedure Post-Validation Neural Ensemble (PVNE). Note that this process discards the neurons that are more weakly connected to the output layer. The activity of these discarded neurons could be more relevant to the computation of the next hidden state than to the construction of the network's output, and hence the construction of the PVNE could have a positive effect on the final predictions. Our results seem to support this hypothesis.

The following section describes how the activation of each of the K-selected neurons is used to determine the neuron's vote, and how the individual votes are combined to compute the final ensemble's decision.

Voting of Individual Neurons. Figure 3 shows the activation of a highly ranked neuron from the recurrent layer of an Elman RNN trained with user 7, for all the target (red lines) and non-target (blue lines) stimuli. Thick lines represent averages over stimuli. It is interesting to note the big difference between target and non-target averages in the *interest interval* defined by the *offset* and the *window size* hyperparameters. We have observed a correlation between the position of a neuron in the ranking and the difference between its average response to the target and the non-target stimuli in the selected interval.

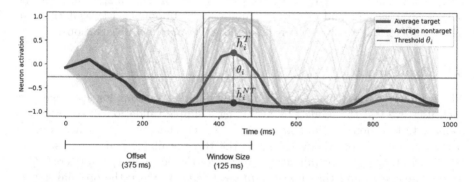

Fig. 3. Activation of a neuron from the hidden layer of an Elman RNN trained with user 7. The blue curve represents the neuron's activation along the time of the corresponding neuron when tested on any of the non-target stimuli, and the red one does the same when tested on any of the target stimuli. Vertical blue lines delimit the *interest interval*. The green horizontal line is a threshold θ_i at the middle point between the target, $\bar{h}_i^T$, and the non-target, $\bar{h}_i^{NT}$, averages for this example neuron. (Color figure online)

Motivated by this observation, we decided to define an activation threshold, θ_i, as the middle point between the target, $\bar{h}_i^T$, and the non-target, $\bar{h}_i^{NT}$, averages for neuron i:

$$\theta_i = \frac{1}{2}(\bar{h}_i^T + \bar{h}_i^{NT}) \tag{2}$$

The average values $\bar{h}_i^T$ and $\bar{h}_i^{NT}$ are evaluated at the middle of the *interest interval*. The neuron is considered to vote in favor of the presence of a P300 event if its activation h_i in the middle point of the *interest interval* lies on the target side of this threshold. That is, neuron's i vote is given by:

$$v_i = \begin{cases} 1, & \text{if } (h_i - \bar{h}_i^{NT})/(\theta_i - \bar{h}_i^{NT}) > 1, \\ 0, & \text{otherwise,} \end{cases} \tag{3}$$

where $v_i = 1$ means preference for a P300 event. Finally, the PVNE prediction is the hard voting of the top K neurons chosen from the defined ranking score:

$$p = \frac{1}{K} \sum_{i=1}^{K} v_i. \tag{4}$$

The model predicts as target (P300 event) if p is greater than 0.5.

3   Analysis and Results

In this work, we present a novel approach by modifying the output layer's activation in the evaluation phase to test the models using Elman and LSTM recurrent networks. In Sect. 3.1, we describe the experiments. In Sect. 3.2, we analyze the output layer weights and discuss the importance of applying L1 regularization. Then, in Sect. 3.3, we show the results and give some final observations.

3.1   Experiments

The complete dataset has 8 users and four different sessions for each one. For each user, we test the models by averaging a simple validation (3 training sessions, 1 test session) of the four available sessions per user. For validation, we perform a 3-fold cross-validation using the three available training sessions (2 sessions for training, 1 for validation) to look for the best hyperparameters (*offset* and *window size*) and thus find the *interest interval*. Once the optimal hyperparameters have been found, a new model is trained using the whole training data and evaluated using the test session. In the particular case of PVNE, the additional hyperparameter K (number of voters in the ensemble) is chosen in two different manners: i) fixed for all users (for instance, PVNE-K5 refers to using the top 5 neurons), or ii) the best K for each user (PVNE-KBest refers this second option).

As a metric for evaluation, we use the balanced accuracy, $BAC = (recall + specificity)/2$, because this problem has an intrinsic imbalance: there are five negative stimuli against only one positive stimulus. The standard classification consists of getting the model's prediction probability for a 1000 ms window to be or not a P300 wave. As our models provide a continuous output (one output for each time step) we use the procedures described in Sects. 2.3 and 2.4 to transform this sample-level output into an event classification.

3.2 Output Layer Analysis

Choosing the appropriate *offset* and *window size* is crucial when training recurrent neural networks to predict P300 events in a sample-level mode [21] because we know that, due to the inter-variability between users, the P300 event does not always appear in the same temporal window. For the experiments, we introduce the L1 regularization penalty with parameter $\gamma = 0.05$ into the model. We use L1 because of its aggressive impact on the neurons' weights, since we want the model to discard those neurons which are not relevant in the output layer.

In this case, the analysis of the output layer takes a significant role since it is crucial to understand the post-validation ensemble model. To analyze the output weights, we show in Fig. 4 two example bar plots for each neuron in the hidden layer with the absolute value of its output weights. The top figure represents the non-regularized settings, and the bottom figure represents the regularized settings. Both plots were obtained with the best *interest interval* (*offset* = 375 ms and *window size* = 125 ms) when the network is trained with User 7 and tested with Session 4. Similar results have been observed with all other users and sessions.

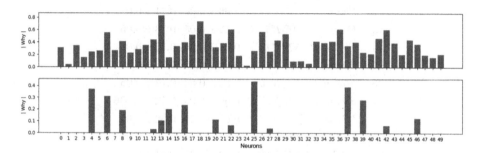

Fig. 4. For each neuron in the hidden layer, the bar plots represent the absolute value of its output weights. The top figure represents the non-regularized settings, and the bottom figure represents the regularized settings with the best *interest interval* (*offset* = 375 ms and *window size* = 125 ms) when the network is trained with User 7 and tested with Session 4. Similar results have been observed with all other users and sessions.

There exists a substantial difference between the two figures. When we train the network without L1 regularization (top figure), almost all neurons influence the model's prediction in its output. However, when applying regularization to the output weights (bottom figure), there are a few neurons that determine the model's prediction. Hence, some neurons are determinant to give a proper prediction, while the rest of the neurons are used to process the previous time steps and keep the relevant information from the temporal sequence. This result lines up with previous research ideas [22,23]. Therefore, if some neurons differ from themselves when identifying P300 or not P300, we confirm that these neurons can somehow classify the data individually, so their voting in the PVNE will be more meaningful.

3.3 Results

In the remaining of this section, we show the test BAC averaged over the eight available users. Please note that the *interest interval* (*offset* and *window size*) is different for each user, as well as the value of K if we refer to PVNE-KBest (see Sect. 3.1). We show in Table 1 the test BAC for different settings and models: the first row is trained with the standard preprocessing since we are replicating the state of the art Hoffman's BLDA model [14], and the rest of them are trained following the sample-level preprocessing.

Table 1. Test Balanced Accuracy obtained with all proposed models when training with and without L1 regularization.

#	Models	L1reg = 0	L1reg = 0.05
1	*BLDA* [14]	0.71 ± 0.05	
2	*Elman*	0.66 ± 0.06	0.71 ± 0.06
3	*Elman-PVNE-K5*	0.62 ± 0.05	0.73 ± 0.06
4	*Elman-PVNE-K10*	0.64 ± 0.05	0.73 ± 0.06
5	*Elman-PVNE-K15*	0.64 ± 0.06	0.73 ± 0.06
6	*Elman-PVNE-K20*	0.65 ± 0.06	0.73 ± 0.06
7	*Elman-PVNE-KBest*	0.66 ± 0.06	**0.75 ± 0.06**
8	*LSTM* [21]	0.69 ± 0.05	0.69 ± 0.06
9	*LSTM-PVNE-K5*	0.67 ± 0.05	0.70 ± 0.06
10	*LSTM-PVNE-K10*	0.68 ± 0.05	0.71 ± 0.06
11	*LSTM-PVNE-K15*	0.68 ± 0.06	0.71 ± 0.07
12	*LSTM-PVNE-K20*	0.68 ± 0.06	0.71 ± 0.07
13	*LSTM-PVNE-KBest*	0.69 ± 0.05	0.72 ± 0.07

From the table, we can extract two main ideas. First, to apply or not L1 regularization notably affects the final performance of the models (compare columns *L1reg = 0* and *L1reg = 0.05*). In the case of the LSTMs, the variation in the results is more modest. However, the performance of Elman networks is strongly affected. Second, the regularization scheme seems to be more relevant than the network architecture. In fact, the Elman network slightly outperforms the LSTM in the best configuration, so we could claim that complex models, such as LSTMs, are not needed to solve this problem. Finally, the Elman-PVNE approach improves the state of the art in more than 4% of test BAC when the best K is chosen for each user (compare rows 1 and 7). Intuitively, we should only perform this experiment if the output layer has been regularized, but it can also be applied if there is no regularization penalty. As expected, the best performance is obtained when L1 regularization turns off the unnecessary neurons. When it is not the case, the use of PVNE has no benefits in the model performance (note that rows 2 and 7 have the same BAC when no L1 regularization is applied).

4   Conclusions and Discussion

In this article, we have introduced a novel approach that consists of a post-validation neural ensemble (PVNE) methodology for detecting the sample-level temporal structure of P300 event-related potentials. This neural ensemble is made by selecting neurons according to the importance of the weights that connect the recurrent layer with the network's output. Subsequently, the individual neural predictions are combined to obtain the final PVNE decision.

We have compared the performance of Elman RNNs against the standard LSTM, and we have shown that, for this particular problem, models as complex as LSTMs are not indispensable since better results are obtained with an Elman network (compare rows 2 and 8 from Table 1 when L1 has been applied). In addition, PVNE with its best settings outperforms the state of the art (BLDA [14]) by 4% (compare rows 1 and 7 from Table 1). Furthermore, applying PVNE on a recurrent network, either Elman or LSTM, improves the standard network (compare rows 2 and 7, and 8 and 13 from Table 1). This last result lines up with other research ideas [22,23] in which a few neurons determine the model's prediction, and the rest are used to process and keep the relevant information from the temporal sequence. L1 regularization reduces the number of active neurons in the output layer, differentiating the decision-maker neurons from the rest.

This sample-level methodology opens the way to a study of the EEG signal in ERP-based BCIs that will improve the information transfer rate, which is a pending challenge [27]. Sample-level prediction allows real-time monitoring of the EEG signal generation related to ERPs since this methodology can help locate the temporal information from a target stimulus. This way, some approaches, such as those presented in this work, help to manage inter- and intrasubject variability, a latent problem in BCIs. Likewise, the proposal of this work helps to gain knowledge into the interpretability of the EEG signal. In a clinical problem (as in any machine learning problem) it is essential to verify that the high-accuracy measurement is the result of an adequate representation of the problem and not of possible artifacts in the data [20].

Our work contributes to techniques that seek to understand how the model has learned. Our analysis of the output layer departs from the importance of applying regularization, described in Sect. 3.2, and could give us more insight into the internal interpretability of the models. Further research could focus on the analysis of the internal behavior of the recurrent layer to ensure confidence in the signal features and get the most relevant input electrodes in the temporal decision-making. Another interesting research could be the addition of some mechanisms for the *offset* and *window size* hyperparameters adjustment as trainable parameters of the network. This way, the potential model could learn specific inter- and intrasubject differences from each user.

Acknowledgements. This work has been partially funded by Spanish project PID2020-114867RB-I00, (MCIN/AEI and ERDF- "A way of making Europe"), Universidad Politécnica Salesiana 034-02-2022-03-31 and by Predoctoral Research Grants 2015-AR2Q9086 of the Government of Ecuador through SENESCYT.

References

1. Abibullaev, B., Zollanvari, A.: A systematic deep learning model selection for P300-based brain-computer interfaces. IEEE Trans. Syst. Man Cybern. Syst. **52**(5), 2744–2756 (2021)
2. Allison, B.Z., Kübler, A., Jin, J.: 30+ years of P300 brain-computer interfaces. Psychophysiology **57**(7), e13569 (2020)
3. Bashivan, P., Rish, I., Yeasin, M., Codella, N.: Learning Representations from EEG with Deep Recurrent-Convolutional Neural Networks (2015)
4. Bishop, C.M.: Pattern Recognition and Machine Learning. Springer (2006)
5. Changoluisa, V., Varona, P., Rodríguez, F.B.: An electrode selection approach in P300-based BCIs to address Inter-and Intra-subject variability. In: 2018 6th International Conference on Brain-Computer Interface (BCI), pp. 1–4. IEEE (2018)
6. Changoluisa, V., Varona, P., Rodriguez, F.B.: A fine dry-electrode selection to characterize event-related potentials in the context of BCI. In: Rojas, I., Joya, G., Català, A. (eds.) IWANN 2021. LNCS, vol. 12861, pp. 230–241. Springer, Cham (2021). https://doi.org/10.1007/978-3-030-85030-2_19
7. Changoluisa, V., Varona, P., Rodríguez, F.B.: A low-cost computational method for characterizing event-related potentials for BCI applications and beyond. IEEE Access **8**, 111089–111101 (2020)
8. Chollet, F., et al.: Keras (2015). https://keras.io
9. Craik, A., He, Y., Contreras-Vidal, J.L.: Deep learning for electroencephalogram (EEG) classification tasks: a review. J. Neural Eng. **16**(3), 031001 (2019)
10. van Dinteren, R., Arns, M., Jongsma, M.L., Kessels, R.P.: P300 development across the lifespan: a systematic review and meta-analysis. PloS One **9**(2), e87347 (2014)
11. Elman, J.L.: Finding structure in time. Cogn. Sci. **14**(2), 179–211 (1990)
12. Havaei, P., Zekri, M., Mahmoudzadeh, E., Rabbani, H.: An efficient deep learning framework for P300 evoked related potential detection in EEG signal. Comput. Methods Programs Biomed. **229**, 107324 (2023)
13. Hochreiter, S., Schmidhuber, J.: Long short-term memory. Neural Comput. **9**(8), 1735–1780 (1997)
14. Hoffmann, U., Vesin, J.M., Ebrahimi, T., Diserens, K.: An effcient P300-based brain-computer interface for disabled subjects. J. Neurosci. Methods **167**, 115–25 (2008)
15. Hu, L., Zhang, Z. (eds.): EEG Signal Processing and Feature Extraction. Springer, Singapore (2019). https://doi.org/10.1007/978-981-13-9113-2
16. Joshi, R., Goel, P., Sur, M., Murthy, H.A.: Single trial P300 classification using convolutional LSTM and deep learning ensembles method. In: Tiwary, U.S. (ed.) IHCI 2018. LNCS, vol. 11278, pp. 3–15. Springer, Cham (2018). https://doi.org/10.1007/978-3-030-04021-5_1

17. Li, F., et al.: Inter-subject P300 variability relates to the efficiency of brain networks reconfigured from resting- to task-state: evidence from a simultaneous event-related EEG-fMRI study. NeuroImage **205**, 116285 (2020)
18. Lotte, F., et al.: A review of classification algorithms for EEG-based Brain-Computer Interfaces: a 10 year update. J. Neural Eng. **15**(3), 031005 (2018)
19. Luck, S.J.: An introduction to the event-related potential technique. MIT press, second edn. (2014)
20. Montavon, G., Samek, W., Müller, K.R.: Methods for interpreting and understanding deep neural networks. Digital Sig. Process. **73**, 1–15 (2018)
21. Oliva, C., Changoluisa, V., Rodríguez, F.B., Lago-Fernández, L.F.: Precise temporal P300 detection in brain computer interface EEG signals using a long-short term memory. In: Farkaš, I., Masulli, P., Otte, S., Wermter, S. (eds.) Artificial Neural Networks and Machine Learning - ICANN 2021, pp. 457–468. Springer International Publishing, Cham (2021)
22. Oliva, C., Lago-Fernández, L.F.: On the interpretation of recurrent neural networks as finite state machines. In: Tetko, I.V., Karpov, P., Theis, F. (eds.) ICANN 2019. LNCS, vol. 11727, pp. 312–323. Springer, Cham (2019). https://doi.org/10.1007/978-3-030-30487-4_25
23. Oliva, C., Lago-Fernández, L.F.: Separation of memory and processing in dual recurrent neural networks. In: Farkaš, I., Masulli, P., Otte, S., Wermter, S. (eds.) ICANN 2021. LNCS, vol. 12894, pp. 360–371. Springer, Cham (2021). https://doi.org/10.1007/978-3-030-86380-7_29
24. Ouyang, G., Hildebrandt, A., Sommer, W., Zhou, C.: Exploiting the intra-subject latency variability from single-trial event-related potentials in the P3 time range: a review and comparative evaluation of methods Neurosci. Biobehav. Rev. **75**, 1–21 (2017)
25. Pedregosa, F., Varoquaux, G., Gramfort, A., Michel, V., Thirion, B., Grisel, O., Blondel, M., Prettenhofer, P., Weiss, R., Dubourg, V., Vanderplas, J., Passos, A., Cournapeau, D., Brucher, M., Perrot, M., Duchesnay, E.: Scikit-learn: Machine learning in Python. J. Mach. Learn. Res. **12**, 2825–2830 (2011)
26. Philip, J.T., George, S.T.: Visual P300 mind-speller brain-computer interfaces: a walk through the recent developments with special focus on classification algorithms. Clin. EEG Neurosci. **51**(1), 19–33 (2020)
27. Ramadan, R.A., Vasilakos, A.V.: Brain computer interface: control signals review. Neurocomputing **223**, 26–44 (2017)
28. Sutton, S., Braren, M., Zubin, J., John, E.R.: Evoked-potential correlates of stimulus uncertainty. Science **150**(3700), 1187–1188 (1965)
29. Tal, O., Friedman, D.: Recurrent Neural Networks for P300-based BCI. CoRR abs/1901.10798 (2019), http://arxiv.org/abs/1901.10798
30. Zhang, X., Yao, L., Wang, X., Monaghan, J., McAlpine, D., Zhang, Y.: A survey on deep learning-based non-invasive brain signals: recent advances and new frontiers. J. Neural Eng. **18**(3), 031002 (2021)

Energy Efficiency of Deep Learning Compression Techniques in Wearable Human Activity Recognition

Chiara Contoli$^{(\boxtimes)}$ [ID] and Emanuele Lattanzi [ID]

Department of Pure and Applied Sciences, University of Urbino, Piazza della
Repubblica 13, 61029 Urbino, Italy
{chiara.contoli,emanuele.lattanzi}@uniurb.it

Abstract. Deploying deep learning (DL) models onto low-power devices
for Human Activity Recognition (HAR) purposes is gaining momentum
because of the pervasive adoption of wearable sensor devices. However,
the outcome of such deployment needs exploration not only because
the topic is still in its infancy, but also because of the wide combination between low-power devices, deep models, and available deployment
strategies. We have investigated the outcome of the application of three
compression techniques, namely lite conversion, dynamic quantization,
and full-integer quantization, that allow the deployment of deep models
on low-power devices. This paper describes how those three compression techniques impact accuracy and energy consumption on an ESP32
device. In terms of accuracy, the full-integer technique incurs an accuracy drop between 2% and 3%, whereas the dynamic quantization and
the lite conversion result in a negligible accuracy drop. In terms of power
efficiency, dynamic and full-integer quantization allow for saving almost
30% of energy. The adoption of one of those two quantization techniques
is recommended to obtain an executable network model, and we advise
the adoption of the dynamic quantization given the negligible accuracy
drop (Chiara Contoli is a researcher co-funded by the European Union -
PON Research and Innovation 2014-2020.).

Keywords: Human Activity Recognition · Compression techniques ·
Deep learning · Microcontroller

1 Introduction

Deep Learning (DL) has become a ubiquitous tool in many modern applications such as computer vision, natural language processing, and speech recognition. However, the computational requirements of DL models are often substantial, hindering their deployment on resource-constrained devices such as mobile
phones or embedded systems. As such, there has been significant research interest in developing efficient techniques to compress DL models without sacrificing
their performance.

I. Maglogiannis et al. (Eds.): AIAI 2023, IFIP AICT 675, pp. 102–113, 2023.
https://doi.org/10.1007/978-3-031-34111-3_10

One approach to address this challenge is to leverage model compression techniques such as pruning [1], quantization [11], and knowledge distillation [9]. These techniques aim to reduce the number of parameters or operations in a DL model while maintaining its accuracy.

Pruning and quantization have been recently surveyed in terms of methods of compression and mathematical formulation by Liang et al. [12]. Pruning consists of removing unnecessary parameters or neurons, and connections because do not provide a significant contribution to resulting accuracy. As of today, pruning can be distinguished depending on various aspects that are considered during the operation. In particular, three categories exist: i) whether the pruned network is symmetric or not, it is classified as structured or unstructured pruning; ii) based on the pruned element type, it is classified as neurons or connections pruning; iii) based on when pruning steps are carried out, i.e., after training but before inference, or during the inference process, it is classified as static pruning or dynamic pruning, respectively.

Quantization, on the other hand, consists of reducing weight representation by reducing bit width numbers, typically from floating point values to integer values. The most widely used quantization techniques are: i) post-training quantization, which envisages the model training followed by weight quantization, and as a last step a model (re)optimization to generate the quantized model; ii) quantization-aware training, which envisages the weight quantization during training, and then the network is re-trained to fine-tune the model precision to compensate the accuracy degradation occurred during the quantization process. Unfortunately, at present, it is not always clear how to balance the trade-off between compression, accuracy, and energy efficiency, and different techniques may perform differently for different models and for different DL tasks [2].

In this work, we carried out a thorough analysis of the energy effectiveness of the most recent quantization-based compression methods applied to a sensor-based Human Activity Recognition (HAR) case study resolved by deep learning models. HAR represents a set of tasks that gained a lot of attention in recent years because of the broad range of real-world applications. Early diagnosis, rehabilitation, and patient assistance can be provided in medical decision processes for healthcare monitoring purposes; industrial applications, gaming, and sport/fitness tracking are of great interest as well. Two main approaches are leveraged for HAR: camera-based and sensor-based recognition. Camera and inertial sensors allow to detect a set of daily human activities via computer vision techniques and acceleration/location sensors, respectively.

In this work, we focus on real-time sensor-based HAR tasks directly executed on top of a low-power wearable device characterized by strong real resource constraints. The contribution of this paper can be summarized as follows:

- We provide a methodology to fine-tune models hyperparameters while taking into account the energy efficiency applied to convolutional neural networks (CNN) and Long short-term memory (LSTM) neural networks.
- We characterize the accuracy-energy trade-off of different quantization-based compression techniques
- We made real energy consumption measurements in a real case study scenario by porting and executing each model on top of a real low-power wearable hardware setup.

2 Related Work

In recent years, researchers have started exploring the interplay between DL model compression techniques and energy efficiency. This includes developing compression techniques that explicitly consider energy consumption as a metric, as well as developing hardware-aware compression techniques that optimize the compressed model's energy consumption on specific hardware platforms [3].

The investigation of HAR on low-power microcontroller units (MCUs) blossomed in the last few years: back in 2020, Novac et al. evaluated the implementation of multi-layer perceptrons and convolutional neural networks for HAR on an ARM-Cortex-M4F-based MCU [15]. They compared the supervised learning methods to the unsupervised and online learning ones, by proving the higher benefits of the latter. Authors refer to online learning as the ability of a neural network to adapt itself to a new set of data, even though the initial learning phase is over. They further explored the deployment of HAR on MCU by proposing a new quantization method, together with a new framework that allows training, quantizing, and deploying deep neural networks [14]. In their work, they only consider convolutional neural networks (specifically, the ResNetv1 model architecture); int8, int16, and float32 were considered as quantization techniques, and SparkFun Edge and Nucleo-L452RE-P were considered as MCU platforms (both belonging to the Cortex-M4F core family).

Daghero et al. applied Binary Neural Networks (BNNs) to HAR to decrease network complexity via an extreme form of quantization [6]; indeed, by using BNNs the precision of data format, both weights and layers input/output, is reduced to 1-bit precision. Authors propose a BNN inference library that targets RISC-V processors. Subsequently, authors extended their work [4,5] by proposing a set of efficient one-dimensional convolutional neural networks (1D CNNs) and testing optimization techniques such as sub-type and mixed-precision quantization. The aim was to find a good trade-off between accuracy and memory occupation. As a target platform, they leveraged again the RISC-V MCU.

Similarly, Ghibellini et al. proposed a CNN model for falling and running detection within an industrial environment for safety purposes [8]. This work shows very preliminary results in terms of accuracy and model size. Dynamic range quantization was applied to reduce the size of the model which is then deployed on the firmware of an Arduino BLE 33 Sense.

Compared to the existing literature, besides the one-dimensional convolutional neural network, which is the only one considered in all the others works, we explore also the deployment, on a target MCU, of another deep neural network (DNN) relevant to the context of HAR. We consider the combination of the one-dimensional convolutional neural network (1D_CNN) with the vanilla long short-term memory (LSTM). The goal of this work is twofold: on the one hand, we want to perform an in-depth analysis that compares the deployment of relevant DNNs on a target MCU; on the other one, we want to provide insights on: i) the feasibility of the deployment of those networks on the target MCU; ii) a comparison in terms of classification performance and power-efficiency.

3   Methodology

In this section, we describe the proposed methodology to characterize in terms of classification accuracy and energy consumption, the state-of-the-art compression techniques applied to two types of deep neural networks. In particular, we considered the one-dimension convolutional network (1D_CNN) and the combined adoption of CNN and LSTM (1D_CNN_LSTM) applied to a HAR case study deployed on an Espressif ESP32-wroom-32 DevKit representing a real resource-constrained wearable device [7]. The ESP32 has two CPU cores that can be individually controlled running at a clock frequency adjustable from 80 MHz to 240 MHz. The chip also has a low-power mode that can be used to save power while performing peripheral I/O tasks that do not require much computing effort. Our version of the ESP32 has 4 MB of flash memory for saving the firmware and 400 KB of RAM memory.

Then we focused on tuning those hyperparameters that impact the complexity, the memory footprint, and the effectiveness of the network. On top of the obtained models, we applied compression techniques to investigate the tradeoff between accuracy loss and energy saving.

3.1   Hyperparameters Tuning

The proposed 1D_CNN network envisages one convolutional 1D layer, followed by a pooling layer and two fully connected dense layers, in which the last one provides the output. It is worth mentioning that: i) a dropout layer is placed after the 1D convolutional layer; ii) a flatten layer is placed after the pooling layer; iii) the softmax function is used in the last layer to infer the activity label. For what concern the combined approach 1D_CNN_LSTM, the network structure is as follows: one convolutional 1D layer followed by a batch normalization and by a ReLU layer, which is then followed by a LSTM layer, followed by a dropout layer and two fully connected dense layers, in which the last one provides the output.

Table 1 lists the network types highlighting the hyperparameters adopted in our investigation. The network ID is used as a shortcut to refer to the network type and its relative structure. The network structure labels are coded by using the xxT notation where xx is the number of units and T represents the type of unit. For instance, in the case of C_8, the string *32F 3K 100D* stays for 32 convolutional filters with a kernel size of 3 followed by a dense layer containing 100 neurons.

Table 1. Network types and structure.

Net Type	Net ID	Net Structure	Net Type	Net ID	Net Structure
1D_CNN	C_8	32F 3K 100D	1D_CNN_LSTM	–	–
	C_7	20F 3K 100D		–	–
	C_6	16F 3K 100D		CL_6	16F 3K 16H 256D
	C_5	10F 3K 100D		CL_5	16F 3K 8H 256D
	C_4	8F 3K 100D		CL_4	16F 3K 4H 256D
	C_3	4F 3K 100D		CL_3	8F 3K 16H 256D
	C_2	2F 3K 100D		CL_2	4F 3K 16H 256D
	C_1	1F 3K 100D		CL_1	2F 3K 16H 256D

The hyperparameter tuning in deep-learning models dedicated to a tiny device must be carefully conducted because of its resource limitations. In particular, the network dimension must be compatible with the device memory characteristics of the device, together with its execution time (i.e. the time needed to make an inference). After a brief manual tuning of the structure parameters, we end up in the network structures listed in Table 1. For each network type, we decide to start from what we expect to be the biggest size capable of fitting inside the device, and from that size, we then decrease one, or two, parameters in order to lower the network complexity.

For (1D_CNN) we made use of 3 kernels because we have seen it is a value typically used in literature; instead, the choice of the filter value is related to the fine-tuning phase. To gradually decrease the network complexity we decide to reduce the number of filters in the convolutional layers while keeping the same number of kernels, planning a total of 8 network models. For the combined network (1D_CNN_LSTM), starting from the bigger network installable in the device memory, we planned 6 network models obtained by reducing the number of filters in the convolutional layer.

3.2 Models Characterization Workflow

The proposed characterization workflow consists of three phases highlighted in Fig. 1. In the first phase, the raw data sampled from a 3-axial accelerometer and gyroscope are extracted from a dataset and are fed into the base network model to perform train and subsequent evaluation. The raw signals have been divided into time windows to generate samples for training and testing purposes. In the second phase, the compression techniques have been applied to the trained models. In particular, first of all, we applied the lite conversion to the trained model, then the post-training dynamic quantization, and the post-training full-integer quantization.

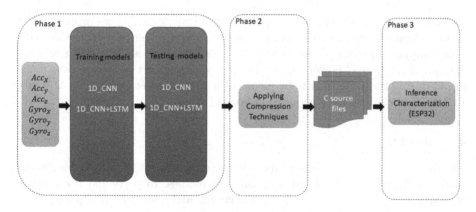

Fig. 1. General workflow.

The application of each compression technique via the TensorFlow lite converter allows us to generate a C source file containing the char array version of the lite. In the third phase, each C source file is compiled into an executable file by means of the ESP-IDF platform (Espressif IoT Development Framework) and moved onto the ESP32 device. Here the execution time and energy have been measured. It is worth mentioning that the proposed workflow has been applied to each network listed in Table 1.

4   Experimental Evaluation

All the deep learning models have been trained and tested using a Keras-TensorFlow application running in a Google Colab environment [16]. TF provides also TensorFlow Lite(TFL) a library for network model deployment on mobile devices, microcontrollers, and edge devices. In particular, TFL allows converting a base TF model into a compressed version via the so-called TFLite converter by applying different compression techniques such as post-training dynamic quantization and full-integer 8-bit quantization.

As a case study we developed a wearable sensor-based HAR application on top of an Espressif ESP32-wroom-32 DevKit [7] connected to an MPU6050 integrated 6-axis motion tracking device that combines a 3-axis gyroscope, and 3-axis accelerometer [10]. The application was entirely developed in C++ using the ESP-IDF platform with the TensorFlow Lite Micro libraries installed.

To train the models and test their accuracy we leveraged the UCI-HAR dataset [17] which is a publicly available dataset where accelerometer and gyroscope signals are sampled 50 Hz. The monitored activities are gathered from 30 subjects aged between 18 and 48 years and are: *walking, walking upstairs, walking downstairs, sitting, standing, and lying down*. In this work, the entire dataset was split into 75% for training and 25% for testing.

To estimate the energy consumption of the ESP32 device, we measured the voltage drop across a sensing resistor (9.8Ω) placed in series with the device's power supply. The device was powered at 3.3V through an NGMO2 Rohde & Schwarz dual-channel power supply [18], and we sampled the signals to be monitored during the experiments by means of a National Instruments NI-DAQmx PCI-6251 16-channel data acquisition board [13].

4.1   Results

This section reports the performance characterization of the compression techniques applied to the proposed deep-learning models. In particular, we provide a comparison in terms of classification accuracy and energy consumption.

Classification Accuracy. Table 2 reports the highest classification accuracy reached by each network type before (base) and after the application of the compression techniques.

Table 2. Highest classification accuracy reached by each network type considering the application of each compression technique. The "base" case refers to a model not subject to any compression techniques.

network		accuracy			
type	configuration	base	lite	dynamic	full-integer
1D_CNN	C_3	0.887	0.884	0.888	0.858
1D_CNN_LSTM	CL_3	0.918	0.917	0.922	0.902

These results, first of all, highlight the already known supremacy of the combined network with respect to the 1D_CNN which scores nearly 3% points more accuracy in the uncompressed configuration. On the other hand, going from the basic model to the lite one, no significant loss of accuracy is found and, even if dynamic compression is applied to the latter, the classification performance still remains the same. Notice that, the negligible increase in accuracy, in the latter case, is due to the different routines used in TensorFlow to characterize lite models with respect to base models. Applying the full-integer quantization to both models, on the other hand, a loss of accuracy ranging from 2 to 3% points is obtained.

Table 3 reports with an ✗ all the network models with respect to the compression technique: Lite (L), Dynamic (D), and Full-integer (F) not fitting inside the device. It is interesting to note that by simply lite converting the 1D_CNN_LSTM we never obtain a fitting and running network model.

Table 3. Network models fitting on the wearable device.

Net Type	Net ID	L	D	F	Net Type	Net ID	L	D	F
1D_CNN	C_8	✗	✓	✓	1D_CNN_LSTM	–	–	–	–
	C_7	✗	✓	✓		–	–	–	–
	C_6	✗	✓	✓		CL_6	✗	✓	✓
	C_5	✓	✓	✓		CL_5	✗	✓	✓
	C_4	✓	✓	✓		CL_4	✗	✓	✓
	C_3	✓	✓	✓		CL_3	✗	✓	✓
	C_2	✓	✓	✓		CL_2	✗	✓	✓
	C_1	✓	✓	✓		CL_1	✗	✓	✓

Figures 2 (a) and (b) show the accuracy provided by each compression technique applied respectively to the 1D_CNN and 1D_CNN_LSTM models when the network complexity is increased. Concerning the 1D_CNN network, the increase in complexity from C_1 to C_2 results in a large increase in the classification accuracy which reaches its maximum value with C_3 and then keeps it at high levels for both Lite and Dynamic models. Notice that, the accuracy of the configurations C_6, C_7, and C_8 of the Lite models are not plotted since they do not fit into the memory device. The significant loss of accuracy due to full-integer quantization is also evident from the graph for each network configuration.

The behavior of the 1D_CNN_LSTM network is almost the same with an increase in accuracy for more complex configurations and a non-negligible accuracy loss in the case of the full-integer quantization.

Energy Consumption. For each network type, all the respective fitting network models reported in Table 3 were deployed one by one on the ESP32 device. Given a running model, the HAR application was run to sample real-time data directly from the gyroscope and the accelerometer and to perform real-time inference measurements. In particular, for each model, we collected 10 consecutive measures in order to get an average of the inference time. Moreover, during execution, the device was connected to the energy measurement setup to sample the corresponding current consumption waveforms form which to derive the inference energy of each model.

Figures 3 (a) and (b) show the inference energy measured respectively for the 1D_CNN and 1D_CNN_LSTM models when varying the hyperparameters configuration. In both cases, increasing the model complexity produces an increase in the energy needed to make an inference. In the 1D_CNN case also the energy consumed by the simple lite model for configurations C_1 to C_5 is reported highlighting a non-negligible energy saving produced by dynamic and full-integer quantization techniques with respect to the raw lite models. On the other hand,

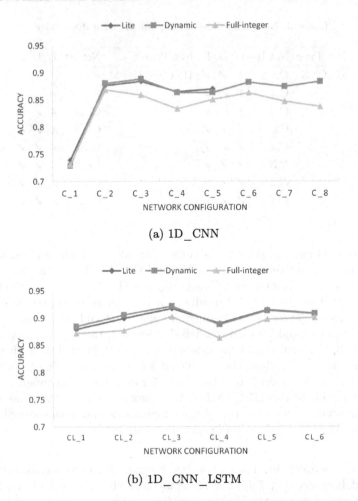

(a) 1D_CNN

(b) 1D_CNN_LSTM

Fig. 2. Classification accuracy of each network type per increasing network complexity, obtained by applying lite conversion, dynamic quantization, and full-integer quantization

the full-integer quantization does not appear to introduce an additional energy advantage over dynamic quantization. Notice that, unfortunately, no configuration of lite models was able to run on the device in the case of the CNN and LSTM combined network so we do have not an energy consumption baseline in this case.

In the case of model 1D_CNN, for the configurations from C_1 to C_5, we have estimated the energy savings induced by the two quantization techniques with respect to the base value of the lite model. Figure 4 shows the corresponding bar graph. Interestingly, for the simplest model (C_1) both techniques do not affect the energy consumption which is always very low. Starting from C_2 to C_5 configurations, the energy saved by the full-integer quantization always

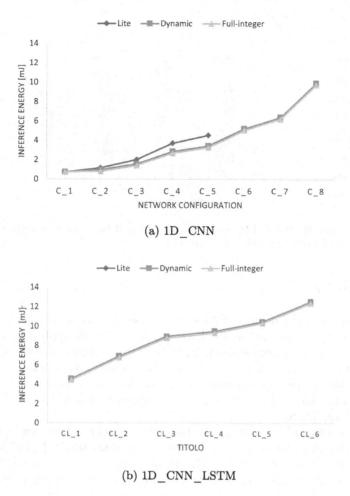

(a) 1D_CNN

(b) 1D_CNN_LSTM

Fig. 3. Energy obtained by applying lite conversion, dynamic quantization and full-integer quantization

overcomes that obtained with the dynamic technique even if, it seems that as the complexity of the models increases, the differences between the two techniques decrease, both reaching around an energy-saving close to 30%.

Considering that, from the classification accuracy point of view, the dynamic quantization technique does not involve a priceable loss, we would like to advise in any case the use of this technique even if the energy savings produced by the full-integer quantization could be slightly greater. Furthermore, we remind you that the application of one of the two quantization techniques is even indispensable for models of considerable size which otherwise would not execute on some extremely low-power platforms such as the ESP32.

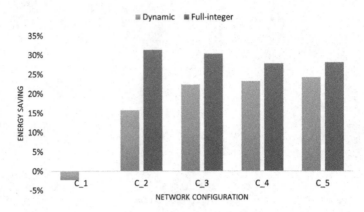

Fig. 4. Energy saving obtained by applying dynamic and full-integer quantization on the 1D_CNN model when varying its complexity.

5   Conclusions

In this paper, we carried out a thorough analysis of the energy effectiveness of the most recent quantization-based compression methods applied to a HAR case study resolved by deep learning models. We specifically looked at CNN models and CNN and LSTM combinations. The models were run on a real low-power wearable device while concurrently monitoring its energy consumption after being converted and compressed from a dataset that is widely used in the field of HAR applications.

From the classification point of view, the dynamic quantization technique and the lite conversion result in a negligible loss of accuracy while the full-integer recorded losses between 2% and 3%. On the other hand, for both dynamic and full-integer compression techniques, we measured an energy saving of close to 30%.

As a final remark, we would like to advise in any case the use of the dynamic quantization technique considering that, from the classification accuracy point of view, it does not involve a priceable loss. Furthermore, we confirm the need of applying one of these quantization techniques for several models of considerable size which otherwise would not execute on some extremely low-power platforms such as the ESP32.

References

1. Augasta, M., Kathirvalavakumar, T.: Pruning algorithms of neural networks-a comparative study. Open Comput. Sci. **3**(3), 105–115 (2013)
2. Chaman, S.: Techniques for compressing deep convolutional neural network. In: 2020 International Conference on Computational Performance Evaluation (ComPE), pp. 048–053. IEEE (2020)

3. Choudhary, T., Mishra, V., Goswami, A., Sarangapani, J.: A comprehensive survey on model compression and acceleration. Artif. Intell. Rev. **53**(7), 5113–5155 (2020). https://doi.org/10.1007/s10462-020-09816-7
4. Daghero, F., et al.: Human activity recognition on microcontrollers with quantized and adaptive deep neural networks. ACM Trans. Embed. Comput. Syst. (TECS) **21**(4), 1–28 (2022)
5. Daghero, F., Pagliari, D.J., Poncino, M.: Two-stage human activity recognition on microcontrollers with decision trees and CNNs. In: 2022 17th Conference on Ph. D Research in Microelectronics and Electronics (PRIME), pp. 173–176. IEEE (2022)
6. Daghero, F., et al.: Ultra-compact binary neural networks for human activity recognition on RISC-V processors. In: Proceedings of the 18th ACM International Conference on Computing Frontiers, pp. 3–11 (2021)
7. Espressif: Esp32-c3-wroom-02 datasheet (2022). https://www.espressif.com/en/support/documents/technical-documents Accessed 07 Feb 2023
8. Ghibellini, A., Bononi, L., Di Felice, M.: Intelligence at the IoT edge: activity recognition with low-power microcontrollers and convolutional neural networks. In: 2022 IEEE 19th Annual Consumer Communications & Networking Conference (CCNC), pp. 707–710. IEEE (2022)
9. Gou, J., Yu, B., Maybank, S.J., Tao, D.: Knowledge distillation: a survey. Int. J. Comput. Vis. **129**, 1789–1819 (2021)
10. InvenSense Inc.: Mpu-6050 product specification (2023). https://invensense.tdk.com/products/motion-tracking/6-axis/mpu-6050/ Accessed 07 Feb 2023
11. Khoram, S., Li, J.: Adaptive quantization of neural networks. In: International Conference on Learning Representations (2018)
12. Liang, T., Glossner, J., Wang, L., Shi, S., Zhang, X.: Pruning and quantization for deep neural network acceleration: A survey. Neurocomputing **461**, 370–403 (2021)
13. National. Instruments: Pc-6251 datasheet (2020). http://www.ni.com/pdf/manuals/375213c.pdf Accessed 07 Feb 2023
14. Novac, P.E., Boukli Hacene, G., Pegatoquet, A., Miramond, B., Gripon, V.: Quantization and deployment of deep neural networks on microcontrollers. Sensors **21**(9), 2984 (2021)
15. Novac, P.E., Castagnetti, A., Russo, A., Miramond, B., Pegatoquet, A., Verdier, F.: Toward unsupervised human activity recognition on microcontroller units. In: 2020 23rd Euromicro Conference on Digital System Design (DSD), pp. 542–550. IEEE (2020)
16. Pang, B., Nijkamp, E., Wu, Y.N.: Deep learning with tensorFlow: a review. J. Educ. Behav. Stat. **45**(2), 227–248 (2020)
17. Reyes-Ortiz, J.L., Oneto, L., Samà, A., Parra, X., Anguita, D.: Transition-aware human activity recognition using smartphones. Neurocomputing **171**, 754–767 (2016)
18. Rohde&Schwarz: Ngmo2 datasheet (2020). https://www.rohde-schwarz.com/it/brochure-scheda-tecnica/ngmo2/ Accessed 07 Feb 2023

Enhancing Medication Event Classification with Syntax Parsing and Adversarial Learning

Zsolt Szántó[✉], Balázs Bánáti, and Tamás Zombori

Institute of Informatics, University of Szeged, Szeged, Hungary
szantozs@inf.u-szeged.hu

Abstract. In this paper, we introduce a method for extracting detailed information from raw medical notes that could help medical providers more easily understand a patient's medication history and make more informed medical decisions. Our system uses NLP techniques for finding the names of medications and details about the changes to their disposition in unstructured clinical notes.

The system was created to extract data from the Contextualized Medication Event Dataset in three subtasks. Our system utilizes a solution based on a large language model enriched with adversarial examples for the medication extraction and event classification tasks. To extract more detailed contextual information about the medication changes, we were motivated by aspect-based sentiment analysis and used the local context focus mechanism to highlight the relevant parts of the context and extended it with information from dependency syntax.

Both adversarial learning and the syntax-enhanced local focus mechanism improved the results of our system.

Keywords: Medication event classification · Dependency parsing · Adversarial learning

1 Introduction

Understanding the complete medication history is necessary for having a fuller picture of the patient, but in many cases, medication-related information is documented only as unstructured clinical notes. This can make it challenging for healthcare providers to obtain a comprehensive view of a patient's medication history including information on medication changes, dosages, and adverse reactions. The automatic analysis of these notes could help medical providers have a fuller background on the patient, better understand the reasons behind medication changes, and identify the healthcare provider who ordered a medication change, as well as the reason for the change. This would allow for more informed medical decisions and improve patient safety.

The Contextualized Medication Event Dataset (CMED) [14] and the National NLP Clinical Challenges 2022 Track 1 aimed at the extraction of these medication events from clinical notes. As well as identifying names of medications, this dataset

© IFIP International Federation for Information Processing 2023
Published by Springer Nature Switzerland AG 2023
I. Maglogiannis et al. (Eds.): AIAI 2023, IFIP AICT 675, pp. 114–124, 2023.
https://doi.org/10.1007/978-3-031-34111-3_11

Table 1. Frequency of event and context classes in the training and test data.

Task	Label	#train	#test	Task	Label	#train	#test
Event	NoDisposition	5260	1326	Temporality	Past	744	173
	Disposition	1412	335		Present	494	132
	Undetermined	557	122		Future	145	29
Action	Start	568	131		Unknown	29	1
	Stop	340	67	Certainty	Certain	1176	281
	Increase	129	22		Hypothetical	134	33
	Decrease	54	13		Conditional	100	15
	UniqueDose	285	88		Unknown	2	6
	OtherChange	1	0	Actor	Physician	1278	311
	Unknown	35	14		Patient	106	17
Negation	Negated	32	6		Unknown	28	7
	NotNegated	1380	329				

allows for the detailed analysis of the context of medication-related events. It aims to extract more detailed information from the text about the mentioned medications: like whether the use of the medication was started or stopped, or identifying the person requesting the change. This is a context classification problem where the goal is to find the information that relates to the specific expression, eg. being able to correctly identify if one medicine was started, but another was stopped for a patient within the same note.

Nowadays the most generic approach for this type of problem is using a pre-trained language model and fine-tuning it for our tasks. We applied two main additions to this standardized framework. One of our modifications is aiming to handle the noisy, error-ridden nature of the clinical notes, for this problem we applied adversarial attacks throughout the training process. The other was used for the context classification task and motivated by the state-of-the-art algorithms of aspect-based sentiment analysis as they both aim to identify the context relevant to the selected phrase. We also used syntactic relations to help find the more closely related parts of the sentences.

2   Dataset

The aim of the shared task was to find new ways to extract information from raw medical notes using NLP techniques. The full Contextualized Medication Event Dataset is comprised of 500 clinical notes that contain a total of 9012 medication mentions. The annotation of these documents can be divided into three levels, each reliant on the last. These three tasks are the following:

- Medication Extraction: The first task is to identify all the medications mentioned in clinical notes; this is a standard sequence labeling task.
- Event Classification: Once we have extracted these mentions, we classify each of them into one of three categories: **Disposition** (meaning a change in the

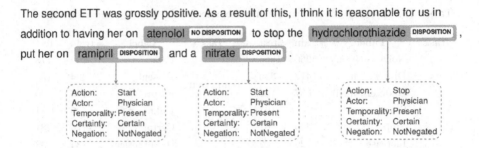

The second ETT was grossly positive. As a result of this, I think it is reasonable for us in addition to having her on atenolol NO DISPOSITION to stop the hydrochlorothiazide DISPOSITION , put her on ramipril DISPOSITION and a nitrate DISPOSITION .

Action:	Start
Actor:	Physician
Temporality:	Present
Certainty:	Certain
Negation:	NotNegated

Action:	Start
Actor:	Physician
Temporality:	Present
Certainty:	Certain
Negation:	NotNegated

Action:	Stop
Actor:	Physician
Temporality:	Present
Certainty:	Certain
Negation:	NotNegated

Fig. 1. The annotation of two sentences in the Contextualized Medication Event Dataset.

medication was discussed), **NoDisposition** (meaning no change was discussed), or **Undetermined** (meaning we need more information to make a determination).
- Context Classification: For medication mentions that fall into the Disposition category, we go a step further and classify them according to five different dimensions: Action (did the medication start or stop?), Negation (was it negated in any way?), Temporality (is it a past or a present change?), Certainty (was it hypothetical or conditional?), and Actor (who initiated the medication change?). This gives us a more complete understanding of the context in which the medication was mentioned.

As we mentioned earlier there are 9012 examples for event classification (the medication mentions) and only 1747 of them are in the **Disposition** category (ones with change in the medication). The detailed sizes of the different classes are shown in Table 1. There are three dimensions - the Actor, the Certainty, and Negation - where one class dominates the dataset: for these their most frequent label makes up more than 80 percent of the data. The distribution of different Actions is more balanced: the **Start**, the **Stop**, and the **UniqueDose** occur in more than 20 percent of the medication event changes.

Figure 1 shows an annotation for two example sentences. The colored boxes show the four different medications mentioned in the text. The color of the mention indicates the classification of the event, there are three with a change in disposition (marked orange) and one with no disposition change (marked blue). All three with a changed disposition are further annotated by the five context categories. We can see that the physician ordered the stop of the *hydrochlorothiazide* and the start of the *ramipril* and *nitrate*. All of these changes are in the present and are not negated, hypothetical, or conditional.

3   Method

Our system consists of two separable components. First, we solve the medication extraction and the event classification tasks in one step. Therefore in this step, we start from the raw text and find the mentions of medications and assign event classes (**Disposition, NoDisposition** and **Undetermined**) to each of them.

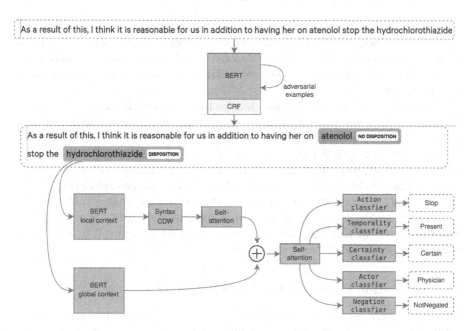

Fig. 2. The architecture of our system with an example document. The dashed line text boxes contain the example sentences and our outputs.

In the second step, we work only with the medications tagged as **Disposition**: we use the related parts of the sentence to assign values to all of the predefined categories of Action, Negation, Temporality, Certainty, and Actor.

The full architecture is shown in Fig. 2.

3.1 Medication Event Recognition

First, we devised a solution for the medication extraction and the event classification tasks in the same step. Our basic architecture was similar to a named entity recognition setup. We handled the problem as a token classification task, annotated the texts with IOB encoding, and used the three event labels as entity types.

To solve this token classification problem, we utilized a large language model and extended it with a CRF layer on top of that. This idea involves merging the transfer learning capabilities of pre-trained language models such as BERT with the structured predictions made by CRF. This method was successfully applied to different token classification tasks, like Portuguese named entity recognition [20] or text anonymization in medical documents [15].

Adversarial Learning. Next, we aimed to handle the error-prone nature of the clinical notes. Previous studies showed that adversarial attacks can increase the generalization abilities of natural language processing systems, especially in the case of medical documents [16].

To apply adversarial attacks we used the iterative version of the fast gradient sign method [5,11] (IFGSM) with text-specific modifications [4]. These modifications were needed as the traditional attacking methods are more often applied to images where the pixels are continuous values, as opposed to words in a document.

The gradient attack could make changes in the embedding layer of the large language model, but generating documents from the attacked embeddings is not a straightforward task. After a gradient attack, we reconstruct the attacked document by searching for the closest word piece to each embedding. We only accept a new adversarial example where the text is changed compared to the original. The size of the changes is controlled by the ϵ parameter of the IFGSM attack. Larger ϵ makes more changes. We started with a small ϵ value (1) and increased it with a fixed step size (1) to a maximum of 10 iterations until we found a change in the text. Every second epoch we generate 200 adversarial examples that we add to the training set.

3.2   Medication Context Classification

For the last subtask, our methods were motivated by the field of aspect-based sentiment analysis. Aspect-based sentiment analysis [2] is a well-researched area that has similarities to these types of problems. In sentiment analysis, the task is to determine which sentiments are associated with which target. For example, in the sentence "I love the last jedi, but not a fan of the rise of skywalker" there is positive sentiment about The Last Jedi Star Wars movie, but for The Rise of Skywalker the writer shared a negative opinion.

Local Context Focus Mechanism. For aspect-based sentiment analysis the local context focus [23] (LCF) mechanism was efficiently used. This method pays more attention to the words that are more closely related to our target.

For the context classification task, we applied this LCF mechanism to prioritize the local context of the given target expressions: in our case the given medication. The architecture of the LCF is shown at the bottom of Fig. 2. First, the text is encoded by two language models, one handles the global and one the local context. The local language model has two extra layers, a context features dynamic weighted (CDW) layer and a multi-headed self-attention, these highlight the tokens that are close to the target medication. The outputs of the local and global model are concatenated and there is another multi-headed self-attention over that. The CDW layer weights the tokens by calculating how many tokens were between the target expression and the given token, the tokens closer to the target get higher weights. This method helps to highlight the context of the medication, but a token that is far from the target is not necessarily irrelevant.

Syntax-Based Weighting. To describe more precisely the context of the medication, we applied syntax-based dynamic weighting [17].

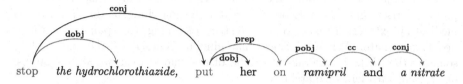

Fig. 3. Dependency structure for a part of a sentence. Blue and red edges indicate the route between the medication mentions and the verb they are the syntactic dependent of. (Color figure online)

Figure 3 shows the dependency tree of a part of a sentence that contains three medication mentions. The medication names are marked in italics, the verbs showing the type of disposition change are colored blue for the **stop** and red for the **start** action; these verbs' dependency relations to the medications are marked the same colors also.

The figure shows that while the name of the medication *hydrochlorothiazide* is equally close to the **start** action verb *put* and the **stop** action verb, in the dependency tree it is directly reachable with one step from *stop*, but not from *put*.

Despite this method's drawback that the dependency trees can only possibly consider one sentence at a time and cannot handle a following sentence referring back to a previously mentioned medication, we found that using the syntactic information improves our results for this task.

So far we have described a method for a single context classification task, but in this dataset, we had five separate classification problems for each of the dispositions.

Like in the two previous tasks, we also applied adversarial learning in the same way. For implementation, we used the PyABSA [22] framework that was initially developed for aspect-based sentiment analysis. We used SpaCy's [9] English transformer model for dependency tree parsing.

4   Results

4.1   Experimental Setup

We used the Contextualized Medication Event Dataset for each of our experiments. The organizers of the National NLP Clinical Challenges 2022 shared task separated 50 clinical notes from the original training set to create a development set. We used that development set to evaluate our intermediate systems. Therefore the training set contains 350, the development set 50 and the test set 100 clinical notes. The training and development set was provided with labels and the test set was released without them.

In the next subsections, we evaluate our system's performance on the development set, then show the results of our final system on the test set as evaluated by the organizers of the shared task.

For evaluation, we applied the official script of the shared task. This script provides strict and lenient scores based on the matching of the spans in the medication extraction task. To achieve strict matching, the span's offsets must be an exact match. While for lenient matching, it is enough for the spans to have some overlap. Like in the official results of the shared task, we always publish our results with lenient matching.

Because of the nondeterministic nature of the training process, we trained all the models three times and selected the best-achieving system from these independent runs. The results of these systems are shown in Table 2 and Table 4, and these are the system that we have submitted for the shared task.

4.2   Event Classification

First, we evaluated the medication extraction and the event classification tasks. We are starting from raw text and annotating the medication mentions and classifying them by the type of events.

We used the BERT large model and applied the following parameters during the training: batch size: 6, learning rate: 1e-05, and trained the model for 20 epochs.

Table 2. Lenient F1-scores on the medication extraction task on the development set.

	Precision	Recall	F1
CRF-BERT	0.9572	0.9752	0.9661
CRF-BERT + adv	0.9573	0.9772	0.9671

In the medication extraction task, we have already achieved good results with the CRF-BERT baseline. Table 2 shows that the adversarial examples didn't give us further improvement. This is because the detection of the medication mentions is more dependent on specific word forms.

Table 3. Lenient macro F1-scores on the event classification tasks on the development set.

	Precision	Recall	F1
CRF-BERT	0.8671	0.8671	0.8670
CRF-BERT + adv	0.8985	0.8631	0.8791

However, in the event classification task, where the labels depend more on the context, the application of adversarial examples increased the results. As we can see in Table 3. there is a 1.2% point increment in the case of the macro F1 score in the development set.

4.3 Context Classification

For context classification experiments we used the provided gold annotation for the medication extraction and event classification tasks. We applied the same parameters as we used in the previous step. Like in the shared task, we provide lenient combined F1 score. The combined F1 score only accepts a prediction when the class is correct in each of the five dimensions.

Table 4. Combined performance of the systems on the event context classification task on the development set.

	Precision	Recall	F1
BERT	0.5920	0.5385	0.5640
BERT + S-LCF	0.6070	0.5520	0.5782

Table 4 describes the effect of the local context focus mechanism with syntax-based context weighting. These context-specific features increased the performance of the baseline system by 1.4% points.

The detailed results of the syntax-enhanced local focus mechanism system are in Table 5. It shows lenient macro scores over all of the five classification tasks.

Table 5. Task level lenient macro F1 scores of the BERT + S-LCF system on the development set.

	Precision	Recall	F1
Action	0.8109	0.7376	0.7725
Temporality	0.8358	0.7602	0.7962
Certainty	0.9502	0.8643	0.9052
Actor	0.8955	0.8145	0.8531
Negation	0.9801	0.8914	0.9336

We can see that the action and temporality detection proved to be the most difficult tasks. These tasks have the most classes and the most balanced label distribution. An interesting type of error in the detection of the action type can be seen in the following example, where for finding the correct solution the model would require mathematical knowledge: *Continue T 40 mg b.i.d. - as 20 mg b.i.d. did not give full control with the generic pills.* In this sentence to decide whether the dose is increased or decreased the model should know if *20* or *40* is larger.

4.4 Shared Task Results

The shared task was evaluated in three steps on the test set that was originally released unlabelled. In the first release, the raw text had to be analyzed, thus the event and the context classification tasks contained the error of the lower-level tasks as well. In the second release, the organizers provided the gold medication mentions, in the third release the gold event annotation was also provided and the only task was the context classification. Since our system performs the first and second tasks in one step, we focused on the first and third releases.

Table 6. Performance of the final system on the test set of Contextualized Medication Event Dataset. Release 1 only contained raw texts that we ran all of our systems on. The gold event classification in Release 3 could be used for evaluating the context classification task.

	Medication F1	Event F1	Context F1
Release 1	0.9714	0.7682	0.4780
Release 3			0.5982

The Table 6 shows our official results on the test set. Among the 32 participant teams, our system achieved 8th place on the context classification task both in the case of release 1 and release 3, also 8th place on the event classification in release 1, and 9th place on the medication mention task.

5   Related Work

Although the use of a local context focus mechanism and its syntax-based extension was developed in recent years, highlighting part of the context and the application of syntax parsing in context classification tasks is not a new concept. In aspect-based sentiment analysis, both dependency and constituent analysis have been applied for feature extraction [6,10] before the spread of large language models. Several different methods have also been developed for the weighting of the features [7].

In the case of large language models, the first solution that comes to mind is the application of sentence pair classification [19] that doesn't make any change to the structure of the neural network, only modifies the input document. It concatenates the full context and the target word with a separator. This allows the model to identify the target in the context. This simple method improved the results over the previous feature- and word-embedding-based solutions.

In each of our experiments, we applied the large version of BERT, but the application of other large language models such as RoBERTa [13] or DeBERTa [8] is a low-hanging fruit for future improvement. As well as utilizing more domain-specific knowledge from biological and clinical text-based pre-trained language models, like the BioBERT [12] or the Clinical BERT [1].

The distinction between the local and global context was also applied to clinical text analysis. In previous works, the combination of CNN and RNN [18] was used for relation classification where the CNN was motivated by their local context extraction capabilities, while RNNs are more suited for long-term dependencies. Earlier work in the Second i2b2 Shared-Task [21] about obesity classification used dictionary-based solutions to analyze the context of diseases for negation and uncertainty [3].

6 Conclusion

Our paper proposes solutions for the extraction and analysis of the medication mentions in clinical notes. For our experiments, we used the Contextualized Medication Event Dataset which contains three tasks. We employed a CRF-BERT-based solution enriched with adversarial examples for the medication extraction and event classification tasks.

In the third task of assigning more detailed context to the medication changes, we implemented a pre-trained language model-based solution that we extended with syntax-based highlighting of the relevant part of the documents. The main motivations of this approach come from the field of sentiment analysis. The usage of the local context focus mechanism and syntax parsing-based weighting successfully improved the results of the context classification as well.

Overall we found that these modifications positively affected the results. In the event classification task, adversarial learning improved our results by 1.2% points while in the context classification task taking syntax into consideration in the local context mechanism resulted in a 1.4% points improvement.

Acknowledgements. This research has been supported by the European Union project RRF-2.3.1-21-2022-00004 within the framework of the Artificial Intelligence National Laboratory.

References

1. Alsentzer, E., et al.: Publicly available clinical BERT embeddings. arXiv preprint arXiv:1904.03323 (2019)
2. Do, H.H., Prasad, P., Maag, A., Alsadoon, A.: Deep learning for aspect-based sentiment analysis: a comparative review. Expert Syst. Appl. **118**, 272–299 (2019)
3. Farkas, R., et al.: Semi-automated construction of decision rules to predict morbidities from clinical texts. J. Am. Med. Inform. Assoc. **16**(4), 601–605 (2009)
4. Gong, Z., Wang, W., Li, B., Song, D., Ku, W.S.: Adversarial texts with gradient methods. arXiv preprint arXiv:1801.07175 (2018)

5. Goodfellow, I.J., Shlens, J., Szegedy, C.: Explaining and harnessing adversarial examples. arXiv preprint arXiv:1412.6572 (2014)

6. Hangya, V., Berend, G., Varga, I., Farkas, R.: SZTE-NLP: aspect level opinion mining exploiting syntactic cues. SemEval **2014**, 610 (2014)

7. Hangya, V., Farkas, R.: Filtering and polarity detection for reputation management on tweets. In: CEUR WORKSHOP PROCEEDINGS. SZTE (2013)

8. He, P., Gao, J., Chen, W.: DeBERTaV3: improving DeBERTa using ELECTRA-style pre-training with gradient-disentangled embedding sharing. arXiv preprint arXiv:2111.09543 (2021)

9. Honnibal, M., Montani, I., Van Landeghem, S., Boyd, A.: spaCy: industrial-strength natural language processing in python. arXiv preprint arXiv:1810.04805 (2020)

10. Kong, L., Schneider, N., Swayamdipta, S., Bhatia, A., Dyer, C., Smith, N.A.: A dependency parser for tweets. In: Proceedings of the 2014 Conference on Empirical Methods in Natural Language Processing (EMNLP), pp. 1001–1012 (2014)

11. Kurakin, A., Goodfellow, I., Bengio, S.: Adversarial machine learning at scale. arXiv preprint arXiv:1611.01236 (2016)

12. Lee, J., et al.: BioBERT: a pre-trained biomedical language representation model for biomedical text mining. Bioinformatics **36**(4), 1234–1240 (2020)

13. Liu, Y., et al.: RoBERTa: a robustly optimized BERT pretraining approach. arXiv preprint arXiv:1907.11692 (2019)

14. Mahajan, D., Liang, J.J., Tsou, C.H.: Toward understanding clinical context of medication change events in clinical narratives. In: AMIA Annual Symposium Proceedings. vol. 2021, p. 833. American Medical Informatics Association (2021)

15. Mao, J., Liu, W.: Hadoken: a BERT-CRF model for medical document anonymization. In: IberLEF@ SEPLN, pp. 720–726 (2019)

16. Moradi, M., Samwald, M.: Improving the robustness and accuracy of biomedical language models through adversarial training. J. Biomed. Inform. **132**, 104114 (2022). https://doi.org/10.1016/j.jbi.2022.104114

17. Phan, M.H., Ogunbona, P.O.: Modelling context and syntactical features for aspect-based sentiment analysis. In: Proceedings of the 58th Annual Meeting of the Association for Computational Linguistics, pp. 3211–3220 (2020)

18. Raj, D., Sahu, S., Anand, A.: Learning local and global contexts using a convolutional recurrent network model for relation classification in biomedical text. In: Proceedings of the 21st Conference on Computational Natural Language Learning (CoNLL 2017), Vancouver, Canada, pp. 311–321. Association for Computational Linguistics (Aug 2017). https://doi.org/10.18653/v1/K17-1032

19. Song, Y., Wang, J., Jiang, T., Liu, Z., Rao, Y.: Attentional encoder network for targeted sentiment classification. arXiv preprint arXiv:1902.09314 (2019)

20. Souza, F., Nogueira, R., Lotufo, R.: Portuguese named entity recognition using BERT-CRF. arXiv preprint arXiv:1909.10649 (2019)

21. Uzuner, O.: Second i2b2 workshop on natural language processing challenges for clinical records. AMIA Ann. Symp. Proc. / AMIA Symp. AMIA Symp. **6**, 1252–1253 (2008)

22. Yang, H., Li, K.: PyABSA: open framework for aspect-based sentiment analysis. arXiv preprint arXiv:2208.01368 (2022)

23. Zeng, B., Yang, H., Xu, R., Zhou, W., Han, X.: LCF: a local context focus mechanism for aspect-based sentiment classification. Appl. Sci. **9**(16), 3389 (2019)

Generating Synthetic Vehicle Speed Records Using LSTM

Jiri Vrany$^{(\boxtimes)}$, Michal Krepelka , and Matej Chumlen

Faculty of Mechatronics, Informatics and Interdisciplinary Studies, Technical
University of Liberec, Liberec, Czech Republic
jiri.vrany@tul.cz

Abstract. Quality assurance testing of automotive electronic components such as navigation or infotainment displays requires data from
genuine car rides. However, traditional static on-site testing methods are
time-consuming and costly. To address this issue, we present a novel
approach to generating synthetic ride data using Bidirectional LSTM,
which offers a faster, more flexible, and environmentally friendly testing
process. In this paper, we demonstrate the effectiveness of our approach
by generating synthetic vehicle speed along a given route and evaluating the fidelity of the generated output using objective and subjective
methods. Our results show that our approach achieves high levels of
fidelity and offers a promising solution for quality assurance testing in
the automotive industry. This work contributes to the growing research
on generative machine learning models and their potential applications
in the automotive industry.

Keywords: LSTM · generative models · vehicle speed · synthetic
data · applied machine learning · digital twin

1 Introduction

Our work focuses on the computers used for vehicle-driver interaction, like the
dashboard, navigation or infotainment. The current approach for their integration testing is either field testing or on-site Hardware-In-The-Loop simulation.
The velocity model described in this paper is part of a larger project that aims
to digitise integration testing and create a digital twin of the vehicle section.

A simulation requires data obtained from actual driving. Getting data in this
way is time, resource and environmentally intensive. Almost every change to the
test scenario then requires another field run. Data synthesis as part of the digital
transformation process can reduce these costs. It will also allow testing on new,
unfamiliar routes. By unfamiliar, we mean that no previously recorded data are
available from rides on such a route.

The primary variable obtained in the measurement is the instantaneous velocity of the vehicle at a given location and time. In addition, the measurement process acquires data from sensors in the car, currently mostly shared via Controller
Area Network (CAN) bus. All data obtained in this way are time series.

Published by Springer Nature Switzerland AG 2023
I. Maglogiannis et al. (Eds.): AIAI 2023, IFIP AICT 675, pp. 125–136, 2023.
https://doi.org/10.1007/978-3-031-34111-3_12

This paper summarises our approach towards vehicle speed data synthesis based on Global Navigation Satellite System (GNSS) coordinates using Long-Short Term Memory Neural Network (LSTM). The primary desired property of the model results is their realism. We are using objective and subjective tests to evaluate the model fidelity.

Our goal is to create the most credible velocity model possible in terms of the perception of the test equipment operator. We do not address typical traffic simulation, the evolution of traffic density during the day, multi-vehicle interaction or local effects on speed. If the test operator cannot distinguish the origin of the testing data, then our goal is fulfilled.

The main contributions of this paper are 1) a description of specific data preparation method to link actual rides and map data, 2) an evaluation of the possibility of using LSTM to generate geo-referenced time series and 3) a summary of the combined approach to verify the result plausibility by objective and subjective criteria.

2   The Problem and Motivation

Vehicle speed is a pseudo-stochastic process influenced by many external phenomena. Specific changes in the recorded velocity cannot be reliably explained by retrospective data analysis as the necessary data might not be available. According to [1], the vehicle speed is, among others, affected by traffic volume during the day, weather or road signals. However, the probe vehicle might not be logging such information.

The measured data gives the instantaneous car speed at a given position. If we have enough training data from a particular route, creating a model to simulate further runs along that route is undoubtedly possible.

We aim to create a more general model capable of generating a velocity waveform for an unfamiliar route. We use the external map data to enrich the training data to achieve this goal. That is, create plausible speed data for any location worldwide, assuming map data is available.

3   Related Work

Predicting the velocity profile along a route could be formulated as a regression problem over a time series. The vehicle velocity model can predict long or short term [3].

Short in this context means a time frame of seconds. For example, the model predicts the speed for the next 10 or 20 s. One of the first works focused on speed prediction using deep learning was [2], where Lemieux and Ma solve short-term prediction even though not precisely named this way. In [5], a feedforward neural network (FNN) can predict short-term vehicle velocity. Furthermore, using road slope data increases the accuracy of the prediction. The [4] states that using LSTM is suitable for vehicle velocity time series and should be preferred over vanilla Recurrent Neural Networks (RNN). In [6], Deufel explores vehicle speed prediction by using encoder-decoder LSTM, OpenStreetMap (OSM) data and slope data computed from Shuttle Radar Topography Mission (SRTM). Also, [8, 9] and [10] report the successful usage of LSTM for short-term velocity prediction in different scenarios.

However, our target is long-term prediction. Long-term in our context means we are trying to predict speed for the entire itinerary. Time frames can vary from minutes to hours. This prediction type is more challenging than short-term prediction because it can be affected by unexpected traffic events. From the studies we know, only [7] combines FNN with LSTM for effective long-term vehicle velocity prediction.

Generally speaking about time series prediction, [11] shows that Bidirectional LSTM (BiLSTM) significantly improves the precision of stock price forecasting compared to Unidirectional LSTM.

Generative Adversarial Networks (GAN) are state-of-the-art in artificial data creation. These works suggest practical testing methods for generated data authenticity, even for works not focused on GANs like ours. To test the generative properties of the model, i.e., prediction over an unknown route, we need to test the realism of the result. The principle is the same as in the case of GAN. Zhou [24], Lucic [13], Xu [14], Yang [15], and Borji [16] have published their approaches to the problem of validating GAN results and finding objective quality metrics.

4   Method

The goal is to create a generalised model to predict the speed profile on a given route. We must create new attributes to train the model to help explain specific speed changes in the measured data. For example, whether the car drives in town, on a motorway or a countryside road, whether the route is straight or contains turns, the radius of those turns, and other information. We denote these new attributes as the geometry of the route. We then use the measured data enriched with these new attributes to train an appropriate machine-learning model. An essential requirement for the resulting synthetic data is then its realism.

Deufel [5] shows that incorporating slope data improves the prediction of short-term vehicle speed and further extends this idea in [6] with map data and encoder-decoder LSTM. A combination of FNN and LSTM was applied in [7] for long-term vehicle speed prediction. Namini [11] shows BiLSTM increases prediction performance over LSTM on stock time series. Combining elevation and map data with BiLSTM could yield good long-term vehicle speed prediction.

4.1   Maps and Spatial Information

We use the OSM as a primary map data source and the Open Source Routing Machine (OSRM) as a routing service. We used the speed profile generated by the OSRM as the baseline model for comparison. The velocity calculation in OSRM is based on a vehicle profile defining the maximum speed on different surfaces and types of roads. At the same time, representing a new profile or modifying an existing one on a local service instance will change the resulting velocity estimate [17].

4.2   Dataset, Preprocessing and Feature Engineering

Our research partner organization provided actual ride measurement data for model training. The dataset consists of 2815 drives with a total length of 22179.5 km and a duration of 455 h. Unfortunately, the dataset is currently not publicly available.

The speed on an arbitrary route should be independent of its exact location in the world. The factors influencing the velocity can be divided into driver-related, route-related and traffic-related. As we mentioned before, traffic simulation is not the goal of this work. Therefore we omit the traffic-related factors. Once all the route-related aspects are known, we can synthesize the speed data. We focus on collecting as much route-related data as possible.

We use map-matching algorithms from OSRM to pair measured spatiotemporal data with OSM geographical data. We can merge data from multiple sources by assigning the car ride data to uniquely identified OSM objects.

With knowledge of OSM identifiers, we then acquire map metadata. For this purpose, we use Overpass API. Further, we add elevation and slope data from Open-Elevation API, an open-source elevation API based on SRTM data. These attributes are then combined with the measured velocity to form the final model training and validation dataset. We also add those features to each specified route at the time of new data prediction. The list of training data attributes is in Table 1.

Table 1. Model input attributes.

Name	Type	Description
azimuth_delta	continuous	first difference of forward azimuth
elevation_delta	continuous	first difference of absolute elevation
way_maxspeed	continuous	OSM speed limit
way_surface	categorical	OSM road surface (asphalt, sett, cobblestone, etc.)
way_type	categorical	OSM road type (primary, highway, residential, etc.)
node	categorical	node specific features (level crossing, traffic sign, intersection, traffic signal, etc.)

The training dataset contains three continuous and three categorical attributes. After one hot encoding, the categorical attributes yield 35 features. The total number of model input attributes is 38. The single target variable is called *target_speed*.

From the input attributes, the *way_maxspeed* attribute seems to be essential for limiting the resulting speed and following the traffic rules. However, this parameter is inconsistent and often missing in the OSM data. To train the model, we filled in the missing values during preprocessing by interpolation and analyzing whether the path passes through the settlement or is outside.

The resulting data are multivariate sequences with data points not equally distributed in distance nor time. The sampling frequency of the measured data and the coarseness of OSM nodes determine the distribution. To solve this issue, we resample the data. Every data point forms a new feature vector describing a 1-meter segment of the road. Output sequences are of shape (N, s) where N is the number of samples and s is the route length in meters.

4.3   Neural Networks

In the case of time series prediction, temporal information plays an important role. RNN can learn context from already processed sequences and are suitable for time series prediction. Vanilla RNNs suffer from vanishing and exploding gradients, making them hard to train, especially considering long-term dependencies [4]. We use a Long Short-Term Memory Network (LSTM) to solve this issue. The LSTM cell can be described by following equations taken from [12]:

$$i_t = \sigma(W_{ii}x_t + b_{ii} + W_{hi}h_{t-1} + b_{hi})$$
$$f_t = \sigma(W_{if}x_t + b_{if} + W_{hf}h_{t-1} + b_{hf})$$
$$g_t = tanh(W_{ig}x_t + b_{ig} + W_{hg}h_{t-1} + b_{hg})$$
$$o_t = \sigma(W_{io}x_t + b_{io} + W_{ho}h_{t-1} + b_{ho})$$
$$c_t = f_t \odot c_{t-1} + i_t \odot g_t$$
$$h_t = o_t \odot tanh(c_t)$$

where t is given time, x_t input, σ is sigmoid function, $\odot$ is element-wise product and $W_{..}$ are matrices mapping input or hidden state to input i_t, forget f_t, cell g_t and output o_t gates respectively. Finally, c_t is cell state and h_t hidden state.

BiLSTM is an extension of LSTM. As the name suggests, we apply LSTM to the input data twice, in standard and reversed order. Output for a given time step t is the concatenation of hidden states from both directions.

4.4   Testing the Fidelity of the Result

To test the plausibility of the result, we have been comparing the synthetic results with measured rides. We used Wasserstein distance - W_p [18,19] and kernel Maximum Mean Discrepancy - *MMD* [20,21] as the discriminative metrics for comparing the similarity of two waveforms.

More studies pointed out that human-based evaluation is insufficient for general conclusions [22,23]. However, the end user of the results of our model will be a human tester working at the testbed. Therefore, we decided also to use a user Turing test to verify the fidelity of the result. In designing our human-based evaluation approach, we followed the rules described in the HYPE work [24].

5 Experiments and Discussion

5.1 The Baseline Model - OSRM Speed

Using OSRM as a part of the data preprocessing gives us the ETA and the calculated travel speed between the nodes of the route. The primary question was if the OSRM result could serve as a speed model for our final goal.

5.2 The LSTM Model

We have complete information about the route's geometry during model training and prediction time. Considering the sequential nature of the data, we decided to use BiLSTM to take advantage of both past and future contexts and implemented it in Python with Pytorch standard LSTM class [12]. We assume this is similar to actual driving, where the driver can see the route situation far ahead or know the route details from the past.

We tested different combinations of hyperparameters, and for the final model, we used 5 layers of LSTM with a hidden dimension of 512 and a single linear output layer. We add an activation function (ReLU) to the output value and found it to improve the training results. The data for training were batches (size 128) of sequences of length 128 sampled with stride 16 from the measured drives. We trained the model for 30 epochs with a fixed learning rate of 1e-5. We used MSE loss function with Adam optimizer.

5.3 Objective Evaluation of the Model

Since many factors affect the resulting speed profile, let's assume that no two rides on an identical route in real life will have an identical speed profile record. And although such two waveforms will be different, both will be real. We first examined how the actual data differ from each other to develop a metric for objectively evaluating the quality and realism of the modelled data.

First, we chose a test route and then found all rides on it using dynamic time warping (DTW) [25] applied to GNSS coordinates. We defined the combined DTW score as follows:

$$dtw_{comb} = dtw(lat) + dtw(lon) \tag{1}$$

We consider two routes similar when $dtw_{comb} < 0.1$. Our dataset's most extensive group of repetitive test drives consists of 20 measurements. This most repetitive route includes urban areas, a main road and a motorway and is approximately 17 km long.

Figure 1 shows five randomly selected measured speed records along the most repetitive route. It is visible that the speed waveforms are different for each ride.

After a series of experiments, we selected Wasserstein distance W_p and Maximum Mean Discrepancy MMD as the primary metrics to describe the similarity of the measurements. We used the Radial-basis function kernel rbf [26] for MMD.

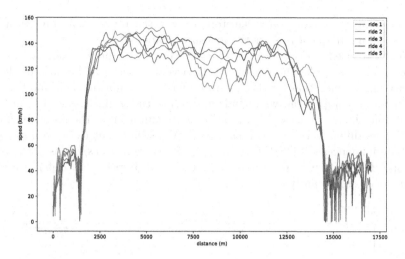

Fig. 1. Captured speed profiles of five randomly selected rides on the test route.

By computing all 2-element non-repeating combinations from 20 rides, we obtained 190 ride pairs. For each ride, we had the measured velocity v and can calculate acceleration a. The acceleration is a significant indicator of the speed profile fidelity because of the car's physical limits. We then calculated W_p and MMD of v and a for each of the 190 ride pairs. This gives four metrics denoted as $W_p v$, $W_p a$, $MMDv$ and $MMDa$.

All four metrics have a normal-like distribution, so we used the basic empirical rule to evaluate if a generated ride can be considered real-like. We consider the generated data realistic if, for each observation X the 3σ-rule is valid:

$$Pr(\mu - 3\sigma \leq X \leq \mu + 3\sigma) \qquad (2)$$

The Table 2 contains the calculated values. It should be noted that the minimum real value for both W_p and MMD is zero, since in this case the two compared rides are identical. Thus, the negative lower bound value of the interval of the 3σ-rule results is replaced by zero.

Table 2. Wasserstein distance and Maximum Mean Discrepancy of actual rides.

Real rides	$W_p\ \mu$	$W_p\ \sigma$	$MMD\ \mu$	$MMD\ \sigma$
acceleration a	0.640031	0.273252	0.00079216	0.00010252
velocity v	6.120097	2.145314	0.019162	0.009737

For the model evaluation, we first generated the coordinates of the test route using the OSM web application and saved the result in KML format. After preprocessing this basic route skeleton, we got the route dataframe with the same sampling frequency as for the measured data (0.1 s).

Next, we used the OSRM speed profile from the route dataframe as the baseline velocity model and computed the acceleration for it. We also predicted velocity and acceleration for the test route with our trained LSTM model.

For visual comparison, we include a graph of the resulting speed from both models and the *way_maxspeed*. From Fig. 2, we can see that the baseline OSRM model gives different results at first glance. We assume that the *way_maxspeed* attribute influences the OSRM speed value. If the *way_maxspeed* is not present in a specific location in the OSM data, the OSRM speed can differ from the actual speed significantly.

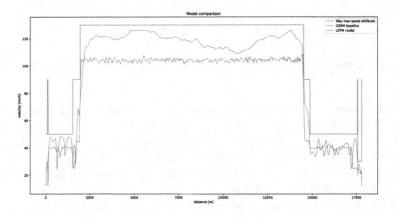

Fig. 2. Comparison of models and way max speed on the test route.

Next we randomly selected 10 routes from the test set, and for each of them, we computed W_p and *MMD* between the actual data and the models for v and a. This gives us $W_p a$, *MMDa*, $W_p v$, *MMDv* for each model. The mean result calculated from 10 tests for each model are shown in Tables 3 and 4.

Table 3. Mean result for 10 random test routes predicted by OSRM model.

$W_p v$	84.598625	0.486241	0.000000 - 12.556039
$W_p a$	2.564519	0.091275	0.000000 - 1.459787
MMDv	0.359960	0.017533	0.000000 - 0.048373
MMDa	0.135979	0.016274	0.000485 - 0.001100

The resulting metrics for the OSRM model were outside the specified range in all ten cases. The mean value in Table 3 shows, that the OSRM results cannot be considered realistic according to our criterion. They do not fit inside the given interval neither for velocity nor for acceleration. Hence the model is insufficient to generate further CAN bus data tied to the car speed. This baseline model is applicable for estimating the ETA during navigation. However, it does not achieve the necessary sensitivity for our purposes.

Table 4. Mean result for 10 random test routes predicted by LSTM model.

LSTM	μ	σ	3σ-rule interval
$W_p v$	6.653617	4.224982	0.000000 - 12.556039
$W_p a$	0.707986	0.538143	0.000000 - 1.459787
$MMDv$	0.021584	0.019176	0.000000 - 0.048373
$MMDa$	0.0008177	0.0002019	0.000485 - 0.001100

The LSTM satisfies the 3σ-rule for all four metrics. In all ten test cases, W_p and MMD for velocity and acceleration were within the defined range. This is demonstrated by the mean result shown in the Table 4. Thus, we consider the LSTM results realistic by objective metrics.

5.4 Subjective Evaluation of LSTM Model

The baseline OSRM model did not pass the objective test. Therefore, we used only the LSTM model for subjective testing with a group of pre-selected and instructed evaluators. Evaluators worked voluntarily, without reward.

Evaluators were shown a plot of randomly selected speed profiles and asked whether the speed was measured or synthesized. Two figures represented each instance: a linear plot of speed over time and a heat map of speed as a route line in the map.

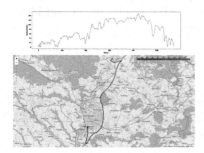

Fig. 3. Example of actual profile.

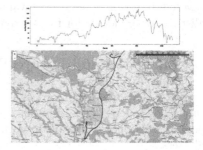

Fig. 4. Example of synthetic profile.

Figures 3 and 4 show examples of the actual and synthetic speed profiles displayed to the testers. For this particular pair of speed profiles, the $W_p v$ and

MMDv values were 5.11879 and 0.036183. However, we did not disclose the objective metrics to the testers.

We used a method similar to the cost-effective approximation from the HYPE paper [24]. Each evaluator got 10 actual and 10 generated velocity profiles randomly selected from 1000 measured and 1000 generated runs.

In selecting the evaluators, we approached the volunteers and personnel who performed component testing on the mentioned testbeds. We first explained the problem and showed several edge cases. Next, all evaluator candidates performed the qualification test. The test aimed to check whether the candidates understood the problem and were sufficiently motivated to solve it. The test consisted of ten pre-selected rides, and candidates must successfully identify at least six to pass.

A total of 23 volunteers passed the qualification test for subjective testing. We obtained ratings for 447 of 460 given profiles, as some volunteers did not rate all given samples. The question for each sample was whether it was an actual measurement. Correctly classifying the displayed profile as measured or synthetic led to true positive and true negative results. Classification of the generated profile as measured resulted in a false positive. And finally, false negatives mean that the measured profile was marked as synthetic.

Table 5. Confusion matrix for the subjective test of LSTM fidelity.

Truth/Prediction	Real	Synthetic
Real	123	109
Synthetic	101	114

Table 5 shows the confusion matrix obtained from this analysis. The Accuracy was 53.02%, Precision 54.91% and Recall 53.01%. This means that the testers were unable to reliably distinguish whether the results were generated or measured. In terms of subjective evaluation, the LSTM results can be considered realistic and applicable for further development.

6   Conclusion and Future Work

We created a system for preprocessing and encoding the georeferenced information usable for general speed profile generation on any given route. The BiLSTM model is functional and realistic both in objective metrics and when tested by real users.

The model will be used to synthesise other CAN bus data in the project. Some of these parameters correlate with speed and route geometry. Using synthetic speed data, we can generate data like wheel rotation speed, brake pressure or throttle pedal pressure.

The developed model generates a single speed profile for each route. Nevertheless, for some simulation scenarios, we need more dynamic behaviour. Therefore, our future work will focus on the GAN domain. We aim to generate multiple velocity profiles for a single route using configurable hyperparameters.

Acknowledgements. This paper was supported by the Technology Agency of the Czech Republic project CK01000020, "Development of a GNSS route generator and CANBUS signal with machine learning using Software Defined Radio."

References

1. Lin, H., Zito, R.: A review of travel-time prediction in transport and logistics. In: Proceedings of the Eastern Asia Society for Transportation Studies, vol. 5 (2005)
2. Lemieux, J., Ma, Y.: Vehicle Speed Prediction Using Deep Learning, 2015 IEEE Vehicle Power and Propulsion Conference (VPPC), (2015), pp. 1–5, https://doi.org/10.1109/VPPC.2015.7353037
3. Bratsas, C., Koupidis, K., Salanova, J.-M., Giannakopoulos, K., Kaloudis, A., Aifadopoulou, G.: A comparison of machine learning methods for the prediction of traffic speed in urban places. Sustainability **12**, 142 (2020). https://doi.org/10.3390/su12010142
4. Du, Y., et al.: The Vehicle's Velocity Prediction Methods Based on RNN and LSTM Neural Network, 2020 Chinese Control And Decision Conference (CCDC), (2020), pp. 99–102, https://doi.org/10.1109/CCDC49329.2020.9164532
5. Deufel, F., Gießler, M., Gauterin, F.: A generic prediction approach for optimal control of electrified vehicles using artificial intelligence. Vehicles **4**(1), 182–198 (2022). https://doi.org/10.3390/vehicles4010012
6. Deufel, F., Jhaveri, P., Harter, M., Gießler, M., Gauterin, F.: Velocity Prediction Based on Map Data for Optimal Control of Electrified Vehicles Using Recurrent Neural Networks (LSTM). Vehicles 4, 808–824. (2022) 10.3390/vehicles4030045
7. Yufang, L., Mingnuo, C., Wanzhong, Z.: Investigating long-term vehicle speed prediction based on BP-LSTM algorithms. IET Intell. Transp. Syst. **13**, 1281–1290 (2019). https://doi.org/10.1049/iet-its.2018.5593
8. Maa, X., et al.: Long short-term memory neural network for traffic speed prediction using remote microwave sensor data. Transportation Research Part C: Emerging Technologies, vol. 54, 2015, pp. 187–197. Elsevier Ltd. https://doi.org/10.1016/j.trc.2015.03.014
9. Yeon, K., Min, K., Shin, J., Sunwoo, M., Han, M.: Ego-vehicle speed prediction using a long short-term memory based recurrent neural network. Int. J. Automot. Technol. **20**(4), 713–722 (2019). https://doi.org/10.1007/s12239-019-0067-y
10. Zhao, J., Gao, Y., Bai, Z., Wang, H., Lu, S.: Traffic Speed Prediction Under Non-Recurrent Congestion: Based on LSTM Method and BeiDou Navigation Satellite System Data, in IEEE Intelligent Transportation Systems Magazine, vol. 11, no. 2, pp. 70–81, Summer (2019) https://doi.org/10.1109/MITS.2019.2903431
11. Siami-Namini, S., Tavakoli, N., Namin, A.S.: The performance of LSTM and BiLSTM in forecasting time series. IEEE Int. Conf. Big Data (Big Data) **2019**, 3285–3292 (2019). https://doi.org/10.1109/BigData47090.2019.9005997
12. Pytorch LSTM Documentation. Accessed 12 Jan 2023. https://pytorch.org/docs/stable/generated/torch.nn.LSTM.html
13. Lucic, M., Kurach, K., Michalski, M., Gelly, S., Bousquet, O.: Are gans created equal? a large-scale study. In: Advances in Neural Information Processing Systems, pp. 700–709 (2019)

14. Xu, Q., et al.: An empirical study on evaluation metrics of generative adversarial networks. arXiv preprint arXiv:1806.07755 (2018)
15. Yang, L., Lerch, A.: On the evaluation of generative models in music. Neural Comput. Appl. **32**(9), 4773–4784 (2020)
16. Borji, A.: Pros and cons of gan evaluation measures. Comput. Vision Image Underst. **179**, 41–65 (2018)
17. Huber, S., Rust, C.: Calculate Travel Time and Distance with Openstreetmap Data Using the Open Source Routing Machine (OSRM). Stata J. **2016/16**(2):416–423 (2016) https://doi.org/10.1177/1536867X1601600209
18. Arjovsky, M., Soumith, C., Bottou, L.: Wasserstein generative adversarial networks. International conference on machine learning, PMLR (2017)
19. Wacha, B., Belilovsky, E., Blaschko, M., Antonoglou, I., Gretton, A.: A test of relative similarity for model selection in generative models. arXiv preprint arXiv:1511.04581 (2015)
20. Vallender, S.S.: Calculation of the Wasserstein distance between probability distributions on the line. Theor. Probab. Appl. **18**(4), 784–786 (1974)
21. Borgwardt, K.M., et al.: Integrating structured biological data by kernel maximum mean discrepancy. Bioinformatics **22**(14), e49–e57 (2006)
22. Ariza, C.: The interrogator as critic: the turing test and the evaluation of generative music systems. Comput. Music. J. **33**(2), 48–70 (2009)
23. Pease, A., Colton, S.: On impact and evaluation in computational creativity: a discussion of the turing test and an alternative roposal. In: Proceedings of the AISB symposium on AI and philosophy, p 39. York, United Kingdom (2011)
24. Zhou, S., et al.: Hype: A benchmark for human eye perceptual evaluation of generative models. In: Advances in Neural Information Processing Systems, vol. 32 (2019)
25. Salvador, S., Chan, P.: FastDTW: toward accurate dynamic time warping in linear time and space. Intell. Data Anal. **11**(5), 561–580 (2007)
26. Rasmussen, C.E., Williams, C.K.I.: Gaussian Processes for Machine Learning, the MIT Press, 2006, ISBN 026218253X. c 2006 Massachusetts Institute of Technology. https://www.GaussianProcess.org/gpml

Measuring the State-Observation-Gap in POMDPs: An Exploration of Observation Confidence and Weighting Algorithms

Yide Yu[1(✉)], Yan Ma[1], Yue Liu[1], Dennis Wong[1], Kin Lei[1],
and José Vicente Egas-López[2]

[1] Faculty of Applied Sciences, Macao Polytechnic University, Macao SAR, China
{yide.yu,yue.liu,cwong,liamli}@mpu.edu.mo, mayan@bupt.edu.cn
[2] RGAI, University of Szeged, Szeged, Hungary
egasj@inf.u-szeged.hu

Abstract. The objective of this study is to measure the discrepancy between states and observations within the context of the Partially Observable Markov Decision Process (POMDP). The gap between states and observations is formulated as a State-Observation-Gap (SOG) problem, represented by the symbol Δ, where states and observations are treated as sets. The study also introduces the concept of Observation Confidence (OC) which serves as an indicator of the reliability of the observation, and it is established that there is a positive correlation between OC and Δ. To calculate the cumulative entropy λ of rewards in $\langle o, a, \cdot \rangle$, we propose two weighting algorithms, namely Universal Weighting and Specific Weighting. Empirical and theoretical assessments carried out in the Cliff Walking environment attest to the effectiveness of both algorithms in determining Δ and OC.

Keywords: Partially Observable Markov Decision Process ·
Reinforcement Learning · Information Theory

1 Introduction

Partially Observable Markov Decision Process (POMDP) has gained significant attention as a research topic in recent years due to its extensive applications in various fields, including Artificial Intelligence, Data Mining, and Data Analysis. In recent years, POMDPs have been applied to various domains, including robotics, autonomous driving, and swarm robotics. For instance, POMDPs have been used for planning under uncertain object compositions [1], devising behavior planning mechanisms that are cognizant of traffic mirrors [2], and modeling the interaction dynamics between human operators and unmanned aerial vehicle teams [3], among others applications.

© IFIP International Federation for Information Processing 2023
Published by Springer Nature Switzerland AG 2023
I. Maglogiannis et al. (Eds.): AIAI 2023, IFIP AICT 675, pp. 137–148, 2023.
https://doi.org/10.1007/978-3-031-34111-3_13

In practice, most real-world scenarios can be described as POMDP problems since it is often impractical to list out all possible states of a complex system. Recent research has focused on developing effective solutions for POMDP problems. For example, Chades et al. [4] introduced three methods to solve the POMDP problem: belief MDP (Markov Decision Process) [5], solution representation [6,7] and interpretation and visualization [8,9].

Nonetheless, it is worth noting that the identification of the POMDP environment cannot be achieved autonomously, as it always necessitates human judgment. Since the development of a POMDP model is heavily reliant on human experience, the model can potentially become unsafe, unpredictable, and unstable. Moreover, distinguishing between fully observable and partially observable environments can pose challenges, as demonstrated by the use of medical devices that monitor patients' physical indicators in operating rooms. It is plausible that there exist valid indicators that cannot be observed, and their nature and quantity are currently unknown.

Similarly, the gap between the state and observation is critical in applying reinforcement learning (RL) algorithms to POMDP problems. To address this challenge, we propose the concept of Observation Confidence (OC) as a measure of the gap between the state and observation. The larger the gap between the state and observation, the lower the OC, and vice versa. We define the state-observation-gap (SOG) problem, and represent states and observations as sets with multiple dimensions to address the discrepancy between the two. We also provide an algorithm to calculate OC and demonstrate its effectiveness through experiments. Our contributions extend the definition of POMDP and provide a novel approach to addressing the SOG problem.

To the best of our knowledge, this paper represents the first effort to provide a metric that measures the gap between states and observation in the POMDP problem.

2   Relative Works and Preliminaries

Definition 1. $\mathcal{P} : \mathbb{S} \times \mathbb{A} \times \mathbb{S} \to [0,1]$ *is a set of conditional transition probabilities between states. Formally, a POMDP is a 7-tuple* $\mathcal{G} = \langle \mathbb{S}, \mathbb{A}, \mathcal{P}, \mathcal{R}, \Omega, \mathbb{O}, \gamma \rangle$*, where* $\mathbb{S}$ *is a finite set of states* s*, and* $\mathbb{A}$ *is a set of actions* a*.* $\mathcal{P} : \mathbb{S} \times \mathbb{A} \times \mathbb{S} \to [0,1]$ *is a set of conditional transition probabilities between states.* $\mathcal{R} : \mathbb{S} \times \mathbb{A} \to \mathbb{R}$ *is the reward function.* Ω *is a set of observations* o*, and* $\mathbb{O}$*: a set of conditional observation probabilities.* $\gamma \in [0,1)$ *is a discount factor.*

$\mathbb{T}$ represents the set of action-observation histories. At each timestep, the environment is in a state $s \in \mathbb{S}$. The agent then selects an action $a \in \mathbb{A}$, and the environment transitions from s to s' with probability $\mathcal{P}(s' \mid s, a)$. Subsequently, the agent observes an observation o from s' with probability $\mathbb{O}(o \mid s', a)$, and receives a reward r according to the reward function $\mathcal{R}(s, a)$. This process is repeated continuously, and all interactions $\langle o^t, a, r_t \rangle$ are recorded in $\mathbb{T}$. The objective is to maximize the expectation of discounted rewards: $E\left[\sum_{t=0}^{\infty} \gamma^t r_t\right]$, where r_t is the reward at time t, and γ is the discount factor.

There are some approaches to measure the belief of every single state on the decision chain. For instance, the belief state [5] is a well-established probability distribution that captures uncertainty over potential environmental states. The FlOw-based Recurrent BElief State model (FORBES) [10] extends this notion to continuous belief states in POMDPs, while the Moore machine with belief state mapping to an external world [11] represents an additional variation. However, this paper distinguishes itself by computing the discrepancy between state and observation in the environment, as opposed to solely characterizing the belief state or its variations.

The linear weighting algorithm has gained considerable traction in the domain of POMDPs. C. Kavaklioglu et al. [12] employ grid-based approximations and linear programming models to generate approximate policies for CPOMDPs, while Y. Yang et al. [13] address the issue of POMDP model learning for linear Gaussian systems. In addition, Optimistic Linear Support with Alpha Reuse (OLSAR) [14] computes a bound approximation of the optimal solution set for all feasible weightings of the objectives. Analogously, this paper adopts the linear weighting method to solve the SOG.

3   Observation Confidence

In this section, we expound on the definition of extended POMDP, OC, and SOG. Following this, we propose two weighting scheme algorithms aimed at quantifying the SOG.

3.1   State-Observation-Gap

The following presents an extended definition of the POMDP.

Definition 2. *The extended POMDP is a* $\mathcal{G}_{extend} = \langle \hat{\mathbb{S}}, \hat{\Omega} \rangle$*, where* $\mathbb{S}$ *is an estimate state set and* $\hat{\Omega}$ *is an estimate observation set.*

Set $\mathbb{D}$ *is a set of dimensions, and* $\mathbb{D}$ *is composed of dimensions* $d \in \mathbb{D}$*.* ω *is a weight, where* $\omega \in \mathbb{R}$*. Then,* $s_{\mathbb{D}}$ *is a state represented by an infinite set of dimensions as*

$$s_{\mathbb{D}} = \{\omega_n d_n \mid \omega_n \geq \omega_{n+1}, n \to \infty, \omega_n d_n \geq 0\}, s_{\mathbb{D}} \subset \mathbb{S}$$

$\hat{s}_{\mathbb{D}}$ *is an estimated state represented by a finite set of dimensions as*

$$\hat{s}_{\mathbb{D}} = \{\omega_m d_m \mid \omega_m \geq \omega_{m+1}, n > m, n > 0, \omega_m d_m \geq 0\}, \hat{s}_{\mathbb{D}} \subset \hat{\mathbb{S}} \subset \mathbb{S}$$

$o_{\mathbb{D}}$ *is an observation represented by a finite set of dimensions as*

$$o_{\mathbb{D}} = \{\omega_k d_k \mid \omega_k \geq \omega_{k+1}, n > k, k > 0\}, o_{\mathbb{D}} \subset \Omega$$

$\hat{o}_{\mathbb{D}}$ *is an estimate observation represented by a finite set of dimensions as*

$$\hat{o}_{\mathbb{D}} = \{\omega_l d_l \mid \omega_{\geq} \omega_{l+1}, k \geq l, l > 0, \omega_l d_l \geq 0\}, \hat{o}_{\mathbb{D}} \subset \hat{\Omega} \subseteq \Omega$$

Definition 2 relies on three implicit assumptions. Firstly, it is assumed that the dimension of state s is infinite, and as such, $s_\mathbb{D}$ also constitutes an infinite set. This assumption is deemed to be more realistic. Secondly, the weight ω of each dimension reflects its relative importance, and for any given task, not all dimensions are of equal significance. Hence, a zero bound l is introduced for ω, such that $\prod_{i=1}^{l} \omega_i d_i > 0$ and $\prod_{i=l}^{m} \omega_i d_i = 0$, where $m > i > 0$. We disregard the part of ω that is 0 and refer to the set comprising the remaining ω as the estimate state $\hat{s}$. Lastly, while it is not always the case in practice, it is assumed that $\Omega \subset \mathbb{S}$. There exist instances where it is feasible to observe all states, particularly in simple scenarios.

In Fig. 1, it is postulated that human agents are restricted in their capacity to observe the complete environment and thus, are unable to obtain the full state space $\mathbb{S}$ (depicted in pink). Additionally, critical information $\hat{\mathbb{S}}$ (depicted in green) is often unobserved, and agents can only perceive a limited set of useful information $\hat{\Omega}$ (depicted in blue). Consequently, agents utilize the blue observable subset to construct a simulation of the environment on the right-hand side.

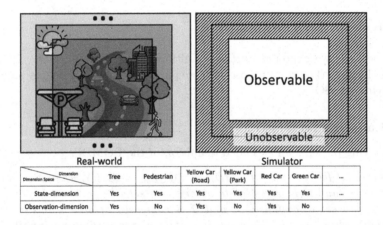

Dimension Space \ Dimension	Tree	Pedestrian	Yellow Car (Road)	Yellow Car (Park)	Red Car	Green Car	...
State-dimension	Yes	Yes	Yes	Yes	Yes	Yes	...
Observation-dimension	Yes	No	Yes	No	Yes	No	

Fig. 1. This image is an account of the unmanned vehicle task, wherein the left figure represents the observable (blue), latent (green), and irrelevant (pink) aspects of the environment in the real-world, while the right figure depicts a simulator constructed by human observers based on their observations of the former. The table shows the observable information. (Color figure online)

3.2   Observation Confidence (OC)

In practical applications, it is frequently uncertain whether the observation corresponds to a complete or partial state, and mistakenly assuming $\hat{\Omega} = \hat{\mathbb{S}}$ can lead to misinterpretation of a single observation o as multiple states $s_1, s_2, \ldots, s_x$. This can result in different rewards $r_1, r_2, \ldots, r_x$ being associated with taking action following the observation, which can cause the RL algorithm to fail and lead to the miscalibration of its $Q(a, s)$ and $\pi(a|s)$ [19].

To evaluate the confidence of an observation o, we define the Observation Confidence (OC), denoted by $OC = p(s|o)$, and we put forth the subsequent proposition to explicate the correlation between Observation Confidence (OC) and the veritable State-Observation-Gap (SOG), denoted as Δ.

Proposition 1. *Let $\Delta = \hat{\mathbb{S}} - \hat{\Omega}$, then $\forall \Delta$, $p(s \mid o) \propto 1/\Delta$.*

Proof. Set $\Delta = \hat{\mathbb{S}} - \hat{\Omega}$ and $p(o \mid s) = 1$ (according to Definition 2). Because $\hat{s}_{\mathbb{D}} \subset \hat{\mathbb{S}}$, $\hat{o}_{\mathbb{D}} \subset \hat{\Omega}$, $s = \hat{s}_{\mathbb{D}}$, $o = \hat{o}_{\mathbb{D}}$. Based on Bayes' theorem, we have the following:

$$
\begin{aligned}
p(s \mid o) &= \frac{p(o \mid s) \cdot p(s)}{p(o)} \\
&= \frac{p(s)}{p(o)} \\
&= \frac{p(\hat{s}_{\mathbb{D}} \mid \hat{\mathbb{S}})}{p(\hat{o}_{\mathbb{D}} \mid \hat{\Omega})} \\
&= \frac{p(\hat{s}_{\mathbb{D}} \mid \hat{\Omega} + \Delta)}{p(\hat{o}_{\mathbb{D}} \mid \hat{\Omega})} \propto 1/\Delta
\end{aligned}
\tag{1}
$$

Proof finished.

To quantify the plausibility of an observation o, we introduce the concept of OC, which measures the discrepancy between the estimated observation space $\hat{\Omega}$ and the estimated state space $\hat{\mathbb{S}}$. We have developed two approaches to measure the value of Δ.

3.3   Weighting

RL algorithms encounter diverse scenarios across various tasks, and consequently, the estimate of the state space $\hat{\mathbb{S}}$, varies accordingly. To account for this variability, we propose two distinct methodologies to adapt the estimate of the state space, $\hat{\mathbb{S}}$, to accommodate different types of scenarios, i.e., specialized and general scenarios. Moreover, we evaluate the discrepancy between the true state and the observed state Δ, denoted by λ.

Universal Weighting. The weighting scheme, whereby the weights are set to Boolean values, can be expressed as follows:

$$
w = \begin{cases} 1 & d \in \mathbb{D} \\ 0 & d \notin \mathbb{D} \end{cases}
\tag{2}
$$

To maintain a generalizable approach, we adopt a straightforward strategy to determine the index set $\hat{o}_{\mathbb{D}}$, as prescribed by (2), which allows for the selection of dimensions to be included in the dimension set. However, in a POMDP, the reward for $\langle a, s, \cdot \rangle$ may vary. Thus, to address this challenge, we introduce the Boolean weighting parameter, which is defined as follows:

$$\lambda = \sum_{j=1}^{J} \sum_{i=1}^{I} \theta_{ji}, \tag{3}$$

where $\theta = 1$. $I \in \mathbb{Z}^+$ is the number of different reward classes in $\langle o, a, \cdot \rangle$, which $\{r_1, r_2, \cdots, r_W\}$ is extracted from $\langle o, a, \cdot \rangle$, and $\{\theta_1, \theta_2, \cdots, \theta_I\} = de-duplicate\{r_1, r_2, \cdots, r_W\}$ (de-duplicate is de-duplication operator). $J \in \mathbb{Z}^+$ is the number of tuples $\langle o, a, \cdot \rangle$ in history, and we give a theorem proving its relation with λ.

Theorem 1. *Let ω be the Boolean Weighting from (9), λ be a metric from (3). Set $\Delta = \hat{\mathbb{S}} - \hat{\Omega}$, then $\exists \alpha \geq 0$ such that $\lambda = \alpha \mid \Delta \mid$.*

Proof. According to Definition 2, we know that:

$$\hat{s}_{\mathbb{D}} = \{\omega_m d_m \mid \omega_m \geq \omega_{m+1}, n > 0, \omega_m d_m \geq 0\},$$
$$\hat{o}_{\mathbb{D}} = \{\omega_l d_l \mid \omega_l \geq \omega_{l+1}, m > l, l > 0, \omega_l d_l \geq 0\}$$

Then, we donate Δ_{sub} to measure the gap between a state s and an observation o :

$$\begin{aligned}
\Delta_{sub} &= \hat{s}_{\mathbb{D}} - \hat{o}_{\mathbb{D}} \\
&= \{\omega_{l+1} d_{l+1}, \omega_{l+2} d_{l+2}, \cdots, \omega_{m-l} d_{m-l}\}
\end{aligned} \tag{4}$$

We assume the $\Theta = \{\theta_1, \theta_2, \cdots, \theta_I\} = de-duplicated\{r_1, r_2, \cdots, r_i\}$, where $\{r_1, r_2, \cdots, r_i\}$ comes from $\langle o, a, \cdot \rangle$ which the number is b in history $\mathbb{T}$ and $u > v$. We know $|\Theta| = 1$ in fully observable MDP because $o = s$. More details are:

$$\begin{aligned}
&s \times a = r \\
&\Rightarrow \hat{s}_{\mathbb{D}} \times a = r \\
&\Rightarrow \{\omega_1 d_1, \omega_2 d_2, \cdots, \omega_m d_m\} \times a = |\theta_1| \\
&\Rightarrow |\Theta| = 1
\end{aligned} \tag{5}$$

So, we have:

$$\begin{aligned}
\Delta_{sub} \times a &= (\hat{s}_{\mathbb{D}} - \hat{o}_{\mathbb{D}}) \times a \\
&= \hat{s}_{\mathbb{D}} \times a \\
&= \{\omega_{l+1} d_{l+1}, \omega_{l+2} d_{l+2}, \cdots, \omega_{m-l} d_{m-l}\} \times a \\
&= \{\theta_1, \theta_2, \cdots, \theta_{m-l}\} \\
&\Rightarrow |\Theta| = m - l \\
&\Rightarrow |\Theta| = |\Delta_{sub}|
\end{aligned} \tag{6}$$

Set $\hat{\mathbb{S}} = \{\hat{s}_{\mathbb{D}_1}, \hat{s}_{\mathbb{D}_2}, \cdots, \hat{s}_{\mathbb{D}_g}\}$ and $\hat{\mathbb{O}} = \{\hat{o}_{\mathbb{D}_1}, \hat{o}_{\mathbb{D}_2}, \cdots, \hat{o}_{\mathbb{D}_h}\}$, where $g > h$. Then:

$$\begin{aligned}
\Delta &= \hat{\mathbb{S}} - \hat{\Omega} \\
&= \{\hat{s}_{\mathbb{D}_1}, \hat{s}_{\mathbb{D}_2}, \cdots, \hat{s}_{\mathbb{D}_g}\} - \{\hat{o}_{\mathbb{D}_1}, \hat{o}_{\mathbb{D}_2}, \cdots, \hat{o}_{\mathbb{D}_h}\} \\
&= \{\Delta_{sub_{h+1}}, \Delta_{sub_{h+2}}, \cdots, \Delta_{sub_{g-h}}\} \\
&= \{\Theta_{sub_{h+1}}, \Theta_{sub_{h+2}}, \cdots, \Theta_{sub_{g-h}}\}
\end{aligned} \tag{7}$$

Thus,

$$\alpha \mid \Delta \mid = \alpha \sum_{c=h+1}^{g-h} \mid \Theta_{sub_c} \mid$$

$$= \alpha \sum_{c=h+1}^{g-h} \sum_{e=l+1}^{m-l} \mid \theta_{sub_{ec}} \mid \propto \lambda_{UW},$$

(8)

where λ_{UW} is the λ from Universal Weighting and $\alpha > 0$. The proof of Theorem 1 finished.

Specific Weighting. The weighting scheme, whereby the weights are assigned continuously, is mathematically expressed as follows:

$$w = \begin{cases} \beta & d \in \mathbb{D} \\ 0 & d \notin \mathbb{D} \end{cases}$$

(9)

where $\beta \geq 0$ represents the importance of the dimension differently in the specific task or agent. The formula for λ is given below:

$$\lambda = -\sum_{j=1}^{J} \sum_{i=1}^{I} p_{ji} \times \log_2 (p_{ji}),$$

(10)

where $J \in \mathbb{Z}^+$ is the number of the tuple $\langle o, a, \cdot \rangle$ in the history $\mathbb{T}$, and $I \in \mathbb{R}$ is the ratio of different reward classes in a tuple $\langle o, a, \cdot \rangle$. p is the proportion of a reward in a rewarding class. The formula is:

$$p = \frac{\mid \{ r_w \mid r_w \in \{ r_1, r_2, \cdots, r_W \}, r_w = \theta_i, i \leq I \} \mid}{\mid \{ r_1, r_2, \cdots, r_W \} \mid}$$

We give a theorem proving its relation with λ.

Theorem 2. *Let ω be the Continuous Weighting from (9), λ to be a metric from (10). Set $\Delta = \hat{\mathbb{S}} - \hat{\Omega}$, then $\exists \mu \geq 0$ such that $\lambda = \mu \mid \Delta \mid$.*

Proof. Because of $\theta = 1$, we know:

$$\{ \theta_1, \theta_2, \cdots, \theta_I \} \propto \{ -p_1 \log_2 p_1, -p_2 \log_2 p_2, \cdots, -p_I \log_2 p_I \},$$

where $p \in (0, 1)$ and $-p_i \log_2 p_i > 0$. According to Eq. (8), we have:

$$\Delta = \hat{\mathbb{S}} - \hat{\Omega}$$

$$= \{ \Theta_{sub_{h+1}}, \Theta_{sub_{h+2}}, \cdots, \Theta_{sub_{g-h}} \}$$

$$\propto \{ -p_1 \log_2 p_1, -p_2 \log_2 p_2, \cdots, -p_I \log_2 p_I \}$$

(11)

Thus, based on Eq. (8),

$$\mu \mid \Delta \mid = \mu \sum_{c=h+1}^{g-h} \mid -p_{sub_c} \log_2 p_{sub_c} \mid$$

$$= \mu \sum_{c=h+1}^{g-h} \sum_{e=l+1}^{m-l} \mid -p_{sub_e c} \log_2 p_{sub_e c} \mid \propto \lambda_{SW}, \tag{12}$$

where λ_{SW} is the λ from Specific Weighting and $\mu > 0$. The proof of Theorem 2 finished.

Theorems 2 and 1 concur on the positive correlation between λ and Δ. With respect to Universal and Specific Weighting schemes, the former solely focuses on ascertaining the relevance of a dimension, without considering its relative importance, in a generic scenario. Meanwhile, the latter weighs the importance of each dimension based on a specific task or agent in a particular scenario. We present algorithms for the realization of both weighting methodologies as outlined in Algorithms 1 and 2.

3.4   Algorithm

Algorithm 1. λ-list Generate Function

Input: $\mathbb{T}, o_{select}, a_{select}$
Output: a λ-table
Process: Function λ-ListGenerate
    Initialisation : Set a empty list λ-list
1: begin
2:   set H is the length of $\mathbb{T}$
3:   for $h := 1$ to $\ldots H$ do
4:      if $o_h == o_{select}$ and $a_h == a_{select}$ then
5:         insert r_h into λ-list
6:      end if
7: end for

Algorithm 1 outlines the methodology for generating the λ-list, which serves as the preparatory stage for computing λ. This algorithm takes a tuple $\langle o_{select}, a_{select}\rangle$ as input, selected from the historical data $\mathbb{T}$, and subsequently outputs the corresponding λ-list. Algorithm 1 iterates through $\mathbb{T}$ to identify all the matching rewards $\langle o_{select}, a_{select}, \cdot \rangle$, and compiles them into the λ-list.

Algorithm 2 delineates the process of computing λ. Initially, it iterates through $\mathbb{T}$ and populates the set U with the unique pairs $\langle o_h, a_h \rangle$, while also ensuring that no duplicates exist in U. Subsequently, it loops through U, utilizing Algorithm 1 to compute the corresponding λ-list, and applies Eq. 3 or Eq. 10 to determine λ.

Algorithm 2. λ Calculation Algorithm

Input: $\mathbb{T}$
Output: λ
Process: λ-Function
 1: begin
 2: set $U \leftarrow$ empty list.
 3: set H is the length of $\mathbb{T}$
 4: **for** $h := 1$ to $\ldots H$ **do**
 5:    **if** $\langle o_h, a_h \rangle$ not in U **then**
 6:      U append $\langle o_h, a_h \rangle$
 7:    **end if**
 8: **end for**
 9: set K is the length of U
10: set $\lambda = 0$
11: **for** $k := 1$ to $\ldots K$ **do**
12:    Set $\lambda_{sub} = 0$
13:    λ-list $\longleftarrow$ λ-ListGenerate$\langle o_k, a_k \rangle$
14:    calculate λ_{sub} using λ-list (by (3) λ for Boolean Weighting, by (10) (λ for Continuous Weighting)
15:    $\lambda \longleftarrow \lambda + \lambda_{sub}$
16: **end for**

4   Experiment

4.1   Preparation

In this study, we conducted experiments utilizing the Cliff Walking problem [15] made available by Gym OpenAI [16]. This environment is one of the standard grid-world [17] examples employed for evaluating the effectiveness of on-policy Sarsa [18] and off-policy Q-learning [19] methods. The environment, as shown in Panel A of Fig. 2, is a 4×12 grid [20] with cliffs in the fourth row. The agent starts at position $[3, 0]$ and aims to reach the goal at position $[3, 11]$. The agent's action space $\mathbb{A}$ is discrete, with four possible actions: up, down, left, and right. If the agent falls off a cliff, it incurs a penalty of -100, and the episode ends, resetting the agent's position. Additionally, each action results in a penalty of -1. The Cliff Walking task's goal is to minimize the agent's cumulative reward during an episode. Notably, the environment has $3 \times 12 + 1$ total states, excluding cliff states $[3, 1 \ldots 10]$. We decompose the state and observation into $\hat{s}\mathbb{D} = \omega 1 d1, \omega_2 d_2, \ldots, \omega_{37} d_{37}$ and $\hat{o}\mathbb{D} = \omega 1 d1, \omega_2 d_2, \ldots, \omega_{37} d_{37}$, respectively.

4.2   Dimension Melting

We created an innovative experimental approach called **Dimension Melting** to comprehensively study Δ. This approach involves systematically eliminating state dimensions to simulate the impact of λ. The evaluation of Δ is achieved by continuously melting dimensions. For the Cliff Walking task, we developed two

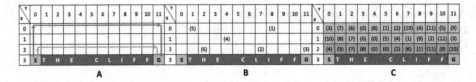

Fig. 2. The explanatory figure portrays the Cliff Walking environment and the experimental design for the Dimension Melting experiments. Panel **A** depicts the base environment of Cliff Walking, with the optimal path for Q-learning and Sarsa illustrated. Panel **B** showcases the experimental design for random melting across six dimensions. In contrast, Panel **C** depicts the row traversal melting methodology with a three-part implementation.

melting schemes for observations. Panel **B** in Fig. 2 randomly selects six dimensions for melting, while Panel **C** gradually and independently melts dimensions along each row.

The experiment comprises 2000 episodes, with a maximum of 50 agent steps per episode. After each episode, we log $\langle s, a, \cdot \rangle$, compute λ using Algorithm 2, and determine the reward sum. We conduct ten runs for each melting experiment and average the results. To facilitate the experiment, we employ a *dimension replacement mechanism*, wherein a melted dimension is replaced by one of its adjacent dimensions or a randomly selected available dimension if no adjacent dimensions exist.

5   Result

In our experimental results, we employ four algorithms in the dimensional melting experiments design. The four algorithms are Q-learning UW (Q-learning-based λ adopting Universal Weighting), Q-learning TW (Q-learning-based λ adopting Specific Weighting), Sarsa UW (Sarsa-based λ adopting Universal Weighting), Sarsa TW (Sarsa-based λ adopting Specific Weighting). Figure 3, the overall trend of λ based on Q-learning and Sarsa increases as the dimension melts more. All the λ for Universal Weighting are almost close, so indicating that Universal Weighting is a universal solution for λ in this task because λ does not change with the agent or task changes. The global dimensional stochastic melting apparently has a greater impact on Q-learning, making the observations obtained by the agent based on it even less confident.

The first graph of Fig. 4 is the result of **C** panel of Fig. 2. All λ is equal to zero in (1) because row 1 is replaced by row 2 in Fig. 2. This change does not affect Q-learning and Sarsa and even makes Sarsa's results better than the base environment. Sarsa does not detect this change because it chooses a shorter path than the original. In the (2) and (3) graphs of Fig. 4, all λ steadily increase with the dimension melting. The reason is that rows 1 and 2 are the critical paths for Sarsa in Fig. 2, so λ for Sarsa goes up. For Q-learning, no doubt, row 2 is the optimal route. However, λ of Q-learning increases because according to

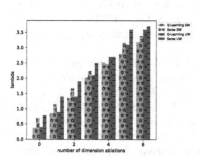

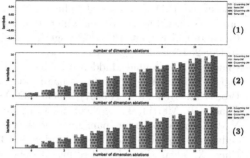

Fig. 3. The result of **B** panel of Fig. 2.

Fig. 4. The result of **C** panel of Fig. 2. (1), (2), (3) represent the result of green. blue, pink rows in panel A Fig. 2, respectively. (Color figure online)

dimension replacement mechanism, when dimensions in row 2 are deleted, they will be replaced with their lower states in row 1. Row 2 is a mandatory route for Q-learning, so Q-learning detects the change in row 2.

Overall, λ performs consistently and can determine λ as the dimension melts. However, the weakness exists in the high algorithm dependence (all $\langle o, a, \cdot \rangle$ need to be explored by algorithms) and *dimension replacement mechanism*, they may lead to the malfunction of λ.

6 Conclusion

In this study, we introduce the State-Observation-Gap (SOG) problem in the context of POMDP and devise two distinct weighting methodologies to compute the cumulative entropy λ. Moreover, we propose two algorithmic approaches and carry out experimental evaluations in the Cliff Walking environment. The extended definition in POMDP serves to enhance the practical applicability of our proposed methodology.

References

1. Pajarinen, J., Lundell, J., Kyrki, V.: POMDP planning under object composition uncertainty: Application to robotic manipulation. IEEE Trans. Robotics (2022)
2. Zhang, C., et al.: Traffic Mirror-Aware POMDP behavior planning for autonomous urban driving. In: 2022 IEEE Intelligent Vehicles Symposium (IV). IEEE (2022)
3. Singh, G., Roy, R.N., Chanel, C.P.C.: Pomdp-based adaptive interaction through physiological computing (2022)
4. Chadès, I., Pascal, L.V., Nicol, S., Fletcher, C.S., Ferrer-Mestres, J.: A primer on partially observable Markov decision processes (POMDPs). Methods Ecol. Evol. **12**(11), 2058–2072 (2021)
5. Åström, K.J.: Optimal control of Markov processes with incomplete state information. J. Math. Anal. Appl. **10**(1), 174–205 (1965)

6. Smallwood, R.D., Sondik, E.J.: The optimal control of partially observable Markov processes over a finite horizon. Oper. Res. **21**(5), 1071–1088 (1973)
7. Cassandra, A.R.: The POMDP Page (2003). https://www.pomdp.org/. (Accessed 10 Dec 2022)
8. Chadès, I., McDonald-Madden, E., McCarthy, M.A., Wintle, B., Linkie, M., Possingham, H.P.: When to stop managing or surveying cryptic threatened species. Proc. Natl. Acad. Sci. **105**(37), 13936–13940 (2008)
9. Chadès, I., Martin, T.G., Nicol, S., Burgman, M.A., Possingham, H.P., Buckley, Y.M.: General rules for managing and surveying networks of pests, diseases, and endangered species. Proc. Natl. Acad. Sci. **108**(20), 8323–8328 (2011)
10. Chen, X., et al.: Flow-based recurrent belief state learning for pomdps. In: International Conference on Machine Learning. PMLR (2022)
11. Biehl, M., Virgo, N.: Interpreting systems as solving POMDPs: a step towards a formal understanding of agency. arXiv preprint arXiv:2209.01619 (2022)
12. Kavaklioglu, C., Helmeczi, R., Cevik, M.: Linear programming-based solution methods for constrained POMDPs. arXiv preprint arXiv:2206.14081 (2022)
13. Yang, Y., Chen, J., Li, S.: Learning POMDP models with similarity space regularization: a linear gaussian case study. In: Learning for Dynamics and Control Conference. PMLR (2022)
14. Roijers, D.M., Whiteson, S., Oliehoek, F.A.: Point-based planning for multi-objective POMDPs. In: Proceedings of the Twenty-fourth International Joint Conference On Artificial Intelligence (IJCAI) (2015)
15. Demin, V.: Cliff walking problem (2009)
16. Brockman, G., et al.: Openai gym. arXiv preprint arXiv:1606.01540 (2016)
17. Meuth, R.J.: A Survay of Reinforcement Learning Methods in the Windy and Cliff-walking Gridworlds
18. Sutton, R.S., Barto, A.G., et al.: Introduction to reinforcement learning (1998)
19. Watkins, C.J., Dayan, P.: Q-learning. Mach. Learn. **8**(3), 279–292 (1992)
20. Sutton, R.S., Barto, A.G.: Reinforcement learning: An introduction. Robotica **17**(2), 229–235 (1999)

Predicting Colour Reflectance with Gradient Boosting and Deep Learning

Asei Akanuma[1,2], Daniel Stamate[1,2(✉)], and J. Mark Bishop[2]

[1] Data Science and Soft Computing Lab, London, UK
[2] Department of Computing, Goldsmiths College, University of London, London, UK
d.stamate@gold.ac.uk

Abstract. Colour matching remains to be a labour-intensive task which requires a combination of the colourist's skills and a time consuming trial-and-error process even when employing the standard analytical model for colour prediction called Kubelka-Munk. The goal of this study is to develop a system which can perform an accurate prediction of spectral reflectance for variations of recipes of colourant concentration values, which could be used to assist the colour matching process. In this study we use a dataset of paint recipes which includes over 10,000 colour samples that are mixed from more than 40 different colourants. The framework we propose here is based on a novel hybrid approach combining an analytical model and a Machine Learning model, where a Machine Learning algorithm is used to correct the spectral reflectance predictions made by the Kubelka-Munk analytical model. To identify the optimal Machine Learning method for our hybrid approach, we evaluate several optimised models including Elastic Net, eXtreme Gradient Boosting and Deep Learning. The performance stability of the models are studied by performing computationally intensive Monte Carlo validation. In this work we demonstrate that our hybrid approach based on an eXtreme Gradient Boosting regressor can achieve superior performance in colour predictions, with good stability and performance error rates as low as 0.48 for average dE_{CMC} and 1.06 for RMSE.

Keywords: Colour Reflectance Prediction · Paints · Coatings · AI-Machine Learning · eXtreme Gradient Boosting · Deep Learning · Elastic Net · Monte Carlo Validation

1 Introduction

Colour matching is a specialised task which requires a colourist to mix a set of colourants in different proportions until a suitable visual match is achieved between the mix and a desired colour. The mix that is produced is a formula

This Work Was Part Funded by InnovateUK Through a Knowledge Transfer Partnership

I. Maglogiannis et al. (Eds.): AIAI 2023, IFIP AICT 675, pp. 149–160, 2023.
https://doi.org/10.1007/978-3-031-34111-3_14

called the 'recipe' which is a list of mixing ratio of the colourants used to obtain the colour match. Colour matching is therefore a considerably laborious task and is achieved through a combination of the colourist's skills and trial-and-error. To assist the colourists and to speed up the process of discovering recipes, Computer Colourant Formulations are often used which utilises various colour prediction software. These software allow for the prediction of colour given a recipe which are often based on analytical models. A relatively common method of Computer Colourant Formulation is to implement an analytical model based on the radiation transfer theory known as Kubelka-Munk (K-M) [1,2] which was originally proposed in 1931 [1]. Briefly, the K-M models allows for the prediction of the spectral reflectance for a mixture of colourants by characterising them according to two coefficients which are absorption (K) and scattering (S). Though the K-M model is favoured for their simplicity and ease of use, in many cases their approximations alone are not sufficiently accurate for real world applications. Subsequently, to overcome some of the limitations of the modelling assumptions made by the K-M models, multi-flux models [3] have been proposed as alternatives. However, the improvements in prediction accuracy from these models have been relatively limited despite their added modelling complexity.

Thus, there have been numerous previous works on the application of Machine Learning methods for colour recipe predictions. In the works by Bishop et al. [4,5] neural network models were used to predict recipes for dye concentrations from CIELAB coordinates. Bezerra and Hawkayard [6] used a neural network to predict the concentrations of florescent dyes from spectral reflectance values. On the other hand, Westland et al. employed a neural network model to predict spectral reflectance for mixtures of inks printed on cards [7]. Furferi and Governi [8] proposed a neural network based approach to correcting the spectral reflectance from an analytical model, to estimate spectrophotometer readings for carded fiber. In the work by Hung et al. [9] a neural network was trained to predict colour properties of cotton fabrics. Jawahar et al. [10] devised a neural network model to predict the tri-stimulus values for leather dyeing, which was shown to perform better than a K-M model. Hemingray and Westland [11] used a number of several separate neural networks to predict the spectral reflectance at each wavelength for fibre blends, while Pan et al. used a similar neural network for the transformation between two Spectral Spaces [12]. On the other hand, Furferi et al. [13] proposed a hybrid K-M-neural network method to predict the reflectance values of a blend. Shen et al. [14] introduced a hybrid model based on the Stearns-Noechel and a neural network model. Also, Zhang et al. [15] proposed a method to improve predictions of K-M using a hybrid of least squares and grid search method, for spectrophotometric colour matching for fiber blend. In [27] the authors of this work proposed a neural network approach to estimating colour reflectance with product independent models.

Recent works have also attempted to solve the inverse problem of spectral reflection prediction. In the works by Tarasov et al. [16,17] and [18], a feedforward neural network was used to predict the colourant recipe values from the observations of spectral data. The work by Zhang et al. proposed a method for dye recipe prediction from colour measurements for cotton fabrics, using a novel recurrent neural network [19].

Our present work focuses on the prediction of spectral reflectance from colourant concentration values for paints recipes. We design a system which is able to perform predictions of spectral reflectance for variations of recipes. However, rather than attempting to model the relationship of the colourants to spectral reflectance directly, we propose a unique solution for colour prediction which is based on a combined approach of the K-M analytical model and Machine Learning. More specifically, our approach uses the Machine Learning models to correct the spectral reflectance approximations made by the K-M analytical models *thereby overcoming some limitations of the traditional analytical models*. Thus, it is a hybrid approach of the analytical and Machine Learning methods which always provides a better predictive performance than the K-M analytical model alone.

In addition, our work includes a comparison of several different varieties of Machine Learning algorithms, including Elastic Net, Extreme Gradient Boosting and Deep Learning. Interestingly, our experimental results demonstrates that the Extreme Gradient Boosting algorithm provides the most stable and best performance among them.

The remainder of the paper is organised as follows. In Sect. 2 we describe the methodology, the data that is used, and the Machine Learning predictive models used for this study. Section 3 discusses the experimental results. Finally Sect. 4 provides the conclusions.

2   Methodology

2.1   Dataset

The data used in this study originates from a commercial database of paint colour recipes used for coatings. The database includes recipes for more than 10,000 colour samples which are mixed from more than 40 different colourants in defined proportions with each having a corresponding spectral reflectance curve measured for their colour by a Spectrophotometer. The measurements of the reflectance spectra include 31 wavelengths of the visual spectrum in the range of 400 to 700 nanometres at each 10 nanometre step intervals under the illuminant D65, measured at 45 °C face angle. The reflectance values are therefore vectors of length 31 which correspond to each wavelength for the measured range of the spectral curve. All variables in the data are numerical and continuous, and thus this work is considered a regression task of predicting 31 target variables.

Data Cleansing: For the data cleansing process we removed samples with incomplete paint recipes and incomplete measurements. Additionally, as a precautionary measure, we excluded some of the data by ranking the samples which have the highest dE_{CMC} [26] errors between the measured colour and a predicted colour from the K-M analytical model, by removing 2 percent of those top ranked samples. The assumption here is that some of the samples may contain errors which may originate from the data collection or from the process of entering the data in the database. Using the K-M analytical model also as a proxy for assessing sample quality, we find this data cleansing process is able to assure better quality of data, resulting in a dataset with a population of reliable and consistent samples.

2.2 A Hybrid Approach to Colour Prediction

The aim of this work is to perform a reliable prediction of the spectral reflectance for any given recipe. Our approach distinguishes itself from most colour prediction approaches in the sense that we combine the analytical K-M model with Machine Learning methods. This can be described as a two step process of (1) making an initial prediction of the spectral reflectance by using a K-M model for the recipe from the colourant concentration values, followed by (2) using the Machine Learning model to correct the initial prediction made in step (1) such that the final estimates are closer to the actual spectral reflectance (measured by the spectrophotometer). This is achieved by optimising the Machine Learning models to predict the residuals of the K-M model's predictions of the measured spectral reflectance values. For the inference of new datapoints, the K-M model's predictions are summed up with the Machine Learning model's predictions.

The following gives a description of the input and output variables for the Machine Learning predictive models used in this work.

Descriptions of Input Variables:

- The paint recipe which are the concentrations of the colourants given by percentage composition values - a sparse vector where each element represents the concentration amount of a colourant (where a value of 0 indicates that the colourant is not in use).
- The spectral reflectance of the K-M model's predictions - a vector of length 31 for each value in the spectral reflectance curve.

Descriptions of the Target Variables: The target variables in this study are the residuals between the measured spectral reflectance values of the 31 wavelengths and the predictions made initially by the K-M model.

2.3 Predictive Models and Fine Tuning

In this study we developed several optimised predictive models in order to compare performances among them. The predictive models that we explored in this work are the Elastic Net, two types of eXtreme Gradient Boosting (linear and tree based models) and Deep Learning.

Elastic Net: Firstly, an Elastic Net model [20] was tuned for each of the 31 target variables individually. Elastic Net is a type of regularized regression model which provides a middle ground between Ridge regression and Lasso regression. Elastic Net uses a regularisation term which is a simple mix or both Ridge and Lasso which is shown in the Eq. 1 below.

$$J(\theta) = MSE(\theta) + r\alpha \sum_{i=1}^{n} |\theta_i| + \frac{1-r}{2}\alpha \sum_{i=1}^{n} \theta_i^2 \qquad (1)$$

The r hyperparameter is a regularisation mix ratio; when $r = 0$, Elastic Net is equivalent to Ridge regression, whereas when $r = 1$, it is equivalent to Lasso regression. The α hyperparameter represents the strength of the regularisation. The Elastic Net was tuned by searching for the optimal hyperparameter values by a using a grid search with a 3 fold-cross validation on the training set in the search ranges shown in Table 1. A final model was then fitted on the entire training set data.

Table 1. Hyperparameter search grid for Elastic Net algorithm

ENet hyperparameters	Hyperarameter Search Range
α	[0.00–100]
r	[0.1–1]

eXtreme Gradient Boosting with Linear Models: Secondly, we applied the eXtreme Gradient Boosting [21] regressor algorithm based on linear models, with the squared error objective. For this implementation, 31 individual eXtreme Gradient Boosting models were tuned with a grid search to find the optimal configurations for the *learning rate, estimator numbers, lambda and alpha* hyperparameters using a 3 fold-cross validation on the training set. After the optimal hyperparameters were found, the final models were fitted on the entire training set data. Table 2 shows the table of the searched hyperparameter ranges.

Table 2. Hyperparameter search grid for eXtreme Gradient Boosting (linear based) algorithm

XGBoost (linear) hyperparameters	Hyperparameter Search Range
learning rate	[0.05–0.2]
n estimators	[500–2500]
lambda	[0.1–100]
alpha	[0.1–100]

eXtreme Gradient Boosting with Tree Models: Thirdly, we tuned the eXtreme Gradient Boosting regressor based on tree models, with the squared error objective. 31 individual eXtreme Gradient Boosting models were tuned with a grid search to find the optimal configurations for the hyperparameters for *learning rate, max depth, subsample rate, min child weight, number of estimators, column sample by node, column sample by tree* for the search ranges shown in Table 3. Once the optimal hyperparameters were found, the final model was fitted on the entire training set.

Table 3. Hyperparameter search grid for eXtreme Gradient Boosting (tree based) algorithm

XGBoost (Tree) hyperparameters	Hyperparameter Search Range
learning rate	[0.05–0.2]
max depth	[5–20]
subsample	[0.5–1]
min child weight	[0.5–1]
n estimators	[500–2500]
colsample bynode	[0.33–1]
colsample by tree	[0.33–1]

Deep Learning: For our Deep Learning approach we experimented with various Multilayer Perceptron (MLP) model architectures including a fully-connected feed-forward model, a Resnet [22] like model (with skip-connections), and a wide-and-deep-learning [23] like model. In all the experiments, the network architecture is a single model which has a fixed number of input nodes which is equal to the number of the variables used, and has 31 output nodes. Different configurations were searched for the optimal number of layers, hidden node numbers, and different hidden node activations such as:

– Logistic Sigmoid:

$$\text{sigmoid}(x) = \frac{1}{1 + \exp(-x)}$$

– Hyperbolic tangent:

$$\tanh(x) = \frac{e^x - e^{-x}}{e^x + e^{-x}}$$

– ReLU (Rectified Linear Unit):

$$\text{ReLU(x)} = \begin{cases} 0 & \text{if } x < 0 \\ x & \text{if } x \geq 0 \end{cases}$$

- SELU and ELU:

$$\text{SELU}_{\alpha,\lambda}(x) = \lambda \begin{cases} \alpha(\exp(x) - 1) & \text{if } x < 0 \\ x & \text{if } x \geq 0 \end{cases}$$

where α and λ are constants 1.6732 and 1.0507 respectively for standard scaled inputs., and

$$\text{ELU}_{\alpha}(x) = \begin{cases} \alpha(\exp(x) - 1) & \text{if } x < 0 \\ x & \text{if } x \geq 0 \end{cases}$$

where value for alpha is picked typically between 0.1 and 0.
- Softplus:

$$\text{Softplus}(a) = \ln(1 + e^a),$$

The Deep Learning model was tuned using the Adam optimiser [25] to minimise various loss functions such as the *MSE, MAE* and *Huber* loss. The Huber loss L_δ, as defined below, was used in particular to prevent the potential impact of any remaining outliers in the data:

$$L_\delta = \begin{cases} \frac{1}{2}(y - f(x))^2 & \text{for } |y - f(x)| \leq \delta \\ \delta(|y - f(x)| - \frac{1}{2}\delta), & \text{otherwise.} \end{cases}$$

The network was trained up to 2000 epochs to minimise the loss. In addition, to control for model overfitting, the L2 regularisation was applied to the hidden layer weights, and an early stopping criteria was used to find the appropriate number of epochs, by observing if a validation loss did not improve within the next 100 epochs based on a validation set which was randomly selected from 10 percent of the training set population. Table 4 shows the searched ranges for hyperparameters values in the Deep Learning algorithm.

Table 4. Hyperarameter search grid for Deep Learning algorithm

Deep Learning params	Hyperparameter Search Range
number of layers	[1–5]
hidden node size	[50–500]
loss functions	[MSE, MAE, Huber]
learning rate	[0.001–0.1]
L2 regularization	[0.0001–0.1]
hidden activations	[sigmoid, tanh, relu, elu, selu, softplus]

2.4 Hardware and Software

Due to the significant computational requirements of the Monte Carlo validation that we use in our framework, the implementation of this work was performed on two servers with Xeon 6-cores processors and 96 GB of RAM each, and one server with a Ryzen 16-cores processor, 128 GB of RAM and an RTX 3080 GPU. The experiments were carried out with Python 3 and Numpy, Pandas, scikit-learn, XGBoost, Tensorflow and Keras packages.

3 Experiments and Results

3.1 Evaluating Performances

From the dataset, 90 percent was used as the training set for optimising and building the predictive models while the remaining 10 percent was used as testing set to evaluate the performance of the modelling.

The main concern of this work is to minimise the visual difference between the spectrophotometer's measured colour and the predicted colour of the recipe samples. Therefore the dE_{CMC} colour distance [26] in the Eq. 2 below is appropriate for measuring the performances of the proposed methods as it takes the colour sensitivities of the human visual system into consideration. For each of the compared models, the performance was measured as the calculated averages of dE_{CMC} for the test set predictions. Additionally, in the Results subsection below we also provide the root mean squared error RMSE for the prediction results.

$$dE_{CMC} = \sqrt{\left(\frac{dL}{lS_L}\right)^2 + \left(\frac{dC}{cS_C}\right)^2 + \left(\frac{dH}{S_H}\right)^2} \qquad (2)$$

3.2 Monte Carlo Validation

To investigate stability of the performance of the models we further evaluate results by running a Monte Carlo validation which consists of repeating the process of randomly splitting the dataset into training and testing sets as described previously, rebuilding the models on the training sets and evaluating them on the test sets. This allows for the variation in model performances to be assessed. For the Monte Carlo validation, the average and the standard deviation (SD) of the performances are provided for each performance measure. Our Monte Carlo validation consists of 30 runs, i.e. 30 data splits with model training and evaluation.

3.3 Results

A summary of the results for the best performances, measured as dE_{CMC} and $RMSE$ errors (smaller figures are better for both measures), can be found in

Table 5. Evaluation of performances for different algorithms for average dE_{CMC} and $RMSE$

Machine Learning Methods	Avg. dE_{CMC}	$RMSE$
Elastic Net	0.675	1.366
Extreme Gradient Boosting (Linear)	0.674	1.326
Extreme Gradient Boosting (Trees)	0.479	1.057
Multilayer Perceptrons	0.539	1.111

Table 6. Evaluation of performances of different algorithms for average dE_{CMC} and $RMSE$ with Monte Carlo validation based on 30 runs

Machine Learning Methods	Avg. dE_{CMC}	$RMSE$
Elastic Net	0.708 ± 0.009	1.400 ± 0.045
Extreme Gradient Boosting (Linear)	0.677 ± 0.018	1.403 ± 0.062
Extreme Gradient Boosting (Trees)	0.477 ± 0.010	1.089 ± 0.047
Multilayer Perceptrons	0.547 ± 0.014	1.188 ± 0.061

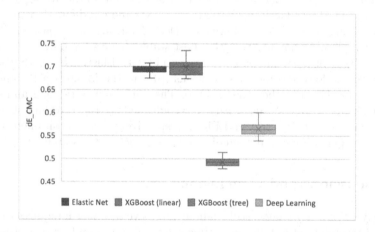

Fig. 1. Box plots for average dE_{CMC} performance results for Monte Carlo validation based on 30 runs

Table 5. Of the 4 compared Machine Learning methods, the best model was obtained using the eXtreme Gradient Boosting with trees, which achieved the best performances of 0.479 and 1.057 for average dE_{CMC} and $RMSE$, respectively. This was followed by the second best model obtained using the Deep Learning method. The latter achieved 0.539 and 1.11 for average dE_{CMC} and $RMSE$, respectively. Elastic Net and the Extreme Gradient Boosting linear based methods however, achieved the two worst performances across the 4 Machine Learning methods.

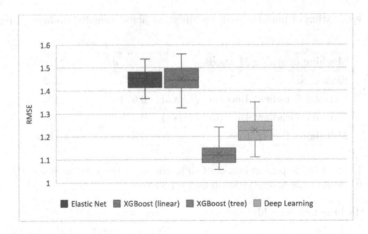

Fig. 2. Box plots for $RMSE$ performance results for Monte Carlo validation based on 30 runs

A similar ranking of performances can be observed from the average results of 30 runs in the Monte Carlo validation, with eXtreme Gradient Boosting based on trees, being on top and followed by Deep Learning, as shown in Table 6. Moreover it should be noted that the most stable models are obtained with the eXtreme Gradient Boosting based on trees, and with Elastic Net methods, since they led to the lowest standard deviations (SD) in the Monte Carlo validation procedure, as shown in the same Table 6. The performance ranking and stability conclusions above are also visually reconfirmed by the boxplots shown for dE_{CMC} and $RMSE$ in Fig. 1 and Fig. 2, respectively (lower positioned boxplot is better for performance, and smaller boxplot is better for stability).

4   Discussions and Conclusions

Currently, colour matching is still a labour-intensive task which requires a combination of the colourist's skills and a time consuming trial-and-error process even when employing one of the most used analytical models for colour prediction, namely Kubelka-Munk (K-M). The goal of this study was to develop a system which can perform an accurate prediction of spectral reflectance for variations of recipes of colourant concentration values, which could be used to assist the colour matching process.

This work explored the prediction of spectral reflectance from colourant concentration values using a dataset of paints recipes, and proposed a combined approach based on the K-M conventionally-employed analytical method and a selection of Machine Learning methods. This hybrid approach involves using optimised Machine Learning models to correct the initial predictions made by a K-M model trained on the data. In particular, the Machine Learning models were used to predict the residuals of the K-M model, computed as the difference between the measured spectral reflectance values of the colour recipes and the K-M predictions. In order to obtain the final reflectance predictions, the Machine Learning predictions were then added to the K-M predictions. We explored 4 Machine Learning methods for our proposed approach, including Elastic Net, two types of eXtreme Gradient Boosting methods (linear and tree based), and Deep Learning. The Machine Learning methods were assessed for their performances (for which lower is better) in terms of the error measures of average dE_{CMC} and $RMSE$. The experiments demonstrated that the best performing model was the tree based eXtreme Gradient Boosting which outperformed all other models tested, achieving the smallest error measures of dE_{CMC} and $RMSE$. Moreover, the same model was also the most stable, together with Elastic Net which in turn was among the two worst performing models with respect to dE_{CMC} and $RMSE$.

References

1. Kubelka, P., Munk, F.: Ein Beitrag zur Optik der Farbanstriche. Technische Physik, Zurich (1931)
2. Nobbs, J.H.: Kubelka-Munk theory and the prediction of reflectance. Rev. Progress Coloration (SDC) **15**, 66–75 (1985)
3. Mudgett, P.S., Richards, L.W.: Multiple scattering calculations for technology. Appl. Opt. **10**(7), 1485–1502 (1971)
4. Bishop, J.M., Bushnell, M.J., Westland, S.: The application of neural networks to computer recipe prediction. Color **16**(1), 3–9 (1991)
5. Bishop, J.M., Bushnell, M.J., Usher, A., Westland, S.: Neural Networks in the Colour Industry. In: Proceedings of AIENG 1991, pp. 423–434, Oxford, UK (1991)
6. Bezerra, C.d.M., Hawkyard, C.J.: Computer match prediction for fluorescent dyes by neural networks. Coloration Technol.**116** (56), 163 –169 (2000)
7. Westland, S., Iovine, L., Bishop, J.M.: Kubelka-Munk or neural networks for computer colorant formulation?. In: Proceedings of the SPIE, vol. 4421, pp. 745–748 (2002)
8. Furferi, R., Governi, L.: Prediction of the spectrophotometric response of a carded fibre composed by different kinds of coloured raw materials: An artificial neural network-based approach. Color Res. Appli. **36**, 179191 (2011)
9. Hung, O.N., et al.: Using artificial neural network to predict colour properties of laser-treated 100% cotton fabric. Fibers Polymers **12**(8), 1069–1076 (2011)
10. Jawahar, M., Kannan, N., Babu, C., Manobhai, M.K.: Artificial neural networks for colour prediction in leather dyeing on the basis of a tristimulus system. Coloration Technol. **131**(1), 48–57 (2015)
11. Hemingray, C., Westland, S.: A novel approach to using neural networks to predict the colour of fibre blends. Color. Technol. **132**(4), 297–303 (2016)
12. Pan, Q., Katemake, P., Westland, S.: Neural Networks for Transformation to Spectral Spaces. In: ACA 2016 China, Color Driving Power, Proceedings. ACA, CFCA, CAC (2016)
13. Furferi, R., Governi, L., Volpe, Y.: Color matching of fabric blends: Hybrid Kubelka-Munk+ artificial neural network based method. J. Electron. Imaging **25**(6), 061402 (2016)

14. Shen, J., Zhou, X., Ma, H., Chen, W.: Spectrophotometric prediction of pre-colored fiber blends with a hybrid model based on artificial neural network and Stearns-Noechel model. Text. Res. J. **87**(3), 296–304 (2017)
15. Zhang, G., Pan, R., Zhou, J., Wang, L., Gao, W.: Spectrophotometric color matching for pre-colored fiber blends based on a hybrid of least squares and grid search method. Textile Res. J. (2021)
16. Tarasov, D., Milder, O., Tyagunov, A.: Inverse problem of spectral reflection prediction by artificial neural networks: Preliminary results. In: Ural Symposium on Biomedical Engineering, p. 2018. Radioelectronics and Information Technology (USBEREIT). IEEE (2018)
17. Tarasov, D., Milder, O.: The Inverse Problem of Spectral Reflection Prediction by Artificial Neural Networks: Neugebauers Primaries vs. Recipes. In: International Multi-Conference on Engineering, p. 2019. Computer and Information Sciences (SIBIRCON). IEEE (2019)
18. Tarasov, D.A., Milder, O.B.: The inverse problem of spectral reflection prediction: Problems of framework selection. In: AIP Conference Proceedings, vol. 2293(1). AIP Publishing LLC (2020)
19. Zhang, J., et al.: Dyeing recipe prediction of cotton fabric based on hyperspectral colour measurement and an improved recurrent neural network. Coloration Technol. **137**(2), 166–180 (2021)
20. Zou, H., Hastie, T.: Regularization and variable selection via the elastic net. J. Roy. Stat. Soc. B **67**(2), 301–320 (2005)
21. Chen, T., Carlos, G.: Xgboost: A scalable tree boosting system. In: Proceedings of the 22nd Acm Sigkdd International Conference on Knowledge Discovery and Data Mining (2016)
22. He, K., Zhang, X., Ren, S., Sun, J.: Identity mappings in deep residual networks. In: Leibe, B., Matas, J., Sebe, N., Welling, M. (eds.) ECCV 2016. LNCS, vol. 9908, pp. 630–645. Springer, Cham (2016). https://doi.org/10.1007/978-3-319-46493-0_38
23. Cheng, H.-T., et al.: Wide & deep learning for recommender systems. In: Proceedings of the 1st Workshop on Deep Learning for Recommender Systems, pp. 7–10 (2016)
24. Géron, A.: Hands-on machine learning with Scikit-Learn, Keras, and TensorFlow: Concepts, tools, and techniques to build intelligent systems. O'Reilly Media Inc. (2019)
25. Kingma, D.P., Jimmy, B.: Adam: A method for stochastic optimization. arXiv preprint arXiv:1412.6980 (2014)
26. Robertson, A.R.: CIE guidelines for coordinated research on colour difference evaluation. Color. Res. Appl. **3**, 149–151 (1978)
27. Akanuma, A., Stamate, D.: A Neural Network Approach to Estimating Color Reflectance with Product Independent Models. In: 31st International Conference on Artificial Neural Networks - ICANN 2022. LNCS vol 13531. Springer. https://doi.org/10.1007/978-3-031-15934-3_66

The Importance of the Current Input in Sequence Modeling

Christian Oliva$^{(\boxtimes)}$ ⓘ and Luis F. Lago-Fernández ⓘ

Universidad Autónoma de Madrid, Madrid 28049, Spain
{christian.oliva,luis.lago}@uam.es

Abstract. The last advances in sequence modeling are mainly based on deep learning approaches. The current state of the art involves the use of variations of the standard LSTM architecture, combined with several adjustments that improve the final prediction rates of the trained neural networks. However, in some cases, these adaptations might be too much tuned to the particular problems being addressed. In this article, we show that a very simple idea, to add a direct connection between the input and the output, skipping the recurrent module, leads to an increase of the prediction accuracy in sequence modeling problems related to natural language processing. Experiments carried out on different problems show that the addition of this kind of connection to a recurrent network always improves the results, regardless of the architecture and training-specific details. When this idea is introduced into the models that lead the field, the resulting networks achieve a new state-of-the-art perplexity in language modeling problems.

1 Introduction

Deep learning models constitute the current state of the art in most artificial intelligence applications, from computer vision to robotics or medicine. When dealing with sequential data, Recurrent Neural Networks (RNNs), specially those architectures with gating mechanisms such as the LSTM [7], the GRU [3] and other variants, are usually the default choice. One of the most interesting applications of RNNs is related to the field of Natural Language Processing, where most tasks, such as machine translation, document summarization or language modeling, involve the manipulation of sequences of textual data. Of these, language modeling has been extensively used to test different innovations in recurrent architectures, mainly due to the ease of obtaining very large datasets that can be used to train neural networks with millions of parameters.

Sequence modeling consists of predicting the next element in a sequence given the past history. In language modeling, the sequence is a text, and hence the task is to predict the next word or the next character. In this context, some of the best performing architectures include the Mogrifier LSTM [12] and different variations of the Averaged SGD Weight-Drop (AWD) LSTM [13], usually combined with dynamic evaluation and Mixture of Softmaxes (MoS) [6,20]. These models

© IFIP International Federation for Information Processing 2023
Published by Springer Nature Switzerland AG 2023
I. Maglogiannis et al. (Eds.): AIAI 2023, IFIP AICT 675, pp. 161–172, 2023.
https://doi.org/10.1007/978-3-031-34111-3_15

obtain the best state-of-the-art performance with moderate size datasets, such as the Penn Treebank [15] or the Wikitext-2 [14] corpora, when no additional data are used during training. When larger datasets are considered, or when external data are used to pre-train the networks, attention-based architectures usually outperform other models [2,18].

In this work we use moderate-scale language modeling datasets to explore the effect of a mechanism recently proposed by [16], when combined with different LSTM-based models in the language modeling context. The idea consists of modifying a recurrent architecture by introducing a direct connection between the input and the output of the recurrent module. This has been shown to improve both the model's generalization results and its readability in simple tasks related to the recognition of regular languages.

In a standard RNN, the output depends only on the network's hidden state, h_t, which in turn depends on both the input, x_t, and the recent past, h_{t-1}. But there is no explicit dependence of the network's output on its input. In some cases this could be a shortcoming, since the transformation of x_t needed to compute the network's internal state is not necessarily the most appropriate to compute the output. However, an explicit dependence of the output on x_t can be forced by adding a *dual* connection that skips the recurrent layers. We claim that this strategy may be of general application in RNN models.

To test our hypothesis we perform a thorough comparison of several state-of-the-art RNN architectures, with and without the *dual* connection, on the Penn Treebank (PTB) and the Wikitext-2 (WT2) datasets. Our results show that, under all experimental conditions, the *dual* architectures outperform their non-dual counterparts. In addition, the Mogrifier-LSTM enhanced with a *dual* connection establishes a new state-of-the-art word-level perplexity for the Penn Treebank dataset when no additional data are used to train the models.

The remainder of the article is organized as follows. First, in Sect. 2, we present the different models we have used and the two possible architectures, the standard recurrent architecture and the *dual* architecture. In Sect. 3, we describe the datasets and the experimental setup. In Sect. 4, we present our results. And finally, in Sect. 5, we extract some conclusions and discuss further lines of research.

2   Models

We start by presenting the standard recurrent architecture which is common to all the models. In absence of a *dual* connection, the basic architecture involves an embedding layer, a recurrent layer and a fully-connected layer with *softmax* activation:

$$e_t = W^{ex}x_t \tag{1}$$

$$h_t = REC(e_t, S_{t-1}) \tag{2}$$

$$y_t = softmax(W^{yh}h_t + b^y), \tag{3}$$

where W^{**} and b^{*} are weight matrices and biases, respectively, and x_t is the input vector at time t. The REC module represents an arbitrary recurrent layer, with S_{t-1} being a set of vectors describing its internal state at the previous time step. In the most general case, this module will simply be an LSTM cell, but we consider other possibilities as well, as described below.

The *dual* architecture introduces an additional layer, with ReLU activation, which is fed with both the output of the embedding layer and the output of the recurrent module:

$$e_t = W^{ex}x_t \tag{4}$$
$$h_t = REC(e_t, S_{t-1}) \tag{5}$$
$$d_t = ReLU(W^{de}e_t + W^{dh}h_t + b^d) \tag{6}$$
$$y_t = softmax(W^{yd}d_t + b^y). \tag{7}$$

This way the network's input can reach the softmax layer following two different paths, through the recurrent layer and through the *dual* connection. In the following we consider different forms for the recurrent module in Eq. 2 and 5.

2.1 The LSTM Module

In the simplest approach the recurrent module consists of an LSTM cell, where the internal state includes both the output and the memory, $S_t = \{h_t; c_t\}$, which are computed as follows:

$$f_t = \sigma(W^{fe}e_t + W^{fh}h_{t-1} + b^f) \tag{8}$$
$$i_t = \sigma(W^{ie}e_t + W^{ih}h_{t-1} + b^i) \tag{9}$$
$$o_t = \sigma(W^{oe}e_t + W^{oh}h_{t-1} + b^o) \tag{10}$$
$$z_t = tanh(W^{ze}e_t + W^{zh}h_{t-1} + b^z) \tag{11}$$
$$c_t = f_t \odot c_{t-1} + i_t \odot z_t \tag{12}$$
$$h_t = o_t \odot tanh(c_t), \tag{13}$$

where, as before, W^{**} are weight matrices and b^{*} are bias vectors. The $\odot$ operator denotes an element-wise product, and σ is the logistic sigmoid function. For convenience, we summarize the joint effect of Eqs. 8–13 as:

$$h_t = LSTM(e_t, \{h_{t-1}; c_{t-1}\}). \tag{14}$$

In the literature it is quite common to stack several LSTM layers. Here we consider a double-layer LSTM, where the output h_t of the recurrent module is obtained by the concatenated application of two LSTM layers:

$$h'_t = LSTM_1(e_t, \{h'_{t-1}; c'_{t-1}\}) \tag{15}$$
$$h_t = LSTM_2(h'_t, \{h_{t-1}; c_{t-1}\}). \tag{16}$$

We refer to this double LSTM module as $dLSTM$:

$$h_t = dLSTM(e_t, \{h_{t-1}; c_{t-1}; h'_{t-1}; c'_{t-1}\}) \tag{17}$$
$$= LSTM_2(LSTM_1(e_t, \{h'_{t-1}; c'_{t-1}\}), \{h_{t-1}; c_{t-1}\}). \tag{18}$$

2.2   The Mogrifier-LSTM Module

The Mogrifier-LSTM [12] is one of the state-of-the-art variations of the standard LSTM architecture achieving the lowest perplexity scores in language modeling tasks. It basically consists of a standard LSTM block, but the input e_t and the hidden state h_{t-1} are transformed before entering Eqs. 8–13. The mogrifier transformation involves several steps where e_t and h_{t-1} modulate each other:

$$e_t^i = 2\sigma(Q^i h_{t-1}^{i-1}) \odot e_t^{i-2}, \quad \text{for odd } i \in \{1, 2, ..., r\} \tag{19}$$
$$h_{t-1}^i = 2\sigma(R^i e_t^{i-1}) \odot h_{t-1}^{i-2}, \quad \text{for even } i \in \{1, 2, ..., r\}, \tag{20}$$

where Q^i and R^i are weight matrices and we have $e_t^{-1} = e_t$ and $h_{t-1}^0 = h_{t-1}$. The linear transformations $Q^i h_{t-1}^{i-1}$ and $R^i e_t^{i-1}$ can also include the addition of a bias vector, which has been omitted for the sake of clarity. The constant r is a hyperparameter whose value defines the number of rounds of the transformation. We refer to this recurrent module, including the mogrifier transformation and the subsequent application of the LSTM layer, as:

$$h_t = mLSTM(e_t, \{h_{t-1}; c_{t-1}\}) = LSTM(e_t^*, \{h_{t-1}^*; c_{t-1}\}), \tag{21}$$

where e_t^* and h_{t-1}^* are the highest indexed e_t^i and h_{t-1}^i in Eq. 19 and 20. Note that the choice $r = 0$ recovers the standard LSTM model.

The original work also explored the use of a double-layer LSTM enhanced with the mogrifier transformation. This strategy can be summarized as follows:

$$h_t = mdLSTM(e_t, \{h_{t-1}; c_{t-1}; h'_{t-1}; c'_{t-1}\}) \tag{22}$$
$$= mLSTM_2(mLSTM_1(e_t, \{h'_{t-1}; c'_{t-1}\}), \{h_{t-1}; c_{t-1}\}). \tag{23}$$

3   Experiments

3.1   Datasets

We perform experiments on two datasets: the Penn Treebank (PTB) corpus [11], as preprocessed by [15], and the WikiText-2 (WT2) dataset [14]. In both cases, the data are used without any additional preprocessing.

The Penn Treebank dataset has been widely used in the literature to experiment with language modeling. The standard data preprocessing is due to [15], and includes transformation of all letters to lower case, elimination of punctuation symbols, and replacement of all numbers with a special token. The vocabulary is limited to the 10,000 most frequent words. The data is split into a training set which contains almost 930,000 tokens, and validation and test sets with around 80,000 words each.

The WikiText-2 dataset, introduced by [14], is a more realistic benchmark for language modeling tasks. It consists of more than 2 million words extracted from Wikipedia articles. The training, validation and test sets contain around 2,125,000, 220,000, and 250,000 words, respectively. The vocabulary includes over 30,000 words, and the data retain capitalization, punctuation, and numbers.

3.2   Experimental Setup

All the considered models follow one of the two architectures discussed in Sect. 2, either the Embedding-Recurrent-Softmax (ERS) architecture (Eqs. 1–3) or the *dual* architecture (Eqs. 4–7). In either case, the recurrent module can be any of *LSTM*, *dLSTM*, or *mdLSTM*. Weight tying [8,17] is used to couple the weight matrices of the embedding and the output layers. This reduces the number of parameters and prevents the model from learning a one-to-one correspondence between the input and the output [13].

We run two different sets of experiments. First, we analyze the effect of the *dual* connection by comparing the performances of the two architectures (ERS vs Dual), using each of the recurrent modules, on both the PTB and the WT2 datasets. In this setting the hyperparameters are tuned for the ERS architecture, and then transferred to the *dual* case. Second, we search for the best hyperparameters for the *dual* architecture using the *mdLSTM* recurrence, and compare the perplexity score with current state-of-the-art values. All the experiments have been performed using the Keras library [4].

The networks are trained using the Nadam optimizer [5], a variation of Adam [9] where Nesterov momentum is applied. The number of training epochs is different for each experimental condition. On one hand, when the objective is to perform a pairwise comparison between *dual* and non-dual architectures, we train the models for 100 epochs. On the other hand, when the goal is to compare the *dual* network with state of the art approaches, we let the models run for 300 epochs. We use batch sizes of 32 and 128 for the PTB and the WT2 problems, respectively, and set the sequence length to 25 in all cases. The remaining hyperparameters are searched in the ranges described in Table 1.

Finally, all the models are run twice, both with and without dynamic evaluation [10]. Dynamic evaluation is a standard method commonly used to adapt the model parameters, learned during training, using also the validation data. This allows the networks to get adapted to the new evaluation conditions, which in general improves their performance. In order to keep the models as simple as possible, no additional modifications have been considered.

Table 1. List of all the hyperparameters and the search range associated with each of them. Those marked with an asterisk (*) refer to the *dual* architectures only.

Name	Description	Values
Num epochs	Number of training epochs	$\{100, 300\}$
Learning rate	Learning rate	$[10^{-6}, 10^{-3}]$
Batch size	Batch size	$\{32, 128\}$
Seq len	Sequence length	$\{10, 25, 50\}$
Embedding units	Size of the embedding layer	$\{400, 850\}$
Recurrent units	Size of the recurrent layers	$\{400, 850, 1150\}$
LSTM layers	Number of recurrent layers	$\{1, 2, 3\}$
*Dual units**	Size of the *dual* layer	$\{400, 850\}$
Embedding L2reg	L2 regularization applied to the Embedding and output layers	$\{0, 10^{-6}, 10^{-5}\}$
Rec. input L2reg	L2 regularization applied to the input weights of the recurrent layer	$\{0, 10^{-6}, 10^{-5}\}$
Rec. L2reg	L2 regularization applied to the recurrent weights of the recurrent layer	$\{0, 10^{-6}, 10^{-5}\}$
Activation L2reg	L2 regularization applied to the recurrent layers output	$\{0, 10^{-6}, 10^{-5}\}$
*Dual L2reg**	L2 regularization applied to *dual* layer	$\{0, 10^{-6}, 10^{-5}\}$
Rec. input Dropout	Dropout before the first recurrent layer	$[0.0, 0.5]$
Rec. Dropout	Dropout for the linear transformation of the recurrent state	$[0.0, 0.5]$
Rec. internal Dropout	Dropout between the recurrent layers	$[0.0, 0.5]$
Rec. output Dropout	Dropout after the last recurrent layer	$[0.0, 0.5]$
*Dual input Dropout**	Dropout before the *dual* layer	$[0.0, 0.5]$
*Dual output Dropout**	Dropout after the *dual* layer	$[0.0, 0.5]$
Mogrifier deep	Mogrifier rounds	$\{0, 2, 3, 4, 5, 6\}$
Mogrifier L2reg	L2 regularization applied to Mogrifier weights	$\{0, 10^{-6}, 10^{-5}\}$
Mogrifier rank	Weight factorization. $Q^i \in R^{m \times n} = Q_l^i Q_r^i$ with $Q_l^i \in R^{m \times k}, Q_r^i \in R^{k \times n}$	$\{0, 50, 100, 200\}$
Mogrifier Dropout	Dropout between the Mogrifier weights	$[0.0, 0.2]$
Learning rate eval	Learning rate when Dynamic evaluation	$[10^{-6}, 10^{-3}]$
Seq len eval	Sequence length when Dynamic evaluation	$[5, 50]$
Clipnorm eval	Gradients clipping to a maximum norm	$[0.0, 1.0]$

4   Results

We first show the results of the comparative analysis ERS vs Dual, then we focus on the search of the optimal hyperparameters for the *dual* architecture with the *mdLSTM* recurrence.

4.1   Dual vs Non-dual Architectures

Table 2 displays the validation and test perplexity scores obtained for each of the experimental configurations on the PTB and the WT2 problems, both with and without dynamic evaluation. To facilitate the comparison, each pair of rows contain the results for one of the recurrent modules (*LSTM*, *dLSTM* or *mdLSTM*) using the two architectures ERS and Dual, with the best values shown in bold. In each case, the hyperparameters are tuned for the standard ERS architecture and then used within the *dual* networks without any additional adaptation. The exceptions are hyperparameters, such as the *dual* dropout, which do not exist in the ERS configuration (those marked with an asterisk in Table 1). To give a measure of the model complexity, Table 2 contains also the approximate number of trainable parameters for each configuration.

Table 2. Validation and test word-level perplexity obtained for each of the experimental configurations on the PTB (top) and the WT2 (bottom) datasets.

Penn Treebank Dataset					
		No. Dyneval		Dyneval	
Model	No. PARAMS	Val.	Test	Val.	Test
LSTM	8.88 M	67.37	64.91	62.31	61.17
Dual LSTM	9.60 M	61.22	59.39	**55.26**	**54.69**
dLSTM	13.62 M	63.44	61.03	57.18	56.01
Dual dLSTM	13.94 M	60.99	59.56	**56.11**	**54.87**
mdLSTM	21.43 M	57.42	55.48	51.16	50.27
Dual mdLSTM	22.88 M	56.08	54.12	**48.82**	**48.00**
mdLSTM+	22.16 M	57.77	56.29	50.42	49.83
WikiText-2 Dataset					
		No. Dyneval		Dyneval	
Model	**No. PARAMS**	Val.	Test	Val.	Test
LSTM	20.23 M	92.84	88.28	74.98	69.42
Dual LSTM	20.95 M	85.88	82.48	**61.94**	**57.61**
dLSTM	29.60 M	78.65	75.60	63.26	59.42
Dual dLSTM	30.32 M	77.01	73.90	**61.10**	**57.10**
mdLSTM	37.51 M	72.05	69.06	57.42	53.93
Dual mdLSTM	38.95 M	71.78	70.83	**53.48**	**50.71**

As expected, dynamic evaluation improves the results regardless of the model or the dataset. The main observation, however, is that networks enhanced with the *dual* connection display lower perplexity scores for almost all the training conditions on both the PTB and the WT2 datasets. The advantage of the Dual vs the ERS architecture is larger for less complex models, and narrows as the model complexity increases. Nevertheless, even for networks with $mdLSTM$ recurrence, the *dual* architectures outperform their non-dual counterparts in more than 2 perplexity points on the test set, when dynamic evaluation is used.

In order to test that this improvement is due to the *dual* connection and not to the presence of an extra processing layer, we performed an additional experiment with a *Dual mdLSTM* model, but removing the term $W^{de}e_t$ from Eq. 6. The results for the PTB dataset are shown in Table 2 as $mdLSTM+$. Note that, in spite of slightly improving the baseline, this enhanced mogrifier model is still well below the result obtained with the full *dual* architecture.

Finally, it is worth noting that all the results presented correspond to our own implementation of the models, and that in most cases we are not including some of the several training or validation adaptations frequently used in the literature (such as AWD or MoS, for example). This can explain the difference with respect to the results reported by [12] for the Mogrifier-LSTM model. We would expect a further improvement of the results if these additional mechanisms were implemented.

4.2   Dual Mogrifier Fine Tuning

The second part of the experiments consists of searching for the best hyperparameters in the configuration that provided the smallest perplexity in the previous setup, that is the *Dual mdLSTM* architecture. We carry out this experiment with the PTB problem. After an extensive search (see Table 1), the best performance is obtained with a model with 850 units in the embedding layer, 850 units in each of the mogrifier LSTM layers, and 850 units also in the *dual* layer. The input, recurrent, internal, and output dropout rates are all set to 0.5, the *dual* input and output dropout rates are set to 0.5 and 0.4, respectively, and the mogrifier dropout rate is set to 0.15. Both the embedding and the *dual* L2 regularization parameters are set to 10^{-5}. The mogrifier number of rounds is set to 4, and the rank to 100. All the remaining hyperparameters are set to 0.

After the training phase, we continue with a fine tuning of some additional hyperparameters, using the validation data. First, we look for the best sequence length in the range [5, 70], and then we fine-tune the softmax temperature in the range [0.9, 1.3]. When using dynamic evaluation, we also look for the best gradient clipping value (in the range [0.0, 1.0]) and, following [12], we repeat the whole procedure with the β_1 parameter of the Nadam optimizer set to 0, which resembles the RMSProp optimizer without momentum. The results are shown in Table 3, together with the top perplexity scores reported in the literature for the same problem.

The state-of-the-art is dominated by several variations of the AWD-LSTM network [13], the most common being the inclusion of a Mixture of Softmaxes

Table 3. Best validation and test word-level perplexity scores reported in the literature for the Penn Treebank dataset, with and without dynamic evaluation. Missing values in the last two columns correspond to works where the dynamic evaluation approach was not considered. The last row in the table displays the results obtained with our *Dual mdLSTM* network.

Model		No Dyneval		Dyneval	
		Val.	Test	Val.	Test
AWD-LSTM [13]	24 M	60.00	57.30	–	–
AWD-LSTM-DOC [19]	23 M	54.12	52.38	–	–
AWD-LSTM [10]	24 M	59.80	57.70	51.60	51.10
mdLSTM - ours	22 M	57.42	55.48	51.16	50.27
AWD-LSTM +PDR [1]	24 M	57.90	55.60	50.10	49.30
AWD-LSTM +MoS [21]	22 M	56.54	54.44	48.33	47.69
AWD-LSTM +MoS +PDR [1]	22 M	56.20	53.80	48.00	47.30
AWD-LSTM-DOC x5 [19]	185 M	48.63	47.17	–	–
AWD-LSTM +MoS +FRAGE [6]	24 M	55.52	53.51	47.38	46.54
AWD-LSTM +MoS +Adv [20]	22 M	54.98	52.87	47.15	46.52
AWD-LSTM +MoS +Adv +PS [20]	22 M	54.10	52.20	46.63	46.01
Mogrifier-LSTM [12]	24 M	51.40	50.10	44.90	44.80
Dual mdLSTM - ours	23 M	52.87	51.19	45.13	**44.61**

(MoS) [21]. Other add-ons include Direct Output Connection (DOC) [19], which is a generalization of MoS, Frequency Agnostic word Embedding (FRAGE) [6], Past Decode Regularization (PDR) [1], or Partial Shuffling (PS) with Adversarial Training (Adv) [20]. The mogrifier-LSTM described in Sect. 2.2 combines many of these ideas with a mutual gating between the input and the hidden state vectors to obtain the best results reported in the literature for the PTB problem, among those obtained by networks that do not use additional data during the training phase. Compared with all these models, our current approach leads the ranking with a perplexity score of 44.61, even though most of the aforementioned adjustments have not been considered.

Finally, it is important to mention that the last two rows in the table do not correspond to comparable models. While the penultimate row shows the results reported by Melis et al. [12] with their *Mogrifier-LSTM* model, the last table row contains the results of our *Dual mdLSTM* model, which uses the mogrifier transformation but lacks many of the additional characteristics of the Melis et al. model. Hence, regarding the improvement associated with fine-tuning the *Dual mdLSTM* model, the fair comparison would be with the results shown in Table 2, which have been also included in Table 3 for the sake of clarity. In this case the dual model outperforms its non-dual equivalent in more than 5 perplexity points (50.27 versus 44.61) on the test set.

5   Discussion

In this work, we have presented a new network design for the Language Modeling task based on the *dual* network proposed by [16]. This network adds a direct connection between the input and the output, skipping the recurrent module, and can be adapted to any of the traditional Embedding-Recurrent-Softmax (ERS) models, opening the way to new approaches for this task. We have based our work on the Penn Treebank [15] and the WikiText-2 [14] datasets, comparing the ERS approach and its *dual* alternative. Regardless of the configuration, the *dual* version performs always better, even though it faces a slight disadvantage, since most of the hyperparameters are tuned using the ERS model. We can expect a much better performance if the complete set of hyperparameters is properly tuned for the *dual* network.

This is in fact the case for the second experiment, where a *Dual mdLSTM*, which includes a simplified version of the mogrifier LSTM [12] within a *dual* architecture, is fine tuned for the Penn Treebank dataset. After a thorough search of the hyperparameter space, we have found a network configuration that establishes a new state-of-the-art score for this problem. Interestingly, this new record has been obtained in spite of leaving aside many of the standard features used in most state-of-the-art approaches, such as *AWD* [13] or *MoS* [21]. The incorporation of these features into the *dual* architecture can be expected to further increase the model performance.

The *dual* architecture was firstly proposed as an alternative that reduces the computational load on the recurrent layer, letting it concentrate on modeling the temporal dependencies only. From a more abstract point of view, it has been argued that the dual architecture can be understood as a sort of Mealy machine, where the output explicitly depends on both the hidden state and the input [16]. Our results show that this explicit dependence on the input can indeed lead to better performance on language modeling tasks. This emphasizes the importance of the current input in RNN models.

Finally, although the new approach has not been tested with large-scale language corpora, we expect that our results scale well to larger datasets. Work in progress contemplates this extension. The *dual* architecture also needs further research concerning the deepness of the specific variations of Language Modeling and other families of problems not necessarily related to Natural Language Processing. This work opens a new line of research to be considered when processing any sequence or time series. The utility of this approach in more general problems will be addressed as future work.

Acknowledgments. This work has been partially funded by Spanish project PID2020-114867RB-I00, (MCIN/AEI and ERDF- "A way of making Europe").

References

1. Brahma, S.: Improved language modeling by decoding the past. In: Proceedings of the 57th Annual Meeting of the Association for Computational Linguistics, pp. 1468–1476. Association for Computational Linguistics, Florence, Italy (Jul 2019)

2. Brown, T., et al.: Language models are few-shot learners. In: Larochelle, H., Ranzato, M., Hadsell, R., Balcan, M.F., Lin, H. (eds.) Advances in Neural Information Processing Systems, vol. 33, pp. 1877–1901. Curran Associates, Inc. (2020)
3. Cho, K., et al.: Learning phrase representations using RNN encoder-decoder for statistical machine translation. In: Moschitti, A., Pang, B., Daelemans, W. (eds.) Proceedings of the 2014 Conference on Empirical Methods in Natural Language Processing, EMNLP 2014, 25–29 October 2014, Doha, Qatar, A meeting of SIGDAT, a Special Interest Group of the ACL, pp. 1724–1734. ACL (2014)
4. Chollet, F., et al.: Keras (2015). https://keras.io
5. Dozat, T.: Incorporating nesterov momentum into adam. In: Proceedings of 4th International Conference on Learning Representations, Workshop Track (2016)
6. Gong, C., He, D., Tan, X., Qin, T., Wang, L., Liu, T.Y.: Frage: Frequency-agnostic word representation. In: Bengio, S., Wallach, H., Larochelle, H., Grauman, K., Cesa-Bianchi, N., Garnett, R. (eds.) Advances in Neural Information Processing Systems, vol. 31. Curran Associates, Inc. (2018)
7. Hochreiter, S., Schmidhuber, J.: Long short-term memory. Neural Comput. 9(8), 1735–1780 (1997)
8. Inan, H., Khosravi, K., Socher, R.: Tying word vectors and word classifiers: A loss framework for language modeling. In: Proceedings of the 5th International Conference on Learning Representations (2017)
9. Kingma, D.P., Ba, J.: Adam: A method for stochastic optimization. In: Bengio, Y., LeCun, Y. (eds.) 3rd International Conference on Learning Representations, ICLR 2015, San Diego, CA, USA, 7–9 May 2015, Conference Track Proceedings (2015)
10. Krause, B., Kahembwe, E., Murray, I., Renals, S.: Dynamic evaluation of neural sequence models. In: Dy, J., Krause, A. (eds.) Proceedings of the 35th International Conference on Machine Learning. Proceedings of Machine Learning Research, 10–15 Jul, vol. 80, pp. 2766–2775. PMLR (2018)
11. Marcus, M.P., Marcinkiewicz, M.A., Santorini, B.: Building a large annotated corpus of english: The penn treebank. Comput. Linguist. 19(2), 313–330 (1993)
12. Melis, G., Kočiský, T., Blunsom, P.: Mogrifier LSTM. In: International Conference on Learning Representations (2020)
13. Merity, S., Keskar, N.S., Socher, R.: Regularizing and optimizing LSTM language models. In: International Conference on Learning Representations (2018)
14. Merity, S., Xiong, C., Bradbury, J., Socher, R.: Pointer sentinel mixture models. In: 5th International Conference on Learning Representations, ICLR 2017, Toulon, France, 24–26 April 2017, Conference Track Proceedings. OpenReview.net (2017)
15. Mikolov, T., Karafiát, M., Burget, L., Cernocký, J., Khudanpur, S.: Recurrent neural network based language model. In: Kobayashi, T., Hirose, K., Nakamura, S. (eds.) INTERSPEECH, pp. 1045–1048. ISCA (2010)
16. Oliva, C., Lago-Fernández, L.F.: Separation of Memory and Processing in Dual Recurrent Neural Networks. In: Farkaš, I., Masulli, P., Otte, S., Wermter, S. (eds.) ICANN 2021. LNCS, vol. 12894, pp. 360–371. Springer, Cham (2021). https://doi.org/10.1007/978-3-030-86380-7_29
17. Press, O., Wolf, L.: Using the output embedding to improve language models. In: Proceedings of the 15th Conference of the European Chapter of the Association for Computational Linguistics: Volume 2, Short Papers, pp. 157–163. Association for Computational Linguistics, Valencia, Spain (Apr 2017)
18. Radford, A., Wu, J., Child, R., Luan, D., Amodei, D., Sutskever, I.: Language models are unsupervised multitask learners (2019)

19. Takase, S., Suzuki, J., Nagata, M.: Direct output connection for a high-rank language model. In: Proceedings of the 2018 Conference on Empirical Methods in Natural Language Processing, pp. 4599–4609. Association for Computational Linguistics, Brussels, Belgium (Oct-Nov 2018)
20. Wang, D., Gong, C., Liu, Q.: Improving neural language modeling via adversarial training. In: Chaudhuri, K., Salakhutdinov, R. (eds.) Proceedings of the 36th International Conference on Machine Learning. Proceedings of Machine Learning Research, 09–15 Jun, vol. 97, pp. 6555–6565. PMLR (2019)
21. Yang, Z., Dai, Z., Salakhutdinov, R., Cohen, W.W.: Breaking the softmax bottleneck: A high-rank RNN language model. In: International Conference on Learning Representations (2018)

Towards Historical Map Analysis Using Deep Learning Techniques

Ladislav Lenc[1,2(✉)], Josef Baloun[1,2], Jiří Martínek[1,2], and Pavel Král[1,2]

[1] Department of Computer Science and Engineering, Faculty of Applied Sciences,
University of West Bohemia, Plzeň, Czech Republic
{llenc,balounj,jimar,pkral}@kiv.zcu.cz
[2] NTIS - New Technologies for the Information Society, Faculty of Applied Sciences,
University of West Bohemia, Plzeň, Czech Republic

Abstract. This paper presents methods for automatic analysis of historical cadastral maps. The methods are developed as a part of a complex system for map digitisation, analysis and processing. Our goal is to detect important features in individual map sheets to allow their further processing and connecting the sheets into one seamless map that can be better presented online. We concentrate on detection of the map frame, which defines the important segment of the map sheet. Other crucial features are so-called inches that define the measuring scale of the map. We also detect the actual map area.

We assume that standard computer vision methods can improve results of deep learning methods. Therefore, we propose novel segmentation approaches that combine standard computer vision techniques with neural nets (NNs). For all the above-mentioned tasks, we evaluate and compare our so-called "Combined methods" with state-of-the-art methods based solely on neural networks. We have shown that combining the standard computer vision techniques with NNs can outperform the state-of-the-art approaches in the scenario when only little training data is available.

We have also created a novel annotated dataset that is used for network training and evaluation. This corpus is freely available for research purposes which represents another contribution of this paper.

Keywords: Historical Maps · Document Image Processing · CNN · Fully-convolutional Neural Networks

1 Introduction

Processing of historical documents is of a great interest. Various archival documents are stored in vast collections and are gradually digitised. The digitisation is the first step in the process of making the documents accessible and easily exploitable.

© IFIP International Federation for Information Processing 2023
Published by Springer Nature Switzerland AG 2023
I. Maglogiannis et al. (Eds.): AIAI 2023, IFIP AICT 675, pp. 173–185, 2023.
https://doi.org/10.1007/978-3-031-34111-3_16

We focus on the processing of cadastral maps from the first half of the nineteenth century. The maps cover parts of the former Austria-Hungary empire – a region currently linked to the Czech Republic. The maps are hand-drawn and are available as a set of individual map sheets. The final goal of the map analysis and processing is to provide a seamless connection of the individual sheets.

The main goal is twofold. The first task is to construct a virtual grid of the map sheet positions to learn which ones are next to each other according to the historical coordinate system. The second goal consists in precise detection of map borders within the map sheets that belong to the same grid cell (map sheets on the border of cadastre areas). Thanks to the detected border, the neighbouring sheets can be seamlessly connected. The outside of the map is masked within this procedure. The final result of the task demonstrated on map sheets covering Pilsen city area is depicted in Fig. 1.

Fig. 1. Example of a composed map of the city of Pilsen constructed from the individual map sheets (https://archivnimapy.cuzk.cz/uazk/pohledy/archiv.html)

The information about the position within the map coordinate system (in the grid) is provided by so-called nomenclature. The nomenclature is basically a label of the map sheet and it is usually located at the top right corner. It contains information about the map area name, relative position from the main meridian (west "W.C." or east "O.C."), and indices (marked by a Roman and Arabic numerals and a pair of letters a–d and e–i) that uniquely identify the position in the coordinate system (Fig. 2). For a more detailed overview of the projection and positioning, see [13].

A related task is detection of a map frame, which is ideally a rectangular area covering the grid cell. However, in reality, in the case of scanned hand-drawn maps, it is slightly curved which brings challenges for its precise detection. The measuring scale of the map is indicated by so-called inches that lie on the map frame and are equidistantly positioned.

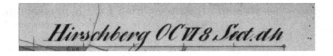

Fig. 2. Example of a nomenclature in Hirschberg cadastre area

This paper deals with several sub-tasks that allow us to achieve the seamless map connection. We concentrate mainly on detection of map frames and precise positions of inches and corners. We also solve map area segmentation. For all the above-mentioned tasks, we compare our so-called "Combined methods" with state-of-the-art methods based solely on neural networks. The proposed approaches combine standard computer vision techniques with neural networks (NNs). We assume that the combination of the standard computer vision techniques with NNs could outperform the state-of-the-art approaches in this particular scenario when only little training data are available.

2 Related Work

Map processing and analysis is usually comprised of segmentation and object detection algorithms. One important direction is the processing of historical maps. Several successful methods for map content segmentation were developed within the MapSeg competition [3]. The methods submitted to the competition are built on traditional computer vision approaches as well as neural network-based methods. IRISA [1] method is a representative of traditional methods while L3IRIS utilises a HSNet network [9]. The winning UWB method then combines both image processing methods and fully convolutional networks (FCN). One important aspect that the methods have in common is the adaptation on small amounts of training data which is common in this domain and hampers larger utilisation of deep learning methods. Lenc et al. [7] concentrated on the segmentation of the cadastre border and the detection of important points on it, so-called landmarks. The algorithms mainly relied on FCN networks and the results were post-processed and refined using image processing techniques such as mathematical morphology, skeletonization, etc. Chen et al. [4] presented a method for segmentation of historical maps. They utilised BiDirectional Cascade Network (BDCN) for detecting edges and at the same time filtering unwanted features such as text. Their dataset is a set of urban map sheets of a central area of Paris from the year 1925.

Another important related part of the map analysis research focuses on remote sensing. With the massive deployment of remote sensing technologies, the automatic processing of the images got a new dimension. Timilsina et al. [14] presented a method based on convolutional networks. It was tailored for detection of tree coverage of cadastre parcels. Another sub-task, road detection from aerial images, was addressed by Kestur et al. [6]. The authors used a novel U-shaped FCN (UFCN) model. Last but not least, Neyns and Canters [10] provided an overview of approaches to map urban vegetation from high-resolution remotely sensed data.

3 Dataset

The dataset used for our experiments comes out of the Map Border Dataset[1]. We have created new annotations for the solved tasks, namely for the inch and the corner detection and also for the map area segmentation. The inch and corner masks allow automatic generation of map frame ground-truths. We utilised the border annotations together with the inch annotations to semi-automatically create the map area ground-truths.

The dataset is split into training, testing and validation sections, which contain 69, 20 and 10 images, respectively and it is available as an extension of the above mentioned Map Border Dataset on the same website.

4 Corner Detection

The map frame detection is important for the connection of the neighbouring map sheets. As mentioned above, the map frame is a bounding rectangle that surrounds the map content. In reality, the shape is slightly distorted, which makes the task more challenging. An example of a map frame with inches (crop of the original map sheet) is shown in Fig. 3.

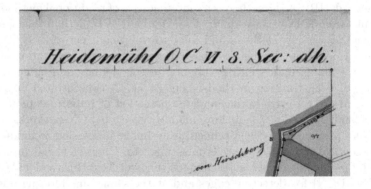

Fig. 3. Detail of a map frame with the inches

A crucial step in the map frame detection is the detection of the map frame corners. The corner positions are essential for the frame representation and the subsequent tasks we have to perform. Namely, we utilize it to detect inches in the next step.

---

[1] https://corpora.kiv.zcu.cz/map_border/.

We proposed and implemented two methods for this task. The first one combines image processing techniques and an FCN while the second one relies solely on an FCN. We will report the approaches as "Combined" and "FCN-based".

4.1 Combined Method

We developed a novel approach that combines standard image processing techniques with neural networks. We first binarize the image using recursive Otsu thresholding method [11]. Next, we apply a fully convolutional network trained for prediction of map frame lines. We utilize the architecture proposed in [2]. The frame lines in the ground-truth masks are enhanced using a Gaussian kernel in order to put more weight to the line itself and gradually lower the weight with increasing distance from the line. This enhancement proved to be better compared to use solely the line in our preliminary experiments. The network prediction is then multiplied by the binarized image which leads to elimination of noise present in the binarization result.

After obtaining the rough map frame mask, the Hough transform is applied to detect horizontal and vertical lines. We filter all other lines with angles differing more than 2o from the vertical and horizontal directions. This way we obtain several line candidates close to each of the map frame lines. Due to the fact that some map sheets may have more than two horizontal/vertical lines, we apply filtering based on the assumed distance of the line candidates. Thus we obtain only the real map frame lines. Intersections of the line candidates are chosen as corner candidates. As a final step, the candidate points are refined. We crop a rectangle surrounding the candidate corner point (see Fig. 4) and construct horizontal and vertical projection profiles. The profile maxima are the coordinates of the actual corner positions.

Fig. 4. Binarized corner candidate region extracted around the candidate corner point

4.2 FCN-based Method

As a competing approach we have selected a method based solely on a neural network. We utilize the FCN network architecture proposed by Wick and Puppe [15] The architecture is shown in Fig. 5. This method is an adaptation of U-Net model proposed by Ronneberger et al. [12]. We chose this network because of its good results and more efficient computation times as shown in [8].

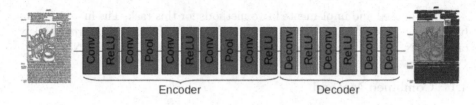

Fig. 5. Modified U-Net architecture proposed by Wick and Puppe [15]

Contrary to the U-Net architecture, it does not use skip connections. The whole architecture of this network is also simpler and the number of parameters is lower. The encoder part is composed of 5 convolutional and two pooling layers. The size of the convolution kernels is set to 5 and padding is used to keep the dimension. The decoder consists of 4 deconvolution layers.

The ground-truth masks for this task have circles at the positions of the corners. We thus predict the frame corner positions directly.

Due to the relatively small size of the ground-truth masks compared to the background, we utilize a patch-based approach that first divides the image into a set of rectangular patches according to a rectangular grid. The patches are then predicted individually and the final result is composed from the partial predictions.

4.3 Results

We have evaluated and compared both methods on the newly annotated map frame dataset. We report precision and recall of the detected corners as well as mean average error (MAE) measuring the average distance of the predicted corner and ground-truth position. Table 1 shows the results of this experiment.

The results indicate that the Combined method achieved better results regardless of the settings of the FCN-based method. The size of patches influences both precision and recall. The best results are obtained with patch sizes of 720×720 pixels. The number of patches per image used for training positively influences the overall results. An advantage of the FCN-based method is slightly better MAE which means that the predicted corners are closer to the ground-truth ones. This fact can be potentially used for refinement of the corner positions.

5 Inch Detection

The task of inch detection follows the corner detection. The inch positions are equidistantly placed on the map frame lines between the corners. In reality, the distances vary slightly because the maps were hand-drawn. However, the known approximate distance can serve as a hint mainly in cases where the inches are not well-marked. There are also issues with false inches because there are usually many lines that can be misinterpreted as inches. We again compare a Combined method with a solely FCN-based one.

Table 1. Comparison of corner detection results of the Combined method and the FCN-based method with different number of patches per image used for training and with different patch sizes

Combined method				
	P	**R**	**MAE**	**IoU**
	100	100	2.06	–

FCN-based method				
Patch Size ($w \times h$)	**P**	**R**	**MAE**	**IoU**
25 patches 240×240	8.1	64.6	1.65	8.4
320×320	11.2	72.9	1.61	11.1
480×480	35.4	18.8	0.53	13.9
640×640	82.0	54.2	1.61	35.8
720×720	46.9	54.2	1.59	27.3
50 patches 240×240	4.8	52.1	1.59	4.7
320×320	21.9	87.5	1.53	21.4
480×480	35.9	43.8	2.72	18.2
640×640	29.6	47.9	1.52	21.4
720×720	64.7	81.3	1.57	46.4
100 patches 240×240	29.4	79.2	1.53	24.7
320×320	33.3	77.1	1.45	28.4
480×480	12.9	72.9	1.72	11.2
640×640	69.2	72.9	1.33	43.3
720×720	78.6	54.2	1.66	36.3
150 patches 240×240	16.8	85.4	1.80	16.1
320×320	8.7	72.9	1.55	8.6
480×480	70.5	83.3	1.23	53.0
640×640	64.7	56.3	1.65	33.7
720×720	86.0	58.3	1.58	42.5

5.1   Combined Method

This method uses the outputs from the corner detection step. We first extract rectangular areas along the map frame lines. The crops are then used as input for an FCN trained for inch prediction. The network output is utilized for obtaining an initial set of inch candidates. Next we perform a check of the inches and try to compute positions of possibly missing ones. Once we have a complete set of candidate inches, a further refinement is applied. The procedure is very similar to the one used for corner position refinement. We again rely on the projection profiles computed in a small neighbourhood of the candidate position. Maxima of the projection profiles are used as the final inch positions.

5.2 FCN-Based Method

The method utilizes the same network architecture and patch-based processing as the one used for corner detection. We mainly wanted to evaluate if it is possible to use only the FCN network and apply it on the whole image. This approach would contribute to the simplification of the overall task and could reduce computational demands of some computationally intensive steps in the corner detection algorithm, mainly the Hough transform and other related computations. In this case, it could fully substitute the corner detection step.

As in the case of corners, we use ground-truth in the form of masks with white dots at the positions of inches.

5.3 Results

Table 2 summarises the results obtained for the inch detection task. As in related studies, we report precision, recall, mean absolute error (MAE) and intersection over union (IoU) values.

Table 2. Comparison of inch detection results of the Combined and FCN-based method with different number of patches per image used for training and with different patch sizes

Combined method		P	R	MAE	IoU
		97.4	97.6	1.98	–
FCN-based method					
Patch Size $(w \times h)$		P	R	MAE	IoU
50 patches	320×320	0.0	0	0	0
	160×640	73.0	34.3	0.93	0.12
	100×1280	70.1	32.6	1.34	0.11
	160×1280	0	0	0	0
100 patches	320×320	69.0	36.3	0.97	
	160×640	77.2	57.2	0.95	0.16
	100×1280	74.5	63.6	1.08	0.17
	160×1280	71.7	60.4	1.13	0.16
150 patches	320×320	65.2	34.8	1.33	0.08
	160×640	0	0	0	0
	100×1280	73.8	39.4	1.08	0.09
	160×1280	72.2	54.6	1.07	0.16

In this experiment, the solely FCN-based method proved relatively inefficient. The precision and recall values are relatively low. In this case, the patch size does not play as important role as in the corner detection. Similarly as in corner detection, the results of the FCN bring slightly more precise location of the points. The comparison proves that it is beneficial to use the pre-computed corner positions and detect inches only near the map frame lines. However, on the other hand, there is room to further improve the localisation accuracy of the Combined method.

6   Map Area Segmentation

The map area segmentation is another crucial step in the pipeline of the seamless map connection. It allows to visualize only the relevant area without blank parts outside the cadastre borders. Moreover, it is useful for attaching the relevant complementary part. Therefore, high demands are placed on the localization accuracy of the contours.

Generally, the map area might consist of several fragments within the map frame. The number of fragments is not limited, but in most cases, the frames contain only one fragment.

6.1   Combined Method

The Combined method utilises an FCN trained for prediction of fragment contours and multiplication with binarized image similarly as in Sect. 4.1. Given the fragment contour, we further use euclidean distance transform to obtain the distance from contour for each pixel. Based on that distance, the watershed is used to close the contour and retrieve the fragment area mask. This process is illustrated in Fig. 6.

Fig. 6. Combined method process. From left: border contour, euclidean distance transform result, watershed result

Since several fragments can occur, we have to set watershed markers for each of them. These markers are decided as local maxima of the distance from the contour. That allows processing several fragments with precise details provided by binarization as illustrated in Fig. 7.

6.2 Mask R-CNN

Mask R-CNN [5] is a state-of-the-art model for image segmentation. It is basically a convolutional network trained for the detection of essential image regions. It is an extension of R-CNN and Faster R-CNN networks which predict solely bounding boxes of segmented objects. On the other hand, Mask R-CNN provides us also with segmentation masks that are necessary for our application. We utilise the implementation from the Detectron2 framework.

6.3 Results

Table 3 and Fig. 8 show the comparison of Mask R-CNN and our Combined method. The performance is measured in terms of intersection over union (IoU). Further we provide Hausdorff distance (H) as error measure to compare the contour localisation accuracy. We can see that the Combined method significantly outperformed Mask R-CNN in this task.

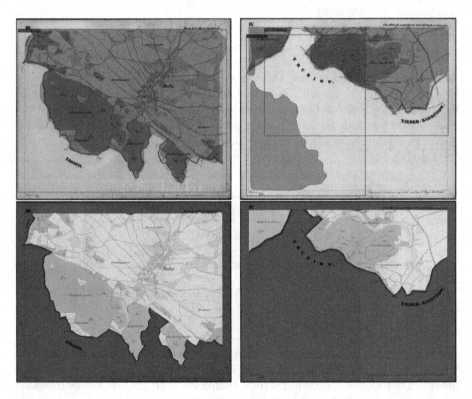

Fig. 7. Example of map area prediction using Mask R-CNN (top) and Combined method (bottom)

Table 3. Map area segmentation results of Combined method and Mask R-CNN

Method	IoU (%)	Hausdorff distance
Mask R-CNN	85.8	616.6
Combined method	97.0	172.9

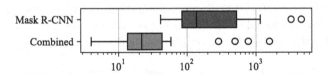

Fig. 8. Hausdorff distance distribution of test samples; smaller values are better

Figure 7 shows two example predictions made by the Mask R-CNN network (top) and by the combined method (bottom). The visualizations confirm the results indicated by IoU and Hausdorff distance. We can observe that the Combined method performs much better mainly near the cadastre borders. This amount of detail is hard to achieve with Mask R-CNN or other FCN-based methods. The Combined method also has less false positive map regions. The differences are caused mainly by the different learning objectives when we predict only the border contours in the case of the Combined method. On the other hand, the Combined method may fail if the binarization or contour prediction is of poor quality. In such a case, a part or the whole fragment may be lost.

7 Conclusions and Future Work

We have presented a set of methods that will be utilized within a larger system for processing and analysis of historical cadastral maps. The final goal of the system is to seamlessly connect individual map sheets into one piece and allow a user-friendly presentation on the web. We have focused on the map frame identification which involves corner and inch marks detection. Another solved task is segmentation of map area where we need to differentiate between the useful map content and the outside area which we want to mask out.

We assumed that standard computer vision methods can improve the results of the deep learning approaches. Therefore, we proposed novel segmentation approaches that combine standard computer vision techniques with neural nets (NNs). For all the solved tasks, we evaluated and compared our so-called "Combined methods" with state-of-the-art methods based solely on neural networks.

The results have shown that it is beneficial to use a combination of neural networks with standard image processing techniques. We can state that utilizing the networks is important mainly in complicated cases where solely the traditional methods fail. On the other hand, using only deep learning is also not sufficient, mainly because of the need of large amounts of annotated data for network training. It is noticeable mainly in the task of map area segmentation, where the complicated state-of-the-art Mask R-CNN gives rather poor results compared to a simple FCN complemented by binarization, distance transform and watershed.

We have also created a novel annotated dataset, that is freely available for research purposes, which represents another contribution of this paper.

In the future, we would like to further improve the developed methods and thus improve the overall system for map connection. We also would like to experiment with networks based on the Transformer architecture, which lately brought interesting results also in the image processing domain.

Acknowledgement. This work has been partly supported by Grant No. SGS-2022-016 Advanced methods of data processing and analysis.

References

1. Aurelie, L., Jean, C.: Segmentation of historical maps without annotated data. In: The 6th International Workshop on Historical Document Imaging and Processing, pp. 19–24 (2021)
2. Baloun, J., Král, P., Lenc, L., Rocha, A., Steels, L., van den Herik, H.: ChronSeg: novel dataset for segmentation of handwritten historical chronicles. In: ICAART (2), pp. 314–322 (2021)
3. Chazalon, J., et al.: ICDAR 2021 competition on historical map segmentation. In: Lladós, J., Lopresti, D., Uchida, S. (eds.) ICDAR 2021. LNCS, vol. 12824, pp. 693–707. Springer, Cham (2021). https://doi.org/10.1007/978-3-030-86337-1_46
4. Chen, Y., Carlinet, E., Chazalon, J., Mallet, C., Duménieu, B., Perret, J.: Combining deep learning and mathematical morphology for historical map segmentation. In: Lindblad, J., Malmberg, F., Sladoje, N. (eds.) DGMM 2021. LNCS, vol. 12708, pp. 79–92. Springer, Cham (2021). https://doi.org/10.1007/978-3-030-76657-3_5
5. He, K., Gkioxari, G., Dollár, P., Girshick, R.: Mask R-CNN. In: Proceedings of the IEEE International Conference on Computer Vision, pp. 2961–2969 (2017)
6. Kestur, R., Farooq, S., Abdal, R., Mehraj, E., Narasipura, O.S., Mudigere, M.: UFCN: a fully convolutional neural network for road extraction in RGB imagery acquired by remote sensing from an unmanned aerial vehicle. J. Appl. Remote Sens. **12**(1), 016020 (2018)
7. Lenc, L., Prantl, M., Martínek, J., Král, P.: Border detection for seamless connection of historical cadastral maps. In: Barney Smith, E.H., Pal, U. (eds.) ICDAR 2021. LNCS, vol. 12916, pp. 43–58. Springer, Cham (2021). https://doi.org/10.1007/978-3-030-86198-8_4
8. Martínek, J., Lenc, L., Král, P.: Building an efficient OCR system for historical documents with little training data. Neural Comput. Appl. **32**, 17209–17227 (2020)
9. Min, J., Kang, D., Cho, M.: Hypercorrelation squeeze for few-shot segmentation. CoRR abs/2104.01538 (2021). https://arxiv.org/abs/2104.01538
10. Neyns, R., Canters, F.: Mapping of urban vegetation with high-resolution remote sensing: A review. Remote Sens. **14**(4), 1031 (2022)
11. Nina, O., Morse, B., Barrett, W.: A recursive OTSU thresholding method for scanned document binarization. In: 2011 IEEE Workshop on Applications of Computer Vision (WACV), pp. 307–314. IEEE (2011)

12. Ronneberger, O., Fischer, P., Brox, T.: U-Net: convolutional networks for biomedical image segmentation. In: Navab, N., Hornegger, J., Wells, W.M., Frangi, A.F. (eds.) MICCAI 2015. LNCS, vol. 9351, pp. 234–241. Springer, Cham (2015). https://doi.org/10.1007/978-3-319-24574-4_28
13. Timár, G., Molnár, G., Székely, B., Biszak, S., Varga, J., Jankó, A.: Digitized maps of the Habsburg Empire - the map sheets of the second military survey and their georeferenced version, January 2006. https://doi.org/10.13140/2.1.1423.7127
14. Timilsina, S., Sharma, S., Aryal, J.: Mapping urban trees within cadastral parcels using an object-based convolutional neural network. ISPRS Ann. Photogramm. Remote Sens. Spat. Inf. Sci. 4, 111–117 (2019)
15. Wick, C., Puppe, F.: Fully convolutional neural networks for page segmentation of historical document images. In: 2018 13th IAPR International Workshop on Document Analysis Systems (DAS), pp. 287–292. IEEE (2018)

Agents/Case Based Reasoning/Sentiment Analysis

Analysis of the Lingering Effects
of Covid-19 on Distance Education

Büşra Kocaçınar[1]([✉])🆔, Nasibullah Qarizada[1], Cihan Dikkaya[1],
Emirhan Azgun[1], Elif Yıldırım[1]🆔, and Fatma Patlar Akbulut[2]🆔

[1] Department of Computer Engineering, Istanbul Kültür University, Istanbul, Turkey
{b.kocacinar,elif.yildirim}@iku.edu.tr
[2] Department of Software Engineering, Istanbul Kültür University, Istanbul, Turkey
f.patlar@iku.edu.tr

Abstract. Education has been severely impacted by the spread of the
COVID-19 virus. In order to prevent the spread of the COVID-19 virus
and maintain education in the current climate, governments have com-
pelled the public to adopt online platforms. Consequently, this decision
has affected numerous lives in various ways. To investigate the impact
of COVID-19 on students' education, we amassed a dataset consisting
of 10,000 tweets. The motivations of the study are; (i) to analyze the
positive, negative, and neutral effects of COVID-19 on education; (ii) to
analyze the opinions of stakeholders in their tweets about the transition
from formal education to e-learning; (iii) to analyze people's feelings and
reactions to these changes; and (iv) to analyze the effects of different
training methods on different groups. We constructed emotion recognition models utilizing shallow and deep techniques, including Convolutional Neural Network (CNN), Recurrent Neural Network (RNN), Long-
short Term Memory (LSTM), Random Forest (RF), Naive Bayes (NB),
Support Vector Machine (SVM), and Logical Regression (LR). RF algorithms with a bag-of-words model outperformed with over 80% accuracy
in recognizing emotions.

Keywords: Deep learning · social media · sentiment analysis · word
embedding · distance education

1 Introduction

Covid-19, also known as SARS-CoV-2, has deeply shaken and altered all aspects
of human life, including working, studying, and participating in social activities.
Education was undoubtedly one of the most affected fields. In so that governments and institutes decided to close schools, courses universities, and education centers which was going to be the main reason for changing their formal
face-to-face education to online platforms under the title of online learning or e-
learning in different ways. This decision would also push the socio-economically

This research is supported by Istanbul Kultur University under ULEP-2022–2023.

disadvantaged groups into obscurity, where serious consequences awaited. Subsequently, this caused educators, families, and academics to be concerned about online learning inequalities. In less than two months, virtually every educational institution has adopted remote operation and e-learning. Recent research indicates that 1.52 billion students [11] are impacted by the closure of educational facilities, putting them at risk for socioeconomic concerns such as academic integrity, homelessness, internet, housing, and student indebtedness.

During the pandemic, students not only lost educational experiences but also social and emotional development. Some experienced the displacement of family members, others lost their employment and levels of revenue, and the vast majority were alienated. In order to alleviate anxiety, it is crucial to comprehend how these changes influence pupils [2,18] and to establish whether they have beneficial or bad consequences on the learning process. These impacts can also vary from person to person, and various learning abilities may react differently. The study of learning is, in a nutshell, the examination of the connections between students and their ecosystems. If considered logical, these insights can have very unique influences on educational practitioners.

Sentiment analysis is a field with the potential to extract and analyze the opinions of individuals regarding a particular case, personality, or concept. Today, machine learning and deep learning are used extensively and effectively in natural language processing and text analysis, the preferred methodologies in this field of study. In this study, we analyzed the perspectives of students, instructors, and families regarding the effects of Covid-19 on their lives, particularly their academic lives. Our aim is to study this topic from multiple perspectives and dimensions and to do sentiment analysis utilizing tweets shared by different users. The main contributions of this study are three-fold follows as;

- To analyze effects of Covid-19 on education within emotions and reactions of people as positive, negative, and neutral forms.
- Analyzing thoughts of individuals' tweets regarding changes from formal education to e-learning.
- To analyze the effects of different educational methods on different groups.

2   Related Work

In recent years, a vast amount of research has been conducted to analyze people's perspectives on particular issues [17]. Unquestionably, one of the most explored issues is how COVID-19 affects our everyday lives. The physical closure of educational institutions and the enforcement of online learning may have an adverse impact on student performance through several touchpoints: clinical signs of stress, fewer hours spent having to learn, and a lack of student commitment. Initial research [1] indicates that only 73% of students have access to the internet, and only 71.4% are fully equipped to access online classes via a mobile device. Due to the interruption of their academic habits, some students reported experiencing poor mental health [7]. In addition, students who are quarantined at home with their parents [6] as a result of COVID-19 may experience increased anxiety and depression. Aside from the discussion of the efficacy of in versus online courses, research shows that fewer hours spent studying can result in having learned decrease. Another issue is the peer effects which are a well-known factor influencing academic performance in the school setting. Participating in a classroom and, thus, having the chance to engage with peers may yield significant positive outcomes [13]. Social impacts may manifest through several routes, such as instructing one another and improving collectively, and individuals may be inspired to work harder by the accomplishments of their peers.

One of the ways to understand the effects of all these factors on people is to examine social media data closely. During a given time period, individuals who were confined to their houses began to make their opinions known using online social media platforms. Numerous individuals have both favorable and negative perceptions of online vs. traditional education [12]. Particularly, tweets are frequently utilized as a source to analyze people's emotions, particularly in terms of online learning during the COVID-19 pandemic [5, 19]. Despite the fact that they contain so many diverse words, abbreviations, informal language, and symbols, it is difficult to determine which words or groups of words produce positive or negative statements. Sentiment analysis solves these problems by organizing unstructured data [10, 14, 15]. Examining the thoughts and emotions that people have concerning COVID-19, based on their perspectives can be accomplished by first transforming the unstructured text-based sequential data that is associated with distance education into structured data. In order to gather structured data, one must first complete a number of pre-processing procedures, including text cleaning, dimension reduction, and transformation, amongst others. In order to investigate the sentiments of posts that are related to education, the quality of the assessment serves as the major yardstick for judging whether or not this organized data is reliable. As a consequence of this, the analysis of these data with up-to-date natural language processing (NLP) technologies is an essential component in the process of determining the impact that the field of education and in providing useful feedback so that educational institutions can improve the quality of education.

Text-based sentiment analysis is an NLP classification operation that generates actionable insights from documented linguistic concepts. This is one of the first NLP topics addressed by many academics fresh to machine learning. This is because of its logical simplicity and applicability, as well as the availability of conventional and deep learning approaches. During COVID-19, several studies [2, 3, 16–18] analyzed the positive, negative, and neutral feelings of tweets pertaining to education with state-of-the-art approaches. Even though people couldn't agree on the results, it was clear that their socioeconomic status affected the results and their points of view.

3   Methodology

To study the impacts of pandemics on education, we gathered a dataset from specified social media tweets and then applied pre-processing techniques such as

Textblob [9], NLTK [4], and Vader [8]. Following that, we conducted an analysis using deep learning approaches. As shown in Fig. 1, the entirety of the analytic technique is suitable for reflecting the findings of the design, which consists of data retrieval, preprocessing, feature engineering, training, and testing.

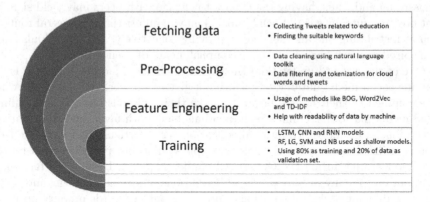

Fig. 1. Procedure of data fetching, preprocessing, feature extraction, and classification of the proposed method

3.1   Fetching Dataset

In order to investigate the effects, we collected 10,000 tweets using Twint[1], an advanced scraping tool for Twitter posts. As the primary objective of the research, the majority of tweets were collected from the days when covid-19 spread peaked ("May of 2020 to June of 2021") in order to conduct a robust analysis. We selected certain keywords to identify individuals who offered their opinion and perspective on the effects of COVID-19 on schooling. COVID-19 education, COVID-19, Education, COVID-19 Schools, distant learning, corona education, online learning, and e-learning are some of the keywords utilized. Another potential issue while generating a dataset is the language of tweets. It can be elusive during the creation of a dataset, but we eliminated it before the primary preparation phase.

3.2   Text Pre-processing

In the raw format of the dataset, it is evident that most tweets contain punctuation marks, images, emoticons, and links. Using datasets in their default format has the potential to mislead the analysis technique and model's performance. Consequently, data must be cleansed and organized prior to further analysis. We

---

[1] available at https://github.com/twintproject/twint.

utilized the NeatText library[2] to conduct filtering and tokenization by removing hashtags, user handles, URLs, and punctuation marks. Tokenization was used to separate the stream of textual input into individual words, phrases, sentences, symbols, or other meaningful units. Data filtering was used to process identifying stop words, such as conjunctions, and prepositions such as "a, are, is, there, would...". Samples of pre-processed tweets can be seen in Table 1.

Table 1. Tweets after being pre-processed

Normal Tweet	Clean Tweet	Tokenization
@■■■ @■■■ @■■ @■■■ @■■ You should put your kids in virtual school and make sure they where a mask whenever on screen.True story, my cousin got covid over the internet.	you should put your kids in virtual school and make sure they where a mask whenever on screen true story my cousin got covid over the internet	['kids', 'virtual', 'school', 'sure', 'mask', 'screen', 'true', 'story', 'cousin', 'got', 'covid', 'internet']
@■■■ @■■ not a single student or staff has died from your precious covid at my sons school since mandates were lifted, they must be following the magic, not THE SCIENCE!	not a single student or staff has died from your precious covid at my sons school since mandates were lifted they must be following the magic not the science	['single', 'student', 'staff', 'died', 'precious', 'covid', 'sons', 'school', 'mandates', 'lifted', 'following', 'magic', 'science']

3.3 Feature Engineering

The results of research conducted in 2020[3] indicate that cleaning and organizing data consumes sixty percent of data scientists' time. The results demonstrate the significance of the datasets' readability and clarity. The process of manipulating, transforming, and choosing data into predefined forms for use in supervised learning is known as feature engineering. In this study, a feature engineering study was carried out with the discretization method. For each tweet, VADER sentimental analysis yielded positive, negative, neutral, and compound outcomes. This information was examined and sentiment tags were assigned. The range for neutral tweets in this method is –0.05 to 0.05. Compound results of less than -0.05 are labeled as negative and those greater than 0.05 are labeled as positive.

---

[2] available at https://jcharis.github.io/neattext.

[3] available at https://www.anaconda.com/state-of-data-science-2020.

3.4   Tweet Sentiment Analysis

In order to gain a complete understanding of the actual scenario and level of satisfaction with online education during the epidemic, 10,000 tweets are evaluated for the sentiment. After purifying the data and making it computer-readable, one of the most important aspects of the research that contributes to the final outcomes is sentiment analysis. There are several pretrained libraries that are compatible with various methodologies. In this study, positive, negative, and neutral tweets were analyzed using the TextBlob and Vader libraries. Textblob, a lexicon-based Python module that is commonly used in sentiment analysis, was the first tool we employed. TextBlob gives a polarity between –1, 0, and 1, which is typically reconstructed as negative, neutral, and positive in sentiment analysis. For instance, in the tweets we analyzed with Textblob, the tweet with a polarity result of 0.6 is labeled as positive, while the tweet with a polarity result of –0.09 is classified as negative. Table 2 shows illustrative sentiment analysis values and their corresponding outcomes from our dataset.

Table 2. Sentiment analysis samples by TextBlob

Tweet	Polarity	Subjectivity	Sentiment
Maybe people would take Covid more seriously if it was as physically evident as chickenpox ormeasles.Both are contagious. You can't just walk around with chickenpox infecting others at work or school. Anyway, long Covid will be a thing	0.1	0.32	Positive
Believe it's airborne Ï went nowhere" people got grocery got gas kids went school live apartment/townhouse live home flu sit surface minute surely Covid	0.26	0.63	Positive

TextBlob is utilized to annotate sentiment data that returns a tuple of sentiment values (polarity and subjectivity). Polarity can take on values between –1 and 1 [9]. Accordingly, tweets with a polarity score below 0 are labeled as "negative," whereas tweets with a polarity score above 0 are labeled as "positive." If it is equal to 0, the tweet is marked as "neutral." As a second option, we favored Vader, a Lexicon and Rule-based library that is functionally equivalent to Lexicon. TextBlob employs a collection of positive, negative, and neutral terms. Vader has the ability to interpret emoticons such as ":),:(", slang, and even short sentences like "LOL." In a different technique, we did sentiment analysis using the Vader library. Initially, the Sentiment Intensity Analyzer was used to generate the polarity score that consists of negative, positive, neutral, and combined findings. Considering the compound results, a labeling procedure was done which has taken into account a particular time frame. Positive tweets have a compound value above 0.05, whereas negative tweets have a value below –0.05. Tweets whose total value falls between these two thresholds are neutral. The positive, negative, neutral, and null distributions of these two techniques are depicted in Table 3. According to the findings of our analysis, TextBlob performed better without providing null data. In the interim, Vader returned 2040 null values.

Table 3. TextBlob vs VADER for Sentiment Analysis

	Positive	Negative	Neutral	Null
TextBlob	4439	3480	2086	0
Vader	4153	2293	1519	2040

The relationship between data analysis outcomes and the methods and procedures employed by the analyst in generating research findings is comprehensive. Simply said, the more diverse methods we employ to achieve an objective, the more resilient the result. Then, we put frequently used words in Fig. 2 to find out what people are going through these days.

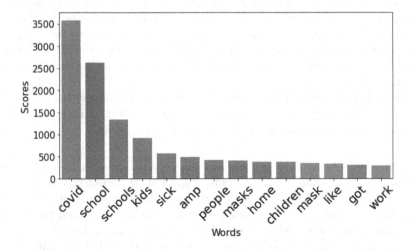

Fig. 2. Most frequently used words from the negative corpus and their distributions

3.5   Word Embedding

Word embeddings bridge human and computer language understanding. They learn to represent text in n-dimensional space such that words with the same meaning seem alike. Comparable words are represented as vectors near together in a vector space. This study included three distinct approaches for word embedding: a bag of words (BoW), Term Frequency Inverse Document Frequency (TF-IDF), and doc2vec. The "bag of words" model is used to extract characteristics from texts and is a textual representation of the occurrence of words in a document. BoW reorganizes its text data by tokenizing k-grams. TF-IDF computes the relevance of a term inside a string or corpus to a text. Doc2Vec vectorizes word association connections.

3.6 Proposed Sentiment Models

To understand the patterns in a long set of data, we need networks that can look at patterns over time. Typically, Recurrent Networks (LSTM, RNN) are utilized for such data learning. They can comprehend long-term and short-term interdependencies and temporal disparities. In addition, 1D CNNs are excellent for processing 1D signals because of their compact architecture and minimal computational requirements. In the proposed study, therefore, three distinct deep models consisting of an LSTM, an RNN, and a CNN were created. In addition, four shallow models were constructed utilizing the naive Bayes, logistic regression, random forest, and support vector machine methods. Textblob and Vader were used in two distinct investigations to identify sentiment labels.

LSTM Model. As a preliminary step, we transformed our data by tokenizing language based on a set of rules. We built our model with five layers. The first layer is the embedding layer, with parameters such as "vocabulary size," "embedding vector length," and "input length = 200." SpatialDropout1D is used as a second layer to prevent overfitting. The LSTM layer is set as the third layer with 50 units, a dropout value of 0.5, and a recurrent dropout value of 0.5. Follow-up layer consisting of dropout with probability p = 0.2 to reduce overfitting. The final layer is the output layer, which has a sigmoid activation function, and the Adam optimizer is used to update the weights of the model.

RNN Model. The RNN model employs seven layers, some of which are utilized in pairs. The embedding layer is initially utilized for the input layer. Then there are two RNN layers with 512 hidden units and "ReLu" for the activation function. Then, 1D global average pooling is utilized as the transition layer before feeding the data to the output layer, which is composed of a dense layer. Dense layers are utilized in two distinct ways. Initially, with 64 hidden units and an activation function that contains "ReLu". Before moving on to the next dense layer, the dropout layer is utilized to prevent overfitting. The second dense layer was then applied, but this time the activation function was "softmax" to scale and normalize output according to probabilities.

CNN Model. The proposed 1D-CNN model employs ten layers to model textual information. The embedding layer is initially utilized for the input layer. Then there is the 1D convolution layer that contains a kernel with size 5 × 5, 512 hidden units, and "ReLu" for an activation function. The following 1D convolution layer consists of a kernel with a size of 3 × 3. Then, we utilized max-pooling to achieve downsampling by dividing the input into 1-D pooling regions.

The subsequent layers are dropout with probability p = 0.4, a 1D global average pooling layer, a dense layer with 64 hidden units and a ReLu activation function, and dropout again with probability p = 0.4. The final dense layer has an input size of 3 and an activation function of softmax.

Naïve Bayes, Logistic Regression, Random Forrest, and Support Vector Machine models. After performing feature engineering approaches such as a BoW, TF-IDF, and Word2Vec, we have preferred widely used classifiers such as support vector machine (SVM), Random Forest (RF), Nave Bayes (NB), and Logistic Regression (LR) to validate the findings and compare them to the proposed deep model. The kernel type for the SVM model is determined as "linear". The regularization parameter of the error term is set to 1 for C. The "probability" parameter is set to True to enable probability estimates. For the RF classifier, the "n_estimators" parameter, which represents the number of trees in the forest, is set to 400.

4   Results

In this section, we investigated and compared the performance of different classifiers for detecting sentiment in the dataset. Table 4 shows the validation accuracy of our LSTM, CNN, and RNN models with Vader and Texblob. A binary classification study was conducted on the LSTM model to determine the positive and negative classes. Textblob achieved a precision of 0.51, whereas Vader achieved 0.48. Using RNN and CNN models, a 3-class study was done to identify negative, positive, and neutral feelings. Comparing the accuracy results for Textblob (Fig. 3), it was found that the CNN model achieved 0.81 accuracies, whereas the RNN model performed 0.70 accuracies overall. When evaluating the RNN and CNN findings for Vader, the validation accuracy was 0.72 and 0.59, respectively. It has been observed that TextBlob produces superior results. We have discovered that our models can be enhanced in numerous ways.

Table 4. Validation accuracy results of CNN, LSTM, and RNN models

	Textblob	Vader
Convolutional Neural Network	0.81	0.72
Recurrent Neural Network	0.70	0.59
Long Short-Term Memory	0.51	0.48

When examining the accuracy results of shallow classification models, we aimed to obtain as many distinct outcomes as feasible. Therefore, we began testing four distinct models: Random Forest, Logistic Regression, Naive Bayes, and Support Vector Machine. In addition, employing alternative approaches as a

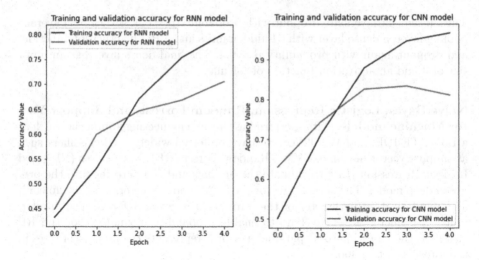

Fig. 3. Training and validation accuracy of RNN and CNN models over four epoch

Table 5. Validation accuracy and F1 Score results of shallow classifiers with three different word embedding methods

		TextBlob		Vader	
		Validation Accuracy	F1 Score	Validation Accuracy	F1 Score
LR	BoW	0.39	0.35	0.34	0.36
	TF-IDF	0.42	0.33	0.37	0.34
	Word2Vec	0.45	0.31	0.36	0.32
NB	BoW	0.39	0.34	0.35	0.34
	TF-IDF	0.39	0.34	0.35	0.34
	Word2Vec	0.37	0.29	0.34	0.29
SVM	BoW	0.39	0.35	0.36	0.36
	TF-IDF	0.39	0.36	0.36	0.36
	Word2Vec	0.39	0.31	0.35	0.31
RF	BoW	0.82	0.82	0.75	0.81
	TF-IDF	0.81	0.82	0.75	0.82
	Word2Vec	0.65	0.64	0.66	0.65

feature engineering technique was yet another way we achieved distinct and more effective outcomes. The results of the comparison are shown briefly in Table 5. Considering the results of limited data, model performance can be increased by expanding the data collection phase.

5   Conclusion

COVID-19 has taken the globe to a state in which all aspects of conventional life have been altered. Education was among the things most affected. Online learning is the new face of education and has been preferred by nearly all governments and institutions to prevent the spread of COVID-19. Among its advantages, online learning had some serious and effective disadvantages. Financial problems, social limitations, a lack of access to technology, and the effectiveness of education were the problems that raised the worries of stakeholders. in order to analyze the reactions of people to find the problems and focus on ways to solve or reduce them. Therefore, to analyze the effects of the pandemic, we focused on the tweets and used several techniques to recognize the sentiments of individuals. After applying feature engineering techniques such as BoW, TF-IDF, and Word2Vec, we categorize inputs with TextBlob and Vader methods and recognize emotions with LSTM, RNN, and CNN. According to the ratio of tweets classified with Textblob, roughly 0.45 tweets are positive, while the ratio of tweets classified by Vader is 0.52 tweets that are positive. We can see that a greater number of people see distance learning under pandemic conditions favorably. We observed that LSTM performed with a value of 0.51 for TextBlob and 0.48 for Vader, while CNN accuracy for TextBlob is 0.81 and RNN is 0.70. In the case of comparing our models with the shallow models, we preferred to use LR, NB, SVM, and RF. RF was the best-performing model by TextBlob, with an accuracy of 0.82 (F1 score = 0.82).

References

1. Althagafi, A.H., Althobaiti, G., Alhakami, H., Alsubait, T.: Arabic tweets sentiment analysis about online learning during Covid-19 in Saudi Arabia. Int. J. Adv. Comput. Sci. Appl. **12**, 620–625 (2021)
2. Ayaz, T.B., et al.: Global impact of the pandemic on education: a study of natural language processing. In: 2022 Innovations in Intelligent Systems and Applications Conference (ASYU), pp. 1–4. IEEE (2022)
3. Bhagat, K.K., Mishra, S., Dixit, A., Chang, C.Y.: Public opinions about online learning during covid-19: a sentiment analysis approach. Sustainability **13**(6) (2021). https://doi.org/10.3390/su13063346, https://www.mdpi.com/2071-1050/13/6/3346
4. Bird, S., Loper, E.: Nltk: the natural language toolkit. Association for Computational Linguistics (2004)
5. Blanco, G., Lourenço, A.: Optimism and pessimism analysis using deep learning on covid-19 related twitter conversations. Inf. Process. Manag. **59**(3), 102918 (2022). https://doi.org/10.1016/j.ipm.2022.102918, https://www.sciencedirect.com/science/article/pii/S0306457322000437
6. Dorman-Ilan, S., et al.: Anxiety and depression symptoms in covid-19 isolated patients and in their relatives. Front. Psychiatry **11**, 581598 (2020)
7. Dorn, E., Hancock, B., Sarakatsannis, J., Viruleg, E.: Covid-19 and education: the lingering effects of unfinished learning. McKinsey Comp. **27**, 1–15 (2021)
8. Hutto, C., Gilbert, E.: Vader: a parsimonious rule-based model for sentiment analysis of social media text. In: Proceedings of the International AAAI Conference on Web and Social Media, vol. 8, pp. 216–225 (2014)
9. Loria, S., et al.: Textblob documentation. Release 0.15 2, 269 (2018)

10. Mathur, A., Kubde, P., Vaidya, S.: Emotional analysis using twitter data during pandemic situation: covid-19. In: 2020 5th International Conference on Communication and Electronics Systems (ICCES), pp. 845–848 (2020). https://doi.org/10.1109/ICCES48766.2020.9138079

11. Miks, J., McIlwaine, J.: Keeping the world's children learning through covid-19. Acesso em **6**(05) (2020)

12. Mujahid, M., et al.: Sentiment analysis and topic modeling on tweets about online education during covid-19. Appl. Sci. **11**(18), 8438 (2021). https://doi.org/10.3390/app11188438

13. Mushtaque, I., Rizwan, M., Dasti, R.K., Ahmad, R., Mushtaq, M.: Students' attitude and impact of online learning; role of teachers and classmate support during the covid-19 crisis. Perf. Improv. **60**(5), 20–27 (2021)

14. Okango, E., Mwambi, H.: Dictionary based global twitter sentiment analysis of coronavirus (COVID-19) effects and response. Ann. Data Sci. **9**, 1–12 (2021). https://doi.org/10.1007/s40745-021-00358-5

15. Priyadarshini, I., Mohanty, P., Kumar, R., Sharma, R., Puri, V., Singh, P.K.: A study on the sentiments and psychology of twitter users during COVID-19 lockdown period. Multimedia Tools Appl., 1–23 (2021). https://doi.org/10.1007/s11042-021-11004-w

16. Relucio, F.S., Palaoag, T.D.: Sentiment analysis on educational posts from social media. In: Proceedings of the 9th International Conference on E-Education, E-Business, E-Management and E-Learning, IC4E 2018, pp. 99–102. Association for Computing Machinery, New York (2018). https://doi.org/10.1145/3183586.3183604

17. Sadigov, R., Yıldırım, E., Kocaçınar, B., Patlar Akbulut, F., Catal, C.: Deep learning-based user experience evaluation in distance learning. Cluster Comput., 1–13 (2023)

18. Sosun, S.D., et al.: Deep sentiment analysis with data augmentation in distance education during the pandemic. In: 2022 Innovations in Intelligent Systems and Applications Conference (ASYU), pp. 1–5. IEEE (2022)

19. Sunitha, D., Patra, R.K., Babu, N., Suresh, A., Gupta, S.C.: Twitter sentiment analysis using ensemble based deep learning model towards covid-19 in India and European countries. Pattern Recogn. Lett. **158**, 164–170 (2022). https://doi.org/10.1016/j.patrec.2022.04.027, https://www.sciencedirect.com/science/article/pii/S0167865522001246

Exploring the Power of Failed Experiences in Case-Based Reasoning for Improved Decision Making

Fateh Boulmaiz[1]([✉]), Patrick Reignier[1], and Stephane Ploix[2]

[1] Université Grenoble Alpes, CNRS, Grenoble INP, LIG, 38000 Grenoble, France
fateh.boulmaiz@univ-grenoble-alpes.fr
[2] Université Grenoble Alpes, CNRS, Grenoble INP, G-SCOP, 38000 Grenoble, France

Abstract. Case-based reasoning (CBR) is a popular approach for problem-solving and decision-making that involves using previous cases as a basis for reasoning about new situations. While CBR has shown promise in many domains, it is not immune to errors and failures. One limitation of the approach is that it tends to focus primarily on successful cases, ignoring the potential value of failed cases as a source of learning and insight. While many studies have focused on the role of successful cases in CBR, less attention has been given to the value of analyzing failed cases. In this paper, we explore the benefits of reasoning from both successful and failed cases in CBR. We argue that by examining both types of cases, we can identify patterns and insights that can help to refine CBR methods, improve their accuracy and efficiency, and reduce the likelihood of future failures. Using a combination of theoretical modeling and empirical analysis, we demonstrate that failed cases can provide valuable insights into identifying potential solutions that might otherwise be overlooked. To illustrate our approach, we present a case study in which we apply our reasoning methodology to a real-world problem in the field of energy management. Our analysis demonstrates that by considering both successful and failed cases, we can identify new and more effective solutions to the problem at hand.

Keywords: Case-based reasoning · adaptation · successful case · failed case

1 Introduction

Case-based reasoning (CBR) is certainly the most intuitive approach of artificial intelligence to solve a problem since it mimics human behavior in problem-solving. A CBR system looks in its memory represented by a base of previously solved experiments called source cases, for cases having similar problems to the target problem to be solved by adapting their solutions if necessary. The target solution is revised to make sure of its adequacy to solve the target problem and finally the base of cases is enriched following the new experiment of resolution of the target

© IFIP International Federation for Information Processing 2023
Published by Springer Nature Switzerland AG 2023
I. Maglogiannis et al. (Eds.): AIAI 2023, IFIP AICT 675, pp. 201–213, 2023.
https://doi.org/10.1007/978-3-031-34111-3_18

case. Each step of the reasoning process is supported by a process of acquiring the necessary knowledge to perform this step. It is worth highlighting the close connection between the knowledge of the different stages of the CBR approach.

Of the four principal stages of the reasoning process, adaptation is a crucial stage since the quality of the solution heavily depends on its performance. Its focus is on fitting the solutions of similar source cases to meet the specific requirements of the target problem. This is particularly important since the source problems usually do not match the target problem, and as a consequence, without this step, the CBR system cannot ultimately generate an appropriate solution to the target problem. Awareness of the pivotal role that adaptation plays was noted from the early days of CBR systems, as a result, there is a large number of studies exploring various approaches to acquiring adaptation knowledge to improve its performance.

Existing adaptation approaches focus exclusively on cases whose solutions are deemed relevant to the corresponding problems (hereafter these cases are referred to as successful cases and are denoted by $C+$). The appreciation of success is subjective to the application domain, e.g., in the context of the CBR application in the elaboration of an energy management system in a building, a successful case would correspond to a scenario satisfying the user's comfort while minimizing the energy expenditure. However, there are also failed cases. A failed case (noted hereafter $C-$) is a case having an unsatisfactory solution to the problem to solve, in particular, these are cases proposed by the adaptation process but rejected during the validation stage. Moreover, the adaptation process often involves the acquisition of the knowledge required to generate the adaptation rules. Usually, such knowledge is strongly dependent on the application domain, making the acquisition process complex and challenging to understand and grasp.

Surprisingly, despite a large number of research studies and an increased interest in the adaptation issue, few works are concerned with the challenge of proposing a domain-independent adaptation approach. Even less studies consider adaptation from the solution quality perspective, i.e., addressing both failed and successful cases. These cases are seldom used by the CBR systems even though they constitute potentially useful source of knowledge.

In this work, we propose a novel perspective on the adaptation process of the CBR paradigm, based on a fully domain-independent approach and drawing on both successful and failed cases. In particular, the present study proposes a new approach to the acquisition of adaptation knowledge exploiting both successful cases and failed ones. The approach takes its inspiration from studies in the planning of the path of a robot moving towards a destination in an unknown and insecure environment (includes obstacles). The originality of this approach consists in applying artificial forces to the solution to be proposed to move away from failed source solutions and move closer to successful source solutions.

The rest of this paper is arranged as follows. Section 2 introduces an illustration of motivation and the background of this work. Section 3 details the contribution to harnessing failed and successful cases for a new adaptation approach.

An evaluation of the proposed approach is presented and discussed in Sect. 4, before drawing conclusions about this work and outlining some guidelines for future work in Sect. 5.

2 Motivating Example and Preliminaries

A CBR-based energy management system (EMS) in a building is a representative case study of the systems relevant to the scope of this study. The objective of an EMS is to fulfill the user's desire for thermal comfort, air quality, etc. while minimizing the energy consumption in the building. Indeed, a building is a complex system whose potential to save energy depends on several factors with dependencies difficult to identify [3], such as climate, building materials, geographical position, and energy rate, but also the occupant of the building exercises a major influence. Findings of earlier work [7] has already highlighted the advantage of acquiring adaptation knowledge in improving the performance of a CBR-based EMS. Furthermore, due to the growing awareness of environmental issues, several studies have focused on the correlation between energy consumption in a building and the comfort of its occupants, leading to the definition of standards [1,2,5] to estimate the comfort of users. Thanks to the norms defined in these standards, the revision process can gauge the quality of the target solution proposed by the adaptation process, allowing the retention process to label this solution as a successful case $C+$ or a failed one $C-$.

In the CBR-based EMS proposed in [3], the objective is to make the user conscious of the influence of his actions on the energy behavior of the building. For this, the system guides the user in his actions by advising him on a set of actions aiming at decreasing the energy waste while considering his comfort. A case describes the energy management scenario of a building for one day. The actions retained in the system case base are the actions effectively carried out by the building occupant, so there is no guarantee that they are actions that generate satisfactory effects for the occupant. For this reason, the system is provided with a function to evaluate the performance of the actions stored in the case base, allowing to label the corresponding cases with the appropriate labels ($C+$ or $C-$).

2.1 Founding Notions and Notations About CBR Approach

The memory of a CBR system is made of a set of source cases C_{sr} which constitute a case base CB.

Case Description. Let $\mathbb{C}$, $\mathbb{A}$, and $\mathbb{E}$ be three mutually disjoint sets. A case is a triplet $(\mathscr{C}, \mathcal{A}, \mathcal{E}) \in \mathbb{C} \times \mathbb{A} \times \mathbb{E}$ where:

- $\mathscr{C}$ is an element of the context domain $\mathbb{C}$, i.e., the imposed elements of the problem over which one cannot exert control. For instance, in a CBR-based disease treatment system, the context data can be the different physiological measures of the patient (blood pressure, glycemic rate, etc.).

- $\mathcal{A}$ is an element of the action domain $\mathbb{A}$, i.e., elements that can be controlled to achieve the relevant outcomes. It represents the solution proposed by the system. For instance, the names and the protocol for administering the drugs prescribed in a CBR-based disease treatment system.
- $\mathcal{E}$ is an element of the effect domain $\mathbb{E}$, i.e., elements describe the state of the system after applying action $\mathcal{A}$ to context $\mathscr{C}$. For instance, the patient's physiological measures after the treatment.

A target context $\mathscr{C}_{tg}$ is a context for which the CBR system tries to predict target actions $\mathcal{A}_{tg}$ to generate target effects $\mathcal{E}_{tg}$ and thus elaborate a target case C_{tg}. Formally, the resolution of a problem in the CBR paradigm is defined by Eq. (1).

$$\text{CBR system: } (CB, \mathscr{C}_{tg}) \longmapsto \mathcal{A}_{tg}$$
$$C_{tg} \triangleq (\mathscr{C}_{tg}, \mathcal{A}_{tg}, \mathcal{E}_{tg}) \tag{1}$$

With CB – the case base.

Retrieving and Adaptation. A full presentation of the reasoning process is beyond the focus of this paper, but due to the particular connection between adaptation and retrieving knowledge, it is usually necessary to present the adaptation process in conjunction with the retrieval process. Indeed, the reasoning process modeled by Eq. (1) is made up of two main steps.

- *retrieval process*: Given a threshold σ for the distance between the context variables of the source cases and the target context, the retrieval process consists of identifying the source cases having a context similar to the target context. The profile of the retrieval function is given in Eq. (2).

$$\text{Retrieve: } \quad \mathscr{C}_{tg} \longmapsto \{\forall C_{sr} \in CB / Distance(\mathscr{C}_{tg}, \mathscr{C}_{sr}) \leq \sigma\} = \mathcal{S}_{C_{tg}} \tag{2}$$

  where $Distance(\mathscr{C}_{tg}, \mathscr{C}_{sr})$ – a metric that computes the distance between the context variable $\mathscr{C}_{tg}$ and the context variable $\mathscr{C}_{sr}$.
  No constraints are imposed on the type of distance to use since it permits handling the context variables. For instance, the Minkowski metric can be used to calculate the context distance in a CBR-based EMS since the context variables are real values.
- *adaptation process*: Since the source contexts usually do not match the target context, it is required to define a function to adapt the source actions to satisfy the requirements of the target context. The profile of the adaptation function is defined by the Formula (3).

$$\text{Adaptation: } \forall C_{sr} \triangleq (\mathscr{C}_{sr}, \mathcal{A}_{sr}, \mathcal{E}_{sr}) \in \mathcal{S}_{C_{tg}},$$
$$(\{(\mathscr{C}_{sr}, \mathcal{A}_{sr}, \mathcal{E}_{sr})\}, \mathscr{C}_{tg}) \longmapsto \mathcal{A}_{tg} \tag{3}$$

  where $\mathcal{S}_{C_{tg}}$ – the set of similar source cases as defined by Eq. (2).
  Note that Eq. (3) does not impose any constraints on the number of similar cases considered in the adaptation process, thus we are dealing with a compositional adaptation (whose single case adaptation is a particular case), where

solutions from several source cases are combined to yield a target solution. Indeed, the experiment indicated that retaining a single case often gives less accurate results [9]. This is explained by the fact that frequently only a part of the problem of the similar source case is relevant for the target problem, which makes the task of adaptation complicated (if not impossible).

2.2   Collisionless Path Planning

Robot path planning study focus on the path planning of an autonomous robot moving in an unknown environment, i.e., guide the robot in its movement from an initial position to a target position by calculating the optimal but moreover the safest path to avoid obstacles that can occur along the path towards the target.

Several approaches were proposed to tackle this challenge, in particular, the Artificial Potential Field (APF) approach originally proposed in [6] is extensively adopted in robot guidance. The APF approach can cope with the reality of the current environment of the robot displacement by considering both the objectives to be reached and the obstacles to be avoided while moving. The key idea of this approach is to consider the robot as a point evolving in a 2-dimensional space (in the basic scenario) subject to the field influences of targets to reach and obstacles to avoid. Consequently, the robot is subjected to two kinds of forces, including an attractive one $\mathbb{F}_{at}$ generated by targets and a repulsive one $\mathbb{F}_{rp}$ generated by obstacles to move the robot further away.

Whereas repulsive forces are disproportional to the distance between the robot and the obstacles, i.e. they are strongest close to the obstacles and are less influential at distance, attractive forces are proportional to the distance between the target and the robot. The combined (total) of all the forces $\overrightarrow{\mathbb{F}} = \overrightarrow{\mathbb{F}_{at}} + \overrightarrow{\mathbb{F}_{rp}}$ applied to the robot defines the movement direction of the robot and its speed whilst avoiding collisions with obstacles. For the sake of simplification, the principle of this method for a robot traveling in a 2-dimensions environment is depicted in Fig. 1.

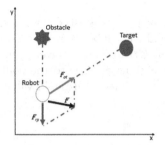

Fig. 1. Artificial potential field.

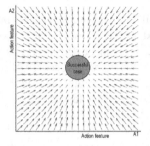

Fig. 2. CBR attractive force

3   Reasoning from Successful and Failed Cases

3.1   Problem Formalization

The adaptation problem considering failed and successful cases can be formalized as follows. Given the following observations:

- the case base CB is divided into two partitions of failed cases $CB\_$ and successful cases CB_+. So, $CB = CB\_ \cup CB_+$.
- by misuse of language, we refer to a target case as the elements of a target context for which we are looking for a solution. The case structure is not completely defined as the elements representing the actions and therefore, the effects are unknown.

Finding a solution for a target case (thus under construction) is to infer, from source cases having similar context, a set of target actions that best satisfy the target context, which leads to the definition of the target effects, and thus to building an effective case containing the three elements: context, actions, and effects.

Similar source cases should be handled differently depending on whether they are failed (member of $CB\_$) or successful (member of CB_+) and on their degree of similarity to the target case. The method to be proposed should provide mechanisms to move towards the solutions of successful similar source cases and away from failed similar source cases while taking into account that the closer the source case to the target case the more influence its solution has on the target solution.

3.2   Principle

The principle of our approach to considering failed cases in the adaptation process is inspired by navigation algorithms originating from the literature on the programming of autonomous robots, in particular, based on the artificial potential field presented in Sect. 2.2.

Before describing the details of our approach in the next section, to ensure the successful implementation of an artificial potential field-like concept in the context of this work, some assumptions are formulated:

- while the labeling process falls outside the scope of this study, we assume that previous experiences (source cases) are already labeled as successful or failed cases. Furthermore, we suppose that the CBR system is given a quality function $\mathcal{Q}$ which scores the efficacy of the actions applied to the context. The highest scores are the best. This implicitly defines a threshold value $\mathcal{P}_s^{\mathcal{E}_i}$ for each effect feature $\mathcal{E}_i$ according to Eq. (4).

$$\forall\, C_i \in CB \;,\; \mathcal{Q} : \mathcal{E}_i \longmapsto \mathbb{R}$$

$$\mathcal{L}(C_i) = \begin{cases} C_i+ & \text{if } \mathcal{Q}(\mathcal{E}_i) \geq \mathcal{P}_s^{\mathcal{E}_i}\;,\; \forall \mathcal{E}_i \in \mathbb{E} \\ C_i- & \text{otherwise.} \end{cases} \tag{4}$$

With $\mathcal{L}$ – the labeling function, $\mathcal{E}_i$ – an effect feature of case C_i.

– classical CBR methods retrieve a defined number of neighboring cases from the case base CB regardless of an optimal number of similar ones regarding the target case. This KNN-like approach poses some issues since the target cases do not necessarily have the same number of similar neighbors, while some target cases should have more similar cases, others less. Furthermore, the configuration where much more source cases with equal distance from a target case than the predefined number, must be handled. In this work, we assume the existence of a retrieval approach that adjusts the number of source cases similar to the target case C_{tr} by dynamically defining a similarity threshold $\sigma_{C_{tr}}$ for the context distance between C_{tr} and the neighboring source cases. For instance, the work presented in [3], provides a method to define this threshold by combining a statistical approach and a genetic algorithm.

The key idea of the approach proposed in this work is to map the type of source cases available in the case base, i.e., successful and failed cases, to the type of objects handled in the context of robot moving, i.e., target and obstacles. Therefore, failed cases are assimilated into obstacles and successful cases into targets. While cases $C_i+ \in S_{C_{tg}}$ with good performances should generate an attractive force $\mathbb{F}_{at}$ that pulls the target solution towards them, the bad cases $C_i- \in S_{C_{tg}}$ should produce a repulsive force $\mathbb{F}_{rp}$ that pushes away the solution from them.

The successful and failed source cases are considered to be sources for generating a potential field representing the properties of the target solution. As in the robotic potential field method, the CBR potential field is still composed of two fields. For instance, regarding the attractive potential field, an attractive force is produced from the target solution to the source solutions of the successful cases by the configuration of the latter, which allows to pull the target solution towards the solutions of these cases.

To illustrate this concept, let's consider, for the sake of presentation, a system with domain knowledge containing only 2 action variables, the attractive potential field generated by any successful case looks like Fig. 2, where at each point of the context space representing the target context, the force vectors are directed towards the successful source case. Concerning the repulsive potential field, a pushback force is generated by the configuration of the failed case towards the target solution, which allows to pull the target solution away from the solutions of these cases. Figure 3 depicts the CBR repulsive force in a similar configuration to the example illustrating the CBR attractive force.

Ultimately, the configuration of the target solution, i.e., the position of the target solution in the space of solutions (actions), is determined by summing all repulsive and attractive forces generated by neighboring failed and successful cases respectively. For the simple case of only two neighbors, a successful case and a failed case, the total potential field has the shape shown in Fig. 4.

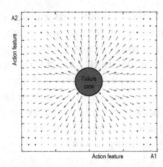
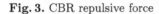
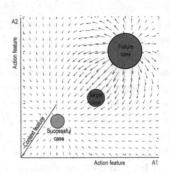

Fig. 3. CBR repulsive force   **Fig. 4.** CBR total potential force

3.3   Local Prediction of the Target Solution

Although we are inspired by the potential artificial field method, its application in the context of this work as applied in the robotics context does not permit determining the solution for many reasons:

- the potential total force in the robotic context depends exclusively on the distance between the goal/obstacles and the robot. In the CBR context, the magnitude of the attraction and repulsion forces are not dependent only on the distance between the target context and the neighboring source contexts but also on the performance (quality solution) of the neighboring source contexts.

- within the robotics context, unlike the attractive force, the magnitude of the repulsive force is at its highest value close to the obstacle and decreases proportionally when moving away from it. Within the context of CBR applications, the magnitude of the two forces should be proportional to the performance of the source solutions but disproportional to the distance between the source contexts and the target one.

- there is usually only one goal to reach in robotic applications, but in the case of a multi-goal environment, one looks for a path that goes through all these goals in sequential order by optimizing some criteria. For CBR systems, the aim is to combine the knowledge of all the neighboring source cases to infer the target solution.

- while the purpose of the robotic potential artificial field is to find the safe path to the goal, its purpose in the CBR application is to acquire new knowledge that guides the adaptation process in the construction of the target solution, i.e., to orient the reasoning process towards the most useful solutions (closest and best-performing cases) and away from the worst cases (farthest away or bad performance).

It is, therefore, necessary to adapt the approach of the artificial potential field to take into consideration the specificities of the CBR adaptation process. To do so, our approach defines the target solution (actions) $\mathcal{A}_{tg}$ by the vectorial sum of

Table 1. Summery of evaluation results.

APPROACH \ TEST SET	S1 METRICS			S2 METRICS			S3 METRICS			S4 METRICS			S5 METRICS			GLOBAL METRICS		
	PER (%)	APR(%)	TIR(%)	PER	APR	TIR	PER	APR	TIR	PER	APR	TIR	PER	APR	TIR	PER	APR	TIR
CBR − S	16.73	59.13	59.13	17.85	48.57	48.57	19.53	60.12	60.12	20.48	56.07	56.07	18.79	64.48	64.48	18.68	57.67	57.67
CBR − B	18.27	57.51	57.51	15.36	63.90	63.90	22.85	59.69	59.69	24.23	65.52	65.52	21.10	662.71	62.71	20.36	61.87	61.87
CBR − P	22.62	42.26	57.10	18.54	48.85	63.71	20.14	50.21	60.10	22.48	52.92	70.19	23.47	39.86	60.09	21.45	46;82	62,24
CBR − R	-2.56	32.18	49.75	9.12	29.89	51.19	14.71	43.07	64.24	17.45	39.52	57.74	12.04	41.26	62.84	10.15	37.18	57.15
CBR − APF	**34.68**	**100**	**100**	**28.85**	**99.76**	**99.76**	**33.91**	**100**	**100**	**31.27**	**100**	**100**	**38.73**	**99.88**	**99.88**	**33.49**	**99.92**	**99.92**

all attractive forces ($\mathbb{F}_{at}^{C_i+}, \forall\, C_i+ \in \mathcal{S}_{C_{tg}}$) and all repulsive forces ($\mathbb{F}_{rp}^{C_i-}, \forall\, C_i- \in \mathcal{S}_{C_{tg}}$) as described in Eq. (5).

$$\forall\, C_i+, C_i- \in \mathcal{S}_{C_{tg}}, \sum_{C_i} \mathbb{F}^{C_i} \overrightarrow{\mathcal{A}_{tg}\mathcal{A}_i} = \sum_{C_i+} \mathbb{F}_{at}^{C_i+} \overrightarrow{\mathcal{A}_{tg}\mathcal{A}_{C_i+}} + \sum_{C_i-} \mathbb{F}_{rp}^{C_i-} \overrightarrow{\mathcal{A}_{tg}\mathcal{A}_{C_i-}} = 0 \tag{5}$$

As already mentioned earlier, the magnitude of the repulsion and attraction forces depends both on the distance of the target context from the context of the similar source case and on the performance of the latter. From Eq. (5), the metric $\mathbb{F}^{C_i}$ defines the magnitude and direction of the associated force to the case C_i. We propose in Eq. (6) a formula to estimate its value.

$$\forall\, C_i \in \mathcal{S}_{C_{tg}}, \mathbb{F}^{C_i} = \begin{cases} \left(1 - \dfrac{\mathcal{D}_C(C_{tg}, C_i)}{\sigma_{C_{tg}}}\right) \times (\mathcal{Q}_i - \mathcal{P}_s) & \text{if } \mathcal{Q}_i \neq \mathcal{P}_s \\ 1 - \dfrac{\mathcal{D}_C(C_{tg}, C_i)}{\sigma_{C_{tg}}} & \text{else} \end{cases} \tag{6}$$

With $\sigma_{C_{tg}}$ – the context distance threshold, $\mathcal{Q}_i$ – the performance of the case C_i, $\mathcal{P}_s$ – the performance threshold, $\mathcal{D}_C(C_{tg}, C_i)$ – the context distance between C_{tg} and its neighbor C_i.

From Eq. (6), one can observe that whatever the type of force, its magnitude progressively decreases at the expense of an increasing context distance until it becomes null when the context distance equals the similarity threshold $\sigma_{C_{tg}}$. Besides defining the magnitude of the force, the operand $\mathcal{Q}_i - \mathcal{P}_s$ specifies the type of the force. When $\mathcal{Q}_i \geq \mathcal{P}_s$, then $\mathbb{F}^{C_i} \geq 0$, and the case C_i generates an attractive force else, it should be a repulsive force.

In this manner, the actions to be proposed $\mathcal{A}_{tg}$ have to satisfy:

$$\mathcal{A}_{tg} = \frac{1}{\sum_{C_i} \mathbb{F}^{C_i}} \sum_{C_i} \mathbb{F}^{C_i} \mathcal{A}_i \, , \ \forall\, C_i \in \mathcal{S}_{C_{tg}} \tag{7}$$

where $\mathcal{S}_{C_{tg}}$ – set of similar cases to the target case C_{tg}.

4   Evaluation

The present section provides an empirical evaluation of our approach. The objective of the evaluation is twofold, i) study the potential impact of considering both failed and successful cases on improving the performance of the CBR system; ii) assess the performance of the artificial potential field approach, this is referred to as CBR-APF in the following, compared to other adaptation approaches.

4.1 Experimental Setup

As mentioned in Sect. 2, the approach is implemented in an EMS whose objective is to make the user aware of the impact of his actions on the energy use in a building. Concretely, the EMS proposes to the occupant a series of actions to improve the comfort while consuming less energy.

To evaluate our approach, we conducted an experiment using semi-synthetic data generated from real-data presented in [4]. The case base contains 15,948 cases, where each case is composed of: 1) the effect variables which represent the temperature and air quality in the building; 2) the action variables which model the opening of the door and window; 3) the context variables which are weather conditions. Each variable is described by a 24-value vector corresponding to one day. We adopted a 5-fold cross-validation where the original case base is randomly split into five equal-sized subsets: $S1$, $S2$, $S3$, $S4$, and $S5$. A single set is selected as a test set CB^T (target cases) while the remaining four sets are used as a learning set CB^L (source cases). The cross-validation procedure is performed five times, each of the five sets being used once as a test set. The results of the metrics adopted to evaluate the performance are averaged to provide a final estimate.

To evaluate case performance we used functions that assess the user's dissatisfaction with the effects of the actions, as presented by Formula (8). To simulate the effects following the application of the proposed actions, a physical model of the building involved in the experiment was developed.

$$
\mathcal{S}_T^h(T) = \begin{cases} 0 & \text{if } T \in [21, 23] \\ \frac{T-23}{26-23} & \text{if } T > 23 \\ \frac{21-T}{21-18} & \text{if } T < 21 \end{cases} \quad , \quad \mathcal{S}_C^h(C) = \begin{cases} 0 & \text{if } C \le 500 \\ \frac{C-500}{1500-1000} & \text{if } C > 500 \end{cases} \quad (8)
$$

With $\mathcal{S}_T^h(T)$ – the dissatisfaction with the temperature in the office, $\mathcal{S}_C^h(C)$ at hour h – the dissatisfaction with the air quality in the office at hour h.

4.2 Baselines and Metrics

Several baselines are considered in the evaluation process:

1. the approach proposed in [4], denoted CBR-S in the following, exploits failed and successful cases but with a null adaptation process as the latter consists in making a vote among the similar cases solutions to select the solution with the best performance (maximizes the quality function) by applying it directly to the target case. The choice of this baseline is to check the relevance of using several source cases to establish the adaptation process.
2. a standard barycentric approach that combines solutions from the set of successful and failed similar source cases without artificial forces, noted CBR-B hereafter. The goal is to validate the efficiency of the artificial forces in improving the adaptation process.

3. a modified variant denoted CBR-P of our approach is tested, it considers only positive cases and thus uses only attractive forces. The objective is to illustrate the advantage of considering both negative and positive cases w.r.t only positive cases.
4. the approach proposed in [8] is used as a further baseline. This approach referred to as CBR-R, is based on a KNN approach to select similar source cases from which a generalized case is generated. Similar cases are used also to train a linear regression model, which is applied to the generalized case to predict the target case solution.

Note that in the experiment, the performance evaluation of all tested approaches is performed by comparison against a reference which is the actions carried out by the user without assistance according to three measures:

- *Performance Enhancement Rate (PER)*: The PER consists of comparing, for each test case C_i, the average of the thermal performances Q_T^*, the air quality performances Q_C^*, and the global performance Q^* of the proposed actions to the corresponding values Q_T^r, Q_C^r, and Q^r of the actions already recorded in the case base. The PER_{C_i} related to the test case C_i, if any, is given by the (9).

$$PER_{C_i} = \frac{Q^* - Q^r}{Q^r} \tag{9}$$

- *Approach Efficiency Rate (APR)*: The APR is defined as the average of the ratio of the number of test cases whose performance is improved by applying the actions recommended by this approach to the total number of test cases.

$$APR = \frac{Z^+}{Z} \tag{10}$$

With $Z = |CB^T|$ – the set of test cases, $Z^+ = \{C_i \in CB^T \ / \ PER_{C_i} > 0\}$
- *True Improvement Rate (TIR)*: This measure is the average of the ratio between the number of test cases whose performance is improved by applying the actions recommended by the approach and the total number of the test cases for which the approach successfully proposed a solution (improving or degrading performance compared to the user's actions).

4.3   Results and Analyse

Whatever the adaptation approach applied in a CBR system, its performance depends partially on the retrieval process. However, analyze the latter goes beyond the scope of the present paper. We use the approach given in [4] to estimate the similarity and define the similar source cases in the training set. It follows that each target case from the test set has at least one similar source case from the training set.

Table 1 summarizes the results of the 5-fold cross-validation of our approach against the four baselines considered. Some important findings from this experiment are:

- while the value of the TIR metric corresponds to the value of APR for the CBR-S, CBR-B, and CBR-APF approaches, the APR value is less than that of TIR for the CBR-P and CBR-R approaches, which is due to the ability of the first three approaches to computing a solution even with a similar set of cases consisting exclusively of failed cases.
- regardless of the test set, our CBR-APF approach is clearly better in performance than all other baselines with also better APR and TIR.
- the number of similar source cases has a significant influence on the quality of the adaptation process, a compositional adaptation systematically gives a better PER, as illustrated by the comparison between PERs of CBR-APF which is a compositional approach and CBR-S which uses a single similar case.
- attraction and repulsion forces have an important impact on the results of the adaptation process. Given the same number of similar cases, by using these forces, our CBR-APF approach outperforms the CBR-B baseline, which does not use them. CBR-APF is 1.64 times more performing than CBR-B regarding the improvement of the cases performances (global PER = 33.49% versus 20.36%) and 1.61 times more efficient according to the number of cases for which it manages to find a solution (CBR-APF improves the performance of the solutions proposed by the user without assistance for 99.92% of cases against 61.87% for CBR-B).
- using failed cases in case-based reasoning significantly influences the performance of a CBR system. By exploiting both successful and failed cases, the system improves the results of the reasoning process. Comparing the performance of the CBR-APF approach with that of the CBR-P and CBR-R approaches (both do not use failed cases in their reasoning), the TIR results show that the CBR-APF approach outperforms the other baselines. CBR-APF approach is more than three times more efficient than CBR-R and more than 1.5 times more than CBR-P in improving the performance (PER).

5   Conclusion

This paper proposed a new approach to the adaptation process in the CBR paradigm by looking at both failed and successful source cases instead of the traditional practice of considering only successful source case. We found inspiration in the studies on planning safe paths for a robot moving in an unknown environment. The concept is that both successful and failed cases generate attraction and repulsion forces respectively on a likely barycentric solution to drive the reasoning towards the best performing solutions and away from the failed ones. The experimentation of this approach in the context of an EMS showed a significant improvement in the system performance by considering both successful cases and failed ones.

In this work we have developed and evaluated an approach considering the whole set of successful and failed similar cases, it would be interesting to perform a deeper evaluation taking into account the number of neighboring successful and failed cases considering only the n cases with the best performances and the m cases with the worst performances. Another line of future research for this work would be to explore the possible impact of a failed case on the domain ontology (if any). It could be useful to suggest new necessary conditions to add to the domain ontology that would avoid the reappearance of such a negative case in the future.

References

1. ASHRAE, editor: ASHRAE Standard Thermal Environmental Conditions for Human Occupancy. American Society of Heating, Refrigerating and Air-Conditioning Engineers, Atlanta, USA (1992)
2. ASHRAE, editor: Indoor air quality guide: best practices for design, construction, and commissioning. American Society of Heating, Refrigerating and Air-Conditioning Engineers, Atlanta, USA (2009)
3. Boulmaiz, F., Alyafi, A.A., Ploix, S., Reignier, P.: Optimizing occupant actions to enhance his comfort while reducing energy demand in buildings. In: 11th IEEE IDAACS (2021)
4. Boulmaiz, F., Reignier, P., Ploix, S.: An occupant-centered approach to improve both his comfort and the energy efficiency of the building. Knowl. Based Syst. **249**, 108970 (2022)
5. CSA Group: Z412–17 Office ergonomics - an application standard for workplace ergonomics (2017)
6. Khatib, O.: Real-time obstacle avoidance for manipulators and mobile robots. In: Proceedings of the IEEE International Conference on Robotics and Automation (1985)
7. Minor, M., Marx, L.: Case-based reasoning for inert systems in building energy management. In: Aha, D.W., Lieber, J. (eds.) ICCBR 2017. LNCS (LNAI), vol. 10339, pp. 200–211. Springer, Cham (2017). https://doi.org/10.1007/978-3-319-61030-6_14
8. Patterson, D.A., Rooney, N.F., Galushka, M.: A regression based adaptation strategy for case-based reasoning. In: AAAI/IAAI (2002)
9. Sizov, G., Öztürk, P., Marsi, E.: Compositional adaptation of explanations in textual case-based reasoning. In: Goel, A., Díaz-Agudo, M.B., Roth-Berghofer, T. (eds.) ICCBR 2016. LNCS (LNAI), vol. 9969, pp. 387–401. Springer, Cham (2016). https://doi.org/10.1007/978-3-319-47096-2_26

Improving Customer Experience in Call Centers with Intelligent Customer-Agent Pairing

Stylianos Filippou[1], Andreas Tsiartas[3], Petros Hadjineophytou[3],
Spyros Christofides[3], Kleanthis Malialis[1]([✉]), and Christos G. Panayiotou[1,2]

[1] KIOS Research and Innovation Center of Excellence, University of Cyprus,
Nicosia, Cyprus
{filippou.stylianos,malialis.kleanthis,christop}@ucy.ac.cy
[2] Department of Electrical and Computer Engineering, University of Cyprus,
Nicosia, Cyprus
[3] Cyprus Telecommunications Authority (CYTA), Nicosia, Cyprus
{andreas.tsiartas,petros.hadjineophytou,spyros.christofides}@cyta.com.cy

Abstract. Customer experience plays a critical role for a profitable organisation or company. A satisfied customer for a company corresponds to higher rates of customer retention, and better representation in the market. One way to improve customer experience is to optimize the functionality of its call center. In this work, we have collaborated with the largest provider of telecommunications and Internet access in the country, and we formulate the customer-agent pairing problem as a machine learning problem. The proposed learning-based method causes a significant improvement in performance of about 215% compared to a rule-based method.

Keywords: customer-agent pairing · machine learning · call center · customer experience

1 Introduction

Organisations or companies set high standards for providing excellent products and services to expand in the market, to retain current customers, and attract new ones. Customer experience significantly affects the loyalty and satisfaction of the customer in relation to a company's products and services [12]. It is a top priority for any company or organisation, and it constitutes a vital component of its commercial and marketing strategy.

Nowadays, there exist multiple channels through which a customer can contact an organisation; one of the most widely used is the call center. A call center is a department within an organisation, that handles a large amount of incoming calls related to their products and services. The organisation through the call center collects and stores a variety of historical information through the different media of interaction with the customer. The main aim of the call center is to

I. Maglogiannis et al. (Eds.): AIAI 2023, IFIP AICT 675, pp. 214–224, 2023.
https://doi.org/10.1007/978-3-031-34111-3_19

assist customers and answer any enquiry, therefore, a good functioning call center can drastically improve customer experience. By keeping customers satisfied, an organization can achieve their objectives, which among others, it includes customer retention through customer satisfaction [12]. Moreover, by successfully assisting customers, an overall positive experience can attract new customers.

An important way of improving customer experience through the call center is by minimizing the waiting time of a customer until an agent (i.e., call operator) assists them. Minimization of the call duration can be achieved by avoiding the traditional interaction via keypad, which redirects the customer after a series of keypad selections to the relevant agent who can assist with their enquiry. Minimizing each call duration offers significant benefits which are: (i) a customer is assisted faster; (ii) a company can assist more customers in the same amount of time; and (iii) a company saves valuable resources, e.g., by re-assigning agents to important problems.

The contributions of this work are as follows. We have collaborated with the Customer Support team of the largest provider of telecommunications and Internet access in the country, and have formulated the customer-agent pairing problem in their call center as a machine learning problem. We have conducted a rich experimental study using realistic data provided by the organisation, and examining various learning models. The proposed learning-based method is statistically 2.15 times better than a rule-based method.

The rest of the paper is organised as follows. Section 2 reviews the related work. The problem formulation and proposed method are discussed in Sect. 3. Section 4 presents the datasets, classification models, and evaluation metrics used in this study. A description of the results and the comparative study are presented in Sect. 5. We conclude in Sect. 6.

2   Related Work

Customer Relationship Management (CRM) is the strategy for building, managing and strengthening loyal and long-lasting customer relationships. According to [12] there are two main objectives of CRM. First, customer retention through customer satisfaction, and second customer development through customer insight. To achieve both objectives, organizations should focus on customer needs, behavior and preferences. Machine learning algorithms have played a major role towards achieving these objectives; many studies use such methods in CRM-related tasks.

Customer identification and segmentation is an important task for any organization because it can identify customer requirements and divide customers into groups using demographic data, such as age, location, gender, occupation etc. In [20] the authors compared various machine learning algorithms in order to group customers using these features: total call duration, frequency of using a service, and money spent during a certain period. In [18] they grouped customers into a number of classes using Naive Bayes, Decision Tree and MLP, while in [11] they used dimensionality reduction (PCA) and clustering (k-mode) to group customers.

Customer attraction is the task of attracting customers to an organization's products and services. In [13] the authors have applied machine learning to predict purchase of services, while in [19] the authors have used machine learning to identify prospect customers.

Customer retention refers to strategies that are, typically, targeted on customers that are most likely to abandon a service. According to [17], retention strategies should be applied by all organizations or companies as they are considered to be cost-effective (e.g., compared to attracting new customers). In [9] the authors have applied various machine learning algorithms on a telecommunication dataset, while authors in [8] used a semi-supervised learning to retain their valuable customers.

Customer churning is the task of identifying the cost of losing customers. In [1], the authors have applied machine learning for churn prediction in the area of telecommunications. Also in the same area, the authors in [15] have proposed deep fully-connected and convolutional neural networks for churn prediction in the area of telecommunications.

Customer lifetime value (CLV) refers to the task of identifying the approaches that can create value to organizations, optimize their resources, and maximize their profits. In [5], the authors used tree-based learning algorithms to define CLV in airline travelers, and classified them as high, medium and low value travelers. In [16] using features such as client loyalty number, recency, frequency and monetary, the authors proposed a customer shopping behavior model using recurrent neural networks.

Customer-agent pairing focuses on the successful communication between agents (i.e., call operators) and customers, thus maximizing customer satisfaction. To enhance the customer's call experience, organizations utilize historical and demographic data to improve the service to the customer by minimising the call duration, from the point a customer contacts the call center to the point the user enquiry is satisfied. To our knowledge, not many studies explored this problem. In [14] the authors used biographic information and historical data to find the best pairing of callers and agents for the call center of an insurance company. This work is closer in spirit to ours, however, the focus of our work is in the area of telecommunications. Lastly, in this study [2], the features that were considered are words, from speech to text conversion system available at the organisation. This method relies on an additional step where the customer is first required to describe the reason for calling, as opposed to interacting with their keypad which is what our proposed method is intended for.

3   Intelligent Customer-Agent Pairing

3.1   Problem Formulation

We consider a centralised call center that aims to provide services to existing or potential customers. The call center consists of many components, from which we will focus on the Interactive Voice Response (IVR) and the available assistance departments. The IVR component is a technology that allows a computer to interact with humans through input via a keypad. It provides an automated first contact with a customer before forwarding the call to the appropriate department. The IVR provides the user with a predefined number of options. Each initial category consists of a subgroup of options for the precise request identification, which will help the IVR to assign the caller to the queue of the appropriate department. Each department consists of a specialized group of personnel (the "agents" or "operators") that are qualified to help the customers with specific enquires. The overview of the current flow in IVR can be seen in Fig. 1. We describe Stages 1–2 here, while the prediction stage is described in the next section.

Stage 1. The customers voice call will be forwarded to the IVR system. At stage 1 the user will receive a welcome audio message, and be presented with the available J options. The user will use the keypad to make their desired choice that fits most their enquiry. Depending on the selection, this process can be repeated. It is assumed that the average duration time of this stage is t_{stage1}.

Stage 2. The user will be assigned to the corresponding N queues, one for each department. Finally, the user is able to communicate with the appropriate personnel. The average duration for this stage is assumed to be t_{stage2}.

The average time duration of any call c at the call center is:

$$T^c = t_{stage1} + t_{stage2} \tag{1}$$

Let the total number of calls be C, the total average duration of all calls is:

$$T^{total} = \sum_{c=1}^{C} T^c \tag{2}$$

3.2   ML-Based Pairing

Intelligent pairing can be achieved by classifying the call of each user before stage 1, and assigning the user to the correct queue department at stage 2. This is shown in red in Fig. 1. By achieving that, the user can skip the time consuming stage 1, and given a quick verification of the user they could directly forward the call to a department's queue, resulting in a faster service and an enhanced customer experience.

Let the identifier (e.g., telephone) of user u that contacts the call center be $id(u) \in \mathbb{Z}^+$. A feature generating process $g : \mathbb{Z}^+ \to \mathbf{R}^d$ creates at each time step d features, such that, $x^u = g(id(u))$ which corresponds to engineered features for the customer using historical data from previous calls to the center, as well as using other information (e.g., demographics).

We consider a learning model (multi-class classifier) $f : \mathbf{R}^d \to \{0, 1, ..., N\}$, such that, $\hat{y}^u = f(x^u)$ where N is the number of departments, and $\hat{y}^u$ is the predicted department to be transferred to. Note that the time taken for feature extraction and model prediction is negligible (i.e., in the order of milliseconds). At this point, the user receives a message to confirm whether or not the prediction

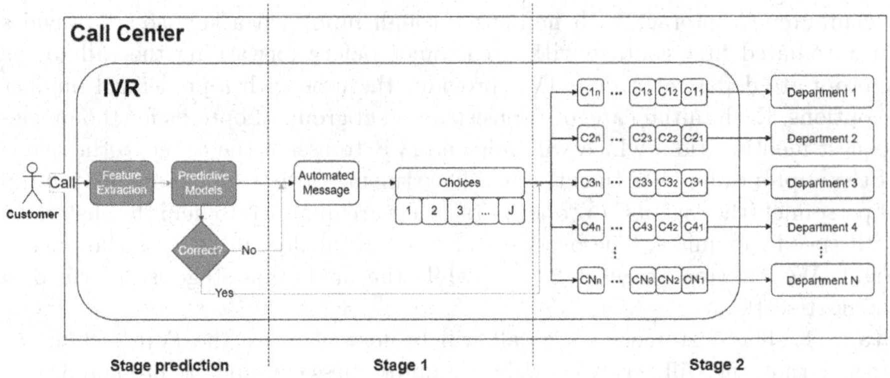

Fig. 1. The proposed solution overview of the Customer's call procedure

is correct (i.e., in the order of a few seconds). Let us assume that the average time required is $t_{stage^{pred}}$.

The main objective is to minimize the average time duration of each call T^c and, as a result, the total average duration time T^{total}, as defined in Eqs. 1 and 2. We define the time duration of a call c for which the model provided a correct prediction as follows:

$$
\begin{aligned}
T^c_{correct} &= t_{stage^{pred}} + t_{stage^2} \\
&= t_{stage^{pred}} + (T^c - t_{stage^1})
\end{aligned}
\tag{3}
$$

where T^c is the original average time taken without any prediction as defined in Eq. 1. In this case $T^c_{correct} << T^c$ as the stage 1 is by-passed which, typically, requires tens of seconds.

Similarly, let us define the average time duration of a call for which the model provided an incorrect prediction as shown below. In this case $T^c_{incorrect} > T^c$.

$$
T^c_{incorrect} = t_{stage^{pred}} + T^c
\tag{4}
$$

Based on the number of calls which correspond to correct and incorrect predictions respectively, the total average duration time is defined as:

$$
T^{total}_{pred} = \sum_{c=1}^{T_P+T_N} T^c_{correct} + \sum_{c=1}^{F_P+F_N} T^c_{incorrect}
\tag{5}
$$

where T_P, T_N, F_P and F_N correspond to the number of True Positives, True Negatives, False Positives, and False Negatives respectively.

Thus far we have considered the general case where a multi-class classifier is used. For completeness, when the task is binary, that is, to predict whether a user is calling for a particular service $SERVICE\_A$ or for any other service $OTHER$, the previous equation is replaced with the following:

$$T_{pred}^{total} = \sum_{c=1}^{T_P} T_{correct}^c + \sum_{c=1}^{F_P} T_{incorrect}^c + \sum_{c=1}^{T_N+F_N} T^c \qquad (6)$$

4 Experimental Setup

4.1 Case Study

We have collaborated with one of the largest telecommunications and Internet provider in the country, to provide a proof-of-concept to our proposed ML-based customer - agent pairing. The objective of this initial case study is to predict whether a user calls to purchase a specific service $SERVICE\_A$, otherwise she/he calls for another reason $OTHER$. To achieve this, we extract the following types of information related to each user.

Demographics: It includes general demographic information, such as, age, language, address, and the user type (e.g., company or individual).

Customer Profile: It contains detailed information about each service or product the customer has used or has been using (e.g., start date, expiration date, description, and status).

Customer Interaction: It includes information about issues that were reported by a user in the past via the Customer Call Center or at a retail store; this source includes information, such as, date and time, and department handled by.

Feature engineering is performed on the extracted features related to customer profile and interaction, for example, "number of previous calls in the last three months for $SERVICE\_A$".

After the dataset creation, we split the dataset into training, validation, and test sets as shown in Table 1.

Table 1. Dataset description

Dataset	Duration (months)	Unique Callers	Service_A Calls	Other Calls	Total Calls
Train	12	162563	18581	822102	849683
Validation	2	56317	2289	118317	120606
Test	1	34128	1378	59407	60785

4.2 Compared Methods

Rule-Based: Combination of rules derived based on domain knowledge, as well as, extensive analysis of historical data.

Logistic Regression (LR) [7]: It is a statistical algorithm that models the probability of an event taking place by analyzing the linear relationship between one or more existing independent variables.

Decision Tree (DT) [21]: It is a classification algorithm that predicts the class of a target variable by learning decision rules inferred from prior data.

Random Forest (RF) [3,4]: It is a tree-based, ensemble learning algorithm, i.e., it depends on multiple tree-based learners which make individual predictions that are then averaged together.

Extreme Gradient Boosting (XGBoost) [6]: It is a machine learning technique that produces a prediction model in the form of an ensemble of weak prediction models, which are typically tree-based. This technique builds a model in a stage-wise fashion and combines weak learners into a single strong learner. As each weak learner is added, a new model is fitted to provide a more accurate estimation. The XGBoost classifier is a tree-based ensemble machine learning algorithm with Gradient Boosting as its main component.

Multilayer Perception (MLP) [3]: It is a feed-forward neural network that consists of an input and an output layer, and can have multiple hidden layers. MLP uses the backpropagation algorithm for training which computes the gradient of the loss function with respect to the weights of the neural network.

4.3 Evaluation Metrics

We analyze the results of the classifier using a **confusion matrix**. The confusion matrix classifies the results into True Positives (T_P), True Negatives (T_N), False Positives (F_P), and False Negatives (F_N).

Classifiers are typically evaluated using the accuracy metric. However, this metric becomes unsuitable as it is biased towards the majority class. In this study we adopt two widely accepted metrics which are less sensitive to imbalance; these are, F1-score (F1) [10] and Geometric Mean (GM).

F1-score (F1) is defined as the harmonic mean of Precision and Recall. Specifically, Precision (P) provides information concerning the rate at which the algorithm detects $SERVICE\_A$ over all detection of $SERVICE\_A$ given by:

$$P = \frac{T_P}{T_P + F_P}. \tag{7}$$

Similarly, Recall (R) is the ratio at which the algorithm detects $SERVICE\_A$ over all possible $SERVICE\_A$ given by:

$$R = \frac{T_P}{T_P + F_N}. \tag{8}$$

Finally, the $F1$-score $(F1)$ is the weighted average of P and R and is the measure of accuracy on the data set given by

$$F1 = 2\left(\frac{P \times R}{P + R}\right). \tag{9}$$

The $F1$-score gets a higher value (near 1) when the F_P and F_N are low. If a system is performing poorly by generating more F_P and F_N, the $F1$-score will be low (near 0).

Geometric Mean (GM) is defined as the geometric mean of Recall and Specificity, and is given by

$$GM = \sqrt{R \times S}, \tag{10}$$

where the Specificity (S), which is defined as the true negative rate, is given by

$$S = \frac{T_N}{T_N + F_P}. \tag{11}$$

Note that GM has the desirable property of being high when both R and S are high, and when their difference is small [10]. For this reason, we introduce a combined metric which is defined as the geometric mean of $F1$ and GM:

$$F1 - GM = \sqrt{F1 \times GM} \tag{12}$$

5   Experimental Results

5.1   Role of the Learning Model

In this section we explore the performance of each model on the validation set. Due to the stochastic nature of the learning models we repeat the experiment 20 times, and report the average performance. An overview of the results can be seen in Table 2. The MLP appears to be the best performing model based on the combined $F1 - GM$ metric; specifically, it produces the highest $F1$ and the second highest GM.

Table 2. Performance of machine learning models on the validation set.

Model	F1	GM	F1-GM
LR	47.69	75.93	60.17
DT	46.74	71.34	57.74
RF	47.31	**77.89**	60.70
XGBoost	50.00	74.25	60.93
MLP	**50.17**	76.39	**61.91**

5.2   Comparative Study

In this section we compare the machine learning algorithm to the manual rules method. We have selected the highest performing machine learning algorithm, MLP and the best rule combination for manual rules method. Table 3 presents the average performance of MLP and manual rules on the test set. The proposed leaning-based method yields an $F1$ and $GM - F1$ scores which are 4.5 and 2.15 times better than the rule-based method. This significant improvement can reduce the waiting times, thus enhancing the customer experience, as well as it allows an organisation to allocate its limited resources more efficiently.

Table 3. Comparative study on the test set.

Algorithm	F1	GM	F1-GM
Manual Rules	10.67	74.04	28.10
MLP	**48.55**	**75.39**	**60.50**

5.3 Empirical Analysis of the Results

Table 4 presents the confusion matrix of Manual Rules and MLP on the test set. In this section, given the numbers presented in Table 4 and the formulated equations in Sect. 3, we analyse three methods. The first one is the traditional way in which a call centre operates, i.e., without any prediction method in-place. The second and third methods are the rule-based and ML-based respectively. MLP achieves a significant improvement over the rule-based method; we notice here the huge difference in the number of true negatives and false positives.

Table 4. Confusion matrix of Manual Rules and MLP algorithms on the test set.

Algorithm	T_N	F_P	F_N	T_P
Manual Rules	41675	17732	301	1077
MLP	58308	1099	579	799

Traditional (No Prediction). Let us now consider the traditional method of not having any prediction method in-place. Given Eq. 2 and the total number of calls which is 60785, the total time duration equals to:

$$T_{trad}^{total} = \sum_{c=1}^{60785} T^c \tag{13}$$
$$= 60785 t_{stage1} + 60785 t_{stage2}$$

Rule-Based. Based on Eq. 6, the total duration time is:

$$T_{pred\_rules}^{total} = \sum_{c=1}^{1077} T_{correct}^c + \sum_{c=1}^{17732} T_{incorrect}^c + \sum_{c=1}^{41976} T_{other}^c$$
$$= 18809 t_{stage^{pred}} + 59708 t_{stage1} + 60785 t_{tstage2}$$
$$= 18809 t_{stage^{pred}} + 59708 t_{stage1} + 877 t_{stage1} - 877 t_{stage1} + 60785 t_{tstage2}$$
$$= T_{trad}^{total} + 18809 t_{stage^{pred}} - 877 t_{stage1} \tag{14}$$

MLP. Based on Eq. 6, the total duration time is:

$$T^{total}_{pred\_MLP} = \sum_{c=1}^{799} T^c_{correct} + \sum_{c=1}^{1099} T^c_{incorrect} + \sum_{c=1}^{58887} T^c_{other}$$

$$= 1898 t_{stage^{pred}} + 59986 t_{stage^1} + 60785 t_{stage^2}$$

$$= 1898 t_{stage^{pred}} + 59986 t_{stage^1} + 799_{stage^1} - 799_{stage^1} + 60785 t_{stage^2}$$

$$= T^{total}_{trad} + 1898 t_{stage^{pred}} - 799_{stage^1}$$

$$(15)$$

We can further derive that the average time required by the traditional method is larger than that of the proposed method if the following condition is true:

$$T^{total}_{trad} > T^{total}_{pred\_MLP}$$

$$\Rightarrow 799 t_{stage^1} - 1898 t_{stage^{pred}} > 0 \qquad (16)$$

$$\Rightarrow t_{stage^1} > 2.38 t_{stage^{pred}}$$

Similarly, the average time required by the rule-based method is larger than that of the proposed method if the following condition is true:

$$T^{total}_{pred\_rules} > T^{total}_{pred\_MLP}$$

$$\Rightarrow 16911 t_{stage^{pred}} - 78 t_{stage^1} > 0 \qquad (17)$$

$$\Rightarrow t_{stage^1} < 216.81 t_{stage^{pred}}$$

In our case study, reasonable values for the average duration of the prediction and first stages are $t_{stage^{pred}} = 5$ s and $t_{stage^1} = 45$ s respectively. Both the above conditions are met. Specifically, the proposed ML-based method reduces the total average waiting time in the test set (1 month) compared to the rule-based method by more than 22 h ($= T^{total}_{pred\_rules} - T^{total}_{pred\_MLP}$), and to the traditional method by more than 7 h ($= T^{total}_{trad} - T^{total}_{pred\_MLP}$).

6   Conclusions and Future Work

We have collaborated with the largest provider of telecommunications and Internet access in the country, and we have formulated the customer-agent pairing problem as a machine learning problem. The proposed learning-based method causes a significant improvement in performance of about 215% (i.e., 2.15 times better) compared to a rule-based method. One future direction is to examine the effect of methods, such as, cost-sensitive learning and resampling, to address the class imbalance problem, in an attempt to further improve our results.

Acknowledgements. This work has been supported by the CYTA-KIOS Research Collaboration Agreement, the European Union Horizon 2020 program under Grant Agreement No. 739551 (KIOS CoE), and the Government of the Republic of Cyprus through the Deputy Ministry of Research, Innovation and Digital Policy.

References

1. Ahmad, A.K., Jafar, A., Aljoumaa, K.: Customer churn prediction in telecom using machine learning in big data platform. J. Big Data **6**(1), 1–24 (2019). https://doi.org/10.1186/s40537-019-0191-6
2. Avdagić-Golub, E., Begović, M., Kosovac, A.: Optimization of agent-user matching process using a machine learning algorithms. TEM J. **9**, 158–163 (2020)
3. Bishop, C.M.: Pattern Recognition and Machine Learning. Information Science and Statistics, Springer, Heidelberg (2006)
4. Breiman, L.: Random forests. Mach. Learn. **45**(1), 5–32 (2001)
5. Chen, S.: Estimating customer lifetime value using machine learning techniques, chap. 2. In: Thomas, C. (ed.) Data Mining. IntechOpen, Rijeka (2018)
6. Chen, T., Guestrin, C.: XGBoost: a scalable tree boosting system. In: Proceedings of the 22nd ACM SIGKDD International Conference on Knowledge Discovery and Data Mining, pp. 785–794 (2016)
7. Cox, D.R.: The regression analysis of binary sequences. J. Roy. Stat. Soc. Ser. B (Methodol.) **20**(2), 215–232 (1958)
8. Emtiyaz, S., Keyvanpour, M.: Customers behavior modeling by semi-supervised learning in customer relationship management. In: Advances in Information Sciences and Service Sciences (AISS), vol. 3 (2012)
9. Sabbeh, S.F.: Machine-learning techniques for customer retention: a comparative study. Int. J. Adv. Comput. Sci. Appl. **9**, 273–281 (2018)
10. He, H., Garcia, E.A.: Learning from imbalanced data. IEEE Trans. Knowl. Data Eng. **21**(9), 1263–1284 (2009)
11. Kamthania, D., Pawa, A., Madhavan, S.S.: Market segmentation analysis and visualization using k-mode clustering. J. Comput. Inf. Technol. **26**, 57–68 (2018)
12. Tsiptsis, K.K., Chorianopoulos, A.: Data Mining Techniques in CRM: Inside Customer Segmentation. Wiley (2009)
13. Martínez, A., Schmuck, C., Pereverzyev, S., Pirker, C., Haltmeier, M.: A machine learning framework for customer purchase prediction in the non-contractual setting. Eur. J. Oper. Res. **281**, 588–596 (2020)
14. Mehrbod, N., Grilo, A., Zutshi, A.: Caller-agent pairing in call centers using machine learning techniques with imbalanced data. In: 2018 IEEE International Conference on Engineering, Technology and Innovation (ICE/ITMC), pp. 1–6 (2018)
15. Mishra, A., Reddy, U.S.: A novel approach for churn prediction using deep learning. In: 2017 IEEE International Conference on Computational Intelligence and Computing Research (ICCIC), pp. 1–4 (2017)
16. Salehinejad, H., Rahnamayan, S.: Customer shopping pattern prediction: a recurrent neural network approach. In: 2016 IEEE Symposium Series on Computational Intelligence (SSCI), pp. 1–6 (2016)
17. Singh, D., Singh, P., Gupta, M.: An inclusive survey on machine learning for CRM: a paradigm shift. Decision **47**, 447–457 (2021)
18. Singh, D., Singh, P., Singh, K.K., Singh, A.: Machine learning based classification and segmentation techniques for CRM: a customer analytics. Int. J. Bus. Forecast. Mark. Intell. **6**, 99 (2020)
19. Singh, P., Agrawal, R.: A customer centric best connected channel model for heterogeneous and IoT networks. J. Organ. End User Comput. **30**, 32–50 (2018)
20. Wassouf, W.N., Alkhatib, R., Salloum, K., Balloul, S.: Predictive analytics using big data for increased customer loyalty: Syriatel Telecom Company case study. J. Big Data **7**(1), 1–24 (2020). https://doi.org/10.1186/s40537-020-00290-0
21. Wu, X., et al.: Top 10 algorithms in data mining. Knowl. Inf. Syst. **14**, 1–37 (2008)

Mind the Gap: Addressing Incompleteness Challenge in Case-Based Reasoning Applications

Fateh Boulmaiz[1(✉)], Patrick Reignier[1], and Stephane Ploix[2]

[1] Université Grenoble Alpes, CNRS, Grenoble INP, LIG, 38000 Grenoble, France
fateh.boulmaiz@univ-grenoble-alpes.fr
[2] Université Grenoble Alpes, CNRS, Grenoble INP, G-SCOP, 38000 Grenoble, France

Abstract. Data quality is a crucial aspect of case-based reasoning (CBR), and incomplete data is a ubiquitous challenge that can significantly affect the accuracy and effectiveness of CBR systems. Incompleteness arises when a case lacks relevant information needed to solve a problem. Existing CBR systems often struggle to handle such cases, leading to sub-optimal solutions, and making it challenging to apply CBR in real-world settings. This paper highlights the importance of data quality in CBR and emphasizes the need for systems to handle incomplete data effectively. The authors provide for the first time a framework for addressing the issue of incompleteness under the open-world assumption. The proposed approach leverages a combination of data-driven and knowledge-based techniques to detect incompleteness. The approach offers a promising solution to the incompleteness dimension of data quality in CBR and has the potential to improve the practical utility of CBR systems in various domains as illustrated by the results of a real data-based evaluation.

Keywords: Case based reasoning · Data quality · Data completeness

1 Introduction

In the era of extensive digitization and ubiquitous computing, ensuring the quality of data manipulation has emerged as a critical challenge for companies and academic research across various fields such as database, artificial intelligence, image processing, information systems, and more. Numerous studies have highlighted the significant impact of data quality on the handling process. For instance, research has shown that the quality of data utilized in machine learning algorithms directly influences their performance [21, 26]. A survey conducted in [1] has also shed light on the adverse effects of poor data quality on a country's economy. It estimates that the US economy alone loses over $3 trillion annually due to poor data quality, and this financial cost is still on the rise [2].

As organizations face increasingly complex data issues that can impact their profitability, and as research proposes more data quality-sensitive algorithms,

© IFIP International Federation for Information Processing 2023
Published by Springer Nature Switzerland AG 2023
I. Maglogiannis et al. (Eds.): AIAI 2023, IFIP AICT 675, pp. 225–239, 2023.
https://doi.org/10.1007/978-3-031-34111-3_20

the importance of accurate and trustworthy data has never been more critical. However, because of the diverse objectives and ways of using data, different data quality dimensions (requirements) exist, which characterize quality properties such as accuracy, completeness, and consistency. Despite the extensive literature devoted to data quality (see [11] for an overview), it is worth noting that: 1) There is no consensus on the properties that should be considered when defining a data quality standard, despite ongoing research in this area [18]. For example, while the authors in [28] identify 179 dimensions for data quality, a more recent study [15] describes more than 300 properties that should be considered for defining data quality; 2) Although some requirements have been universally identified as important, there is no agreement on their precise definitions. The same requirement name may have different meanings in different studies; 3) Because of the diversity of data sources, the multitude of quality dimensions, and the specificity of the application domain, data quality assessment is a domain-specific process. Therefore, it is not possible to propose a generic data quality assessment approach that can be applied to all data-intensive applications.

Although data quality has been extensively studied by the database and data mining communities, it has been overlooked in the machine learning domain, where the focus is on developing learning algorithms and reasoning approaches that assume high-quality data. This paper aims to address this gap by exploring the issue of data quality in the context of machine learning, with the goal of improving the robustness of learning algorithms and reducing the impact of poor quality data on overall results. However, due to the broad scope of both data quality and machine learning, certain limitations were necessary to make this work feasible. Specifically, we restrict our research to approaches based on the case-based reasoning paradigm, as the machine learning domain is too vast to provide a single data quality assessment method that is valid for all approaches. Furthermore, we only investigate the data completeness dimension, which is still largely unexplored in the context of case-based reasoning. In this paper, we propose a heuristic based on the change point detection method to address the issue of data incompleteness in the CBR approach.

The remainder of the paper is organized along the following lines: Sect. 2 reviews the existing literature on the topic. Section 3 describes the background of the research. Section 4 outlines the problem statement through an motivating example followed by a formulation of the problem. Section 5 details the proposed approach to address the problem under consideration. Section 6 evaluates the proposed approach through a real case study and discusses the results. Section 7 concludes the paper and presents future work.

2   Related Work

Data incompleteness is a common problem in various domains, and many methods have been proposed to address this issue. However, traditional methods for handling missing data assume a closed-world assumption, which means that any unobserved value is assumed to be missing at random from the same distribution as the observed data. This assumption can be problematic in some cases where data is incompletely observed under an open-world assumption, where unobserved values can be missing because they are not present in the data-generating process. One of the early works in this area is the paper [24], which introduced the concept of the open world assumption in the context of incomplete data. This challenge has been studied in several domains, and various approaches have been proposed to handle data incompleteness under the OWA. One approach is to use probabilistic models to reason about missing values, such as Bayesian networks and Markov logic networks (MLNs). For example, in the domain of natural language processing (NLP), there has been extensive work on using probabilistic models to handle data incompleteness in text corpora [17]. MLNs have also been used to handle incomplete data in other domains, such as bioinformatics [20] and image analysis [4].

Recently, deep learning methods have also been proposed for handling data incompleteness under the open world assumption. For instance, DeepProbLog [19] is a probabilistic programming language that combines deep learning with logic programming to handle data incompleteness in relational domains. Another example of such technique is DeepImpute method [3], which is a deep learning-based imputation method that has been applied in various domains, such as genomics and biomedical data analysis. Other deep learning approaches for handling incomplete data include generative models [6] and adversarial training [29]. Works [9,23] demonstrate the effectiveness of deep learning models for imputing missing data.

In addition to these methods, there have been several studies focused on understanding the causes and consequences of data incompleteness. For instance, The authors in [30] analyzed the impact of missing data on the medical domain and concluded that the missingness mechanism (i.e., the reason why data is missing) plays a critical role in determining the appropriate analysis strategy.

Overall, the literature on data incompleteness is vast, and a wide range of techniques have been developed to address this challenge. However, there is no one-size-fits-all solution. Each approach has its strengths and weaknesses, and the appropriate method depends on the characteristics of the data and the objectives being addressed by the application.

Surprisingly, despite the pervasiveness of incomplete data issue in real-world applications and the importance of addressing this issue in various fields, there has been a lack of attention given to incomplete data in case-based reasoning. Thus, there is a need for further research in CBR to address the issue of incomplete data and develop approaches that can detect, handle, and reason with incomplete information effectively.

3   Background

3.1   Case-Based Reasoning and Data Completeness

Case-based reasoning (CBR) is a reasoning paradigm based on a case base $\mathbb{CB}$ representing a collection of source cases. A case $\mathbb{C}$ represents an experience of problem-solving, usually defined by a couple $(\mathfrak{p}, \mathfrak{s})$ wherein $\mathfrak{p}$ is a problem in the considered application domain and s is its solution. In the following, we assume a finer representation of the case $\mathbb{C}$ as a triplet $(\mathtt{C}^\mathtt{C}, \mathtt{A}^\mathtt{C}, \mathtt{E}^\mathtt{C})$ [8]. Let $\mathbb{C}^S$, $\mathbb{A}^S$, and $\mathbb{E}^S$ be three sets. The context $\mathtt{C}^\mathtt{C}$ is an element of $\mathbb{C}^S$ representing the phenomena undergone by the application domain. The actions $\mathtt{A}^\mathtt{C}$ is an element of $\mathbb{A}^S$ modeling controllable phenomena of the application domain. The effects $\mathtt{E}^\mathtt{C}$ is an element of $\mathbb{E}^S$ describing the consequence of the application of the actions $\mathtt{A}^\mathtt{C}$ to the context $\mathtt{A}^\mathtt{C}$. The intuition underlying the CBR paradigm is formulated by Hypothesis 1. The process of solving a target case $\mathbb{C}_{tg}$, which is formed initially from the context only, consists in calculating the relevant actions, which once applied will produce effects, generating a new source case in the case base.

Assumption 1 (Consistency). *The effects of applying similar actions to similar contexts are similar.*

Precisely, the reasoning strategy starts by looking for the set $\mathtt{SIM}^{\mathbb{C}_{tg}}$ of source cases $\mathbb{C}_{sr}$ similar to the target case $\mathbb{C}_{tg}$ (retrieval stage), followed by the modification of the actions of the cases $\mathbb{C}_{sr}$ to match the specificity of the context of the case $\mathbb{C}_{tg}$, generating thus the actions $\mathtt{A}^{\mathtt{C}_{tg}}$ (adaptation stage). According to the adopted validation stage, the effects $\mathtt{E}^{\mathtt{C}_{tg}}$ of the application of $\mathtt{A}^{\mathtt{C}_{tg}}$ to the context $\mathtt{C}^{\mathtt{C}_{tg}}$ are generated, and thus the new target case $\mathbb{C}_{tg}(\mathtt{C}^{\mathtt{C}_{tg}}, \mathtt{A}^{\mathtt{C}_{tg}}, \mathtt{E}^{\mathtt{C}_{tg}})$, if approved, is integrated into the case base $\mathbb{CB}$ (memorization stage). This can be formalized as follows:

CBR system : Memorization ∘ Validation ∘ Adaptation ∘ Retrieval

Retrieval function : $\mathtt{C}^{\mathtt{C}_{tg}} \longmapsto \mathtt{SIM}^{\mathbb{C}_{tg}} = \{\mathbb{C}_{sr}\} \subseteq \mathbb{CB}$

Adaptation function : $\mathtt{SIM}^{\mathbb{C}_{tg}} \cup \mathtt{C}^{\mathtt{C}_{tg}} \longmapsto \mathtt{A}^{\mathtt{C}_{tg}} \cup \{\mathtt{failure}\}$

Validation function : $\mathtt{A}^{\mathtt{C}_{tg}} \longmapsto \mathbb{C}_{tg}(\mathtt{C}^{\mathtt{C}_{tg}}, \mathtt{A}^{\mathtt{C}_{tg}}, \mathtt{E}^{\mathtt{C}_{tg}})$

Memorization function : $(\mathbb{CB}, \mathtt{C}^{\mathtt{C}_{tg}}) \longmapsto \mathbb{CB} \cup \mathbb{C}_{tg}(\mathtt{C}^{\mathtt{C}_{tg}}, \mathtt{A}^{\mathtt{C}_{tg}}, \mathtt{E}^{\mathtt{C}_{tg}})$

To conduct the different steps of the reasoning process, a CBR system draws on a set of knowledge spread over four containers: domain, case, similarity, and adaptation knowledge [25]. Usually, each stage of the reasoning process is supported by several knowledge containers because of the close connections existing between them.

Completeness. In keeping with existing literature on Knowledge bases [12] and databases [14], we consider completeness through an ideal reference domain knowledge container $\mathtt{K}_R^D$, which captures all the real-world aspects of the application domain. The domain knowledge $\mathtt{K}^D$ of CBR system is complete if the application of any actions (defined in $\mathtt{K}^D$) to any context (likewise defined in $\mathtt{K}^D$) generates the same effects on $\mathtt{K}^D$ as on $\mathtt{K}_R^D$.

Definition 1 *[Completeness]. Completeness refers to the ability of the domain knowledge container of a CBR system to describe every relevant state of the domain application environment.*

The principal barrier to assessing and achieving completeness, as stated in Definition 1, is the Open World Assumption. The latter states that if a given piece of real-world knowledge is not represented in the Knowledge domain K^D, then that knowledge is not necessarily false, it may be real-world true but not included in the K^D.

A plethora of work has been done on data quality assessment, which continues to be an intense research domain in such diverse fields as relational databases, big data, machine learning, data mining, etc. Data quality verification remains a challenging process for several reasons:

- *Data quality verification is a permanent process.* This is due to the data nature (particularly, their velocity) on one side and the different processings performed on the data (e.g., data cleaning) on the other side.
- *Data quality verification is strongly dependent on the application-task domain.* The different dimensions of data quality are evaluated by metrics whose specification strongly depends on the needs of the user/expert, the application domain (the aeronautics domain does not have the same requirements in terms of data quality as the education domain, for example) but also on the task (in the health domain, there are different requirements for the diagnostic phase and the treatment phase).

3.2 Change Point Analysis

Change points in a data set modeling a system are defined by abrupt shifts in the data. These change points can represent transitions that occur between states of the modeled system due to hidden changes in the properties of the data set. Determining the change points in a data set is the objective of the change point analysis approaches, which have sparked an increasing work in statistics [27] as well as in several application domains such as climate [13], medical [31], finance [10].

More formally, consider a system characterized by non-stationary random phenomena and modeled by a multivariate vector $\Omega = \{\omega_1, \ldots, \omega_m\}$ whose values are defined in $\mathbb{R}^{d \geq 1}$ and consisting of m samples. It is further supposed that the vector Ω is piecewise stationary, i.e., certain phenomena of the system change abruptly at unknown instants $t_1, t_2, \ldots, t_m$. The detection of the change points consists in solving a model detection problem whose objective is to determine the optimal segmentation S based on a quantitative criterion to be minimized. Specifically, it consists in identifying the number m of changes and finding the indices $t_{i_{(1 \leq i \leq m)}}$.

4 Problem Setting

4.1 Motivating Example

We motivate the need to guarantee the completeness of data in a CBR system through a concrete scenario. Let's consider the scenario of a CBR-based energy management system (EMS) that monitors a building equipped with an air-conditioning (AC) system, but the EMS designer has not envisaged any means to discover the AC system function. On two days with a similar context (e.g., the same weather conditions) and the same actions, if the AC system was turned on one day but not on the other (this phenomenon cannot be detected by the system), the two days would have different effects (e.g., different indoor temperatures), which calls into question the founding assumption of the CBR technique.

4.2   Problem Statement

Existing CBR systems exploit directly the case base to carry out the different steps of the CBR cycle, assuming that the domain knowledge is consistent. Indeed, by adopting the consistency assumption (Assumption 1), it is implicitly admitted that the completeness hypothesis is valid. However, it is arguably not warranted, especially considering the modeling of a complex domain with many dependent variables. The violation of the completeness assumption poses some substantive issues:

- the system has no guarantee that the principle of the CBR approach (Assumption 1) is respected.
- the CBR system cannot identify incomplete data and therefore cannot determine which data reflects reality for use in the reasoning process.
- as a consequence of the previous statements, the performance of the reasoning process may degrade as the case base includes cases that are wrongly judged as similar.

The failure of one of four knowledge containers to be adequately defined (incomplete) can be overwhelming to the whole CBR system unless any of the remaining knowledge containers can fill the missing knowledge. As a result, either the CBR system will fail to respond or provide inaccurate solutions. In particular, it was established that incomplete domain knowledge generates such a critical dysfunction of a CBR system [5]. Incomplete domain knowledge in a CBR system most likely leads to the generation of incomplete cases. Moreover, the retrieval process is burdened by the absence of missing data since the similarity evaluation is biased by the incompleteness of the data. Furthermore, incomplete cases can also degrade the adaptation process when the adaptation knowledge is acquired automatically from the case base.

It is obvious that the problem of incompleteness verification can be reformulated as a hidden variable detection problem. Indeed, an incompleteness situation occurs in a case base when a group of similar cases produces different effects, which is necessarily a consequence of the existence of context and/or action variables that are not considered in the similarity evaluation process.

Formally, consider a case base $\mathbb{CB} = \{\mathbb{C}_i\}_{1 \leq i \leq n}$ consisting of a finite number n of cases $\mathbb{C}_i$. Each element of the latter is described by a set of features. The context $\mathbf{C}^{\mathbb{C}_i}$ of case $\mathbb{C}_i$ is specified by $\mathbf{C}^{\mathbb{C}_i} = \{O_{Cj}^{\mathbb{C}_i}\}_{1 \leq j \leq n_1}$, where the observed features O_C are defined on the knowledge domain $\mathbb{K}_C^D$. The actions $\mathbf{A}^{\mathbb{C}_i}$ are modeled by the features $\{O_{Aj}^{\mathbb{C}_i}\}_{1 \leq j \leq n_2}$ which are defined on the knowledge domain $\mathbb{K}_A^D$, and the effects are specified on the knowledge domain K_E^D by the features $\{O_{Ej}^{C_i}\}_{1 \leq j \leq n_3}$. The knowledge domain K^D of the CBR system is defined by $K^D = K_C^D \cup K_A^D \cup K_E^D$. Let's also assume, $\{H_{Cj}\}_{1 \leq j \leq m_1}$, $\{H_{Aj}\}_{1 \leq j \leq m_2}$, and $\{H_{Ej}\}_{1 \leq j \leq m_3}$ are the hidden features of the context, action, and effect elements respectively. We denote the reference knowledge domain by $K_R^D = K^D \cup \{H_{Cj}\}_{1 \leq j \leq m_1} \cup \{H_{Aj}\}_{1 \leq j \leq m_2} \cup \{H_{Ej}\}_{1 \leq j \leq m_3}$.

The completeness evaluation problem of a CBR system against K_R^D consists in identifying eventual incompleteness situations in the case base. An incompleteness situation is formalized as:

$$\text{Incompleteness situation} \Leftrightarrow \exists\, \mathbb{C}_1, \mathbb{C}_2 \in \mathbb{CB}/$$

$$(\{O_{Cj}^{C_1}\} = \{O_{Cj}^{C_2}\})_{1 \leq j \leq n_1} \wedge (\{O_{Aj}^{C_1}\} = \{O_{Aj}^{C_2}\})_{1 \leq j \leq n_2} \wedge (\{O_{Ej}^{C_1}\} \neq \{O_{Ej}^{C_2}\})_{1 \leq j \leq n_3}$$

$$\implies \exists f \in \{H_{Cj}\}_{1 \leq j \leq m_1} \cup \{H_{Aj}\}_{1 \leq j \leq m_2}$$

For effectiveness reasons, we argue that is a prerequisite to check the completeness of the data as early as possible in the problem-solving process, i.e., before starting the reasoning cycle. Furthermore, the incompleteness assessment process must be launched whenever the case base is updated.

5   Incompleteness Checking in the CBR System

In this section, we detail the workflow of our I2CCBR (InCompleteness Checking CBR) algorithm to evaluate data incompleteness in a CBR system. This section is divided according to the global architecture of the I2CCBR algorithm into two parts. In this workflow, starting from splitting the case base into the best possible segmentation by grouping the cases according to their effects, we exploit the resulting partitions to search for possible incomplete situations by relying on an effective method based on context and action knowledge.

5.1   Case Base Partitioning

The process of partitioning the case base aims to identify possible patterns in the cases' effects, i.e., detecting and estimating changes in the statistical properties of the effects, so that cases having similar effects can be grouped into the same cluster. In this section, a hybrid method based on the change point detection approach is proposed to achieve this objective. This is a mixture of two techniques: the cumulative sum (CUMSUM) technique proposed in [22] and the bootstrapping mechanism introduced in [16]. In short, the detection of change points in the case effects model is an iterative process involving the following two steps:

Step 1: Cumulative Sums. Considering the notation introduced in Sect. 3.1, cumulative sums CS_i of the effect variables are calculated by the recursive formula described in Eq. (1). Note that the cumulative sums do not represent the cumulative sums of the effect variables but rather they represent the cumulative sums of the differences between the values and the average $\overline{\mu}$. Consequently, the last cumulative sum (CS_n) is always null.

By plotting the chart of cumulative sums CS_i, potentials change points in the effect variables could be identified as changes in the direction of the diagram. However, the cumulative sums chart cannot determine with certainty either the existence of these change points or the indices of the cases corresponding to these changes. These two problems are the focus of the second step. For the sake of the second step, it will be necessary to estimate the change magnitude CS_M of cumulative sums CS_i. One way to do so is to apply Formula (2).

$$\forall\, i \le n, \; CS_i = \begin{cases} CS_{i-1} + (E^{C_i} - \overline{\mu}) \\ 0, \qquad \text{if } i = 0 \end{cases} \tag{1}$$

With n – the number of cases, $\overline{\mu}$ – the average of the effect variable given as $\overline{\mu} = \frac{1}{n}\sum_{i=1}^{n} E^{C_i}$.

$$CS_M = \max_{1 \le i \le n} CS_i - \min_{1 \le i \le n} CS_i \tag{2}$$

Step 2: Bootstrapping. The first objective of the this step is to determine a confidence level for the observed change points. In the following, this issue is addressed with a bootstrapping approach. The rationale underlying the bootstrapping is to imitate the behavior of the cumulative sums CS_i^b in the case where there is no change in the patterns of effects. The resulting cumulative sums will provide a baseline for comparing the cumulative sums CS_i of the effects of the cases in their original order (as calculated in step 1). The bootstrapping process consists in applying the same process from step 1 to the randomly reorganized case base, which produces the cumulative sums CS_i^b and the change magnitude CS_M^b.

When the plot of the cumulative sums CS_i^b is likely to remain closer to zero than the chart of the original cumulative sums CS_i, a change has probably taken place. The estimation of the index of confidence in the existence of a change point includes conducting a significant k number of bootstraps and determining the number (let l be this number) of situations for which the magnitude of change CS_M^b is smaller than the change magnitude CS_M of the original case base. The confidence index CI that a shift in the pattern of effects is given by Formula (3).

$$CI = \frac{l}{k} \times 100 \tag{3}$$

Change Point Position. If the confidence level is high enough (typically around 90%) to confirm the existence of a change point, one way to estimate the case index corresponding to the change in the model of effects is to use the mean square error (MSE) metric. The case base is divided into two parts containing z and $n - z$ cases, where z is the index of the last case preceding the change in effect model. The estimation of the index z consists in solving an optimization problem whose objective is to minimize Function 4.

$$MSE = \sum_{i=1}^{z} (E^{C_i} - \overline{\mu}_1)^2 + \sum_{i=z+1}^{n} (E^{C_i} - \overline{\mu}_2)^2 \tag{4}$$

With $\overline{\mu}_1 = \frac{1}{z}\sum_{i=1}^{z} E^{C_i}$, $\overline{\mu}_2 = \frac{1}{n-z}\sum_{i=z+1}^{n} E^{C_i}$.

Once a change point is identified, the case base is divided into two case bases, a first case base including cases from 1 to z and the remaining cases composing the second case base. The process described in steps 1 and 2 is then iteratively applied on each of the case bases until there are no other change points in the case bases. As a result, more changes, if existing, are detected.

5.2 Incompleteness Detection

Let $m \neq 0$ be the number of change points detected in the case base $\mathbb{CB}$. Let $\mathcal{I}$ denotes the set of indices of the cases whose effects represent a change in the model, such as $|\mathcal{I}| = m$ and $\mathcal{I} = \{I_j\}_{1 \leq j \leq m}$. Precisely, index I_j corresponds to the index of the case preceding the jth change in the model of the effect variables. Then, the case base $\mathbb{CB}$ can be broken into $m + 1$ groups $\mathbb{G}_{1 \leq j \leq m+1}$ Such that constraints (5) are satisfied.

$$\mathbb{CB} = \bigcup_{j=1}^{m+1} \mathbb{G}_j$$

$$\mathbb{G}_j = \begin{cases} \{\mathbb{C}_t\}_{I_{j-1} < t \leq I_j}, & \text{if } 2 \leq j \\ \{\mathbb{C}_t\}_{1 \leq t \leq I_j}, & \text{if } j = 1 \end{cases} \tag{5}$$

The idea behind the completeness evaluation is to detect situations where two cases with similar actions and similar contexts but different effects. Specifically, the investigation of possible incompleteness situations is performed as follows.

1. given the set of groups $\{\mathbb{G}_j\}$, for each group $\mathbb{G}_j$, which represents the set of cases with similar effects, compute the maximum context-action distance $D_{CA,j}^{max}$ and minimum one $D_{CA,j}^{min}$ between cases. Let S_j^{CA} denote the interval $[D_{CA,j}^{min}, D_{CA,j}^{max}]$. Let $S_j^{E} = [E_j^{min}, E_j^{max}]$ be the effect variable interval of group $\mathbb{G}_j$.
2. a situation of incompleteness is reliably identified if there exist two cases $\mathbb{C}_1$ and $\mathbb{C}_2$, located respectively in two different groups $\mathbb{G}_1$ and $\mathbb{G}_2$ whose effect models differ, such that the context-action distance between $\mathbb{C}_1$ and $\mathbb{C}_2$ belongs to one of the intervals S_1^{CA}, S_2^{CA}. Formally:

$$\exists \, \mathbb{C}_{i'} \in \mathbb{G}_i, \mathbb{C}_{j'} \in \mathbb{G}_j, k \in \{i, j\}/$$
$$D_{CA}(\mathbb{C}_{i'}, \mathbb{C}_{j'}) \in S_k^{CA} \implies S_i^E \cap S_j^E = \emptyset \, \vee (E^{\mathbb{C}_1} \notin S_i^E \cap S_j^E \wedge E^{\mathbb{C}_2} \notin S_i^E \cap S_j^E)$$
$$\vee \, (E^{\mathbb{C}_m} \notin S_i^E \cap S_j^E, m \in \{i', j'\} \wedge \mathbb{C}_m \notin \mathbb{G}_k)$$

6   Evaluation

The objective of the experiment is to investigate the reliability and efficiency of the I2CCBR algorithm to discover incompleteness in a case base. First, we describe the dataset used in the experimentation, then we present the experimental setup, and finally, we report the results.

Dataset. To investigate the effectiveness of the I2CCBR approach, we conducted experiments using real word dataset. We used the real dataset from [7] that resulted from the experiment of the motivation example (see Sect. 4.1). More precisely, the authors proposed a CBR-based approach to improve the energy efficiency of buildings considering the comfort of the occupants. The approach is evaluated through a case study where data are collected from numerous sensors deployed in an academic research office.

Collected data are classified into three categories according to the casec structure presented in Sect. 3.1. The context data, which besides the meteorological data, includes the number of occupants. The action data model opening/closing of doors/windows. The effect data concern the temperature and the concentration of CO_2 in the office. A case corresponds to one-day measurements. The case base used in the present evaluation consists of 98 cases ordered by their measurements' dates. In this experiment, we are restricted to the incompleteness evaluation regarding the indoor temperature as the only effect variable.

Experimental setup. To avoid biasing the results of the similarity assessment due to the dominant influence of variables with large values, the context and action data are rescaled between 0 and 1 using the MinMax strategy.

In this experiment, the weighted Euclidean distance is used as a similarity function to evaluate the context-action-based similarity between two cases. It is beyond the scope of this work to detail the process of weighting context and action variables. We adopted the approach developed in [8] to estimate these weights.

The experiments were performed on a 13" MacBook Pro laptop equipped with an Intel® Core™ i7-8559U CPU 2.70 GHz, 16 GB of RAM, powered by Windows 10 pro 64 bit. The I2CCBR algorithm is implemented in Python 3.9. The code was ran in Jupyter Notebook 6.4.

Case Base with Random Incompleteness. At this stage, we do not know whether the case base is complete since the modeling of the building environment is difficult due to the high number and the complex interactions between the phenomena influencing the energetic behavior of a building. To check the efficiency of the I2CCBR algorithm, we need a baseline for which it certainly presents incompleteness situations.

We constructed an incomplete case base $\mathbb{CB}^I$ from the case base $\mathbb{CB}$. The process of generating the incompleteness situations is described as follows:

- we introduced incompleteness in $\mathbb{CB}$ by randomly choosing and modifying 5% of the cases (5 cases).
- as the office where the experimentation took place was not equipped with an air-conditioning system, the modification of the chosen cases consists in integrating a new action variable modeling the air conditioning in the office. This variable simulates the presence of a hidden variable in the CBR sys-

tem. Values of this variable are sampled from a discrete uniform distribution between 18 °C and 23 °C.
– the effects following the application of the new actions (turn on the air conditioner) to the context of the chosen cases are generated using the physical model of the office. For consistency, the real effects of the other cases are simulated by the physical model too.

Empirical Results. Figure 1 plots the average of the real effect variable (temperature) of the 98 cases (green curve) and the corresponding simulated values (red curve). Note that the simulated effects of cases C_6, C_{19}, C_{25}, C_{59}, and C_{71} are far from their original ones. The significant discrepancy between the original values and the simulated ones is due to the influence of the hidden variable (modeling air conditioning) on the effects of these cases, i.e., these cases correspond to the five randomly chosen and modified cases. Note also that the two curves overlap almost all along the plot. The Mean Absolute Percentage Error (MAPE) analysis, excluding the modified cases, indicates that the variation of the simulated data from the real data is less than 2.50%, showing the robustness of the physical model used in the simulation of the effect variables.

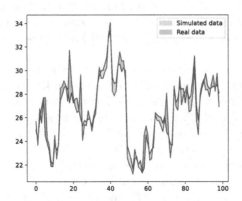

Fig. 1. Real and simulated effect.

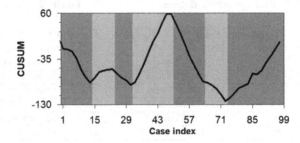

Fig. 2. Change point detection

The results of the first step of the C2CBR algorithm, which consists in detecting changes in the model of effects (temperature), are depicted in Figs. 2 and 3. In Fig. 2 plotting the cumulative sums of the effect variable, each color change in the background corresponds to an abrupt change in the direction of the chart indicating the occurrence of a pattern change, i.e., each swap between the yellow and turquoise colors models a change point. It emerges that there are 6 permutations of background colors, which correspond to 6 change points.

The 6 identified change points serve to split the case base into 7 disjointed groups according to the chronological recording of case effects, as presented in Fig. 3. Each change point is displayed by a shift in the turquoise-colored background and corresponds to a case index in the case base. A turquoise-shaded segment depicts a group containing all cases based on the current effect variable model formed by two successive change points. Each row of Table 1 provides detailed information on each change point. The index of the change case from which a model change is detected is assigned a confidence interval estimated at a 95% probability of being accurate. For instance, with a probability of 95%, the 6th change point is estimated to be between cases 75 and 77. Furthermore, using Formula 3, a confidence index in each detected change point is reported to qualify the quality of the analysis. For instance, the system is 99% confident that the 6th change point took place. Further information is also provided as averages of the groups' effect variables before and after a change point. Table 2 gives the values of the S^{CA} and S^E metrics (defined in Sect. 5.2) for each of the seven groups.

After applying the proposed heuristic, The five incompleteness situations that were artificially generated in the previous step have been correctly identified, as shown in Table 3. Each probable incompleteness situation is described by the two cases $\mathbb{C}_1^I$ and $\mathbb{C}_2^I$ generating this situation. Note that the cases in column $\mathbb{C}_1^I$ of Table 3 correspond to the five modified cases. For instance, the incompleteness situation S5 is observed between the cases $\mathbb{C}_{71}$ and $\mathbb{C}_{79}$ since the distance $D_{CA}(\mathbb{C}_{71}, \mathbb{C}_{79})$ is lower than the distance D_{CA}^{max} of the group $\mathbb{G}_7$ to which the case $\mathbb{C}_{79}$ belongs but the effect variable of the case $\mathbb{C}_{71}$ belongs to the group $\mathbb{G}_6$ knowing that $E^{\mathbb{C}_6} = 24.77 \notin S_6^E \cap S_7^E$ and $E^{\mathbb{C}_7} = 28.43 \notin S_6^E \cap S_7^E$.

Table 1. Change points details.

Index	Confidence interval	Confidence index	From	To	Level
15	(11,15)	96%	24.49	27.814	4
25	(25,25)	94%	27.814	25.725	5
33	(33,37)	99%	25.725	29.733	3
51	(51,51)	100%	29.733	22.745	2
65	(65,67)	98%	22.745	25.305	3
75	(75,77)	99%	25.305	28.355	1

Table 2. Groups' properties.

Group	S^{CA}	S^E
G_1	$[0.138, 0.526]$	$[21.88, 27.25]$
G_2	$[0.199, 0.550]$	$[26.61, 28.70]$
G_3	$[0.156, 0.516]$	$[25.26, 26.14]$
G_4	$[0.166, 0.390]$	$[23.65, 33.42]$
G_5	$[0.188, 0.377]$	$[21.35, 24.54]$
G_6	$[0.155, 0.440]$	$[23.64, 26.42]$
G_7	$[0.126, 0.602]$	$[25.79, 31.23]$

Table 3. Change points details.

Situation	C_1^J	C_2^J	D_{CA}
S1	$C_6 \in G_1$	$C_{85} \in G_7$	0.531
S2	$C_{19} \in G_2$	$C_{39} \in G_4$	0.184
S3	$C_{25} \in G_3$	$C_{18} \in G_2$	0.275
S4	$C_{59} \in G_5$	$C_{69} \in G_6$	0.369
S5	$C_{71} \in G_6$	$C_{79} \in G_7$	0.545

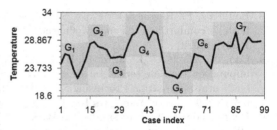

Fig. 3. Change points detection.

7 Conclusion

This study introduces a novel approach, called I2CCBR, which aims to tackle the challenge of data incompleteness in a CBR system based on the open-world assumption. The authors employed a combination of a change point detection technique and a heuristic strategy to detect possible incompleteness in the case base. To the best of the authors' knowledge, this is the first attempt to address this issue. The effectiveness of the proposed approach was evaluated in a real-world experiment, and the results demonstrate its potential for practical implementation with promising outcomes.

The next phase of this study involves expanding the experimental evaluation of the I2CCBR algorithm by testing it on more extensive datasets. This will enable the researchers to verify the findings obtained in the initial study.

References

1. Extracting business value from the 4 v's of big data. techreport, IBM (2016). http://www.ibmbigdatahub.com/infographic/extracting-business-value-4-vs-big-data. Accessed 31 May 2022
2. 2019 Global data management research. Taking control in the digital age. Benchmarkreport, Experian UK&I, February 2019
3. Arisdakessian, C., Poirion, O., Yunits, B., Zhu, X., Garmire, L.X.: DeepImpute: an accurate, fast, and scalable deep neural network method to impute single-cell RNA-seq data. Genome Biol. **20**, 211 (2019)
4. Barker, S.A., Rayner, P.J.W.: Unsupervised image segmentation using Markov random field models. Pattern Recogn. **33**(4), 587–602 (2000)
5. Bergmann, R., Wilke, W., Vollrath, I.: Integrating general knowledge with object-oriented case representation and reasoning. In: 4th German Workshop: Case-Based Reasoning - System Development and Evaluation (1996)
6. Bernal, E.A.: Training deep generative models in highly incomplete data scenarios with prior regularization. In: 2021 IEEE/CVF Conference on Computer Vision and Pattern Recognition Workshops (CVPRW), pp. 2631–2641 (2021)
7. Boulmaiz, F., Ploix, S., Reignier, P.: A data-driven approach for guiding the occupant's actions to achieve better comfort in buildings. In: IEEE 33rd International Conference on Tools with Artificial Intelligence (ICTAI) (2021)

8. Boulmaiz, F., Reignier, P., Ploix, S.: An occupant-centered approach to improve both his comfort and the energy efficiency of the building. Knowl. Based Syst. **249**, 108970 (2022)

9. Cao, W., Wang, D., Li, J., Zhou, H., Li, Y., Li, L.: BRITS: bidirectional recurrent imputation for time series. In: Proceedings of the 32nd International Conference on Neural Information Processing Systems, NIPS 2018, Red Hook, NY, USA, pp. 6776–6786. Curran Associates Inc. (2018)

10. Charakopoulos, A., Karakasidis, T.: Backward degree a new index for online and offline change point detection based on complex network analysis. Phys. A **604**, 127929 (2022)

11. Cichy, C., Rass, S.: An overview of data quality frameworks. IEEE Access **7**, 24634–24648 (2019)

12. Galárraga, L., Razniewski, S., Amarilli, A., Suchanek, F.M.: Predicting completeness in knowledge bases. In: Proceedings of the Tenth ACM International Conference on Web Search and Data Mining. ACM, February 2017

13. Getahun, Y.S., Li, M.-H., Pun, I.-F.: Trend and change-point detection analyses of rainfall and temperature over the Awash river basin of Ethiopia. Heliyon **7**(9), e08024 (2021)

14. Grohe, M., Lindner, P.: Probabilistic databases with an infinite open-world assumption. In: Proceedings of the 38th ACM SIGMOD-SIGACT-SIGAI Symposium on Principles of Database Systems, PODS 2019. ACM Press (2019)

15. Haug, A.: Understanding the differences across data quality classifications: a literature review and guidelines for future research. Ind. Manage. Data Syst. **121**(12), 2651–2671 (2021)

16. Hinkley, D.V., Schechtman, E.: Conditional bootstrap methods in the mean-shift model. Biometrika **74**, 85–93 (1987)

17. Khot, T., Balasubramanian, N., Gribkoff, E., Sabharwal, A., Clark, P., Etzioni, O.: Exploring Markov Logic Networks for question answering. In: Proceedings of the 2015 Conference on Empirical Methods in Natural Language Processing, September 2015, Lisbon, Portugal, pp. 685–694. Association for Computational Linguistics (2015)

18. Liaw, S.-T., Rahimi, A., Ray, P., Taggart, J.: Towards an ontology for data quality in integrated chronic disease management: a realist review of the literature. Int. J. Med. Inform. **82**, 10–24 (2013)

19. Manhaeve, R., Dumančić, S., Kimmig, A., Demeester, T., De Raedt, L.: Neural probabilistic logic programming in DeepProbLog. Artif. Intell. **298**, 103504 (2021)

20. Margolin, A., et al.: ARACNE: an algorithm for the reconstruction of gene regulatory networks in a mammalian cellular context. BMC Bioinform. **7**(Suppl. 1), S7 (2006)

21. Nguyen, P.T., Di Rocco, J., Iovino, L., Di Ruscio, D., Pierantonio, A.: Evaluation of a machine learning classifier for metamodels. Softw. Syst. Model. **20**(6), 1797–1821 (2021)

22. Pettitt, A.N.: A simple cumulative sum type statistic for the change-point problem with zero-one observations. Biometrika **67**(1), 79–84 (1980)

23. Phung, S., Kumar, A., Kim, J.: A deep learning technique for imputing missing healthcare data. In: 2019 41st Annual International Conference of the IEEE Engineering in Medicine and Biology Society (EMBC) (2019)

24. Reiter, R.: A theory of diagnosis from first principles. Artif. Intell. **32**(1), 57–95 (1987)

25. Richter, M.M.: The knowledge contained in similarity measures. In: International Conference on Case-Based Reasoning, ICCBR 1995, Sesimbra, Portugal (1995)

26. Sessions, V., Valtorta, M.: The effects of data quality on machine learning algorithms. In: Talburt, J.R., Pierce, E.M., Wu, N., Campbell, T. (eds.) Proceedings of the 11th International Conference on Information Quality, MIT, Cambridge, MA, USA, 10–12 November 2006. MIT (2006)

27. Truong, C., Oudre, L., Vayatis, N.: Selective review of offline change point detection methods. Signal Process. **167**, 107299 (2020)

28. Wang, R.Y., Strong, D.: Beyond accuracy: what data quality means to data consumers. J. Manage. Inf. Syst. **12**(4), 5–33 (1996)

29. Wang, W., et al.: Learning from incomplete labeled data via adversarial data generation. In: 2020 IEEE International Conference on Data Mining (ICDM) (2020)

30. Wilcox, C., Djahel, S., Giagos, V.: Identifying the main causes of medical data incompleteness in the smart healthcare era. In: 2021 International Symposium on Networks, Computers and Communications (ISNCC) (2021)

31. You, S.-H., et al.: Change point analysis for detecting vaccine safety signals. Vaccines **9**(3), 206 (2021)

Sentiment Analysis of Tweets on Online Education during COVID-19

Elif Yıldırım[1]([✉]) [iD], Harun Yazgan[1], Onur Özbek[2], Ahmet Can Günay[2],
Büşra Kocaçınar[1] [iD], Öznur Şengel[1] [iD], and Fatma Patlar Akbulut[3] [iD]

[1] Department of Computer Engineering, Istanbul Kültür University, Istanbul, Turkey
{elif.yildirim,b.kocacinar,o.sengel}@iku.edu.tr
[2] Department of Electrical-Electronic Engineering, Istanbul Kültür University,
Istanbul, Turkey
[3] Department of Software Engineering, Istanbul Kültür University, Istanbul, Turkey
f.patlar@iku.edu.tr

Abstract. The global coronavirus disease (COVID-19) pandemic has
devastated public health, education, and the economy worldwide. As
of December 2022, more than 524 million individuals have been diagnosed with the new coronavirus, and nearly 6 million people have per-
ished as a result of this deadly sickness, according to the World Health
Organization. Universities, colleges, and schools are closed to prevent
the coronavirus from spreading. Therefore, distance learning became a
required method of advancing the educational system in contemporary
society. Adjusting to the new educational system was challenging for
both students and instructors, which resulted in a variety of complica-
tions. People began to spend more time at home; thus, social media usage
rose globally throughout the epidemic. On social media channels such
as Twitter, people discussed online schooling. Some individuals viewed
online schooling as superior, while others viewed it as a failure. This
study analyzes the attitudes of individuals toward distance education
during the pandemic. Sentiment analysis was performed using natural
language processing (NLP) and deep learning methods. Recurrent neural network (RNN) and one-dimensional convolutional neural network
(1DCNN)-based network models were used during the experiments to
classify neutral, positive, and negative contents.

Keywords: Deep Learning · Sentiment Analysis · Social Media ·
COVID-19 · Distance Education

1 Introduction

The COVID-19 disease, which started to spread over the globe in late February
2019, plunged the entire planet into a pandemic. Globally, It had an impact
on every subject of human life, including science, sports, entertainment, transportation, social interactions, politics, and commercial operations. The reality of

This research is supported by Istanbul Kultur University under ULEP-2022-2023.

I. Maglogiannis et al. (Eds.): AIAI 2023, IFIP AICT 675, pp. 240–251, 2023.
https://doi.org/10.1007/978-3-031-34111-3_21

the situation is difficult to bear as a result of threats, and the education sector continues to be one of the worst affected by the coronavirus pandemic. No country or race on the globe is currently immune to the coronavirus pandemic, and COVID-19's rapid expansion and catastrophic effects seem to be overwhelming the whole planet. As the COVID-19 threat increased, it became harder to manage this situation, especially in areas in which the disease can spread quickly, for example, schools. After only a few months since the sickness first appeared, it has already significantly altered everyone's way of life, forcing billions of people to "remain at home," "observe self-isolation," and conduct work and school from their homes. It has restricted people's freedom to move around, work, and socialize.

Numerous lessons about pandemics' sociological, ethical, scientific, and medical aspects can be learned from history. The current pandemic is taking place against a backdrop of increased skepticism toward science, which is occasionally purposefully fostered for political purposes. There has never been a greater need to teach the public and future scientists how to think critically, base their arguments on evidence, and be active and socially responsible citizens. Global education systems urgently need to adopt curriculum, instruction, and assessment strategies to enable students to develop scientific habits of thought. The quality of online learning settings is under intense pressure because of the present health crisis. When students are unable to appear in person for exams, high-stakes assessment systems confront major accountability issues in getting accurate measures of learning outcomes. Over 1.5 billion students, or 87% of all students worldwide, have been impacted by the COVID-19 pandemic-related school closures, according to UNESCO [11]. Global health systems have found it extremely challenging to handle the educational disruptions and global health issues brought on by the COVID-19 pandemic.

Another issue is that COVID-19 increases social inequality in classrooms. Parents with greater financial resources send their children to schools with superior digital infrastructure and teachers who may be more efficient in using advanced technology. Some schools may be well-stocked with digital resources and teaching aids. Students from disadvantaged backgrounds attend institutions with inadequate ICT infrastructure and instructional resources. More privileged students are enrolling in schools and using online learning as a result of COVID-19. Institutions in underprivileged rural locations lack the necessary infrastructure to deliver instruction remotely. In terms of technology and instructional resources, private and public schools differ significantly from one another. According to the Tadesse et al. survey [18], students experience high levels of stress, anxiety, and depression disorders while schools are closed.

The COVID-19 pandemic may endure for a considerable amount of time, and its effects on modern science and society are likely to be felt for a significant period of time. Thus, the papers focus on understanding how society has been perceiving online education during the COVID-19 outbreak period by analyzing tweets. This paper presents a sentimental analysis of Twitter comments based on sequential models to find out what people think about online education during the COVID-19 pandemic.

2   Related Work

Today, social media, in which individuals express their emotions and thoughts through information technology while getting information about the emotions and thoughts of others, creates a robust network of information, communication, and engagement. People have made social media the primary source of information by expressing their emotions and thoughts to the public via their social media accounts. On the basis of this circumstance, it can be stated that social media has vast data [12, 13, 15].

The rapid growth of information sharing and access in social media networks has spawned the concept of transforming information into informatics in this industry. In this context, the concept of sentiment analysis or opinion mining is on its way to becoming the bright star of the growing information industry with technological developments [2]. Sentiment analysis continues to be developed by identifying problems in the studies carried out [17]. In their works, Fang and Zhan [6] attempted to assist by investigating the issue of categorizing emotion polarity and contributing to various stages of emotion analysis. They provided a new technique for identifying negative statements and a method for generating feature vectors for polarity classification in sentiment analysis.

This epidemic process has been the subject of an extensive investigation involving both coronavirus and artificial intelligence technology. Among these works, research focusing on sentiment analysis of COVID-19 using social media data stands out [1,3] (Fig. 1). This is because individuals, corporations, and governments are communicating through social media about the COVID-19 outbreak. Following the increase of dread linked with the rapid spread of COVID-19 infections, Samuel et al. [16] offered a systematic method for analyzing Twitter data in order to determine public mood. According to the findings of this study, the Naive Bayes approach delivers roughly 91% accuracy for short tweets, whereas the logistic regression method provides approximately 74% accuracy for shorter tweets. In another study [8], researchers aimed to undertake a novel NLP study based on an LSTM model to find important hidden themes and classify emotion-related comments in COVID-19-related topics. Their LSTM model performed better than well-known machine learning techniques, with an accuracy of 81.15 percent.

One of the high-performing methods in recent years develop for processing natural language, Bidirectional Encoder Representations from Transformers (BERT) has started to garner attention alongside all the other innovations. BERT is a deep learning method for NLP that helps artificial intelligence programs understand the context of ambiguous words in a text. In a study conducted on the tweets of Indian citizens [4], the BERT model outperformed the more established logistic regression (LR), support vector machine (SVM), and LSTM models with an accuracy of 89%. Based on their analysis of 3090 tweets, they found that the BERT model performed the best, while the LR and SVM models both obtained roughly 75% accuracy, and the LSTM model performed at only 65% accuracy.

Fig. 1. Word cloud showing some words of the subject

3 Sentiment Analysis

Increased internet usage and technological advancements have led to an expansion in the amount of information. People use social media even more during pandemic restrictions, such as staying at home. The increasing popularity of social media has created new academic topics. Clustering [5,9,14], automatic text summarization [7,20], and sentiment analysis are only a few of the study subjects generated by this data deluge. When seen from this angle, it is simple to observe people's comments, likes and dislikes, desires, concerns, health and financial issues, and many other features when perusing social media posts on popular platforms such as Twitter, Facebook, or Instagram. These kinds of approaches establish the foundation for sentiment analysis or idea mining [10]. The process of automatically extracting subjective information from a text is called sentiment analysis. Using sentiment analysis, we may detect whether a text's subjective orientation is positive or negative. Sentiment analysis in social media posts is one of the most essential approaches [19]. However, with the explosion of user-generated material on the Internet, particularly in recent years, it has become a universe unto itself. The way individuals share their ideas and beliefs has also altered as a result of this atmosphere. Individuals may now submit their thoughts about a product they purchased on their website, as well as in internet forums, discussion groups, blogs, and social media about nearly anything. Long forum messages and blogs are frequently a source of inspiration. As a result, finding relevant sources, extracting phrases about concepts, reading, summarizing, and organizing them into usable formats is tough [19]. As a result, systems that automatically find and summarize opinions are required. While the fundamental foundations of emotion analysis are created by processing this information, removing subjectivity, and classifying emotion, this also involves problems owing to its structure.

4   Proposed Sentiment Model

The task initially consisted of collecting tweets that were in some way relevant to the subject of distance education. We gathered the tweets dataset using Twint[1]. We utilized the search terms "covid and education" to narrow the output. During the data collecting procedure, numerous irrelevant details such as id, username, location, date, geo, and mentions were also gathered. Such information as that depicted in Fig. 2 is undesirable since it consumes memory and processing time.

Fig. 2. Data reduction with eliminating unnecessary features

Since preprocessing was the initial step in the NLP model-building procedure, during the early round of data collection, we realized cleaning and arranging the raw data. Data preparation is an essential step since it influences the performance of the chosen model, and the results depend on how well the data has been preprocessed. In the final phase, we completed the data processing portion by tokenizing the data. The details of all stages are explained hereafter.

4.1   Preprocessing

The removal of punctuation marks and stopwords, which is used to divide the text into sentences, paragraphs, and phrases, affects the results of any text processing technique, particularly those that rely on word and phrase occurrence

---

[1] Twint - Twitter intelligence tool, 2022.

frequencies, as punctuation marks are often employed in the text. Stop words are a collection of commonly used words without further contexts, such as articles, determiners, and prepositions. Some of the terms frequently used in texts that need to be removed are "a," "an," "the," etc. These terms have no actual meaning because they don't help distinguish between the contexts. By removing these commonly used words from the text, we have been able to focus on the relevant concepts. Case sensitivity is another point of text data to keep in mind. Although "Book" and "book" have the same meaning, they are represented as separate words in the vector space model if they are not converted to lowercase. It also results in the production of additional dimensions. As a result, it has an effect on our processing speed and the accuracy of our deep learning models. Therefore, we converted every letter into lowercase. Tokenization, or dividing a sentence into words, is a fundamental step in NLP. This is a crucial stage since the text's meaning may be deduced from an examination of the words in the text. Tokenization is the process of separating source text into distinct tokens for examination. Tokens are fragments of the original text that have not been reduced to their simplest form. Figure 3 depicts a sample tweet following the application of preprocessing processes.

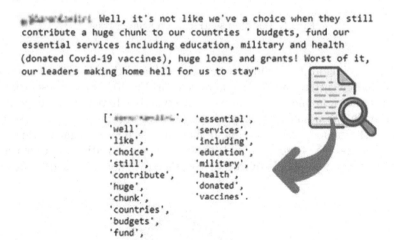

Fig. 3. Sample before and after applying preprocessing steps

4.2   Sentiment Labelling

The polarity[2] is a decimal value ranging from -1 to 1 that measures the intensity of the text's emotion. We generated a polarity value for the collected records

---

[2] Sentiment analysis with textblob and vader.

by TextBlob. In order to determine the polarity (positive or negative) and subjectivity of a given piece of text, it employs a pre-trained Naive Bayes classifier. Positive emotions with polarity values between 0 and 1 are represented by the number 1, whilst negative emotions with polarity values between −1 and 0 are represented by the number −1. A tweet with a polarity rating of 0 is neutral and contains no subjective information. Labeled samples are shown in Fig. 4.

	0	text	polarity	subjectivity	sentiment
0	Well, it's not like we've a choi...	well its not like weve a choice when they sti...	-0.060000	0.640000	negative
1	The fact that u have to defend your...	the fact that u have to defend yourself speak...	0.050000	0.550000	negative
2	Ok, I own 0 guns, a...	ok i own 0 guns and im somewhat proud of tha...	0.633333	0.833333	negative
3	The pro death ...	the pro death cult pro covidpro rape party a...	0.200000	0.550000	negative
4	Covid related lockdowns in 2020 added to our w...	covid related lockdowns in 2020 added to our w...	0.234470	0.609091	positive
5	Antivax idiots now think monkey pox is really ...	antivax idiots now think monkey pox is really ...	-0.128571	0.317857	negative
6	We appeared on the second draft of our Educati...	we appeared on the second draft of our educati...	0.000000	0.000000	positive
7	It came sharply into focus when not ONE of the...	it came sharply into focus when not one of the...	-0.231250	0.737500	negative
8	Congratulations to Dr. MaryKate Conboy for rec...	congratulations to dr marykate conboy for rece...	0.250000	0.450000	positive
9	Today marks the one-year anniversary of the CO...	today marks the oneyear anniversary of the cov...	-0.405000	0.715000	negative

Fig. 4. Textblob sentiment on sample tweet

After labeling all tweets in the dataset, we found that 42.86% were positive, 46.72% were negative, and 10.42% were neutral (Fig. 5). This suggests that individuals are not immune to the pandemic lifestyle they have recently experienced. Even though the number of people with positive and negative views seems to be about the same, it has been found that there are more negative views. This means that distance education, which was the main education strategy the government imposed on people during the pandemic, is not well-liked by people.

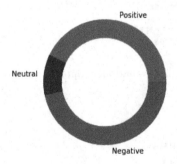

Fig. 5. Sentiment model class distribution

4.3 Deep Model

After labeling the data with the unsupervised approach, we evaluated deep learning models to predict the target variable. Then, we developed and trained an algorithm to categorize the emotions of tweets. Using a sequential network, we deployed RNN and 1D-CNN models. We utilized Python version 3.9 and TensorFlow API Core version 2.7 with Keras to generate models[3]. The proposed architecture has been subjected to a categorization of positive, negative, and natural sentiments stated by Twitter users. In the established model, first we incorporated words from tweets into the model's embedding layer. During the training phase, the word embedding layer contained 284,700 parameters for mapping a sequence of word indices (xn) to embedding vectors ($varepsilon$) and learning the word embedding. The subsequent layers comprise simple RNN units with shapes of 97×256 and parameters of 78,592. The last layer consists of three classes arranged in a dense layer. In the final stage, we configured the model using the Softmax activation function and SGD optimizer. The architecture of the proposed RNN-based model is given in detail in Fig. 6.

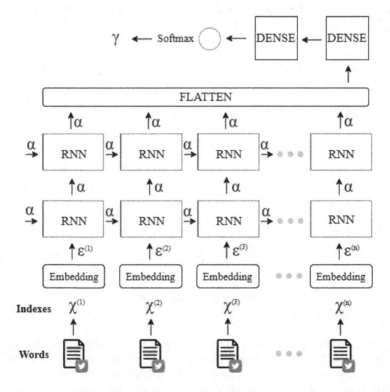

Fig. 6. RNN Model's Architecture used for Twitter sentiment analysis

---

[3] Francois Chollet et al. Keras, 2015.

The 1D-CNN architecture has been designed as a second model that contains eight 1D convolutional layers in total. Each of the two consecutive convolutional layers uses the same number of units. For each pair of convolutional layers, 64, 128, and 512 units, respectively, were used. The maximum pooling layer has been applied after each of the two convolutional layers. Following the last layer of maximum pooling, a 256-unit dense layer was applied. The last layer has a dense layer with three classes that employ the softmax activation function.

5 Experimental Results

Because the primary objective of this study is to develop deep learning models that are capable of analyzing the emotions that individuals have regarding education obtained through distance learning, we have developed a variety of models and built them with accuracy and loss metrics. These two algorithms, one-dimensional Convolutional Neural Networks (1D-CNN) and Recurrent Neural Networks (RNN), produced the best results for us out of all the ones we tested. To evaluate the proposed models' performance, we trained them with 30 epochs. Figures 7 and 8 depict the accuracy and loss scores of the proposed RNN and 1D-CNN models, respectively.

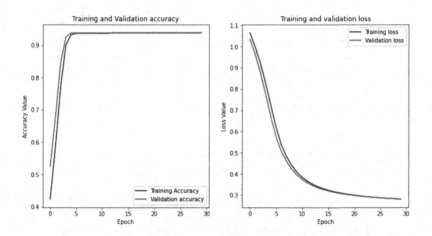

Fig. 7. Performance results of RNN model

Table 1 provides an overview of the results of the proposed models' respective performances. The Table reveals that the validation accuracies for the RNN model are 93%, while those for the 1D-CNN model are 92%.

Performances of the two models are similar to each other as it is seen from Table 1. When compared to the performance of proposed models, RNN's training and validation set accuracy values are closer together, indicating that it learned from the training set well and could perform similarly in the validation set.

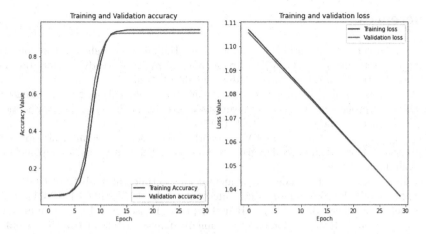

Fig. 8. Performance results of 1D-CNN model

Table 1. Performance metrics of the proposed deep sentiment models

Model	Training Accuracy	Validation Accuracy	F1 Score
1D-CNN	0.9420	0.9243	0.9420
RNN	0.9387	0.9379	0.9386

6   Conclusion

It will likely take some time to comprehend the true impact of the COVID-19 epidemic. Clearly, it is not difficult to foresee that our lives, altered by the pandemic, will never be the same again. Changes in fundamental areas such as health and education had a profound impact on everyone's lives. In order to comprehend the emotional returns and reflections in the sphere of education, we have developed this study. We evaluated people's tweets to comprehend the implications of shifting education to online platforms and continuing it at home rather than in institutions as a result of COVID-19 and to determine how it impacted daily life. We presented sentiment analysis methodologies for modeling emotions based on Twitter data. Using sophisticated models, we determined the proportions of positive, negative, and neutral posts. In the experiments, the RNN model had the highest performance and accuracy (93.79%). As a consequence of our investigation, we discovered that although the dataset we collected was rather small, there was no apparent consensus among individuals; nonetheless, we did identify the presence of students who viewed the effects of the adjustments as nearly equally favorable and unfavorable.

References

1. Abd-Alrazaq, A., Alhuwail, D., Househ, M., Hamdi, M., Shah, Z.: Top concerns of Tweeters during the COVID-19 pandemic: infoveillance study. J. Med. Internet Res. **22**(4), 19016 (2020). https://doi.org/10.2196/19016
2. Ayaz, T.B., et al.: Global impact of the pandemic on education: a study of natural language processing. In: 2022 Innovations in Intelligent Systems and Applications Conference (ASYU), pp. 1–4. IEEE (2022)
3. Bilen, B., Horasan, F.: LSTM network based sentiment analysis for customer reviews. Politeknik Dergisi **25**, 959–966 (2021). https://doi.org/10.2339/politeknik.844019
4. Chintalapudi, N., Battineni, G., Amenta, F.: Sentimental analysis of COVID-19 tweets using deep learning models. Infect. Dis. Rep. **13**(2), 329–339 (2021)
5. Coletta, L.F.S., da Silva, N.F.F., Hruschka, E.R., Hruschka, E.R.: Combining classification and clustering for tweet sentiment analysis. In: 2014 Brazilian Conference on Intelligent Systems, pp. 210–215 (2014). https://doi.org/10.1109/BRACIS.2014.46
6. Fang, X., Zhan, J.: Sentiment analysis using product review data. J. Big Data **2**(1) (2015). https://doi.org/10.1186/s40537-015-0015-2
7. Gupta, P., Tiwari, R., Robert, N.: Sentiment analysis and text summarization of online reviews: a survey. In: 2016 International Conference on Communication and Signal Processing (ICCSP), pp. 0241–0245 (2016). https://doi.org/10.1109/ICCSP.2016.7754131
8. Jelodar, H., Wang, Y., Orji, R., Huang, S.: Deep sentiment classification and topic discovery on novel coronavirus or COVID-19 online discussions: NLP using LSTM recurrent neural network approach. IEEE J. Biomed. Health Inform. **24**(10), 2733–2742 (2020). https://doi.org/10.1109/JBHI.2020.3001216
9. Li, G., Liu, F.: A clustering-based approach on sentiment analysis. In: 2010 IEEE International Conference on Intelligent Systems and Knowledge Engineering, pp. 331–337 (2010). https://doi.org/10.1109/ISKE.2010.5680859
10. Liu, B.: Sentiment analysis and subjectivity. In: Handbook of Natural Language Processing (2010)
11. World Health Organization: Coronavirus disease 2019 (COVID-19): situation report, 73 (2020)
12. Porreca, A., Scozzari, F., Di Nicola, M.: Using text mining and sentiment analysis to analyse Youtube Italian videos concerning vaccination. BMC Pub. Health **20**(1), 1–9 (2020)
13. Raghupathi, V., Ren, J., Raghupathi, W.: Studying public perception about vaccination: a sentiment analysis of tweets. Int. J. Environ. Res. Public Health **17**(10), 3464 (2020)
14. Rehioui, H., Idrissi, A.: New clustering algorithms for Twitter sentiment analysis. IEEE Syst. J. **14**(1), 530–537 (2020). https://doi.org/10.1109/JSYST.2019.2912759
15. Sadigov, R., Yıldırım, E., Kocaçınar, B., Patlar Akbulut, F., Catal, C.: Deep learning-based user experience evaluation in distance learning. Cluster Comput., 1–13 (2023)
16. Samuel, J., Ali, G.G.M.N., Rahman, M.M., Esawi, E., Samuel, Y.: COVID-19 public sentiment insights and machine learning for Tweets classification. Information **11**(6) (2020). https://doi.org/10.3390/info11060314. www.mdpi.com/2078-2489/11/6/314

17. Sosun, S.D., et al.: Deep sentiment analysis with data augmentation in distance education during the pandemic. In: 2022 Innovations in Intelligent Systems and Applications Conference (ASYU), pp. 1–5. IEEE (2022)

18. Tadesse, A.W., Mihret, S., Biset, G., Muluneh, A.: Psychological impacts of COVID-19 among college students in Dessie town, Amhara region, Ethiopia; cross-sectional study (2020)

19. Xiao, Y., Yin, Y.: Hybrid LSTM neural network for short-term traffic flow prediction. Information **10**, 105 (2019). https://doi.org/10.3390/info10030105

20. Yadav, N., Chatterjee, N.: Text summarization using sentiment analysis for DUC data. In: 2016 International Conference on Information Technology (ICIT), pp. 229–234 (2016). https://doi.org/10.1109/ICIT.2016.054

Biomedical - Image Analysis

Image Classification Using Class-Agnostic Object Detection

Geoffrey Holmes[(✉)] , Eibe Frank , and Dale Fletcher

University of Waikato, Hamilton, New Zealand
{geoff,eibe,dale}@waikato.ac.nz

Abstract. Human-in-the-loop interfaces for machine learning provide a promising way to reduce the annotation effort required to obtain an accurate machine learning model, particularly when it is used with transfer learning to exploit existing knowledge gleaned from another domain. This paper explores the use of a human-in-the-loop strategy that is designed to build a deep-learning image classification model iteratively using successive batches of images that the user labels. Specifically, we examine whether class-agnostic object detection can improve performance by providing a focus area for image classification in the form of a bounding box. The goal is to reduce the amount of effort required to label a batch of images by presenting the user with the current predictions of the model on a new batch of data and only requiring correction of those predictions. User effort is measured in terms of the number of corrections made. Results show that the use of bounding boxes always leads to fewer corrections. The benefit of a bounding box is that it also provides feedback to the user because it indicates whether or not the classification of the deep learning model is based on the appropriate part of the image. This has implications for the design of user interfaces in this application scenario.

Keywords: Human-in-the-loop Machine Learning · Convolutional Neural Networks · Image Classification · Object Detection

1 Introduction

Image classification using deep convolutional networks is one of the most prominent practical applications of machine learning. The learning algorithms for these networks require labelled images as training data. Often, obtaining these labels requires access to sophisticated domain expertise (e.g., in the medical domain), which can be costly. Thus, it is important to provide mechanisms to obtain correct labels for images in the most efficient manner possible.

It is important to note that this applies even when the total amount of labelled data required can be reduced by applying transfer learning so that the

---

This work is part of a user-friendly deep learning project funded by the New Zealand Ministry for Business, Innovation and Employment.

I. Maglogiannis et al. (Eds.): AIAI 2023, IFIP AICT 675, pp. 255–266, 2023.
https://doi.org/10.1007/978-3-031-34111-3_22

learning of a neural network does not have to start with random parameter settings. For example, a standard strategy for transfer learning in convolutional neural networks is to take a network that has been pre-trained on a large collection of images, such as the well-known ImageNet database consisting of more than a million images, each furnished with one of 1,000 class labels, and fine-tune the parameters of this network on the labelled target domain data that is available once the classification "head" of the network has been replaced to feature as many classes as are present in the target domain. Even though this standard form of transfer learning can dramatically decrease the amount of labelled data required to achieve a satisfactory level of accuracy, there generally remains a substantial amount of labelling effort that must be applied to obtain a sufficient amount of labelled data for the target domain. Hence, even if transfer learning is applied—and we do apply it in this paper—a procedure for efficiently generating correct labels for this data is very useful.

A central idea in this context is to apply a form of human-in-the-loop machine learning, where the expert provides a small initial set of labelled examples for training a classifier, which is subsequently applied to *pre*-label batches of unlabeled data before they are passed for inspection to the expert, who then simply needs to *correct* the provided labels rather than determining labels from scratch for unlabeled images. Crucially, a proxy for the human effort required in this process is the number of *corrections* that the expert must perform, not the total number of examples to be labelled.

Earlier work [5] has investigated how best to order the batches of unlabeled data to minimise the number of corrections that need to be performed to train the image classifier to a satisfactory level. A key outcome of this work is that so-called "active" learning strategies [10] (e.g., uncertainty sampling) are inappropriate when the desired outcome is to minimise this measure of required effort: random example ordering generally yields a lower number of required corrections regardless of the image classification dataset and neural network architecture applied. Another strategy that performed well in [5] is to select a representative sample of unlabeled data *a priori* (i.e., before labelling/learning starts) using an algorithm called kernel herding [2], which attempts to improve on random sampling by ensuring good coverage of the full population. Intuitively, the poor performance of active learning can be understood by considering that it is based on selecting those examples for labelling that "surprise" the classifier the most (e.g., by considering its predictive uncertainty). These are clearly often examples where the predicted label is incorrect and must therefore be corrected by the human involved.

In this paper, building on these findings, we investigate whether the labelling effort can be further reduced by enabling the expert to provide additional information to speed up machine learning in the human-in-the-loop system. More specifically, we consider whether the use of a bounding box that the expert draws around the part of the image that is deemed responsible for its class label can help to reduce the number of corrections that this expert must perform during the learning process—focusing again on the number of times that a predicted class label must be corrected in the human-in-the-loop process, *not* the total number of class labels required. Two strategies of supplying bounding boxes are applied in conjunction with the two *a priori* sampling methods from the previous study—random sampling and kernel herding—to determine whether the use of this additional information can assist in the overall goal of reducing the number of corrections a user has to make. With both strategies, a standard object detection model is trained in a class-agnostic manner based on the bounding boxes provided by the expert. The expert-provided or, when available, a predicted bounding box is used to extract the part of the image that is passed to the image classification model to enable the association with a class label. This is compared to the set-up from [5], where the entire image is associated with a label.

2   Related Work

There is a vast amount of literature on human-in-the-loop object detection that looks at how interactive machine learning can reduce the number of annotations such as bounding boxes that the human must provide to enable learning of an accurate object detection model. Some of this work is surveyed in [11]. It is important to note that this is not the problem that is the focus of this paper. Instead, we apply object detection as a tool to improve the efficiency of human-in-the-loop learning for image classification.

Our use of an object detection method can be viewed as a form of class-agnostic object detection, a concept that has been introduced fairly recently in the literature in [7]. According to [7], in class-agnostic object detection, "the goal is to predict bounding boxes for all objects in an image but not their object-classes". We focus on the special case where a single object is present in the image and the detector provides a single bounding box for this object. This bounding box is subsequently used to crop the image before it is passed to the learning algorithm for the image classification model.

Related to our work are approaches that attempt to use auxiliary information to improve the accuracy of image classification. [8] consider the use of bounding boxes as auxiliary information and provide a learning algorithm and neural network architecture that can exploit this information, looking primarily at whether this improves the quality of the explanations of predictions given in the form of saliency maps because accurate explanations are important for establishing trust.

Interestingly, [6] finds that enabling users to provide feedback to a simulated object detection system by providing the ability to correct bounding boxes based on the human-in-the-loop process *lowers* their trust in the machine learning system, regardless of whether the accuracy of object detection improves or not. Considering the potential use of object detection in safety-critical applications, this quite plausibly more realistic assessment of the algorithms' ability may be appropriate.

Fig. 1. Ground truth bounding boxes (Color figure online)

We are unaware of any work in the literature that investigates the use of class-agnostic object detection to improve the efficiency of human-in-the-loop machine learning for image classification.

3   Set-up for the Experiments

For each of the image classification datasets considered in our experiments, we start with a pre-trained image classification model that has been trained on ImageNet. Subsequently, data is provided to the learning algorithms in batches. Assuming the base case considered in [5], where no object detection is performed, only labels need to be provided for the images in a batch. For the first batch, the human in the loop is required to label all the images in this batch. Subsequently, the pre-trained image classification model is fine-tuned on this batch (details are given below) and applied to pre-label the images in the next batch, which the user must then (potentially) correct. Once the labels have been finalized, the pre-trained model is fine-tuned on the extended dataset, comprising both the first and the second batch of data, before the third batch of data is processed in the same manner. This is repeated until a sufficient level of accuracy is achieved or the data is exhausted. We examine two approaches to ordering training images into batches: random selection and kernel herding (both are described in [5]). Both approaches can be applied before the loop starts because they do not require knowledge of any class labels.

This base case approach to human-in-the-loop learning for image classification does not apply object detection and does not use bounding boxes. We introduce bounding boxes into the process and investigate whether this improves efficiency.

Figure 1 shows some ground-truth bounding boxes for the datasets used in the experiments. These bounding boxes must also be generated by using the human in the loop. However, once at least some of the training data has been furnished with bounding boxes, one can train a standard object detection model on these boxes. In this paper, we build a model of the bounding boxes from the training data for each dataset using Faster RCNN [9] by applying a ResNet101 base network. This was chosen simply because it is popular and effective. The model is trained in a class-agnostic manner: it is simply configured to detect "the object" in the image, regardless of the class of the object. As the model can output multiple bounding boxes for an image, we simply pick the one for which the model exhibits the greatest confidence.

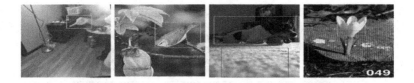

Fig. 2. Model misunderstandings (Color figure online)

Once trained, the model can be used to predict bounding boxes for new images. It is important to note that this can happen as soon as the first batch of data has been annotated with boxes (and class labels) in the human-in-the-loop process, and the object detection model has been trained on this batch. Thus, in the second and subsequent batches, we can use the object detection model to predict bounding boxes, which the user may or may not correct—we investigate both approaches in the experiments.

In many cases, bounding boxes can explain why classification fails. For illustration, Fig. 2 shows predicted bounding boxes, in blue, for images where the ground truth is also shown in yellow. It should be noted that each of these images involves the correct classification of the class label by the corresponding image classification model. However, given the blue bounding boxes, the reason for the classification is erroneous. The object detection model predicts, for the leftmost image, a dark area of a small chest of drawers instead of the hand. The next image to the right is easier to understand, as the bird does share a lot with the fruit in the predicted bounding box. The confusion in the dog image, between the carpet and the dog, may well be due to the similarity of the white part of the dog and the carpet. For the final image, there is some overlap between the flower and the predicted area, which does at least contain the stem and some of the petals of the flower.

The last image illustrates why a measure of overlap between predicted and ground-truth bounding boxes is used to evaluate object detectors. The intersection over union (IoU) provides such a measure, and Fig. 3 shows the relationship between two boxes based on this measure as the degree of overlap moves from 0.0 (no overlap in the top left image) to 1.0 (fully overlapped in the bottom right). Object detection methods are commonly evaluated using this measure by considering IoU values above a certain threshold (e.g., 0.5) as a match. FasterRCNN with a ResNet101 backbone is known to yield high performance according to this metric (see, e.g., [1]) and this is why it is used in our experiments.

The predicted bounding boxes for the second and subsequent batches of data can be used to crop the images so that they can be fed to the image classifier. In line with the above discussion, our experiments in this paper involve two update strategies for the object detection model. One method simulates the user correcting the bounding boxes every iteration (referred to as BB) and the other simulates the user only providing correct bounding boxes for the first batch of data (referred to as BB-1). The latter strategy aims to determine the effectiveness of a minimalist approach, where the user only needs to correct the bounding

Fig. 3. Intersection over Union in increments 0.0, 0.2, 0.4 on the top row from left to right, and 0.6, 0.8, 1.0 on the bottom row from left to right

boxes available for the very first batch of data, and the object detection model remains fixed afterwards throughout the human-in-the-loop process.

Whether corrected or uncorrected bounding boxes are used, the bounding box generated for an image is used to crop the image before it is passed to the image classifier to obtain a label. The image classification model—we evaluate pre-trained MobileNet, ResNet50, and ResNet152 models—is fine-tuned on the cropped training dataset, and evaluated against the cropped test and validation datasets. For the test and validation datasets, the cropping is based on the predicted bounding boxes produced by the current state of the bounding box prediction model: corrected boxes are obviously not available when the trained image classification system—incorporating both the object detection model and the image classifier—is deployed in practice, and thus measures of predictive performance must be based on predicted bounding boxes only.

3.1   Dataset Descriptions

We conducted experiments using the four publicly available datasets listed in Table 1. These datasets exhibit various collection sizes (ranging from 1300 to 20,000), class counts (17 to 200), and modeling complexity (easy to difficult). All datasets contain bounding box annotations, which are rectangles around the object of interest that identify the image's label. Whenever a "corrected" bounding box is required in our experiments, we use the corresponding ground-truth box provided by the annotations: we assume that the user makes perfect corrections in the simulated human-in-the-loop process we use in our experiments. This applies to both bounding boxes and labels. Ground-truth bounding boxes are shown in yellow for examples from each dataset in Fig. 1.

The 17 Flowers dataset[1] contains 80 images per class with varying backgrounds, but each image displays a centrally placed flower.

The American Sign Language dataset[2] comprises 50 to 90 images per label. Each image depicts a hand forming the sign of a single letter of the English

---

[1] https://www.robots.ox.ac.uk/~vgg/data/flowers/17/.

[2] https://public.roboflow.com/object-detection/american-sign-language-letters.

Table 1. Datasets

Name	Number of Examples	Number of Classes
`17Flowers`	1360	17
`American Sign Language`	1728	26
`Stanford Dog Breeds`	20,580	120
`Birds`	11,788	200

alphabet, and the hand appears in the same location in each image under relatively consistent lighting conditions, rendering this dataset relatively uniform.

The Dog Breeds dataset[3] contains 120 classes with between 100 to 200 images per class, classified by breed. The position of the dog and the background differ substantially in this dataset.

The Birds dataset[4] contains 200 categories, most of which include 59 or 60 images, with some categories having fewer, and the smallest class containing 41 images. Each image shows a single bird, classified by species, with the bird typically positioned centrally, but with varying backgrounds.

3.2 Methodology

Our experimental methodology aims to simulate the human-in-the-loop training process. We implement our experiments in Python, utilizing the Keras deep-learning library, which provides pre-trained models [3]. We chose three pre-trained models: Mobilenet, Residual Networks [4] (ResNets) with 50 layers, and ResNets with 152 layers. Mobilenet is preferred for lightweight applications, particularly for mobile applications, while ResNets are typically used in medium to heavyweight applications. We use Docker images to control the GPU environment (Nvidia GeForce GTX 1080Ti).

The experimental process consists of generating a stratified holdout dataset comprising 15% of the images from each class at random. This dataset is used to evaluate the model at each iteration of the training loop. The remaining 85% is considered the training dataset and is ordered according to the ordering approach (kernel herding or random order). We then fine-tune the chosen pre-trained model iteratively with successively larger portions of the training dataset, increasing by 50 examples per iteration.

Within each iteration of this experimental process, the images are cropped according to the current object detector model. For the BB strategy, we train an object detector each iteration on all current training images, whereas for BB-1 we train the object detector only once on the first iteration of 50 images.

The networks are optimized using gradient descent employing a validation set for early stopping. Once the training dataset for the next iteration has been assembled, we remove a randomly-selected 15% for internal validation.

---

[3] http://vision.stanford.edu/aditya86/ImageNetDogs/main.html.

[4] http://www.vision.caltech.edu/visipedia/CUB-200-2011.html.

The remaining training items are randomly shuffled and used to fine-tune the pre-trained model using gradient descent.

The initial weights for the pre-trained models are obtained by training on ImageNet, with fine-tuning using the sparse categorical cross-entropy loss function, the ADAM optimizer with an initial learning rate of 0.0001 and a decay of 0.000001, and accuracy as the only metric for early stopping. Fine-tuning is applied for a maximum of 100 epochs of mini-batch stochastic gradient descent with 5 images at a time in each mini-batch used for computing gradients.

After fine-tuning, we evaluate the model against the holdout dataset to estimate the predictive accuracy of the model at that point in the simulated human-in-the-loop training process. Additionally, we evaluate the current model against the 50 selected examples for the next iteration as a measure of how well it performs when pre-labelling those items. This allows us to estimate the number of examples that would need to be corrected if an actual human were involved in the experiments. We can compare the ground-truth labels and the predicted labels in our simulated human-in-the-loop set-up because all the benchmark data used in our experiments is fully labelled.

4   Results of the Experiments

As the random and kernel herding methods were generally superior in the previous experiments [5], which evaluated human-in-the-loop training for image classification without bounding boxes, we use them as baselines. Figure 4 shows the overall accuracy of each model on each dataset as the number of iterations progresses, as judged by the holdout test set. All curves tend to the same level of accuracy. Where there are differences, these are typically due to better performance by the BB strategy. Random ordering and kernel herding without object detection, as used in [5], are worse. However, the differences are generally small.

Considering the number of corrections required in each iteration, as in Fig. 5, the graphs are generally again quite similar, but the kernel herding set of results shows significant instability. Cumulative corrections, as shown in Fig. 6, show more separation in the graphs. This shows that the previous high-performing ordering methods from [5] are improved significantly by the addition of bounding boxes. The best methods are random BB and random BB-1. This pattern is repeated in Fig. 7, where the top-left results, indicating high accuracy over the fewest iterations, are generally those same methods. Encouragingly, the two BB-1 methods often perform quite well.

An overview of the total user effort required to fix the labels is shown in Table 2. The table shows that regardless of ordering method, it is always better to use a bounding box strategy than not. The best bounding box strategies are random BB and kernel herding BB. Random BB-1 and kernel herding BB-1 are generally worse than their BB counterparts but perform similarly. These results are promising in the sense that the differences between fully corrected bounding boxes (BB) and single-iteration corrected bounding boxes (BB-1) is not that

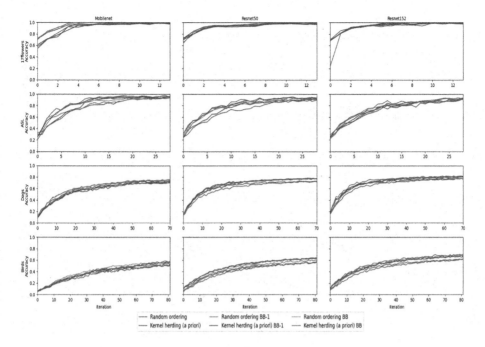

Fig. 4. Holdout accuracy

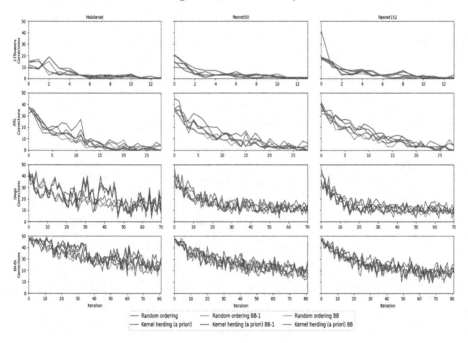

Fig. 5. Corrections needed per iteration

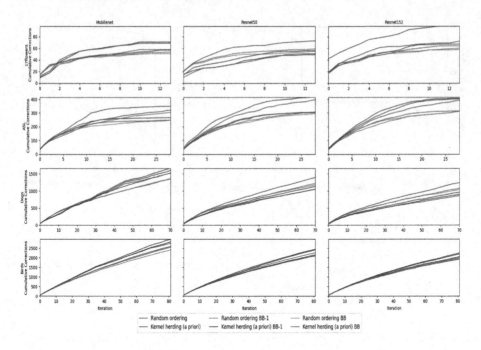

Fig. 6. Cumulative correction counts

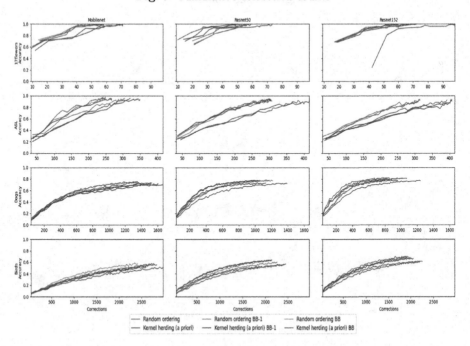

Fig. 7. Accuracy versus number of corrections

Table 2. Total corrections per method and model with and without bounding boxes

Model	Random	Random BB	Random BB-1	KH	KH BB	KH BB-1
17F-mnet	57	51	54	71	58	69
17F-resnet50	73	55	59	56	51	49
17F-resnet152	72	58	60	98	64	67
ASL-mnet	321	248	305	349	248	266
ASL-resnet50	397	295	308	415	302	305
ASL-resnet152	392	311	312	406	314	402
Dogs-mnet	1517	1348	1358	1664	1528	1604
Dogs-resnet50	1390	1219	1178	1133	1048	1054
Dogs-resnet152	1241	1038	1078	963	857	903
Birds-mnet	2603	2419	2554	2972	2768	2832
Birds-resnet50	2453	2147	2269	2415	2090	2148
Birds-resnet152	2255	1974	2003	2201	1926	2055

great. This also suggests that a user interface designed to encourage the user to only correct the worst cases of bounding box error is likely to lead to good results.

5 Conclusion

A combination of using passive sampling methods alongside class-agnostic object detection for image classification shows that bounding boxes help to reduce the number of class labels a user has to correct in a human-in-the-loop training scenario. Two strategies were adopted representing the maximal and minimal bounding box correction effort that could be made in the loop. While the maximal approach outperformed the minimal approach, the difference in terms of numbers of corrections needed was not significant. This is important because correcting bounding boxes obviously also requires user effort; thus, constructing a human-in-the-loop system for image classification that only requires minimal correction of bounding boxes, namely in the first batch of data, can be recommended as a practical approach.

There are a number of avenues for future work. Our results suggest that effective and simple user interfaces can be constructed using a passive sampling method coupled with a click-on-the-object-of-interest strategy for worst-case bounding box errors. The proposed system also offers the possibility of monitoring and potentially correcting model bias. Investigating different object detection methods in the setting considered in this paper could also be a fruitful undertaking.

References

1. Cassidy, B., et al.: The DFUC 2020 dataset: analysis towards diabetic foot ulcer detection. touchREVIEWS Endocrinol. **17**(1), 5–11 (2021)
2. Chen, Y., Welling, M., Smola, A.: Super-samples from kernel herding. In: Proceedings of the Twenty-Sixth Conference on Uncertainty in Artificial Intelligence, pp. 109–116 (2010)
3. Gulli, A., Pal, S.: Deep learning with Keras. Packt Publishing Ltd. (2017)
4. He, K., Zhang, X., Ren, S., Sun, J.: Deep residual learning for image recognition. In: Proceedings of the IEEE Conference on Computer vision and Pattern Recognition, pp. 770–778 (2016)
5. Holmes, G., Frank, E., Fletcher, D., Sterling, C.: Efficiently correcting machine learning: considering the role of example ordering in human-in-the-loop training of image classification models. In: 27th International Conference on Intelligent User Interfaces, pp. 584–593 (2022)
6. Honeycutt, D., Nourani, M., Ragan, E.: Soliciting human-in-the-loop user feedback for interactive machine learning reduces user trust and impressions of model accuracy. In: Proceedings of the AAAI Conference on Human Computation and Crowdsourcing, vol. 8, pp. 63–72 (2020)
7. Jaiswal, A., Wu, Y., Natarajan, P., Natarajan, P.: Class-agnostic object detection. In: Proceedings of the IEEE/CVF Winter Conference on Applications of Computer Vision, pp. 919–928 (2021)
8. KC, D., Zhang, C.: Improving the trustworthiness of image classification models by utilizing bounding-box annotations. arXiv preprint arXiv:2108.10131 (2021)
9. Ren, S., He, K., Girshick, R., Sun, J.: Faster R-CNN: towards real-time object detection with region proposal networks. In: Advances in Neural Information Processing Systems, vol. 28 (2015)
10. Settles, B.: Active Learning. Synthesis Lectures on Artificial Intelligence and Machine Learning. Morgan & Claypool Publishers (2012)
11. Wu, X., Xiao, L., Sun, Y., Zhang, J., Ma, T., He, L.: A survey of human-in-the-loop for machine learning. Futur. Gener. Comput. Syst. **135**, 364–381 (2022)

Ince-PD Model for Parkinson's Disease Prediction Using MDS-UPDRS I & II and PDQ-8 Score

Nikos Tsolakis[1(✉)], Christoniki Maga-Nteve[1], Georgios Meditskos[1,2], Stefanos Vrochidis[1], and Ioannis Kompatsiaris[1]

[1] Centre for Research & Technology Hellas, Information Technologies Institute, Marousi, Greece
{tsolakin,chmaga,stefanos,ikom}@iti.gr, gmeditsk@csd.auth.gr
[2] School of Informatics, Aristotle University of Thessaloniki, 54124 Thessaloniki, Greece

Abstract. Parkinson's disease (PD) is one of the most prevalent and complex neurodegenerative disorders. Timely and accurate diagnosis is essential for the effectiveness of the initial treatment and improvement of the patients' quality of life. Since PD is an incurable disease, the early intervention is important to delay the progression of symptoms and severity of the disease. This paper aims to present Ince-PD, a new, highly accurate model for PD prediction based on Inception architectures for time-series classification, using wearable data derived from IoT sensor-based recordings and surveys from the mPower dataset. The feature selection process was based on the clinical knowledge shared by the medical experts through the course of the EU funded project ALAMEDA. The algorithm predicted total MDS-UPDRS I & II scores with a mean absolute error of 1.97 for time window and 2.27 for patient, as well as PDQ-8 scores with a mean absolute error of 2.17 for time window and 2.96 for patient. Our model demonstrates a more effective and accurate method to predict Parkinson Disease, when compared to some of the most significant deep learning algorithms in the literature.

Keywords: Deep Learning models · Parkinson's Disease · MDS-UPDRS · PDQ-8 · Wearable Sensors · Convolution Networks

1 Introduction

Parkinson's disease (PD) is a progressive, chronic and common neurodegenerative disease that affects more than 10 million people worldwide [1]. The prevalence of PD has been increased in recent decades, and it's estimated that almost 1% of people above 60 years old in industrialized societies are affected by the condition. However, the symptoms of PD can often go unnoticed in the early stages, which might delay early diagnosis and accurate treatment [2, 3]. Usually, the symptoms are both motor and non-motor, but in the early stages, they are mostly linked with dyskinesia, tremor and muscle stiffness. Severity of PD is commonly assessed using the Movement Disorder Society-Unified

© IFIP International Federation for Information Processing 2023
Published by Springer Nature Switzerland AG 2023
I. Maglogiannis et al. (Eds.): AIAI 2023, IFIP AICT 675, pp. 267–278, 2023.
https://doi.org/10.1007/978-3-031-34111-3_23

Parkinson's Disease Rating Scale (MDS-UPDRS) and Parkinson's disease Questionnaire (PDQ-8). The MDS-UPDRS is a revision of Unified Parkinson's Disease Rating Scale (UPDRS) and developed to resolve some flaws of the original scale [4]. The MDS-UPDRS consists of 4 different parts, MDS-UPDRS I, II, III and IV, which are used to monitor and evaluate motor and non-motor aspects of experiences and activities of daily living (ADL), mood and mental state, complication in treatment and more. Moreover, PDQ-8 is an 8-item questionnaire and a shortened version of PDQ-39. It requires the patient to answer eight questions relevant to their mood, physical condition, Activities of Daily Living (ADL) and mental state where a high accumulated score signifies poor quality of life. Overall, both of these assessment tools are considered as reliable and valid measures and are widely used in clinical practice and research settings [5, 6].

In recent years, the extensive use of Artificial Intelligence (AI) and Internet of Things (IoT) technologies to monitor patients with Parkinson's disease has been gaining traction in the healthcare industry [7]. Especially during the COVID-19 pandemic era, the advanced need for PD patients to continue their treatment in a riskless way highlighted the necessity for personalized and remote monitoring [8, 9]. To achieve that, sensors such as magnetometers, accelerometers, gyroscopes, are increasingly being used in wearable devices like smartwatches and smart insoles to collect real-time data on patients with the aim of providing better health services and improving their living conditions [10–12]. This data can be used in combination with Machine Learning (ML) and Deep Learning (DL) techniques to predict disease stage, severity, symptoms or medical test scores, providing more flexible ways of handling large medical datasets, minimizing the costs of medical care and assisting healthcare professionals to make timely decisions [13].

The ALAMEDA project[1], funded by the EU, aims to provide personalized rehabilitation treatment assessments for patients with neurological disorders such as Parkinson's, Multiple Sclerosis and Stroke, using AI. One of the key goals of the project is to assist healthcare professionals in making timely and accurate decisions (e.g. diagnosis) without requiring patients to make physical visits to a clinic or hospital. To achieve this goal, the project is using various wearable sensors, such as accelerometers, to collect real-time data on patients' movements and other physical indicators. This paper presents a deep learning-based algorithm for estimating total MDS-UPDRS (parts I and II) and PDQ-8 score from data collected from wearable sensors. More specifically, we present Ince-PD, a highly accurate model for PD prediction based on the InceptionTime architecture for time-series classification [14]. For comparison purposes, we implemented a number of deep learning models based on LSTM and CNN architectures.

The rest of this paper is organized as follows. In Sect. 2, a literature review on previous related works on Parkinson's disease prediction using wearable sensors and deep learning techniques is presented. In Sect. 3, the Ince-PD architecture and the implementation of the model for PD prediction is introduced. In Sect. 4, the experimental setup, the comparative and evaluation methods are described. Finally, in Sect. 5 the results obtained of the proposed framework are discussed and in Sect. 6, the conclusions and future research directions are presented.

---

[1] https://alamedaproject.eu/.

2 Related Work

In the existing literature, there are numerous studies on the PD detection, the stage and severity of the disease and the prediction of variables pertinent to the use case. Some of the most common machine learning and deep learning models for Parkinson's disease are logistic regression, k-nearest neighbors, Support Vector Machine, classification trees and neural networks [15–19]. Nilashi et al. [20] used supervised and unsupervised learning methods to perform PD diagnosis through UPDRS prediction. Their study's results demonstrated that Expectation-Maximization (EM) with Support Vector Regression (SVR) ensembles provide better performance than decision trees and SVR combined with other clustering approaches. An ensemble deep model for continuously estimating UPDRS III based on free-body motion data was presented by Hssayeni et al. [21]. The evaluation with Leave-One-Out Cross-Validation (LOOCV) indicated high correlation and a low Mean Absolute Error (MAE) of 5.95. Rehman et al. [22] applied Deep Learning techniques to wearable-based gait data to predict MDS-UPDRS III scores. Their proposed DL Convolutional Neural Network (CNN) achieved a MAE of 6.29. A gait analysis-based PD auxiliary diagnosis system proposed by Chen et al. [23]. The system collected data from embedded devices, which was then analyzed by a 1D CNN model. The system achieved a high recognition accuracy of 91.4% for abnormal gait. Setiawan et al. [24] also implemented a DL algorithm based on Vertical Ground Reaction Force (VGRF) time frequency features for PD detection and severity classification. The best average accuracy of this algorithm was 96.52% using ResNet-50. Papadopoulos et al. [25] focused on the unobtrusive detection of PD from multi-modal and in-the-wild sensor data using a deep learning model that consists of three parts: the feature extraction module, the attention module and the final classifier module. Asuroglu et al. [26] presented a deep learning model, which combines CNNs and Locally Weighted Random Forest (LWRF) for PD severity assessment using wearable sensor data and achieved 3.009 MAE. Zhao et al. [27] presented a deep learning architecture that combines CNN and Long shot-term memory (LSTM) that outperforms other previous studies in terms of accuracy in Parkinson's Disease prediction. In a recent study, Yang et al. [28] developed an objective method to automatically classify patients with Parkinson's Disease and Health Controls (HC) using PD-ResNet from gait data. Interestingly, they achieved better results than previous methods in terms of accuracy, precision, F1-Score and recall. Balaji et al. [29] presented an automatic and non-invasive method for PD diagnosis, using LSTM network for severity rating of PD. Finally, Bobic et al. [30] introduced a predictive model for bradykinesia in PD, using CNN architectures.

Even though Time Series Classification (TSC) is considered as a complex problem, the arise of deep learning showed promising results for its solution. The InceptionTime, as presented by [14], is an ensemble of deep CNN models, which provide great results for TSC. The core parts of an inception network are the two residual blocks, each of one consists of three Inception modules, which replace the traditional fully convolutional layers. Each inception module is composed of multiple layers like the Bottleneck layer, the convolution layer, the max pooling layer and the depth concatenation layer. A linear shortcut connection is used to transfer the input of every residual block to the next block's input. After deploying the residual blocks, a Global Average Pooling (GAP) is utilized which computes the average of the output multivariate time series of the whole

dimension. Lastly, a traditional fully connected Softmax layer is used. Figure 1 presents
the basic structure of the InceptionTime network.

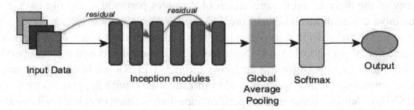

Fig. 1. The Inception network of InceptionTime model.

The present study uses several residual connections and modified inception modules
as key components of its architecture to predict PD stage using total MDS-UPDRS I &
II and PDQ-8 scores. To the best of our knowledge, this is the first regression model
for PD prediction that is based on the InceptionTime network and the efficiency of the
model provides great potential for future work. As in most cases the DL algorithms
perform better in PD prediction, we utilized some of the most efficient architectures as
the comparison base for our approach.

3   Methodology

Machine Learning and Deep Learning techniques have shown great potential in predicting and diagnosing diseases, including Parkinson's disease. This study utilizes the
InceptionTime architecture, a novel architecture for Time Series Classification (TSC),
to build Deep Learning models able to diagnose Parkinson's Disease through predicting total MDS-UPDRS I & II and total PDQ-8 scores. InceptionTime architecture is
presented in Sect. 2 and our proposed Ince-PD is presented in detail in Sect. 3.3. The
proposed framework for deep learning modeling for Parkinson's disease diagnosis, as
shown in Fig. 2 can be highlighted in 3 specific stages:

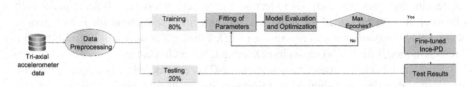

Fig. 2. Flow of the proposed Ince-PD framework for PD prediction.

- *Data acquisition*, where the data is acquired and evaluated based on the clinical
  requirements and the needs of the project.
- *Data preprocessing*, where the data is converted into defined sets.
- *Model implementation and total MDS-UPDRS I & II and total PDQ-8 prediction*,
  where the model architecture is built and the target labels are predicted.

3.1 Data Acquisition

This study used data acquired from the mPower Public Research Portal [31]. The mPower is a clinical observation study on PD that collected data from sensor-based recordings and surveys over a large number of participants. The whole study carried out through a mobile application interface and its 7 tasks are divided in activities (walking, memory, tapping and voice) and survey questionnaires (demographic survey, MDS-UPDRS survey and PDQ-8 survey).

Based on the suggestions from the medical experts, we utilized four out of seven tasks (the walking task, the demographics survey, the PDQ-8 and MDS-UPDRS survey). The walking test consists of three different segments: outbound, rest and return. The accelerometer and gyroscope of the smartphone capture the three-dimensional linear and angular acceleration of each participant during this test. The purpose of utilizing these data is the evaluation of any movement limitation that is relevant to PD and discriminating PD patients from healthy control subjects, while predicting disease stage using the scores of the questionnaires. Table 1 summarizes the number of participants and the unique tasks per activity in the mPower dataset.

Table 1. Data availability in mPower dataset.

Activity	Number of Unique Participants	Unique Tasks
Demographics	6805	6805
PDQ-8	1334	1641
MDS-UPDRS	2024	2305
Walking total	3101	35410
Walking outbound acc	3101	35407
Walking return acc	2807	23883
Walking rest acc	3101	35407

3.2 Data Preprocessing

Numerous studies have shown that pre-processing the data is necessary for MDS-UPDRS and PDQ-8 prediction to be more accurate [32, 33]. In the preprocessing stage, missing values, noise and inconsistencies in the dataset are addressed. The first step was to determine which of the available data is useful for the requirements of the project and the management of the missing values, as they can be an essential obstacle for Deep Learning Algorithms. Feature selection aims to reduce model's complexity and provides faster and easier training and interpretation. In this work, participants who performed both surveys and specific walking tasks were selected by utilizing information derived from the clinicians of the project. Converting the raw data to appropriate input format for training models was important part of the preprocessing, while the definition of the common keys addressed the overlapping values of the dataset. The following step was the segmentation of the time sequences into smaller fragments by using sliding windows of 5 s (500 rows given a sampling rate of 100 Hz), corresponding to 50% overlap. For the dataset partitioning, the 80% of the data was the training sample, while the 20% was utilized for testing purposes.

3.3 Proposed Model Architecture and Implementation

In this study, the InceptionTime, a novel architecture for TSC, is utilized for total MDS-UPDRS I & II and PDQ-8 prediction. The main parts of the Inception network architecture are described in Sect. 2. Several significant modifications have been implemented in the architecture, which are classified into two distinct categories: Firstly, alterations pertaining to the Bottleneck layer inside the inception modules. Secondly, changes have been made to the overall framework, including the addition of dropout and batch normalization layers, as well as the utilization of different activation functions. The residual blocks are essential parts as the connection at every third inception module provides better optimization capabilities and overall performance. Thus, they remained as proposed in the original work. The Bottleneck layer inside the inception module is removed, as experiment results suggested that without it, better efficiency is achieved. After the modified inception modules, a batch normalization layer is deployed, followed by a Rectified Linear activation function (ReLU). The output from the ReLU activation function is passed on to an one-dimensional Global Average Pooling before passing to the output layer where instead of the Softmax layer, a Rectified Linear activation function (ReLU) is deployed to achieve faster learning and better performance. To overcome overfitting problems, tuning of the kernel size of the convolution has been implemented, while adding a Dropout layer with 0.5 rate after Inception modules improve the generalization of the model and prevent it from relying too heavily on any set of features. Other parameters that needed to be modified were the depth and the number of filters. The final stage of the implementation process was the prediction stage. At this point, the models predicted the total MDS-UPDRS I & II and PDQ-8 according to the input data. The proposed Ince-PD model is built by utilizing InceptionTime and differentiating essential components, as detailed above. In Fig. 3, a schematic diagram of the proposed Inception model for PD prediction is depicted.

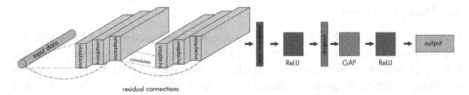

Fig. 3. The architecture of the proposed Ince-PD model for total-MDS-UPDRS I & II and PDQ-8 prediction.

After implementing several experiments, we concluded that the use of convolution layers between the inception modules is a sensible decision with respect to performance and computational complexity.

4 Experiments

4.1 Model Performance Evaluation

The performance evaluation of the Inception model was carried-out by using the Mean Absolute Error (MAE) and Mean Square Error (MSE) per-window and per-patient basis. The mathematical formulas of MAE and MSE are presented in Eq. 1 and Eq. 2, respectively, where $\hat{y}_i$, y_i are the predicted value and the actual value. The character n represents the entire set of the samples.

$$\text{MAE} = \frac{1}{n} \sum_{i=1}^{n} |\hat{y}_i - y_i| \tag{1}$$

$$\text{MSE} = \sum_{i=1}^{n} \frac{(\hat{y}_i - y_i)^2}{n} \tag{2}$$

To further evaluate our model, a variety of different approaches in literature for estimating the total MDS-UPDRS I & II and PDQ-8 were used for comparison purposes. The proposed method was compared to the same dataset for both target labels with the architectures that will be introduced in the next sections.

4.2 Experimental Setup

The Inception model that is presented in this study was developed with "Python 3.8" and operated on a PC with an Intel(R) Xeon(R) Silver 4210 CPU @ 2.20 GHz processor. The developed network was implemented in TensorFlow [34] and the models trained on 10 epochs, allowing the model to demonstrate better performance by learning from the training data. During the training process, the fit method was applied to the training data and target labels, and the Adam optimizer, an adaptive learning rate optimizer, was used for efficiency and speed purposes [35]. The model's hyperparameters tuning was implemented heuristically, using TensorFlow's HParams library. The optimization and tuning processes utilized MAE and MSE to define the effectiveness of the model and were important for the optimal configuration of the model. The aim was to minimize the MAE and MSE without sacrificing the speed and complexity of the model, while comparing our results with optimized models that achieved efficient results on the same dataset. In the following Table 2, some essential parameters of our model are presented.

4.3 Comparative Methods

In order to facilitate comparisons, we trained some models based on CNN and LSTM architectures described in the literature. All the models were trained and evaluated on the same train and test set to achieve meaningful comparison. The first model is an 1D Convolutional Neural Network (1D-CNN) that consists of four convolutional layers, two pooling layers and two fully connected layers proposed in [23]. The second model is introduced in [21] and describes a 1-D CNN-LSTM (1D-CNN-LSTM) network, consisted of three convolutional blocks with a max pooling layer deployed between each block. The third model, which is presented in [22], is based on CNN architecture (CNN),

Table 2. Specification of parameters of the model.

Parameters	Specification
Activation function	ReLu
Batch size	256
Epochs	10
Optimizer	Adam
Metric	Mean Absolute Error (MAE)
Loss function	Mean Squared Error (MSE)

where the first block of the convolutional layers (each one consists of four 1-D Convolutional layers) is followed by a fully connected layers block. Between each 1-D convolutional layer a Rectified Linear Activation Function (ReLU) is deployed. The fourth model that was implemented is based on [29] and was a class of recurrent neural network, a Long Short-Term Memory (LSTM), which is followed by a Fully Connected Layer and a Softmax layer. The last model that designed was a Convolutional Neural Network (CONV-1-CONV-2) proposed by [30] which comprised of a convolutional layer (CONV-1) with 16 filters followed by a batch normalization layer, a ReLU activation function layer, and a max-pooling layer and convolutional layer (CONV-2) with 32 filters size, followed by the same architecture.

5 Results

5.1 Total MDS-UPDRS I & II and PDQ-8 Results

The first step of evaluating our model was the verification of its superiority against the previously described models. Due to the combination of inception modules with ReLU function, residual connections and dropout layer the Ince-PD provide better learning capabilities, while being computationally efficient and speeding up the training process. Despite optimizing the parameters of the comparative methods, our proposed model demonstrates the best performance compared to them, achieving a MAE of 1.97 on per-window and 2.27 on per-patient basis for total MDS-UPDRS I & II and a MAE of 2.17 on per-window and 2.96 on per-patient basis for total PDQ-8. Table 3 lists the results for MDS-UPDRS I & II and PDQ-8.

After implementing multiple experiments, it was concluded that the appropriate number of epochs is 10, as the model reached saturation. To verify this, we run our experiments for 13 epochs, but the performance of the models did not show significant improvement, comparing to 10. Figure 4 depicts the comparative results in MAE for the different models for PDQ-8 after running experiments for 10 and 13 epochs.

Table 3. MAE for Total MDS-UPDRS I & II and PDQ-8 on per-window and per-patient basis.

Model	Total MDS-UPDRS I & II		Total PDQ8	
	MAE (window)	MAE (patient)	MAE (window)	MAE (patient)
1-D CNN	5.02	6.19	3.11	3.6
1-D CNN-LSTM	5.73	6.93	2.94	3.29
CNN	5.22	6.38	3.04	3.44
LSTM	5.08	5.80	3.62	3.57
CONV-1-CONV-2	5.46	5.12	3.21	3.36
Ince-PD	1.97	2.27	2.17	2.96

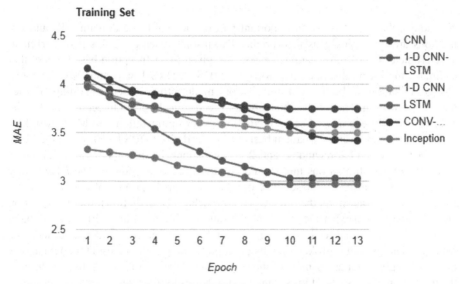

Fig. 4. MAE for PDQ-8 for 10 and 13 epochs.

To observe the model's loss during the training process, we examine the value of the Mean Squared Error during 10 epochs. As seen in Table 4, Ince-PD achieves significant improvement in its performance for both target labels. The MSE of the model steadily decreases from 9.32 to 6.91 for total MDS-UPDRS I & II and from 9.49 to 8.23 for total PDQ-8. This reduction indicates the ability of the proposed method to effectively predict the score of the surveys.

Table 4. The MSE of Ince-PD for total MDS-UPDRS I & II and PDQ-8 for 10 epochs.

Epochs	MDS – UPDRS I & II	PDQ-8
	MSE	MSE
2	9,3224	9,4992
4	9,1288	9,0174
6	8,6521	8,7637
8	7,874	8.4439
10	6,9102	8,2354

6   Conclusion

Nowadays, the use of AI is an important part of the healthcare domain. ML and DL methods are increasingly used to predict Parkinson's disease. In this paper, tri-axial accelerometer data from wearable sensors are given to an Inception based model that estimates the mean absolute error for total MDS-UPDRS I & II and PDQ-8 scores. The combination of the different units of our model provides better learning abilities and generalization. The results obtained far exceed some basic architectures used in the field of neurodegenerative disease prediction. After optimization, the MAE was 1.97 and 2.27 for window and for patient basis for total MDS-UPDRS I & II, while the MAE for PDQ-8 was 2.17 for window and 2.96 for patient. Despite its great performance though, there are limitations that should be addressed in the future. The adaptability of the model to different datasets is a concern, as a small amount of data may affect its efficiency. Furthermore, the framework approaches PD prediction through regression and no classification experiments executed for its evaluation. Future work should expand the model for more target labels (e.g. Hoehn & Yahr) and more neurodisorders like Multiple Sclerosis and Stroke. With its great performance, the Ince-PD model enables an increasingly better assessment of the stage of a patient's Parkinson's disease through the prediction of the score of important questionnaires for medical experts. Experiments show that with proper optimization the MAE is minimized and thus this work provides great potential in the field of PD prediction, helping to minimize costs and to make diagnosis by physicians more efficient.

Acknowledgements. This project has received funding from the European Union's Horizon 2020 research and innovation programme under grant agreement No GA101017558.

References

1. Nussbaum, R.L., Ellis, C.E.: Alzheimer's disease and Parkinson's disease. New England J. Med. **348**(14), 1356–1364 (2003)
2. Tysnes, O.-B., Storstein, A.: Epidemiology of Parkinson's disease. J. Neural Transm. (Vienna, Austria: 1996) **124**(8), 901–905 (2017)

3. Pringsheim, T., Jette, N., Frolkis, A., Steeves, T.D.L.: The prevalence of Parkinson's disease: a systematic review and meta-analysis. Mov. Disord. **29**, 1583–1590 (2014)
4. Goetz, C.G., et al.: Movement disorder society-sponsored revision of the unified Parkinson's disease rating scale (MDS-UPDRS): scale presentation and clinimetric testing results. Mov. Disord. Official J. Mov. Disord. Soc. **23**(15), 2129–2170 (2008). https://doi.org/10.1002/mds.22340
5. Franchignoni, F., et al.: Rasch analysis of the short form 8-item Parkinson's disease questionnaire (PDQ-8). Qual. Life Res. Int. J. Qual. Life Aspects Treat. Care Rehabil. **17**(4), 541–548 (2008)
6. Katsarou, Z., et al.: Assessing quality of life in Parkinson's disease: can a short-form questionnaire be useful? Mov. Disord. Official J. Mov. Disord. Soc. **19**(3), 308–312 (2004)
7. Giannakopoulou, K.-M., et al.: Internet of things technologies and machine learning methods for Parkinson's disease diagnosis, monitoring and management: a systematic review. Sensors (Basel, Switzerland) **22**(5), 1799 (2022)
8. Miele, G., et al.: Telemedicine in Parkinson's disease: how to ensure patient needs and continuity of care at the time of COVID-19 pandemic. Telemedicine J. E-Health Official J. Am. Telemed. Assoc. **26**(12), 1533–1536 (2020)
9. Podlewska, A.M., van Wamelen, D.J.: Parkinson's disease and Covid-19: the effect and use of telemedicine. Int. Rev. Neurobiol. **165**, 263–281 (2022)
10. Ossig, C., et al.: Wearable sensor-based objective assessment of motor symptoms in Parkinson's disease. J. Neural Transm. **123**(1), 57–64 (2015). https://doi.org/10.1007/s00702-015-1439-8
11. Tong, K., Granat, M.H.: A practical gait analysis system using gyroscopes. Med. Eng. Phys. **21**(2), 87–94 (1999)
12. Suzuki, M., et al.: Quantitative analysis of motor status in Parkinson's disease using wearable devices: from methodological considerations to problems in clinical applications. Parkinson's Dis. **2017**, 6139716 (2017)
13. Bates, D.W., et al.: Big data in health care: using analytics to identify and manage high-risk and high-cost patients. Health Aff. (Proj. Hope) **33**(7), 1123–1131 (2014)
14. Fawaz, H.I., et al.: InceptionTime: finding AlexNet for time series classification. Data Min. Knowl. Discov. **34**, 1936–1962 (2019)
15. Senturk, Z.K.: Early diagnosis of Parkinson's disease using machine learning algorithms. Med. Hypotheses **138**, 109603 (2020)
16. Li, A., Li, C.: Detecting Parkinson's disease through gait measures using machine learning. Diagnostics **12**(10), 2404 (2022)
17. Moradi, S., Tapak, L., Afshar, S.: Identification of novel noninvasive diagnostics biomarkers in the Parkinson's diseases and improving the disease classification using support vector machine. BioMed. Res. Int. **2022**, 8 (2022). Article ID 5009892
18. Templeton, J.M., Poellabauer, C., Schneider, S.: Classification of Parkinson's disease and its stages using machine learning. Sci. Rep. **12**, 14036 (2022)
19. Alzubaidi, M.S., et al.: The role of neural network for the detection of Parkinson's disease: a scoping review. Healthcare (Basel, Switzerland) **9**(6) 740 (2021)
20. Nilashi, M.: Predicting Parkinson's disease progression: evaluation of ensemble methods in machine learning. J. Healthcare Eng. **2022**, 17 (2022). Article ID 2793361
21. Hssayeni, M.D., Jimenez-Shahed, J., Burack, M.A., et al.: Ensemble deep model for continuous estimation of Unified Parkinson's disease rating scale III. BioMed. Eng. OnLine **20**, 32 (2021)
22. Zia Ur Rehman, R., et al.: Predicting the progression of Parkinson's disease MDS-UPDRS-III motor severity score from gait data using deep learning. In: Annual International Conference of the IEEE Engineering in Medicine and Biology Society. IEEE Engineering in Medicine and Biology Society. Annual International Conference, vol. 2021, pp. 249–252 (2021)

23. Chen, F., Fan, X., Li, J., Zou, M., Huang, L.: Gait analysis based Parkinson's disease auxiliary diagnosis system. J. Internet Technol. **22**(5), 991–999 (2021). Web 26 Feb. 2023
24. Setiawan, F., Lin, C.-W.: Implementation of a deep learning algorithm based on vertical ground reaction force time-frequency features for the detection and severity classification of Parkinson's disease. Sensors (Basel, Switzerland) **21**(15) 5207 (2021)
25. Papadopoulos, A., Iakovakis, D., Klingelhoefer, L., et al.: Unobtrusive detection of Parkinson's disease from multi-modal and in-the-wild sensor data using deep learning techniques. Sci. Rep. **10**, 21370 (2020)
26. Aşuroğlu, T., Oğul, H.: A deep learning approach for Parkinson's disease severity assessment. Health Technol. **12**, 943–953 (2022)
27. Zhao, A., et al.: A hybrid spatio-temporal model for detection and severity rating of Parkinson's disease from gait data. Neurocomputing **315**, 1–8 (2018)
28. Yang, X., Ye, Q., Cai, G., Wang, Y., Cai, G.: PD-ResNet for classification of Parkinson's disease from gait. IEEE J. Transl. Eng. Health Med. **10**, 2200111 (2022)
29. Balaji, E., Brindha, D., Elumalai, V.K., Vikrama, R.: Automatic and non-invasive Parkinson's disease diagnosis and severity rating using LSTM network. Appl. Soft Comput. **108** (2021)
30. Bobić, V., Djurić-Jovičić, M., Dragašević, N., Popović, M.B., Kostić, V.S., Kvaščev, G.: An expert system for quantification of bradykinesia based on wearable inertial sensors. Sensors. **19**(11), 2644 (2019)
31. Bot, B., Suver, C., Neto, E., et al.: The mPower study, Parkinson disease mobile data collected using ResearchKit. Sci. Data **3**, 160011 (2016)
32. Kotsiantis, S., Kanellopoulos, D., Pintelas, P.: Data preprocessing for supervised leaning. World Academy of Science, Engineering and Technology, Open Science Index 12. Int. J. Comput. Inf. Eng. **1**(12), 4104–4109 (2007)
33. Misra, P., Yadav, A.S.: Impact of preprocessing methods on healthcare predictions. In: ICACSE 2019: Proceedings (2019)
34. Abadi, M., Agarwal, A., et al.: Large-scale machine learning on heterogeneous systems (2015)
35. Kingma, D.P., Ba, J.: Adam: a method for stochastic optimization. CoRR abs/1412.6980 (2014)

Medical Knowledge Extraction from Graph-Based Modeling of Electronic Health Records

Athanasios Kallipolitis[1]([✉]) [iD], Parisis Gallos[2] [iD], Andreas Menychtas[1,2] [iD],
Panayiotis Tsanakas[3] [iD], and Ilias Maglogiannis[1] [iD]

[1] Department of Digital Systems, University of Piraeus, Piraeus, Greece
{nasskall,imaglo}@unipi.gr, amenychtas@bioassist.gr
[2] BioAssist S.A, Kastritsiou 4, Rion, Greece
parisgallos@bioassist.gr
[3] School of Electrical and Computer Engineering, National Technical University, Athens,
Greece
panag@cs.ntua.gr

Abstract. The variety and dimensionality of health-related data cannot be addressed by the human perception to arrive at useful knowledge or conclusions for proposing individualized treatment, diagnosis, or prognosis for a disease. Treating this wealth of heterogeneous data in a tabular manner deprives us of the knowledge that is hidden in interactions between the different types of data. In this paper, the potentials of graph-based data modeling and management are explored. Entities such as patients, encounters, observations, and immunizations are structured as graph elements with meaningful connections and are, consequently, encoded to form graph embeddings. The graph embeddings contain information about the graph structure in the vicinity of the node. This vicinity contains multiple low-level graph embeddings that are further encoded into a single high-level vector for utilization in downstream tasks by applying higher-order statistics on Gaussian Mixture Models With reference to the Covid-19 pandemic, we make use of synthetic data for predicting the risk of a patient's fatality with a focus to prevent hospital overpopulation. Initial results demonstrate that utilizing networks of health data entities for the generation of compact medical representations has a positive impact on the performance of machine learning tasks. Since the generated Electronic Health Record vectors are label independent, they can be utilized for any classification or clustering task words.

Keywords: Graph Embeddings · Electronic Health Records · Fisher Vector · Heterogenous Graphs

1 Introduction

The transformation of health records into their electronic equivalent has given birth to numerous applications related to the management of information in databases and the production of valuable, health-related insights. These refer among others to selective

© IFIP International Federation for Information Processing 2023
Published by Springer Nature Switzerland AG 2023
I. Maglogiannis et al. (Eds.): AIAI 2023, IFIP AICT 675, pp. 279–290, 2023.
https://doi.org/10.1007/978-3-031-34111-3_24

retrieval, visualization, and the use of machine learning [1] as well as deep learning techniques [2, 4]. Starting from the adoption of electronic health records (EHRs) in healthcare organizations, a huge amount of information is collected and used for administrative, financial, and clinical purposes [3]. The variety and dimensionality of this information cannot be addressed by human perception. Moreover, it should be taken into consideration that EHRs contain a variety of interconnected medical entities that share valuable information among them and in turn, form networks of information exchange. Storing such entities in tabular form deprives the possibility of maximally exploiting the knowledge that is hidden in the network's structure and the included interconnections. This whole ecosystem of health-related information along with the included interconnections is an ideal set-up for graph theory to kick in. Utilizing the existing graph knowledge in medical data modeling can make a positive contribution in extracting usable knowledge in forecasting, risk assessment, and population grouping on personalized or population health issues.

Due to the Covid-19 pandemic, one of the major problems that Emergency Departments (ICUs) face in a worldwide spectrum is the phenomenon of "crowding", in the sense that the demand for emergency medical services exceeds the available resources for care and treatment of patients. One of the causes is the visits of patients to the ICU, which are characterized as "inappropriate", "non-urgent" or "potentially avoidable". In this paper, we explore the potential of managing and analyzing EHR that form graphs on the use case scenario of classifying the incoming patients into two classes, "urgent" and "non-urgent". By creating compact representations of medical entities and their interconnections that are stored as nodes and edges in a graph, we show that the classification task can be performed more efficiently by exploiting the structure and hidden connections of the EHR network. Towards this end, we propose a novel method for representing health-related nodes and their corresponding relations into vectors by extending the metapath2vec paradigm [5]. Furthermore, multiple instances of embeddings that are related to specific entities are encoded into a single vector per entity by utilizing the Fisher Vector technique [6] to enable their utilization for downstream tasks. The whole methodology improves the classification results in comparison to treating the data in their initial tabular form and is unsupervised in order to maintain a task-independent character.

2   Related Work

The early steps of health data analysis focused mainly on tabular data and their processing through simple statistical techniques or machine learning techniques limited by handcrafted features [7]. The data are transformed into solid encodings via neural networks and are therefore used as tabular data for inference tasks. However, potentials are confined by the fact that each category of information is treated as an isolated island. To overcome these limitations, graph representations have recently been added to this research landscape. Graphs can store health data with the advantage that they are treated as interconnected entities. Each category of information (patients, appointments, observations, organizations, drugs) can be coded as part of the neighborhood in a way similar to word2vec [8].

Transferring the scenario from word2vec to node2vec [9] and health-related data, we consider a patient with the accompanying information regarding his demographics and a series of laboratory tests, or the drugs administered per appointment in a health-care structure as a graph. Then, the information surrounding the patient's neighborhood (i.e., laboratory tests, vaccinations, appointments in health facilities, treatments) can be summarized in a vector representation of reduced space by mapping the neighborhood of the patient to the patient. Starting from the Word2Vec paradigm, which in the graph contextual environment can be referred to as Node2Vec, several approaches have been proposed in the literature for the representation of graphs into embeddings. A large family of these approaches depends on the Deep Graph Infomax [10] training procedure and includes Graph Convolutional Networks (GCNs) [11], Graph Attention Networks (GATs) [12], Approximate Personalized Propagation of Neural Predictions (APPNPs) [13], GraphSAGE [14], Relational Graph Convolutional Networks (RGCNs) [15] and ClusterGCN [16]. This procedure is unsupervised and is guided by the maximization of the mutual information between the whole graph and parts of the graph. It consists of five steps as depicted in the workflow in Fig. 1. The first step concerns the mutation of the original graph where the data is stored through a function C. The function C changes the position in the contents of the nodes. The second step codes the information of each node based on its neighborhood using a graph2vec algorithm (E). A summary vector of the original graph is created using the Summary R (eg global average pooling). The next step uses a neural network of discriminator type, which receives the nodes of both graphs as inputs and is trained based on a cost function that is maximized for samples of the original graph and minimized for samples of the corrupted graph.

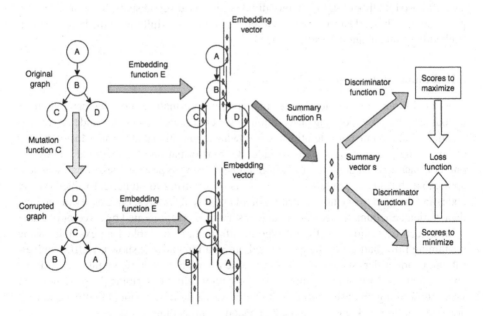

Fig. 1. Deep Graph Infomax workflow presentation.

While GCN is an extension of Convolutional Neural Networks for graph components and exploits graph convolutions to predict node features from the features of the surrounding nodes, GATs utilize an attention mechanism that learns the importance of each node feature for the specific node and RGCNs generalize the GCN notion to heterogeneous graphs with multiple edge types. APPNPs emphasize the insight that is gained by GCNs concerning the nodes that do not participate in the neighborhood and utilize the relationship between GCNs and PageRank to derive an improved scheme for the node-to-node propagation procedure.

Extracting knowledge from medical data is a dynamic process that is constantly evolving as new trends in disease, treatment plans, communicating populations, and new generation drugs are discovered. During this ever-changing process, prior knowledge of a prediction algorithm requires updating to provide knowledge that corresponds to the real state of the world rather than an outdated version. This requirement for continuous updating is in line with the need for a knowledge mechanism that does not require the updating of the entire graph upon insertion of a new node. Therefore, the use of the GraphSAGE algorithm is preferred over others that require updating the embedding model in each new node integration [17]. The calculation of each node encoding is performed by a neural network that tries to predict each node from each surrounding node neighborhood. An important drawback of the mentioned approaches is that in their majority they cannot handle heterogeneous graphs.

3 Methodology

The proposed methodology is mainly divided into six discrete steps: Tabular Data preprocessing, Tabular Data to graph, Graph embeddings, Multiple embeddings vector, Embedding fusion, and Classification (Fig. 2).

3.1 Tabular Data Preprocessing

The initial inputs are simple.csv files that contain information about the patients, their encounters, the corresponding observations registered at each encounter, and their immunizations. Taking into consideration the following assumption that the data do not require cleaning, the preprocessing steps include the transformation of categorical features to one-hot encoded features, the transformation of string type variables to dates, where applicable (birthdate, deathdate), the conversion of string to numerical values (value, code) and the zero to one normalization of all numerical features. Each entity of medical data, patient, encounter, medication, and observation is represented by a vector of many values, each describing a different type of information. In Table 1 an example of the containing information for the patient and observation entity is shown. UUID (Universal unique identifier) stands for a 128-bit value to uniquely identify an instance. All the above-mentioned variables result in a vector with n values describing the patient and m values describing an observation. If the initial variables of the patient entity are k, they are extended to n > k due to the one hot encoding procedure.

3.2 Tabular Data to Graph

Each category of health entity (patient, encounter, observation) contains common keys, upon which the rows of the entities are connected to form meaningful graphs. Graphs are formed by joining data frames. A single patient in his EHR is connected to many encounters and immunizations. In turn, each encounter is connected to observations and medications. All relationships have equal to one weight and are considered undirected. In this context, a graph is formed that contains patients, encounters, observations, and immunizations as nodes and their relationships as edges. The tabular data are stored as attributes, internally in each node.

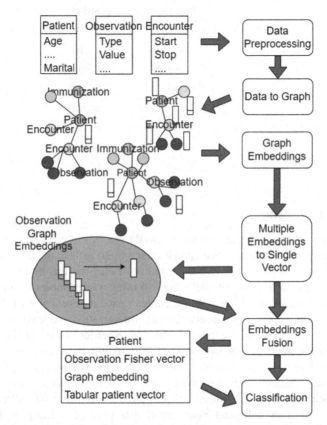

Fig. 2. General workflow architecture. The main steps of proposed methodology on the right side with the corresponding byproducts on the left.

Table 1. Description and type of variables contained in the initial dataset.

Entity	Variable	Type
Patient	Id	UUID
	Birthdate	String
	Deathdate	String
	Marital	String
	Race	String
	Ethnicity	String
	Gender	String
Observation	Patient	UUID
	Encounter	UUID
	Category	String
	Code	String
	Description	String
	Value	String
	Unit	String
	Type	String

3.3 Graph Embeddings

Once the graph is formed, the next step concerns the creation of meta-path random walks that can be applied in heterogeneous graphs since these walks take into consideration the different types of nodes and avoid the pitfall of bias towards highly concentrated and visible nodes. In the case of EHR, the following are examples of meta-paths: a) observation, encounter, observation, b) encounter – patient - encounter, c) observation – encounter – patient – encounter - observation, d) immunization – patient – immunization. The generated random walks are the equivalent of sentences in the word2vec paradigm and are utilized to transform the structure of the graph into the skip-gram analog. Up to this point, the steps are inspired by the implementation in [5]. However, instead of utilizing the plain skip-gram model to form node embeddings, the implementation is enhanced to utilize Doc2Vec [18] and Fasttext [19]. Doc2Vec expands the Word2Vec algorithm by the utilization of an additional input feature that represents meta-path information. On the other hand, the Fasttext embedding model exploits intra-node meaningful information to describe each node of the health-related heterogeneous graph with a single vector. Both manage to incorporate information concerning the structure and attributes of the surrounding nodes regardless of their entity type. A critical difference between the two approaches is that Fasttext requires no retraining for the updating of new nodes in contradiction to Doc2Vec and Word2Vec. Each health entity patient, observation, and encounter is encoded to a vector containing w values which is a hyperparameter of each implementation and for the use case scenario it is set to 64 by a trial-and-error process to achieve better classification results. This vector encapsulates knowledge about the graph that is missing from the initial tabular representation and can be concatenated to the n or m-valued vector of the 3.1 subsection. Although there is redundancy in the concatenated information, experimentation has demonstrated that concatenating both vectors is beneficial.

3.4 Multiple Embeddings Vector

Since our classification tasks concern patients, multiple low-level observation graph embeddings need to be encoded into a high-level vector for each patient. For this purpose, the Fisher vector technique [6]. Unlike other works where the temporal information is encoded by neural network configurations such as Recurrent Neural Networks or Long Short-Term Memories, the technique is based on the utilization of Gaussian distributions for modeling the generation procedure of the graph embeddings and their encoding by higher-order statistics. The Gaussian Mixture model consists of k Gaussian distributions and their parameters are the following $\lambda = \{w_i, \mu_i, \Sigma_i, i = 1,...,k\}$, where w is the height, μ the mean and Σ the covariance matrix of the distribution. The probability that a random descriptor x_r is generated by the GMM is described by Eq. (1). Before the passing of the graph embeddings to the model, the embeddings are concatenated with the initial one-hot encoded observation vector that contains the node attributes.

$$p_r(\lambda) = \sum_{i=1}^{k} w_i N(x_i; \mu_i \Sigma_i) \tag{1}$$

The algorithm attempts to compute the gradient of the sample's likelihood with respect to λ parameters and results in a $k(1 + 2w)$ representation. The Fisher vector embedding technique is a far more sophisticated approach from the Bag of Words paradigm that applies hard assignment to each cluster and ignores higher order statistics such as the covariance matrix Σ. Since our data consists of entities that occur during various periods in time, each set of instances that belong to an entity can be encoded into a single vector that incorporates the information during time efficiently.

3.5 Embeddings Fusion

The patient vector that derives from the graph embedding process is concatenated with the tabular patient attribute vector and the Fisher observations vector to form a compact and meaningful representation.

3.6 Classification

To predict the fatality event, the XGBoost classifier is selected as an efficient ensemble classification scheme that bases its success on the exploitation of the gradient boosting technique in combination with decision trees. The use of an ensemble based on decision trees provides the ability to explore explainability properties of the above-mentioned classification scheme by calculating the sum of gini inpurity or info gain metric.

4 Experimental Results

The utilization of synthetic health data is a popular choice for researchers since real health data is accompanied by specific legal restrictions, privacy, security, and intellectual property restrictions. One of the most popular datasets available due to COVID-19 is the homonymous dataset [20] available in both 10k and 100k versions. For the use case of avoiding overpopulation in COVID-19 clinics, the entity data frames are filtered to exclude any information that will favor the predictive model. Therefore, encounters and observations after the date of the Covid-19 diagnosis are removed. The ground truth for the binary classification task is provided by selecting all patients that suffered from the disease and dividing them into a positive and negative class according to the fatality event. The predicted probability can be utilized to make decisions for keeping a patient in a hospital. Since the dataset is highly imbalanced towards the negative class, samples from this class are reduced to contain only double (IMB2) or triple (IMB3) or four times (IMB4) the number of positive samples. It is split into a training and test set with proportion a of 66.6 - 33.3% and a three-fold cross-validation scheme is applied. The classification task is performed with a) the tabular patient attributes (PA), b) the Fasttext graph embeddings (FE), c) the Word2Vec (WV) graph embeddings, d) the Doc2Vec (DV) graph embeddings, e) the tabular patient attributes vector that is concatenated with the Fasttext embedding (PAFE), f) the tabular patient attributes vector that is concatenated with the Word2Vec embedding (PAWV), g), the tabular patient attributes vector that is concatenated with the Doc2Vec embedding (PADV), h) the tabular patient attributes vector that is concatenated with the Fasttext graph embedding and the Fisher vector (PAFEFV), i) the patient attributes vector that is concatenated with the Word2Vec embedding and the Fisher vector (PAWVFV), j) the patient attributes vector that is concatenated with the Doc2Vec embedding and the Fisher vector (PADVFV). The utilized metrics for classification performance include accuracy and balanced accuracy. Results for all the above-mentioned scenarios are depicted in Table 2. The review of the presented results demonstrates that the best results are achieved by the PAFEFV implementation and as the imbalance increases, the PADVFV proves better. The plain Fasttext graph embeddings are worst in predicting the classification task than the tabular data, in contrast to Doc2Vec and Word2Vec approaches that show improved results. In most cases, the Doc2Vec embedding demonstrates strong resilience to imbalance bias.

To assess the performance of a clustering technique, we apply k-means clustering in three configurations (k = 3, 4, 5) to the generated embeddings in the IMB4 dataset. The clustering experiment in k = 3,4 and 5 aims to verify the effectiveness of the proposed methodology in an unsupervised manner. The selection of the k parameter has been done arbitrarily, however there exist techniques that can indicate the optimal k value based on the intra/ inter cluster characteristics such as Elbow score and Silhouette index. The utilized metrics for evaluation of the clustering performance are the homogeneity, completeness, v measurement, adjusted rand index, mutual info, and silhouette index scores. The results are presented in Table 3. The best score for all clustering metrics is one. By reviewing the clustering results, it is inferred that in most cases the implementations that exploit the Doc2Vec embeddings provide better results. However, it should be noted that extending the patient vector with additional information from the Fisher vector is not always beneficial for clustering as it is for the classification task. There are some

Table 2. Binary Classification results. Accuracy is labelled as Acc, balanced accuracy as Bacc.

Case	Classification Results					
	IMB2		IMB3		IMB4	
	Acc	Bacc	Acc	Bacc	Acc	Bacc
PA	0.70	0.67	0.77	0.69	0.78	0.66
FE	0.71	0.60	0.75	0.52	0.80	0.51
WV	0.77	0.72	0.80	0.67	0.80	0.58
DV	0.84	0.84	0.80	0.72	0.80	0.62
PAFE	0.80	0.75	0.82	0.69	0.83	0.60
PAWV	0.83	0.81	0.85	0.77	0.86	0.70
PADV	0.86	0.86	0.87	0.81	0.88	0.76
PAFEFV	**0.95**	**0.95**	**0.96**	**0.94**	0.95	0.90
PAWVFV	**0.95**	**0.94**	0.95	0.93	0.95	0.90
PADVFV	0.93	0.92	0.94	0.92	**0.96**	**0.93**

implementations with the Fisher vectors that demonstrate a significant decrease in the clustering metrics when compared to vectors with less information.

Table 3. Clustering Results.

Case	k	Clustering Results					
		Homogeneity	Completeness	V measurement	Adjusted random	Mutual info	Silhouette index
PA	3	0.007	0.004	0.005	0.003	0.004	0.322
	4	0.008	0.003	0.004	0.001	0.003	0.356
	5	0.013	0.045	0.007	0.016	0.005	0.42
FE	3	0.003	0.001	0.002	0.010	0.001	0.041
	4	0.003	0.001	0.002	0.004	0.001	0.039
	5	0.003	0.013	0.019	0.004	0.001	0.043
WV	3	0.168	0.126	0.143	0.332	0.143	0.443
	4	0.168	0.112	0.135	0.337	0.133	0.408
	5	0.21	0.080	0.116	0.112	0.115	0.130
DV	3	0.154	0.111	0.129	0.307	0.128	**0.530**
	4	0.159	0.103	0.126	0.323	0.125	0.534
	5	0172	0.106	0.131	**0.344**	0.130	0.55

(continued)

Table 3. (*continued*)

Case	k	Clustering Results					
		Homogeneity	Completeness	V measurement	Adjusted random	Mutual info	Silhouette index
PAFE	3	0.169	0.001	0.002	0.010	0.001	0.035
	4	0.175	0.001	0.001	0.007	0.001	0.034
	5	0.151	0.002	0.003	0.0016	0.002	0.033
PAWV	3	0.003	0.106	0.131	0.233	0.130	0.094
	4	0.002	0.073	0.102	0.130	0.101	0.015
	5	0.007	0.054	0.080	0.092	0.079	0.030
PADV	3	0.152	0.110	0.128	0.307	0.127	0.447
	4	0.160	0.084	0.11	0.231	0.109	0.128
	5	0.173	0.070	0.1	0.128	0.099	0.052
PAFEFV	3	0.368	0.169	0.232	0.166	0.231	0.201
	4	0.38	0.138	0.203	0.091	0.202	0.14
	5	0.38	0.12	0.182	0.039	0.182	0.122
PAWVFV	3	0.353	0.173	0.234	0.194	0.231	0.236
	4	0.356	0.136	0.201	0.099	0.205	0.173
	5	0.348	0.110	0.199	0.078	0.191	0.166
PADVFV	3	0.36	**0.177**	**0.242**	0.229	**0.242**	0.248
	4	0.37	0.143	0.210	0.087	0.209	0.180
	5	**0.39**	0.128	0.187	0.079	0.186	0.168

5   Conclusions and Future Work

In this paper, we propose an unsupervised embedding approach that extracts meaningful information from networks of electronic health records to improve the initial tabular data for downstream tasks. The extension of the Word2Vec paradigm to Doc2Vec and Fasttext leads to better classification performance, while the Fasttext approach has the advantage of requiring no retraining upon insertion of new nodes. By utilizing the Fisher vector approach, which is a rare case in the EHR literature for low to high-level representation, information from multiple nodes can be concatenated to the final classification vector to boost the performance in high numbers. Clustering results are also improved by the graph structure information and demonstrate much higher performance with the addition of fisher vectors. It is important to mention that since the proposed methodology is label independent, the provided vectors can be utilized for different supervised or unsupervised ML tasks. Future work is focused on the handling of big data, the integration of an interpretability mechanism that will provide reasonable explanations of the predicted results, and the quantitative comparison with state-of-the-art approaches.

Acknowledgment. This research has been co-financed by the European Union and Greek national funds through the Operational Program Competitiveness, Entrepreneurship, and Innovation, under the call RESEARCH – CREATE –INNOVATE (project code: MediLudus - Personalized home care based on research has based on game and gamified elements T1EDK-03049).

References

1. Ghassemi, M., Naumann, T., Schulam, P., Beam, A.L., Chen, I.Y., Ranganath, R.: A review of challenges and opportunities in machine learning for health. AMIA Jt Summits Transl, Sci, Proc, **2020**, 191–200 (2020)
2. Xiao, C., Choi, E., Sun, J.: Opportunities and challenges in developing deep learning models using electronic health records data: a systematic review. J. Am. Med. Inf. Assoc.: JAMIA **25**, 1419–1428 (Oct2018)
3. Lee, D., Jiang, X., Yu, H.: Harmonized representation learning on dynamic EHR graphs. J. Biomed. Inform. **106**, 103426 (2020)
4. Poongodi, T., Sumathi, D., Suresh, P., Balusamy, B.: Deep learning techniques for electronic health record (EHR) analysis. In: Bhoi, A.K., Mallick, P.K., Liu, C.-M., Balas, V.E. (eds.) Bio-inspired Neurocomputing. SCI, vol. 903, pp. 73–103. Springer, Singapore (2021). https://doi.org/10.1007/978-981-15-5495-7_5
5. Dong, Y., Chawla, N.V., Swami, A.: Metapath2vec: scalable representation learning for heterogeneous networks. In: Proceedings of the 23rd ACM SIGKDD International Conference on Knowledge Discovery and Data Mining (KDD 2017). Association for Computing Machinery, New York (2017)
6. Perronnin, F., Dance, C.: Fisher Kernels on Visual Vocabularies for Image Categorization. In: 2007 IEEE Conference on Computer Vision and Pattern Recognition, pp. 1–8 (2007)
7. Solares, J.R.A., et al.: Deep learning for electronic health records: a comparative review of multiple deep neural architectures. J. Biomed. Inf. **101**, 103337 (2020)
8. Grohe, M.: Word2vec, node2vec, graph2vec, X2vec: towards a theory of vector embeddings of structured data. In: Proceedings of the 39th ACM SIGMOD-SIGACT-SIGAI Symposium on Principles of Database Systems (PODS 2020) , pp. 1–16. Association for Computing Machinery, New York (2020)
9. Grover, A., Leskovec, J.: node2vec: scalable feature learning for networks. In: KDD : proceedings. International Conference on Knowledge Discovery & Data Mining, vol. 2016, pp. 855–864 (2016)
10. Velickovic, P., Fedus, W., Hamilton, W.L., Lio', P., Bengio, Y., Hjelm, R.D.: Deep Graph Infomax. ArXiv, abs/1809.10341 (2019)
11. Kipf, T., Welling, M.: Semi-Supervised Classification with Graph Convolutional Networks. ArXiv, abs/1609.02907 (2017)
12. Velickovic, P., Cucurull, G., Casanova, A., Romero, A., Lio', P., Bengio, Y.: Graph Attention Networks. ArXiv, abs/1710.10903 (2018)
13. Klicpera, J., Bojchevski, A., Günnemann, S.: Predict then propagate: graph neural networks meet personalized PageRank. In: ICLR (2019)
14. Hamilton, W.L., Ying, Z., Leskovec J.: Inductive representation learning on large graphs. In: NIPS (2017)
15. Schlichtkrull, M., Kipf, T., Bloem, P., Berg, R.V., Titov, I., Welling, M.: Modeling Relational Data with Graph Convolutional Networks. ArXiv, abs/1703.06103 (2018)
16. Chiang, W., Liu, X., Si, S., Li, Y., Bengio, S., Hsieh, C.: Cluster-GCN: an efficient algorithm for training deep and large graph convolutional networks. In: Proceedings of the 25th ACM SIGKDD International Conference on Knowledge Discovery & Data Mining (2019)

17. Perozzi, B., Al-Rfou, R., Skiena, S.: DeepWalk: online learning of social representations. In: Proceedings of the 20th ACM SIGKDD International Conference on Knowledge Discovery and Data Mining (KDD 2014) , pp. 701–710. Association for Computing Machinery, New York (2014)
18. Le, Q., Mikolov, T.: Distributed representations of sentences and documents. In: Proceedings of the 31st International Conference on International Conference on Machine Learning, vol. 32, pp. II-1188–II-1196 (2014)
19. Bojanowski, P., Grave, E., Joulin, A., Mikolov, T.: Enriching Word Vectors with Subword Information. Trans. Assoc. Comput. Linguist. 5, 135–146 (July2016)
20. Walonoski, J., et al.: Synthea™ novel coronavirus (COVID-19) model and synthetic data set. Intell.-Based Med. 1, 100007 (2020)

Predicting ALzheimer's Disease with AI and Brain Imaging Data

Chun-Cheng Peng, Guan-Wei Lin$^{(\boxtimes)}$, Jian-Min Lin, Guan-Ting Chen, and Wei-Chen Liu

Department of Information and Communication Engineering, Chaoyang University of Technology, Taichung City, Taiwan (ROC)
goudapeng@cyut.edu.tw, {s10830015,s11130623,s10830075, s10830011}@gm.cyut.edu.tw

Abstract. According to the latest estimates, one in three elderly people will suffer from dementia in 2050, with the majority of cases being Alzheimer's disease. This study proposes a novel deep-learning CNN architecture for the prediction of Alzheimer's disease, utilizing the OASIS-2 dataset. On average, the proposed approach achieves a testing accuracy of 96.37% for 100-fold cross validation, outperforming related works such as VGG-19 [4], AlexNet [3], and GoogLeNet [3] by 0.55%, 4.97%, and 3.35%, respectively. Experimental results provide positive evidence that the proposed approach, with much fewer parameters, has strong potential to tackle the prediction problem of Alzheimer's disease. In the future, a specialized system can be developed to handle Alzheimer's disease and alleviate the diagnostic burden of doctors. This intelligent system can collaborate with doctors in the early stages of diagnosis, reducing the burden of consultations. If the system achieves higher accuracy, it can enable early detection and treatment, delaying the progression of symptoms. Such a system can detect Alzheimer's disease early, monitor the patient's condition over time, provide personalized treatment plans, and achieve better results.

Keywords: Alzheimer's Disease · OASIS · Prediction · Convolutional Neural Networks · Adam Optimizer

1 Introduction

Being the most common dementia, Alzheimer's disease (AD) originated in 1906 when the German psychiatrist and pathologist Eros Alzheimer first published senile dementia [1]. More than a hundred years later, as with no radical cure, AD is now believed to be a brain disease that causes problems with memory, thinking, and behavior, where both courses of medication and diseases are possible to be impeded. Under the assumption of early-discovery, early medical treatment and relative healthcare are extremely important to the AD patients and their families. As a result, plenty of AI approaches in smart healthcare were proposed [2–4] in order to tackle this issue.

© IFIP International Federation for Information Processing 2023
Published by Springer Nature Switzerland AG 2023
I. Maglogiannis et al. (Eds.): AIAI 2023, IFIP AICT 675, pp. 291–301, 2023.
https://doi.org/10.1007/978-3-031-34111-3_25

The progress and development of the medical industry in today's society plays a crucial role in modern people's lives. In the past, many diseases could have irreversible consequences due to a lack of timely and effective diagnosis and treatment. However, today, with the development of technologies such as artificial intelligence [5] and deep learning [6], intelligent medical treatment has become one of the important ways to improve the medical industry.

The development of deep learning technology has brought great help to intelligent medical treatment. Through technologies such as deep learning and machine learning, patients' data can be effectively collected, analyzed, and processed to provide doctors with more accurate diagnosis and treatment plans. In this case, the accuracy and completeness of the data are essential for the training and learning of the artificial intelligence model. Incorrect data will have a negative impact on the model's learning and diagnosis, even leading to incorrect diagnosis and treatment plans.

The application of intelligent medical treatment can not only improve the efficiency and accuracy of the medical industry but also help people better manage their health. For example, in daily life, many people may overlook some abnormal phenomena in their bodies due to busyness or other reasons. However, if intelligent medical treatment technology is used, the patient's data can be used to monitor the body's condition in real-time, and diseases can be detected and treated in a timely manner, thereby better protecting their health.

In summary, the application of intelligent medical treatment is a field worthy of attention and development. Through continuously advancing the development and application of technology, it is believed that in the future, intelligent medical treatment will become more widespread and improved, bringing more benefits to people's health and lives.

This paper adopts deep-learning convolutional neural networks (CNN) [7], and the experimental dataset uses the Open Access Series of Imaging Studies (OASIS). Regarding the application of CNN in medical imaging assistance, current medical image data analysis mostly relies on doctors' naked eye. The observation and reading inspection of medical images, as well as differences based solely on doctor experience, will affect the accuracy of diagnosis to some extent, and the increase in clinical image data has brought a lot of workload to doctors. In recent years, deep learning technology is used to automatically extract features and analyze medical images to provide auxiliary diagnosis, provide doctors with judgment, and reduce the workload of doctors.

2 Related Works

Alzheimer's disease is a cognitive impairment that is degenerative and irreversible. It deteriorates over time, leading to a gradual loss of physical function. In recent years, with the development of smart medical care, many scholars have used deep learning to identify Alzheimer's disease, with good results in recognition accuracy.

There are several common methods for diagnosing AD, including medical history, physical examination, psychological testing, MRI and CT scans, and biomarker testing. Among them, fMRI [8] is a new diagnostic method that also has potential in AD diagnosis. Research by Samuel L. Warren et al. [9] has shown that fMRI and deep learning can be used for AD diagnosis. However, due to the complexity and noise issues of fMRI, further exploration is needed for its clinical applications. To address fMRI noise, Quan Mai et al. [10] used the BrainVGAE neural network for data processing, while Xuan Kan et al. [11] used the FBNetGen neural network to predict clinical outcomes. Tianren Yang et al. [12] conducted related research using fMRI and proposed new architectures and methods that could be used for Alzheimer's disease classification and biomarker research, potentially becoming an important diagnostic tool in the future. The OASIS is a project that aims to make brain neuroimaging datasets freely available to the scientific community. This experiment utilized OASIS-2 [13], which includes MRI scans of elderly individuals aged 60 years and above, with each participant undergoing 2 or more scans separated by at least 1 year. As a result, a total of 373 MRI scans were obtained.

Junxiu Liu et al. [3] proposed a deep separable CNN model for AD classification. In their work, depthwise separable convolution (DSC) was used to replace the traditional network, and the parameter setting and calculation costs were greatly reduced. Figure 1 displays the network architecture proposed in [3]. Experimental results indicate that the DSC algorithm based on OASIS AD detection in this dataset is very successful, and AlexNet and GoogLeNet are also used for migration learning, with an average classification rate of 91.40% and 93.02%. L. Sathish Kumar et al. [2] proposed the use of the OASIS brain dataset for testing. The proposed model used all parts of the human brain, such as axial and shape loss, to detect AD, and applied more than 100,000 MRI images for training, while the final accuracy rate reaches 98.35%. Figure 2 exhibits the methods proposed by [2]. Manimurugan S suggested [4] that early diagnosis is very important; the study utilized a pre-trained deep transfer learning model VGG-19 for MRI images. The main processes are preprocessing, feature extraction, and classification, and 373 MRI images were obtained from the OASIS dataset for evaluation. For 80% training and 20% testing, compared with existing CNN models (such as AlexNet, GoogLeNet, and VGG-16), the evaluation process uses 5 evaluation indicators to test the performance of the model. The final model achieves 96.04% training accuracy and a 95:82% test rate, which is 1.90% to 5.30% higher than the AlexNet and GoogLeNet models in performance. Figure 3 shows the network architecture model proposed by the author. Table 1 summarizes the aforementioned relevant findings.

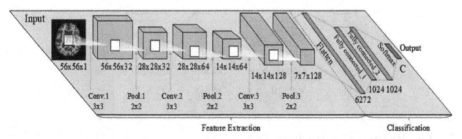

Fig. 1. The author used this model as a reference and basis

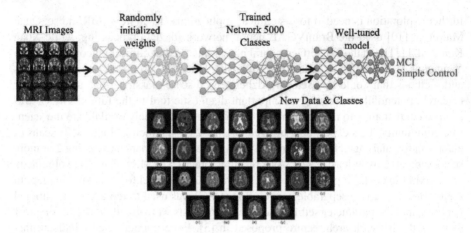

Fig. 2. Proposed Methodology and Framework

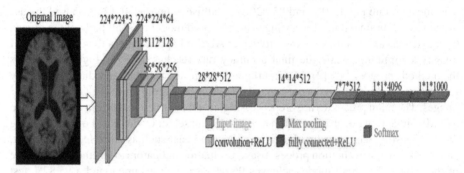

Fig. 3. A Detailed Look at the Proposed VGG-19 Architecture

Table 1. Synthesis of Related Research Results

Paper	Module	Dataset	Accuracy
[3]	Alexnet	OASIS	98.35%
[4]	Alexnet	OASIS	91.40%
[4]	GoogLeNet	OASIS	93.02%
[5]	Vgg-19	OASIS	95.82%

3   The Proposed Approach

In order to convert medical files into visualized PNG images, this study utilized the powerful NIFTI Image Converter [14], which offers various practical features. For example, with this converter we can easily change the angle of medical files, including 90, 180, and 270 degrees. Before outputting the image, we can also determine the dimension of the file, whether it is 3D or 4D. To optimize computing resources and further adjust the models and corresponding free parameters, we resize the images to 32 × 32 pixels. The reason behind using such small images is that it reduces the computational complexity of the model and enables faster training, ultimately shortening the time required for model development. In Fig. 4, we present an example of a medical file converted using the NIFTI Image Converter, demonstrating its efficiency and usefulness.

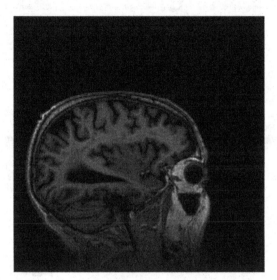

Fig. 4. MRI Image with 256 × 256 Pixel Matrix Size

Figure 5 shows the network architecture used in this experiment. The design of this CNN architecture aims to extract features from images through multiple layers of convolution and pooling, and map these features to different classes. Before the convolution operation, the image is transformed into a matrix form, and convolution is performed by setting different convolution kernels. In this CNN architecture, each convolutional layer uses different convolution kernels to detect different features.

After the convolution operation, pooling layers are added to the model to reduce the size of the feature map. Two different pooling methods are used here, namely max pooling and average pooling. Max pooling selects the maximum value in each region, while average pooling calculates the average value of each region. These pooling operations can reduce the size of the feature map while retaining the most important features.

After extracting the features of the image, these features need to be mapped to different classes. To achieve this goal, two fully connected layers are added to the model. In these fully connected layers, each neuron is connected to all neurons in the previous layer, and its output value is adjusted by weight matrices. These fully connected layers can find the best weights and biases through learning to achieve image classification.

To further improve the performance of the model, Rectified Linear Units (ReLU) are added after the convolution, pooling, and fully connected layers. ReLU is a nonlinear function that can convert negative numbers to 0 while retaining positive numbers. This can effectively reduce the computation and parameter numbers, while improving the accuracy and generalization ability of the model. In addition, since ReLU can effectively avoid the gradient vanishing problem, it has been widely used in deep learning.

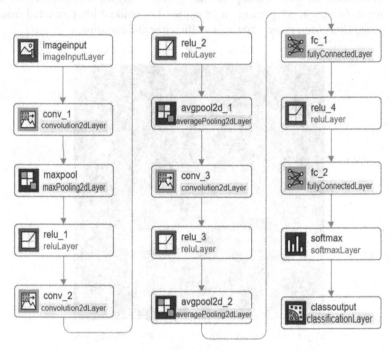

Fig. 5. Components and Layers of the CNN Model Architecture

Proper optimization algorithms and hyperparameter selection are crucial when training deep learning models, as they can have a significant impact on the model's performance and training speed. In this study, the Adam optimizer was used to optimize the parameters of a CNN model for better training results. The Adam optimizer [15] is an adaptive learning rate optimization algorithm that combines the advantages of the AdaGrad and RMSProp algorithms and dynamically adjusts the learning rate based on the gradient and update history of each parameter. Compared to traditional gradient descent algorithms, the Adam optimizer can converge faster and avoid problems such as vanishing or exploding gradients, making it widely used in the field of deep learning.

In addition to the Adam optimizer, other hyperparameters need to be appropriately set in the experiment, such as learning rate, batch size, and iteration times. The choice of these hyperparameters affects the model's training speed and performance. A larger learning rate can lead to faster training speed, but may also cause the model to oscillate or not converge. A larger batch size can use more samples for training, but it also increases memory overhead and computation time. Iteration times is also an important hyperparameter, as too many iterations can lead to overfitting, while too few iterations can prevent the model from converging. Therefore, choosing the appropriate hyperparameters is crucial, and optimization needs to be performed through experiments and parameter tuning. In this study, the authors continuously adjusted the values of hyperparameters and finally obtained the best combination of parameters to maximize the model's accuracy and generalization performance. Table 2 summarizes the modified parameters used in this experiment, including learning rate, batch size, training rounds, and other relevant hyperparameters.

Table 2. Adam Optimizer Parameters Used in the Model

Parameter name	Parameter value
InitialLearnRate	0.001
LearnRateDropFactor	0.01
LearnRateDropPeriod	30
L2Regularization	0.0000004
MaxEpochs	50
MiniBatchSize	128
Shuffle	every-epoch

4   Experimental Results and Discussions

All simulations of this paper are implemented via the Deep Learning Toolbox, MATLAB 2020a, on a MS-Windows 10 platform equipped with Intel® Core™ i7-2600 CPU @ 3.40 GHZ. For the sake of cross validation, the 50- run and 100-run simulation results are conducted, with the ratio between training, validation and testing 70%, 15% and 15%. Figures 6 and 7 respectively display the simulation curves and corresponding confusion matrices.

It can be observed that, from Table 3, the averaged testing accuracies for our 50- and 100-run cross validations are 96.24% and 96.37%, respectively, which outperform the latest related works, i.e., VGG-19 [4], AlexNet [3] and GoogLeNet [3], by 0.55%, 4.97% and 3.35%, respectively. As a result, our preliminary experimental results provide promising performance for AD prediction, in terms of higher accuracy and low computational complexity.

Table 3. Summary of Averaged Simulation Outcomes

RUN	Training (%)	Validation (%)	Testing (%)
50-RUN	98.79	96.29	96.24
100-RUN	99.18	96.42	96.37

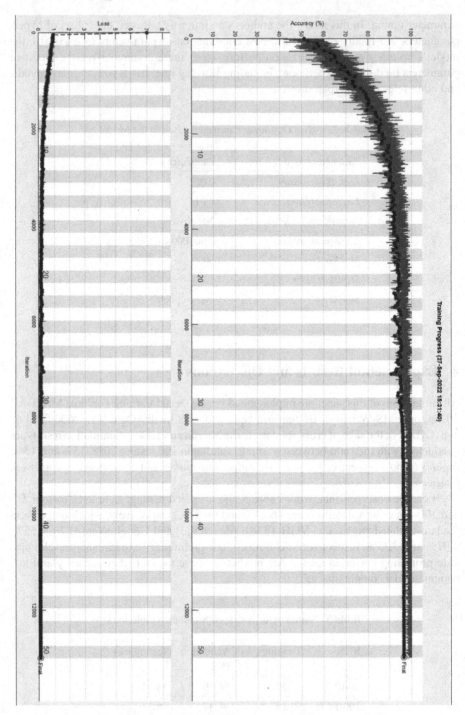

Fig. 6. Learning Curve for a Single Training Run

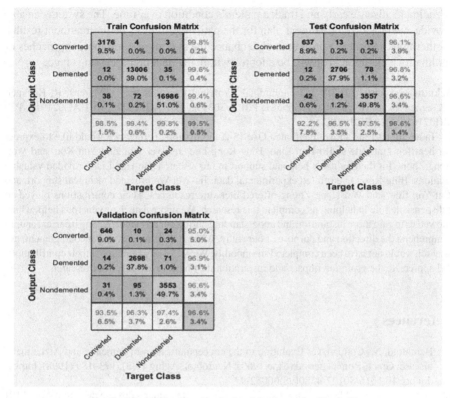

Fig. 7. Model Testing: Confusion Matrices of a Single Run

5 Conclusions and Future Works

Being a no-radical-cure disease, AD diagnosis is limited to the proper and precise interpretation of the specific questionnaires and examinations by medical personnels. In this
study, a revised CNN-like deep-learning approach for AD prediction is proposed in order
to develop medical assistant systems for effective healthcare. Experimental comparison
on the OASIS-2 dataset shows that, the proposed approach achieved the averaged training and testing accuracies of 99.18% and 96.37%, under 100-fold cross validation, which
is with strong potential to surmount other related deep-learning methods. In the coming
future, other OASIS datasets will be taken into consideration in order to further verify the
generalization ability and continuously enhance performance of our proposed system.

In the future, we will develop a specialized system for Alzheimer's disease. This intelligent system can collaborate with doctors in the first stage of diagnosing Alzheimer's
disease, thus reducing the burden of doctors' consultations. The conducting system will
apply intelligent technologies to analyze a patient's vast amount of data, such as blood
tests, electroencephalograms, and imaging tests, to provide a comprehensive assessment
of the patient's condition.

If the system has a higher accuracy rate, it can also achieve the effect of early detection
and early treatment, delaying the deterioration of symptoms. Such a system can detect

Alzheimer's disease early and track a patient's condition over time. The system can also provide a personalized treatment plan for the patient, providing better treatment results. Furthermore, in order to progressively enhance the system performance, approaches of cardinality estimation [16] will be adopted within the data preprocessing stage.

Acknowledgments. OASIS-2: Longitudinal: Principal Investigators: D. Marcus, R, Buckner, J. Csernansky, J. Morris; P50 AG05681, P01 AG03991, P01 AG026276, R01 AG021910, P20 MH071616, U24 RR021382.

In addition to the above-mentioned OASIS-2 contributors, hereby, we would like to express our heartfelt gratitude to Bo-Han Liao, Bing-Rong Lee, Jia-Wei Wu, Zhu-Yun Kou, and Wei-Hong Zhong for their valuable help and support in our research. Bo-Han Liao provided valuable opinions, Bing-Rong Lee offered experimental data, Jia-Wei Wu provided technical support, and Zhu-Yun Kou, and Wei-Hong Zhong offered literature resources. Their contributions played an indispensable role in helping us complete this research. We appreciate their generous help, which allowed us to gain more inspiration and understanding during our research, making it easier for us to comprehend the direction and purpose of our study. Without their support and encouragement, our research would not have been completed so smoothly. We will always remember their contributions and appreciate the profound impact and inspiration they have given us for our research.

References

1. Berchtold, N., Cotman, C.: Evolution in the conceptualization of dementia and Alzheimer's disease: Greco-Roman period to the 1960s. Neurobiol. Aging **19**(3), 173–189 (1998). https://doi.org/10.1016/S0197-4580(98)00052-9
2. Kumar, L., et al.: AlexNet approach for early stage Alzheimer's disease detection from MRI brain images. Mater. Today: Proc. **51**(1), 58–65 (2022). https://doi.org/10.1016/j.matpr.2021.04.415
3. Luo, Y., et al.: Alzheimer's disease detection using depthwise separable convolutional neural networks. Comput. Methods Programs Biomed. **203**, 106032 (2021). https://doi.org/10.1016/j.cmpb.2021.106032
4. Manimurugan, S.: Classification of Alzheimer's disease from MRI Images using CNN based Pre-trained VGG-19 Model. J. Comput. Sci. Intell. Technol. **1**(2), 15–21 (2020). https://doi.org/10.53409/mnaa.jcsit20201205
5. Russell, S., Norvig, P.: Artificial Intelligence: A Modern Approach, 4th edn. Pearson, Boston (2021)
6. LeCun, Y., Bengio, Y., Hinton, G.: Deep learning. Nature **521**, 436–444 (2015). https://doi.org/10.1038/nature14539
7. Alzubaidi, L., et al.: Review of deep learning: concepts, CNN architectures, challenges, applications, future directions. J. Big Data **8**(1), 1–74 (2021). https://doi.org/10.1186/s40537-021-00444-8
8. Singleton, M.: Functional magnetic resonance imaging. Yale J. Biol. Med. **82**(4), 233 (2009)
9. Warren, S., Moustafa, A.: Functional magnetic resonance imaging, deep learning, and Alzheimer's disease: a systematic review. J. Neuroimaging **33**(1), 5–18 (2023). https://doi.org/10.1111/jon.13063
10. Quan, M., Nakarmi, U., Huang, M.: BrainVGAE: end-to-end graph neural networks for noisy fMRI dataset. In: Proceedings on 2022 IEEE International Conference on Bioinformatics and Biomedicine (BIBM), pp. 3852–3855. IEEE (2022). https://doi.org/10.1109/BIBM55620.2022.9994963

11. Xuan, K., Cui, H., Lukemire, J., Guo, Y., Yang, C.: FBnetgen: task-aware gnn-based fmri analysis via functional brain network generation. In: Proceedings on International Conference on Medical Imaging with Deep Learning, pp. , 618–637. PMLR (2022)

12. Yang, T., Al-Duailij, M., Bozdag, S., Saeed, F.: Classification of autism spectrum disorder using rs-fMRI data and graph convolutional networks. In: 2022 IEEE International Conference on Big Data (Big Data), pp. 3131–3138. IEEE (2022). https://doi.org/10.1109/BigData55660.2022.10021070

13. Marcus, D., et al.: Open access series of imaging studies: longitudinal MRI data in nondemented and demented older adults. J. Cogn. Neurosci. **22**(12), 2677–2684 (2010). https://doi.org/10.1162/jocn.2007.19.9.1498

14. Laurence, A.: NIfTI Image Converter (2022). https://github.com/alexlaurence/NIfTI-Image-Converter. GitHub. Accessed 9 Dec 2022

15. Kingma, D., Ba, J.: Adam: a method for stochastic optimization. arXiv preprint arXiv:1412.6980 (2014). https://doi.org/10.48550/arXiv.1412.6980

16. Drakopoulos, G., Kontopoulos, S., Makris, C.: Eventually consistent cardinality estimation with applications in biodata mining. In: Proceedings of the 31st Annual ACM Symposium on Applied Computing, pp. 941–944 (2016)

Pre-trained Model Robustness Against GAN-Based Poisoning Attack in Medical Imaging Analysis

Pakpoom Singkorapoom and Suronapee Phoomvuthisarn[✉]

Department of Statistics, Chulalongkorn University, Bangkok, Thailand
pakpoom.singkora@gmail.com, suronapee@cbs.chula.ac.th

Abstract. Deep learning revolutionizes healthcare, particularly in medical image classification, with its analysis performance aided by public architectures and transfer learning for pre-trained models. However, these models are vulnerable to adversarial attacks as they rely on learned parameters, and their unexplainable nature can make it challenging to identify and fix the root cause of the model after an attack. Given the increasing use of pre-trained models in life-critical domains like healthcare, testing their robustness against attacks is essential. Evasion and poisoning attacks are two primary attack types, with poisoning attacks having a broader range of poison sample-generating methods, making testing model robustness under them more critical than under evasion attacks. Poisoning attacks do not require an attacker to have a complete understanding to corrupt the model, making them more likely to occur in the real world. This paper evaluates the robustness of the famous pre-trained models trained as binary classifiers under poisonous label attack. The attacks use GANs to generate mislabeled fake images and feed poison samples to the model in a black box manner. The amount of performance degradation using classification metrics evaluates the model's robustness. We found that ConvNeXt architecture is the most robust against this type of attack, suggesting that transformer architecture can be used to build a more robust deep-learning model.

Keywords: adversarial machine learning · poisoning attack · medical image classification · generative adversarial networks (GANs)

1 Introduction

We have seen tremendous development in deep learning-powered applications in almost every field of business in the past few years. Healthcare and the medical field have also benefitted from this rise for some time. Nevertheless, a thorough analysis of the model's robustness and security must be considered for life-critical applications. The topic of adversarial attacks in deep learning has been a concern in the research field since the discovery of [1]. "Adversarial examples," tiny input modifications imperceptible to humans, can cause neural networks to make prediction errors, posing security risks for machine

© IFIP International Federation for Information Processing 2023
Published by Springer Nature Switzerland AG 2023
I. Maglogiannis et al. (Eds.): AIAI 2023, IFIP AICT 675, pp. 302–313, 2023.
https://doi.org/10.1007/978-3-031-34111-3_26

learning due to the unpredictable behavior they cause. In healthcare, medical images acquired from different modalities, such as X-ray radiography, computed tomography (CT), and magnetic resonance imaging (MRI), are crucial in healthcare data analysis as they serve as the essential source of data, accounting for 90% [2] and provide important anatomical information used in the detection/localization and diagnosis of abnormalities [3]. However, recent research has revealed that medical images can be susceptible to modification and utilized in adversarial attacks, which raises significant concerns regarding the use of such technology in applications that impact human lives [4].

An adversarial attack against the model's security aspect can be divided into two types of attacks, evasion attack, and poisoning attack [5–8]. The evasion attack occurs during the inference phase of the model life cycle, where we want to use the model to predict unseen samples, whereas poisoning attack occurs in the training phase. While an evasion attack solely affects prediction results, a poisoning attack can potentially modify the learning process and produce a suboptimal classifier due to the insertion of contaminated samples. The attacker may use different methods to generate poisoned samples, including advanced deep learning technologies such as generative adversarial networks or GANs [9–12] frequently employed in medical data augmentation [13–16]. This type of attack can be executed with limited knowledge about the target model. Furthermore, the attacker may take advantage of the necessity to update or retrain an existing model by surreptitiously introducing poison samples into the system [3, 7] without the requirement to directly manipulate the samples, as is the case with evasion attacks. In light of these factors, poisoning attacks pose a more significant threat to healthcare than evasion attacks.

In this paper, we conduct an experiment to study the robustness of various deep learning pre-train models in medical image classification against a poisoning attack. First, we consider the poisonous label attack scheme proposed by [17], a black box attack that uses GANs to generate fake images and mislabel them from the true class label. The black-box attack is more realistic than the white-box attack, requiring only limited knowledge about the dataset. Next, we simulate the attack on five different binary classifiers and find that the ConvNeXt architecture is the most robust, while VGG16 is the weakest. This paper's contribution is the demonstration that advanced pre-trained deep learning models can be vulnerable to attacks, especially in healthcare. This highlights the need for robust and secure medical image classifiers that can resist such attacks. The suggested models in this study serve as a starting point for developing more reliable and secure classifiers, ultimately enhancing patient care and safety.

2 Related Work

Existing research has identified two types of adversarial attacks depending on the timing of the attack: evasion and poisoning attacks. In evasion attacks, the attacker manipulates the input to the model during inference time by adding a carefully crafted perturbation, leading to incorrect predictions. For instance, in [18], the author demonstrates that GoogLeNet misclassifies a perturbed panda image as a gibbon with high confidence. On the other hand, a poisoning attack occurs during the training or update phase, whereby the attacker creates poison samples that look realistic but typically with inconsistent labels, leading to changes in decision boundaries [5, 7]. These attacks can be further categorized into white-box and black-box attacks. In white-box attacks, the attacker is assumed to understand the target model, which is unrealistic, but developers can use this setting to test the worst-case performance of the target model. Whereas a black-box attack does not require an attacker to have complete information about the system, only the input and output formats of the target system are sufficient [5]. In healthcare, poisoning attacks are more relevant than evasion attacks because poisoning attacks only need an attacker to stealthily add poison samples to the dataset compared to direct manipulation of unseen samples at the inference time of evasion attacks which could require more skill and effort of an attacker [3]. Additionally, an attacker can launch poisoning attacks using various methods of poison sample generation, which can increase the chance of the attack's success and affect the entire learning process, resulting in a poor classifier. In contrast, evasion attacks rely on adding perturbations to inference samples and only affect the prediction result.

There have been many studies on poisoning attacks in deep neural networks. In one study [19], the authors investigated poisoning attacks in three tasks: sample and malware detection and hand digit recognition. They proposed a back gradient optimization algorithm that can trace the gradient computation process and solve the bi-level optimization problem to obtain poison samples that can degrade the performance of the target model. In spam and malware detection, they showed that the test set error rate of one-layer neural networks with ten neurons could be increased up to 25% in a white-box attack setting. However, the method slightly increased classification errors in handwritten digit recognition using CNN as the target model. The authors in [9] proposed a solution to the computational intensity issue of [19] by utilizing generative adversarial networks with an autoencoder as the generator and the target model serving as the discriminator. They experimented with MNIST and CIFAR-10 datasets, using a two-layer feed-forward neural network and the LeNet model as the target models. They achieved at least a 16.59% decrease in accuracy for the two-layer feed-forward neural network on MNIST and a 20.74% decrease in accuracy for the LeNet model on CIFAR-10, with a 200-fold improvement in poison generation time. Although these methods are effective, their white-box nature is also a drawback. In contrast, the authors in [17] proposed a poisonous label attack method that uses DCGAN with reconstruction loss to generate poison samples that look realistic and are mislabeled with a probability transition vector. This method was tested on the MNIST dataset with a LeNet model, resulting in a 65.4% decrease in accuracy after injecting 900 poison samples. Although this result is slightly worse than the previous two studies, the poisonous label attack is a black-box attack, making it more realistic and easier to deploy in real-world applications.

Although the experiments discussed used deep neural networks, the methods described so far report their results with standard datasets, e.g., MNIST, and CIFAR-10, which are not representative of real-world or healthcare-domain datasets. Also, the target model architecture used in these experiments is relatively simple and not state-of-the-art. The study [20] conducted an algorithm-independent poisoning attack on five healthcare tabular datasets and six machine learning algorithms, including multilayer perceptrons (MLPs). By adjusting the degree of performance degradation, poison samples were added to the dataset and were shown to compromise the performance of the models. The study found that adding 30% poison samples to the training data led to a 20% and 26% decrease in accuracy for the thyroid disease and breast cancer datasets when used to train MLPs, respectively. Other studies [4, 21] demonstrated the susceptibility of deep learning pre-trained models in healthcare and medical images. [4] explained that pre-trained models in this domain are uniquely susceptible to these attacks due to monetary incentives and technical vulnerability. They stated that the ground truth in this domain is often ambiguous and that without the eyes of the expert, it is almost impossible to diagnose data correctly, and if a malicious attacker perturbs data even the expert may have a tough time. Moreover, medical images are highly standardized compared to raw images because these images are captured by pre-defined and well-established positioning and exposure. This high-standard property is the potential to be attacked because the dynamic nature of natural images can mitigate the effects of the attack. They also demonstrated the attack across three datasets, i.e., diabetic retinopathy, pneumothorax chest x-ray, and dermoscopic melanoma photographs, against ResNet50 architecture and reported that the attacks could completely fool the model. Under three white and black box attack types, [21] analyzed two CNN models trained on the chest x-ray dataset against Inception-ResNet-V2 and Nasnet-Large. The result is not entirely different from previous works. Although [4, 21] have shown that deep learning pre-trained models used in medical image classification can be compromised, they only studied evasion attacks, which we believe will have less impact than poisoning attacks in the healthcare domain, as we stated before. This paper explores the impact of error-generic performance degradation caused by a black box poisoning attack, specifically a poisonous label attack. We conduct experiments using five binary deep learning classifiers trained on a chest x-ray images dataset and investigate how each model's performance changes due to poison samples injected during update time.

3 Methods

3.1 Overview

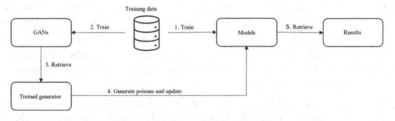

Fig. 1. Overview of the experiment

The experimental framework is illustrated in Fig. 1. Initially, a dataset is collected, and a training set is used to train five binary classifiers. Next, GANs are also trained using the training set. Then, the generator component of GANs is extracted to generate fake images with mislabeled attributes. Poison samples are then applied to update the trained classifiers. Afterward, performance degradation data is gathered and plotted to visualize the results.

3.2   Dataset

We use the chest x-ray dataset from [22], which contains chest x-ray images of three classes, including covid-19, pneumonia, and normal lung. Since we focused on binary classifiers, we used only pneumonia and normal images. The dataset consists of 14,507 images for training, with 6,849 images depicting normal lungs and 7,208 images depicting pneumonia. The dataset also contained 3,514 validation images, including 1,712 normal lung images and 1,802 pneumonia images, and 4,393 test images, comprising 2,140 normal lung images and 2,253 pneumonia images. All images were preprocessed and scaled to 128 x 128 pixels, and the dataset did not exhibit any signs of class imbalance.

3.3   Models

To evaluate the robustness of models, we trained five deep learning pre-trained models as binary classifiers: VGG16, ResNet50V2, MobileNetV2, InceptionV3, and ConvNetX-Tiny. These models differ in various aspects, such as architecture, number of layers, number of learned parameters, technique employed, and hyperparameters, and should behave differently under attack. We hypothesize that VGG16 may suffer the most because of its simple architecture of stacking convolution layers. Next, each model was trained consistently using transfer learning. We used parameters learned from the ImageNet dataset and replaced the old classifier portion with our new classifier. We used Adam optimizer with a learning rate of 0.0001 and batch size of 64, and an early stopping strategy to halt training before overfitting. Once all models were trained, we fine-tuned the weight of each network by unfreezing all weights and trained each network for another 16 epochs using a small learning rate of 0.00001 [23]. In these 16 epochs, we only saved the model that achieved the best validation metric for each architecture.

3.4   Attack Method

In this study, we use a poisonous label attack purposed by [17] as an attack method. The poisonous label attack is a black box, meaning the attacker does not need complete information about the attacked or victim model. It is also a performance degradation type that aims to cause classification errors. Initially, this attack is targeted, which means it aims to cause misclassification on a specific set of samples but can be adjusted to attack indiscriminately. It is also error-generic that will have samples misclassified as any other class except the actual class. This attack is feasible because conditional GANs [24] generate fake images for each class and a probability transition vector to mislabel those images from the true class. We also use the FID score [25] to evaluate the quality of generated images.

First, we build a conditional DCGAN [26] to generate fake images of normal and pneumonia lungs. In this process, we build the conditional DCGAN using only training data to prevent GANs from learning information about the image in the validation set and test set. We use the architecture of the generator and discriminator proposed in [15] as our initial idea and make modifications. As reported in [17, 27], adding reconstruction loss to the GANs' primary objective function can improve the quality of the generated image, so we mount L1 reconstruction loss to it. We also employ a two-time scale update rule [25], which uses different learning rates in the generator and discriminator and can stabilize the training process. For the generator, we use a learning rate of 0.0001, and for the discriminator, we use a learning rate of 0.0003. In the generator, instead of using a convolutional transpose layer as in [26], we use a convolutional layer along with the nearest neighbor upsampling method, which can reduce the checkerboard artifact in generated images [28]. To make DCGAN conditional as described in [24], we use an embedding layer to transform the integer representing the label to a matrix and pass this matrix along with the corresponding image. In training time, we train our networks for 200 epochs and use a batch size of 16. For every five epochs, we compute the FID score, a metric measuring distance between data distribution and generated distribution. The FID score is the most popular metric for evaluating the quality of generated images; the lower the score the better the quality. In our work, we use the FID implementation of [29] which takes into account the effect of resizing images before feeding them to InceptionV3 network. For each FID computation, we compute three values of FID due to the random property of input to the generator using an equal number of images between images in the training data of two classes and generated data and take the average of three values. Figure 2 shows the average FID score for every five epochs.

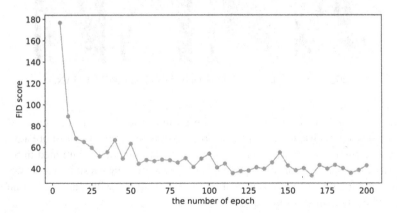

Fig. 2. The average FID score for every five epochs in training.

Once the training is finished, we investigate the epoch with the lowest average FID score and find that at the end of epoch 165th, the average FID score is 33.58. Therefore, we save the generator at this epoch and use it in the attacking experiment. Figure 3 shows examples of generated images of normal and pneumonia lungs from our 165th epoch generator.

After we have obtained the generator, another part of the poisonous label attack is mislabeling these generated samples. In [17], the authors use the probability transition vector or poisoning vector called by the authors. The poisoning vector has two versions: the symmetric and asymmetric poisoning vectors. The probability of the symmetric poisoning vector is a uniform distribution that changes the label of generated samples to other labels randomly and uniformly. In contrast, the probability distribution of the asymmetric poisoning vector is a two-point distribution that alters the label of generated

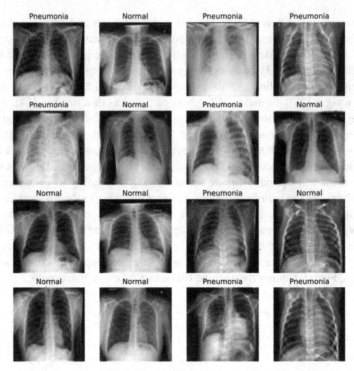

Fig. 3. Example of images generated by conditional DCGAN.

samples to a single label different from the ground truth label. In this case, we only consider the asymmetric poisoning vector reported by the authors to be more aggressive than the symmetric poisoning vector. As our five victim models mentioned in Sect. 3.2 are binary classifiers, we only swap the label of these two classes so that after we create fake typical lung images with 0 as the ground truth label, we will change it to 1 and vice versa for fake pneumonia images.

4   Result

4.1   Performance Evaluation

Before we perform the attack experiment, we evaluate the test set performances of our models using the following classification metrics: accuracy, sensitivity, and specificity. The result is shown in Table 1.

For the attack experiment, we updated our models with poison samples generated by conditional DCGAN. We first generated 32 images of normal and pneumonia lungs, 64 images in total which equate to our train batch size, and mislabeled them as described in Sect. 3.3. We then fed these poison samples to our models using the same learning as a training phase. We only update our models with less than 14,000 poison samples as 14,000 is roughly our training data size, and for each model, we repeated the update

Table 1. Test set performances for three classification metrics of models

Model	Accuracy	Sensitivity	Specificity
VGG16	0.9463	0.9387	0.9542
ResNet50v2	0.9313	0.9387	0.9234
MobileNetv2	0.9360	0.9316	0.9406
InceptionV3	0.9367	0.9348	0.9388
ConvNext-Tiny	0.9369	0.9243	0.9489

three times to get the average value of performance drop. Figures 4, 5 and 6 show the performance drop trends for each model's classification metric.

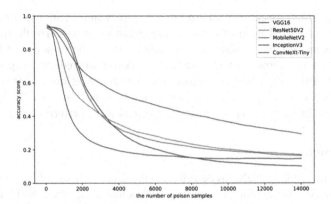

Fig. 4. Average accuracy drops for each model

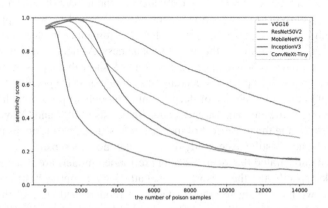

Fig. 5. Average sensitivity drops for each model

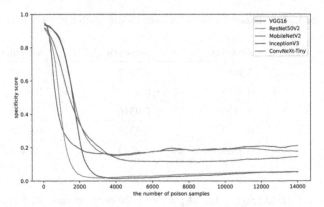

Fig. 6. Average specificity drops for each model

From Fig. 4, 5, 6, we can see that in terms of accuracy and sensitivity, ConvNeXt-Tiny is the most robust model against the poisonous label attack, followed by the ResNet50V2. As we hypothesized, the VGG16 model cannot restrain the poisonous label attack's effect. Figure 5 also shows that all models tend to suffer in predicting negative class as all lines go down rapidly when the number of poison samples is around 2,000. There is an interesting behavior in Fig. 5 where poison samples can help improve the sensitivity of models, but as the number of poison samples increases, the performance still decreases.

4.2 Discussion

The architecture of ConvNeXt, as described in the paper [30], closely resembles that of ResNet. However, the authors incorporate various techniques from Swin Transformer into the ResNet body, which may explain why ResNet50V2 performs as the second-best model in our experiment. As ConvNeXt employs Swin Transformer technology, we can infer that Transformer technology may help alleviate the impact of poison samples and may be more secure than the traditional convolutional neural network approach. Furthermore, both ConvNeXt and ResNet50V2 share a dominant characteristic: the residual connection that can contribute to the model's robustness. As demonstrated in Fig. 6, our experiments on a binary chest x-ray classification task show that a poisoning attack can significantly increase false positives, leading to a sudden drop in specificity scores. This result highlights the vulnerability of deep learning models to poisonous label attacks, even when using well-established architectures like ResNet50V2 and ConvNeXt. However, it is worth noting that the effect of increasing false negatives is not as pronounced, even though the attack still successfully degrades the model's sensitivity.

We have demonstrated that deep learning pre-trained models are susceptible to poisoning attacks, specifically the poisonous label attack. Our approach differs from prior works in that we have evaluated these attacks on modern and state-of-the-art model architectures using a real-world dataset from the healthcare domain. The findings of this study have significant implications for the medical community, as the results highlight the importance of developing robust medical image classifiers resistant to adversarial attacks. Furthermore, our suggested models can serve as a starting point for researchers and practitioners to develop more secure and reliable medical image classifiers, which can ultimately improve patient care and safety.

5 Conclusion and Future Work

In this paper, we conduct an experiment showing that the poisonous label attack can compromise various CNN models used for medical image classification tasks. We use conditional DCGAN with an average FID score of 33.58 to generate fake images of normal and pneumonia lungs. After that, we update the five-trained CNN model with generated images with the wrong label and observe the performance degradation. We found that ConvNeXt is the most robust model among five others, followed by Resnet50v2. These might suggest that the technology in the Transformer and residual connection, the main characteristic of convnext and resnet, can be adapted to create a more secure classification model in the medical images domain, and the simple architecture of stacking convolution layers model like VGG16 should be avoided.

In the future, with more time and resources, we could try experimenting with more types of attacks, e.g., targeted poisoning attack and back door attack, and we could use the SOTA models in the medical image domain and also general SOTA models for example, Swin Transformer, Vision Transformer, and other attention-based models as our victim model. Additionally, it is worthwhile to explore the model's interpretability under attacks, such as evaluating the effect of attacks on Grad-CAM's visualization or Transformer's attention maps.

References

1. Szegedy, C., et al.: Intriguing properties of neural networks. arXiv preprint arXiv:1312.6199 (2013)
2. Zhou, S.K., et al.: A review of deep learning in medical imaging: Imaging traits, technology trends, case studies with progress highlights, and future promises. Proc. IEEE **109**(5), 820–838 (2021)
3. Qayyum, A., et al.: Secure and robust machine learning for healthcare: a survey. IEEE Rev. Biomed. Eng. **14**, 156–180 (2020)
4. Finlayson, S.G., et al.: Adversarial attacks against medical deep learning systems. arXiv preprint arXiv:1804.05296 (2018)
5. Bae, H., et al.: Security and privacy issues in deep learning. arXiv preprint arXiv:1807.11655 (2018)
6. Biggio, B., Roli, F.: Wild patterns: ten years after the rise of adversarial machine learning. Pattern Recogn. **84**, 317–331 (2018)
7. Liu, Q., et al.: A survey on security threats and defensive techniques of machine learning: a data driven view. IEEE access **6**, 12103–12117 (2018)
8. Liu, X., et al.: Privacy and security issues in deep learning: a survey. IEEE Access **9**, 4566–4593 (2020)
9. Yang, C., et al.: Generative poisoning attack method against neural networks. arXiv preprint arXiv:1703.01340 (2017)
10. Shi, Y., et al.: Generative adversarial networks for black-box API attacks with limited training data. In: 2018 IEEE International Symposium on Signal Processing and Information Technology (ISSPIT). IEEE (2018)

11. Muñoz-González, L., et al.: Poisoning attacks with generative adversarial nets. arXiv preprint arXiv:1906.07773 (2019)

12. Kasichainula, K., Mansourifar, H., Shi, W.: Poisoning attacks via generative adversarial text to image synthesis. In: 2021 51st Annual IEEE/IFIP International Conference on Dependable Systems and Networks Workshops (DSN-W). IEEE (2021)

13. Zhang, Q., et al.: Medical image synthesis with generative adversarial networks for tissue recognition. In: 2018 IEEE International Conference on Healthcare Informatics (ICHI). IEEE (2018)

14. Bhagat, V., Bhaumik, S.: Data augmentation using generative adversarial networks for pneumonia classification in chest Xrays. In: 2019 Fifth International Conference on Image Information Processing (ICIIP). IEEE (2019)

15. Kora Venu, S., Ravula, S.: Evaluation of deep convolutional generative adversarial networks for data augmentation of chest x-ray images. Future Internet 13(1), 8 (2020)

16. Kim, D., Joo, J., Kim, S.C.: Fake data generation for medical image augmentation using GANs. In: 2022 International Conference on Artificial Intelligence in Information and Communication (ICAIIC). IEEE (2022)

17. Liu, H., Li, D., Li, Y.: Poisonous label attack: black-box data poisoning attack with enhanced conditional DCGAN. Neural Process. Lett. 53(6), 4117–4142 (2021). https://doi.org/10.1007/s11063-021-10584-w

18. Goodfellow, I.J., Shlens, J., Szegedy, C.: Explaining and harnessing adversarial examples. arXiv preprint arXiv:1412.6572 (2014)

19. Muñoz-González, L., et al.: Towards poisoning of deep learning algorithms with back-gradient optimization. In: Proceedings of the 10th ACM Workshop on Artificial Intelligence and Security (2017)

20. Mozaffari-Kermani, M., et al.: Systematic poisoning attacks on and defenses for machine learning in healthcare. IEEE J. Biomed. Health Inf. 19(6), 1893–1905 (2015)

21. Taghanaki, S.A., Das, A., Hamarneh, G.: Vulnerability analysis of chest X-ray image classification against adversarial attacks. In: Stoyanov, Danail, Taylor, Zeike, Kia, Seyed Mostafa, Oguz, Ipek, Reyes, Mauricio, Martel, Anne, Maier-Hein, Lena, Marquand, Andre F., Duchesnay, Edouard, Löfstedt, Tommy, Bennett Landman, M., Cardoso, Jorge, Silva, Carlos A., Pereira, Sergio, Meier, Raphael (eds.) Understanding and Interpreting Machine Learning in Medical Image Computing Applications: First International Workshops, MLCN 2018, DLF 2018, and iMIMIC 2018, Held in Conjunction with MICCAI 2018, Granada, Spain, September 16-20, 2018, Proceedings, pp. 87–94. Springer International Publishing, Cham (2018). https://doi.org/10.1007/978-3-030-02628-8_10

22. Tahir, A.M., et al.: COVID-19 infection localization and severity grading from chest X-ray images. Comput. Biol. Med. 139, 105002 (2021)

23. Aggarwal, S., et al.: Automated COVID-19 detection in chest X-ray images using fine-tuned deep learning architectures. Expert. Syst. 39(3), e12749 (2022)

24. Mirza, M., Osindero, S.: Conditional generative adversarial nets. arXiv preprint arXiv:1411.1784 (2014)

25. Heusel, M., et al.: Gans trained by a two time-scale update rule converge to a local nash equilibrium. In: Advances in Neural Information Processing Systems, vol. 30 (2017)

26. Radford, A., Metz, L., Chintala, S.: Unsupervised representation learning with deep convolutional generative adversarial networks. arXiv preprint arXiv:1511.06434 (2015)

27. Isola, P., et al.: Image-to-image translation with conditional adversarial networks. In: Proceedings of the IEEE Conference on Computer Vision and Pattern Recognition (2017)

28. Odena, A., Dumoulin, V., Olah, C.: Deconvolution and checkerboard artifacts. Distill 1(10): e3 (2016)

29. Parmar, G., Zhang, R., Zhu, J.-Y.: On aliased resizing and surprising subtleties in gan evaluation. In: Proceedings of the IEEE/CVF Conference on Computer Vision and Pattern Recognition (2022)
30. Liu, Z., et al.: A convnet for the 2020s. In Proceedings of the IEEE/CVF Conference on Computer Vision and Pattern Recognition (2022)

Semi-supervised Brain Tumor Segmentation Using Diffusion Models

Ahmed Alshenoudy[1]([✉]) [iD], Bertram Sabrowsky-Hirsch[1] [iD], Stefan Thumfart[1] [iD],
Michael Giretzlehner[1] [iD], and Erich Kobler[2] [iD]

[1] Research Department Medical Informatics, RISC Software GmbH, Softwarepark
32a, 4232 Hagenberg, Austria
{ahmed.alshenoudy,bertram.sabrowsky-hirsch,stefan.thumfart,
michael.giretzlehner}@risc-software.at
[2] Department of Neuroradiology, University Hospital Bonn, Venusberg-Campus 1,
53127 Bonn, Germany
erich.kobler@ukbonn.de

Abstract. Semi-supervised learning can be a promising approach in
expediting the process of annotating medical images. In this paper, we
use diffusion models to learn visual representations from multi-modal
medical images in an unsupervised setting. These learned representations
are then employed for the challenging downstream task of brain tumor
segmentation. To avoid feature selection when using pixel-level classifiers, we propose fine-tuning the noise predictor network for semantic
segmentation. We compare these methods against a supervised baseline
over a varying number of training samples and evaluate their performance on a substantially larger test set. Our results show that, with
less than 20 training samples, all methods outperform the supervised
baseline across all tumor regions. Additionally, we present a practical
use-case for patient-level tumor segmentation using limited supervision.
The code we used and our trained diffusion model are publicly available
(https://github.com/risc-mi/braintumor-ddpm).

Keywords: Denoising Diffusion Probabilistic Models · Medical Image
Segmentation · Few Shot Semantic Segmentation

1 Introduction

Medical image annotation is a very challenging, costly and time-consuming task
that requires expert knowledge. Manual delineation for different regions of interest is still the standard practice, which is prone to errors and sometimes subject
to inter- and intra-rater variability [7,26]. To expedite this annotation process,
deep learning-based algorithms can be used, as they currently hold state-of-
the-art performance on various medical image segmentation tasks [12]. However,
these algorithms require large and representative datasets to achieve good performance, which is often impractical and tedious to acquire in the medical domain.

© IFIP International Federation for Information Processing 2023
Published by Springer Nature Switzerland AG 2023
I. Maglogiannis et al. (Eds.): AIAI 2023, IFIP AICT 675, pp. 314–325, 2023.
https://doi.org/10.1007/978-3-031-34111-3_27

Therefore, creating a bottleneck for employing deep learning-based algorithms in the medical domain where expert annotations are scarce.

Semi-supervised learning has emerged as a promising approach to address this challenging issue. It attempts to tackle the practical situation where a significant amount of unlabeled data is available in parallel with a few labeled samples [20]. This is often the case in the medical domain, as thousands of image acquisitions are carried out on patients daily and tight resources permit only the labeling of a few exemplar annotations in contrast to annotating full datasets. A common approach is to learn visual representations from the data in an unsupervised setting and then learn a mapping between learned visual representations and the available labeled samples. Different approaches have been explored to learn visual representations, from constructing self-supervised tasks [9,32] to using generative models [14,33]. With the recent success of diffusion models [6] and their straightforward training, they are gaining more attention and are explored in different application domains. Additionally, diffusion models have also been used in unsupervised visual representation learning [4] and currently hold state-of-the-art performance for few-shot semantic segmentation on multiple segmentation tasks.

In this paper, we leverage learned visual representations from diffusion models to tackle the challenging task of brain tumor segmentation. We also compare the segmentation performance against a supervised baseline over a varying degree of training samples. Instead of using a pixel-level classifier for the downstream task, we propose fine-tuning the noise predictor network of the diffusion model. Finally, we present a practical use-case, where we automatically annotate tumor regions across different axial slices within the same patient. This is achieved by using an exemplar tumor slice and two healthy tissue slices for training.

2   Related Work

Denoising Diffusion Probabilistic Models, or Diffusion models for brevity, are a class of likelihood-based generative models [10,18,27]. Dhariwal et al. [6] showed that they outperform state-of-the-art Generative Adversarial Networks (GANs) in terms of sample quality and diversity on multiple datasets. Because of this success, they have gained a lot of interest from the research community and have been explored in multiple applications such as super-resolution [25], in-painting [15], semantic segmentation [1,4,29], anomaly detection [21,28,31] and text-to-image generation [19]. A growing interest in using diffusion models for medical image analysis has also been observed, as outlined in a recent survey by Kazerouni et al. [13]. Other methods such as latent diffusion [23], inverse heat dissipation models [22] and blurring diffusion [11] have been motivated by denoising diffusion probabilistic models.

The core idea behind diffusion models is the transformation of a complex data distribution into a simpler one, that is tractable through a defined forward process. Thus, learning to approximate the reverse of this forward process would define the distribution of the generative model [10,27]. For diffusion models, this target data distribution is typically a standard Gaussian, which is achieved by a forward process that gradually adds noise over a fixed amount of T time steps. A trained diffusion model would transform noise $x_T \sim \mathcal{N}(\mathbf{0}, \mathbf{I})$ to a sample x_0 by gradually denoising x_T. Additionally, diffusion models are latent variable models where latents $x_1, \ldots, x_T$ share the same dimensionality as the original data $x_0 \sim q(x_0)$. The forward process is a Markov chain that gradually adds Gaussian noise according to a fixed variance schedule $\beta_1, \ldots, \beta_T$:

$$q(x_t|x_{t-1}) := \mathcal{N}(x_t; \sqrt{1 - \beta_t}x_{t-1}, \beta_t \mathbf{I}), \tag{1}$$

Forward sampling an input x_0 to any time-step x_t can be done in closed form using $\alpha_t := 1 - \beta_t$ and $\bar{\alpha}_t := \prod_{s=1}^{t} \alpha_s$. The forward process can be rewritten as:

$$q(x_t|x_0) = \mathcal{N}(x_t; \sqrt{\bar{\alpha}_t}x_0, (1 - \bar{\alpha}_t)\mathbf{I}), \tag{2}$$

$$x_t = \sqrt{\bar{\alpha}_t}x_0 + \sqrt{1 - \bar{\alpha}_t}\epsilon, \quad \epsilon \sim \mathcal{N}(\mathbf{0}, \mathbf{I}). \tag{3}$$

Diffusion models learn to approximate the reverse process:

$$p_\theta(x_{t-1}|x_t) := \mathcal{N}(x_{t-1}; \mu_\theta(x_t, t), \Sigma_\theta(x_t, t)), \tag{4}$$

where in practice, this is done by predicting the noise component at each step t, using a noise predictor network $\epsilon_\theta(x_t, t)$, which is typically a U-Net architecture [24]. The mean of the distribution $\mu_\theta(x_t, t)$ in Eq. 4 is then calculated from a linear combination between predicted noise and x_t. For $\Sigma_\theta(x_t, t)$, it can be fixed to time-dependent constants or learned, where the latter was shown to improve likelihood-scores and allow for faster sampling [18]. Baranchuk *et al.* [4] showed that diffusion models are capable of learning visual representations and exploited these representations for semantic segmentation. Learned visual representations are acquired by forward sampling an image x_0 using Eq. 2 and extracting the intermediate activations of $\epsilon_\theta(x_t, t)$. These activations are then scaled to the original input size and are considered pixel-wise visual representations. For semantic segmentation, a Multi-layer Perceptron (MLP) is trained to classify these pixel-level visual representations to target classes.

Diffusion models and GANs have been previously explored for medical image segmentation. GANs have been used for segmenting 3D brain tumors by Cirillo *et al.* [5], who used it to generate segmentation maps, while also punishing the model for producing non-realistic segmentations. Diffusion models have been used for 2D brain tumor segmentation before by Wolleb *et al.* [29], where a diffusion model generates binary segmentation maps conditioned on the anatomical structure. Guo *et al.* [8] accelerated this by incorporating pre-segmentation results from another segmentation network. Wu *et al.* [30], added key improvements to address step-wise regional attention and the negative effects of high-frequency noise. Therefore, inspired by these works, specifically [4], we explore the use of diffusion models in a semi-supervised setting that replicates a practical scenario for medical image segmentation.

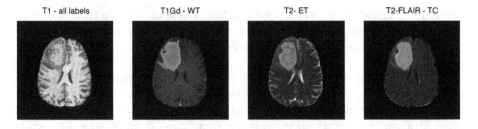

Fig. 1. An exemplar axial slice illustrating different modalities, tumor labels and regions. Tumor labels are shown for ED, ET and NCR in blue, green and yellow, respectively. Tumor regions are overlayed on different modalities, where from left to right are the WT, ET and TC. (Color figure online)

3 Method

Our primary goal is to evaluate how learned visual representations from a diffusion model transfer to the downstream task of medical image segmentation. We designed an experiment that replicates a practical scenario, in which annotated data are scarce. The goal is learning to extend knowledge from a few annotated samples to the full dataset. We derived our method based on the approach presented by Baranchuk *et al.* [4] and tuned the hyper-parameters to our dataset as outlined in our published documentation.

3.1 Experimental Design

In our experiments, we employ data from the Brain Tumor Segmentation (BraTS) 2021 challenge [2,3,17]. The dataset contains multi-parametric Magnetic Resonance Imaging (mpMRI) scans from 2,040 patients, of which 1,251 are provided with ground-truth segmentations for algorithm development and training. For each patient, the mpMRI scan comprises four MRI modalities, which are T1-weighted (T1), post-contrast T1-weighted (T1Gd), T2-weighted (T2) and T2 Fluid Attenuated Inversion Recovery (T2-FLAIR). Each MRI volume has a size of $155 \times 240 \times 240$, with uniform isotropic resolution ($1\ mm^3$). The ground-truth segmentations have three tumor labels, which are Necrotic Tumor Core (NCR), Peritumoral Edematous (ED) and Non-enhancing tumor (ET). For the challenge evaluation, metrics are reported based on different tumor regions. These regions are Whole Tumor (WT), which is a combination of all tumor labels, Tumor Core (TC), which results from ET ∪ NCR and the last region is the ET itself. Figure 1 illustrates the different MR sequences, tumor labels and regions.

We define a dataset $\mathcal{D} = \mathcal{D}_u \cup \mathcal{D}_p$, where $\mathcal{D}_u$ denotes the set of unlabeled samples and $\mathcal{D}_p$ denotes an available pool of annotated samples with a ratio to $\mathcal{D}_u$ of $\approx 9.5\%$. The entire dataset $\mathcal{D}$ was used to train a diffusion model for extracting visual representations. We then sample different training subsets $\mathcal{D}_n$ from $\mathcal{D}_p$, with varying training samples n, which we use to train different downstream models and a supervised baseline. These models are then evaluated on the entire $\mathcal{D}_u$. Additionally, we define an upper-bound to the task, where we trained a state-of-the-art supervised method on the entire $\mathcal{D}_p$ and also evaluated on $\mathcal{D}_u$.

For our experiments, we extract axial slices from the original 3D MRI volumes and the ground-truth segmentations. The longitudinal locations were stratified to increase the proportion of slices containing a segmented tumor: we chose seven locations to extract slices, starting from slice 70 up to slice 100, while skipping four slices in between. Axial slices are ordered in the superior direction through this paper. Afterwards, we normalized each extracted axial slice between [-1, 1] and down-sampled it to 128×128 using bilinear interpolation. Labels were down-sampled using nearest neighbors interpolation. This resulted in a dataset $\mathcal{D}$ of 8,757 axial slices, which we split into a training pool and a test dataset. The training pool $\mathcal{D}_p$ (757 slices), was used to randomly sample (without replacement) training datasets $\mathcal{D}_n$ of varying size $n \in \{10, 20, 30, 40, 50\}$ for conducting different experiments. The test dataset $\mathcal{D}_u$ comprised the remaining 8,000 slices, which we used to evaluate the different segmentation approaches in our experiments.

3.2 Diffusion Model Training

The training was based on the pipeline used in [18]. The model was trained for 360,000 iterations, with a learning rate of 2×10^{-4}, a batch size of eight images and an exponential moving average (EMA) over model weights of 0.995. We used a diffusion process with $T = 4,000$ steps and a cosine noise schedule, as both have been shown to boost model performance [18]. For simplicity, we kept $\Sigma_\theta(x_t, t)$ to untrained time-dependent constants. The $\epsilon_\theta(x_t, t)$, or ϵ-predictor network, is based on a U-Net architecture, we use a down-sampling stack comprising six stages, where each stage has three residual blocks. The down-sampling stages had layer widths of $[C, C, 2C, 2C, 4C, 4C]$, where we set $C = 64$ and the up-sampling stack mirrored this down-sampling stack. We also use multi-head attention with four attention heads, however, applied only to resolutions of 32×32.

3.3 Semantic Segmentation Methods

Pixel-Level Classifier. We use the same multi-layer perceptron (MLP) architecture used in [4], which we call Simple MLP and another variant architecture which we name Deep MLP. These models learn to classify pixel-level visual representations to target classes. Visual representations are extracted from decoder layers $\{16, 17, 18\}$ after sampling an input to $t = 250$, where each layer had an output shape of $64 \times 64 \times 64$. Through empirical experiments, we found out that this configuration was a good choice for extracting visual representations for our downstream segmentation task. This configuration was founded on a visual analysis of learned visual representations, but also different configurations can be used. All pixel-level classifiers were trained for 6 epochs, with a batch size of 64 and a learning rate of 10^{-3}.

Noise Predictor Network. Instead of extracting intermediate representations from the ϵ-predictor network, we propose to fine-tune this network on the available labeled data and use it for prediction. This is possible, as the latent space of the diffusion model shares the same dimensionality as the original data. We train this network with two configurations, one with fixed weights in the encoder and the other with trainable weights. The final convolutional block was adjusted to the number of output classes. Model training was carried out on a batch of five images and a learning rate of 3×10^{-3} for 150 epochs. We used a decay factor of 0.95 for the learning rate, employed whenever training loss plateaued and limited the learning rate to a minimum of 10^{-6}. We incorporated random flipping, rotations, affine transformations and random adjustments of brightness and gamma to augment the images. Predictions were performed in the latent space, after sampling inputs to $t = 100$.

Supervised Baseline and Upper-bound. The nnU-Net architecture [12], currently holds state-of-the-art performance on various medical image segmentation tasks and was incorporated in the winning submission for BraTS 2021 challenge [16]. For training the nnU-Net architecture, we only use the 2D U-Net model as we are dealing with 2D axial slices. Models were trained with the default configuration, except for a few modifications. The overall training was restricted to 500 epochs instead of 1,000. Images were fed to the 2D U-Net in full resolution of 128×128 and post-processing of predictions was disabled. Models were trained directly on the entire data and not in the standard 5-fold cross-validation, except for the upper-bound model. The idea was to have a model-to-model comparison, as ensembling or post-processing can be applied to any model and would only skew the performance if not applied equally. Baseline models were trained on different $\mathcal{D}_n$ and the upper-bound model was trained on $\mathcal{D}_p$. Therefore, we provide an estimate for the upper and lower bounds of this task for the extracted dataset.

4 Results

Learned visual representations from our trained diffusion model are shown in Fig. 2. Earlier decoder layers capture high-level visual representations, which gradually increase in detail as we progress through different decoder layers. However, representations become noisier towards later decoder layers and as we sample to later time steps in the forward diffusion process, which aligns with the findings of Baranchuk *et al.* [4]. As our primary goal was to extract visual representations, we did not evaluate the generative quality of the model. In our downstream task evaluation, we include two commonly reported segmentation metrics, the Dice Similarity Coefficient (DSC) and Hausdorff Distance at the 95th percentile (HD95), besides we also report the standard deviation across different experiments. Results for our experiments are presented in Fig. 3, where we outline segmentation metrics for different methods while varying the number of training samples. For each $\mathcal{D}_n$, results are plotted for five different experiments. Additionally, we report an upper-bound DSC of 79.36 ± 0.23, 71.76 ± 0.15, 74.85 ± 0.32 for WT, ET and

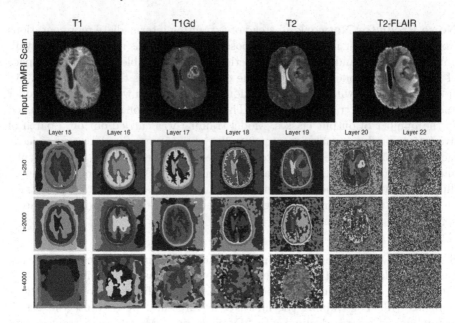

Fig. 2. Learned visual representations for sample input. Extracted from ϵ-predictor network decoder layers $\{15, 16, \ldots, 20, 22\}$ and $t = \{250, 2000, 4000\}$ for BraTS_00489 axial slice 95. To visualize learned representations, we apply K-means clustering across different feature maps for each layer, with $K = 10$.

TC, respectively, while the upper-bound HD95 was 4.50 ± 0.10, 3.81 ± 0.07 and 3.21 ± 0.04 for WT, ET and TC, respectively. All methods surpassed the nnU-Net baseline in terms of DSC performance when only 10 samples were available for training. In terms of HD95 scores, the nnU-Net baseline and fine-tuned ϵ-predictor network had an advantage over both pixel-level classifiers. This is evident for the Whole Tumor region, where the nnU-Net baseline and fine-tuned ϵ-predictor network had consistently better HD95 scores. This difference can be attributed to pixel-level classifiers falsely predicting individual pixels, as they do not directly consider neighborhood information. As HD95 scores for ET and TC had a narrower gap between different methods, scores for WT region were better for the nnU-Net baseline and retrained ϵ-predictor network because of better ED predictions. The performance gap narrows between all methods as more training samples are used, which we did expect. We detail the exact results for experiments with $\mathcal{D}_{10}$ and $\mathcal{D}_{50}$ in Tables 1 and 2. We show some exemplar predictions for all methods on three different cases in Fig. 4.

A practical use-case is shown in Fig. 5, in which we predict axial slices within the same 3D volume given only a few support slices. The support slices serve as exemplary segmentations to train the model, which then predicts the other axial slices. This could save time during the annotation process as correcting good estimates usually consumes less time than annotating from scratch. We used the Simple MLP architecture and trained on three sample slices, where only one

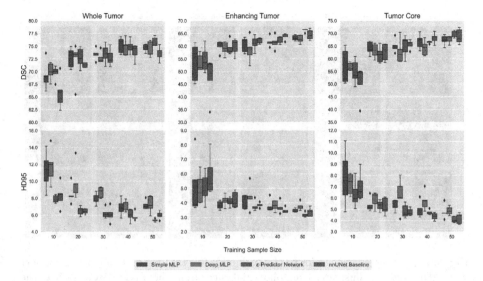

Fig. 3. Segmentation scores for different tumor regions against varying training sample counts. The top row shows Dice scores, while the bottom row shows Hausdorff Distance 95 percentile metric.

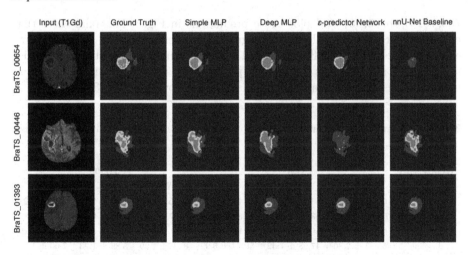

Fig. 4. Prediction examples from different methods for training dataset $\mathcal{D}_{10}$, showing axial slices for BraTS_00654, BraTS_00446 and BraTS_01393 from top to bottom and slices 95, 70 and 100, respectively. ED, ET and NCR are shown in blue, yellow and green, respectively.

slice contained a tumor section and the other two healthy tissue. Representations were extracted from decoder layers $\{15, 16, 17, 18\}$, to include more high-level semantic features from layer 15. Training was done on slices $\{5, 60, 100\}$ after sampling inputs to time-step $t = 100$. We evaluate predictions for slices

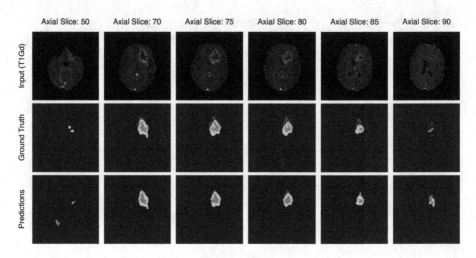

Fig. 5. Predicting axial slices for the full volume, after training with only three support slices. The top row illustrates exemplar axial slices from the T1Gd MR sequence, the middle row and the last row contain ground-truth segmentations and Simple MLP predictions, respectively.

$\{50, 70, 75, 80, 85, 90\}$ and plot those predictions in Fig. 4. For axial slices that contain larger sections of the tumor, segmentation performance is excellent. However, for slices that the diffusion model was not trained on, which also comprise a very small area of pixels to segment, performance drops significantly. Segmentation metrics of these predicted axial slices are shown in Table 3.

Table 1. Segmentation scores on different metrics for different architectures trained on 10 samples.

Architecture	DSC			HD95		
	WT	ET	TC	WT	ET	TC
Simple MLP	69.20 ± 2.47	53.95 ± 6.75	56.32 ± 6.42	11.25 ± 1.99	5.07 ± 1.81	7.78 ± 2.21
Deep MLP	**70.02 ± 1.54**	53.47 ± 3.00	**56.83 ± 1.41**	11.77 ± 1.83	**4.97 ± 0.95**	7.24 ± 0.85
Retrained ϵ_θ	69.72 ± 1.24	**54.78 ± 4.55**	54.83 ± 4.33	**7.89 ± 0.40**	5.04 ± 0.93	**6.33 ± 1.08**
Baseline	65.83 ± 2.80	47.98 ± 7.42	50.73 ± 5.99	8.30 ± 1.29	5.89 ± 1.23	7.00 ± 1.14

Table 2. Segmentation scores on different metrics for different architectures trained on 50 samples.

Architecture	DSC			HD95		
	WT	ET	TC	WT	ET	TC
Simple MLP	74.70 ± 0.67	63.24 ± 0.94	67.34 ± 1.78	7.18 ± 0.47	3.50 ± 0.11	4.77 ± 0.55
Deep MLP	74.79 ± 1.43	62.76 ± 1.39	67.62 ± 1.31	7.27 ± 0.90	3.76 ± 0.24	4.87 ± 0.34
Retrained ϵ_θ	**75.86 ± 0.84**	**66.19 ± 0.60**	**69.89 ± 1.25**	**5.39 ± 0.14**	**3.18 ± 0.14**	**4.09 ± 0.24**
Baseline	73.66 ± 1.24	64.46 ± 1.84	68.75 ± 2.63	5.99 ± 0.41	3.37 ± 0.27	4.21 ± 0.43

Table 3. Segmentation metrics for exemplar axial slices within the same case BraTS_00000. Axial slices with larger tumor sections have excellent segmentation scores for both DSC and HD95.

Axial Slice	Dice			HD95		
	WT	ET	TC	WT	ET	TC
50	21.31	39.39	22.03	47.98	39.51	47.99
70	92.43	86.06	95.97	2.00	1.10	1.00
75	86.94	74.30	91.63	3.00	2.44	2.00
80	87.26	73.35	89.12	3.00	2.83	2.23
85	83.65	79.88	87.47	3.78	2.89	5.00
90	51.63	34.04	19.05	4.24	8.35	8.60
mean	70.54	64.50	67.54	10.67	9.52	11.38

5 Conclusion

We showed that diffusion models can be used for extracting visual representations from mpMRI data. We exploited these representations for the downstream task of semantic segmentation, utilizing different approaches. Pixel-level classifiers were used and we proposed fine-tuning the ϵ-predictor network. This results in better HD95 scores in comparison to pixel-level classifiers. Fine-tuning is used to avoid selecting specific layers to extract visual representations. With limited training data, both pixel-level classifiers and ϵ-predictor network performed much better than the nnU-Net baseline with fewer training samples. Furthermore, we illustrated a practical use-case, where a single axial slice with annotated tumor region and other slices with only healthy tissue are used to predict other tumor-containing axial slices with competitive segmentation performance. Given the current research progress in diffusion models, we expect to see even improved approaches based on our experiments and using alternative models such as blurring diffusion models. Our approach could be further improved by adapting a 3D architecture for the diffusion model and further adapting the fine-tuning approach of the ϵ-predictor network. We suggest using our method in an active learning pipeline, such that most informative axial slices are sampled, annotated and then extended to the rest of the volume.

Acknowledgments. This project is financed by research subsidies granted by the government of Upper Austria. RISC Software GmbH is Member of UAR (Upper Austrian Research) Innovation Network.

References

1. Amit, T., Shaharbany, T., Nachmani, E., Wolf, L.: Segdiff: Image segmentation with diffusion probabilistic models (2021)

2. Baid, U., et al.: The RSNA-ASNR-miccai brats 2021 benchmark on brain tumor segmentation and radiogenomic classification (2021)

3. Bakas, S., et al.: Advancing the cancer genome atlas glioma MRI collections with expert segmentation labels and radiomic features. Scientific Data **4**, 170117 (2017)

4. Baranchuk, D., Voynov, A., Rubachev, I., Khrulkov, V., Babenko, A.: Label-efficient semantic segmentation with diffusion models. In: International Conference on Learning Representations (2022)

5. Cirillo, M.D., Abramian, D., Eklund, A.: Vox2Vox: 3D-GAN for brain tumour segmentation. In: Crimi, Alessandro, Bakas, Spyridon (eds.) BrainLes 2020. LNCS, vol. 12658, pp. 274–284. Springer, Cham (2021). https://doi.org/10.1007/978-3-030-72084-1_25

6. Dhariwal, P., Nichol, A.: Diffusion models beat GANS on image synthesis. In: Advances in Neural Information Processing Systems, vol. 34, pp. 8780–8794. Curran Associates, Inc. (2021)

7. Fiez, J.A., Damasio, H., Grabowski, T.J.: Lesion segmentation and manual warping to a reference brain: Intra- and interobserver reliability. Human Brain Mapping **9**(4), 192–211 (2000)

8. Guo, X., Yang, Y., Ye, C., Lu, S., Xiang, Y., Ma, T.: Accelerating diffusion models via pre-segmentation diffusion sampling for medical image segmentation (2022)

9. He, K., Chen, X., Xie, S., Li, Y., Dollár, P., Girshick, R.: Masked autoencoders are scalable vision learners. In: Proceedings of the IEEE/CVF Conference on Computer Vision and Pattern Recognition (CVPR), pp. 16000–16009 (2022)

10. Ho, J., Jain, A., Abbeel, P.: Denoising diffusion probabilistic models. In: Advances in Neural Information Processing Systems, vol. 33, pp. 6840–6851. Curran Associates, Inc. (2020)

11. Hoogeboom, E., Salimans, T.: Blurring diffusion models (2022)

12. Isensee, F., Jaeger, P.F., Kohl, S.A.A., Petersen, J., Maier-Hein, K.: nnu-net: A self-configuring method for deep learning-based biomedical image segmentation. Nat. Methods **18**, 203–211 (2021)

13. Kazerouni, A., et al.: Diffusion models for medical image analysis: A comprehensive survey (2022)

14. Li, D., Yang, J., Kreis, K., Torralba, A., Fidler, S.: Semantic segmentation with generative models: Semi-supervised learning and strong out-of-domain generalization. In: Proceedings of the IEEE/CVF Conference on Computer Vision and Pattern Recognition (CVPR), pp. 8300–8311 (2021)

15. Lugmayr, A., Danelljan, M., Romero, A., Yu, F., Timofte, R., Van Gool, L.: Repaint: Inpainting using denoising diffusion probabilistic models. In: Proceedings of the IEEE/CVF Conference on Computer Vision and Pattern Recognition (CVPR), pp. 11461–11471 (2022)

16. Luu, H.M., Park, S.H.: Extending nn-UNet for brain tumor segmentation. In: Brainlesion: Glioma. Multiple Sclerosis, Stroke and Traumatic Brain Injuries, pp. 173–186. Springer International Publishing, Cham (2022). https://doi.org/10.1007/978-3-031-09002-8_16

17. Menze, B.H., et al.: The multimodal brain tumor image segmentation benchmark (brats). IEEE Trans. Med. Imaging **34**(10), 1993–2024 (2015)

18. Nichol, A.Q., Dhariwal, P.: Improved denoising diffusion probabilistic models. In: Meila, M., Zhang, T. (eds.) Proceedings of the 38th International Conference on Machine Learning. Proceedings of Machine Learning Research, vol. 139, pp. 8162–8171. PMLR (2021)

19. Nichol, A.Q., et al.: GLIDE: Towards photorealistic image generation and editing with text-guided diffusion models. In: Proceedings of the 39th International Conference on Machine Learning. Proceedings of Machine Learning Research, vol. 162, pp. 16784–16804. PMLR (2022)

20. Ouali, Y., Hudelot, C., Tami, M.: An overview of deep semi-supervised learning (2020)

21. Pinaya, W.H.L., et al.: Fast unsupervised brain anomaly detection and segmentation with diffusion models. In: Medical Image Computing and Computer Assisted Intervention - MICCAI 2022, pp. 705–714. Springer Nature Switzerland, Cham (2022). https://doi.org/10.1007/978-3-031-16452-1_67

22. Rissanen, S., Heinonen, M., Solin, A.: Generative modelling with inverse heat dissipation (2022)

23. Rombach, R., Blattmann, A., Lorenz, D., Esser, P., Ommer, B.: High-resolution image synthesis with latent diffusion models. In: Proceedings of the IEEE/CVF Conference on Computer Vision and Pattern Recognition (CVPR), pp. 10684–10695 (2022)

24. Ronneberger, O., Fischer, P., Brox, T.: U-Net: Convolutional networks for biomedical image segmentation. In: Navab, N., Hornegger, J., Wells, W.M., Frangi, A.F. (eds.) MICCAI 2015. LNCS, vol. 9351, pp. 234–241. Springer, Cham (2015). https://doi.org/10.1007/978-3-319-24574-4_28

25. Saharia, C., Ho, J., Chan, W., Salimans, T., Fleet, D.J., Norouzi, M.: Image super-resolution via iterative refinement. IEEE Trans. Pattern Anal. Mach. Intell. $45(4)$, 4713–4726 (2023)

26. Sharp, G.C., et al.: Vision 20/20: Perspectives on automated image segmentation for radiotherapy. Med Phys. $41(5)$, 050901 (2014)

27. Sohl-Dickstein, J., Weiss, E., Maheswaranathan, N., Ganguli, S.: Deep unsupervised learning using nonequilibrium thermodynamics. In: Proceedings of the 32nd International Conference on Machine Learning. Proceedings of Machine Learning Research, vol. 37, pp. 2256–2265. PMLR, Lille (2015)

28. Wolleb, J., Bieder, F., Sandkühler, R., Cattin, P.C.: Diffusion models for medical anomaly detection. In: Medical Image Computing and Computer Assisted Intervention - MICCAI 2022, pp. 35–45. Springer Nature Switzerland, Cham (2022). https://doi.org/10.1007/978-3-031-16452-1_4

29. Wolleb, J., Sandkühler, R., Bieder, F., Valmaggia, P., Cattin, P.C.: Diffusion models for implicit image segmentation ensembles. In: Proceedings of the 5th International Conference on Medical Imaging with Deep Learning. Proceedings of Machine Learning Research, vol. 172, pp. 1336–1348. PMLR (2022)

30. Wu, J., et al.: Medsegdiff: Medical image segmentation with diffusion probabilistic model (2022)

31. Wyatt, J., Leach, A., Schmon, S.M., Willcocks, C.G.: Anoddpm: Anomaly detection with denoising diffusion probabilistic models using simplex noise. In: 2022 IEEE/CVF Conference on Computer Vision and Pattern Recognition Workshops (CVPRW), pp. 649–655 (2022)

32. Zhang, R., Isola, P., Efros, A.A.: Colorful image colorization. In: Leibe, B., Matas, J., Sebe, N., Welling, M. (eds.) ECCV 2016. LNCS, vol. 9907, pp. 649–666. Springer, Cham (2016). https://doi.org/10.1007/978-3-319-46487-9_40

33. Zhang, Y., et al.: Datasetgan: Efficient labeled data factory with minimal human effort. In: Proceedings of the IEEE/CVF Conference on Computer Vision and Pattern Recognition (CVPR), pp. 10145–10155 (2021)

Classification

A Methodology for Emergency Calls Severity Prediction: From Pre-processing to BERT-Based Classifiers

Marianne Abi Kanaan[1,2]([✉]) [iD], Jean-François Couchot[1]([✉]) [iD],
Christophe Guyeux[1] [iD], David Laiymani[1] [iD], Talar Atechian[2] [iD],
and Rony Darazi[2] [iD]

[1] FEMTO-ST Institute, CNRS, Université de Franche-Comté, Besançon, France
{marianne.abi_kanaan,jean-francois.couchot,christophe.guyeux,
david.laiymani}@univ-fcomte.fr
[2] TICKET Lab, Université Antonine (UA), Baabda, Lebanon
{marianne.abikanaan,talar.atechian,rony.darazi}@ua.edu.lb

Abstract. Emergency call centers are often required to properly assess and prioritise emergency situations pre-intervention, in order to provide the required assistance to the callers efficiently. In this paper, we present an end-to-end pipeline for emergency calls analysis. Such a tool can be found useful as it is possible for the intervention team to misinterpret the severity of the situation or mis-prioritise callers. The data used throughout this work is one week's worth of emergency call recordings provided by the French SDIS 25 firemen station, located in the Doubs. We pre-process the calls and evaluate several artificial intelligence models in the classification of callers' situation as either severe or non-severe. We demonstrate through our results that it is possible, with the right selection of algorithms, to predict if the call will result in a serious injury with a 71% accuracy, based on the caller's speech only. This shows that it is indeed possible to assist emergency centers with an autonomous tool that is capable of analysing the caller's description of their situation and assigning an appropriate priority to their call.

Keywords: Emergency Calls · Text Classification · Transformers · Speech-To-Text · Machine Learning · Audio Processing

1 Introduction

Speech is the main form of communication in human conversations. The analysis of speech can provide many insights that characterize a conversation's intent, nature, emotions... and many more indicators. As such, a speech analysis system can prove to be useful in various contexts.

One such domain is emergency call centers, as they can sometimes face an overload of calls, which in turn leads to mis-prioritisation of the cases. Given that early medical interventions can lead to less fatalities in the cases of severe

I. Maglogiannis et al. (Eds.): AIAI 2023, IFIP AICT 675, pp. 329–342, 2023.
https://doi.org/10.1007/978-3-031-34111-3_28

injuries, it seems that the assistance of operators in their job is essential. This is the case of French Emergency centers for example. In France, just as 911 operators handle emergency situations in the U.S., this work is handled by the SDIS (Service Départemental d'Incendie et de Secours) department of a specific region. They are call centers operated by firemen, and they handle emergency situations in that area 24/7. Following emergency calls, some situations often require the intervention of an emergency team, and as such, there is always a risk of misinterpreting the needs of the intervention i.e. number and nature of resources needed, etc.

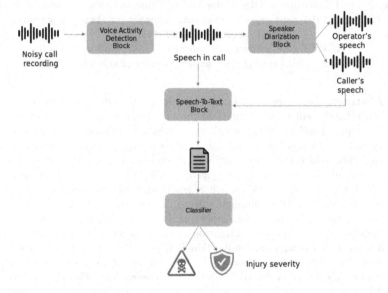

Fig. 1. Emergency phone calls processing pipeline.

Therefore, in this work, our goal is to implement a speech analysis system for emergency centers, and eventually answer the following question: Is it possible to manage incidents more efficiently through a system that can process a phone call, and thereby provide a relevant assessment of the emergency at-hand?

This article describes our attempt to develop a prototype (illustrated in Fig. 1) that aims at assisting operators in handling emergency situations by automatically analysing incoming phone calls and assessing the severity of the caller's situation. The emergency calls used in this work are equivalent to one week's worth of real-life calls provided by the French SDIS 25 firemen station, located in the Doubs region of France.

The starting point of our pipeline is a "voice activity detection" block. This allows us to extract intervals that contain speech activity in the audio streams and discard segments where speech is absent. The next step is the application of speaker diarization on each audio file to extract the caller's speech into a separate signal. Two speech-to-text systems are then evaluated in the automatic transcription of the audio files into text. And finally, we implement an analysis block, which consists of a classifier that labels the transcribed text as a "high severity" case or a "low-severity" case. Our experiments show that it is possible to predict the severity of an emergency call with a 71% accuracy based on the caller's speech only. This result is highly influenced by the choice of classifier and speech-to-text system.

The remainder of the paper is structured as follows: Sect. 2 covers related works that tackle emergency calls categorisation. The proposed methodology for labeling the calls is described in detail in Sect. 3. The experiments and their evaluation are reported in Sect. 4. Finally, a conclusion, some limitations of the work and possible future directions are summarized in Sect. 5.

2   Related Work

Various works have attempted to use speech analysis in healthcare applications, specifically in diagnosing callers to an emergency department with a specific condition. The work in [8] uses a machine learning framework developed by a Danish company to predict cardiac arrests based on automatic transcriptions of a call. The framework achieved a higher sensitivity compared to the medical dispatcher (84.1% vs 72.5%). In [6], the authors describe their study with multiple machine learning classifiers in the classification of manually annotated emergency calls transcriptions into a pre-hospital diagnosis. They do not use the text as is, but rather extract descriptors such as TF-IDF embeddings [33], and train several machine learning algorithms (SVM, Linear Regression...) using these feature vectors. Their most accurate model, an SVM using TF-IDF, achieves a 95% accuracy on unseen data. In our work, we attempt to provide a more generalised analysis of the situation at-hand and assess its risk regardless of the diagnosis. The work in [30] attempts to automate the prioritisation of 911 calls using SVM algorithms with written transcriptions of the calls provided by a security service, using techniques such as lemmatization and pruning. Their model labels the call as either high-priority or low-priority. Its best result is a recall rate of 86%, a precision rate of 75%, and an f1-score of 80%. In our case, considering that our aim is to predict the severity of the call as quickly as possible before the intervention of the firemen's team, using deep learning methods would provide a better performance as they can act as feature extractors without the need for an additional pre-processing step [22].

With the emergence of transformer-based language models, most works have shifted their focus on models such as GPT [35] and BERT [36], which require less text pre-processing, and are available in pre-trained versions on various language-understanding work. One such use of transformers is [17], where the authors attempt to associate a diagnosis to each transcription of an emergency call in a French medical emergency department. The authors pre-train the generative model GPT-2 in an unsupervised manner on a subset of the dataset, then re-train this model on the classification of another part of the annotations. The used dataset is a collection of reports made by intervening physicians, medical assistants, and paramedics. Their f1-scores on each class range from 47.9% to 80%. Similarly, [37] use a pre-trained Chinese BERT to automatically categorise emergency reports with a 91.55% weighted f1-score. The model is trained with a custom loss function in an attempt to overcome the data imbalance issue in their dataset. In our work, given that we are in a binary classification scenario, the data imbalance issue can be resolved by randomly and manually removing samples from the dominating class, which leaves us with a well-balanced dataset.

What sets our work aside from the previously described papers is, first, to the best of our knowledge, no work has attempted to develop an end-to-end pipeline to assess emergency calls' severity in a center. Furthermore, our aim is to detect potentially severe calls, regardless of the diagnosis of the caller. A fall for example can at times seriously injure an individual, while at other times lead to minor or no injuries. This aspect of our data increases the difficulty of our task. We hope that our text analysis component will be able to pick up on specific cues, terms, or patterns in the caller's speech that can go undetected by the operator, in order to predict the possible outcome of the situation. As such, we attempt to perform classification of automatically annotated call recordings, which poses an additional challenge compared to the previously described works, as the transcribed text can contain many errors. To implement the analysis block of our pipeline, transformer-based models seem to be more suitable in our case, as they require less text pre-processing, which is ideal for a future real-time implementation of the system. In addition, we lean towards pre-trained BERT models as opposed to GPT models as in [17], since GPT is originally a generative model [35], and requires an additional step of unsupervised learning on our dataset.

3   Methods

3.1   Dataset

As previously mentioned, the emergency calls used in this work were provided by the SDIS 25, an emergency department in the Doubs region in France. The dataset consists of one week's worth of data, i.e. 904 audio recordings of phone calls in the French language in WMA format. This dataset was constructed by filtering out some of the calls provided by the SDIS: calls between operators, calls between operators and policemen, calls between medical professionals and dispatchers... These conversations are irrelevant to our task since they often discuss the details of a specific intervention on site, whereas our goal is to evaluate the needs of the intervention before the team goes through with it, and based only on the analysis of a non-professional's speech.

Some statistics regarding the duration and number of words of the calls on each version of the dataset post-processing (Callers-Only/Callers-Operators, see next section), are reported in Table 1. A typical conversation consists of the operator interrogating the caller to gather information and provide help to the victim. The recordings are accompanied by a file that includes the reason of the

call (e.g. car accident, loss of consciousness...) and the state of the victim after
the intervention, which consists of three possibilities: lightly injured, severely
injured, or deceased. Since "deceased" is a minority class, it was grouped with
the "severely injured" category. As such, a "lightly injured" label describes minor
injuries such as scratches, small fractures, small wounds... and so on, whereas
a "severely injured" label can mean the victim is either deceased or severely
wounded. It should be noted that the level of injury does not always depend on
the diagnosis in some cases. If, for example, a victim was drowning and the team
was able to intervene early, the victim would likely have no injuries. Similarly,
a minor fire in a caller's kitchen could grow and result in major injuries in case
the team arrives late on site. This is one imperfection in our dataset that makes
the prediction of the severity more challenging.

A confidentiality agreement was signed with the SDIS that restricts us from
sharing the dataset and the text classification model, since the latter could leak
callers' data if shared with a third-party.

In this work, we are interested in labeling a call as either "low-severity",
which consists of the "lightly injured" cases, or "high-severity" which includes
the "severely injured" calls. In the cases where the same call is related to several
victims (in the case of a car accident for example), where each victim has a
different level of injury, we include the call once with the most severe injury
as the label. We balance out the dataset by manually removing some examples
that are labeled "lightly injured", since these types of injuries are more common
than the severe ones. The resulting dataset is therefore made up of 49.78% "low-
severity" calls, and of 50.22% "high-severity" calls.

Table 1. Statistics about the datasets used in this work.

		Min	Max	Average
Callers-Only	Call length (seconds)	4.25	410.77	136.84
	Number of words in call	76	8257	2502
Callers-Operators	Call length (seconds)	8.5	540.91	207.88
	Number of words in call	144	8985	3814

3.2   Audio Pre-processing

Speech Detection and Speaker Diarization. The emergency calls recordings in question contain many parts that are irrelevant to our task and could
introduce additional noise. Such parts include the answering machine and the
waiting music sounds, or the parts where the caller is waiting for someone to
answer their call and there isn't any voice activity. For this reason, we apply
Voice Activity Detection (VAD) on these recordings to extract the segments
that contain voices. VAD allows the detection of speech regions in a given audio
recording. Many studies [5,10,27] have shown that the application of voice activity detection in speech-analysis systems can produce cleaner data and achieve a

higher performance. We implement this using Pyannote.audio, an open-source collection of neural building blocks for speaker diarization [9]. In addition, since the aim of this work is to predict if a caller is seriously injured or not through the analysis of their speech, our work requires an additional step of extracting the caller's speech into a separate signal. As such, we created a Speaker Diarization block with the use of Pyannote.audio [9].

Fig. 2. Emergency call recordings pre-processing phase.

The reason for choosing the aforementioned solution is that it is open-source and can be used offline, meaning that the data will remain protected and uncompromised. In addition, Pyannote.audio provides a pre-trained model for speaker diarization, which eliminates the need to train a model from scratch. It also provides the lowest recorded diarization error rate (DER) in the literature, when tested on French "ETAPE" corpus [9]. Once we obtained the segments for each speaker, we manually separate the segments of the caller and the operator. We aim to automate this process for the real-world application of our method by training a model that could automatically recognize the operator's speech.

We finally re-join the segments of each speaker to obtain one complete audio recording for each speaker. The audio pre-processing phase is illustrated in Fig. 2.

As illustrated in Fig. 3, we later train several classifiers separately on two versions of the dataset: one with the callers-operators dialogues, and one with only the caller's speech. We then evaluate the trained models and compare the results obtained on each version of the dataset.

Speech to Text. For the Automatic Speech Recognition (ASR) component, we compare two speech-to-text systems: Whisper [34] and Vosk API [2]. Whisper is a simple encoder-decoder Transformer [34], trained on 680,000 h of diverse multilingual data collected from the web. VOSK API is a speech recognition toolkit based on Kaldi [2]. It offers various language-specific models, in both large and lightweight versions of the models. The first reason for choosing both of these systems is that they are open source and offline, which ensures that the privacy of our dataset remains protected. A second reason is the proven efficiency of both of these systems on the French language. Whisper has achieved low word error rates (WER) on several French datasets [34], as the highest WER for the large version is 14.7%. Vosk API has been equally successfully used in French speech transcription applications [15], achieving decent word error rates compared to Google Cloud's Speech-To-Text [1]. We select the large version of the multilingual Whisper and the French Vosk.

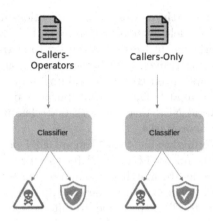

Fig. 3. Training of classifiers on callers-operators speech vs. callers-only speech.

3.3 Emergency Call Severity Prediction

In this section, we describe the implementation of machine learning and deep learning algorithms to predict the severity of a call, equivalent to the level of injury of the victim. On the one hand, we attempt to analyse the audio calls as they are, by training machine learning algorithms on their acoustic features. On the other hand, we use NLP methods to analyse the transcriptions of these audio calls. These methods range from simple models such as LSTMs and CNNs, to more advanced models such as transformers. We then compare the results obtained using each approach.

Audio Classification. For this implementation, we fragment each audio file into 10 s long fragments, as in several speech classification works [21,25]. The fragments are overlapped by 5 s in order to minimise the loss of context in the speech post-fragmentation. We then extract a set of acoustic feature vectors for each audio fragment using Librosa [28] at a sample rate of 8000 Hz Hz. We choose to extract 40 Mel Frequency Cepstral Coefficients (MFCCs) for each fragment. MFCCs are frequently used to represent speech [7,24], as they can represent sound as it is heard by the human ear.

We train our machine learning model in a speaker-independent manner, meaning we completely separate all fragments and avoid fragments leaking from speakers that are included in the test set. As for our audio classifier, and given the fact that our dataset is of a relatively small size for complex audio applications, we opt for machine learning algorithms instead of deep neural networks, as they can achieve decent results on limited data. We train and evaluate an XGBoost model [11] on the MFCC features, since it has been proven that they can achieve competitive results in several audio classification tasks in a clinical context [18,24].

Transcriptions Classification. Most NLP applications nowadays have moved from using RNN-based models, such as LSTMs and GRUs, to using transformers, a type of neural network that utilizes self-attention to learn context in text [29]. CamemBERT [26] is a pre-trained French transformer, based on the RoBERTa architecture (robustly optimized BERT pretraining approach) [23], a variant of BERT [36]. The BERT models [36] are multipurpose pre-trained models that can be trained on several NLP tasks such as text classification, named entity recognition, and many more tasks.

Several steps are required to fine-tune CamemBERT on our dataset. The text is first tokenized with the uncased CamemBERT tokenizer. All transcriptions are either truncated or padded to match a maximum length that we set based on the results of a hyperparameters search (described in the next section). Finally, we use attention masks to allow the model to differentiate between padded and real tokens. We use the base CamemBERT model, and fine-tune it with a single linear classification layer.

In order to obtain a better idea of the difficulty of our text classification task, we establish additional baselines that can be compared to our BERT-based approach. A first baseline is a simple LSTM network, that consists of an embedding input layer, followed by three LSTM layers of size 256, and a 30% dropout layer to reduce the effect of overfitting. The second baseline is an optimized version of the well-known TextCNN model [19]. Some works, such as [16], have demonstrated that CNNs or Hierarchical Neural Networks, can sometimes achieve better results in clinical text classification tasks, compared to BERT. For this reason, we implement a state-of-the-art version of the TextCNN architecture [38]. The network consists of three Convolutional 2D layers, each with 512 filters of sizes 2,3,5 respectively. Once convolution is applied on the text matrix, it is followed by a 1-max pooling layer, which extracts the largest number from each feature map. The resulting feature vectors are concatenated into one, and followed by a final layer with sigmoid activation function to output one of the two labels. We use the GloVe multilingual 300 dimensional embedding [32] to represent our vocabulary in both the LSTM and TextCNN. Our final test is a multi-lingual approach using the XLM-RoBERTa model in its base version [12]. XLM-RoBERTa was pre-trained on a massive corpus from 100 languages, making it a strong candidate for use in multilingual applications and in the support of cross-lingual language processing tasks.

4   Experiments and Evaluation

4.1   Experiments and Hyperparameter Tuning

The training computations are completed using the PyTorch [31] and XGBoost [3] frameworks on an NVIDIA Tesla V100 GPU with 32 GB of memory. Across all our experimentations, we split the dataset using the 80/10/10 method: 80% training data, 10% for validation, and 10% for testing, and report the mean accuracy of 10-fold cross-validation runs. First, we perform a hyperparameters selection for our deep learning models through the Grid Search approach, using Optuna library [4]. For the optimisation of CamemBERT, we base our search on the range of values recommended by BERT's authors [14]. The obtained hyperparameters for all models are reported in Table 2. Developed models are not necessarily the same depending on whether the operators' speech is integrated or not. Consequently, their parameters also change. The operators line of this table indicates if, in this model, the operator's speech is present ("w" for with), absent ("wo" for without). In the case where the same hyperparameters have been chosen, independently of the presence of the operator's speech, w/wo (for with or without) is shown.

Table 2. Optimized hyperparameters of the classifiers obtained using a Grid Search.

Hyperparameters	CamemBERT		XLM-RoBERTa	TextCNN	LSTM	XGBoost	
Operators	w	wo	w/wo	w/wo	w/wo	w	wo
Sequence Length	384	512	512	512	512	–	–
Learning Rate	3e−5	5e−5	5e−5	6e−4	1e−4	1e−4	1e−3
Epsilon	1e−7	1e−5	1e−5	–	–	–	–
Decay	–	–	–	1e−6	1e−6	–	–
Batch Size	16	8	8	8	8	–	–
Estimators	–	–	–	–	–	1e4	1e4
Max Depth	–	–	–	–	–	9	9

Given that the maximum supported sequence length in CamemBERT is 512, we process our text to match this length for the training of the TextCNN and the LSTM, in order to allow all models to learn from the same context. This leads to the discarding of words beyond the 512th word, since the average sequence length ranges from 2502 to 3812 (see Sect. 3.1). Even though some informative parts are lost, we don't consider this a limitation, since our end goal is to assist emergency center operators before the end of the call, with a minimal amount of speech content. We train CamemBERT on each run for 15 epochs instead of the recommended number of 4, since we found that training the network for longer led to higher accuracies on the test set. For each run, we evaluate the model on the test set after each epoch, and select the model with the highest accuracy among all 15 epochs. The same procedure is applied to XLM-RoBERTa.

As mentioned in Sect. 3.2, we separately train our models twice: first on the callers-operators transcriptions, and then on the callers-only transcriptions. Finally for the training of the LSTM and TextCNN, we use early stopping to interrupt training when the validation loss stops decreasing, and checkpoint the model with the lowest validation loss. We use the Adam optimizer [20] as all the networks' optimiser.

4.2 Results

We report in Table 3 the mean accuracy with a 95% confidence interval of the 10-fold cross validation runs for each model. The scores are reported for each combination of data type, speech-to-text system, model, and version of the dataset.

The results show that among the tested models, the CamemBERT one that was trained on the complete caller-operator transcriptions provided the highest accuracy. It achieved a slightly better result compared to the callers-only CamemBERT. In fact, CamemBERT was able to provide approximately the same performance with or without the operator's part of the conversation. This shows that in a scenario where the emergency center is trying to automatically prioritise a call, the caller's description of their situation would be enough for the system to assign them a priority and assess their situation. The audio XGBoost models obtained the lowest scores, ranging from 49.56 to 50.5%, close to the accuracy of random binary guesses. This proves that in an emergency context, acoustic features in a call recording on their own are not informative enough of a caller's situation.

Table 3. Classification accuracies for the models with a 95% confidence interval.

Data Type	Speech-To-Text system	Model	Callers-Only Accuracy	Callers-Operator Accuracy
Audio (MFCCs)	-	XGBoost	49.56 ± 2.25%	50.5 ± 0.90%
Text	Whisper	LSTM	57.83 ± 2.93%	58.22 ± 5.49%
	Whisper	TextCNN	57.56 ± 6.21%	63.96 ± 4.01%
	Whisper	XLM-RoBERTa	55.55 ± 3.2%	56.0 ± 2.14%
	Vosk API	CamemBERT	68 ± 4.29%	69.55 ± 4.64%
	Whisper	CamemBERT	**71.2 ± 3.02%**	**72.3 ± 2.66%**

As for the baseline LSTM and TextCNN trained on the GloVe embeddings, they both underperfom compared to CamemBERT. They achieve similar accuracies on the callers-only dataset, whereas the TextCNN performs better on the callers-operators dataset. This demonstrates the robustness of BERT-based models in text classification tasks, as unlike the LSTM and TextCNN, Camem-BERT was able to achieve decent results on automatically transcribed noisy textual data. Additionally, the Whisper-transcribed text has surprisingly led to higher scores compared to the Vosk API transcriptions, knowing that Whisper is a multilingual model, while the Vosk model was specifically fine-tuned on French language data. This indicates that the multilingual Whisper is a suitable choice for a speech-to-text component in a call center. We can also note that the combination of Whisper/CamemBERT achieves the most stable results, since it has a lower margin of error (confidence interval) compared to other text models. Finally, note that the multi-lingual XLM-RoBERTa delivers sub-par results and seems to have difficulties to generalize good performances with a small french dataset.

Table 4 represents the confusion matrices for the CamemBERT model for callers-only dataset and the complete callers-operators data. The matrices show that it is easier for both models to predict the "Low-Severity" cases than the "High-Severity" ones. Surprisingly, the callers-only model tends to predict severe cases slightly more accurately, whereas the callers-operators model performs better on the non-severe cases. We plan to evaluate this further with a larger dataset in a future work.

Table 4. Confusion matrix of CamemBERT with 71% and 72% accuracy respectively on each testing set.

		High-Severity	Low-Severity
Callers-Only	High-Severity	TP=27	FN=18
	Low-Severity	FP=8	TN=38
Callers-Operators	High-Severity	TP=26	FN=19
	Low-Severity	FP=6	TN=40

5 Conclusion

In the present work, it was concluded that with the appropriate system design choices, it is possible to predict the severity of an emergency call based on only the caller's description of their situation. It is worth noting that the reported severity is the one resulting from the intervention of the emergency team, and may not always conform to the diagnosis of the caller. This, alongside the absence of accurately annotated calls, poses an additional challenge in this work.

The results in this study imply that the feasibility of such an application depends on an adequate analysis of the call's transcriptions through a BERT-based model, preferably specific to the language of the dataset, CamemBERT [26] for instance in the case of this work. The choice of the speech-to-text system also highly influences the accuracy of the predictions, as unlike the classifier, a multilingual model such as Whisper [34] is robust enough to transcribe phone calls with a higher accuracy compared to other language-specific systems [2].

One of the main limitations of this study is that the performance of the system was evaluated based on the accuracy of its predictions, whereas an interesting additional evaluation would be one concerning its computational efficiency, in terms of speed and resources consumption. As such, we plan on implementing several improvements to the system in the future. On the one hand, we aim to improve our system's predictions accuracy by augmenting CamemBERT with the emotional features of the phone calls obtained through speech emotion recognition models. We also aim to attempt the treatment of longer sequences of text, using models such as Longformers [13]. On the other hand, we will evaluate the system's performance in terms of efficiency and inference speed, as we plan to obtain an analysis of an emergency call as the conversation is going. To do so, we will evaluate and optimise each of the pipeline's components performance separately (VAD, Speech-To-Text, CamemBERT).

Acknowledgements. We would like to thank the SDIS 25 (Service Départemental d'Incendie et de Secours du Doubs) for their invaluable assistance, for sharing their needs and ideas, and for trusting us with the dataset used in this work. Computations have been performed on the supercomputer facilities of the "Mésocentre de calcul de Franche-Comté". This work is (partially) supported by the EIPHI Graduate School (contract ANR-17-EURE-0002). It is also supported by the Safar scholarship program, co-funded by the French embassy in Lebanon, and the Agence Universitaire de la Francophonie AUF-BMO, in the framework of the Interuniversity Scientific Cooperation Project WeBel.

References

1. Google cloud speech to text. https://cloud.google.com/speech-to-text. Accessed 30 Sept 2022
2. Vosk offline speech recognition api. https://alphacephei.com/vosk/. Accessed 30 Sept 2022
3. Xgboost extreme gradient boosting. https://github.com/dmlc/xgboost. Accessed 01 Nov 2022
4. Akiba, T., Sano, S., Yanase, T., Ohta, T., Koyama, M.: Optuna: A next-generation hyperparameter optimization framework. In: Proceedings of the 25th ACM SIGKDD International Conference on Knowledge Discovery & Data Mining, pp. 2623–2631 (2019)
5. Alghifari, M.F., et al.: On the use of voice activity detection in speech emotion recognition. Bullet. Electric. Eng. Informat. 8(4), 1324–1332 (2019)
6. Anthony, T., Mishra, A.K., Stassen, W., Son, J.: The feasibility of using machine learning to classify calls to South African emergency dispatch centres according to prehospital diagnosis, by utilising caller descriptions of the incident. In: Healthcare, vol. 9, p. 1107. MDPI (2021)
7. Bhavan, A., et al.: Bagged support vector machines for emotion recognition from speech. Knowl. Based Syst. **184**, 104886 (2019)
8. Blomberg, S.N., et al..: Machine learning as a supportive tool to recognize cardiac arrest in emergency calls. Resuscitation **138**, 322–329 (2019)
9. Bredin, H., et al.: pyannote.audio: Neural building blocks for speaker diarization. In: ICASSP 2020, IEEE International Conference on Acoustics, Speech, and Signal Processing (2020)

10. Cen, L., Wu, F., Yu, Z.L., Hu, F.: A real-time speech emotion recognition system and its application in online learning. In: Emotions, technology, design, and learning, pp. 27–46. Elsevier (2016)

11. Chen, T., et al.: Xgboost: extreme gradient boosting. R package version 0.4-2 1(4), 1–4 (2015)

12. Conneau, A., et al.: Unsupervised cross-lingual representation learning at scale. CoRR abs/1911.02116 (2019). http://arxiv.org/abs/1911.02116 http://arxiv.org/abs/1911.02116

13. Dai, X., Chalkidis, I., Darkner, S., Elliott, D.: Revisiting transformer-based models for long document classification. arXiv preprint arXiv:2204.06683 (2022)

14. Devlin, J., Chang, M.W., Lee, K., Toutanova, K.: Bert: Pre-training of deep bidirectional transformers for language understanding. arXiv preprint arXiv:1810.04805 (2018)

15. Fadel, W., Araf, I., Bouchentouf, T., Buvet, P.A., Bourzeix, F., Bourja, O.: Which French speech recognition system for assistant robots? In: 2022 2nd International Conference on Innovative Research in Applied Science, Engineering and Technology (IRASET), pp. 1–5. IEEE (2022)

16. Gao, S., et al.: Limitations of transformers on clinical text classification. IEEE J. Biomed. Health Informat. 25(9), 3596–3607 (2021)

17. Gil-Jardiné, C., et al.: Trends in reasons for emergency calls during the covid-19 crisis in the department of gironde, France using artificial neural network for natural language classification. Scand. J. Trauma Resuscit. Emerg. Med. 29(1), 1–9 (2021)

18. Irawati, M.E., Zakaria, H.: Classification model for covid-19 detection through recording of cough using xgboost classifier algorithm. In: 2021 International Symposium on Electronics and Smart Devices (ISESD), pp. 1–5. IEEE (2021)

19. Kim, Y.: Convolutional neural networks for sentence classification. In: Proceedings of the 2014 Conference on Empirical Methods in Natural Language Processing (2014). https://doi.org/10.3115/v1/D14-1181

20. Kingma, D.P., Ba, J.: Adam: A method for stochastic optimization. arXiv preprint arXiv:1412.6980 (2014)

21. Kong, Q., Cao, Y., Iqbal, T., Wang, Y., Wang, W., Plumbley, M.D.: Panns: Large-scale pretrained audio neural networks for audio pattern recognition. IEEE/ACM Trans. Audio Speech Lang. Process. 28, 2880–2894 (2020)

22. Liang, H., Sun, X., Sun, Y., Gao, Y.: Text feature extraction based on deep learning: A review. EURASIP J. Wirel. Commun. Netw. 2017(1), 1–12 (2017)

23. Liu, Y., et al.: Roberta: A robustly optimized bert pretraining approach. arXiv preprint arXiv:1907.11692 (2019)

24. Long, J.M., Yan, Z.F., Shen, Y.L., Liu, W.J., Wei, Q.Y.: Detection of epilepsy using mfcc-based feature and xgboost. In: 2018 11th International Congress on Image and Signal Processing, BioMedical Engineering and Informatics (CISP-BMEI), pp. 1–4. IEEE (2018)

25. Luz, S., Haider, F., de la Fuente, S., Fromm, D., MacWhinney, B.: Alzheimer's dementia recognition through spontaneous speech: The adress challenge. arXiv preprint arXiv:2004.06833 (2020)

26. Martin, L., et al.: Camembert: A tasty French language model. arXiv preprint arXiv:1911.03894 (2019)

27. McDuff, D., Rowan, K., Choudhury, P., Wolk, J., Pham, T., Czerwinski, M.: A multimodal emotion sensing platform for building emotion-aware applications. arXiv preprint arXiv:1903.12133 (2019)

28. McFee, B., et al.: librosa: Audio and music signal analysis in python. In: Proceedings of the 14th Python in Science Conference, vol. 8, pp. 18–25 (2015)
29. Minaee, S., Kalchbrenner, N., Cambria, E., Nikzad, N., Chenaghlu, M., Gao, J.: Deep learning-based text classification: A comprehensive review. ACM Comput. Surv. (CSUR) **54**(3), 1–40 (2021)
30. Orellana, M., Trujillo, A., Acosta, M.I.: A methodology to predict emergency call high-priority: Case study ecu-911. In: 2020 Seventh International Conference on eDemocracy & eGovernment (ICEDEG), pp. 243–247. IEEE (2020)
31. Paszke, A., et al.: Pytorch: An imperative style, high-performance deep learning library. Adv. Neural Inf. Process. Syst. **32** (2019)
32. Pennington, J., Socher, R., Manning, C.D.: Glove: Global vectors for word representation. In: Proceedings of the 2014 Conference on Empirical Methods in Natural Language Processing (EMNLP), pp. 1532–1543 (2014)
33. Qaiser, S., Ali, R.: Text mining: use of tf-idf to examine the relevance of words to documents. Int. J. Comput. Appl. **181**(1), 25–29 (2018)
34. Radford, A., Kim, J.W., Xu, T., Brockman, G., McLeavey, C., Sutskever, I.: Robust speech recognition via large-scale weak supervision. arXiv preprint arXiv:2212.04356 (2022)
35. Radford, A., et al.: Improving language understanding by generative pre-training (2018)
36. Tenney, I., Das, D., Pavlick, E.: Bert rediscovers the classical NLP pipeline. arXiv preprint arXiv:1905.05950 (2019)
37. Wang, Z., Wang, L., Huang, C., Luo, X.: Bert-based chinese text classification for emergency domain with a novel loss function. arXiv preprint arXiv:2104.04197 (2021)
38. Zhang, Y., Wallace, B.: A sensitivity analysis of (and practitioners' guide to) convolutional neural networks for sentence classification. arXiv preprint arXiv:1510.03820 (2015)

A Temporal Metric-Based Efficient Approach to Predict Citation Counts of Scientists

Saumya Kumar Dewangan$^{(\boxtimes)}$, Shrutilipi Bhattacharjee, and Ramya D. Shetty

Department of Information Technology, National Institute of Technology Karnataka, Surathkal, Mangaluru, India
{saumyakumardewangan.212it025,shrutilipi, ramyadshetty.207it004}@nitk.edu.in

Abstract. Citation count is one of the essential factors in understanding and measuring the impact of a scientist or a publication. Estimating the future impact of scientists or publications is crucial as it assists in making decisions about potential awardees of research grants, appointing researchers for several scientific positions, etc. Many studies have been proposed to estimate publication's future citation count; however, limited research has been conducted on forecasting the citation-based influence of the scientists. The authors of the scientific manuscripts are connected through common publications, which can be captured in dynamic network structures with multiple features in the nodes and the links. The topological structure is an essential factor to consider as it reveals important information about such dynamic networks, such as the rise and fall in the network properties like in-degree, etc., over time for nodes. In this work, we have developed an approach for predicting the citation count of scientists using topological information from dynamic citation networks and relevant contents of individual publications. This framework of the citation count prediction is formulated as the node classification task, which is accomplished by using seven machine learning-based classification models for various class categories. The highest average accuracy of 85.19% is achieved with the XGBoost classifier on the High Energy Physics - Theory citation network dataset.

Keywords: Citation networks · Citation count · Node classification · Directed and weighted networks · Temporal networks

1 Introduction

Citation analysis is a method of measuring the importance or influence of an author or published articles by counting the number of times other works cite this author or publication. It is analyzed for various purposes, such as to evaluate the impact of a particular work or a scientist, how much the related research

© IFIP International Federation for Information Processing 2023
Published by Springer Nature Switzerland AG 2023
I. Maglogiannis et al. (Eds.): AIAI 2023, IFIP AICT 675, pp. 343–355, 2023.
https://doi.org/10.1007/978-3-031-34111-3_29

area is impactful in the future. An essential objective of citation analysis is to make decisions about giving grants, accepting appointments, etc. Citation count is a well-known measure of such scientific impact. The h-index and i10-index are crucial metrics for the impact analysis of researchers or research outcomes, which are based on the citation count [1]. The citation is a consequence of referring to some article and can be thought of as directed links between the referred and the referencing objects and eventually constructing networks. Citation networks can be broadly categorized into two networks; in a paper-based citation network, the graph is always acyclic because an article can refer to another article that is already published. However, in an author-based citation network, the graph can be cyclic also, as two authors can cite each other's work reciprocally in the same time frame. A self loop may also exist if authors cite their previously published work. These networks are dynamic in nature, such that nodes may get added/removed, and the structure and the weights on the links change from one time frame to the other. The existing works on citation count prediction [2–4] mainly use the content information in the publication, such as *abstract, title, keywords*, etc., for the analysis. However, since such networks are evolving over time, the topological properties [5,6] of such networks are also changing, which can reveal an essential pattern for the citation count prediction task. It also tells about the increasing and decreasing trends in the citation count of the authors over time. In this work, a new approach is proposed for predicting the citation count of the scientists by utilizing the temporal metrics from the topological properties of the author-based citation network. Then, the prediction of citation count is formulated as a node classification problem, accomplished using various machine learning (ML)-based classification models, such as logistic regression, decision tree, random forest, nearest neighbor, support vector machine, multilayer perceptron, and XGBoost.

1.1   Background Study

It is found from the existing literature that the dynamic and complex citation networks have drawn a lot of interest in fields like mining and evaluating scientific activities, promoting authors and papers to researchers, estimating the number of citations an author or paper will receive, etc.

Some studies [2–4] have considered the content present in the published articles for the task of citation count prediction. They use the information in the papers, like *title, abstract, index terms*, etc., for the prediction. Bhat *et al.* [4] proposed methods based on classification and created a predictive technique for predicting the citation count of scientists based on classification models. Using different characteristics, they analyzed how *author influence, author interdisciplinarity, and title terms* affected citation counts. They achieved a training accuracy of 88.7% with the classification tree model.

Some studies [7,8] have used the information present in the graph structure of the citation networks. They have used features like closeness centrality, betweenness centrality, etc., to predict citation counts. Zhu *et al.* [8] suggested a citation count forecasting model based on academic network characteristics.

They have considered multiple features, such as the paper feature, author feature, network feature, etc., and examined the importance of each feature for the task of citation count prediction. Then, they compared the performance with different prediction algorithms and found that the SVM was the best model for their dataset and achieved an 88.87% coefficient of determination.

Some studies [9,10] have addressed the problem of citation count prediction in dynamic citation networks. They have used the link prediction technique for the prediction of citation count. Kaya *et al.* [9] proposed an approach for predicting the citation count of the scientist in a directed, weighted, and dynamic citation network. They introduced a dynamic proximity metric for the classifiers to predict citation count and some basic topological properties. The dynamic metric is based on rising and falling trends in citation networks throughout transitional time frames. They achieved an area under curve (AUC) score of 0.836 with a random forest classifier for the Aminer-Citation network. Bütün *et al.* [10] presented an approach based on the link prediction problem for the scientist's citation count prediction using a supervised learning method. They have developed a temporal link prediction measure using topological properties in complex networks at the local and global levels. Additionally, they compared how well the suggested link prediction measure performed in anticipating new links in complex networks with five other widely used link prediction measures. The highest area under the receiver operating characteristic curve (AUROC) value of 0.872 was achieved with a random forest model for the Aminer-Citation network.

It has been found that many studies are reported for the citation analysis of the papers, and limited studies have addressed the citation analysis of the authors or scientists. Many works [2–4] have considered the content information in the publications to predict its future impact and did not utilize the network's topological properties. Some studies [7,8] have also examined the dynamic network's structural characteristics for predicting the scientists' citation count. Few works [9,10] have used the link prediction method for citation count prediction. In this study, we have made the following contributions:

1. Our study has considered the dynamic structure of the citation networks and relevant contents of the publications to predict the citation count of the scientists.
2. We have created a temporal metric based on various temporal events happening in the dynamic citation network.
3. The problem of predicting the citation count of scientists is formulated into a node classification problem. The temporal metric is used for the node classification task. The node classification task is accomplished by using and comparing different ML-based models.
4. The citation count prediction is also considered a regression task and analyzed for different feature sets using a linear regression model.

The rest of the paper is organized as follows. Section 2 discusses the proposed methodology, and Sect. 3 consists of the empirical setup and results. Finally, Sect. 4 concludes the work.

2   Proposed Methodology

This study has a sequence of stages for predicting the citation counts of scientists. Figure 1 represents the outline of the proposed approach for solving the problem step by step. In the first stage, we have a paper-based citation network. Then, it is converted to an author-based citation network in the second stage. The temporal metric is calculated for all the authors in the third stage, as discussed in Sect. 2.3. The past citation count of the scientists is utilized over time for creating the temporal metric. The temporal metric and the content based information from the publications, such as *title and abstract*, are utilized as the features of an author. In the fourth stage, the problem is framed as a node classification problem, which is achieved using ML-based classification models. A thorough description of these steps are discussed in the following subsections.

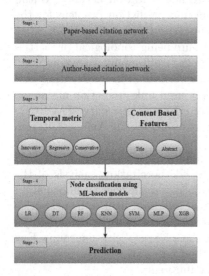

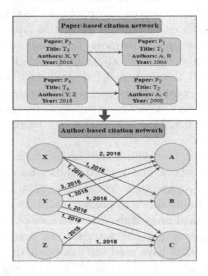

Fig. 1. Proposed methodology for the prediction of citation counts of the scientists

Fig. 2. Conversion of paper-based citation network to author-based citation network

2.1   Paper-Based Citation Network

In a paper-based citation network, the papers published in various conferences, journals, etc., constitute the network nodes, and the directed edges show the citation among the papers. The details present in an article are the *paper title, authors, year of publication, etc.*, which act as the node's features in the paper-based citation network. An example is shown in Fig. 2, consisting of four papers, P_1, P_2, P_3, and P_4, and there is a directed link from paper P_3 to paper P_1, which indicates the paper P_3 has cited paper P_1. The papers as the nodes and their mutual citations as the links construct the entire paper-based citation network from the given datasets. Since our objective is to predict the citation counts of the scientists rather than predicting the citation count of the articles, the paper-based network is converted into an author-based citation network.

2.2   Author-Based Citation Network

To predict the citation count of the scientists, the author-based citation network is generated from the paper-based citation network. In an author-based citation network, the scientists are represented as vertices, and the directed edges show the citations between authors. The directed links include multiple properties, such as weight and time, as shown in Fig. 2. The weight attribute indicates the number of times a scientist has cited the papers of another scientist. Consider an example paper-based citation network shown in Fig. 2. There is an edge from author X to author A with weight and time attributes as 2 and 2016, respectively; it indicates that author X has cited author A two times in the year 2016. The author-based citation network is defined as $G_t(N, E')$ in the time frame t, which is a directed and weighted network, where N is the set of scientists and E' is the set of edges. Each link (i, j) present in E' represents a quadruple of the form (i, j, w, t), where $i, j \in N$, w is the weight attribute, and t is the time instance. Here, every i^{th} node in N is represented by N_i. The citation count of each node i in time frame t is represented by $CC(N_i)_t$. $G_{t,t'}(N, E)$ is the author-based citation network from time frame t to t'; hence it is a directed, weighted, and temporal network. There will be a total of T time frames (where, T depends on the time frame considered in a given dataset) in $G_{t,t'}(N, E)$, each with a window size of s.

The approach to making an author-based citation network from the paper-based network (as shown in Fig. 2) is explained in the following example. If there is an edge from the paper P_3 to a paper P_1, then there will be an edge from all the authors of paper P_3 to all the authors of paper P_1, and the time attribute for the edges will be the time of publication of the paper P_3. Considering the network with four papers, P_1, P_2, P_3, and P_4. For each unique author present in the paper-based citation network, there is a node in the author-based citation network, represented as authors A, B, C, X, Y, and Z. Let us consider the relationship between the authors Y and A. Author Y is present in two papers, P_3 and P_4, published in the year 2016 and 2018, respectively. The weight attribute corresponding to the edge in the year 2016 is 2 because author A is present in the 2 papers cited by Y in 2016, and the time attribute is 2016. Similarly, the weight attribute for the edge in 2018 is 1 because author A is present in 1 paper cited by Y in 2018.

2.3   Temporal Metric (M)

The concept of temporal events is studied in [11], mainly for the link prediction task, where temporal events are based on the increase or decrease in the weights of the links over time. In this work, the idea of temporal events is extended for the nodes, and variation in temporal events is based on the rise and fall in citation count of a node over time. The temporal metric calculates the score for a node which is based on the temporal events occurring to the node in the network. The various temporal events, with respect to a node, are described as follows:

- **Innovative Event (I):**
  An innovative event states that the node (the author) has gained citations in the current time frame t while it did not have any citations in the previous time frame $t - 1$. Hence, this event is positively scored by multiplying with a positive constant i, and the innovative score, $I(N_i, t)$, is formulated as follows:

$$I(N_i, t) = i * CC(N_i)_t \qquad if \quad CC(N_i)_{t-1} = 0 \wedge CC(N_i)_t > 0 \quad (1)$$

- **Regressive Event (R):**
  A regressive event shows that a node has gone through a complete loss in its citation count (zero in the current time frame t) compared to the last state (citation count greater than zero in the time frame $t - 1$). This event is negatively scored by multiplying with a negative constant r because the node has lost all its value in the ongoing time frame, and the regressive score, $R(N_i, t)$, is calculated as follows:

$$R(N_i, t) = r * CC(N_i)_{t-1} \qquad if \quad CC(N_i)_{t-1} > 0 \wedge CC(N_i)_t = 0 \quad (2)$$

- **Conservative Event (C):**
  Conservative event shows the continuation of acquiring the citations by a node from other nodes in the current state from the previous state. If a node has a citation count greater than zero in the current time frame t and a citation count greater than zero in the last time frame $t - 1$, this kind of event is considered a conservative event. Since no complete loss in the node's citation occurs in this event, it is positively scored by multiplying with a positive constant c. In this event, three cases may arise, citation count of a node may increase, decrease, or remain the same in the transition from the time frame $t - 1$ to time frame t. If the citation count increases, then the event is rewarded by the proportion of the increase in the citation count from time frame $t - 1$ to t, and the conservative score is calculated from Eq. (3). If the citation count decreases, a penalty with the proportion of decrease in the citation count is applied due to this event, and the conservative score is calculated from Eq. (4). If the citation count remains the same, then the event is scored positively, and conservative score is calculated from Eq. (5).

$$C_i(N_i, t) = c * (CC(N_i)_{t-1} + \frac{CC(N_i)_t}{CC(N_i)_{t-1}})$$
$$if \quad CC(N_i)_t > CC(N_i)_{t-1} \quad (3)$$

$$C_d(N_i, t) = c * [CC(N_i)_{t-1} + \frac{CC(N_i)_{t-1} - CC(N_i)_t}{CC(N_i)_{t-1}}]$$
$$if \quad CC(N_i)_t < CC(N_i)_{t-1} \quad (4)$$

$$C_u(N_i, t) \quad = \quad c * CC(N_i)_t \qquad if \quad CC(N_i)_{t-1} \quad = \quad CC(N_i)_t \quad (5)$$

The total score for a node, N_i at time frame t is calculated as follows:

$$T(N_i, t) = I(N_i, t) \ or \ R(N_i, t) \ or \ C(N_i, t) \qquad (6)$$

The temporal metric for each node, N_i is calculated as follows [10]:

$$M(N_i) = \sum_{t=2}^{n} log(t+1) * T(N_i, t) \qquad (7)$$

2.4   Content-Based Features

This study also considers the content-based information in the publications for the citation count prediction. The content present in the papers, i.e., *title and abstract*, are also taken as features of the authors, along with the temporal metric. NLP-based text preprocessing tasks have been carried out for these feature extraction, such as tokenization, removal of stop words, and stemming [12].

2.5   Node Classification

This work is formulated as a classification problem of the scientists based on their citation count. The ML-based classification models are used for the node classification task. The class categories are established at various citation count intervals, as shown in Table 1. The temporal metric is calculated for every single node that acts as a feature for the classification models, and class categories act as labels for the classifiers. The task is to predict the class of a node (author) for a time frame according to the temporal metric for that node, which is calculated based on the events with respect to that node over time frames.

Table 1. Class Categories

Citation count interval	Class category
0	C_0
[1, 50]	C_1
>50	C_2

The idea for deciding the citation count intervals for the class categories is to distinguish between the nodes based on their citation counts. If a node falls in the class category C_0, it means it has not received any citation(i.e., it has a citation count of zero) and is significantly less influential for the time being. If a node belongs to the class category C_1, it is an effective node with a citation count between 1 and 50, both inclusive. If a node exists in category C_2, it has citations above 50 and is highly influential. As required, the number of class categories can vary according to the citation count intervals.

3   Empirical Set-up and Results

This section briefly discusses the dataset, and different machine learning algorithms used in our study and analyzes the results of various machine learning models.

3.1   Dataset Details

1. HEP-TH (High Energy Physics - Theory):
   This network dataset [13] consists of 352,807 links and 27,770 nodes. The paper information is available from January 1993 to April 2003. It also provides meta-information descriptions of the articles like *paper title, abstract, author details, publication date, etc.* The statistics of the dataset are shown in Fig. 3. It shows that citation among scientists has increased over time except for 2003 because of the partial data availability. The dataset has 27,770 papers, but we have obtained meta information of around 26,600 papers from [14].

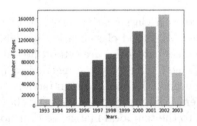

Fig. 3. Statistics of the HEP-TH dataset

3.2   ML-Based Models

The task is to predict the class to which the nodes belong based on the temporal metric and content based features. In this study, we have used seven models, such as logistic regression, decision tree, random forest, nearest neighbor, support vector machine, multilayer perceptron, and XGBoost [15], for the node classification task.

3.3   Experimental Results

Four resampled datasets, DS_1, DS_2, DS_3, and DS_4, are created from the HEP-TH datasets by taking six consecutive years for training and the next one year for prediction. Each resampled dataset has the same time window of size of one year and has different time frames in creating the temporal metric and predicting the citation count. The details of the sampled datasets are given in Table 2.

Table 2. Sampled Datasets Generated from HEP-Th Network

Dataset	Training years for predicting Temporal Metric	Prediction year	Time window (year)
DS_1	1993–1998	1999	1
DS_2	1994–1999	2000	1
DS_3	1995–2000	2001	1
DS_4	1996–2001	2002	1

The experiments are conducted for a different combination of features. The feature set FS_1 consists of the *title* and *abstract* of the publications by the authors, FS_2 consists of the *title, abstract,* and *citation count* of all the previous time frames, and FS_3 contains *title, abstract,* and *temporal metric*. The metrics utilized to evaluate the performance of classifiers are accuracy, precision, recall, and F1 score [16]. There are ten experiments conducted for each of the four resampled datasets, as mentioned in Table 2 with three feature sets. All experiments' train test split is taken as a 75:25 ratio. The average values of the evaluation metrics are taken from the four resampled datasets for each of the three feature sets, and the results are shown in Table 3 and Table 4.

After experimenting with different sets of values of the constants, i, r, and c, we have reported the results with the following values of constants i, r, and c (please refer to Sect. 2.3):

- For the innovative events, the positive constant $i = 1$ is used to score the event positively.
- For the regressive events, the negative constant $r = -0.5$ is used to score the event negatively.
- For the conservative events, the positive constant $c = 0.5$ is used to score the event positively.

The results of the experiments are recorded in Table 3 and Table 4. The average of the results obtained with feature set FS_1 for all the four resampled datasets is presented in Table 3. The XGBoost classifier has given the highest accuracy and precision of 76.39% and 68.32%, respectively, and multilayer perceptron has given the highest recall and F1 score of 61.08% and 61.34%, respectively.

Table 3. Result obtained with FS_1 and FS_2

Models	Results with FS_1				Results with FS_2			
	Accuracy (%)	Precision (%)	Recall (%)	F1 score (%)	Accuracy (%)	Precision (%)	Recall (%)	F1 score (%)
Logistic Regression	74.51	67.38	52.99	56.20	82.45	82.97	70.45	74.96
Decision Tree	73.90	60.39	57.28	58.53	82.05	75.50	73.06	74.14
Random Forest	68.58	65.91	37.32	34.21	74.05	73.77	44.28	44.75
Nearest Neighbor	67.41	66.70	37.51	34.68	81.69	79.98	71.78	74.92
Support Vector Machine	74.18	63.55	54.50	57.21	80.17	70.49	56.70	57.97
Multilayer Perceptron	75.25	61.87	61.08	61.34	83.18	77.73	74.75	76.02
XGBoost	76.39	68.32	57.67	61.03	85.19	83.49	75.76	79.00

The average of the results obtained with feature set FS_2 for the four resampled datasets are given in Table 3. It has been observed that the XGBoost classifier has performed better than the other models in terms of accuracy, precision, recall, and F1 score and has given the highest accuracy of 85.19%. The results of citation count prediction have improved with the feature set FS_2, as compared with the results of the feature set FS_1.

The average of the results obtained with feature set FS_3 are recorded in Table 4. The XGBoost model has outperformed the rest of the classifiers in terms of all the evaluation metrics used. The XGBoost model has achieved the highest accuracy of 84.09% with feature set FS_3, which consists of the *title, abstract,* and *temporal metric.*

Table 4. Result obtained with FS_3

Models	Accuracy (%)	Precision (%)	Recall (%)	F1 score (%)
Logistic Regression	81.95	80.00	67.29	71.80
Decision Tree	80.69	71.50	69.12	70.15
Random Forest	70.11	68.47	39.09	36.99
Nearest Neighbor	80.75	76.26	66.21	69.86
Support Vector Machine	79.80	64.66	53.31	53.16
Multilayer Perceptron	81.97	74.19	71.50	72.65
XGBoost	84.09	80.64	71.92	75.41

Confusion matrix is displayed to analyze the performance of the classifiers for each of the three classes considered in this study. Figure 4 represents the combined confusion matrix obtained from the XGBoost model over all the four resampled datasets. The confusion matrix corresponding to feature set FS_1 is shown in Fig. 4a. With FS_1, the accuracy achieved for class C_0 is 91.15%, but the accuracy for class C_1 and C_2 is comparatively less. It can be inferred from Fig. 4b with FS_2 that the results are better than FS_1. With FS_2, accuracy for all the classes, i.e., C_0, C_1, and C_2, have better accuracies of 94.04%, 69.27%, and 64.47%. However, results with the feature set FS_3 are comparable with FS_2 for all the classes, and better than the results of FS_1, as shown in Fig. 4c.

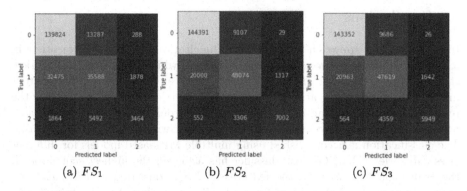

(a) FS_1 (b) FS_2 (c) FS_3

Fig. 4. Confusion matrix for the feature sets FS_1, FS_2 and FS_3 respectively

Table 5. Results of a linear regression model with previous six years' *citations* as the features

Dataset	MAE	RMSE
DS_1	4.88	16.76
DS_2	7.30	24.48
DS_3	5.99	16.65
DS_4	7.33	23.43
Average	6.38	20.33

Table 6. Results of a linear regression model with the *temporal metric* as feature

Dataset	MAE	RMSE
DS_1	6.31	26.24
DS_2	9.05	31.93
DS_3	8.67	27.05
DS_4	9.40	29.55
Average	8.36	28.69

From the experiments, it has been found that the results with feature set FS_3 are better than the results with the feature set FS_1, with an increase in accuracy of 7.7%. However, results with the feature set FS_2 and FS_3 have marginal difference in accuracy (1.1%), with FS_2 having better results. The feature set FS_2 has more features as it has *citation count* of all the time frames, and FS_3 has a single feature *temporal metric*, other than *title* and *abstract*. Therefore, FS_3 is better as compared to FS_2 in terms of reduced number features and time complexity for classification models, incurring similar accuracy.

The prediction of citation count of the scientist is also considered as a regression problem, and a linear regression model is used for this task. The metrics used for the performance evaluation of the regression model are mean absolute error (MAE) and root mean squared error (RMSE). These errors, MAE and RMSE, represent the comparison between the predicted and the actual citation counts. The results are reported in Table 5 and Table 6, respectively.

The average MAE of 6.38, and RMSE of 20.33 is achieved with the citation counts of previous six years as the features, and the average MAE of 8.36, and RMSE of 28.69 is achieved with temporal metric as the feature.

4   Conclusions

In this study, an approach for predicting the citation count of the scientists in a dynamic citation network has been developed, which utilizes the topological structure of the dynamic citation network using temporal metric, and content information of the publications. The temporal metric is created to capture the temporal events occurring in the network. The problem is conceptualized as a node classification task to understand the future citation classes of the scientists. The classification is accomplished using multiple ML-based models for different class categories. The XGBoost classifier has achieved the highest scores for all the evaluation metrics with the feature set FS_2, consisting of *title, abstract, and citation count* of previous years, and FS_3, consisting of *title, abstract, and temporal metric*. The XGBoost model has achieved the highest average accuracy of 85.19% with FS_2. It is observed that the best score for different evaluation metrics is obtained from the feature set FS_2. However, results with feature set FS_3 are better than those with FS_1, and also comparable with FS_2. Since FS_3 has *title, abstract, and temporal metric* as its features and FS_2 has *citation count* of every time frame as its feature along with *title and abstract*, FS_3 is advantageous over FS_2 in terms of less number of features and time complexity for classification. The task of citation count prediction is also considered as a regression problem, and linear regression model is used for the prediction. The average MAE of 6.38 and 8.36 is achieved with the previous year's citation count and temporal metric as the features, respectively. These results are also comparable, having a difference of 2.02 of MAE. Hence, the temporal metric can be an essential feature for the prediction of the citation count of scientists. The author-based features like the number of publications, area of research, etc., can also be used along with the temporal metric, and deep learning models can be applied in the future to enhance the accuracy of the citation count prediction process.

References

1. Ibáñez, A., Larrañaga, P., Bielza, C.: Predicting the h-index with cost-sensitive naive Baye. In: 11th International Conference on Intelligent Systems Design and Applications, pp. 599–604 (2011). https://doi.org/10.1109/ISDA.2011.6121721
2. Fu, L.D., Aliferis, C.F.: Using content-based and bibliometric features for machine learning models to predict citation counts in the biomedical literature. Scientometrics **85**, 257–270 (2010). https://doi.org/10.1007/s11192-010-0160-5
3. Chakraborty, T., Kumar, S., Goyal, P., Ganguly, N., Mukherjee, A.: Towards a stratified learning approach to predict future citation counts. In: IEEE/ACM Joint Conference on Digital Libraries, pp. 351–360 (2014). https://doi.org/10.1109/JCDL.2014.6970190
4. Bhat, H.S., Huang, L.H., Rodriguez, S., Dale, R., Heit, E.: Citation prediction using diverse features. IEEE Int. Conf. Data Mining Worksh. (ICDMW) **2015**, 589–596 (2015). https://doi.org/10.1109/ICDMW.2015.131

5. Shetty, R.D., Bhattacharjee, S., Dutta, A., Namtirtha, A.: GSI: An influential node detection approach in heterogeneous network using covid-19 as use case. IEEE Trans. Comput. Soc. Syst. (2022). https://doi.org/10.1109/TCSS.2022.3180177
6. Shetty, R. D., Bhattacharjee, S.: A weighted hybrid centrality for identifying influential individuals in contact networks. In: 2022 IEEE International Conference on Electronics, Computing and Communication Technologies (CONECCT), Bangalore, India, pp. 1–6 (2022). https://doi.org/10.1109/CONECCT55679.2022.9865749
7. Chen, J., Zhang, C.: Predicting citation counts of papers. In: 2015 IEEE 14th International Conference on Cognitive Informatics & Cognitive Computing (ICCI*CC), pp. 434–440 (2015). https://doi.org/10.1109/ICCI-CC.2015.7259421
8. Zhu, X.P., Ban, Z.: Citation count prediction based on academic network features. In: 2018 IEEE 32nd International Conference on Advanced Information Networking and Applications (AINA), pp. 534–541 (2018). https://doi.org/10.1109/AINA.2018.00084
9. Bütün, E., Kaya, M., Alhajj, R.: A supervised learning method for prediction citation count of scientists in citation networks. IEEE/ACM Int. Conf. Adv. Soc. Netw. Anal. Mining (ASONAM) **2017**, 952–958 (2017)
10. Bütün, E., Kaya, M.: Predicting citation count of scientists as a link prediction problem. IEEE Trans. Cybernet. **50**(10), 4518–4529 (2020). https://doi.org/10.1109/TCYB.2019.2900495
11. Soares, P.R.S., Prudêncio, R.B.C.: Proximity measures for link prediction based on temporal events. Exp. Syst. Appl. **40**(16), 6652–6660 (2013). https://doi.org/10.1016/j.eswa.2013.06.016. ISSN 0957-4174
12. P. Ganeshkumar, A. K. BR, S. Padmanabhan and V. A, "Social Media Personal Event Notifier Using NLP and Deep Learning", 2022 International Conference on Power, Energy, Control and Transmission Systems (ICPECTS), Chennai, India, 2022, pp. 1–5, doi: 10.1109/ICPECTS56089.2022.10047710
13. HEP-Th Dataset. https://snap.stanford.edu/data/cit-HepTh.html. Accessed Sept 2022
14. HEP-Th Dataset Metadata. https://www.kaggle.com/datasets/tayorm/arxiv-papers-metadata. Accessed Sept 2022
15. Sarker, I.H.: Machine learning: Algorithms, real-world applications and research directions. SN Comput. Sci. **2**, 160 (2021). https://doi.org/10.1007/s42979-021-00592-x
16. Nikam, U.V., Deshmuh, V.M.: Performance evaluation of machine learning classifiers in malware detection. In: IEEE International Conference on Distributed Computing and Electrical Circuits and Electronics (ICDCECE) 2022, pp. 1–5 (2022). https://doi.org/10.1109/ICDCECE53908.2022.9793102

Comparing Vectorization Techniques, Supervised and Unsupervised Classification Methods for Scientific Publication Categorization in the UNESCO Taxonomy

Neil Villamizar[ID], Jesús Wahrman[ID], and Minaya Villasana[(✉)][ID]

Universidad Simón Bolívar, Caracas, Venezuela
{15-11523,15-11540,mvillasa}@usb.ve

Abstract. A comparison of classification strategies for scientific articles using the UNESCO taxonomy for categorization is presented. An annotated set of articles were vectorized using TF-IDF, Doc2Vec, BERT y SPECTER and it was established that among those options SPECTER provided the best separability properties using quantitative metrics as well as qualitative inspection of 2D projections using t-SNE. When pairing the best performing vectorization strategy with classical machine learning strategies for the classification task, such as multiple layer perceptron and support vector machines, comparable results are found, concluding that the choice of text representation strategy exerts a greater impact over the choice of classifier. The most problematic areas for classification were identified and a cascading classification strategy was implemented and evaluated. Unsupervised methods were also tested to consider the case when annotated data is not readily available and test their suitability. Two different unsupervised methods were used and it was determined that k-means yielded the best results when considering 3 times the number of categories as the optimal number of clusters.

Keywords: Classification · Natural language processing · Scientific texts · Machine learning

1 Introduction

A fundamental problem in natural language processing is text classification as it helps sort and categorize large text samples. The National Science Foundation reported in 2019 that global research output for peer reviewed science and engineering articles and conference papers, grew 4% annually over the last decade reaching 2.6 million in 2018 [17]. Classification of scientific documents can be a

Supported by ACALconecta project.

powerful tool for information filtering and although most scientific journal can be categorized according to a particular taxonomy, it is also true that several taxonomies or nomenclatures exist such as ASJC, MAG or UNESCO fields. On the other hand, many scientific articles are published in conference proceedings or in electronic archives with broad or no classification.

In this article we show an application and the evaluation of several techniques in a pipeline for a real world system, where the corpus of scientific research outputs from Latin America are classified according to the science and engineering UNESCO field taxonomy [20] and is used within the ACALconecta system (app.acalconecta.org). The UNESCO taxonomy has labeling for fields as well as disciplines and sub-disciplines within these fields, providing greater specificity to document labeling. One can establish an equivalence between the nomenclatures for scientific outputs, and given that the corpus available used the ASJC taxonomy [3], a dictionary was constructed at the UNESCO field level to have annotated documents for training. However, at the discipline (there are 248 disciplines in this taxonomy) and subdiscipline (with 2238 subdisciplines available) level requires manual expert annotation. Therefore an evaluation of alternatives for avoidance of manual annotation for document classification at these taxonomy levels is also conducted.

This article is organized as follows: On Sect. 2 the main techniques are presented as well as the work pipeline. Section 3 details the main results obtained and the comparison between the various methods. The effect over classification power of each element in the pipeline is established, while Sect. 4 ends with final remarks and path forward.

1.1   Related Works

One of the initial text representation strategies was the bag-of-words (BoW) approach, which uses one-hot encoding to represent each word in a document. However, BoW has several limitations, as it fails to capture the context and relationship between words in a document. Term Frequency-Inverse Document Frequency (TF-IDF) [7] improves on BoW by weighing the relevance of each word for a document in a corpus, but still lacks proximity information.

Doc2Vec [8] is a generalization of the Word2Vec [10] model that represents complete documents and uses proximity information in training. It has shown promising results in various NLP tasks, including document classification, sentiment analysis, and topic modeling.

Attention and transformer-based models have taken text representation to the next level by incorporating position encoding and proximity information to capture contextual information. BERT [6] is a pre-trained transformer-based model that generates multiple representations for the same word depending on its context. SciBERT [1] and SPECTER [4] are Transformer-based models, specifically trained on scientific literature. SPECTER includes positive and negative citation paths to capture relationships between documents.

The choice of a representation model depends on the type and amount of information available. Selecting a representation model that fits the specific task and available data is important.

2 Methodology

2.1 Data Collection and Processing

A data set of scientific papers comprised of title, abstract and publishing journal was available, following the distribution in Table 1. From the table one can see that the data is not balanced in the different categories. Classification with unbalanced data affects the performance of classifiers, so a balanced subset was constructed by random sampling on each class. In this work classifiers using the unbalanced data and a balanced subset are constructed, thus showing the effects of unbalanced data on classification.

Table 1. Data distribution in UNESCO fields, the number inside parenthesis represents the UNESCO code for that field.

UNESCO field	Number of samples
Life Sciences (24)	12488
Agricultural Sciences (31)	10923
Chemistry (23)	4957
Mathematics (12)	4599
Astronomy and Astrophysics (21)	4583
Earth and Space Sciences (25)	3396
Physics (22)	2782
Technological Sciences (33)	2506
Medical Sciences (32)	1774

The dataset was processed using the following procedures: First stopwords and punctutation marks were removed and all letters were converted to lower case. Then each word was lemmatized, where the word is replaced by it's correspondent lemma, that is the canonical form, dictionary form, or citation form of a word. Finally, samples were built concatenating the title, abstract and the name of the journal for each article.

2.2 Text Representation

In this work four methods of text representation were used: TF-IDF, Doc2Vec, BERT and SPECTER. This is a mix between classic and some state of the art methods. TF-IDF, Doc2Vec and BERT are very well known methods for text representation while SPECTER is specialized in representing scientific documents, based on transformers like BERT but adds a citation graph in their training process for better results, because a document citing another suggests that these documents have some similarity; it uses a loss function that induces the transformer to generate closer vectors when a document cites another and codifies that relationship on the vectors generated by SPECTER.

The representation methods were evaluated using metrics that are normally used to measure the quality of a clustering. This is based on the fact that a good representation should help distinguish between the various contexts in which documents are produced. These metrics are: Separability Index [11], Silhouette Coefficient [18], Calinski-Harabasz Score [2] and Davies-Bouldin Score [5]. It's important to note that the results of these metrics serve as a heuristic to help select an appropriate representation method. t-SNE [9] was used to project the vectors in two dimensions for visualization.

2.3   Supervised and Unsupervised Classification Methods

Once a text representation method has been selected, the task of classifying the texts was performed using methods from supervised learning for documents annotated at the field level. Also, unsupervised methods were employed as a way to address the classification of documents with no known category, which is the case for classification at the discipline or sub-discipline level in the UNESCO taxonomy.

For supervised learning multiple layered perceptron (MLP) [14] and support vector machines (SVM) [12] were used, with accuracy as the main performance metric and confusion matrix to analyse results. Training was done using cross-validation techniques with the two sets considered: the complete data set (see Table 1) and a balanced subset that has 1774 samples per category.

For unsupervised learning, K-Means [19] and Gaussian Mixture [16] were tested. To predict the category of a sample, the annotated category that appears the most in the cluster is the classification assigned to the samples belonging to the cluster. Results with a balanced and the unbalanced complete data set are presented.

3   Results and Discussion

3.1   Text Representation

In this subsection the methods of representation are evaluated using the validation metrics mentioned above. For these experiments a subset of 5400 samples was used in which each category has 600 instances taken randomly. The complete data set was not used because the computational cost of calculating the validation metrics was high and this suffices to conclude on the best text representation.

Two dimensional representations of the data is shown in Fig. 1 using t-SNE, where it can be seen how the vectors generated by SPECTER form well-defined groups in the 2D projection, in contrast to TF-IDF, Doc2Vec and BERT in which groups are very overlapping. In TF-IDF, Doc2Vec and BERT groupings are not very separated from each other and only a few fields have well recognizable groups, such as the field of Medicine (UNESCO field 32, colored in purple) or the field of Mathematics (UNESCO field 12, colored in dark brown) when using TF-IDF and BERT. Using Doc2Vec, the only recognizable group is the field of Medicine (UNESCO field 32, colored in purple). Libraries for various methods were imported from scikit-learn [13,15].

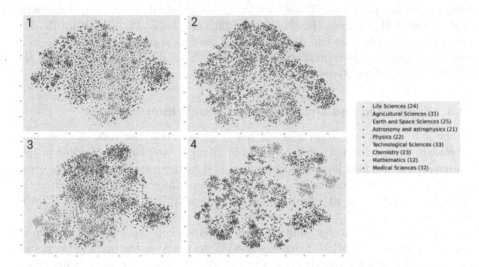

Fig. 1. Two dimensional representations using t-SNE for TF-IDF (1), Doc2Vec (2), BERT (3) and SPECTER (4). Categories are represented with different colors specified in the leyend

Some fields such as Physics (UNESCO field 22) and Astronomy and Astrophysics (UNESCO field 21) are quite overlapping regardless of the representation used. Rather than a deficiency in the rendering algorithm, this may be due to the nature of the data. For example, both Physics and Astrophysics have terms and topics in common, so it makes sense that they are close in representation. A situation similar to this can occur between other fields, such as: life sciences (which includes animal biology) and agricultural sciences (which includes breeding).

Table 2 summarizes the metrics that help to quantitatively investigate the adequacy of a particular representation model. These results confirm that SPECTER surpasses the other models in all metrics except on the Calinski-Harabasz coefficient, where it has the second best value. Therefore, henceforth SPECTER is used as the language representation model.

Table 2. Evaluation metrics compared for each representation method. Best values for each metric are in bold.

Evaluation metrics	TF-IDF	Doc2Vec	BERT	SPECTER
Separability Index	0.712	0.484	0.664	**0.751**
Silhouette Coefficient	0.003	−0.036	0.017	**0.035**
Calinski-Harabasz	8.721	**305.04**	141.967	170.927
Davies-Bouldin	16.637	5.919	6.471	**5.421**

3.2 Supervised Methods

Different methods of supervised learning were evaluated on the task of text classification while using SPECTER as the vectorization technique.

When working with supervised methods, the balance of the data set is important. A model trained with unbalanced data will tend to favor certain predictions, according to the distribution of the data; this can be beneficial if the distribution of the data set is the actual distribution of the data in the real world. On the other had, a model trained with balanced data avoids bias when classifying. Therefore the methods in this section will be tested with the complete data set (unbalanced) and a balanced subset with 1774 samples per category chosen randomly, and trained using cross-validation (with $k = 5$) to determine the error. When using the complete data set, MLP obtained an overall accuracy of 77% and SVM 78%. Meanwhile, using the balanced subset both methods obtained an accuracy of 76% with cross-validation.

Having these estimates, each data set was split in 80% training and 20% test data, chosen randomly. Then both methods were trained with this partition of the data set to look for any possible improvement. With this data partition over the complete data set both methods obtained an accuracy of 79% on test data, close to the expected 77% and 78%. Whereas with the balanced data set the MLP model obtained a classification accuracy of 76% and the SVM 77%, both close to the initial estimations. In Tables 3, 4 and 5 the accuracy for each class and the matrix of confusion of each method can be seen on both data sets.

Table 3 shows that the 3 categories that produce more failed predictions are: Physics (22), Astronomy and Astrophysics (21), and Technological Sciences (33).

For Technological Sciences (33) Tables 4 and 5 show that the failed predictions in this category are distributed in almost all other categories because of the amplitude of this field, that includes disciplines like: Biotechnology, Chemical Engineering, Computer Technology, and others; which can easily be confused with other fields, so the low accuracy is expected.

In the case of Physics (22) and Astronomy and Astrophysics (21), these are related fields and in some taxonomies one is a subset of the other, thus the confusion is almost expected since they share many keywords and the classification could be confusing even for a human.

Table 3. Accuracy obtained in both classification models by category when training with a balanced subset and the complete data set

UNESCO field	Balanced set		Complete set	
	MLP	SVM	MLP	SVM
Mathematics (12)	90%	88%	89%	90%
Physics (22)	65%	69%	60%	57%
Earth and Space Sciences (25)	90%	91%	85%	87%
Agricultural Sciences (31)	70%	71%	79%	79%
Astronomy and Astrophysics (21)	68%	68%	74%	74%
Life Sciences (24)	71%	74%	81%	82%
Technological Sciences (33)	67%	68%	61%	62%
Chemistry (23)	71%	73%	78%	78%
Medical Sciences (32)	94%	94%	89%	88%

Table 4. Confusion matrices for MLP (using UNESCO codes). Rows correspond to the true category while columns are the predicted classes.

	Trained with balanced data set									Trained with complete data set								
	12	22	25	31	21	24	33	23	32	12	22	25	31	21	24	33	23	32
12	321	1	4	2	12	0	13	0	2	848	7	7	2	27	5	17	3	4
22	2	213	1	1	84	0	25	27	1	4	322	4	12	151	2	12	48	1
25	4	1	323	13	5	5	2	1	1	10	2	550	57	4	44	3	9	0
31	0	0	13	252	0	57	13	16	4	5	3	20	1776	0	316	11	47	7
21	21	54	4	0	247	2	16	11	0	37	134	5	4	682	8	23	24	0
24	3	0	13	60	0	246	5	25	3	11	3	26	336	6	2038	10	55	13
33	30	20	2	19	12	7	238	25	2	56	20	5	48	38	15	263	54	2
23	0	14	5	13	10	14	40	257	2	4	23	4	55	26	67	27	783	2
32	4	1	1	6	2	8	1	2	330	8	2	0	11	1	23	0	5	305

Table 5. Confusion matrix for SVM (using UNESCO codes). Rows correspond to the true category while columns are the predicted classes.

	Trained with balanced data set									Trained with complete data set								
	12	22	25	31	21	24	33	23	32	12	22	25	31	21	24	33	23	32
12	326	1	3	2	7	0	13	0	3	843	2	10	2	32	5	19	2	5
22	4	245	1	1	58	0	19	26	0	4	286	5	9	177	2	21	51	1
25	2	2	331	11	2	6	1	0	0	7	0	595	40	2	29	2	4	0
31	0	0	18	258	0	49	12	13	5	2	1	32	1739	0	350	12	37	12
21	18	75	4	0	229	1	16	10	2	28	111	6	4	706	5	31	24	2
24	2	0	9	58	0	254	4	24	4	10	4	32	316	4	2065	11	42	14
33	28	24	3	20	12	3	238	25	2	57	14	4	47	38	9	282	46	4
23	1	13	6	12	8	16	40	259	0	4	19	8	71	29	62	32	763	3
32	2	1	1	5	3	7	2	2	332	5	2	0	9	1	23	0	2	313

When Physics and Technological Science are eliminated from the complete data set both classification methods achieve an accuracy of 83%, thus errors on those categories have a great influence of the final model accuracy. A similar experiment on the balanced data set where the three most failed categories are eliminated from the data set, the results of the cross-validation provide an accuracy of 86% for both models. Thus, for the two classes: Physics (22) and Astronomy and Astrophysics (21), a binary classifier was built to discern documents among them so that this model could be used in cascade; that is bundling those two classes into one for the first model while the second model is responsible for differentiating them. Both MLP and SVM were tested using the previously described training techniques on the cascade classification scheme, selecting the best model among the trained ones. The best results obtained for this experiment were attained with a MLP as primary classifier and an SVM as secondary classifier (to discern between Physics and Astronomy and Astrophysics). When training the main classifier, an 80% success rate was obtained, while the secondary one obtained 76%. By putting them to work together, a success rate of 76% was achieved, with 66% and 65% in Physics (22) and Astronomy and Astrophysics (21), respectively over the balanced data set, thus no real improvement was obtained.

3.3   Method of Representation Vs Method of Classification

Is the power of the classification in the method of representation of the texts or in the method of classification? To answer this, the classification methods were tested again with the balanced data set, using the text representation given by Doc2Vec and BERT, and tuning the hyperparameters of the models in each case. TF-IDF was discarded due to the high dimensionality of the vectors it generates.

Table 6 shows the overall accuracy of the several pairs of classifier with the different text vectorization strategies. From these results it can be seen that the representation method used exerts a great influence in the classification results compared to the choice of the classification method, since by changing the representation method the accuracy varies considerably. Not so when changing the classification method, where the accuracy between the two methods is relatively close when not the same.

Table 6. Accuracy of classifiers for several representation methods, pointing out the best result of each row in bold letters.

	Doc2Vec	BERT	SPECTER
SVM	66%	71%	**76%**
MLP	67%	70%	**76%**

3.4 Unsupervised Methods

To classify texts at the discipline and sub-discipline levels with supervised methods, annotated data for the over 700 categories present would have to be available, which can be prohibitive. This section explores the idea of classification using unsupervised methods that can be applied in those cases, but using the annotated data available at the field level to obtain evaluation metrics. K-Means and Gaussian Mixture were explored and while it's not expected that these outperform the supervised methods, it serves as a preliminary study for future research involving classification at the discipline and sub-discipline level.

In the tests with K-Means the complete data set and a balanced subset are used. After training the model for 9 groups with the complete data set, an accuracy of 54.71% was obtained. Accuracy improved when augmenting the number of groups, reaching up to 65.9% for 45 groups. In the case of Gaussian Mixture, after training the model for 9 groups with the complete data set, an accuracy of 55.27% was obtained, while increasing to the same number of groups did not improve the accuracy (see Table 7 for $\delta = 0$), it is clear that $k = 18$ is favorable.

Upon inspection of the clusters generated with these methods it can be seen that there is no clear classification of the cluster samples since a big percentage of the documents can be classified into the trailing category for that cluster. Again, this could be due to the interdisciplinary nature of some research articles. A second prediction is considered to enhance the performance of the unsupervised classifiers. By defining δ as the difference in the proportions of the two main categories in a cluster, consider a positive category prediction for the trailing category if the difference between the proportions of the main category and the second to main category is lower than δ. Therefore, the classifier uses both results to predict, and if one of them is the correct label it is considered as a correct prediction.

Adding the possibility of double prediction described above to the tests, an accuracy of 76.57% is achieved in the case of K-means (for k = 45 and $\delta = 0.20$). The inclusion for a double prediction did not benefit the predictions for Gaussian Mixture since most accuracy were below 65%. The results with the complete data set can be seen at Table 7 for various values of δ.

When the methods were trained with the balanced subset, K-means obtained a 52.69% accuracy with 9 groups while Gaussian Mixture obtained an accuracy of 55.27%. When the number of groups was increased in the training of this data set, the best result was obtained with 45 groups, with a 67.63% accuracy in the case of K-means, while in the case of Gaussian Mixture the best accuracy was 61.4% (also with 45 groups), in sharp contrast with the results presented in Table 3. To obtain a comparable accuracy, a threshold of $\delta = 0.20$ must be used, implying that there is at least 20% of the data in the cluster not assigned to any of the leading categories.

Table 7. Accuracy of K-Means and Gaussian Mixture, highlighting in bold the best result of each row. Each method is trained with the complete data and with the balanced set, also the accuracy for various δ thresholds.

	Trained with balanced data set						Trained with complete data set				
δ	k = 9	k = 18	k = 27	k = 36	k = 45	δ	k = 9	k = 18	k = 27	k = 36	k = 45
	K-means						K-means				
0.00	52.69%	61.71%	60.49%	66.69%	67.63%	**0.00**	54.71%	63.32%	63.78%	65.18%	65.9%
0.05	56.29%	63.15%	65.28%	68.47%	69.25%	**0.05**	56.18%	65.54%	67.68%	69.63%	68.79%
0.10	63.9%	70.07%	70.35%	69.1%	71.98%	**0.10**	56.87%	67.26%	68.07%	69.4%	71.69%
0.15	64.03%	70.44%	69.88%	70.19%	72.29%	**0.15**	59.84%	70.35%	70.43%	72.54%	71.47%
0.20	63.9%	69.51%	72.23%	71.35%	73.76%	**0.20**	63.05%	72.65%	72.23%	75.03%	76.57%
	Gaussian Mixture						Gaussian Mixture				
0.00	53.94%	36.07%	23.61%	58.36%	61.4%	**0.00**	55.27%	62.67%	60.95%	58.45%	53.74%
0.05	60.39%	43.49%	23.61%	61.52%	62.77%	**0.05**	56.79%	64.78%	62.88%	63.81%	53.74%
0.10	64.53%	51.5%	23.61%	65.87%	62.77%	**0.10**	56.79%	68.12%	65.98%	64.98%	53.74%
0.15	67.85%	51.5%	23.61%	66.72%	63.18%	**0.15**	56.79%	69.03%	68.02%	67.2%	53.74%
0.20	70.76%	60.55%	23.61%	66.88%	63.18%	**0.20**	62.26%	74.82%	70.61%	67.6%	54.22%

4 Conclusions and Discussion

This article set out to evaluate solutions to author classification using their scientific products so that they can be labeled in a platform that offers a scientific directory for Latin America (ACALconecta.org). The multiple classification problem was posed as a supervised learning task but also as an unsupervised one to test the methodology for the discipline classification. The best classifier overall resulted with an accuracy of 79% on test data using SPECTER as the language representation model. The training for SPECTER was done over a corpus of scientific documents. It was shown that pairing this representation model with SVM or MLP provided equivalent accuracy results in the classification task, however SVM improved the classification of 4 UNESCO fields, while MLP resulted in better classification in 2 fields. Therefore, SVM seemed better suited for the task.

Some scientific vocabulary may be exclusive to certain areas, for example, vocabulary pertinent to certain fields in mathematics are seldom used in other areas of science (e.g., Sobolev spaces, diffeomorphism, symplectic manifold), while other words are more universal and span out to various disciplines (e.g. simulation, analysis, data, etc.). Scientific articles that used specialized vocabulary were easily classified within their respective fields. In contrast, the use of ample cross-discipline vocabulary or research that is interdisciplinary in nature (e.g. mathematical biology research or applications of machine learning techniques) can deem the classification task difficult even for a human. A proof of the widespread interdisciplinary research is the fact that out of all SCOPUS classified journals, only 33% of them are classified in one of the UNESCO areas, and although articles published in cross-discipline journals were not considered, much of the research in the remaining journals still share common scientific vocabulary that can span two or more fields.

The interdisciplinary nature of research was made evident in our classifier's difficulty discerning between physics and astronomy and astrophysics, that are very much interrelated areas and share common terms. In MAG taxonomy those two areas are bundled together while areas such as computer science holds its own category as opposed to the UNESCO taxonomy where it is a discipline within mathematics. One could pose the question of whether classification under one taxonomy is better than another, considering it as future work.

When analyzing the confusion matrices for the models trained with balanced data, it is evident that the categories that are difficult for the models to classify correctly are physics, astronomy and astrophysics and technological sciences. In the last case, failed predictions are distributed in the various fields and this is expected due to the wide range of topics covered and the intersections that exist with other areas. In the case of MLP 84 physics labelled data points are classified as Astronomy and Astrophysics while 54 of the latter are classified as the former, similar situation occurs with SVM. If the 3 categories are eliminated from the data set, the models achieve an 86% accuracy in both classification models (MLP and SVM), thus confirming that these areas are affecting the general classification results.

Pooling together similar areas (physics and astronomy and astrophysics) and applying a cascade model such that the first model predicted amongst the 8 remaining areas after pooling and the second model discerned within the pooled category is applicable, was unsuccessful in terms of a greater prediction accuracy overall in each of the pooled categories. However, a significant improvement in accuracy was observed when trained to separate the pooled categories with respect to other areas (an 80% accuracy as opposed to the 76% for when trained using all the data), while the accuracy obtained in other fields remained similar. This could again reinforces the idea that the classification of certain areas using a different taxonomy may be beneficial.

One key aspect that has been noted both here and in other articles is the relevance of the vectorization method used. Table 6 clearly demonstrates the fact that using the same vectorization strategy both classifiers yield similar precision on test data. However, the precision varies greatly when the vectorization method is exchanged. Text representation is an active area, and new transformer based embeddings may increase the classification precision on this data set.

The availability of annotated data for a large corpus is rare, therefore the possibility of using unsupervised methods was explored for classification purposes. Our findings demonstrate that among the methods evaluated K-means showed the greatest potential for classification, requiring 45 groups for a reasonable classification with no double prediction on the complete and balanced data set. The inclusion of the double prediction improved the accuracy as expected consistently maintaining the number of groups at larger values. K-Means and Gaussian mixture benefit from training with the complete data set, but it was more evident in the case of Gaussian Mixture that achieved good accuracy with fewer groupings.

Training a classification model with bias in the data composition can be troublesome as that bias is learned as well. However, there are instances in which the trends in the training sample mimic the underlying distribution of the data, and can provide insight to the model as well, thus this prompted to train all models for the two types of sets, balanced and complete set, obtaining two models for each strategy. In the case of supervised methods, the overall accuracy was greater in the complete data set, due to the bias induced by the data. In Table 3, clearly the over expressed categories (Life Science and agricultural sciences) in the data benefit from the unbalanced training samples, while the underrepresented categories (Medical Sciences) require a balance set in order to achieve better classification metrics.

References

1. Beltagy, I., Lo, K., Cohan, A.: Scibert: A pretrained language model for scientific text. arXiv preprint arxiv:1903.10676 (2019). https://doi.org/10.48550/ARXIV.1903.10676
2. Caliński, T., Harabasz, J.: A dendrite method for cluster analysis. Commun. Statist. Theory Methods **3**(1), 1–27 (1974)
3. Cascajares, M., Alcayde, A., Garrido-Cárdenas, J., Manzano-Agugliaro, F.: The contribution of Spanish science to patents: Medicine as case of study. Int. J. Environ. Res. Publ. Health **17**, 3638 (2020). https://doi.org/10.3390/ijerph17103638
4. Cohan, A., Feldman, S., Beltagy, I., Downey, D., Weld, D.S.: Specter: Document-level representation learning using citation-informed transformers. arXiv preprint arxiv:2004.07180 (2020). https://doi.org/10.48550/ARXIV.2004.07180
5. Davies, D.L., Bouldin, D.W.: A cluster separation measure. IEEE Trans. Pattern Anal. Mach. Intell. PAMI **1**(2), 224–227 (1979). https://doi.org/10.1109/TPAMI.1979.4766909
6. Devlin, J., Chang, M.W., Lee, K., Toutanova, K.: Bert: Pre-training of deep bidirectional transformers for language understanding (2018). arXiv preprint arxiv:1810.04805. https://doi.org/10.48550/ARXIV.1810.04805
7. Klabunde, R.: Daniel jurafsky/james h. martin, speech and language processing. Zeitschrift für Sprachwissenschaft **21**(1), 106–108 (2002)
8. Le, Q.V., Mikolov, T.: Distributed representations of sentences and documents. arXiv preprint arxiv:1405.4053 (2014). https://doi.org/10.48550/ARXIV.1405.4053
9. Van der Maaten, L., Hinton, G.: Visualizing data using t-sne. J. Mach. Learn. Res. **9**(11) (2008)
10. Mikolov, T., Chen, K., Corrado, G., Dean, J.: Efficient estimation of word representations in vector space. arXiv preprint arxiv:1301.3781 (2013). https://doi.org/10.48550/ARXIV.1301.3781
11. Mthembu, L., Marwala, T.: A note on the separability index. arXiv preprint arxiv:0812.1107 (2008). https://doi.org/10.48550/ARXIV.0812.1107
12. Noble, W.S.: What is a support vector machine? Nat. Biotechnol. **24**(12), 1565–1567 (2006)

13. Pedregosa, F., et al.: Scikit-learn: Machine learning in Python. J. Mach. Learn. Res.**12**, 2825–2830 (2011)
14. Popescu, M.C., Balas, V., Perescu-Popescu, L., Mastorakis, N.: Multilayer perceptron and neural networks. WSEAS Trans. Circuits Syst. **8** (2009)
15. Reimers, N., Gurevych, I.: Sentence-bert: Sentence embeddings using siamese bert-networks. In: Proceedings of the 2019 Conference on Empirical Methods in Natural Language Processing. Association for Computational Linguistics. arXiv preprint arxiv:1908.10084 (2019)
16. Reynolds, D.A.: Gaussian mixture models. Encyclopedia. Biometrics **741**, 659–663 (2009)
17. Schneegans, S., Lewis, J., Straza, T.: Informe de la unesco sobre la ciencia: La carrera contra el reloj para un desarrollo más inteligente - resumen ejecutivo (2021)
18. Shahapure, K.R., Nicholas, C.: Cluster quality analysis using silhouette score. In: 2020 IEEE 7th International Conference on Data Science and Advanced Analytics (DSAA), pp. 747–748 (2020). https://doi.org/10.1109/DSAA49011.2020.00096
19. Singh, S., Gill, N.S.: Analysis and study of k-means clustering algorithm. Int. J. Eng. Res. Technol. **2** (2013)
20. UNESCO: Proposed international standard nomenclature for fields of science and technology (1988)

Decoding Customer Behaviour: Relevance of Web and Purchasing Behaviour in Predictive Response Modeling

Sunčica Rogić$^{(\boxtimes)}$ ⬤ and Ljiljana Kašćelan ⬤

Faculty of Economics, University of Montenegro, Jovana Tomaševića 37, 81000 Podgorica, Montenegro
{suncica,ljiljak}@ucg.ac.me

Abstract. In this paper, an approach is presented to improve the online direct marketing process regarding predictive customer response modeling. Namely, customer response models are usually faced with a class imbalance problem, due to a low conversion rate, in relation to the entire number of targeted offers. To avoid the bias towards the negative class in machine learning process, this paper proposes a combination of random undersampling and Support Vector Machine method for data pre-processing and increasing the predictive performances of subsequently used classifiers – Decision Tree and Random Forest. In addition, different attribute groups are tested in terms of their influence to the model performance, which enables marketing decisions makers to better understand which attributes have the highest impact in determining the customer's response to a direct marketing campaign. The results showed that the proposed method successfully solved the class imbalance and significantly increased the accuracy of the response prediction, as well as that web behavior is the most significant when predicting the customer's response.

Keywords: Customer Response Model · Class Imbalance · Web Metrics · Customer Behaviour Metrics · Predictive analytics · Support Vector Machine

1 Introduction

Technology and the digital domain are expanding quickly, and customer lifestyles are changing in practically every aspect, which makes marketing in the 21st century unique. In particular, consumer behavior has evolved and been redefined, as have the ways in which individuals find information and spend their leisure time [1]. Therefore, it is evident that businesses cannot remain unaffected and that they must reevaluate their everyday operations and marketing strategies. As of October 2022, the average online time for users globally was six hours and 37 min, with an increasing tendency [2]. Therefore, there is an evident desire and need for businesses to move some of their activities (if not all of them) online and use online media for customer communication, product promotion, and brand building.

© IFIP International Federation for Information Processing 2023
Published by Springer Nature Switzerland AG 2023
I. Maglogiannis et al. (Eds.): AIAI 2023, IFIP AICT 675, pp. 369–380, 2023.
https://doi.org/10.1007/978-3-031-34111-3_31

According to previous research, using big data opportunities and technologies accelerates changes in marketing through the implementation of precise strategies, the efficient use of limited marketing resources, and the targeting of valuable customers. This has a significant impact on the market's development in the era of new retail [3]. Direct marketing became more significant as Internet technologies advanced and communication costs dropped quickly. The ability for businesses to establish a direct connection with thousands of customers in a way that was previously unthinkable with the use of middlemen has emerged as a result of the low cost of Internet access [4]. In the context of direct marketing, some of the primary objectives include identifying and selecting customers for targeting in future campaigns as well as assessing their needs and behavior patterns in order to tailor future marketing efforts based on this information.

When it comes to prediction of customer response, the number of positive instances is typically much smaller than the negative ones, therefore, class imbalance is one of the major issues. The number of customers that make a purchase in response to a campaign, i.e. the response rate or conversion rate, is, as a consequence very low when compared to the entire group of potential customers who were targeted and notified of the offer. With a response rate often less than 5%, we can say that a minor class problem exists in this context. In the literature that addresses this issue, it is noted that bias and misclassification of the minor class exist in the most of predictive classification algorithms [5, 6].

In relation to the aforementioned, earlier research has demonstrated the benefits of the Support Vector Machine (SVM) method for resolving the issue of class imbalance, by complementing the minor class with new, relevant instances from the bigger class [7–10]. Additionally, it is demonstrated that the SVM approach performs substantially better than undersampling and oversampling at class balancing, and that SVM may be used to improve the performance of other classifiers by refining the data they utilize.

Thus, SVM was used as a pre-processor to balance the data and improve overall classification accuracy. The SVM is biased in favor of the major class when there is a severe class imbalance, as there is in our data (response rate of 0.41%). In order to avoid bias, SVM in combination with random undersampling (balanced SVM) was employed as a pre-processor during the training of the SVM pre-processor. Following the SVM data balancing procedure, two classification algorithms will be applied on different subsets of attributes – Decision Tree (DT) and Random Forest (RF), with the aim to uncover groups of attributes that have the most significant impact in predictive customer response modeling.

The suggested models are developed with the aim to improve the effectiveness of the decision-making process in direct marketing, which should lead to a more profitable campaign, better communication with the most crucial customers, smoother development of a particular offer, and a higher level of customer retention.

The paper is structured as follows: the second section provides a literature review, focusing on the class imbalance problem in direct marketing, as well as customer response modeling. Data and methods are presented in the third section, followed by the Results and Discussion in the fourth part of the paper. Finally, the Conclusion is given in the last, fifth section.

2 Literature Review

When allocating marketing resources to consumers that are active and have a high potential value to the company information from the campaign response model is extremely vital. After the era of direct mail, the emergence of the Internet and social networks, along with the possibilities for online marketing campaigns, has created a space for investigation into the efficiency of this medium. The Internet has made it easy to gather a lot of data and has emerged as one of the best systems for storing it. Since it incorporates information technology capable of producing and storing a significant amount of complicated and complex data, the idea of direct marketing becomes particularly important in that virtual world [11].

Many types and forms of data are used as inputs when modeling the response to a social media campaign, but the goal of this process is always the same - correctly identifying respondents [12]. The lowering of the overall costs of marketing operations is influenced by the proper selection of the target group of respondents. This suggests that, in comparison to conventional, descriptive models, improved predictive models and methodologies can help marketers make decisions that are more cost-effective [13]. It's important to note that the problem of low response rate, or conversion rate, is evident in online direct marketing, as it was in traditional direct marketing which utilized direct mail. In the digital sphere, it is even more emphasized, having in mind that it's relatively less expensive for companies to target a larger group of customers than ever before. Hence, class imbalance occurs as the count of online sessions that resulted in completed purchases being far lower than the overall session count [14]. When the predictive model is trained using a small number of positive instances, the class imbalance problem results in biased results of the predictive model. Such biased models typically perform poorly in classification tasks since they frequently assign all test instances to the dominating class [15], which is, in this case, the segment of customers that did not respond to the campaign, or that did not complete the purchase.

According to Sun et al. [16], to tackle the problem of class imbalance in classification models, solutions were developed at the level of data, at the level of algorithms, as well as cost-sensitive solutions. At the data level, the goal is to balance the classes with resampling, which can be random or targeted under-sampling and over-sampling. At the algorithm level, the solutions tend to adapt the algorithm, in order to improve training for small classes. Cost-sensitive solutions, both at the data level and at the algorithm level, will attach higher misclassification costs to examples from the minor class. During the last few years, this problem has been addressed in several studies [17–20].

This issue was tackled in the literature using different approaches. Kurniawan et al. [21] proposed a method in their paper that combines feature selection from Particle Swarm Optimization (PSO) with data-level techniques like Random Under-Sampling (RUS) and Synthetic Minority Over-sampling Technique (SMOTE), implemented through the AdaBoost algorithm, and assessed using 10-fold cross-validation. In Noviantoro and Huang's study [22], they used clickstream data from online businesses to explore customer behavior and purchase prediction and employed DT, Random Forest, Neural Networks, Deep Learning, Naive Bayes, k-NN, Logistic Regression, and Rule Induction. The neural network model outperformed the Random Forest model, which had slightly lower accuracy. Rogić and Kašćelan [23] evaluated the degree to which the problem of the minor class (the most valuable consumers) may be solved by a hybrid model integrating SVM and DT. According to the findings, this method can predict the segment of the most valued consumers with an accuracy of 77%, which is 44% better than the DT model used alone. As a result, SVM worked successfully as a preprocessor to improve the minor class's prediction accuracy. Furthermore, SVM was put to the test by Farquad and Bose [7] as a preprocessor for class balancing of insurance customer data. They emphasized how applying classifiers to the refined set results in considerably higher sensitivity, or the number of real instances of the minor class that the model properly categorizes.

Besides solving the class imbalance issue, the aim of this paper is to determine which attribute groups have the highest effect on the model performance in terms of predicting the customer's response. The researchers have previously employed a variety of datasets and databases when choosing data for analysis and predicting campaign responses. Hauser et al. [24] examined the effectiveness of combining "soft" data (demographic and psychographic information) from secondary sources with "hard" data (information on previous purchases) from the company's database. According to the study's findings, "hard" data were selected as predictors to a substantially greater extent than the other kind. These results suggest that accurate campaign response models can be developed without the use of demographic and psychographic data using only historical customer-level transaction data [24]. This eliminates the extra expense of gathering and processing additional data from secondary sources. Kaatz et al. [25] combined clickstream and customer survey data to analyze the effect of using various devices, such as desktop computers, tablets, and smartphones, on conversion rate. According to their survey findings, purchase decisions made by computer users are mostly influenced by cognitive aspects of the shopping experience, but those made by smartphone users are primarily influenced by emotive and behavioral factors. In addition, Rho et al. [26] merged demographic data with web log data to segment clients and determine their value using clustering and the DT approach.

This group of attributes was also employed in earlier research by Lee et al. [27], which aimed to establish associative rules to create marketing strategies based on patterns in consumer behavior. Web attributes have been used in prior studies to model online search, assess consumer behavior, estimate and anticipate campaign reactions, as well as identify purchasing trends and customer segmentation. Based on metrics like visits to specific pages, time spent, and frequency of visits, Hofgesang and Kowalczyk [28] divided users into three groups: browsers, searchers and purchasers. Such categorization of potential customers is crucial from a marketing perspective because it allows for the development of targeted advertising campaigns that will maximize the value of each individual customer or group of customers.

Therefore, based on the review of the previous literature, the assessment of the influence of previous purchasing and web behavior on prediction using the response model, based on SVM class balancing, has not been considered so far.

3   Data and Methods

3.1   Data

For the purpose of testing the proposed customer response model empirically, and to assess the influence of different attributes, a dataset was acquired from a renowned Montenegrin sports distributor. For a period of four months, from October 2018 to January 2019, the dataset included visits to e-commerce websites from paid social media posts (sponsored posts from Facebook and Instagram). 9660 different website visitors who exhibited interest in the offered deal during the monitored period clicked on a link from a targeted Instagram or Facebook post, making them potential consumers. 33,662 sessions were recorded across six online direct marketing programs on social media, with a response rate of 0.41. The dataset included the following attribute groups: Recency, Frequency, Monetary (RFM) attributes - previous purchase history data, where Recency represents the length of the time period since the last purchase, Frequency indicates the number of purchases made in the observed period, while Monetary determines the total monetary value of the customer's transactions in that period (R1 - recency obtained by splitting the dataset into five equal parts from least to most recent transactions, R2 - recency obtained by assigning numbers from 2 to 5 based on the last campaign the customer ordered from, F1 - number of campaigns with orders, F2 - total number of orders in all campaigns, F3 - number of orders in the last campaign, M1 - the average transaction amount in all campaigns, M2 - average amount of transactions in the last campaign and M3 - total sum of realized transactions); Web metrics (the average number of sessions in all campaigns, the average session duration in all campaign, the average bounce rate for all selected campaign visits, number of sessions from the Central, Southern and Norther, number of sessions using desktop, mobile device and tablet, number of sessions using Android OS, iOS and Windows); and product description data (number of purchased products in apparel sector, footwear and equipment, number of purchased products for boys, girls, men, women and unisex products, number of purchased products for performance, lifestyle or outdoor, number of purchased products from A brands (high end) and License brands (low end), number of purchased products for adults, kids, teens and for all ages, number of purchased products on discount less than 30% and between 30% and 50%).

As the main aim of the paper was predicting the customer response to the direct marketing campaign on social media, only a completed transactions were taken as positive instances, which were marked as respondents. In line with that, initial customer action – following the link to find out more information regarding the offer, was not recorded as a response.

The final dataset was divided into training and test datasets. The training dataset included data from Campaign 1 to 5, with Campaign 5 being the indicator of their response. The data for the test set included 7929 visitors from Campaigns 1 through 5 and the response indicating whether a consumer responded to Campaign 6. However, new website visitors who first appeared in Campaigns 5 or 6 were not included in the database. Additionally, all targeted customers which had a website session shorter than 30 s were excluded from the database in the initial preparation for the analysis.

3.2 Methods

In this paper, a combination of Support Vector Machine and random undersampling was applied, with the aim to overcome the problem of class imbalance and perform data pre-processing. In the data set provided for this research, there is an extremely high level of class imbalance, with only 0.41% of respondents. With this in mind, balanced SVM was applied, i.e. a combination of 1:1 random undersampling and SVM method. After data pre-processing, two classifiers, DT and RF, were trained on the training data, and then applied for the prediction of the respondents on unknown, test data. In order to determine the impact of different attribute groups on the model performance, each group was, during several iterations, individually excluded from the model training and testing. Such results can indicate which customer features are the most relevant in predicting the response to the direct marketing campaign. The proposed procedure is presented in Fig. 1 [20].

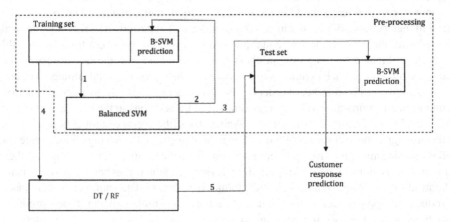

Fig. 1. Proposed predictive procedure

The SVM approach, proposed by Vapnik [29] in the 90s for the tasks of pattern recognition, is a supervised machine learning method that successfully seeks to solve overlapping and imbalanced classes, by establishing a hyperplane between examples from various classes, which can differentiate the class to the maximum distance, despite the quantity of available examples for training. By moving the margin to the examples of the major class that are closest and most similar examples to the minor class, and placing them into the smaller class, SVM completes the minor class with the most relevant examples. This led to the adoption of SVM as a data pre-processor to balance the data and provide higher accuracy for classifiers that are subsequently applied. In situations of significant class imbalance, such as the one present in this paper, the SVM is predisposed to favor the dominant class. Therefore, in this paper, balanced SVM was used as pre-processor, by applying it in combination with 1:1 random undersampling, as stated above.

Following this procedure, DT and RF classifiers were tested on balanced data. The DT method divides the data based on attribute values, selecting the attribute that produces the purest subsets in respect to the target class. For the purity of data subsets obtained by division, many measurements such as information gain, gain ratio, and Gini index are utilized [30, 31]. The division technique is recursively repeated on the produced data subsets until totally pure subsets are acquired or some user-defined requirement, such as maximum tree depth, is met. Concurrently with the divisions, a model in the form of a tree-shaped structure is generated, with the nodes representing the attributes by which the division is made and the branches representing the values of those attributes. The root-to-leaf path defines if-then classification rules in terms of predictive attributes. On the other hand, Random Forest is based on a combination of bootstrap training dataset, random selection of predictors and DT method [32]. For each randomly chosen subset of data, Random Forest creates a "forest" of DT models, and optimization entails determining the ideal number of DT models to use. The following phases make up the RF model development process [33]: selecting a bootstrap sample and initiating tree construction; selecting a random selection of predictors for division at each node (without pruning the tree); Repeating this process several times, until a forest of trees is created; Completing a prediction for each tree and selecting the class that received the most votes, in order to categorize the new example.

4   Results and Discussion

In this section, the results of the proposed procedure will be presented, focusing on the data preprocessing and balancing procedure, followed by the influence of different attribute groups on the model performance. Each classifier (SVM, DT and RF) was applied to test data after undergoing cross-validation on an initial, pre-processed training set. Table 1 shows the predictive performance of both models before and after SVM pre-processing on the test data.

Table 1. Predictive performance of classification algorithms without and with SVM pre-processing.

Model	Accuracy	Sensitivity	AUC	Fallout
DT	99.43%	12.50%	0.608	0.13%
SVM + DT	90.36%	80.54%	0.898	8.16%
RF	99.48%	0.00%	0.827	0.01%
SVM + RF	89.27%	75.99%	0.921	8.74%

It is apparent from the results that approach with SVM pre-processing outperforms standalone classifier approaches in class balancing, i.e. finding solutions for minor class problem. Table 1 demonstrates that after data pre-processing, sensitivity and AUC were enhanced across both models. For instance, SVM + RF obtained 75.99% while standalone RF obtained 0% sensitivity prior to data balancing. Also, standalone DT models' AUC metric was quite low, coming in at 0.608, which is too close to a model being unable to effectively distinguish between the positive and negative classes, while the improvement of the metric can be observed after applying SVM pre-processing.

This performance increase operationally means that the proposed approach will recognize about 70% more respondents compared to stand-alone classifiers. Bearing in mind that most of the classifiers applied in the existing solutions largely misclassify the minor class (especially when it is extremely small), and therefore the most likely respondent, it is obvious that the proposed approach can significantly increase the chances of generating income from campaigns.

Table 2 contains the prediction performance metrics for DT and RF models, tested on all attributes, as well as by excluding specific attribute groups.

Table 2. Prediction Models of DT and RF Classification Algorithms

Model	Performance metric	All attributes	Web attributes excluded	Product attributes excluded	RFM attributes excluded	Recency excluded	Frequency excluded	Monetary excluded
DT	Accuracy	90.36%	88.47%	90.36%	90.20%	90.36%	90.36%	90.36%
	AUC	0.898	0.567	0.898	0.852	0.898	0.898	0.898
	Fallout	8.16%	0.09%	8.16%	8.29%	8.16%	8.16%	8.16%
	TP	832	125	832	828	832	832	832
	Sensitivity	80.54%	12.10%	80.54%	80.15%	80.54%	80.54%	80.54%
	FP	563	6	563	572	563	563	563
RF	Accuracy	89.27%	88.54%	88.38%	88.88%	89.38%	89.10%	88.42%
	AUC	0.921	0.567	0.931	0.929	0.924	0.921	0.918
	Fallout	8.74%	0.23%	10.37%	9.74%	8.60%	8.98%	9.74%
	TP	785	140	827	823	784	788	787
	Sensitivity	75.99%	13.55%	80.06%	79.67%	75.90%	76.28%	76.19%
	FP	603	16	715	672	593	619	672

All classification algorithms were applied on the entire test set (all attributes), and also on the subset of attributes, by excluding each of the attribute groups separately (Web attributes, Product attributes and RFM attributes). In addition, to determine the potential influence of individual Recency, Frequency and Monetary attributes on the model performance, they were excluded both as a group and individually.

From Table 2, it can be observed that both DT and RF models achieved overall good predictive performance. The first, DT model, achieved Accuracy of 90.36%, Sensitivity of 80.54% and AUC of 0.898. On the other hand, RF model achieved slightly lower Accuracy and Sensitivity, of 89.27% and 75.99%, respectively, but a higher AUC of 0.921. Taking into account the AUC result, we can conclude that the DT model can distinguish between the positive and negative class in 89.8% chances, while the RF model improves this metric to 92.1%. The higher the AUC, the better differentiation capacity between classes in the observed model.

Since the aim of the paper is to determine and predict customer response in terms of purchase in a direct marketing campaign, this paper focuses on Sensitivity metric, rather than Accuracy. Sensitivity provides more relevant information regarding the potential respondents with greater probability of purchase intention. Testing the model on all attributes in DT model, the obtained Sensitivity result was of 80.54%, and it keeps the same value when Product attributes are excluded, as well as all individual RFM attributes, while it slightly reduces by excluding RFM attributes as a group. Hence, we can state that these two sets of attributes do not have a significant influence in predicting the potential respondents in a direct marketing campaign. However, excluding the Web attributes influences this result greatly, as this metric falls to 12.10%. This shows the most significant influence on the DT model performance, where, in this case, only 12.10% of expected respondents would be targeted.

Impact of Web attributes on the DT model performance can also be seen by looking at the TP metric, as well as AUC. When these attributes are excluded from the analysis, only 125 potential respondents may be targeted, compared to 832 when the model is tested on all attributes. Also, the AUC is reduced to 0.567, which is very close to 0.5, i.e. the situation where the model cannot differentiate between the positive and negative class at all.

Testing on the second model (RF) shows almost identical scenario. Sensitivity obtained on all attributes is 75.99%, and is improved by three percentage points when Product attributes are excluded (80.06%) and when RFM attributes are excluded as a group (79.67%), but only shows a slight difference when they are excluded individually. Similar to testing on DT model, excluding Web attributes leads to significant decreasing of Sensitivity in RF model to only 13.55%. Same level of AUC, 0.567, is obtained in RF model when Web attributes are excluded.

In this case of excluding the Web attributes, the overall Accuracy remained high in both DT and RF models – 88.47 and 88.54, respectively and the Fallout is reduced to as much as 0.09% and 0.23%, which demonstrates a very high accuracy of the classification of non-respondents, i.e. algorithm bias towards a majority class. Based on the reported results, we can conclude that, when Web attributes are excluded, both classifiers underperform, highlighting the relevance of web metrics in the development of the customer response model.

This strong influence of web variables is consistent with previous research, which has found that clickstream data and web metrics play an essential role in forecasting customer behavior [22, 34–36]. The results presented in this section point to the conclusion that Product attributes, as well as RFM attributes (as a group and individually) do not have a significant influence in the predictive model performance. With the increased use of online marketing, it appears that the prior relevance of purchase behavior for predicting responses is being replaced by web activity, which is demonstrated in previous research as well [36].

5   Conclusion

One of the most complex challenges of predictive segmentation is class imbalance. Although the problem of class imbalance is not new in research, it is becoming increasingly significant in direct marketing as a result of the increased use of very inexpensive and global channels for interaction with customers (such as social networks and online customer targeting). In reality, this means that the number of consumers who respond to the campaign by making a purchase, or the conversion rate, is very small compared to the whole set of prospective customers to whom the offer was made. In this regard, bias and misclassification of the minor class occur with the greatest number of predictive classification algorithms in that situation.

One of the goals that affects the effectiveness of a direct marketing campaign is determining the number and structure of consumers who will respond to the campaign, which is exactly the problem that campaign response models address. These models classify potential consumers into responders and non-respondents, i.e., those who are more likely to respond to a direct marketing campaign by purchasing, in relation to those who are less likely to respond. Modeling customer reaction to a campaign is a key area of direct marketing in this regard, since identifying consumers who are more likely to respond may save marketing expenditures and improve campaign traffic. In line with this, as there are several data streams available to companies, both internal external, and this research aimed to determine the most relevant data types for customer response prediction. Results of such research can point to the use of selected attribute groups for customer response modeling, which have the greatest impact on the model performance. In practical terms, companies could avoid merging several databases when trying to address this issue, and focus on most important attributes in response prediction, which have, in this research, as well as several previous papers, shown to be web metrics, or clickstream data.

The accuracy of the prediction of possible respondents and the adequate interpretation of the results allow decision makers to segment and target potential consumers with greater precision, as well as to identify attributes that can have a significant impact on the response rate to the campaign.

In this paper, both aims were successfully achieved – the data was balanced using undersampling with SVM method, thus solving the class imbalance issue, and also, it was determined that web metrics have the most impact on the model performance, making this attribute group the most significant in predicting the customer response.

References

1. Jackson, G., Ahuja, V.: Dawn of the digital age and the evolution of the marketing mix. J. Direct, Data Digit. Mark. Pract. **17**, 170–186 (2016) https://doi.org/10.1057/dddmp.2016.3
2. Kemp, S.: DIGITAL 2022: OCTOBER GLOBAL STATSHOT REPORT https://datareportal.com/reports/digital-2022-october-global-statshot
3. Zhu, G., Gao, X.: The digital sales transformation featured by precise retail marketing strategy. Expert J. Mark. **7**, 72–76 (2019)
4. Palmer, A., Koenig-Lewis, N.: An experiential, social network-based approach to direct marketing. Direct Mark. An Int. J. **3**, 162–176 (2009). https://doi.org/10.1108/17505930910985116
5. Kim, G., Chae, B.K., Olson, D.L.: A support vector machine (SVM) approach to imbalanced datasets of customer responses: comparison with other customer response models. Serv. Bus. **7**, 167–182 (2013). https://doi.org/10.1007/s11628-012-0147-9
6. Miguéis, V.L., Camanho, A.S., Borges, J.: Predicting direct marketing response in banking: comparison of class imbalance methods. Serv. Bus. **11**(4), 831–849 (2017). https://doi.org/10.1007/s11628-016-0332-3

7. Farquad, M.A.H., Bose, I.: Preprocessing unbalanced data using support vector machine. Decis. Support Syst. **53**, 226–233 (2012). https://doi.org/10.1016/j.dss.2012.01.016
8. Rogic, S., Kascelan, L.: Class balancing in customer segments classification using support vector machine rule extraction and ensemble learning. Comput. Sci. Inf. Syst. **18**, 893–925 (2020). https://doi.org/10.2298/csis200530052r
9. Martens, D., Huysmans, J., Setiono, R., Vanthienen, J., Baesens, B.: Rule extraction from support vector machines: an overview of issues and application in credit scoring. Stud. Comput. Intell. **80**, 33–63 (2008). https://doi.org/10.1007/978-3-540-75390-2_2
10. Djurisic, V., Kascelan, L., Rogic, S., Melovic, B.: Bank CRM optimization using predictive classification based on the support vector machine method. Appl. Artif. Intell. **00**, 1–15 (2020). https://doi.org/10.1080/08839514.2020.1790248
11. Aliabadi, A.N., Berenji, H.: Hybrid model of customer response modeling through combination of neural networks and data pre-processing. In: IEEE International Conerence Fuzzy Systems (2013)
12. Sun, M., Chen, Z.Y., Fan, Z.P.: A multi-task multi-kernel transfer learning method for customer response modeling in social media. Procedia Comput. Sci. **31**, 221–230 (2014). https://doi.org/10.1016/j.procs.2014.05.263
13. Olson, D.L., Chae, B.: Direct marketing decision support through predictive customer response modeling. Decis. Support Syst. **54**, 443–451 (2012). https://doi.org/10.1016/j.dss.2012.06.005
14. Behera, R.K., Gunasekaran, A., Gupta, S., Kamboj, S., Bala, P.K.: Personalized digital marketing recommender engine. J. Retail. Consum. Serv. **53**, 1–24 (2020). https://doi.org/10.1016/j.jretconser.2019.03.026
15. Wang, B., Pineau, J.: Online bagging and boosting for imbalanced data streams. IEEE Trans. Knowl. Data Eng. **28**, 3353–3366 (2016). https://doi.org/10.1109/TKDE.2016.2609424
16. Sun, Y., Wong, A.K.C., Kamel, M.S.: Classification of imbalanced data: a review. Int. J. Pattern Recognit. Artif. Intell. **23**, 687–719 (2009). https://doi.org/10.1142/S0218001409007326
17. Liu, J., Zio, E.: Integration of feature vector selection and support vector machine for classification of imbalanced data. Appl. Soft Comput. J. **75**, 702–711 (2019)
18. Wong, M.L., Seng, K., Wong, P.K.: Cost-sensitive ensemble of stacked denoising autoencoders for class imbalance problems in business domain. Expert Syst. Appl. **141**, 112918 (2020)
19. Lopez-Garcia, P., Masegosa, A.D., Osaba, E., Onieva, E., Perallos, A.: Ensemble classification for imbalanced data based on feature space partitioning and hybrid metaheuristics. Appl. Intell. **49**(8), 2807–2822 (2019). https://doi.org/10.1007/s10489-019-01423-6
20. Rogić, S., Kašćelan, L., Pejić Bach, M.: Customer response model in direct marketing: solving the problem of unbalanced dataset with a balanced support vector machine. J. Theor. Appl. Electron. Commer. Res. **17**, 1003–1018 (2022)
21. Kurniawan, I., Abdussomad, Akbar, M.F. Saepudin, D.F., Azis, M.S., Tabrani, M.: Improving the effectiveness of classification using the data level approach and feature selection techniques in online shoppers purchasing intention prediction. J. Phys. Conf. Ser. 1641(1), 012083 (2020) https://doi.org/10.1088/1742-6596/1641/1/012083
22. Noviantoro, T., Huang, J.-P.: Applying Data Mining Techniques to Investigate Online Shopper Purchase Intention Based on Clickstream Data. Rev. Business, Account. Financ. **01**, 130–159 (2021)
23. Rogic, S., Kascelan, L.: Customer Value Prediction in Direct Marketing Using Hybrid Support Vector Machine Rule Extraction Method. In: Welzer, T., et al. (eds.) ADBIS 2019. CCIS, vol. 1064, pp. 283–294. Springer, Cham (2019). https://doi.org/10.1007/978-3-030-30278-8_30
24. Hauser, W.J., Orr, L., Daugherty, T.: Customer response models: what data predicts best, hard or soft? Mark. Manag. J. **21**, 1–15 (2011)

25. Kaatz, C., Brock, C., Figura, L.: journal of retailing and consumer services are you still online or are you already mobile ? – Predicting the path to successful conversions across different devices. J. Retail. Consum. Serv. **50**, 10–21 (2019). https://doi.org/10.1016/j.jretconser.2019.04.005

26. Rho, J.J., Moon, B.-J., Kim, Y.-J., Yang, D.-H.: Internet customer segmentation using web log data. J. Bus. Econ. Res. **2**, 59–74 (2011). https://doi.org/10.19030/jber.v2i11.2940

27. Lee, K.C., Kim, J.S., Chung, N.H., Kwon, S.J.: Fuzzy cognitive map approach to web-mining inference amplification. Expert Syst. Appl. **22**, 197–211 (2002). https://doi.org/10.1016/S0957-4174(01)00054-9

28. Hofgesang, P.I., Kowalczyk, W.: Analysing clickstream data: From anomaly detection to visitor profiling. Belgian/Netherlands Artif. Intell. Conf. 2006

29. Vapnik, V.N.: The nature of statistical learning theory. Springer, New York (2010)

30. Breiman, L.; Friedman, J.; Stone, C.J.; Olshen, R.A. Classification and regression trees; CRC press (1984)

31. Quinlan, J.R.: C4.5 - programs for machine learning; Kaufmann: San Mateo, CA (1992)

32. Breiman, L.: Random Forests. Mach. Learn. **45**, 5–32 (2001)

33. Varian, H.R.: Big data: New tricks for econometrics. J. Econ. Perspect. **28**, 3–28 (2014). https://doi.org/10.1257/jep.28.2.3

34. Esmeli, R., Mohasseb, A., Bader-El-Den, M.: Analysing the Effect of Platform and Operating System Features on Predicting Consumers' Purchase Intent using Machine Learning Algorithms. In: 12th International Joint Conference Knowledge Discovery SciTePress, pp. 333–340 (2020)

35. Liao, S.H., Chen, Y.J., Hsieh, H.H.: Mining customer knowledge for direct selling and marketing. Expert Syst. Appl. **38**, 6059–6069 (2011). https://doi.org/10.1016/j.eswa.2010.11.007

36. Rogić, S., Customer, K.L., Ensemble, R.M.U., of Balanced Classifiers: Significance of Web Metrics. In Intelligent Computing. SAI,: Lecture Notes in Networks and Systems, vol 506; Arai, K., Ed.; Springer. Cham **2022**, 433–448 (2022)

Exploring Pairwise Spatial Relationships for Actions Recognition and Scene Graph Generation

Anfel Amirat[1(✉)], Nadia Baha[1], and Lamine Benrais[2]

[1] Computer Science Faculty, University of Science and Technology Houari
Boumediene, Algiers, Algeria
{aamirat,anbahatouzene}@usthb.dz
[2] Faculty of Arts, KU Leuven, 3000 Leuven, Belgium
lamine.benrais@kuleuven.be

Abstract. Visual scene understanding is a fundamental problem and
a complex task in computer vision, which not only requires identifying
objects in isolation, but also the ability to understand and recognize the
relationships between them. These relationships can be abstracted into
a semantic representation of $< subject, predicate, object >$, resulting in
a scene graph that captures much of the visual information and semantics in the scene. In recent years, scene graph generation with message-
passing mechanism [1] has been an active area of research, as it has the
potential to capture global dependencies between objects and their relationships. Inspired by these developments, this paper introduces a novel
scene graph generation approach based on spatial relationships. Our approach performs a classification of the spatial relationship between each
pair of objects to generate the initial scene graph. Then, based on the
semantic features, the model detects action relationships in the scene
and updates the scene graph by applying the message-passing mechanism. We conclude this paper by comparing the proposed method with
the state-of-the-art approaches [1–7] and demonstrate the effectiveness
of our method over the Visual Genome [1] dataset.

Keywords: Scene understanding · scene graph · visual relationships
detection · spatial relationships · message-passing

1 Introduction

A scene graph is a structured representation of image content that encodes spatial and semantic information of each object and the relationship between each
pair of them. Recently, inferring such a graph has gained more attention since
it provides a deep understanding of the scene and improves various vision tasks
such as Image Retrieval [8,9], Image Generation [10,11], Image/Video Captioning [12,13], and Visual Question Answering [14,15].

The major challenge of generating scene graphs is reasoning about relationships. Earlier works [16,17] aimed to produce a local prediction of object

© IFIP International Federation for Information Processing 2023
Published by Springer Nature Switzerland AG 2023
I. Maglogiannis et al. (Eds.): AIAI 2023, IFIP AICT 675, pp. 381–392, 2023.
https://doi.org/10.1007/978-3-031-34111-3_32

relationships in order to simplify the process of generating visually-grounded scene graphs. The approach was to independently predict relationships between pairs of objects without considering the scene's context. In contrast, co-reasoning with contextual information could often resolve the ambiguity due to local predictions in isolation [18].

Message passing between individual objects or triplet is valuable for visual relationship detection [18]. Since objects with visual relationships are semantically related to each other, and relationships that share objects partially also have semantic relations, message passing between related elements is beneficial as it can improve the quality of visual relationship detection [2]. However, this mechanism is expensive and requires much computation time due to the numerous features to handle [19]. Moreover, visual appearance of the same relation varies significantly from one scene to another [20], making the features extraction phase more challenging. Thus, many methods focus on semantic features [21], trying to compensate for the lack of visual features.

To address these challenges and overcome the obstacle of variability in visual appearance, this work proposes a novel message-passing approach based on pairwise semantic spatial relationships. The concept is to replicate the human capacity to predict the relations between objects in a scene using their pairwise semantic spatial relationships.

In this paper, we first review past works related to message-passing scene graph generation and spatial relationships classification. Then, we introduce the proposed method in Sect. 3. In Sect. 4, the experimental results are shown and discussed. Finally, Sect. 5 concludes the paper by summarizing the obtained results.

2   Related Work

To contextualize our approach and evaluate its performance against the existing methods, we review the related work on message-passing scene graph generation and spatial relationships applications.

2.1   Message Passing

There are three levels to understanding and perceiving the context [18]: **first**, the interdependence between the different phrase components in a triplet is fundamental, the prediction of one component, such as the subject, predicate, or object, depends on the others. **Second**, triplets are not isolated, objects with relations are semantically dependent, and the relations that partly share object(s) are also semantically linked. **Third**, Visual relationships are specific to the scene, and global view features help predict relationships. Hence, message passing between objects and triplets is significant in detecting visual relationships.

The literature divides message-passing technique into two types:

Local Message Passing Within Triplet. Li et al. [22] proposed a phrase-guided visual relationship detection framework that first extracts three feature branches for each triplet proposal (subject, predicate, and object). Then, it uses a phrase-guided message-passing structure to exchange information between the three branches. Dai et al. [23] proposed an efficient framework known as the Deep Relational Network (DR-Net). By using multiple units of inference that capture the statistical relationships between triplet components, the DR-Net produces the posterior probabilities of the subject, object, and relationship. Zoom-Net [2] is another interesting model. It uses a Spatiality-Context-Appearance Module consisting of 2 spatiality-aware feature alignment cells to pass messages between the different triplet components. This type of message passing ignores the global context, whereas joint reasoning using contextual information can often resolve ambiguities caused by isolated local predictions [18].

Global Message Passing Across All Elements. Li et al. [3] developed a Multi-level Scene Description Network (MSDN) in which the passage of the message is guided by a dynamic graph constructed from objects and caption region proposals. F-Net, proposed by Li et al. [24], clusters the fully-connected graph into several subgraphs. Next, it uses a Spatial-weight Message Passing structure for passing messages between subgraph and object features. MSDN and F-Net considered a subgraph as a whole when sending and receiving messages. Liao et al. [25] proposed semantics-guided graph relation neural network (SGRNN). In their approach, the target and the source must be an object or a predicate within a subgraph. When considering all other objects as carriers of global contextual information for each object, they will pass messages to each other throughout a fully-connected graph. However, propagating many types of features and inferencing on a densely connected graph is very expensive and time-consuming to train [19].

2.2 Spatial Pairwise Relationships

Apprehending the spatial relationships between objects and how they are positioned and related to one another is imperative for a deep understanding of the scene. The application of spatial relation detection is useful in visually situated dialog and Human-robot interaction. For example, when instructing a robot in a household environment to accomplish a specific task [26] or when self-driving cars are designed to provide a textual explanation for their actions [27]. Likewise, the explicit use of spatial prepositions is also helpful in automatic image captioning [28].

For the proposed approach, we decide to stimulate the human capacity to infer much information by knowing the spatial relations between the different objects in the scene to detect and infer activities and action relations between image entities.

In this work, we propose a novel approach for scene graph generation based on the global message-passing mechanism. By incorporating semantic spatial relationships, our approach aims to overcome the challenge of variability in visual appearance and make more robust predictions about the relationships between objects in a scene.

3   Proposed Method

The proposed approach for scene graph generation is divided into pairwise spatial relationships classifications and scene graph update, as Fig. 1 shows. Our model tackles the visually-grounded scene graph generation from an image by generating a graph with a spatial relationship between each object pair. Then, recognize the action relationship and update the scene graph by applying the message-passing mechanism using only semantic features (objects and spatial relations labels). To achieve this, we use two neural network architectures that focus on each task independently and stack both architectures together once they have been trained. We use ground truth objects for object detection and recognition to evaluate the approach appropriately.

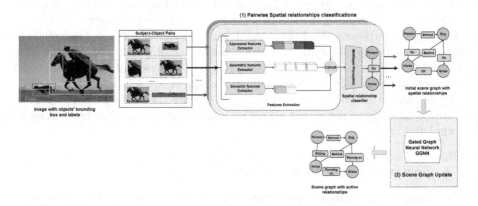

Fig. 1. An overview pipeline of our image scene graph generation model.

Before delving into the proposed model, we describe the scene graph structure. Formally, a scene graph is a structured representation of a scene's content. It comprises the objects' labels with bounding box coordinates and the relationship between each object pair.

A scene graph is defined as a 3-tuple set $G = \{B, O, R\}$:

$B = \{b_1, b_2, ..., b_n\}$ is the bounding box set, $b_i \in R^4$ corresponds to the bounding box of the ith region.

$O = \{o_1, o_2, ..., o_n\}$ object's label set, o_i corresponds to the label class of the region b_i.

$R = \{r_{1 \to 2}, r_{1 \to 3}, ..., r_{n \to n-1}\}$ relationship triplet set, where $r_{i \to j}$ is a triplet of the object (o_j, b_j), the subject (o_i, b_i), and the relationship class $a_{i \to j}$.

3.1   Pairwise Spatial Relationships Classifications

Features Extraction. This module aims to get the objects' appearance, semantic cues, and relative spatial locations between pairwise objects. This approach is inspired by [29] to extract three types of features to classify the semantic spatial relationship between each object's pair in the scene.

Geometric Features: we exploit the spatial contextual information from the subject, object, union, and intersection boxes. For each box (x_1, y_1, x_2, y_2), a 9-dimensional vector is calculated as (1) shows:

$$V = (\frac{c_x}{W}, \frac{c_y}{H}, \frac{w}{W}, \frac{h}{H}, \frac{x_1}{W}, \frac{h_1}{H}, \frac{x_2}{W}, \frac{h_2}{H}, \frac{w*h}{W*H}) \tag{1}$$

where $(c_x, c_y) = (\frac{x_1+x_2}{2}, \frac{y_1+y_2}{2})$ is the box's centroid, $(w, h) = (x_2 - x_1, y_2 - y_1)$ denotes the width and the height of the box, and (W, H) the width and the height of the image. For an empty intersection box, a zero vector represents the intersection box's geometric features. Then, all four vectors are concatenated to compose the geometric features.

Appearance Features: for the subject bounding box region, object bounding box region, union box, and intersection box, we use the FC7 layer from VGG16 [30] pre-trained on ImageNet [31] to extract the appearance feature vector (4096-d). For an empty intersection box, a zero vector represents the intersection box's appreance features. Then we concatenate all four vectors to compose the appearance features of the spatial relationship.

Semantic Features: glove [32] is used as a word embedding engine to encode objects' label names for the subject and the object. For phrase names, the mean vector is calculated. By concatenating the two encoded name features, the semantic relation features are composed.

Finally, the relation features are obtained by concatenating geometric, appearance, and semantic features.

Spatial Relationship Classification. After concatenating the extracted features described in 3.1 for each object's pair, we feed them to a multilayer perceptron neural network architecture (MLP) to classify the spatial relationships. Then, the initial scene graph with only pairwise spatial relationships is generated.

3.2   Scene Graph Update

We aim to update the scene graph relationships generated in 3.1 by applying the message-passing mechanism to have more meaningful semantic information with activities and action relationships.

Action Relationship Recognition. This step aimes to update edge representation while keeping node representations constant by using a variant of GGNN [33] to propagate information among edges. For each edge $a_{s \to o}$, three steps, as Fig. 2 shows, are needed: pass preparation, information aggregation, and edge update.

Pass Preparation: for each node from the subject node (o_s, b_s), and the object (o_o, b_o), its set of neighbors (o_i, b_j) is selected .

Information Aggregation: for each node from subject node (o_s, b_s) and object node (o_o, b_o), information is summarized by computing incoming information from its neighbors as shown in (2) :

$$m_k = o_k + \sum a_{i \to k} \cdot o_i - \sum a_{k \to j} \cdot o_j \tag{2}$$

Edge Update: after information aggregation, we concatenate m_s and m_o. Then it is passed with the current state $a_{S \to O}$ to Gated Recurrent Unit (GRU) to update the edge label. Finally, a scene graph with, in addition, pairwise action relationships is obtained.

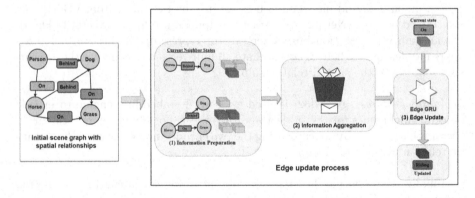

Fig. 2. Relation update process. After computing the information *(Informations Aggregation)* from the selected neighbors *(Information Preparation)*, the state of the edge **(on)** is updated to **(riding)** by passing both the information computed and the current state **(on)** to the GRU *(Edge Update)*.

4   Test and Results

This section presents a details evaluation of the proposed model. First, an evaluation of the spatial relationship classifier is processed. Then, we pass to the model of scene graph generation. Tests are conducted on a personal computer with an i7 processor, 16 GB memory, and a 2 GB Nvidia GPU.

4.1 Pairwise Spatial Relationships Classifications

Dataset. We conduct the experiments and evaluate the Spatial relationships classifier on the SpatialSense dataset [34], a collected benchmark for spatial relation recognition that contains 17498 spatial relations on 11596 images. All images are collected from Flickr and NYU [37]. The annotated spatial relation in the dataset covers 3679 unique object classes and 9 unique predicates (i.e., above, behind, in, in front of, next to, on, to the left of, to the right of, under). The SpatialSense dataset provides positive and negative examples of spatial relationships. To train the spatial relationship classifier, only positive triplets are considered. Following the official split in [34], we take 65% of relations for training, 15% for validation, and 20% for testing.

Evaluation Metric. The proposed classifier's ability to classify pairwise spatial relationships can be evaluated using classification accuracy [35] as a reliable and fair measure.

Compared with State-of-the-art Methods. We compare our classifier with various recent methods.

Table 1. Classification accuracy comparison on the test split of the SpatialSense dataset (All Values Expressed as Percentages). IFO = in front of, TTFO = to the left of, TTRO = to the right of. **Bold** font represents the highest accuracy; underline means the second highest.

Model	overall	above	behind	in	IFO	next to	on	TTFO	TTRO	under
Vip-CNN [22]	67.2	55.6	68.1	66.0	62.7	62.3	72.5	69.7	73.3	66.6
Peyre et al. [36]	67.5	59.0	67.1	69.8	57.8	65.7	75.6	56.7	69.2	66.2
PPR-FCN [38]	66.3	61.5	65.2	70.4	64.2	53.4	72.0	69.1	71.9	59.3
DRNet [23]	71.3	**62.8**	**72.2**	69.8	66.9	59.9	79.4	63.5	66.4	75.9
VTranE [30]	69.4	61.5	69.7	67.8	64.9	57.7	76.2	64.6	68.5	76.9
Language-only [34]	60.1	60.4	62.0	54.4	55.1	56.8	63.2	51.7	54.1	70.3
2D-only [34]	68.8	58.0	66.9	70.7	63.1	62.0	76.0	66.3	74.7	67.9
Language+2D [34]	71.1	61.1	67.5	69.2	66.2	64.8	77.9	**69.7**	74.7	77.2
DSRR [40]	**72.7**	61.5	71.3	**71.3**	**67.8**	65.1	79.8	69.4	**75.3**	**78.6**
The proposed approach	71.6	62.1	67.0	70.2	66.6	64.5	**79.9**	65.9	73.2	72.6

Table 1 shows the performance of different approaches on the SpatialSense dataset. Vip-CNN [22], Peyre et al. [36], PPR-FCN [38], DRNet [23], and VtransE [39], initially designed for visual relationship detection, are based only on visual appearance. Language-only, 2D-only, and Language+2D [34], designed for spatial relation recognition, are based on 2D/Language features. Our classifier takes into consideration the three main types of features: appearance features, semantic features, and geometric features. Overall, the results of the accuracy score indicate that our proposed classifier outperforms almost all existing

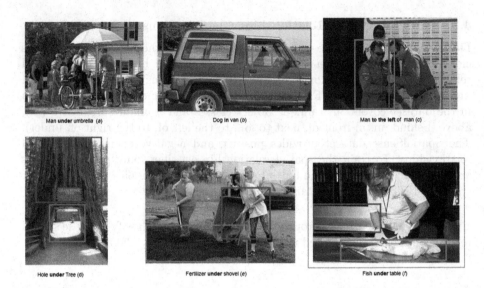

Fig. 3. Classification examples of spatial relationships by the proposed classifier on the SpatialSense dataset: *a, b, c, d,* and *e* are correct classifications, and in contract *f* is a misclassification. We believe that with depth information, our classifier could predict the proper label *in front of* instead of *under* for the misclassification *f*.

approaches in terms of overall accuracy, except DSRR (by only 1.1%) [40], which exploits depth information with an additional depth estimation model. With the additional depth, we expect our classifier to gain another performance boost and correctly classify complex cases that were previously misclassified, as Fig. 3 shows.

4.2   Scene Graph Generation

After training and testing our classifier for spatial relationships between pairs of objects, this sub-section evaluates the whole scene graph generation process.

Dataset. To evaluate the proposed approach, we use VG150 [1]. It is a widely adopted subset of Visual Genome for evaluating scene graph generation tasks. It contains 108073 images and covers 150 object categories and 50 predicate categories. We follow the same split in [1] for evaluating our approach.

Evaluation Metric. We aim to generate the scene graph for images. The key points are relationship classification and graph generation, while we no longer evaluate the accuracy of object detection or recognition. We evaluate the model performance from the aspect of predicate classification (PredCls) as we use both ground truth boxes and object labels directly. We use R@50 and R@100 to evaluate the performance. R@K computes the fraction of times a true relationship is predicted in an image's top k confident relation predictions.

Compared with State-of-the-art Methods. We report predicate classification on Visual Genome [1] in Table 2. This experiment is meant to serve as a benchmark against existing message-passing scene graph approaches.

Table 2. Evaluation results of the predicate classification task on the visual Genome dataset [1].

Model	R@50	R@100
MP [1]	41.8	55.5
Zoom-Net [2]	67.25	77.51
MSDN [3]	67.03	71.01
AGGNN [4]	65.1	67.2
ReRN* [5]	62.1	63.7
Dornadula et al. [6]	56.65	57.21
SGRN [7]	64.2	66.4
Proposed Approach	73.09	78.1

The experiments prove the effectiveness of our proposed method. We outperform existing models that use Visual Genome supervision for PredCls by 6,06 recall@50 and 0.51 recall@100. Message Passing [1], and Zoom-Net [2] are local message-passing-based methods. In contrast, the rest are all global message-passing-based methods.

Visual features for the same relation vary greatly from scene to scene, making relation predicting more challenging, especially for rare and unseen configurations and relations. For example, the visual features that represent the "riding" relation between a person and a horse can be very different from one image to another, depending on the pose, the background, the lighting condition, etc. In contrast, considering the semantic pairwise spatial relationships between the objects in the scene, we can infer from "the man on the horse and horse on the grass" that the action relation between man and horse is "riding". That is why focusing on semantic features like semantic pairwise spatial relationships can improve predicate classification tasks.

5   Conclusion

This paper investigates a novel message-passing scene graph generation approach based on semantic spatial relationships. First, we classify the spatial relationship between each pair of objects in the scene by extracting geometric, appearance, and semantic features and then passing them to an MLP architecture. After, we apply the message-passing mechanism as a second step to detect action relationships and update the scene graph.

Experimental results demonstrate its efficiency and competitiveness compared to the state-of-the-art approaches with 73.09 for R@50 and 78.1 for R@100. However, there are several prospective paths for improving this approach further. Firstly, incorporating additional depth information into the spatial relationship classifier can improve the accuracy and robustness of the model. Moreover, training the spatial relationships classifier on datasets with other spatial relationship classes, such as between, near, and far can be useful in scenes with more diverse spatial configurations. Furthermore, extending the proposed method to work with multi-spatial relations instead of single-spatial relations can boost our model, as it can capture more nuanced relationships between objects.

By incorporating these improvements, the proposed method can be enhanced and upgraded to achieve even better performance.

These prospective paths can be explored in future research and can contribute to advancing the field of scene understanding.

References

1. Xu, D., Zhu, Y., Choy, C. B., Fei-Fei, L.: Scene graph generation by iterative message passing. In: Proceedings of the IEEE Conference on Computer Vision and Pattern Recognition, pp. 5410–5419 (2017)
2. Yin, G., et al.: Zoom-net: Mining deep feature interactions for visual relationship recognition. In: Proceedings of the European Conference on Computer Vision (ECCV), pp. 322–338 (2018)
3. Li, Y., Ouyang, W., Zhou, B., Wang, K., Wang, X.: Scene graph generation from objects, phrases and region captions. In: Proceedings of the IEEE International Conference on Computer Vision, pp. 1261–1270 (2017)
4. Li, S., Tang, M., Zhang, J., Jiang, L.: Attentive gated graph neural network for image scene graph generation. Symmetry 12(4), 511 (2020)
5. Tian, P., Mo, H., Jiang, L.: Exploring correlation of relationship reasoning for scene graph generation. Int. J. Mach. Learn. Cybern. 13(9), 2479–2493 (2022)
6. Dornadula, A., Narcomey, A., Krishna, R., Bernstein, M., Li, F.F.: Visual relationships as functions: Enabling few-shot scene graph prediction. In: Proceedings of the IEEE/CVF International Conference on Computer Vision Workshops, pp. 0–0 (2019)
7. Liao, W., Lan, C., Zeng, W., Yang, M.Y., Rosenhahn, B.: Exploring the semantics for visual relationship detection. arXiv preprint arXiv:1904.02104 (2019)
8. Johnson, J., et al.: Image retrieval using scene graphs. In: Proceedings of the IEEE Conference on Computer Vision and Pattern Recognition, pp. 3668–3678 (2015)
9. Ramnath, S., Saha, A., Chakrabarti, S., Khapra, M.M.: Scene Graph based Image Retrieval-A case study on the CLEVR Dataset. arXiv preprint arXiv:1911.00850 (2019)
10. Fang, F., Yi, M., Feng, H., Hu, S., Xiao, C.: Narrative collage of image collections by scene graph recombination. IEEE Trans. Visual Comput. Graph. 24(9), 2559–2572 (2017)
11. Herzig, R., Bar, A., Xu, H., Chechik, G., Darrell, T., Globerson, A.: Learning canonical representations for scene graph to image generation. In: Vedaldi, A., Bischof, H., Brox, T., Frahm, J.-M. (eds.) ECCV 2020. LNCS, vol. 12371, pp. 210–227. Springer, Cham (2020). https://doi.org/10.1007/978-3-030-58574-7_13

12. Gu, J., Joty, S., Cai, J., Zhao, H., Yang, X., Wang, G.: Unpaired image captioning via scene graph alignments. In: Proceedings of the IEEE/CVF International Conference on Computer Vision, pp. 10323–10332 (2019)
13. Xu, N., Liu, A.A., Liu, J., Nie, W., Su, Y.: Scene graph captioner: image captioning based on structural visual representation. J. Vis. Commun. Image Represent. **58**, 477–485 (2019)
14. Yang, Z., Qin, Z., Yu, J., Hu, Y.: Scene graph reasoning with prior visual relationship for visual question answering. arXiv preprint arXiv:1812.09681 (2018)
15. Qian, T., Chen, J., Chen, S., Wu, B., Jiang, Y.G.: Scene graph refinement network for visual question answering. In: IEEE Transactions on Multimedia (2022)
16. Lu, C., Krishna, R., Bernstein, M., Fei-Fei, L.: Visual relationship detection with language priors. In: Leibe, B., Matas, J., Sebe, N., Welling, M. (eds.) ECCV 2016. LNCS, vol. 9905, pp. 852–869. Springer, Cham (2016). https://doi.org/10.1007/978-3-319-46448-0_51
17. Yu, R., Li, A., Morariu, V.I., Davis, L.S.: Visual relationship detection with internal and external linguistic knowledge distillation. In: Proceedings of the IEEE International Conference on Computer Vision, pp. 1974–1982 (2017)
18. Zhu, G., et al.: Scene graph generation: A comprehensive survey. arXiv preprint arXiv:2201.00443 (2022)
19. Zellers, R., Yatskar, M., Thomson, S., Choi, Y.: Neural motifs: Scene graph parsing with global context. In: Proceedings of the IEEE Conference on Computer Vision and Pattern Recognition, pp. 5831–5840 (2018)
20. Cong, W., Wang, W., Lee, W.C.: Scene graph generation via conditional random fields. arXiv preprint arXiv:1811.08075 (2018)
21. Lu, C., Krishna, R., Bernstein, M., Fei-Fei, L.: Visual relationship detection with language priors. In: Leibe, B., Matas, J., Sebe, N., Welling, M. (eds.) ECCV 2016. LNCS, vol. 9905, pp. 852–869. Springer, Cham (2016). https://doi.org/10.1007/978-3-319-46448-0_51
22. Li, Y., Ouyang, W., Wang, X., Tang, X.O.: Vip-cnn: Visual phrase guided convolutional neural network. In: Proceedings of the IEEE Conference on Computer Vision and Pattern Recognition, pp. 1347–1356 (2017)
23. Dai, B., Zhang, Y., Lin, D.: Detecting visual relationships with deep relational networks. In: Proceedings of the IEEE Conference on Computer Vision and Pattern Recognition, pp. 3076–3086 (2017)
24. Li, Y., Ouyang, W., Zhou, B., Shi, J., Zhang, C., Wang, X.: Factorizable net: an efficient subgraph-based framework for scene graph generation. In: Proceedings of the European Conference on Computer Vision (ECCV), pp. 335–351 (2018)
25. Liao, W., Lan, C., Zeng, W., Yang, M.Y., Rosenhahn, B.: Exploring the semantics for visual relationship detection. arXiv preprint arXiv:1904.02104 (2019)
26. Fasola, J., Mataric, M.: Using spatial language to guide and instruct robots in household environments. In: 2012 AAAI Fall Symposium Series (2012)
27. Kim, J., Rohrbach, A., Darrell, T., Canny, J., Akata, Z.: Textual explanations for self-driving vehicles. In: Proceedings of the European Conference on Computer Vision (ECCV), pp. 563–578 (2018)
28. Ghanimifard, M., Dobnik, S.: What goes into a word: generating image descriptions with top-down spatial knowledge. In: Proceedings of the 12th International Conference on Natural Language Generation, pp. 540–551 (2019)
29. Zhang, Y., Pan, Y., Yao, T., Huang, R., Mei, T., Chen, C.W.: Boosting scene graph generation with visual relation saliency. ACM Trans. Multimed. Comput. Commun. Appl. **19**(1), 1–17 (2023)

30. Simonyan, K., Zisserman, A.: Very deep convolutional networks for large-scale image recognition. arXiv preprint arXiv:1409.1556 (2014)

31. Deng, J., Dong, W., Socher, R., Li, L.J., Li, K., Fei-Fei, L.: Imagenet: A large-scale hierarchical image database. In: 2009 IEEE conference on computer vision and pattern recognition, pp. 248–255. IEEE (2009)

32. Pennington, J., Socher, R., Manning, C.D.: Glove: Global vectors for word representation. In: Proceedings of the 2014 Conference on Empirical Methods in Natural Language Processing (EMNLP), pp. 1532–1543 (2014)

33. Li, Y., Tarlow, D., Brockschmidt, M., Zemel, R.: Gated graph sequence neural networks. arXiv preprint arXiv:1511.05493 (2015)

34. Yang, K., Russakovsky, O., Deng, J.: Spatialsense: An adversarially crowdsourced benchmark for spatial relation recognition. In: Proceedings of the IEEE/CVF International Conference on Computer Vision, pp. 2051–2060 (2019)

35. Japkowicz, N., Shah, M.: Evaluating learning algorithms: a classification perspective. Cambridge University Press (2011)

36. Peyre, J., Sivic, J., Laptev, I., Schmid, C.: Weakly-supervised learning of visual relations. In: Proceedings of the IEEE International Conference on Computer Vision, pp. 5179–5188 (2017)

37. Silberman, N., Hoiem, D., Kohli, P., Fergus, R.: Indoor segmentation and support inference from rgbd images. In: ECCV (5) 7576, 746–760 (2012)

38. Zhuang, B., Liu, L., Shen, C., Reid, I.: Towards context-aware interaction recognition for visual relationship detection. In: Proceedings of the IEEE International Conference on Computer Vision, pp. 589–598 (2017)

39. Zhang, H., Kyaw, Z., Chang, S.F., Chua, T.S.: Visual translation embedding network for visual relation detection. In: Proceedings of the IEEE Conference on Computer Vision and Pattern Recognition, pp. 5532–5540 (2017)

40. Ding, X., Li, Y., Pan, Y., Zeng, D., Yao, T.: Exploring depth information for spatial relation recognition. In: 2020 IEEE Conference on Multimedia Information Processing and Retrieval (MIPR), pp. 279–284. IEEE (2020)

Fake News Detection Utilizing Textual Cues

Vasiliki Chouliara, Paraskevas Koukaras, and Christos Tjortjis[(⊠)]

The Data Mining and Analytics Research Group, School of Science and Technology,
International Hellenic University, Thessaloniki, Greece
{vchouliara,p.koukaras,c.tjortjis}@ihu.edu.gr

Abstract. Easy and quick information diffusion on the web and especially in social media has been rapidly proliferating during the past decades. As information is posted without any kind of verification of its veracity, fake news has become a problem of great influence in our information driven society. Thus, to mitigate the consequences of fake news and its propagation, automated approaches to detect malicious content were created. This paper proposes an effective framework that utilizes only the text features of the news. We evaluate several features for differentiating fake from real news and we identify the best performing feature set that maximizes performance, using feature selection techniques. Text representation features were also explored as a potential solution. Additionally, the most popular Machine Learning and Deep Learning models were tested to conclude to the model that achieves the maximum accuracy. Our findings reveal that a combination of linguistic features and text-based word vector representations through ensemble methods can predict fake news with high accuracy. eXtreme Gradient Boosting (XGB) outperformed all other models, while linear Support Vector Machine (SVM) achieved comparable results.

Keywords: Fake news · Text classification · Linguistic features · Word embeddings · Machine Learning (ML) · Ensemble Machine Learning (EML) · Deep Learning (DL)

1 Introduction

Social media have become the main source of information transmission during the past years, as most people have access to news via online channels avoiding the interaction with traditional sources of information. Social networks provide easy access and circulation of information published, but there is no verification of the news that propagate the network. Thus, social media offer a breeding ground for developing and spreading malicious content. It is apparent that people are exposed to a huge amount of fake news daily while the quality of news in general becomes questionable [1].

Fake news is unreliable content that intends to deliberately manipulate public opinion on different subjects, especially political affairs. It is of great concern though, that malevolent content seems to spread faster, compared to real news, and has greater impact on aspects of life, politics, and economy [2]. A more recent example of the huge influence of disinformation in our everyday lives was during the COVID-19 outbreak, which

© IFIP International Federation for Information Processing 2023
Published by Springer Nature Switzerland AG 2023
I. Maglogiannis et al. (Eds.): AIAI 2023, IFIP AICT 675, pp. 393–403, 2023.
https://doi.org/10.1007/978-3-031-34111-3_33

made the work of health professionals more difficult, while confusing the public and placing millions of individuals at risk [3–5].

Due to the immense impact that fake news has, of critical interest is the ability to detect and distinguish fake from real news in real time. This is challenging for many reasons. First of all, through social media, content is generated and spread fast, which leads to huge amounts of information that need to be validated. Moreover, content is diverse, referring to many different subjects, which makes the task even more complex [6]. It is an established fact that people lack the ability to effectively discern fake content. Studies in social psychology and communications have manifested that human's ability to differentiate fake from real topics is slightly better than chance [7].

On the other hand, fact-checking organizations that try to combat the proliferation of fake news, have limited applicability due to time latency and the quick propagation of information in social media. In recent years, extensive research on establishing an automated framework for online fake news detection has been made, to counter the misinformation diffusion [6]. Many ML models have been proposed in association with text-relevant features (i.e., TF-IDF), text-based linguistic features, visual and social features to automatically detect malicious content adequately.

The main contributions of this work are the following: i) to perform an extensive feature set evaluation aiming at finding the best feature set able to detect fake news, and ii) to evaluate and compare several ML and Deep Learning (DL) models leading to a robust methodology that addresses the fake news classification problem using the best performing feature set.

The following is an outline of the remaining research. Section 2 provides information from the literature related to fake news. Section 3 presents the dataset, data preprocessing, as well as the feature extraction techniques that were utilized to provide a solution to the problem. Section 4 focuses on evaluating the performance of the experiments conducted. Section 5 discusses the findings. Section 6 presents the conclusions of this research and sets some future work suggestions.

2 Background

2.1 Fake News Related Areas

A plethora of scientific studies on the field of Fake News identifies a variety of false information types. Rashkin, H., et al., in their research, use two dimensions to classify fake news, the quality of the article and the intention of the writer to deceive [8]. This approach is also adopted by many other researchers. In the next section, some of the most common fake news categories are presented.

Propaganda. The term propaganda is used to describe the premeditated attempt to manipulate and influence public perceptions. This endeavor to affect the common belief, is achieved through the activation of strong emotions of the targeted audience, the breeding of fear and the projection of simplified ideas [9]. Propaganda is mainly utilized by political entities to impose damage to a particular political party [10]. In recent years, a new term has been widely used, the computational propaganda. The term refers to the usage of political bots to propagate specific opinions through major social networking applications and manipulate conversations.

Conspiracy Theories. Refer to stories that try to interpret an event or situation that invokes a conspiracy. These stories are based on insufficient or false evidence, though they appear to be relatively widespread among citizens, as they can offer a coherent explanation of the given situation. Studies relate belief in conspiracy theories with low self-esteem, distrust in authority and political cynicism [11]. Conspiracy theories have a wide range of topics, from science, health and economy to politics.

Rumors. A rumor can be described as a story or a statement whose truth value is unverified [12]. This does not always mean that a rumor is a false piece of information, but rather that its veracity is unconfirmed at the time of posting. The importance and the interest of a topic is highly correlated with the spread of the rumor. Sensitive topics can be a fertile ground for rumors to be generated and spread across social media networks. A great percentage of the research aims to develop systems to detect rumors using supervised, unsupervised and hybrid methods.

News Satire. Satire is a form of fake news which employs exaggeration and humor to present a story. Satire news is produced to entertain the audience and not to deliberately spread misinformation. However, this type of news is perceived as credible from many people who usually don't read beyond the headlines. Horne & Adali in their research examined correlations among satire, fake and real news and they concluded that satire news is more closely related to fake than real ones [13].

2.2 Fake News Detection Approaches

According to many researchers the methods used for fake news detection can be classified in three categories: a) knowledge-based, b) content-based and c) social context-based.

Knowledge-Based. When it comes to the knowledge-based approach, one uses a procedure called fact-checking. The scope of this approach is to compare the knowledge extracted from news articles with known facts to determine its veracity. Existing fact-checking approaches can be classified as expert-oriented, crowdsourcing-oriented and automatic. Expert and crowdsourcing-oriented are manually processes that rely on domain experts or the 'wisdom of the crowd' respectively to annotate news articles [7, 14]. Automatic fact-checking is based on NLP and ML techniques as well as network theory and can be segmented into two stages, fact extraction and fact verification [7].

Content-Based. Content-based analysis tries to capture the different writing styles between legitimate users and deceivers. Though the deceivers make great efforts to present a story as credible, the style of their language, can often expose them [15]. The goal of this method is to exploit linguistic features from different levels of intricacy of the text or extract information from visual content such as images. The linguistic characteristics can be categorized as follows.

Stylistic Features: Try to measure the news creator's language proficiency by examining the syntax, text style and grammar of the article. Common ways of investigating the differences in syntax is using "Bag-of-words" [6], part of speech tagging (POS) as well as counting the frequency of function words, punctuation, and sensory words [13].

Complexity Features: The complexity features are studied in two levels of elaborateness: word and sentence level. On a sentence level, the number of words per sentence and the number of clauses per sentence can be examined. Regarding the word level complexity, one can count the total number of words or use the readability indexes, which measure if a reader of a certain level of literacy could understand the text [13].

Psychological Features: These features try to captivate the emotions and behaviors of the creators of the news. They are based on well-researched word counts that are associated with psychological processes and sentiment analysis [13].

Social Context-Based. Social context analysis is the study that analyzes the characteristics of information diffusion in social media and tries to identify anomalous information. Information can be distilled by user-based features, like the registration age and the number of followers/ followees [16] and post-based features that utilize the text of the post to infer the validity of news articles and obtain user stance [14]. Moreover, propagation-based features that utilize context information such as, how fake news propagates in social media platforms can be used to track down fake news [17].

2.3 The Impact of Concept Drift

When data interpretation changes over time, this leads to an impact on performance of previously trained models [18]. This notion is referred to as concept drift in Machine Learning (ML) literature. There are two types of drift in the news. The natural drift that can be caused because news differentiates radically over time, and the artificial drift where the writing style used in misleading news can change, as an effort to create content that is equivalent to verified news [19]. Many researchers provided a thoroughly examined survey on the impact of concept drift incorporating content-based features [18, 19]. They concluded that the performance of content-based models declined over time, but in a slower pace than they considered, which led to the deduction that hand-crafted content-based features that are not topic-specific, are robust to changes.

3 Research Design

The proposed methodology concerns the amelioration of the state-of-the-art techniques for detecting fake news by utilizing linguistic features and word vector features from the text of news articles. Various ML models were trained and evaluated to find the best performing one. An overview of the analysis framework presented in this paper is illustrated in Fig. 1. All steps are detailed in the following subsections.

3.1 Data Collection

The ISOT Fake News dataset provided by Ahmed et al. [20, 21] was used to investigate the issue of fake news detection. The dataset consists of 21,417 real and 23,481 fake news. Different types of articles on different topics are presented in the dataset, with most of them focusing on political and World news topics.

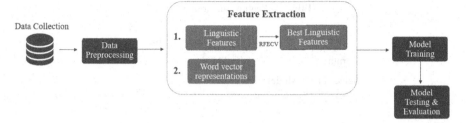

Fig. 1. Flowchart of the overall methodology outline

3.2 Data Pre-processing

Raw text is an unstructured form of data that contains noisy content, and its quality can directly affect the performance of our models. Thus, data preprocessing is required in order to ensure robust results and avoid overfitting. Here, we utilized many Natural Lnaguage Processing (NLP) techniques to preprocess the ISOT dataset, like converting the articles into lowercase and removing URLs, punctuation, numbers, and stop-words that do not convey significant information. Finally, we applied tokenization and stemming to ensure dimensionality reduction. The cleaned text after pre-processing was used to create word vector representations, while the raw text was used to create the linguistic features.

3.3 Feature Extraction

Linguistic Features. Taking into consideration the works of [1, 22, 23] a linguistic-based cue of 35 features were extracted from the available dataset to investigate the fake news problem. The features explored are conceptually divided into seven categories that measure the quantity, complexity, uncertainty etc. and try to capture adequately the characteristics of deceptive and truthful language.

Best Linguistic Features. As a next step, we attempted to limit the dimensions of the examined dataset. The dimensionality reduction results in shorter training times and more efficient algorithms that can perform equally well with other unknown datasets. Additionally, many ML algorithms exhibit a decrease in accuracy when the number of features is significantly higher than the optimal [24]. To find the best combination of features, we investigated three approaches: a) Boruta algorithm, b) Select-From-Model algorithm and c) Recursive Feature Elimination with Cross Validation (RFECV).

All three approaches train a baseline Random Forest and calculate the importance of each feature. Then each algorithm returns the features deemed as important following a different process. The number of features returned by each method is presented in Table 1.

The reduced feature sets produced by these three methods, were tested upon the classifiers under investigation and their performance was evaluated in terms of accuracy. The best linguistic feature subset that yielded the highest accuracy scores among most of the classifiers, was obtained by the RFECV and consists of 28 variables.

Table 2 presents the optimal subset of features.

Table 1. Feature selection results

Approach	Number of features
Boruta	34
Select-From-Model	30
RFECV	28

Table 2. Best Linguistic feature set obtained by using the RFECV

Best Linguistic Features		
# words	avg noun phrase length	Emotiveness index
# syllables	Pausality	Lexical diversity
# sentences	# short sentences	Content word diversity
# verbs	# long sentences	Redundancy
# noun phrases	Flesch reading ease	Typographical error rate
# big words	Sentence complexity	Rate of adjectives & adverbs
avg syllables per word	Modifiers	# affective terms
avg # clauses	% other-reference	Spatio-temporal information
avg word length	Subjectivity	
avg sentence length	% self-reference	

Text Representations. A very popular approach to fake news detection is the use of text representation techniques and word embeddings. Driven by that, we conducted experiments using three text representation techniques: a) TF-IDF, b) word2vec and c) GloVe. In the TF-IDF approach, the vocabulary size was limited to the 10,000 most frequent words to overcome the dimensionality problems. Additionally, the pre-trained word2vec vectors trained on part of Google News dataset were used. The model includes a total of 3 million words and phrases in a 300-dimension vector representation. Finally, we utilized the Wikipedia 2014 pre-trained GloVe[1] embeddings and tested both the 100-dimension and 300-dimension vectors.

All these text representation methods were tested upon a linear Support Vector Machine (SVM) classifier using a 10-fold cross validation. The results presented in Table 3 indicate that TF-IDF achieved the best accuracy scores and thus selected as the one that will be used in the rest of the analysis.

---

[1] https://nlp.stanford.edu/projects/glove/

Table 3. SVM results using text representations

Method	SVM Accuracy (%)
TF-IDF	**98.8**
Word2vec	94.3
Glove 100 dim	92.8
Glove 300 dim	94.2

The best accuracy value is in bold text

4   Results and Evaluation

In our research, we selected the most prevailing ML algorithms found in literature related to fake news classification, to successfully evaluate the given dataset. A variety of traditional and ensemble models with different parametrization were tested. Moreover, DL models were also employed to tackle the problem of fake news detection. Subsequently, we provide some additional information about the experiments conducted.

4.1   Performance Results for the ML Models

Many different feature extraction techniques were investigated along with linguistic features extraction as described in Sect. 3.3. Then, the word representation features were enhanced with the best feature set, to verify the claim that linguistic features improve the model performance.

Furthermore, we performed an extensive classification algorithm study for introducing a robust model that effectively detects fake news articles, utilizing the best performing feature set. Traditional learning models (SVM, KNN, etc.) and ensemble models (Random Forest, etc.) were trained using 10-fold cross validation. Moreover, the grid search approach was implemented to determine the optimal parameters of each classifier and increase its performance.

Results of the experiments are illustrated in Table 4.

Table 4. Accuracy for different feature sets and models

Method	Model Accuracy (%)					
	SVM	KNN	NB	RF	GB	XGB
All Linguistic features	94.1	89.1	69.8	96.2	97.3	97.5
Best Linguistic features	94.1	89.3	72.2	96.3	97.3	97.5
TF-IDF	98.8	90.4	92.8	98.3	98.7	99.0
Best Linguistics & TF-IDF	99.3	94.3	92.8	98.4	99.3	**99.6**

The best accuracy value is in bold text

4.2 Performance Results for the Deep Learning Models

We also performed experiments with DL models, and we evaluated their performance. We tested the Convolutional Neural Network (CNN) and Long-Short Term Memory (LSTM) which are widely used in text classification problems across the research community [25]. Each DL model was trained upon multiple architectures, while some common layers were used in both models to avoid overfitting the training set. We applied Batch Normalization and Dropout to overcome overfitting.

Convolutional Neural Network (CNN). Many experiments were conducted using CNN to reach an optimal network. The CNN model described in Table 5, returned 96.81% accuracy and is the one with the highest performance compared to the rest of the trained CNNs.

Additionally, we examined the influence of feeding the model with pretrained word embeddings, instead of using the ones produced directly by the neural network. By utilizing word2vec and GloVe embeddings in the embedding layer of the CNN we observed degradation in accuracy.

Table 5. Best Performing CNN architecture

Layer	Embedding Layer	Convolutional Layer	Global Avg Pooling	Dense Layer	Batch Normalization	Dropout	Dense Layer
Output dimension	300	128	128	100	100	100	1

Long-Short Term Memory (LSTM). Another extensively used algorithm for fake news detection that was also tested here, is a variation of LSTM called Bi-directional LSTM. Various layers with different number of neurons were employed to conclude to the architecture that yielded the best results. 95.78% was the highest accuracy obtained using Bi-LSTM; its architecture is shown in Table 6.

Table 6. Best Performing LSTM architecture

Layer	Embedding Layer	Bi-LSTM Layer	Dense Layer	Batch Normalization	Dropout	Dense Layer
Output dimension	300	32	100	100	100	1

5 Discussion

The outcomes of this study, support the findings in the literature about linguistic features improving the performance of the classifiers when used as an enhancement to text representations and word embeddings. During the experimental process, we extracted 35 linguistic features which resulted in 97.5% accuracy produced by training an XGB classifier. Subsequently, we searched for a subset of the feature set aiming at reducing the dimensions of the dataset without lowering the accuracy. This was achieved by the RFECV algorithm that deemed 28 features as important. Again, XGB performed best in this dataset preserving the same accuracy as the one obtained by using the whole feature set.

Additionally, text representations and word embeddings were utilized as feature extraction techniques. It is worth noting that when the article's text was represented using pre-trained word embeddings like word2vec and GloVe, the accuracy scores of all models were reduced compared to the scores returned by the TF-IDF text representation method. There can be several reasons to explain these findings. One might say that it is possible that word embeddings cannot represent efficiently the news articles due to their large length. The TF-IDF method obtained 99% accuracy with an XGB method. Furthermore, the combination of the best linguistic feature set with the enhancement of TF-IDF features, reinforced the performance of all the classifiers acquiring an accuracy of 99.6%.

The experimental results on traditional and ensemble models, indicate that ensemble methods overshadowed traditional models in terms of performance. Both Random Forest and Gradient Boosting achieved high accuracy scores, while XGB surpassed all other models in all cases examined. Another remarkable observation is that linear SVM yielded quite impressive results and can compete with ensemble methods.

The results of the DL models were quite promising, despite lacking any explicit linguistic features. CNN and LSTM were trained deploying different architectures, with CNN outperforming LSTM with an accuracy of 96.8%.

6 Conclusions and Future Work

The objective of this paper was to propose an effective way to remedy the issue of dissemination of misinformation using linguistic cues. Several supervised classifiers were trained using linguistic features, word vector representations and their combination, with the latter scheme outshining in all models. Ensemble learners have shown the greatest performance compared to individual learners. DL algorithms were also explored as a potential solution, but they did not manage to overcome the performance of ensemble models, due to the size of the dataset. The promising results returned by the deep neural networks indicate that there is potential for further experimentation to improve performance.

In this study, content-based approaches were utilized to explore patterns in text that differentiate fake from real news, as we aimed to detect fake news in real time before this propagate to social media platforms. For that reason, a possible object of future research could be to employ meta-data about the source and the author of the news, as well as information about the diffusion of the news in social media platforms. Additional information could also be exploited by images and videos included in the articles, employing Transfer learning and pre-trained models. Another future direction involves experimentation with more open access datasets for testing the generalization of the results.

Acknowledgements. This research is co-financed by Greece and the European Union (European Social Fund-SF) through the Operational Program "Human Resources Development, Education and Lifelong Learning 2014–2020" in the context of the project "Support for International Actions of the International Hellenic University", (MIS 5154651).

References

1. Gravanis, G., Vakali, A., Diamantaras, K., Karadais, P.: Behind the cues: a benchmarking study for fake news detection. Expert Syst Appl. **128**, 201–213 (2019). https://doi.org/10.1016/j.eswa.2019.03.036

2. Verma, P.K., Agrawal, P., Amorim, I., Prodan, R.: WELFake: word embedding over linguistic features for fake news detection. IEEE Trans Comput Soc Syst. **8**, 881–893 (2021). https://doi.org/10.1109/TCSS.2021.3068519

3. Kasseropoulos, D.P., Tjortjis, C.: An approach utilizing linguistic features for fake news detection. In: Maglogiannis, I., Macintyre, J., Iliadis, L. (eds.) AIAI 2021. IAICT, vol. 627, pp. 646–658. Springer, Cham (2021). https://doi.org/10.1007/978-3-030-79150-6_51

4. Kasseropoulos, D.P., Koukaras, P., Tjortjis, C.: Exploiting textual information for fake news detection. Int J Neural Syst. **32**, 2250058 (2022). https://doi.org/10.1142/S0129065722500587

5. Chouliara, V., Kapoteli, E., Koukaras, P., Tjortjis, C.: Social media sentiment analysis related to COVID-19 vaccinations. In: Peng, L.C., Vaidya, A., Chen, Y.-W., Jain, V., Jain, L.C. (eds.) Artificial Intelligence and Machine Learning for Healthcare: Vol. 2: Emerging Methodologies and Trends, pp. 47–69. Springer, Cham (2023). https://doi.org/10.1007/978-3-031-11170-9_3

6. Zhang, X., Ghorbani, A.A.: An overview of online fake news: Characterization, detection, and discussion. Inf. Process Manag. **57**, 102025 (2020). https://doi.org/10.1016/j.ipm.2019.03.004

7. Zhou, X., Zafarani, R.: A survey of fake news: fundamental theories, detection methods, and opportunities. ACM Comput Surv. **53**, 1–40 (2020). https://doi.org/10.1145/3395046

8. Rashkin, H., Choi, E., Jang, J.Y., Volkova, S., Choi, Y.: Truth of varying shades: analyzing language in fake news and political fact-checking. In: Proceedings of the 2017 Conference on Empirical Methods in Natural Language Processing, pp. 2931–2937. Association for Computational Linguistics, Copenhagen (2017)

9. Hobbs, R.: Propaganda in an age of algorithmic personalization: expanding literacy research and practice. Read Res Q. **55**, 521–533 (2020). https://doi.org/10.1002/rrq.301

10. Zannettou, S., Sirivianos, M., Blackburn, J., Kourtellis, N.: The web of false information: rumors, fake news, hoaxes, clickbait, and various other shenanigans. J. Data Inf. Qual. **11**, 1–37 (2019). https://doi.org/10.1145/3309699

11. Swami, V.: Social psychological origins of conspiracy theories: the case of the Jewish conspiracy theory in Malaysia. Front Psychol. **3** (2012). https://doi.org/10.3389/fpsyg.2012.00280

12. Alkhodair, S.A., Ding, S.H.H., Fung, B.C.M., Liu, J.: Detecting breaking news rumors of emerging topics in social media. Inf. Process Manag. **57** (2020). https://doi.org/10.1016/j.ipm.2019.02.016

13. Horne, B., Adali, S.: This just in: fake news packs a lot in title, uses simpler, repetitive content in text body, more similar to satire than real news. In: Proceedings of the International AAAI Conference on Web and Social Media, vol. 11 (2017). https://doi.org/10.1609/icwsm.v11i1. 14976

14. Shu, K., Sliva, A., Wang, S., Tang, J., Liu, H.: Fake news detection on social media: a data mining perspective. SIGKDD Explor. Newsl. **19**, 22–36 (2017). https://doi.org/10.1145/313 7597.3137600

15. de Beer, D., Matthee, M.: Approaches to identify fake news: a systematic literature review. In: Antipova, T. (ed.) ICIS 2020. LNNS, vol. 136, pp. 13–22. Springer, Cham (2021). https://doi.org/10.1007/978-3-030-49264-9_2

16. Castillo, C., Mendoza, M., Poblete, B.: Information credibility on twitter. In: Proceedings of the 20th International Conference on World Wide Web, pp. 675–684. Association for Computing Machinery, New York (2011)

17. Jin, Z., Cao, J., Zhang, Y., Luo, J.: News verification by exploiting conflicting social viewpoints in microblogs. In: Proceedings of the AAAI Conference on Artificial Intelligence, vol. 30 (2016). https://doi.org/10.1609/aaai.v30i1.10382

18. Raza, S., Ding, C.: Fake news detection based on news content and social contexts: a transformer-based approach. Int. J. Data Sci. Anal. **13**, 335–362 (2022). https://doi.org/10.1007/s41060-021-00302-z

19. Horne, B.D., NØrregaard, J., Adali, S.: Robust fake news detection over time and attack. ACM Trans. Intell. Syst. Technol. **11** (2019). https://doi.org/10.1145/3363818

20. Ahmed, H., Traore, I., Saad, S.: Detecting opinion spams and fake news using text classification. Secur. Priv. **1**, e9 (2018). https://doi.org/10.1002/spy2.9

21. Ahmed, H., Traore, I., Saad, S.: Detection of online fake news using N-gram analysis and machine learning techniques. In: Traore, I., Woungang, I., Awad, A. (eds.) ISDDC 2017. LNCS, vol. 10618, pp. 127–138. Springer, Cham (2017). https://doi.org/10.1007/978-3-319-69155-8_9

22. Zhou, L., Burgoon, J.K., Nunamaker, J.F., Twitchell, D.: Automating linguistics-based cues for detecting deception in text-based asynchronous computer-mediated communications. Group Decis. Negot. **13**(1), 81–106 (2004). https://doi.org/10.1023/B:GRUP.0000011944. 62889.6f

23. Burgoon, J.K., Blair, J.P., Qin, T., Nunamaker, J.F.: Detecting deception through linguistic analysis. In: Chen, H., Miranda, R., Zeng, D.D., Demchak, C., Schroeder, J., Madhusudan, T. (eds.) ISI 2003. LNCS, vol. 2665, pp. 91–101. Springer, Heidelberg (2003). https://doi.org/10.1007/3-540-44853-5_7

24. Kursa, M.B., Rudnicki, W.R.: Feature selection with the boruta package. J. Stat Softw. **36**, 1–13 (2010). https://doi.org/10.18637/jss.v036.i11

25. Zervopoulos, A., Alvanou, A.G., Bezas, K., Papamichail, A., Maragoudakis, M., Kermanidis, K.: Deep learning for fake news detection on Twitter regarding the 2019 Hong Kong protests. Neural Comput. Appl. **34**(2), 969–982 (2021). https://doi.org/10.1007/s00521-021-06230-0

Fusion of Learned Representations for Multimodal Sensor Data Classification

Lee B. Hinkle[ID], Gentry Atkinson[(✉)][ID], and Vangelis Metsis[ID]

Department of Computer Science, Texas State University,
San Marcos, TX 78666, USA
{leebhinkle,gma23,vmetsis}@txstate.edu

Abstract. Time-Series data collected using body-worn sensors can be used to recognize activities of interest in various medical applications such as sleep studies. Recent advances in other domains, such as image recognition and natural language processing have shown that unlabeled data can still be useful when self-supervised techniques such as contrastive learning are used to generate meaningful feature space representations. Labeling data for Human Activity Recognition (HAR) and sleep disorder diagnosis (polysomnography) is difficult and requires trained professionals. In this work, we apply learned feature representation techniques to multimodal time-series data. By using signal-specific representations, based on self-supervised and supervised learning, the channels can be evaluated to determine if they are likely to contribute to correct classification. The learned representation embeddings are then used to process each channel into a new feature space that serves as input into a neural network. This results in a better understanding of the importance of each signal modality as well as the potential applicability of newer self-supervised techniques to time-series data.

Keywords: self-supervised learning · learned representations · physiological sensor data · polysomnography · human activity recognition · multimodal

1 Introduction

Multimodal, time-series data is generated by various types of sensors that record movement, electrical potentials, temperature, sound, and other information. It is widely used, and various methods for collecting and fusing the data, including signal processing, feature engineering, and feature extraction, have been utilized [13,21]. The focus of this work is on the exploration of self-supervised techniques such as nearest-neighbor contrastive learning (NNCLR) [5], which learn representations from unlabeled image data to multimodal time-series data. Specifically, the data from sensors collecting human attributes such as movement, heart rate, and respiration in the area of Human Activity Recognition (HAR) and sleep disorder diagnosis is used as input to deep neural networks with supervised and self-supervised learning configurations.

© IFIP International Federation for Information Processing 2023
Published by Springer Nature Switzerland AG 2023
I. Maglogiannis et al. (Eds.): AIAI 2023, IFIP AICT 675, pp. 404–415, 2023.
https://doi.org/10.1007/978-3-031-34111-3_34

Diagnosing sleep apnea using polysomnography (PSG) data is an important but expensive task. These data must currently be collected in a controlled environment and interpreted by trained professionals. Machine learning (ML) could potentially make apnea diagnoses cheaper and more widely available. One difficulty with applying ML to the classification of apneic events in sleep data is the wide variety of sensors involved. ML models may struggle to correctly represent and identify the wide range of signals which include: electroencephalography (EEG), electromyography (EMG), electrooculography (EOG), thoracic and abdominal belts, electrocardiography (ECG), and temperature sensors.

In this work, we propose an ML architecture for detecting apneic events in PSG data. This architecture can leverage unlabeled data to drive representation learning of individual signal channels. The importance of these channels is determined during training, meaning that the model's architecture is not tied to any set of sensors but can be easily adapted to fit different data sets and even domains. Signal channels that are more useful to the prediction outcome automatically receive a higher weight at the fusion layer. To demonstrate the flexibility of the model, we use a small labeled HAR dataset and a larger unlabeled dataset collected with the same device. This shows that our system is highly adaptable to its inputs and can be trained on a small set of labeled data by using a larger, unlabeled dataset to boot-strap the feature learners.

The contributions of this work are as follows. An Empatica E4 Wristband (UE4W) dataset containing over 250 h of unlabeled data for evaluating semi-supervised learning data pipelines. A methodology and code[1] for efficiently processing the physiological signal data in the publicly available PSG-Audio dataset [11]. A Tensorflow adaptation of NNCLR for use with time series. A data pipeline that allows for the seamless fusion of different signal modalities. An evaluation of the predictive performance of three architectures: 1) Concatenation of all channels at the input level. 2) Late fusion of convolutional layers trained on each individual channel. 3) Pretraining on unlabeled data of each signal type, and late fusion and fine-tuning on smaller labeled datasets.

2   Background and Related Work

Collecting physiological data from sleeping subjects is important for diagnosing irregularities in breathing and heart rate. The need to collect this data in a controlled environment and the requirement that it be interpreted by trained experts makes the process expensive and time-consuming. ML can improve this process by automatically interpreting collected data. Apnea detection by convolutional neural networks (CNNs) using a face-mounted nasal pressure device has achieved 96.2% accuracy [3]. Approaches using body-worn belt-type sensors have achieved 84% accuracy [19]. Other studies have shown that ML techniques for apnea detection generalize across humans, rats, and pigeons [1].

In addition to the challenges of collecting a large number of signals while a subject is trying to sleep in a clinical site, manually detecting and labeling

---

[1] https://github.com/imics-lab/fusion-of-learned-representations.

the episodes of apnea (cessation of breathing in excess of 10 s) and hypopnea (a reduction in airflow measured directly or reflected in lowered blood oxygen saturation) is difficult [14]. The PSG-Audio dataset [11,12] used in this work contains data recorded on 212 individuals in a hospital setting for sleep apnea syndrome (SAS) diagnosis. Five categories of abnormal events were annotated by a medical team. At this time of this writing, two studies have applied machine learning techniques and published results for the PSG-Audio dataset. In [4] Mel-spectrograms of the audio signals were input into a pre-trained VGG19 (19-layer deep CNN+Max Pooling) model followed by a long-short-term memory (LSTM) fused model. The leave-one-out subject accuracy was 66.29%. In [10], the three EEG signals are converted into spectrograms which are input into a model with three 1D-CNN layers followed by a Gated Recurrent Unit (GRU) with a goal to determine the start and stop time of each episode as the duration of the apnea is significant for diagnosis.

A common shortcoming of ML approaches to PSG data processing is that they rely on the presence of a large body of labeled data and the burden of professionally labeling these data makes them expensive and difficult to publish. Unsupervised and self-supervised approaches that do not rely on labeled data have only recently been applied to diagnosing sleep apnea. Clustering has been used to demonstrate an association between PSG data and the risk of future cardiovascular events [24]. Representation learning of PSG data using self-supervised learning has also been investigated [23]. This approach is very promising, but the remaining difficulty is the heterogeneous nature of the channels. The PSG signals are physically dissimilar and may not have much to contribute to the disorder being predicted.

Self-supervised learning removes the need for labeled data by training models to recognize labels that are generated automatically by the algorithm. A sub-field of self-supervised learning, contrastive learning, generates these labels by augmenting anchor samples of data and training an encoder to recognize augmented copies of the same instance [17]. This work has applied a deep representation learner called NNCLR [5], which was originally developed as a tool for image classification. NNCLR maintains knowledge of nearest neighbors in the learned feature space to improve the process of augmenting data. Other works have had success in adapting NNCLR to time series data [20], but this technique has not been tested in the field of PSG. SimCLR and the accompanying analysis [2] show that for image processing, contrastive learning results for image recognition are improved by: proper data augmentations, learnable non-linear transformations, larger batch sizes, and longer training. The SeqCLR framework [16] applies contrastive learning to time-series EEG signals for Emotion Recognition, EEG classification, and sleep-scoring tasks. LIMU-BERT [22] builds upon the concepts of the natural language model BERT to process inertial measurement unit (motion) data for HAR. Our data pipeline and learned representation model utilize these promising techniques for multimodal HAR and PSG data.

3   Methodology

3.1   Data Processing

To demonstrate our data processing pipeline two multimodal datasets were used. The TWristAR dataset [7] consists of multimodal channels recorded with an Empatica E4 Wristband [6]. The channels are acceleration (movement), blood volume pulse (BVP), electrodermal activity (EDA), and peripheral skin temperature. Per Empatica "the BVP signal is obtained from the PPG sensor by a proprietary algorithm that combines the light signals observed during both green and red exposure." All of the signals were re-sampled to 32 Hz. The TWristAR dataset is small with only three subjects performing six common HAR activities in a scripted manner for ease of labeling and to produce a balanced dataset. The data were split into sliding windows of three-second duration (96 samples) with a step size of one second. For early evaluation of channel contributions, subject three was reserved for testing only, while subjects one and two are used for training and validation. Due to the presence of both subjects in the validation set and the overlapping windows, the validation result represents subject-dependent accuracies and the expected test accuracy is lower as described in our previous work [8]. An associated dataset, the unlabeled E4 wristband (UE4W) dataset [9] provides significantly more unlabeled data for self-supervised training. Figure 1 shows an example of signals collected by the four sensors in the E4 wristband.

As described earlier, the second dataset used, PSG-Audio [11,12] contains data recorded in a hospital setting for SAS diagnosis. Several elements of this dataset that led us to use it in this work: it is fully open-access, multimodal, and the labeling was completed and reviewed by trained personnel. It should be noted that the namesake signals, two channels of high-definition audio, were not used in this work. The 12 channels that were used are shown in Fig. 2b. Nine of the channels (3 x EEG, 2 x EMG, 2 x EOG, 2 leg sensors, and ECG) were downsampled from 200 Hz to 100 Hz to match the remaining three sensors used (flow thermistor plus thoracic and abdominal respiratory belts). Each subject's data, contained within a standard format EDF file were segmented into non-overlapping sliding windows with 500 samples each representing five seconds of time. The event data for labeling were derived from the provided "clean" rml file for patients 995-1494 (not all numbers are present). The respiratory events for "Obstructive Apnea", "Central Apnea", "Mixed Apnea", "Hypopnea", and three other categories were treated as "abnormal". All subject data is labeled, so for the purposes of this work data from the first 50 subjects were treated as labeled and data from the second 50 subjects were treated as unlabeled and only used to train the self-supervised models. For supervised learning, the train and validation sets were better balanced by discarding a portion of the normal samples. Neither the test set nor the unlabeled data could be rebalanced without incurring data leakage.

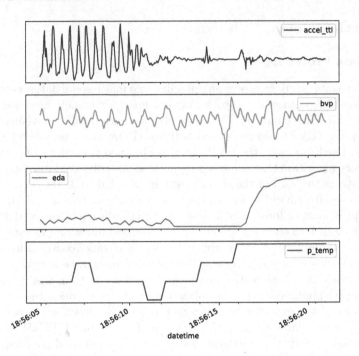

Fig. 1. A 15-s sample of the Empatica E4 sensor data. For this work, the 64 Hz BVP data is downsampled and the 4 Hz EDA and peripheral temperature signals are upsampled so that all signals match the 32 Hz sampling rate of the acceleration data.

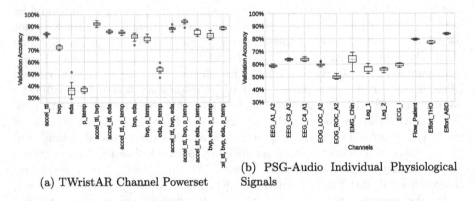

(a) TWristAR Channel Powerset

(b) PSG-Audio Individual Physiological Signals

Fig. 2. Boxplots showing the accuracy of individual channels. In the case of TWristAR with four channels, the powerset of all combinations concatenated was evaluated. For PSG-Audio each of the 12 channels was evaluated individually.

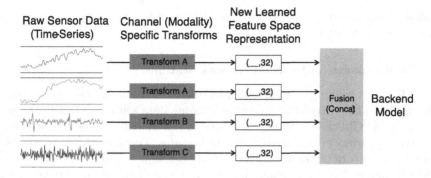

Fig. 3. Each time-series signal is transformed into a new n-dimensional feature space by a learned representation model. The models can be trained in a supervised or in a self-supervised manner on labeled or unlabeled data, respectively.

3.2 Fusion of Multimodal Sensor Data

ML models can learn from several channels of data simultaneously, but when those channels are dissimilar from one another or non-uniform in their contribution to the output of the model, it may not be beneficial to apply the same process of representation learning to every channel. To test this hypothesis, a baseline classifier was trained that applied separate convolutional layers to subsets of the available channels from our investigated datasets. The outputs of these convolutional layers were concatenated and then passed a global average pooling layer, and finally classified by dense layers.

The baseline classifier was also used to conduct a per-channel analysis. Since the network architecture other than shape does not vary with the number of input channels it is possible to run this classifier with one or a subset of multiple channels. For the four channels in the TWristAR dataset, the full powerset (all possible channel combinations) were run. The results of 10 runs in Fig. 2 show that the accuracy with the acceleration and blood volume pulse are much higher than the electro-dermal activity and peripheral temperature signals. The subject-dependent accuracy was highest with all signals except EDA. Figure 2 also shows channel data for PGS-Audio. Due to the number of possible combinations the powerset was not run. The highest accuracies for respiration classification were the airflow and respiration band signals which serve as the basis for the subsequent model evaluations. The EMG_Chin signal showed much greater variability across the 10 runs for unknown reasons.

The models trained as our baseline for comparison were trained using standard back-propagation of the loss relative to the assigned labels. While they will still benefit from learning channel-wise representations of the input data, they cannot capitalize on the large body of unlabeled data that we had available for the two datasets. For the final comparison between the concatenated, multi-headed, and self-supervised experiments sklearn [18] GroupKFold was used to perform hold-one-subject-out cross-validation. For the PSG-Audio dataset, a similar methodology was used but the 192 subjects were split group-wise for 5-fold cross-validation.

3.3   Self-supervised Learned Representations

NNCLR [5] is a training method that uses labels automatically generated at train time to fit feature extraction layers to training data with or without assigned labels. As NNCLR is a training technique, not a model architecture, it can be applied to a variety of neural network architectures. The model architecture used to learn the feature representations is usually called an encoder. For this project, NNCLR was used as the training platform for an encoder composed of two layers of 1D convolutional networks. This CNN-based encoder architecture was chosen because it is simple, effective, and highly flexible for time-series data.

Each feature encoder was trained on one channel of the unlabeled and labeled training data. A validation group was held out, and the loss on that set was used for early stopping. The trained encoders were then used as pre-trained models to generate feature vectors for one channel of the labeled training data, with a fixed output vector dimensionality of 32 elements (Fig. 3). Pairs of channels that were univariate, such as the left and right eye in the EOG data, were encoded using a single encoder and represented by a single vector. The output of all encoders is fused together and fed to dense layers for supervised learning. The weights of the encoder can be frozen or allowed to continue to be trained during the supervised training of the fused model. In our case, we did not freeze the encoder. Due to data availability limitations, especially for the PSG dataset, the encoders were trained on roughly twice as much data as the labeled dataset, in other domains considerably more unlabeled data are typically used.

Figure 4 shows the UMAP [15] 2D projection of the 32-dimensional self-supervised learned representation feature vectors for the TWristAR dataset. The encoder model used to produce the feature vectors was trained on the unlabeled E4 wristband (UE4W) dataset [9]. The labels were used to color code each data point for the figure, but not during the training of the encoder. The features learned from the acceleration channel create a separation of the different classes in the feature space. The data points of "standing", "sitting", and "jogging" are far apart from the points of the other classes, which suggests they would be easy to classify. The points of "walking", "upstairs", and "downstairs" are closer together, which would make them harder to separate. The BVP channel appears to be the second best, although there is some overlap between different classes they do not completely overlap. The EDA and Temperature channels seem to be the worst with points with all classes scattered around.

Figure 5 shows similar plots for the different channels of the PSG dataset. The projected features were processed in a similar manner. The PSG-Audio dataset contains a larger number of instances, and thus the graphs are much denser. The distribution of data points coming from the two classes (normal and abnormal breathing) largely overlap for most channels. The channels for which the point distributions overlap the least are the airflow and the thoracic plus abdominal effort. This is expected, as these channels are directly associated with breathing

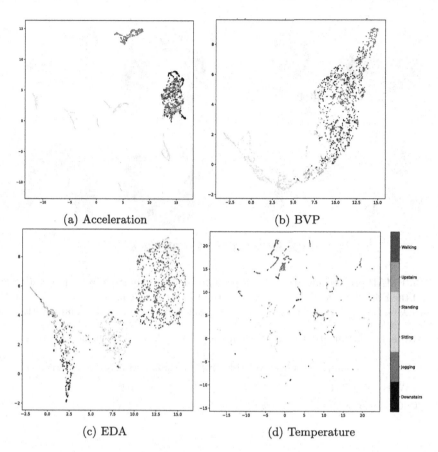

(a) Acceleration   (b) BVP

(c) EDA   (d) Temperature

Fig. 4. UMAP projections of self-supervised learned representations of sequences from the different channels of the TWristAR dataset.

patterns. These three channels also produced the highest classification accuracy when used individually to detect abnormal breathing, as shown in Fig. 2b.

3.4   Model Comparisons

To demonstrate the strength of channel-specific representation learning using self-supervised learning, a classifier was trained on the fused feature vectors output by the NNCLR feature learners. The three encoders used for three different channels share the same network architecture, but their weights have been separately pre-trained on unlabeled data of that channel. Figure 6 shows the architecture of the model that utilizes the self-supervised learning encoders.

Table 1 shows the final comparison of the three architectures evaluated for the TWristAR and PSG-Audio datasets. The train/test split was made using GroupKfold, with each subject/patient representing a different group, with three

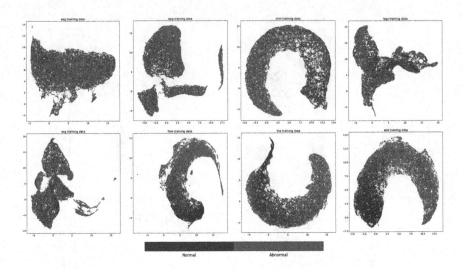

Fig. 5. UMAP projections of learned representations of sequences from different channels of the PSG dataset. From left to right, top to bottom the images show EEG, EOG, Chin EMG, Legs EMG, ECG, Air Flow, Thoracic Effort, and Abdominal Effort.

Table 1. Classification percent accuracies of the three different architectures.

	Simple Concat	Multi-head Supervised	Multi-head Pretrained
TWristAR	79.1	80.9	80.6
PSG-Audio	88.9	88.3	86.3

and five-fold cross-validation, respectively. The results show that the Multi-head Supervised model slightly outperforms the simple concatenation of the inputs. This is likely due to the ability to have different hyperparameters for each channel which is not possible in the concatenated model. The results with PSG-Audio show that the simple concatenation slightly outperformed the multi-headed model. Further tuning may be required. For both datasets, the pre-training did not improve the performance compared to fully supervised training. Based on the usage of self-supervised models in image recognition, it is possible that a much larger set of unlabeled data than is provided by these two datasets is required along with potentially more tuning, including alternate augmentations. Note that the CNN model architecture was initially tuned for the single-head model and was subsequently copied and used as an encoder for each of the different heads of the pre-trained model.

On the left of Fig. 7 is the confusion Matrix for the Concatenated Model, which uses accelerometer and BVP channels as flat inputs into a single CNN. On the right is the confusion Matrix for the Multihead Model, which uses two separately tuned CNNs for the accelerometer and BVP channels. Input is the TWristAR dataset evaluated with hold-one-subject out. The TWristAR dataset

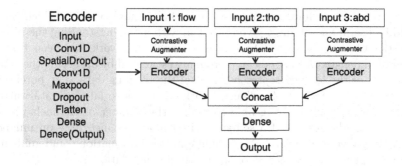

Fig. 6. The self-supervised model architecture

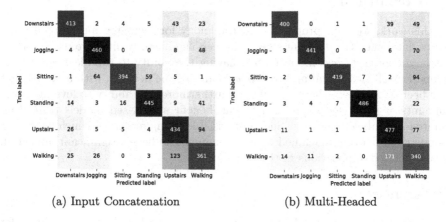

(a) Input Concatenation   (b) Multi-Headed

Fig. 7. The confusion matrices for the Concatenated Input model and the Multihead Model.

is balanced, so the accuracy is reflective of the classifiers' performance. Both architectures struggle to differentiate between some instances of similar activities.

4   Discussion

This work focuses on wearable sensors because of the heterogeneous nature of the signals. A breath flow sensor is much more dissimilar from an ECG signal than the RGB channels of an image. This means that apnea and activity detection can benefit from selecting the information-dense channels and either discarding the others or using ML techniques such as attention to minimize the weights of low-value channels. But this observation is not limited to these specific problem spaces. The methods described in this work could also be applied to other varieties of time-series data with non-uniformly informative channels.

Some degree of domain expertise is still essential when selecting channels of data for training. Ideally, an ML approach to data analysis should rely as little as possible on human expertise. It is challenging to assess which sensors should be useful for solving a given problem without understanding the physical properties of those sensors. One observation of this work has been that the information density of a signal can be roughly estimated by observing the UMAP projections of the learned representations of the training data. The potential of evaluating the usefulness of a channel without access to labeled data warrants further investigation as being able to reduce the number of channels required by examining the results of a self-supervised model trained only on unlabeled data would be very beneficial. At a minimum, this information could guide more targeted experiments using less of the costly labeled data.

5   Conclusion

In this work, we have proposed a methodology for modeling multimodal time-series data when the different signal channels significantly differ from each other. As larger datasets become available, having the ability to tune learning to the properties of each signal and to replace parts of the network with a model that has been trained elsewhere, is crucial. Furthermore, the ability to leverage large amounts of unlabeled training data can benefit supervised models trained on limited-size labeled datasets. Self-supervised learning methods, which have been popularized in other machine learning domains, can have a significant impact on health-related applications in the near future.

References

1. Allocca, G., et al.: Validation of 'Somnivore', a machine learning algorithm for automated scoring and analysis of polysomnography data. Front. Neurosci. **13**, 207 (2019)
2. Chen, T., Kornblith, S., Norouzi, M., Hinton, G.: A simple framework for contrastive learning of visual representations. In: International Conference on Machine Learning, pp. 1597–1607. PMLR (2020)
3. Choi, S.H., et al.: Real-time apnea-hypopnea event detection during sleep by convolutional neural networks. Comput. Biol. Med. **100**, 123–131 (2018)
4. Ding, L., Peng, J., Song, L., Zhang, X.: Automatically detecting Apnea-Hypopnea snoring signal based on VGG19+ LSTM. Biomed. Sig. Process. Control **80**, 104351 (2023)
5. Dwibedi, D., Aytar, Y., Tompson, J., Sermanet, P., Zisserman, A.: With a little help from my friends: nearest-neighbor contrastive learning of visual representations. In: Proceedings of the IEEE/CVF International Conference on Computer Vision, pp. 9588–9597 (2021)
6. Empatica: E4 wristband user's manual, rev. 2.0. https://empatica.app.box.com/v/E4-User-Manual (2020). Accessed 09 Jun 2022
7. Hinkle, L.B., Atkinson, G., Metsis, V.: TWristAR - wristband activity recognition, January 2022, Online. https://doi.org/10.5281/zenodo.5911808
8. Hinkle, L.B., Metsis, V.: Model evaluation approaches for human activity recognition from time-series data. In: Tucker, A., Henriques Abreu, P., Cardoso, J., Pereira Rodrigues, P., Riaño, D. (eds.) AIME 2021. LNCS (LNAI), vol. 12721, pp. 209–215. Springer, Cham (2021). https://doi.org/10.1007/978-3-030-77211-6_23

9. Hinkle, L.B., Metsis, V.: Unlabeled Empatica E4 Wristband Data (UE4W) Dataset, July 2022, Online. https://doi.org/10.5281/zenodo.6898244

10. Kokkalas, L., Korompili, G., Tatlas, N.A., Mitilineos, S.A., Potirakis, S.M.: Severe obstructive sleep apnea event detection from EEG recordings. In: Presented at 2nd International Electronic Conference on Applied Sciences, vol. 15, p. 31 (2021)

11. Korompili, G., et al.: PSG-audio, a scored polysomnography dataset with simultaneous audio recordings for sleep apnea studies. Sci. Data 8(1), 1–13 (2021)

12. Korompili, G., et al.: PSG-Audio, March 2022. https://doi.org/10.11922/sciencedb.00345

13. Lahat, D., Adali, T., Jutten, C.: Multimodal data fusion: an overview of methods, challenges, and prospects. Proc. IEEE 103(9), 1449–1477 (2015)

14. Levy, P., Pépin, J.L., Deschaux-Blanc, C., Paramelle, B., Brambilla, C.: Accuracy of oximetry for detection of respiratory disturbances in sleep apnea syndrome. Chest 109(2), 395–399 (1996)

15. McInnes, L., Healy, J., Melville, J.: UMAP: uniform manifold approximation and projection for dimension reduction. arXiv preprint arXiv:1802.03426 (2018)

16. Mohsenvand, M.N., Izadi, M.R., Maes, P.: Contrastive representation learning for electroencephalogram classification. In: Machine Learning for Health, pp. 238–253. PMLR (2020)

17. Mondal, A., Jain, V., Siddiqi, K.: Mini-batch similarity graphs for robust image classification (2012)

18. Pedregosa, F., et al.: Scikit-learn: machine learning in Python. J. Mach. Learn. Res. 12, 2825–2830 (2011)

19. Piorecky, M., et al.: Apnea detection in polysomnographic recordings using machine learning techniques. Diagnostics 11(12), 2302 (2021)

20. Qian, H., Tian, T., Miao, C.: What makes good contrastive learning on small-scale wearable-based tasks? arXiv preprint arXiv:2202.05998 (2022)

21. Sleeman IV, W.C., Kapoor, R., Ghosh, P.: Multimodal classification: current landscape, taxonomy and future directions. arXiv preprint arXiv:2109.09020 (2021)

22. Xu, H., Zhou, P., Tan, R., Li, M., Shen, G.: LIMU-BERT: unleashing the potential of unlabeled data for IMU sensing applications. In: Proceedings of the 19th ACM Conference on Embedded Networked Sensor Systems, pp. 220–233 (2021)

23. Zhao, A., Dong, J., Zhou, H.: Self-supervised learning from multi-sensor data for sleep recognition. IEEE Access 8, 93907–93921 (2020)

24. Zinchuk, A.V., et al.: Polysomnographic phenotypes and their cardiovascular implications in obstructive sleep apnoea. Thorax 73(5), 472–480 (2018)

Hyperspectral Classification of Recyclable Plastics in Industrial Setups

Georgios Alexakis and Michail Maniadakis[✉]

Foundation for Research and Technology Hellas, Heraklion, Crete, Greece
{geosalexs,mmaniada}@ics.forth.gr

Abstract. The development of the circular economy has attracted significant research interest in recent years. The present work explores the use of HyperSpectral Imaging (HSI) sensors and Machine Learning (ML) techniques for the categorization of recyclable plastics in challenging industrial conditions. Specifically, we present the pipeline for the pre- and post- processing of the spectral signals and we compare four well-known classifiers in categorizing plastics into seven material types, according to the international standards of the circular economy and material recycling in particular. The obtained results show that hyperspectral technology can contribute to the successful categorization of plastics in industrial conditions.

Keywords: Hyperspectral Imaging · Machine Learning · Classifier · Industrial Application · Material Recovery

1 Introduction

Waste management is a significant global issue which we hope to successfully address by following the circular economy model. Essentially, the recycling of materials is where the loop is closed for circular waste management. The sorting of post-consumer waste in different material types is a complicated and expensive task that, to date, has been mostly done manually. However, in recent years there have been several activities focused on automating the treatment of recyclables for material recovery, which leverage recent advances in artificial intelligence and robotics [1,7,9,10].

Interestingly, the classification of recyclables into different material types can be significantly enhanced by HyperSpectral Imaging (HSI) sensors that collect a whole spectrum at each individual pixel of an image [4,8]. Hyperspectral cameras have the ability to collect data outside the human "visible spectrum" which

This work is co-financed by the European Union's Horizon Europe Research and Innovation program under project RECLAIM GA: 101070524, and additionally by the European Union and national resources of Greece and Cyprus within the framework of the INTERREG V-A Cooperation Program "Greece - Cyprus" 2014–2020, project InterRecycle MIS: 5047863.

© IFIP International Federation for Information Processing 2023
Published by Springer Nature Switzerland AG 2023
I. Maglogiannis et al. (Eds.): AIAI 2023, IFIP AICT 675, pp. 416–428, 2023.
https://doi.org/10.1007/978-3-031-34111-3_35

greatly enhances our observation capacity. Especially, when it comes to the classification of recyclables, HSI enables the direct identification of the material from which each package is made.

While very different recyclable materials, for example paper and aluminum, have distinct "spectral signatures" (i.e. the variation of reflectance of a material with respect to wavelengths) which facilitates sorting. However, when we turn to plastics, things are much more complicated [3], because plastics share common material characteristics which makes their spectral signatures similar, and thus the distinction between them is very challenging. Nevertheless, recycling applications assume the classification of plastics into 7 sub-categories namely Polyethylene Terephthalate (PET), High Density Polyethylene (HDPE), Polyvinyl Chloride (PVC), Low Density Polyethylene (LDPE), Polypropylene (PP), Polystyrene (PS), and Others.

Recent works have investigated the combined use of hyperspectral imaging and Artificial Intelligence to categorize plastics in controlled laboratory environments [3,4,8]. The present study explores the applicability of hyperspectral imaging in a real material recovery facility which can be largely affected by weather conditions and humidity, while at the same time, plastic recyclables suffer from uncontrolled dirt. In particular, we compare four well-known supervised classification algorithms in identifying and classifying plastics in waste streams. The obtained results verify the applicability and the potential of hyperspectral imaging for sorting recyclable plastics in real world industrial applications. From a methodological perspective the current work highlights the importance of pre- and post- processing steps that are essential to reveal the value of spectral data and make them useful in for industrial applications.

By moving hyperspectral imaging to the particularly challenging domain of recyclable categorization the present work aims to provide valuable guidelines that facilitate the wider use of hyperspectral imaging in a range of different industrial applications.

2   Experimental Setup

A key objective of the present study is the development of a hyperspectral imaging approach for plastics classification, which would be applicable in real material recovery facilities. To meet this requirement, we exploit the industrial research setup that is available at the Heraklion MRF on the island of Crete, Greece. This setup is open on two opposite sides and therefore 24/7 connected to the open space, which means our approach has to deal with significant fluctuations in air-humidity and dirt, which is known that both affect hyperspectral imaging.

The experimental configuration used in the present study consists of three main parts (see Fig. 1). The first is the hyperspectral camera and the illumination unit, as the sensing part of the equipment. The second is the conveyor belt, that carries recyclable materials for sorting (the current work focuses on plastics). The last part is the computer that actually processes the acquired hyperspectral data to classify the observed objects in different material types.

The hyperspectral imaging camera is a Specim FX17e which has been installed 1.2 m above the conveyor belt. The camera is in fact a line scanner that scans vertically to the flow of the belt. An industrial 80 cm wide conveyor belt is used to transfer recyclables at a constant speed, which in our case is set to 35 cm/s. The illumination unit consists of 4 × 500 W Quartz, 8550 Lumens halogen lamps that are positioned 40 cm above the conveyor belt with 45° inclination, so that the acquired data is minimally affected by the variations of ambient light. We use an industrial fan-less PC that can safely operate in humid and dirty environments. The processing of the hyperspectral data is summarized below.

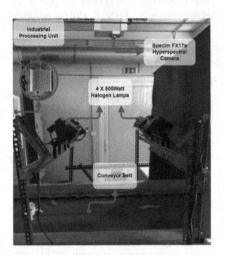 

Fig. 1. Overview of the experimental setup

3   Hyperspectral Processing Pipeline

Given that the implemented system is applied in industrial conditions, it is crucial to enhance its robustness against potential variations in the operating environment, such as ambient lighting, air humidity, dust/dirt and other parameters that cannot be fully controlled. Similar to previous works [6], we have implemented a pipeline for processing hyperspectral images that consists of seven steps, as illustrated in Fig. 2. The implementation of the relevant modules is summarised in the following sections.

3.1   Image Acquisition

We use a hyperspectral line scanner that captures 640 pixels per line. Each pixel consists of 224 spectral bands with a 12 bit representation, which spans

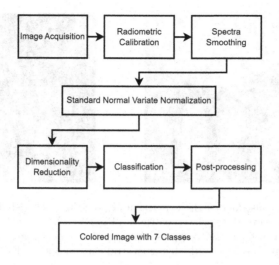

Fig. 2. HSI Pipeline

between 900–1700 nm. Therefore, in analogy to standard RGB cameras where each pixel is represented by 3 values, in the hyperspectral camera case each pixel is represented by 224 values.

The camera's frame rate and exposure time have been experimentally set to 190 fps and 4 ms respectively, following a trial and error procedure which aimed to minimize the visually observed noise in the collected data.

During operation, line scans are processed in batches. Typically, we capture 1000 lines to construct a hyperspectral cube consisting of (1000 lines) × (640 pixels) × (224 bands), that is used for material detection, localization and categorization. Early visualization of the recorded data can be achieved by following a pseudo-coloring approach that uses 3 bands (out of the 224 recorded) to construct and visualise an ordinary RGB image, as shown in Fig. 3.

3.2 Radiometric Calibration

After the acquisition of raw image data, radiometric calibration is essential to ensure the accuracy and repeatability of the data provided by the hyperspectral camera. Relative radiometric calibration is adopted in the present work which means that the output of the sensor is normalized in relation to a reference frame so that a uniform response is obtained for the subsequent frames [5]. Typically, the performance of a hyperspectral camera is characterized by the white and dark frames it captures. These two frames are used as references in radiometric calibration, to enhance the integrity and validity of the obtained data [13,14].

To record the white reference frame, we use a wooden stick wrapped 10 times with white PTFE, which is a handy and low-cost alternative of the spectralon calibration board. The dark frame is obtained by closing the shutter of the

 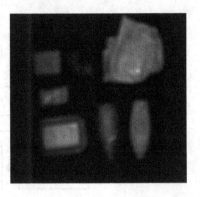

Fig. 3. Indicative snapshot of the experimental procedure. The left image shows the arrangement of 7 recyclables (plastic categories PP, PVC, LDPE, OTHERS, PS, PET, HDPE) using an ordinary RGB representation. The right image shows the pseudo-colored raw image captured by the hyperspectral camera Specim FX17e.

camera. In both cases 100 frames are captured and then the 2D mean frame is calculated by taking, for each spectral band, the mean of the corresponding values in all 100 frames.

Then, at run time, each line scan capturing raw (R) data is normalized against the corresponding spectral band values in the dark (D) and the white (W) reference frames according to the following formula:

$$Refl. = \frac{R - D}{W - D} \qquad (1)$$

which represents the normalised reflectance at the given spectral band.

3.3 Smoothing via Savitzky-Golay Filter

Savitzky-Golay filtering, also called the Digital Smoothing Polynomial (DISPO) filtering, is a smoothing method used to remove noise from a signal [12]. It is a finite impulse response filter that is based on a least squares polynomial fit over a moving window of data. The re-sampling of the fitted polynomial corrects the original recorded data without distorting the information content of the signal.

The Savitzky-Golay filter is frequently used in absorption spectroscopy, [2,11] because it places more emphasis on preserving spectral properties than eliminating noise. In the current work, Savitzky-Golay filtering is used with a moving window of 8 spectral bands and polynomial order 2 to avoid essential information loss. Indicative results of Savitzky-Golay filtering are shown in Fig. 4.

3.4 Standard Normal Variate (SNV)

The Standard Normal Variate (SNV) normalization aims at eliminating the effect that environmental conditions may have on data collection, and thus to make all

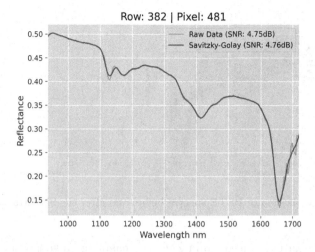

Fig. 4. Smoothing via Savitzky-Golay filter to PETE spectrum (raw data with red and Savitzky-Golay filtered data with blue) (Color figure online)

gathered spectra more comparable. This is achieved by subtracting each spectrum by its own mean and dividing it by its own standard deviation. After this transformation, every spectrum will have 0 mean, and 1 standard deviation.

In detail, the SNV is implemented by the following equation, where $y_{i,j}$ are the calibrated pixel elements, i represents the pixel, j represents the spectral bands, y_i is the mean value of the spectral signature of the pixel i, and n is the number of spectral bands:

$$SNV_{i,j} = \frac{y_{i,j} - y_i}{\sqrt{\sum_{j=1}^{n} \frac{(y_{i,j}-y_i)^2}{n-1}}} \tag{2}$$

SNV is necessary for the correction of the spectra due to light scattering, changes in surface roughness and other environment disturbances. As shown in Fig. 5, SNV normalization can crucially facilitate spectrum comparison and the development of spectrum classifiers.

3.5 Dimensionality Reduction

We use Principal Component Analysis (PCA) to reduce the dimension of the 224 measurements included in each hyperspectral observation, while preserving the maximum amount of the information encoded in the recorded spectrum. In short, PCA aims to reduce the size of a dataset through a linear transformation that approximately describes the original data with fewer dimensions, with the algorithm focused on minimizing the loss of information.

In this paper PCA is used to project the recordings obtained in 224 spectral bands onto only the first 4 principal components that can sufficiently preserve most of the data's variation. In that way, the dimension of the hyperspectral

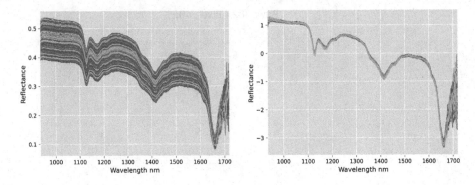

Fig. 5. Normalization of PETE spectra before and after the SNV transformation.

data is significantly reduced (from 224 to 4) enabling all subsequent processing steps to be implemented more efficiently and in less time.

3.6   Classification

To enable the identification of objects and their categorization to one of the available material types, we examine four different supervised classification methods, applied to categorize separately each pixel of the hyperspectral image. The classification methods considered in the present work are summarized below.

Support Vector Machines (SVM). The objective of the SVM algorithm is to find a hyperplane in the N-dimensional space (N is the number of input features) that distinctly classifies the data points. The SVM marks every training data as belonging to one side of the Hyperplane. Therefore, SVM operates as a binary classification method. For multi-class classification, the same principle is used by dividing the multi-class problem into multiple binary problems.

The current work uses the Radial Basis kernel function which is very common in spectral imaging due to its ability to ignore outliers. The algorithm is applied with a dynamic "gamma" which controls the effect of samples near the separation line and a relatively high "penalty" parameter value which enforces the correction of mis-classified pixels.

Random Forest (RF). Random Forest is another supervised machine learning method that is used in classification problems. RF builds inference mechanisms by constructing a multitude of decision trees. During training, the decision tree grows incrementally using randomly selected subspaces of data to improve decision accuracy.

The RF approach aggregates the results of the individual decision trees through a voting mechanism to provide a single output. In that way RF can effectively tackle the well known over-fitting problem of decision trees. In the current work we use forests populated with 10 decision trees each one having a maximum depth of 60. This configuration seems to balance effectively between training speed and high classification accuracy.

K-Nearest Neighbors (KNN). This is a relatively simple, instance-based supervised learning algorithm that is very popular in tackling classification problems. According to the KNN algorithm a new data point is assigned to the most common class among its nearest neighbors, where k refers to the number of nearest neighbours to include in the majority voting process.

The KNN algorithm has been extensively used in classification problems due to its simplicity and ability to work with multi-class problems dealing with both linear and non-linear data. Still, it is computationally expensive to find the k nearest neighbours for new samples and this can affect the use of KNN in hyperspectral imaging applications where the number of pixels (data samples) is very high. In the current work we have used neighborhoods of $k = 3$ neighbors.

Multi-layer Perceptron Classifier (MLP). The Multi-layer Perceptron is a well-known feedforward artificial neural network that uses layers of interconnected neurons to transform inputs to targeted values. Each neuron transforms the outputs of the preceding layer using a non-linear activation function, such as the sigmoid function or the rectified linear unit (ReLU) function. The functionality of the network is tuned using the so called "back-propagation" gradient descent optimization algorithm, which aims to adapt neuron parameters and interconnection weights across layers, in the direction that minimizes the output error in relation to a targeted value. In the present work, we develop an MLP classifier with 3 layers of neurons consisting respectively of 150, 100, 50 neurons that use the ReLU function.

3.7 Post-processing

The output of the classifiers is used to construct a 2D image, where each material type is visualized with a different color. In this image, several outlier pixels appear as noise which should be cleared out. This is accomplished by implementing a binary image separately for each examined material type (i.e. different colour). Then, connected component analysis is performed to find sufficiently large regions that correspond to the examined material. Regions below 1000 pixels are omitted. Finally, the morphological operations of the dilation and erosion are applied for hole filling and region smoothing. After applying the above steps separately for each examined material, the obtained images are united back into the composite image that is recolored using the original, material specific color map.

4 Experimental Results

The data acquisition process took place in the industrial material recovery facility of Heraklion, Crete, Greece, using real recyclables, which were dirty and deformed. On a daily basis, prior to the recording of data, dark and white reference images were acquired, which have been used for radiometric calibration to compensate for environmental variations (see Sect. 3.2).

The dataset captured is associated with all seven plastics categories considered in recycling (PET, HDPE, PVC, LDPE, PP, PS, Others) plus the belt background. Multiple objects for each material type have been used for data acquisition. As mentioned earlier, all captured images consist of 1000 lines, 640 pixels per line, and 224 spectral bands per pixel. The data samples to be processed are collected as individual pixels in the form of a 224-values vector, which are manually associated to the targeted material type represented as a scalar with 8 available options (7 types of plastics + background). In particular, the composition of the dataset is as follows, 6814 pixels for Background, 4507 for PET, 4752 for HDPE, 3337 for PVC, 4224 for LDPE, 4510 for PP, 3852 for PS and 2416 for Others. Following the approach proposed in the current work, all captured pixels are examined one-by-one to be classified into one of the 8 available options.

To minimize execution time, Radiometric Calibration, Spectra Smoothing and Standard Normal Variate normalization are applied per line in parallel running threads. Then, PCA implements dimensionality reduction to compress the initial 224-long vectors to much smaller four-values long vectors that are used as input to the classifiers.

The input-output pairs are randomly divided into two separate sets to be used for the training (70% of samples) and the testing (30% of samples) of the four classifiers discussed above. To facilitate comparisons, all classifiers are optimized and assessed with the same training and testing dataset.

After training, the classifiers are used to separately classify each pixel of the test set. The obtained results are summarised in Table 1, which shows the scores of the algorithms in terms of classification accuracy and the processing time for the whole test set. MLP and SVM have the highest accuracy, as well as the lowest execution times. The Random Forest classifier has the worst results in terms of both the classification accuracy and execution time. Clearly our results do not favour the applicability of HSI in real time applications, since the minimum processing time achieved was 3 s. However, minimizing processing time was not a priority for the current work and there is likely room for further improvement (e.g. by adopting GPU processing).

Table 1. Accuracy of the classifiers on the testing dataset.

Algorithm	Accuracy	Execution Time
SVM	98.05%	3 s
RF	93.16%	54 s
KNN	97.55%	22 s
MLP	99.50%	7 s

Furthermore, we assess the performance of the classifiers in real-world previously unseen images. The classifiers are again applied pixel-wise, and the output is reconstructed as a 2D image to facilitate visual inspection. To estimate classification accuracy we contrast the result of each classifier with the ground truth image. The obtained results are visually illustrated in Fig. 6. We can easily see that the pixels of the different objects are mostly successfully categorized, with the exception of some edges, which are miss-categorized because of the 3D shape of the objects, which affects light reflectance at the border of the objects.

To improve the classification accuracy, the post-processing steps summarized in Sect. 3.7 are applied on each one of the images shown in Fig. 6. To quantify the improvement accomplished by post-processing, we contrast the accuracy of the result in relation to the ground-truth, before and after post-processing. We consider the commonly used Peak Signal-to-Noise Ratio (PSNR), which quantifies the similarity between the targeted and the actually obtained image. The comparative results are summarised in Table 2. Even if the quantitative comparison do not show drastic improvements in terms of accuracy and PSNR, this is mainly because post-processing is focused on local scale corrections.

Table 2. The pixel-wise classification accuracy and PSNR for the whole image, "before" and "after" post-processing, in relation to the ground-truth data.

Classifier	Before Post-Processing		After Post-Processing	
	Accuracy	PSNR	Accuracy	PSNR
SVM	95.62%	41.39 dB	95.83%	41.98 dB
RF	95.05%	40.25 dB	95.27%	40.94 dB
KNN	95.65%	40.81 dB	95.86%	41.22 dB
MLP	95.33%	41.12 dB	95.72%	41.89 dB

Finally, the current work assumes that the recyclables are spread out on the conveyor belt with minimum overlap, so when two (non-background) materials touch each other with an edge that is longer than the 1/3 of the perimeter of the object, they are consolidated into one object with its material determined by the type of the largest area. This facilitates correct identification and masking of all objects (due to space limitations this is not visualized, as we preferred to dedicate the space to the intermediate steps).

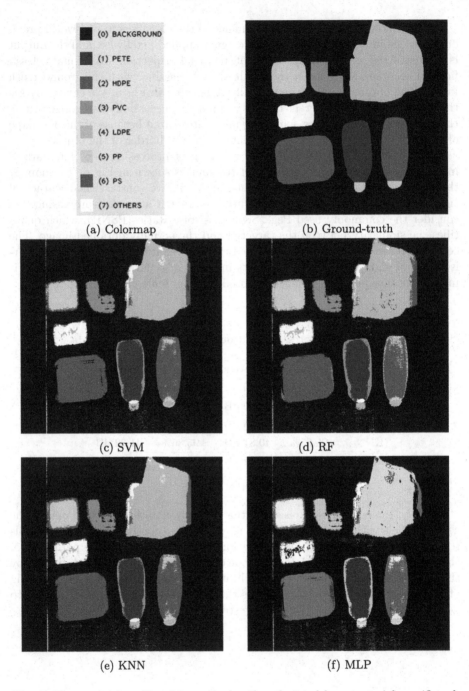

(a) Colormap

(b) Ground-truth

(c) SVM

(d) RF

(e) KNN

(f) MLP

Fig. 6. The material predicted by each classifier, depicted by a material-specific colormap.

5   Conclusions

The current work investigates the applicability of hyperspectral imaging in industrial application and specifically in the challenging environment of recyclable material recovery. We compare four well-known classifiers in sorting plastic packages to the categories officially used in waste recycling. The obtained results demonstrate the high potential of hyperspectral imaging in the given application domain.

Our ongoing work focuses on the integration of the developed technology with the robotic system already installed at the material recovery facility, which will enable the full-day assessment of the composite system.

References

1. Bashkirova, D., et al.: ZeroWaste dataset: towards deformable object segmentation in cluttered scenes. In: Proceedings of the IEEE/CVF Conference on Computer Vision and Pattern Recognition, pp. 21147–21157 (2022)
2. Beitollahi, M., Hosseini, S.A.: Using Savitsky-Golay smoothing filter in hyperspectral data compression by curve fitting. In: Iranian Conference on Electrical Engineering (ICEE), pp. 452–457 (2018). https://doi.org/10.1109/ICEE.2018.8472702
3. Capobianco, G., Bonifazi, G., Serranti, S., Palmieri, R.: Hyperspectral imaging applied to the waste recycling sector. Spectro. Eur. **31**, 8–11 (2019)
4. Henriksen, M.L., Karlsen, C.B., Klarskov, P., Hinge, M.: Plastic classification via in-line hyperspectral camera analysis and unsupervised machine learning. Vib. Spectrosc. **118**, 103329 (2022)
5. Honkavaara, E., et al.: Digital airborne photogrammetry-a new tool for quantitative remote sensing?-A state-of-the-art review on radiometric aspects of digital photogrammetric images. Remote Sens. **1**(3), 577–605 (2009)
6. Karaca, A.C., Ertürk, A., Güllü, M.K., Elmas, M., Ertürk, S.: Automatic waste sorting using shortwave infrared hyperspectral imaging system. In: 2013 5th Workshop on Hyperspectral Image and Signal Processing: Evolution in Remote Sensing (WHISPERS), pp. 1–4 (2013). https://doi.org/10.1109/WHISPERS.2013.8080744
7. Koskinopoulou, M., Raptopoulos, F., Papadopoulos, G., Mavrakis, N., Maniadakis, M.: Robotic waste sorting technology: toward a vision-based categorization system for the industrial robotic separation of recyclable waste. IEEE Robot. Autom. Mag. **28**(2), 50–60 (2021). https://doi.org/10.1109/MRA.2021.3066040
8. Kraśniewski, J., Dąbała, Ł., Lewandowski, M.: Hyperspectral imaging for analysis and classification of plastic waste. In: 2020 25th International Conference on Pattern Recognition (ICPR), pp. 4805–4812 (2021). https://doi.org/10.1109/ICPR48806.2021.9412737
9. Leveziel, M., Laurent, G.J., Haouas, W., Gauthier, M., Dahmouche, R.: A 4-DoF parallel robot with a built-in gripper for waste sorting. IEEE Robot. Autom. Lett. **7**(4), 9834–9841 (2022)
10. Raptopoulos, F., Koskinopoulou, M., Maniadakis, M.: Robotic pick-and-toss facilitates urban waste sorting. In: 2020 IEEE 16th International Conference on Automation Science and Engineering (CASE), pp. 1149–1154 (2020). https://doi.org/10.1109/CASE48305.2020.9216746

11. Ruffin, C., King, R.: The analysis of hyperspectral data using Savitzky-Golay filtering-theoretical basis. 1, vol. 2, pp. 756–758, February 1999. https://doi.org/10.1109/IGARSS.1999.774430
12. Savitzky, A., Golay, M.J.E.: Smoothing and differentiation of data by simplified least squares procedures. Anal. Chem. **36**(8), 1627–1639 (1964). https://doi.org/10.1021/ac60214a047
13. Shaikh, M.S., Jaferzadeh, K., Thörnberg, B., Casselgren, J.: Calibration of a hyperspectral imaging system using a low-cost reference. Sensors **21**(11), 3738 (2021)
14. Shuqiang, L., Huang, C., Hou, M.: Reflectance reconstruction of hyperspectral image based on gaussian surface fitting. In: International Archives of the Photogrammetry, Remote Sensing and Spatial Information Sciences (ISPRS), pp. 1365–1369, August 2020

Mining the Discussion of Monkeypox Misinformation on Twitter Using RoBERTa

Or Elroy[1] , Dmitry Erokhin[2] , Nadejda Komendantova[2] ,
and Abraham Yosipof[1(✉)]

[1] Faculty of Information Systems and Computer Science, College of Law and Business,
Ramat-Gan, Israel
aviyo@clb.ac.il
[2] International Institute for Applied Systems Analysis, Laxenburg, Austria

Abstract. The monkeypox outbreak in 2022 raised uncertainty leading to misinformation and conspiracy narratives in social media. The belief in misinformation leads to poor judgment, decision making, and even to unnecessary loss of life. The ability of misinformation to spread through social media may worsen the harms of different emergencies, and fighting it is therefore critical.

In this work, we analyzed the discussion of misinformation related to monkeypox on Twitter by training different classifiers that differentiate between tweets that spread and tweets that counter misinformation.

We collected over 1.4M tweets related to the discussion of monkeypox on Twitter from over 500K users and calculated word and sentence embeddings using Natural Language Processing (NLP) methods. We trained multiple machine learning classification models and fine-tuned a Robustly Optimized BERT Pretraining Approach (RoBERTa) model on a set of 3K hand-labeled tweets. We found that the fine-tuned RoBERTa model provided superior results and used it to classify the complete dataset into three categories, namely misinformation, counter misinformation and neutral.

We analyzed the behavioral patterns and domains that were used in misinformation and counter misinformation tweets. The findings provide insights into the scale of misinformation within the discussion on monkeypox and the behavior of tweets and users that spread and counter misinformation over time. In addition, the findings allow us to derive policy recommendations to address misinformation in social media.

Keywords: Misinformation · Monkeypox · Classification · RoBERTa · NLP

1 Introduction

The worldwide outbreak of the monkeypox virus in 2022 was declared a global health emergency by the World Health Organization (WHO) [1]. Social media platforms are a primary source of information at times of emergency. The outbreak of the monkeypox virus is accompanied by the spread of misinformation and conspiracy theories on social

© IFIP International Federation for Information Processing 2023
Published by Springer Nature Switzerland AG 2023
I. Maglogiannis et al. (Eds.): AIAI 2023, IFIP AICT 675, pp. 429–438, 2023.
https://doi.org/10.1007/978-3-031-34111-3_36

media platforms, similarly to the COVID-19 pandemic. Twitter is one of the largest and most prominent social networks today and is therefore a fertile ground for the growth and distribution of misinformation and conspiracy theories.

Misinformation is false or inaccurate information according to the best factual evidence that is available at a given point in time, regardless of an intention to mislead or deceive [2]. Misinformation and conspiracy theories offer people with explanations and a sense of control over a situation of uncertainty [3]. A conspiracy theory is misinformation according to which a group of people are secretly trying to cause harm or achieve something, when other explanations are more probable. A conspiracy theory typically opposes the consensus among qualified professionals.

Misinformation is spread by way of rumors, conspiracy theories, fake news, and fear mongering, and can significantly affect what people perceive as a risk, and how they believe they should react to it [4]. The ability of misinformation to spread globally and easily through social media raises the risk of worsening the harms of different types of emergency situations [5–8].

The belief in conspiracy theories is motivated by a humane need to rationalize events. The lack of authoritative sources with reliable information regarding the outbreak of the virus, combined with circumstantial evidence, fosters uncertainty and thus misinformation and conspiracy narratives [9, 10]. Believing in misinformation and conspiracy theories led to the unnecessary loss of life during the COVID-19 pandemic. Hence, fighting the spread of misinformation and conspiracy theories, and countering it with reliable information, is critical.

In attempt to fight misinformation, the WHO advised for the monitoring of the public's sentiment and the timely addressing of misinformation using health information that avoids stigmatization of certain groups [11]. Twitter adopted strict policy towards misinformation during the COVID-19 pandemic, though the number of tweets and accounts removed, as reported by Twitter, is negligible.

Analyzing the discussion on monkeypox during the recent outbreak supports the effort to control and manage the spread of misinformation and conspiracy theories on social media. However, such an analysis presents several challenges, including the collection of enough relevant data, and the development of a classifier for automated detection of tweets that spread and counter misinformation or conspiracy theories. Finally, an analysis of the classified tweets is needed to gain knowledge and insights on how to better fight misinformation and conspiratory narratives.

The objective of this study is to analyze the discussion related to monkeypox on Twitter and differentiate between tweets that spread and counter misinformation. Understanding the evolvement and behavior of misinformation on social media enables a better and faster reaction to misinformation and conspiracy theories in the future. This study achieves a better understanding of the life cycle of misinformation and conspiracy theories using Natural Language Processing (NLP) and inspection of behavioral patterns.

We address these challenges and make the following contributions. We collected 1,440,475 tweets that are relevant to the discussion on monkeypox from 505,163 users on Twitter. We manually labeled 3,218 tweets into three categories, namely misinformation, counter misinformation, and neutral. We fine-tuned a Robustly Optimized Bidirectional Encoder Representations from Transformers Pretraining Approach (RoBERTa) model for the classification task and compared its performance to several other machine learning classifiers. We analyzed the classified dataset to find and compare behavioral patterns in the data. Finally, we offer policy suggestions to reduce unwanted behavior of misinformation and conspiracy spreading, and support wanted behavior that counters misinformation and conspiratory narratives.

This study is structured as follows. The second section presents previous related works that used NLP to analyze misinformation and conspiracy theories using different methodologies and approaches. The third section presents the dataset that was collected and preprocessed. The fourth section discusses the classification process, the models that were compared and their performance. The fifth section presents the analysis results. The last section discusses the conclusion of this study and future work.

2 Related Work

Analyses of misinformation and conspiracy theories have compared between different conspiracy theories [4] and analyzed the behavior of different groups within the same conspiracy [3]. Erokhin et al. [4] analyzed COVID-19 conspiracy theories to identify patterns and categorize them into groups. Batzdorfer et al. [3] investigated the dynamics of tweets that discuss COVID-19 conspiracy theories, by comparing tweets from a group of users that talked about conspiracy theories and a group of users that participated in the general discussion on the virus.

A key task in analyzing tweets related to conspiracy theories or misinformation is to label and classify the tweets. A set of embeddings and labels are needed for the training of a classifier.

BERT, a Bidirectional Encoder Representations from Transformers [12], provides superior results for different NLP tasks including word embedding [13, 14]. Multiple variations of BERT with different strengths and weaknesses are available for a variety of tasks. RoBERTa was pretrained using different design decisions than BERT that improve the performance and state of the art results on different datasets [15]. Previous studies evaluated the performance of RoBERTa and found that it provides better results than BERT [16–18]. Certain models were pretrained on domain specific data to provide better embeddings [19].

Micallef et al. [20] used BERT embeddings to investigate and counter misinformation in tweets related to COVID-19 over a period of five months. Elroy and Yosipof [21] transformed BERT word embeddings to sentence embedding using Sentence-BERT [22] to train a classifier and classify a dataset of over 300K COVID-19 5G conspiracy theory related tweets.

The metadata and characteristics of tweets and their authors are useful to achieve a better understanding of behavioral patterns. Beskow and Carley [23] used the number of users that follow the author and the number of users the author follows as an indication of whether the author is a robot or not. O'Donovan et al. [24] and Gupta et al. [25] found that metadata of tweets, such as URLs, mentions, retweets and tweet length may serve as indicators for credibility. Elroy and Yosipof [21] found that certain features such as the presence of a URL and the sentiment score of a tweet, can help identify conspirative tweets.

3 Dataset

We collected a dataset of tweets using Twitter's academic research API, which enables access to the full archive of Twitter. The search query includes all tweets in English that contain the term "monkeypox" between May 1, 2022 and August 24, 2022, and excludes retweets. The query is simple yet very effective in filtering tweets related to the discussion on monkeypox, and the very wide search query enables us to collect a large amount of data without much noise.

We applied a preprocessing methodology similar to [26]. For performance optimization, we limited the dataset to tweets that were 350 characters or shorter after preprocessing. After preprocessing, the final dataset consists of 1,440,475 tweets related to discussion on monkeypox that were posted by 505,163 users.

In order to train a classifier to classify the full dataset into three categories, namely misinformation, counter-misinformation, and neutral, we hand-labeled 3,218 tweets based on and according to facts provided by the World Health Organization [1]. Table 1 presents the number and examples of tweets in each category.

Table 1. Number and examples of tweets in each category.

Category	# of Tweets	Example Tweets
Misinformation	1,090	*"The monkeypox travel with Pfizer vaccines. It can cover big distances quickly. Stop the vaccine traveling and that will stop the "monkeypox" virus also..."*
Counter misinformation	739	*"Monkeypox is a potentially serious disease caused by infection with the monkeypox virus. Anyone can get monkeypox and it's important for everyone to take precautions to stop the spread."*
Neutral	1,389	*"#India confirms Asia's first #monkeypox death."*

4 Classification

To train the machine learning classifiers, we calculated the word embeddings and transformed to sentence embeddings using RoBERTa and Sentence-BERT, respectively, resulting in 768 features for each tweet. We tested the performance of several machine learning classifiers. We trained a Random Forest model (RF) with 1,000 trees, a k-Nearest Neighbors (k-NN) model with 9 nearest neighbors, a Support Vector Machine (SVM) model with a linear kernel and 5,000 max iterations, a Naïve Bayes model, an XGBoost model, and a Voting Ensemble combining all five models. We evaluated the models using stratified 5-fold cross-validation.

We further fine-tuned a RoBERTa model with a classification layer. We evaluated the model with the same stratified 5-fold cross-validation, except that each 20% test was further split to 10% test and 10% validation for the fine-tuning. We fine-tuned the model for 10 epochs with a dropout of 0.2, weight decay of 0.01, learning rate of 2e−5, and batch size of 16. The model converged at epoch 5 with an average validation loss of 0.631 and an average F1 score of 0.77 on the test sets.

Table 2 presents the average F1, precision, and recall scores of each model on the test sets in all five folds. The performance results shows that the fine-tuned RoBERTa model achieves the best results with an average F1 score of 0.767, average precision of 0.774, and an average recall of 0.774. We therefore used the fine-tuned RoBERTa model to classify the unlabeled dataset.

Table 2. Comparison of performance with other models.

Methods	F1	Precision	Recall
Random Forest	0.674 ± 0.018	0.694 ± 0.020	0.678 ± 0.018
k-NN	0.607 ± 0.008	0.622 ± 0.009	0.611 ± 0.009
SVM	0.717 ± 0.014	0.718 ± 0.015	0.717 ± 0.014
Naïve Bayes	0.616 ± 0.009	0.631 ± 0.006	0.620 ± 0.009
XGBoost	0.693 ± 0.022	0.696 ± 0.022	0.694 ± 0.022
Voting Ensemble	0.712 ± 0.012	0.713 ± 0.012	0.712 ± 0.012
RoBERTa	**0.767 ± 0.021**	**0.774 ± 0.015**	**0.774 ± 0.015**

5   Results Analysis and Discussion

We assigned the unlabeled dataset to the RoBERTa model. The results of the classifier can be seen in Table 3. The results show that 180,259 of the tweets spread or support misinformation related to the monkeypox virus, and 152,522 of the tweets counter misinformation related to the monkeypox virus.

The results indicate that 1,107,694, most of tweets, are neutral or irrelevant to the discussion on misinformation. This methodology allows us to quantify the scale of the discussion on misinformation in relation to the general discussion on monkeypox. The results show that only 30% of the tweets discuss misinformation related to the monkeypox virus.

Analyses of the misinformation and counter-misinformation categories indicate that for each tweet that spreads misinformation there are only 0.85 tweets that counter it. For each user that spreads misinformation there are 0.84 users that counter them. However, users that counter the conspiracy theories tweet slightly more per user than users that spread misinformation.

We examined the behavioral patterns in and between the misinformation and counter-misinformation categories. Figure 1 presents the weekly frequency of tweets in each group.

Table 3. The number of tweets and users in each category.

Category	# of Tweets	# of Users	Tweets/User
Spread misinformation	180,259	112,765	1.599
Counter misinformation	152,522	94,748	1.610
Neutral	1,107,694	401,458	2.759

Two major peaks are observed, and are likely related to the epidemiological evolvement of the virus. The first peak is during May 2022, when according to data from the WHO, the number of new cases reported globally started growing exponentially [27]. The second peak of July and August 2022 took place during a peak of new confirmed cases.

Tweets that spread misinformation have dominated the conversation since the beginning of the outbreak. However, a shift in dominance took place at the beginning of the second peak, possibly marking the last cycle of misinformation [21].

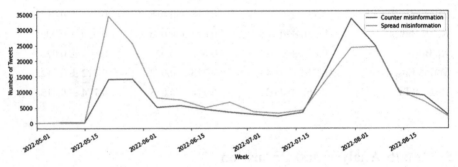

Fig. 1. Weekly frequency time series of tweets spreading misinformation and tweets countering misinformation. The blue line represents the spreading tweets and the red line represents the countering tweets.

We analyzed the users that participated in the conversation over time. Figure 2 presents the number of unique users that participated in the discussion each week, as well as the number of new unique users who participated in the discussion for the first time. The results show that the discussion is mostly driven by users that participate in the discussion for the first time. This behavior indicates that the interest in the discussion on misinformation related to the monkeypox virus is authentic and not artificially created by a small number of users.

To investigate patterns in the behavior of users, we analyzed the domains that were linked in the misinformation and counter-misinformation categories. Domains that do not provide any value to the analysis, such as social media websites and URL-shortening services were ignored.

Both the spreading and countering categories started by referencing news agencies based in the United Kingdom when the outbreak started. The reason for this behavior

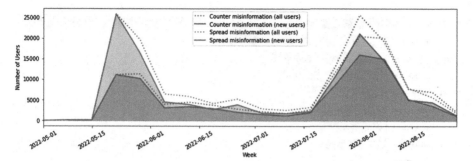

Fig. 2. The weekly number of unique participating users and new unique users.

is likely because the first cases of the outbreak were reported in the United Kingdom and Ireland [27]. The categories have quickly diverged and started referencing different websites from that point onwards.

Figure 3 and Fig. 4 show the top 10 most referenced domains in each category and their percentage in the respective category. The most referenced domains in the category that counters misinformation are of authorities such the U.S. Centers of Disease Control and Prevention (CDC), globally acknowledged entities such as the WHO, and established news agencies such as the NBC and the New York Times (see Fig. 3).

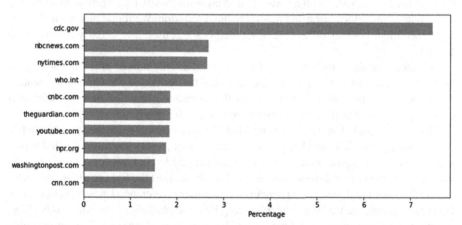

Fig. 3. Top 10 most referenced domains in the counter-misinformation category and their percentage in the category.

On the other hand, the domains referenced in the category that spreads misinformation are mostly of websites that allow users to upload and publish their own content. YouTube leads the list, followed by other platforms that are often associated with extreme free speech and conspiracy theories (see Fig. 4).

These findings are in line with the findings of Micallef et al. [20] that investigated misinformation on COVID-19 and found that YouTube is the most frequently referenced website in both misinformation and counter-misinformation.

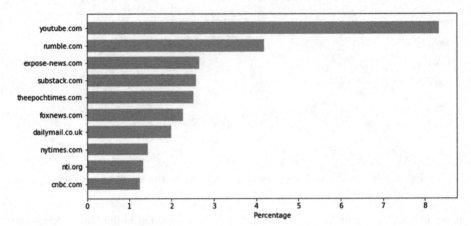

Fig. 4. Top 10 most referenced domains in the misinformation category and their percentage in the category.

6 Conclusion

In this work, we investigated the discussion on misinformation related to monkeypox virus on Twitter. We trained multiple machine learning classification models and fine-tuned a RoBERTa model with a classification layer to classify the tweets as misinformation, counter-misinformation and neutral to the discussion. We found that the RoBERTa fine-tuned model outperformed the other methods and used it to classify the complete dataset.

We analyzed the classified dataset and found that only a third of the tweets related to monkeypox discuss misinformation, whereas two thirds of the tweets are neutral. Analysis of the users that participated in the discussion revealed that the interest is driven by users that participate in the discussion for the first time.

We also found that tweets countering misinformation referenced authoritative sources such as the CDC and WHO more often. As such, it may be recommended to provide more frequent updates on authoritative websites with reliable information for use by the users countering misinformation and indirectly support the fight in misinformation.

On the other hand, tweets that spread misinformation referenced mostly websites that host user content, such as YouTube. Encouraging these platforms to monitor content and adopt stricter community guidelines, would likely reduce the amount of misinformation to be shared. Additionally, it may be recommended to notifying users of social media platforms about the sources of the content and their credibility, to minimize unaware echoing of misinformation.

The data used in this work is limited to the discussion related to monkeypox on Twitter, over a relatively short period, during which the level of uncertainty is unclear and the discussion is still on-going. Future works may make use of data available from other social media platforms and analyze the discussion over a longer period.

Acknowledgements. This research has received funding from the European Union's Horizon 2020 research and innovation program under grant agreement No. 101021746, CORE (science and human factor for resilient society).

References

1. World Health Organization. https://www.who.int/news-room/questions-and-answers/item/monkeypox. Accessed 2 Feb 2023

2. Komendantova, N., et al.: A value-driven approach to addressing misinformation in social media. Human. Soc. Sci. Commun. **8**, 1–12 (2021)

3. Batzdorfer, V., Steinmetz, H., Biella, M., Alizadeh, M.: Conspiracy theories on Twitter: Emerging motifs and temporal dynamics during the COVID-19 pandemic. Int. J. Data Sci. Analyt. 1–19 (2021)

4. Erokhin, D., Yosipof, A., Komendantova, N.: COVID-19 conspiracy theories discussion on Twitter. Soc. Med. Soc. **8**, 20563051221126052 (2022)

5. Peng, Z.: Earthquakes and coronavirus: How to survive an infodemic. Seismol. Res. Lett. **91**, 2441–2443 (2020)

6. Zhou, C., Xiu, H., Wang, Y., Yu, X.: Characterizing the dissemination of misinformation on social media in health emergencies: An empirical study based on COVID-19. Inf. Process. Manage. **58**, 102554 (2021)

7. Kwanda, F.A., Lin, T.T.: Fake news practices in Indonesian newsrooms during and after the Palu earthquake: a hierarchy-of-influences approach. Inf. Commun. Soc. **23**, 849–866 (2020)

8. Peary, B.D., Shaw, R., Takeuchi, Y.: Utilization of social media in the east Japan earthquake and tsunami and its effectiveness. J. Nat. Dis. Sci. **34**, 3–18 (2012)

9. Aschwanden, A., Demir, C., Hinselmann, R., Kasser, S., Rohrer, A.: Zika and travel: Public health implications and communications for blood donors, sperm donors and pregnant women. Travel Med. Infect. Dis. **21**, 77 (2018)

10. Ortiz-Martínez, Y., Garcia-Robledo, J.E., Vásquez-Castañeda, D.L., Bonilla-Aldana, D.K., Rodriguez-Morales, A.J.: Can Google® trends predict COVID-19 incidence and help preparedness? The situation in Colombia. Travel Med. Infect. Dis. **37**, 101703 (2020)

11. World Health Organization. https://www.who.int/emergencies/disease-outbreak-news/item/2022-DON385. Accessed 2 Feb 2023

12. Devlin, J., Chang, M.-W., Lee, K., Toutanova, K.: Bert: Pre-training of deep bidirectional transformers for language understanding. arXiv preprint arXiv:1810.04805 (2018)

13. Piskorski, J., Haneczok, J., Jacquet, G.: New benchmark corpus and models for fine-grained event classification: To BERT or not to BERT? In: Proceedings of the 28th International Conference on Computational Linguistics, pp. 6663–6678 (2020)

14. González-Carvajal, S., Garrido-Merchán, E.C.: Comparing BERT against traditional machine learning text classification. arXiv preprint arXiv:2005.13012 (2020)

15. Liu, Y., et al.: Roberta: A robustly optimized bert pretraining approach. arXiv preprint arXiv:1907.11692 (2019)

16. Adoma, A.F., Henry, N.-M., Chen, W.: Comparative analyses of bert, roberta, distilbert, and xlnet for text-based emotion recognition. In: 2020 17th International Computer Conference on Wavelet Active Media Technology and Information Processing (ICCWAMTIP), pp. 117–121. IEEE (2020)

17. Tarunesh, I., Aditya, S., Choudhury, M.: Trusting roberta over bert: Insights from checklisting the natural language inference task. arXiv preprint arXiv:2107.07229 (2021)

18. Naseer, M., Asvial, M., Sari, R.F.: An empirical comparison of bert, roberta, and electra for fact verification. In: 2021 International Conference on Artificial Intelligence in Information and Communication (ICAIIC), pp. 241–246. IEEE (2021)

19. Müller, M., Salathé, M., Kummervold, P.E.: Covid-twitter-bert: A natural language processing model to analyse covid-19 content on twitter. arXiv preprint arXiv:2005.07503 (2020)

20. Micallef, N., He, B., Kumar, S., Ahamad, M., Memon, N.: The role of the crowd in countering misinformation: A case study of the COVID-19 infodemic. In: 2020 IEEE International Conference on Big Data (Big Data), pp. 748–757. IEEE (2020)

21. Elroy, O., Yosipof, A.: Analysis of COVID-19 5G conspiracy theory tweets using Sentence-BERT embedding. In: Pimenidis, E., Angelov, P., Jayne, C., Papaleonidas, A., Aydin, M. (eds.) Artificial Neural Networks and Machine Learning – ICANN 2022: 31st International Conference on Artificial Neural Networks, Bristol, UK, September 6–9, 2022, Proceedings, Part II, pp. 186–196. Springer Nature Switzerland, Cham (2022). https://doi.org/10.1007/978-3-031-15931-2_16

22. Reimers, N., Gurevych, I.: Sentence-bert: Sentence embeddings using siamese bert-networks. arXiv preprint arXiv:1908.10084 (2019)

23. Beskow, D.M., Carley, K.M.: Bot-hunter: A tiered approach to detecting & characterizing automated activity on twitter. In: Conference paper. SBP-BRiMS: International conference on social computing, behavioral-cultural modeling and prediction and behavior representation in modeling and simulation, p. 3 (2018)

24. ODonovan, J., Kang, B., Meyer, G., Höllerer, T., Adalii, S.: Credibility in context: An analysis of feature distributions in twitter. In: 2012 International Conference on Privacy, Security, Risk and Trust and 2012 International Conference on Social Computing, pp. 293–301. IEEE (2012)

25. Gupta, A., Kumaraguru, P., Castillo, C., Meier, P.: Tweetcred: Real-time credibility assessment of content on twitter. In: Aiello, L.M., McFarland, D. (eds.) SocInfo 2014. LNCS, vol. 8851, pp. 228–243. Springer, Cham (2014). https://doi.org/10.1007/978-3-319-13734-6_16

26. Nguyen, D.Q., Vu, T., Nguyen, A.T.: BERTweet: A pre-trained language model for English Tweets. arXiv preprint arXiv:2005.10200 (2020)

27. World Health Organization. https://www.who.int/emergencies/disease-outbreak-news/item/2022-DON381. Accessed 2 Feb 2023

Multi-feature Transformer for Multiclass Cyberbullying Detection in Bangla

Zaman Wahid[1]([✉]) and Abdullah Al Imran[2]

[1] University of Calgary, Calgary, AB, Canada
zaman.wahid@ucalgary.ca
[2] University of Liverpool, Liverpool, UK
a.al-imran@liverpool.ac.uk

Abstract. Cyberbullying detection is a global issue that must be addressed to improve the cyberspace for millions of online users, services, and organizations. Online harassment of the general public and celebrities is now commonplace on social media, particularly in Bangladesh. In this paper, we present a novel multi-feature transformer followed by a deep neural network for multiple-dimensional cyberbullying detection. Using online Bangla textual data, we introduce the user's social profile, the lexical features, the contextual embedding, and the semantic similarities among word associations in Bangla in order to develop an effective and robust cyberbullying detection system. Our proposed method can detect cyberbullying in Bangla with a 98% detection accuracy for threats and a 90% detection accuracy for sarcastic comments. The aggregate accuracy of all six multiclass labels is 86.3%. In addition, the experimental results find that the proposed technique outperforms the state-of-the-art methods for detecting cyberbully in Bangla.

Keywords: Cyberbullying Detection from Text · Online Harassment Detection in Bangla · Natural Language Processing

1 Introduction

In the context of social media in Bangladesh, cyberbullying has become a daily occurrence for individuals and celebrities. Women are more vulnerable to cyberbullying, which can be motivated by body shaming, sexuality, religious fanaticism, and other factors. While it may seem typical to experience smaller impacts on a daily basis, the repercussions for those who do so routinely are dangerous. Despite Bangladesh's claims to be a digitally advanced nation, it is cautioned in recent national news [26] that there are increasingly more instances of cyberbullying nowadays. Defamation and victim shaming are the two most common

---

Z. Wahid and A. Al Imran—Both authors contributed to this work equally.

© IFIP International Federation for Information Processing 2023
Published by Springer Nature Switzerland AG 2023
I. Maglogiannis et al. (Eds.): AIAI 2023, IFIP AICT 675, pp. 439–451, 2023.
https://doi.org/10.1007/978-3-031-34111-3_37

forms of cyberbullying. The connection between a close-knit communal culture and anonymous harassment, as well as the lack of victim support infrastructure, are two of the most important factors for the increasing prevalence of cyberbullying in Bangladesh [23]. Computer-based Artificial Intelligence (AI) systems to aid in the identification of these potential cyberbullying activities have become essential, as it is nearly impossible to detect cyberbullying and take appropriate action using manual labor, especially given the massive volume of cyberspace and social network profiles in Bangladesh. Policymakers, scientists, social activists-even social media-based companies offering a variety of services in Bangla-are realizing and adapting to AI technologies that can combat online abuse in Bangla and identify simple countermeasures. In recent years, machine learning-based solutions have exhibited promising results in detecting online rumors and fake news [4,33], sexual predators [34], assessing trustworthiness [19], etc. However, Bangla is a low-resource language, which increases the difficulty of dealing with Bangla textual data and developing machine learning models in general [29]. While there has been recent research on online harassment (cyberbullying) in Bangla, the quantity of state-of-the-art works is yet minimal. Therefore, to contribute to this critical and contemporary problem domain specific to Bangla, we introduce a multi-feature transformer approach for cyberbullying detection, in this study. These are the research questions posed in this paper:

- Can we design a multi-feature transformer-based deep learning architecture for cyberbullying detection in Bangla?
- Can a multi-feature transformer-based deep learning architecture perform similarly or better than the state-of-the-art cyberbullying detection methods in Bangla?

By pursuing the above-mentioned research questions in this paper, we add the following contributions to the problem domain of cyberbullying detection in Bangla.

- A novel multi-feature transformer-based deep learning architecture is proposed and implemented for cyberbullying detection in Bangla.
- A set of experimentations is performed using a bunch of different unimodal and multi-feature architectures, followed by a thorough analysis of the performance of the models for cyberbullying detection in Bangla.
- It is demonstrated that the proposed method outperforms the state-of-the-art methods in this problem domain.

In the sections that follow, the related works, dataset description, proposed methodology, experimental result analysis, etc. are discussed in detail.

2   Related Works

Online cyberbullying detection has been a research domain for some time, since the field of study has attracted substantial interest from researchers and government-crime-handling agencies worldwide. However, cyberbullying detection research in the context of Bangla language-specific domains still requires improvement, as Natural Language Processing (NLP) is still evolving its technologies for dealing with non-English languages, notably Bangla. A recent research [11] has introduced a transformer-based technique for detecting online harassment, expressing it as a multilabel classification problem. To better recognize abusive and hateful remarks from Online Social Network (OSN) users, the labels are divided into five categories: threat, sexual, troll, religious, and not bully. Three transformer models have been utilized: Bangla Bidirectional Encoders Representations from Transformers (BERT) [16], Bengali DistilBERT [28], and XLM-RoBERTa [36]. The best accurate model was the XML-RoBERTa model, with a maximum accuracy of 85%. A binary and multiclass classification model employing a Hybrid Neural Network [25] is proposed in [2]. The authors of [2] collected a large sample of Bangla cyberbullying data-Facebook user comments-and curated a large dataset with 44001 records and five annotated class labels. Their initial multiclass classification accuracy was 79.29%. However, by employing ensemble-based classical Machine Learning (ML) techniques such as Support Vector Machine (SVM) [31], K-nearest Neighbors (KNN) [24], Random Forest (RF) [8], and Naive Bayes (NB) [35], the performance was somewhat improved. Another recent study [7] on Bangla cyberbullying detection developed a novel approach that employs Efficiency Learning, an Encoder that Classifies Token Replacements Accurately (ELECTRA) [22], and BERT multi-lingual [10] pre-trained architectures. Using the same dataset as [2,11], the experiment was conducted. With ELECTRA, the performance of the model with the highest accuracy was 84.92%. The authors of [6] proposed Convolutional Neural Network (CNN) [5] and Long Short Term Memory (LSTM) [12] based techniques for online detection of abusive Bangla comments. Their models can recognize offensive Bangla comments based on religious, personal, geopolitical, and political motivations. Using networks such as CNN, Bi-LSTM [14], Conv-LSTM [20], and SVM models, the model with the highest reported performance is 78% accurate. Regarding the current and future trends of cyberbullying detection in all languages, Talpur et al. [32] provides a summary of the obstacles that must be surmounted in order to design a more effective cyberbullying detection system. Jahan et al. [15] created a Bangla cyberbullying detection system comprised of unigrams, bigrams, emojis, and sentiment words, among others. This study utilizes both transliterated and code-mixed Bangla and English text, in addition to the Bangla language. On a proprietary dataset, the authors trained SVM, Random Forest, and Adaboost algorithms and reported an accuracy of 72.14%. The paper [27] proposes a method for identifying abusive Bangla comment emanating from a radio broadcast gateway in real-time. The system uses Multinomial Naive Bayes (MNB) [35], RF, and Logistic Regression (LR) [17] to detect whether a radio broadcast gateway message is abusive. By filtering offensive comments, the proposed method can compare and map real-time communications to the dataset and isolate the positive comments or messages. The maximum reported accuracy for this proposed approach is 75.50%. A comprehensive comparative study [3] of methods used for cyberbullying detection in Bangla revealed that the number of works is limited when comparing classical machine learning-based algorithms to deep learning-based algorithms, and the performance of the models ranges from 75% to 85% for both binary and multiclass classification. Almost all systems used unimodal approaches for cyberbullying detection in Bangla; however, multi-feature transformer-based approaches were never investigated. Multi-feature transformers can capture a more comprehensive understanding of the input data by utilizing multiple modalities that contribute to extracting more useful information and making more accurate predictions compared to unimodal approaches. Therefore, to develop a superior, more robust, and more effective system for cyberbullying detection in Bangla, we propose a multi-feature transformer approach for this research problem. To the best of our knowledge, we propose and investigate a multi-feature transformer approach for detecting cyberbully in Bangla for the first time.

3   Methodology

The proposed methodology introduce a multi-feature transformer based approach for cyberbullying detection in Bangla. The process of feature engineering includes contextual sentence embedding, baseline profiles, word embedding, and lexical profiles. Figure 1 illustrates the overall process of the proposed architecture for detecting cyberbully in Bangla.

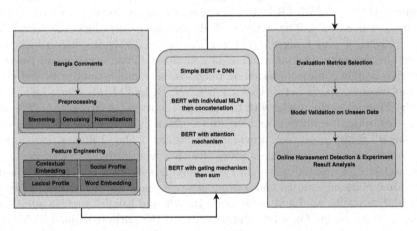

Fig. 1. Workflow of the proposed methodology for cyberbullying detection in Bangla

3.1   Data Preprocessing

Data preprocessing is a crucial component for improving the development of machine learning models, particularly in the field of Natural Language Processing. It is essential when dealing with languages with limited resources, such as

Bangla. Since the majority of training samples are informal Bangla Facebook comments, the following three textual data preparation techniques are used. In this step, three preprocessing tasks-denoising, normalizing, and stemming-have been performed. When data is extracted from many web sites, HTML tags, extra spaces, character encoding, and escape codes often appear. To make the data useable, these excessive noises must be removed, a process known as "denoising" [18]. A hard-coded program is implemented to automate the denoising process by removing noises, HTML tags, and extra white spaces. Text data should be normalized in various ways depending on the language, including case conversion, elimination of punctuation, accent marks, diacritics, stop words, and sparse terms. The Bangla text data were therefore normalized. In particular, a Bengali rule-based stemmer [21] is utilized for stemming.

3.2   Feature Engineering

In a machine learning pipeline, feature engineering plays a key role. From Bangla textual data, four dimensions of features are extracted: contextual sentence embedding, baseline profile, word embedding vectors, and lexical profile.

Contextual Embedding: In contrast to conventional word embedding vector representation techniques, we extract contextual information from online Bangla comments. The context is essential, particularly when it comes to comprehending and identifying cyberbully in Bangla. The Bi-directional Encoder Representations from Transformers (BERT) [16] pre-trained model is used to extract context from Bangla text. A multi-layer, bidirectional transformer designed for this model's architecture enables it to learn the context from both the left and right sides of unlabeled text. Due to its unified architecture, BERT distinguishes itself from other traditional algorithms in that the pre-trained BERT model may be improved to produce cutting-edge models for a variety of NLP applications with only one additional output layer. The unsupervised learning techniques Masked Language Modeling (MLM) and Next Sentence Prediction (NSP) are used to pre-train BERT. From the sequence output layer, the contextual embedding information was extracted to be used for cyberbullying detection in Bangla.

Social Profile: OSN users' social profile is considered a feature set for cyberbullying detection in Bangla because the baseline information is found relevant for whether a person has the potential to be harassed online or not. Gender, user category, and reaction counts are the baseline profile of users. In the user's category, there are categories like Singer, Politician, Actor, etc. The number of reactions to a particular comment is also counted.

Word Embedding: For word embedding, we utilized the Word2vec [9] algorithm. It is a two-layer neural network technique that "vectorizes" words by employing a neural network model to learn word relationships from a large corpus of text. It accepts a text corpus as input and generates a collection of 300-length feature vectors that collectively describe the corpus' words. Word2Vec keeps track of the sequence in which words appear in a sentence; this additional context helps to clarify the meaning of certain terms. It is a compilation of model architectures and optimizations that have proven successful for a number of subsequent NLP tasks. Using this Word2Vec word embedding technique, the Bangla texts' corresponding features are extracted.

Lexical Features: The lexical characteristics of Bangla comments of OSN users are extracted. In addition to word length, frequency, and high-frequency terms, additional lexical properties are incorporated. Language, genre, and other factors can influence the lexical features and collocation of a language. A total of 33 lexical characteristics are extracted and employed.

3.3   Experimental Design

This section describes the different types of multi-feature transformer architectures utilized for cyberbullying detection in Bangla. A multi-feature transformer is a deep learning architecture that operates on multiple input features to generate an output. Recent empirical studies have demonstrated the efficacy of multi-feature transformers for NLP tasks, leading to more accurate outputs [13]. Figure 2 depicts the workflow of the multi-feature transformer architecture used in this study.

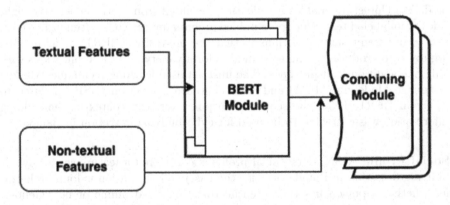

Fig. 2. Workflow of the multi-feature transformer architecture

We proposed to utilize multi-feature transformer architecture for cyberbullying detection in Bangla because, typically, these models include an encoder that processes each modality and a decoder that combines the encoder's representations to produce the final output. Subsequently, multiple modalities can offer the model with a more comprehensive grasp of the input data, resulting in enhanced performance. In this research problem, the online Bangla comments are the input for the BERT transformer module that processes the textual data and extract the corresponding contextual features. On the other hand, the non-textual features, including social profile and lexical features, directly pass through the combining module of the multi-feature transformer architecture. It should be noted that additional modules can be incorporated as well to handle textual data as necessary. For instance, alongside the BERT module, we utilize the Word2Vec module to generate the features of the Bangla textual data, followed by passing the features to the combining module altogether. For the BERT module, we use three distinct architecture of BERT to produce better deep features. The architectures of the BERT module are: BERT with individual MLPs on categorical and numerical features then concat, BERT with attention on categorical and numerical features, and BERT with gating on categorical and numerical features then sum.

BERT with Individual MLPs Then Concat: In this architecture, BERT is used to encode the text data into a vector representation and the Multilayer Perceptrons (MLPs) are used to encode the categorical and numerical features into different vector representations. Finally, these representations are concatenated to form a combined representations, which is used as input to a final layer to predict the target variable. This architecture is useful when the data contains both text and non-text information, and the goal is to utilize both types of information in a unified model. To refer this architecture, we use the term MF01.

BERT with Attention Mechanism: The attention mechanism in BERT allows the model to focus on the most relevant features and assign different weights to different features based on their importance. The attention-weighted representation of the categorical and numerical features is then combined with the representation from BERT to make the final classification. This architecture is effective when the objective is to combine both forms of features in a unified model while providing greater weight to the relevant characteristics. To refer this architecture, we use the term MF02.

BERT with Gating Mechanism Then Sum: The gating mechanism in BERT helps to control the flow of information in the network and decide which information to pass on to the next layer. The final representations produced by the BERT model, with the added gating mechanism, are then summed to produce the final output. This is quite useful in this research as the Bangla comments are converted as sequence of tokens to produce a representation that captures the semantic meaning of the input sequence as well. To refer this architecture, we use the term MF03.

Besides the multi-feature transformer architectures, we additionally designed a unimodal architecture with a simple BERT and DNN only. A total of 10 distinct

Table 1. Experimental Design of the Proposed Methodology

Experiment Name	Architecture	Feature Set
UM00	Simple BERT + DNN	*BC
MF01	BERT with **iMLPs + concat	*BC + *SP
MF02	BERT with **ATT	*BC + *SP
MF03	BERT with **GCM + sum	*BC + *SP
MF01-Ext	BERT with **iMLPs + concat	*BC + *SP + *LP
MF02-Ext	BERT with **ATT	*BC + *SP + *LP
MF03-Ext	BERT with **GCM + sum	*BC + *SP + *LP
MF01-Ext-W2V	BERT with **iMLPs + concat	*BC + *SP + *LP + Word2Vec
MF02-Ext-W2V	BERT with **ATT	*BC + *SP + *LP + Word2Vec
MF03-Ext-W2V	BERT with **GCM + sum	*BC + *SP + *LP + Word2Vec

*BC = Bangla Comments, *SP = Social Profile, *LP = Lexical Profile
**iMLPs = Individual MLPs on categorical and numerical features, **ATT = Attention mechanism on categorical and numerical features, **GCM = Gating mechanism on categorical and numerical features

architectures is designed and experimented combining these architectures with different feature sets. Table 1 demonstrates the experimental design of the study.

4   Experimental Results and Analysis

This section thoroughly presents the experimental results produced by the different sets of architectures experimented with, in this study. Primarily, the result analysis is divided into two parts. The first one discusses the performances of all the different experiments conducted with several multi-feature transformer architectures. The latter demonstrates a comparative analysis of the performance of the proposed method with the state-of-the-art methods.

4.1   Dataset

We have used a publicly available benchmark dataset [1] for cyberbullying detection in Bangla. The size of the dataset is 44001 consisting of online users' comments on Facebook, labeled in five different harassment and threat-wise classes. In addition to having users' comments in Bangla language, the baseline profile information of users is recorded. The dataset is spilt into 80:10:10 with a stratified sampling technique [30] for training, validating, and testing the models. The optimal parameters of the best performing architecture are: learning rate $= 5 \times 10^{-5}$, epochs = 500, activation function = Gaussian Error Linear Unit (GELU) with Adam optimizer.

4.2 Performance Analysis of the Proposed Method

Each model with a unique collection of architectures is validated with a validation set prior to being tested on unobserved original data. Table 2 depicts both the validation and test performance on validation and test data.

Table 2. Validation and Test Performance on different set of multi-feature architectures

Experiment Name	Validation Performance			Test Performance		
	Accuracy	F1 Micro	F1 Macro	Accuracy	F1 Micro	F1 Macro
UM00	0.839286	0.839286	0.825081	0.840076	0.840076	0.836686
MF01	0.841340	0.841340	0.824784	0.839760	0.839760	0.834561
MF02	0.843394	0.843394	0.826053	0.840392	0.840392	0.836593
MF03	0.842446	0.842446	0.829549	0.838654	0.838654	0.830090
MF01-Ext	0.839286	0.839286	0.825081	0.840076	0.840076	0.836686
MF02-Ext	0.837705	0.837705	0.825023	0.836915	0.836915	0.833955
MF03-Ext	0.839602	0.839602	0.826920	0.836125	0.836125	0.829774
MF01-Ext-W2V	0.848205	0.848205	0.833927	0.861839	0.861839	0.846454
MF02-Ext-W2V	0.850174	0.850174	0.834462	0.860021	0.860021	0.846516
MF03-Ext-W2V	0.851841	0.851841	0.836650	**0.863051**	**0.863051**	**0.850946**

The table demonstrates that the models are well-fitted, with little chance of overfitting or underfitting, as the performance of validation and test data is nearly identical. The experiment UM00, which has a simple BERT architecture with simply comments as a feature, scores the worst with an F1 Macro score of 84% and an accuracy of 84% on the test. In contrast, the performance of multi-feature techniques with a variety of BERT architectures and features appears to be superior. Interestingly, the performance of experiments MF01, MF02, and MF03 with both user comments and social profiles as the feature set, but with different BERT architectures, is similar to when only the feature 'user comments' is employed. It indicates that the social-profile feature set of individuals do not necessarily contribute significantly to cyberbullying detection performance. It implies that the textual comments of users are essential for detecting harassment. In experiments MF02-Ext and MF03-Ext, which follow the following architectures: BERT with attention mechanism on categorical and numerical features, and BERT with gating mechanism on categorical and numerical features then sum, the lexical characteristics of users' Bangla comments demonstrate even slightly poorer performance with an accuracy of 83%. The range of lexical features in the Bangla language is considerably fewer than in the English language, which may be a contributing factor to the inferior performance with lexical features. Moreover, the lexical features do not contribute considerably to the model improvement. Focusing more on the Bangla comments and employing both the contextual embedding and word embedding vectors collected from the Bangla comments has a substantial impact on the performance of models with identical topologies. In the architectures of MF01-Ext-W2V, MF02-Ext-W2V, and MF03-Ext-W2V, the accuracy is improved to 86.2%, 86.0%, and 86.3%, respectively. Nonetheless, the experiment MF03-Ext-W2V with the architecture BERT with gating followed by sum performs even better, as the F1 micro and F1 macro scores are superior to those of the other experiments. Table 3 provides more information about the class-wise harassment detection performance of MF03-Ext-W2V.

Table 3. Class-wise performance of the proposed method for cyberbullying detection

	Not Bully	Religious	Sexual	Troll	Threat
Accuracy	0.92	0.98	0.94	0.91	0.98
Precision	0.88	0.93	0.86	0.80	0.75
Recall	**0.94**	**0.99**	**0.97**	**0.94**	**0.99**
F1-Score	0.88	0.93	0.86	0.80	0.78
AUC Score	0.91	0.97	0.92	0.87	0.88

The performance of harassment-wise detection is greatly improved, with a detection accuracy of 98% for potential threats. With an accuracy of 91%, the identification rate for sarcastic comments is the lowest. The AUC Score exceeds 90% for nearly all classes except threat and troll, who have respective scores of 0.88 and 0.87. The religious class has the highest performance scores for accuracy and AUC, with 0.98 and 0.97, respectively. Overall, the performance table by class suggests that the proposed multi-feature transformer technique for detecting Bangla cyberbully performs significantly well.

Table 4. Performance comparison of the proposed method with state-of-the-art

Method	Precision	Recall	F1 Score	Accuracy
RoBERT [11]	0.84	0.84	0.86	85%
SVM [2]	0.85	0.85	0.84	85%
ELECTRA [7]	–	–	–	84.92%
BERT [7]	–	–	–	85%
Proposed*	**0.86**	**0.96**	**0.86**	**86.3%**

Now, consider the most recent state-of-the-art methods for detecting cyberbully in Bangla. Classical machine learning and deep learning techniques, particularly with unimodal approaches, are among the recently proposed methodologies. Table 4 depicts the comparison result of the proposed method with state-of-the-art method. In [2,7,11], the maximum rate of cyberbullying detection accuracy is 85%. ELECTRA [22] performs relatively poorly, with an accuracy of 84.92%. Our proposed method, on the other hand, outperforms the state-of-the-art methods with an accuracy of 86.3%. Moreover, when comparing the precision, recall, and F1 score of all approaches, the maximum score is 0.86, whereas the proposed method has the lowest precision score of 0.863 and the highest recall score of 0.96. Consequently, based on all contemporary evaluation parameters, our proposed technique performs much better than the state-of-the-art with a 12.94% improvement in recall.

5   Conclusion

Cyberbullying detection is a worldwide open problem that is required to be dealt with to provide a better cyber world to millions of online users, services, and entities. In this research, a novel multi-feature transformer-based technique for detecting multiclass cyberbully in Bangla is proposed. The proposed multi-feature transformer-based deep learning architecture uses the extracted contextual meaning, lexical attributes, user's social profile, and semantic similarity of the words from the raw Bangla comments on social media as inputs. With an overall accuracy of 86.3% and class-wise cyberbullying detection accuracy ranging from 92% to 98%, troll to threat, the proposed method outperforms existing methods. Additionally, the performance of cyberbullying detection in Bangla is improved across all performance evaluation-metrics, at least by 12.94% improvement in recall and 1.17% improvement in accuracy. The proposed method is superior to all recently published state-of-the-art techniques. In the future, the deep linguistic profiles of users' Bangla comments will be extracted to investigate the effect of deep linguistic profiles in designing an cyberbullying detection system. Another new avenue of research can be the study of clustering the potential type of users prone to be involved in cyberbullying online in Bangla.

References

1. Ahmed, M.F., Mahmud, Z., Biash, Z.T., Ryen, A.A.N., Hossain, A., Ashraf, F.B.: Bangla online comments dataset. Mendeley Data 1 (2021)
2. Ahmed, M.F., Mahmud, Z., Biash, Z.T., Ryen, A.A.N., Hossain, A., Ashraf, F.B.: Cyberbullying detection using deep neural network from social media comments in bangla language. arXiv preprint arXiv:2106.04506 (2021)
3. Ahmed, M.T., Rahman, M., Nur, S., Islam, A., Das, D.: Deployment of machine learning and deep learning algorithms in detecting cyberbullying in bangla and romanized bangla text: a comparative study. In: 2021 International Conference on Advances in Electrical, Computing, Communication and Sustainable Technologies (ICAECT), pp. 1–10. IEEE (2021)
4. Al Imran, A., Wahid, Z., Ahmed, T.: BNnet: a deep neural network for the identification of satire and fake bangla news. In: Chellappan, S., Choo, K.-K.R., Phan, N.H. (eds.) CSoNet 2020. LNCS, vol. 12575, pp. 464–475. Springer, Cham (2020). https://doi.org/10.1007/978-3-030-66046-8_38

5. Albawi, S., Mohammed, T.A., Al-Zawi, S.: Understanding of a convolutional neural network. In: 2017 International Conference on Engineering and Technology (ICET), pp. 1–6. IEEE (2017)
6. Aporna, A.A., Azad, I., Amlan, N.S., Mehedi, M.H.K., Mahbub, M.J.A., Rasel, A.A.: Classifying offensive speech of bangla text and analysis using explainable AI. In: Advances in Computing and Data Sciences: 6th International Conference, ICACDS 2022, Kurnool, India, 22–23 April 2022, Revised Selected Papers, Part I. pp. 133–144. Springer, Heidelberg (2022). https://doi.org/10.1007/978-3-031-12638-3_12
7. Aurpa, T.T., Sadik, R., Ahmed, M.S.: Abusive bangla comments detection on facebook using transformer-based deep learning models. Social Netw. Anal. Min. **12**(1), 24 (2022)
8. Biau, G., Scornet, E.: A random forest guided tour. TEST **25**(2), 197–227 (2016). https://doi.org/10.1007/s11749-016-0481-7
9. Church, K.W.: Word2vec. Nat. Lang. Eng. **23**(1), 155–162 (2017)
10. Devlin, J., Chang, M.W., Lee, K., Toutanova, K.: Bert: pre-training of deep bidirectional transformers for language understanding. arXiv preprint arXiv:1810.04805 (2018)
11. Emon, M.I.H., Iqbal, K.N., Mehedi, M.H.K., Mahbub, M.J.A., Rasel, A.A.: Detection of bangla hate comments and cyberbullying in social media using nlp and transformer models. In: Advances in Computing and Data Sciences: 6th International Conference, ICACDS 2022, Kurnool, India, 22–23 April 2022, Revised Selected Papers, Part I, pp. 86–96. Springer, Heidelberg (2022). https://doi.org/10.1007/978-3-031-12638-3_8
12. Graves, A., Graves, A.: Long short-term memory. In: Supervised Sequence Labelling with Recurrent Neural Networks, pp. 37–45 (2012)
13. Han, X., Yue, Q., Chu, J., Han, Z., Shi, Y., Wang, C.: Multi-feature fusion transformer for chinese named entity recognition. In: 2022 41st Chinese Control Conference (CCC), pp. 4227–4232. IEEE (2022)
14. Huang, Z., Xu, W., Yu, K.: Bidirectional lstm-crf models for sequence tagging. arXiv preprint arXiv:1508.01991 (2015)
15. Jahan, M., Ahamed, I., Bishwas, M.R., Shatabda, S.: Abusive comments detection in bangla-english code-mixed and transliterated text. In: 2019 2nd International Conference on Innovation in Engineering and Technology (ICIET), pp. 1–6. IEEE (2019)
16. Kowsher, M., Sami, A.A., Prottasha, N.J., Arefin, M.S., Dhar, P.K., Koshiba, T.: Bangla-bert: transformer-based efficient model for transfer learning and language understanding. IEEE Access **10**, 91855–91870 (2022)
17. LaValley, M.P.: Logistic regression. Circulation **117**(18), 2395–2399 (2008)
18. Liu, B., et al.: Web Data Mining: Exploring Hyperlinks, Contents, and Usage Data, vol. 1. Springer, Heidelberg (2011). https://doi.org/10.1007/978-3-642-19460-3
19. Liu, G., Li, C., Yang, Q.: Neuralwalk: trust assessment in online social networks with neural networks. In: IEEE INFOCOM 2019-IEEE Conference on Computer Communications, pp. 1999–2007. IEEE (2019)
20. Liu, Y., Zheng, H., Feng, X., Chen, Z.: Short-term traffic flow prediction with conv-lstm. In: 2017 9th International Conference on Wireless Communications and Signal Processing (WCSP), pp. 1–6. IEEE (2017)
21. Mahmud, M.R., Afrin, M., Razzaque, M.A., Miller, E., Iwashige, J.: A rule based bengali stemmer. In: 2014 International Conference on Advances in Computing, Communications and Informatics (ICACCI), pp. 2750–2756. IEEE (2014)

22. Meng, Y., et al.: Pretraining text encoders with adversarial mixture of training signal generators. arXiv preprint arXiv:2204.03243 (2022)
23. Nova, F.F., Rifat, M.R., Saha, P., Ahmed, S.I., Guha, S.: Online sexual harassment over anonymous social media in Bangladesh. In: Proceedings of the Tenth International Conference on Information and Communication Technologies and Development, pp. 1–12 (2019)
24. Peterson, L.E.: K-nearest neighbor. Scholarpedia 4(2), 1883 (2009)
25. Psichogios, D.C., Ungar, L.H.: A hybrid neural network-first principles approach to process modeling. AIChE J. 38(10), 1499–1511 (1992)
26. Rezwana Rashid, T.T.: Laws protecting victims from cyber harassment (2021). https://www.thedailystar.net/law-our-rights/news/laws-protecting-victims-cyber-harassment-2196491
27. Ritu, S.S., Mondal, J., Mia, M.M., Al Marouf, A.: Bangla abusive language detection using machine learning on radio message gateway. In: 2021 6th International Conference on Communication and Electronics Systems (ICCES), pp. 1725–1729. IEEE (2021)
28. Sanh, V., Debut, L., Chaumond, J., Wolf, T.: Distilbert, a distilled version of bert: smaller, faster, cheaper and lighter. arXiv preprint arXiv:1910.01108 (2019)
29. Sen, O., et al.: Bangla natural language processing: a comprehensive analysis of classical, machine learning, and deep learning based methods. IEEE Access 10, 38999–39044 (2022)
30. Sharma, G.: Pros and cons of different sampling techniques. Int. J. Appl. Res. 3(7), 749–752 (2017)
31. Suthaharan, S.: Support vector machine. In: Machine Learning Models and Algorithms for Big Data Classification. ISIS, vol. 36, pp. 207–235. Springer, Boston, MA (2016). https://doi.org/10.1007/978-1-4899-7641-3_9
32. Talpur, K.R., Yuhaniz, S.S., Amir, N.: Cyberbullying detection: current trends and future directions. J. Theor. Appl. Inf. Technol. 98, 3197–3208 (2020)
33. Wahid, Z., Imran, A.A., Rifat, M.R.I.: BNnetXtreme: an enhanced methodology for Bangla fake news detection online. In: Computational Data and Social Networks: 11th International Conference, CSoNet 2022, 5–7 December 2022, Proceedings, pp. 157–166. Springer, Heidelberg (2023). https://doi.org/10.1007/978-3-031-26303-3_14
34. Wani, M.A., Agarwal, N., Bours, P.: Sexual-predator detection system based on social behavior biometric (ssb) features. Procedia Comput. Sci. 189, 116–127 (2021)
35. Webb, G.I., Keogh, E., Miikkulainen, R.: Naïve bayes. Encycl. Mach. Learn. 15, 713–714 (2010)
36. Zhao, Y., Tao, X.: ZYJ123@ DravidianLangTech-EACL2021: offensive language identification based on xlm-roberta with dpcnn. In: Proceedings of the First Workshop on Speech and Language Technologies for Dravidian Languages, pp. 216–221 (2021)

Optimizing Feature Selection and Oversampling Using Metaheuristic Algorithms for Binary Fraud Detection Classification

Mariam M. Biltawi[1], Raneem Qaddoura[1(✉)], and Hossam Faris[2,3]

[1] Al Hussein Technical University, Amman 11831, Jordan
{mariam.biltawi,raneem.qaddoura}@htu.edu.jo
[2] Research Centre for Information and Communications Technologies (CITIC-UGR),
University of Granada, Granada, Spain
inv.hfaris@ugr.es
[3] King Abdullah II School for Information Technology, The University of Jordan,
Amman 11942, Jordan
hossam.faris@ju.edu.jo
http://evo-ml.com/

Abstract. Identifying fraudulent transactions and preventing unauthorized individuals from revealing credit card information are essential tasks for different financial entities. Fraud detection systems are used to apply this task by identifying the fraudulent transactions from the normal ones. Usually, the data used for fraud detection is imbalanced, containing many more instances of normal transactions than fraudulent ones. This causes diminished classification task results because it is hard to train a classifier that distinguishes between them. Another problem is caused by many features under study for the fraud detection task. This paper utilizes different metaheuristic algorithms for feature selection to solve the problem of unneeded features and uses the Synthetic Minority Oversampling TEchnique (SMOTE) to solve the imbalance problem of the data using different classification algorithms. The metaheuristic algorithms include Particle Swarm Optimization (PSO), Salp Swarm Algorithm (SSA), Grey Wolf Optimizer (GWO), and A Multi-Verse Optimizer (MVO), whereas the classification algorithms include Logistic Regression (LR), Decision Tree (DT), and Naive Bayes (NB) algorithms. The results show that applying the oversampling technique generated better results for the G-Mean and Recall values, while the feature selection process enhanced the results of almost all the classification algorithms.

Keywords: Fraud Detection · SMOTE · Oversampling · Classification · Metaheuristic Algorithms · Optimization

© IFIP International Federation for Information Processing 2023
Published by Springer Nature Switzerland AG 2023
I. Maglogiannis et al. (Eds.): AIAI 2023, IFIP AICT 675, pp. 452–462, 2023.
https://doi.org/10.1007/978-3-031-34111-3_38

1 Introduction

Fraud detection is the process of analyzing, identifying, and preventing unauthorized financial activities. Identify theft, fraudulent credit card transactions, and cyber hacking are examples of fraudulent activities. To avoid such fraudulent activities, different actions can be considered by targeted companies, such as providing employees training on fraud detection or incorporating fraud detection into websites [1]. Generally, fraud areas include bank fraud, insurance fraud, telecommunication fraud, and internet marketing fraud. Credit card fraud, which is the focus of this paper, is a subcategory of bank fraud, which can be transnational fraud or application fraud [1].

Credit card fraud occurs when someone's credit card information is acquired by an unauthorized user, which uses this information to perform purchases [3]. Recently, Machine Learning (ML) algorithms were used to help with credit card fraud detection through creating ML models [20], trained on datasets collected from real transactions. These models can then recognize unusual transactions and detect whether the credit card transaction is fraudulent or not [27].

Metaheuristic algorithms provide sufficiently good solutions to optimization problems through high-level procedures. The advantage of using metaheuristic algorithms is that they are considered generic optimizers that can be implemented not for a specific problem but for almost all problems [2]. That is, the metaheuristic algorithms find the most suitable solutions by encoding the candidate solution and applying this process to the different problems because finding the solutions is independent of the problem type [17]. Different metaheuristic algorithms can be found in the literature. However, these algorithms can be categorized using different taxonomies based on their characteristics. For example, population-based vs. single-point and nature-inspired vs. non-nature inspired. Moreover, metaheuristic algorithms can be used for feature selection and parameter tuning in fraud detection.

Feature selection is the process of selecting relevant features from the dataset to reduce noise and redundant data, thus, creating an effective model. Implementing feature selection's main advantages are simplifying the created models, reducing training time, and avoiding the curse of dimensionality problem [12]. Metaheuristic algorithms can work as optimization algorithms to select the most effective features for generating the model during the preprocessing step of the classification task [18]. Sometimes, experimented datasets contain imbalanced data, which means unequal distribution of examples in each class. To overcome such a problem, a researcher can perform oversampling or undersampling to equalize the number of examples in each class. Oversampling can be defined as the process of increasing the number of examples within the minimum class, while undersampling is the process of decreasing the number of examples within the maximum class [24].

This paper aims to optimize feature selection using metaheuristic algorithms for binary fraud detection classification with and without oversampling. The experimented oversampling method is Synthetic Minority Oversampling TEchnique (SMOTE). While the experimented metaheuristic algorithms for feature selection are Particle Swarm Optimization (PSO) [10], Salp Swarm Algorithm (SSA) [13], Grey Wolf Optimizer (GWO) [15], and Multi-verse Optimizer (MVO) [14]. These metaheuristic algorithms are nature-inspired; for example, PSO is a well-known simple metaheuristic algorithm that mimics the behavior of swarms, SSA mimics salps, and GWO imitates the leadership hierarchy and hunting mechanism of grey wolves. While MVO is based on the concept of multi-verse. Moreover, three well-known classification algorithms were used to compare the results with and without feature selection. These algorithms are; Logistic Regression (LR) [4], Decision Tree (DT) [28], and Naive Bayes (NB) [16].

The remaining of this paper is organized as follows; Sect. 2 presents the related work, Sect. 3 presents the problem and data description, Sect. 4 illustrates the proposed approach with the feature selection methods using metaheuristic algorithms, Sect. 5 presents the experiments and results, and finally, Sect. 6 is the conclusion and future work.

2   Related Work

This section presents research papers experimenting with fraud detection, metaheuristic algorithms, oversampling techniques, and feature selection. The problem with the credit card fraud detection dataset is that it has only a few fraud examples compared to the non-fraud available examples, which reflect a highly imbalanced dataset, to solve this problem, Duman and Elikucuk [5] developed Migrating Birds Optimization algorithm (MBO) which is a neighborhood search technique. The authors also experimented with Genetic Algorithms (GA) and Scattered Search (SS) [6], and results showed that MBO outperformed GA and SS. Similarly, Jovanovic et al. [9] proposed a group search firefly metaheuristic algorithm to solve the problem of credit card fraud detection problem. Results showed that the proposed algorithm outperformed all other experimented algorithms.

Different metaheuristic algorithms were proposed for feature selection. For example, Taghian et al. [25] proposed a Wrapper-based Binary Sine Cosine Algorithm (WBSCA) for feature selection. WBSCA was experimented on seven UCI datasets and against Binary Bat Algorithm (BBA), and Binary Gravitational Search Algorithm (BGSA). The results showed that WBSCA is a competitive algorithm. On the other hand, Taghian et al. [26] conducted a comparison between three transfer function-based binary metaheuristic algorithms for feature selection; BBA, binary Grey Wolf Optimization (bGWO), and BGSA. Experimental results showed that BGSA outperformed both BBA and bGWO. Yusta [29] conducted a comparison, as well, between the three metaheuristic algorithms; Tabu Search, Greedy Randomized Adaptive Search Procedure (GRASP), and Memetic Algorithm, GA and traditional feature selection methods. Experimental results showed that Tabu Search and GRASP outperformed all other algorithms.

Metaheuristic algorithms for feature selection can be found in the literature. For example, Sayed et al. [23] worked on three phases, preprocessing the data, performing feature selection, and building the classification model. In the pre-processing phase, the authors implemented SMOTE for oversampling. Next, feature selection was implemented using the Chaotic Dragonfly Algorithm (CDA), and then the Support Vector Machine (SVM) classifier was built and evaluated. Moreover, Gharehchopogh et al. [8] experimented with different chaotic maps to improve Vortex Search Algorithm (VSA) for feature selection on 24 UCI datasets.

The difference between the current work and the work presented in this section is that the current work focuses on comparing the results of using different metaheuristic algorithms for feature selection, with and without oversampling, rather than using only one metaheuristic algorithm. Moreover, this work also experimented SSA algorithm in fraud detection, and to the best of the authors' knowledge, has not been experimented with in fraud detection till now.

3   Problem and Data Description

The experimented dataset contains data from transactions made by credit cards of European cardholders within two days of September 2013 from the Kaggle website[1]. The number of fraud transactions is only 492 out of 284,807 transactions (around 0.002%), which makes this dataset highly imbalanced. The features of this dataset are the results of the Principal Component Analysis (PCA) transformation. The only original features are the time and amount, noting that the total number of features is 30. The class is represented with 1, which indicates the transaction is fraudulent, and 0, which indicates the opposite.

The credit card fraud detection problem includes building a model to detect whether the transaction is fraudulent. Initially, this model should be trained on past credit card transactions. The complexity of this problem depends on different perspectives, such as the number of examples in the dataset within each class and the number of features within the dataset.

In this paper, the credit card fraud detection dataset is highly imbalanced. The solution of this problem can be solved using either oversampling or under-sampling. However, oversampling was chosen because the number of fraud examples is very small compared to the non-fraud examples. On the other hand, dimensionality reduction can be performed using feature selection methods. The authors of this paper experimented with different metaheuristic algorithms for feature selection.

4   Proposed Approach

The approach followed in this work is presented in Fig. 1. As observed from the figure, the preprocessing step of the approach includes handling the missing data, converting the categorical values to numerical ones, and oversampling the dataset using the SMOTE technique. The second step, which is the main step

---

[1] https://www.kaggle.com/datasets/mlg-ulb/creditcardfraud.

of the approach, considers using the metaheuristic algorithms to optimize the classification process by selecting the features that give the best geometric mean (G-Mean) value for the classification model. This step works as follows:

1. A random population is generated for the first iteration of the optimization process. The population includes individuals with values indicating the existence or absence of each feature. The values direct the selection process of the features.
2. A classification model is generated for the training data with the selected features based on the values of each individual.
3. Fitness evaluation for the validation data using the complement of the G-Mean measure is used to evaluate the generated model. G-mean is commonly used to evaluate the quality of the model for imbalanced datasets.
4. The best individual with the fitness function's best value is recorded for the iteration.
5. The next iteration is performed by modifying the values of the individuals based on the metaheuristic algorithm to generate an enhanced population.
6. Step 2 to Step 5 is repeated until the maximum iteration is reached. This generates the best individual for the optimization process.

The last step includes evaluating the optimization process using the testing data by applying the classification process and evaluating the model using different evaluation measures: Precision, Recall, F1-score, and G-Mean.

5 Experiments and Results

The approach followed in this study is discussed in this section. The different settings are presented here with the results obtained from the experiment using the oversampling technique and the feature selection optimization of the metaheuristic algorithms.

Different classification algorithms, including the LR, NB, and DT with default parameters' values, and different metaheuristic algorithms, including PSO, SSA, GWO, and MVO, are used in the experiments. The EvoloPy framework [7] is extended to include the classification task and the feature selection optimization of the implemented metaheuristic algorithms. The scikit-learn Python library [19] is used for the classification algorithms and the precision, recall, and f1-score evaluation measures, while the imbalanced-learn Python library [11] is used for the SMOTE and the G-mean methods. Fifty individuals and fifty iterations are applied by each metaheuristic algorithm and 30 independent runs are considered.

Table 1 presents the fraud detection results for feature selection optimization using different metaheuristic algorithms and classification algorithms regarding Recall, Precision, F1-score, and G-Mean. The Recall values for the LR and NB show advanced results for all the metaheuristic algorithms compared to the results shown by these algorithms without applying the feature selection

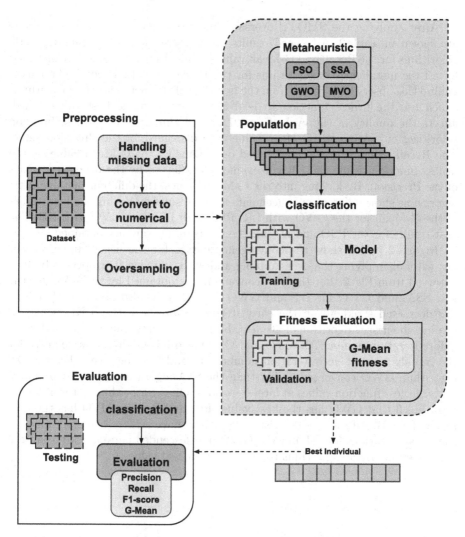

Fig. 1. Feature selection using metaheuristic algorithms for fraud detection

optimization. In contrast, the DT shows decreased Recall values for the meta-heuristic algorithms. The precision and F1-score results show advancement for the LR for all the metaheuristic algorithms but only show advanced results for GWO and MVO for the DT and SSA, GWO, and MVO for the NB. In addition, the G-Mean results show advancement for the different classification algorithms. The SSA shows the best results compared to the other metaheuristic algorithms for the DT in terms of G-Mean, while the MVO and GWO show the best results for the LR and NB, respectively. The best results for the SSA and DT for the G-Mean measure are obtained.

After applying the SMOTE oversampling technique, different observations are shown in Table 2. Advanced results are observed for all the metaheuristic algorithms for the Recall and G-Mean values, while decreased values are observed for all the metaheuristic algorithms for the Precision and F1-score. The reason behind this observation comes from the behavior of the metaheuristic algorithms, which use the fitness function to lead the solution to the best value, which affects the quality of the evaluation [21,22]. In this case, the fitness function prioritizes enhancing the G-Mean value with disregard for the Precision value. The Recall values are enhanced based on enhancing the G-Mean value by the fitness function, while the F1-score values are affected by the decreased values of the Precision. By looking into the G-Mean values, the different metaheuristic algorithms show different enhancements in the results by having the best values of the G-Mean for the GWO with LR, PSO with DT, and MVO with NB. The best results for the PSO and DT for the G-Mean measure are obtained.

Figures 2 and 3 show the convergence curves for the fitness function values without applying the oversampling and with applying it, respectively. It is observed from Fig. 2 that the best convergence is obtained by the MVO for the LR, SSA, and GWO for DT and GWO for NB. It is also observed that SSA has decreased strikingly in the early iterations for the LR and NB, while all the metaheuristic algorithms have a stability of the drop value to a fixed value before iteration number 20. MVO and GWO also have a dramatic decrease for the NB algorithm before iteration numbers 15 and 5, respectively. For the DT algorithm, GWO converged earlier than the SSA algorithm, but SSA obtained better fitness function values at later iterations. On the other hand, it is observed from Fig. 3 that GWO has the best values for the LR while MVO has the best results for NB. All the metaheuristic algorithms have achieved similar values at the latest iterations for DT but the GWO has descended more quickly than the other metaheuristic algorithms to achieve optimized value.

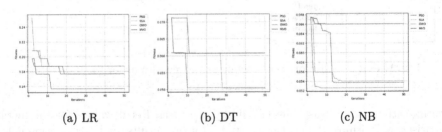

(a) LR   (b) DT   (c) NB

Fig. 2. Convergence curves for the fitness function for LR, DT, and NB without oversampling.

Table 1. Fraud detection results for feature selection optimization using different metaheuristic algorithms and different classification algorithms

Recall

Algorithm	Without FS	FS-PSO	FS-SSA	FS-GWO	FS-MVO
LR	0.500	0.837	0.860	0.860	0.884
DT	0.820	0.720	0.720	0.760	0.760
NB	0.820	0.905	0.881	0.833	0.881

Precision

Algorithm	Without FS	FS-PSO	FS-SSA	FS-GWO	FS-MVO
LR	0.581	0.766	0.771	0.787	0.792
DT	0.732	0.720	0.692	0.776	0.760
NB	0.149	0.132	0.197	0.313	0.230

F1-Score

Algorithm	Without FS	FS-PSO	FS-SSA	FS-GWO	FS-MVO
LR	0.538	0.800	0.813	0.822	0.835
DT	0.744	0.720	0.706	0.768	0.760
NB	0.252	0.231	0.322	0.455	0.365

G-Mean

Algorithm	Without FS	FS-PSO	FS-SSA	FS-GWO	FS-MVO
LR	0.707	0.8232	0.8129	0.8233	0.8436
DT	0.905	0.9393	0.9497	0.9495	0.9393
NB	0.252	0.9340	0.9460	0.9474	0.9463

Table 2. Fraud detection results for feature selection optimization using different metaheuristic algorithms and different classification algorithms with oversampling

Recall

Algorithm	Without FS	FS-PSO	FS-SSA	FS-GWO	FS-MVO
LR	0.500	0.950	0.917	0.967	0.967
DT	0.760	0.868	0.811	0.868	0.868
NB	0.820	0.860	0.880	0.880	0.860

Precision

Algorithm	Without FS	FS-PSO	FS-SSA	FS-GWO	FS-MVO
LR	0.581	0.073	0.057	0.060	0.081
DT	0.576	0.426	0.417	0.393	0.359
NB	0.139	0.076	0.086	0.087	0.087

F1-Score

Algorithm	Without FS	FS-PSO	FS-SSA	FS-GWO	FS-MVO
LR	0.538	0.136	0.108	0.112	0.149
DT	0.655	0.571	0.551	0.541	0.508
NB	0.237	0.139	0.156	0.159	0.158

G-Mean

Algorithm	Without FS	FS-PSO	FS-SSA	FS-GWO	FS-MVO
LR	0.707	0.9521	0.9503	0.9541	0.9497
DT	0.871	0.9680	0.9677	0.9679	0.9678
NB	0.9000	0.9036	0.9041	0.9042	0.9043

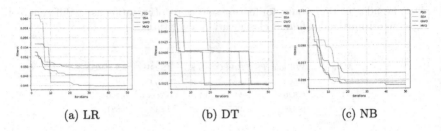

(a) LR   (b) DT   (c) NB

Fig. 3. Convergence curves for the fitness function measure for LR, DT, and NB with oversampling.

6   Conclusion and Future Work

This study experiments with different metaheuristic algorithms by optimizing the feature selection process of the fraud detection task using different classification algorithms, including the LR, DT, and NB. PSO, SSA, GWO, and MVO are selected as metaheuristic algorithms and the SMOTE oversampling technique is used to solve the imbalanced problem of the dataset. The results show that the different metaheuristic algorithms enhanced the classification task for most of the recorded results compared to applying the classification task without feature selection. Oversampling the dataset generated better results in terms of Recall and G-Mean compared with the results obtained without oversampling. The Precision and F1-score results were affected with decreased values when oversampling the dataset and applying the feature selection process.

For future work, the values of the Precision and F1-score can be enhanced by applying a multi-objective fitness function to evaluate the generated individuals at each iteration with G-Mean, Precision, Recall, and F1-score, and not only the G-Mean values. The approach followed in this study can be experimented with using different datasets for fraud detection. In addition, the optimization process can be extended to enhance the parameters' values for the different classification algorithms.

References

1. Abdallah, A., Maarof, M.A., Zainal, A.: Fraud detection system: a survey. J. Netw. Comput. Appl. **68**, 90–113 (2016)
2. Abdel-Basset, M., Abdel-Fatah, L., Sangaiah, A.K.: Metaheuristic algorithms: a comprehensive review. In: Computational Intelligence for Multimedia Big Data on the Cloud with Engineering Applications, pp. 185–231 (2018)
3. Chaudhary, K., Yadav, J., Mallick, B.: A review of fraud detection techniques: credit card. Int. J. Comput. Appl. **45**(1), 39–44 (2012)
4. Cox, D.R.: The regression analysis of binary sequences. J. Roy. Stat. Soc. Ser. B (Methodol.) **20**(2), 215–232 (1958)

5. Duman, E., Elikucuk, I.: Solving credit card fraud detection problem by the new metaheuristics migrating birds optimization. In: Rojas, I., Joya, G., Cabestany, J. (eds.) IWANN 2013. LNCS, vol. 7903, pp. 62–71. Springer, Heidelberg (2013). https://doi.org/10.1007/978-3-642-38682-4_8
6. Duman, E., Ozcelik, M.H.: Detecting credit card fraud by genetic algorithm and scatter search. Expert Syst. Appl. **38**(10), 13057–13063 (2011)
7. Faris, H., Aljarah, I., Mirjalili, S., Castillo, P.A., Guervós, J.J.M.: Evolopy: an open-source nature-inspired optimization framework in python. IJCCI (ECTA) **1**, 171–177 (2016)
8. Gharehchopogh, F.S., Maleki, I., Dizaji, Z.A.: Chaotic vortex search algorithm: metaheuristic algorithm for feature selection. Evol. Intell. **15**(3), 1777–1808 (2022)
9. Jovanovic, D., Antonijevic, M., Stankovic, M., Zivkovic, M., Tanaskovic, M., Bacanin, N.: Tuning machine learning models using a group search firefly algorithm for credit card fraud detection. Mathematics **10**(13), 2272 (2022)
10. Kennedy, J., Eberhart, R.: Particle swarm optimization. In: Proceedings of ICNN'95-International Conference on Neural Networks, vol. 4, pp. 1942–1948. IEEE (1995)
11. Lemaître, G., Nogueira, F., Aridas, C.K.: Imbalanced-learn: a python toolbox to tackle the curse of imbalanced datasets in machine learning. J. Mach. Learn. Res. **18**(17), 1–5 (2017). http://jmlr.org/papers/v18/16-365.html
12. Miao, J., Niu, L.: A survey on feature selection. Procedia Comput. Sci. **91**, 919–926 (2016)
13. Mirjalili, S., Gandomi, A.H., Mirjalili, S.Z., Saremi, S., Faris, H., Mirjalili, S.M.: Salp swarm algorithm: a bio-inspired optimizer for engineering design problems. Adv. Eng. Softw. **114**, 163–191 (2017)
14. Mirjalili, S., Mirjalili, S.M., Hatamlou, A.: Multi-verse optimizer: a nature-inspired algorithm for global optimization. Neural Comput. Appl. **27**(2), 495–513 (2016)
15. Mirjalili, S., Mirjalili, S.M., Lewis, A.: Grey wolf optimizer. Adv. Eng. Softw. **69**, 46–61 (2014)
16. Murphy, K.P., et al.: Naive bayes classifiers. Univ. Br. Columbia **18**(60), 1–8 (2006)
17. Obiedat, R., Harfoushi, O., Qaddoura, R., Al-Qaisi, L., Al-Zoubi, A.: An evolutionary-based sentiment analysis approach for enhancing government decisions during covid-19 pandemic: the case of Jordan. Appl. Sci. **11**(19), 9080 (2021)
18. Obiedat, R., et al.: Sentiment analysis of customers' reviews using a hybrid evolutionary svm-based approach in an imbalanced data distribution. IEEE Access **10**, 22260–22273 (2022)
19. Pedregosa, F., et al.: Scikit-learn: machine learning in Python. J. Mach. Learn. Res. **12**, 2825–2830 (2011)
20. Qaddoura, R., Biltawi, M.: Improving fraud detection in an imbalanced class distribution using different oversampling techniques. In: Engineering International Conference on Electrical, Energy, and Artificial Intelligence (EICEEAI). IEEE (2022)
21. Qaddoura, R., Faris, H., Aljarah, I., Castillo, P.A.: EvoCluster: an open-source nature-inspired optimization clustering framework in python. In: Castillo, P.A., Jiménez Laredo, J.L., Fernández de Vega, F. (eds.) EvoApplications 2020. LNCS, vol. 12104, pp. 20–36. Springer, Cham (2020). https://doi.org/10.1007/978-3-030-43722-0_2
22. Qaddoura, R., Faris, H., Aljarah, I., Castillo, P.A.: Evocluster: an open-source nature-inspired optimization clustering framework. SN Comput. Sci. **2**(3), 1–12 (2021)

23. Sayed, G.I., Tharwat, A., Hassanien, A.E.: Chaotic dragonfly algorithm: an improved metaheuristic algorithm for feature selection. Appl. Intell. **49**(1), 188–205 (2019)
24. Sharma, S., Gosain, A., Jain, S.: A review of the oversampling techniques in class imbalance problem. In: Khanna, A., Gupta, D., Bhattacharyya, S., Hassanien, A.E., Anand, S., Jaiswal, A. (eds.) International Conference on Innovative Computing and Communications. AISC, vol. 1387, pp. 459–472. Springer, Singapore (2022). https://doi.org/10.1007/978-981-16-2594-7_38
25. Taghian, S., Nadimi-Shahraki, M.H.: A binary metaheuristic algorithm for wrapper feature selection. Int. J. Comput. Sci. Eng. (IJCSE) **8**, 168–172 (2019)
26. Taghian, S., Nadimi-Shahraki, M.H., Zamani, H.: Comparative analysis of transfer function-based binary metaheuristic algorithms for feature selection. In: 2018 International Conference on Artificial Intelligence and Data Processing (IDAP), pp. 1–6. IEEE (2018)
27. Varmedja, D., Karanovic, M., Sladojevic, S., Arsenovic, M., Anderla, A.: Credit card fraud detection-machine learning methods. In: 2019 18th International Symposium INFOTEH-JAHORINA (INFOTEH), pp. 1–5. IEEE (2019)
28. Wu, X., et al.: Top 10 algorithms in data mining. Knowl. Inf. Syst. **14**(1), 1–37 (2008)
29. Yusta, S.C.: Different metaheuristic strategies to solve the feature selection problem. Pattern Recogn. Lett. **30**(5), 525–534 (2009)

Predicting Student Performance with Virtual Resources Interaction Data

Alex Martínez-Martínez(✉) ⓘ, Raul Montoliu ⓘ, Jesús Aguiló Salinas,
and Inmaculada Remolar ⓘ

Institute of New Imaging Technologies (INIT), Universitat Jaume I, Avda. de Vicent
Sos Baynat, s/n, 12071 Castelló de la Plana, Spain
{alemarti,montoliu,al395312,remolar}@uji.es

Abstract. E-learning can be able to act where traditional education
cannot, thanks to its ease of interaction with virtual resources. In this
work, the possibility of predicting the final outcome of students based
solely on their interaction with virtual resources will be tested. The study
aims to evaluate the effectiveness of various machine learning and deep
learning models in predicting the performance of students based on their
interactions with these virtual resources. The OULA dataset will be used
to evaluate the proposed models to predict not only whether the student
will pass or fail, but also whether the student will receive a distinction or
will drop out of the course prematurely. Some of the models trained in
this paper, such as Random Forest, have achieved high accuracy levels,
up to 96% for binary classification and up to 80% for multiclass classification. These results indicate that it is possible to predict the performance
of students based exclusively on their interactions during the duration of
the course and to make predictions for each course individually. They also
demonstrate the effectiveness of the proposed models and the potential
of virtual resources in predicting the performance of students.

Keywords: Performance Prediction · E-learning · Machine Learning

1 Introduction

Recent years have shown the importance of distance learning (e-learning) as it
can be used in a variety of contexts, such as higher education and corporate
training [20]. Its use has spread throughout the world thanks to its time and
geographical flexibility. It allows both, teachers and students, to be connected
whenever they need it and allows them to use more educational resources than
in traditional learning. E-learning also provides the opportunity to improve students' engagement and learning experiences by using different digital tools [19].

Its increasing popularity has motivated the research of different learning
analytics, whose objectives encompass other goals, such as behavioral or performance predictions [22]. This has given rise to educational data mining, a new
field of data analysis [4], supported by the use of various techniques for its study,
including deep learning and machine learning [1,15].

ⓒ IFIP International Federation for Information Processing 2023
Published by Springer Nature Switzerland AG 2023
I. Maglogiannis et al. (Eds.): AIAI 2023, IFIP AICT 675, pp. 463–474, 2023.
https://doi.org/10.1007/978-3-031-34111-3_39

Although distance education is starting to become a feasible option for learning, it still has many challenges to overcome [16]. Currently, there are sufficient virtual resources that allow the student to be able to complete the teaching and learning process. However, unlike traditional education, distance education allows a larger number of students to be brought together, which complicates the interaction between students and teachers. Despite the advantages that virtual education can offer, the dropout rate is usually higher than face-to-face education [13].

Having tools to help students in their learning process is important. Each student may have specific needs, so it can be difficult for a teacher to be able to adapt the teaching to each student during classes. This problem is the focus of most research carried out, which tries to solve it by recognizing the characteristics of each student to complement the teacher's work [2].

This work proposes to predict the final result of a student using only the interactions carried out during the course with the available virtual resources. It is likely that a greater number of interactions or visiting certain key resources is important in deciding the student's final outcome. In order to achieve this, the Open university learning analytics dataset (OULAD) will be used [12], which contains information on 22 different courses and the interaction of more than 30,000 students. This work focuses on predicting all four possible outcomes of the student's final results, which are, distinction, pass, fail, or withdraw.

This research aims to measure the effectiveness of using different prediction models to predict the outcome of students using the interaction data of virtual resources. It also aims to find models that work well regardless of the course they evaluate. Each course may have a different set of resources and present different structures, so it may be important to design a model that is able to work in any situation. Then, the objectives to be achieved in this study are as follows:

- To determine the effectiveness of machine and deep learning models in predicting students' performance.
- To analyze the generated interaction data of the students with the virtual resources to evaluate their performance.
- To determine the effectiveness of learning models for early prediction of student performance.

The proposed contribution of this work is to achieve the listed objectives but to study and make predictions for each course separately. As far as we know, this is the first work evaluating all four possible outcomes in the same learning process for each course individually. Most of the work using the OULAD for predictions is focused on other problems, such as binary classification or withdrawn prediction [8].

The rest of the paper has been organized as follows. Section 2 describes existing performance prediction literature. Section 3 describes the dataset and discusses the machine and deep learning models used for the prediction. Sections 4 and 5 present the experimental results and discussion. Finally, Sect. 6 provides the concluding remarks and proposes possible future directions.

2   Related Work

Student performance is a broad area of research as it covers various criteria, such as predicting dropouts or withdrawals, identifying at-risk students, and evaluating final course outcomes. The first step in creating prediction models is to conduct a data analysis process. Some works, such as Waheed et al. [23] have explored different analytics applicable to e-learning.

Early predictions are crucial in this domain due to the lower retention rate of learners in virtual environments compared to traditional ones. Xing et al. [24] identified the factors contributing to the existing dropout rates. Hone and El Said [9] studied how course content, teacher-student interaction, and the platform used to deliver the course impact student performance.

Marbouti et al. [17] used several models to predict at-risk students as early as possible during a course, including Logistic Regression, Support Vector Machines, Multi-Layer Perceptron, and others. Hassan et al. [8] used a Long Short Term Memory model, a version of Recurrent Neural Networks, to predict student withdrawals using the clickstream data to make the predictions. Katarya [11] used a derivative of an autoencoder, combined with techniques like feature selection, to predict the final result of a student. Li et al. [14] used a Graph Neural Network to predict the final result of the student by combining interaction data and student attributes.

The research on the OULA dataset is similar to the previously mentioned works, mostly focusing on performance prediction. Hussain et al. [10] used the dataset to predict student engagement. Some works, like Chen et al. [2] used the dataset to create a recommender system. Waheed et al. [21] used a Generative Adversarial Network to simulate student behavior and generate synthetic data.

Most papers tend to group interactions and make predictions for all courses together, which may pose a problem since courses may differ from one another. This paper will make predictions for each course separately and focus on the classification of the four possible outcomes. Additionally, this paper will only use student interactions and not include demographic data.

3   Material and Methods

This section will describe the data, its pre-processing, and the different models used for the predictions.

3.1   Dataset

The OULA dataset gathers information about the demographic, clickstream behavior, and assessment performance of 32,593 students [12]. There are 22 different courses, from 2013 to 2014, where each course consists of a series of assessments and virtual resources. Each student has a bunch of graded evaluations, from which the final grade for the course can be obtained. The interactions they have had with each virtual resource are also available.

This work aims to predict the final result of each student using only the interactions with the virtual resources. The required information can be found in the *student info* and *student vle* tables. No other student data or type of virtual resource accessed is required for this work. The final result of the students is classified into four labels; distinction (3,024), pass (12,361), fail (7,052), and withdrawn (10,156), the problem to be solved is, therefore, a multiclass classification.

3.2   Problem Definition

For this problem, a set of courses, C, is considered, each with a set of enrolled students, S^i. Each course is defined as:

$$c_i \in C \qquad i \; in[1, ..., n_c] \tag{1}$$

and each student is defined as:

$$s_j^i \in S^i \qquad j^i \in [1, ..., n_s^i] \tag{2}$$

Here, n_c is the number of courses and n_s^i is the number of students enrolled in the i-th course. Each course contains a set of activities, A^i, with each activity defined as:

$$a_k^i \in A^i \qquad k^i \in [1, ..., n_a^i] \tag{3}$$

where n_a^i is the number of activities for the i-th course.

Each student has a set of interactions, x_j^i, with the activities of each given course. These interactions, also called feature or input vectors, can be defined as:

$$x_j^i = [a_{1(j)}^i, ..., a_{k^i(j)}^i] \tag{4}$$

For each feature vector, there is an associated label y_j^i, called output, which represents the final result of the student. The task is to find a model f that maps the input vector x_j^i to a predicted output $\hat{y}_j^i$, i.e.,

$$f \rightarrow \hat{y}_j^i = f(x_j^i, \Omega) \tag{5}$$

where Ω represents the model parameters chosen by hyperparameter tuning.

The predicted label $\hat{y}_j^i$ must be equal to the original label, y_j^i, corresponding to the input vector x_j^i. The effectiveness of each model is measured through accuracy, defined as the ratio of the number of correct predictions to the total number of predictions:

$$acc^i = \frac{\sum_{j=1}^{n_s^i} \left(y_j^i = \hat{y}_j^i \right)}{n_s^i} \tag{6}$$

In addition, the area under the ROC curve (AUC) is also considered. It is defined as the ratio between the true positive rate (well-predicted positives) and the false positive rate (wrongly predicted positives) against original positives and negatives, respectively. The objective of the model f is to maximize the accuracy across all courses:

$$\max \left(\frac{\sum_i acc^i}{n_c} \right) \tag{7}$$

3.3   Data Preparation

The data on student interaction is collected by tracking the number of clicks made by each student for each resource. However, since a student can access a resource multiple times, it is important to determine how to collect the information for each resource. Two options are available. The first one is adding up the number of clicks on the same resource, which can represent the time spent on the resource. The second one is counting the number of times a student returns to the same resource after visiting a new one, which may represent the student's behavior. For this study, the second option has been chosen.

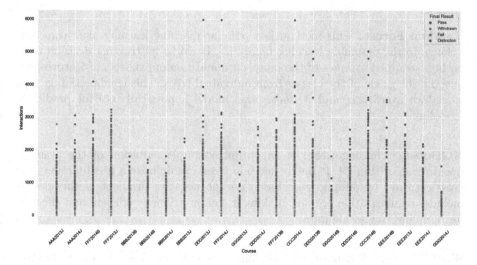

Fig. 1. Relation for course interaction grouped by the final result of each student.

Figure 1 shows the relationship between the course-interaction pair and the final result obtained by each student. The figure indicates that the number of interactions is dependent on both the course and the final result. Therefore, it is justifiable to use a machine learning model for predictions and to separate the learning processes for each course. Since the data for each course may be different, the results obtained may not always be satisfactory.

To verify this, an analysis was conducted to evaluate the relationship between interactions and the final result obtained as well as the course. The interaction data were grouped by course and the final result, and the normality and variance were checked. The analysis indicated that the data was not normal and had unequal variance. Therefore, the Kruskal-Wallis method was used to determine if there were significant differences between the populations. The analysis confirmed that there were significant differences between the interaction populations with more than 95% confidence, with a p-value lower than 0.05 and very close to 0, justifying the separation of the courses on an individual basis.

3.4   Classifiers

This section will describe all the different machine learning models that have been used to make predictions.

KNN. This method is a non-parametric, instance-based supervised learning algorithm [7]. It classifies an instance based on the majority class of its K-nearest data points in the training set using a defined distance metric (e.g. Euclidean). It is popular due to its simplicity and effectiveness on large datasets but has a high computational cost and can be sensitive to the choice of K and distance metrics.

Random Forest. This method is a popular machine learning algorithm that belongs to the ensemble learning family [3]. It works by training decision trees on bootstrapped samples of the input data and random subsets of features and outputs the mode of the classes from individual trees. This combination is used to reduce overfitting and it makes this model a powerful tool for predictive modeling.

XGBoost. This algorithm is an optimized implementation of the gradient boosting algorithm [5]. It builds decision trees to minimize a loss function (e.g. cross-entropy) by adding trees based on the negative gradient of the loss. It includes regularization options, making it computationally efficient and effective for handling large-scale data.

SVM. This method finds a hyperplane that separates linearly separable data into classes by maximizing the margin, and distance between hyperplane and support vectors, in classification problems [18]. To solve non-linearly separable problems it uses the kernel trick by projecting data into a higher dimensional space where a linear separation is possible. The algorithm can handle high-dimensional data and is robust to outliers.

CNN. This type of neural network is a deep learning algorithm [6]. It uses learnable filters to extract local features from some input data through a process called convolution. The data is then reduced in spatial dimension through pooling in order to build a hierarchy of features. Then normalized through batch normalization for faster and more stable training. Finally, it ends with a fully connected layer that outputs the final prediction.

4   Experiments and Results

Two large test batteries were conducted in the study. The first consisted of binary classification of the results, grouping pass and distinction on the one hand, and fail and withdrawn on the other. The second consisted of performing a multiclass classification for each of the results. For each test battery all the models listed in Sect. 3.4 have been carried out.

4.1 Experimental Setup

Once the data and models to be used were established, the next step was to define the structure of the CNN model and the hyperparameters to be obtained for each model. The CNN architecture, shown in Fig. 2, consists of two convolutional layers followed by normalization layers, with a max pooling layer added afterward. The output of these layers is then passed through a series of fully connected layers to produce predictions for both two-class and four-class classification problems. Each model was fitted with its respective tuning process, carried out in combination with a 10-fold cross-validation process. The parameters to be tuned for each model can be observed in Table 1 and the values tested were the most common and reasonable values that are usually used.

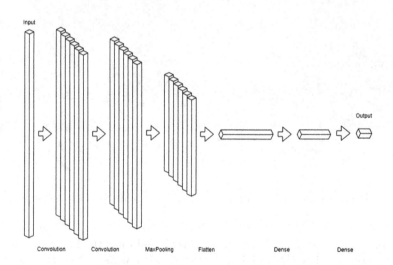

Fig. 2. CNN built for predictions.

4.2 Binary Classification

The binary classification aims to predict if the student will pass the course or not. The final results were converted to 'Pass', composed of 'Distinction' and 'Pass' and 'Fail', composed of 'Withdrawn' and 'Fail'. The results obtained with each model can be observed in Fig. 3.

The results indicate that all five models perform similarly, with KNN being the worst performer in most cases and the Random Forest having the highest mean accuracy of 92%. Figure 4 displays the results of the accuracy and

Table 1. Parameters tuned for each machine learning model.

Model	Parameters
KNN	Number of neighbors, Distance metric
Random Forest	Number of estimators, Max depth, Criterion
SVM	Regularization parameter (C), Kernel, Degree of poly kernel
XGBoost	Number of estimators, Max depth, Learning rate
CNN	Layer Neurons, Normalization, Layer activation

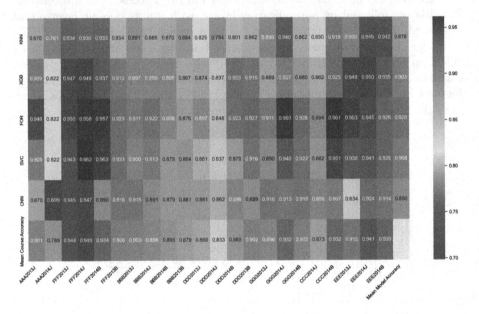

Fig. 3. Accuracies obtained by all binary models for each course.

AUC for each binary model. The SVM classifier obtains the highest accuracy of 96.19%, proving that the Random Forest is not always the best model for all courses. The Kruskal-Wallis test was performed to confirm the independence of the results obtained by the models. The test results reveal that the models are not independent, with a confidence of 95% and a p-value close to 0, indicating that each model can yield completely different results. Therefore, it is important to evaluate each model's performance for each course independently.

4.3   Multiclass Classification

The multiclass classification aims to predict all four possible final results of the students. The classifiers were used to predict 'Distinction', 'Pass', 'Withdrawn', and 'Fail'. The results obtained can be observed in Fig. 5.

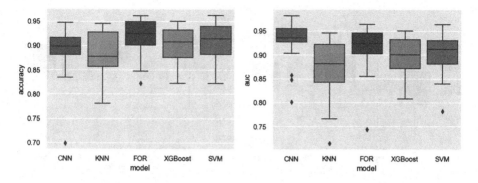

Fig. 4. Results of accuracy and AUC for each binary model.

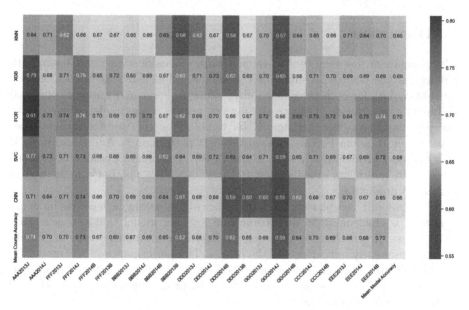

Fig. 5. Accuracies obtained by all multiclass models for each course.

The results indicate that all five models perform similarly, with KNN and CNN being the worst performers in most cases and the Random Forest having the highest mean accuracy of 70.18%. Although the highest accuracy is obtained by the Random Forest, for some of the courses this is not the case and other models achieve better results. Figure 6 displays the results of the accuracy and AUC for each binary model. These results suggest that there is no significant difference between the results for each model, so an ANOVA test was performed to verify this. The result of this test confirms that the results obtained by the models are not independent, with a confidence of 95% and a p-value close to 0, so that each model can assume completely different results.

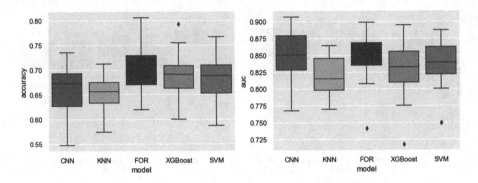

Fig. 6. Results of accuracy and AUC for each multiclass model.

5 Discussion

The comparison between multiclass and binary classification reveals some differences in the results. In multiclass prediction, classifiers deal with a smaller amount of data for each possible result, leading to lower performance compared to binary classification. Despite the uneven results, some models show consistency across tasks. For instance, KNN tends to be the worst model in most cases, while Random Forest achieves the best performance. Additionally, SVM and XGboost yield similar results in both cases. One major distinction between binary and multiclass classification is that CNN does not perform as well in multiclass prediction.

Figures 3 and 5 emphasize the importance of evaluating each course independently. It is challenging to find a machine learning model that can generalize well across different courses. None of the models used in either type of classification consistently outperformed the others. The performance of the models in binary and multiclass classification was relatively similar, with no clear winner. However, Random Forest seems to be the most promising model, as it achieved the best results in most cases.

6 Conclusions

Predicting a student's performance is essential for both students and teachers. Identifying students who are struggling can be extremely beneficial. This study proposes predicting a student's final result using only their interaction data with virtual resources, using machine learning and deep learning models.

The results of this study reveal that it is possible to predict a student's performance by analyzing their interaction data with virtual resources. It can help identify whether the student will pass or fail, or if they will drop out of the course. Furthermore, this study highlights that each course should be evaluated independently, as different courses may have unique structures and information. These predictions can be achieved using both machine learning and deep learning models, with up to 80% accuracy in some multiclass classification and up to 96% in binary classification. These results demonstrate the effectiveness of predicting student performance; however, there are still limitations that need to be addressed, such as the size and quality of data, which need to be studied in greater depth to enhance the accuracy of predictions.

In the future, a wider range of models should be evaluated to determine if there is an algorithm that can improve the predictions further for each course. It would also be interesting to examine different databases that include student interactions with virtual resources, to see if other types of interactions or structures can help determine a student's potential final performance. It would also be valuable to make predictions for different stages of the course, limiting the number of interactions to those carried out up to those points, instead of utilizing all the data to make predictions.

Acknowledgement. Research supported by the e-DIPLOMA, project number 101061424, funded by the European Union. Views and opinions expressed are, however, those of the authors only and do not necessarily reflect those of the European Union or the European Research Executive Agency (REA). Neither the European Union nor the granting authority can be held responsible for them.

Funded by
the European Union

Research is also supported by the Valencian Graduate School and Research Network of Artificial Intelligence (valgrAI).

References

1. Bhardwaj, P., Gupta, P., Panwar, H., Siddiqui, M.K., Morales-Menendez, R., Bhaik, A.: Application of deep learning on student engagement in e-learning environments. Comput. Electr. Eng. **93**, 107277 (2021)
2. Chen, H., Yin, C., Li, R., Rong, W., Xiong, Z., David, B.: Enhanced learning resource recommendation based on online learning style model. Tsinghua Sci. Technol. **25**(3), 348–356 (2019)
3. Dietterich, T.G., et al.: Ensemble learning. Handb. Brain Theory Neural Netw. **2**(1), 110–125 (2002)
4. Dutt, A., Ismail, M.A., Herawan, T.: A systematic review on educational data mining. IEEE Access **5**, 15991–16005 (2017)
5. Friedman, J.H.: Stochastic gradient boosting. Comput. Stat. Data Anal. **38**(4), 367–378 (2002)
6. Gu, J., et al.: Recent advances in convolutional neural networks. Pattern Recogn. **77**, 354–377 (2018)
7. Guo, G., Wang, H., Bell, D., Bi, Y., Greer, K.: KNN model-based approach in classification. In: Meersman, R., Tari, Z., Schmidt, D.C. (eds.) OTM 2003. LNCS, vol. 2888, pp. 986–996. Springer, Heidelberg (2003). https://doi.org/10.1007/978-3-540-39964-3_62
8. Hassan, S.U., Waheed, H., Aljohani, N.R., Ali, M., Ventura, S., Herrera, F.: Virtual learning environment to predict withdrawal by leveraging deep learning. Int. J. Intell. Syst. **34**(8), 1935–1952 (2019)
9. Hone, K.S., El Said, G.R.: Exploring the factors affecting mooc retention: a survey study. Comput. Educ. **98**, 157–168 (2016)

10. Hussain, M., Zhu, W., Zhang, W., Abidi, S.M.R.: Student engagement predictions in an e-learning system and their impact on student course assessment scores. Comput. Intell. Neurosci. **2018** (2018)
11. Katarya, R.: Deep auto encoder based on a transient search capsule network for student performance prediction. Multimedia Tools Appl., 1–25 (2022)
12. Kuzilek, J., Hlosta, M., Zdrahal, Z.: Open university learning analytics dataset. Sci. Data **4**(1), 1–8 (2017)
13. Lee, Y., Choi, J.: A review of online course dropout research: implications for practice and future research. Educ. Technol. Res. Dev. **59**, 593–618 (2011)
14. Li, M., Wang, X., Wang, Y., Chen, Y., Chen, Y.: Study-GNN: a novel pipeline for student performance prediction based on multi-topology graph neural networks. Sustainability **14**(13), 7965 (2022)
15. Lykourentzou, I., Giannoukos, I., Nikolopoulos, V., Mpardis, G., Loumos, V.: Dropout prediction in e-learning courses through the combination of machine learning techniques. Comput. Educ. **53**(3), 950–965 (2009)
16. Maatuk, A.M., Elberkawi, E.K., Aljawarneh, S., Rashaideh, H., Alharbi, H.: The covid-19 pandemic and e-learning: challenges and opportunities from the perspective of students and instructors. J. Comput. High. Educ. **34**(1), 21–38 (2022)
17. Marbouti, F., Diefes-Dux, H.A., Madhavan, K.: Models for early prediction of at-risk students in a course using standards-based grading. Comput. Educ. **103**, 1–15 (2016)
18. Noble, W.S.: What is a support vector machine? Nat. Biotechnol. **24**(12), 1565–1567 (2006)
19. Pan, Z., Cheok, A.D., Yang, H., Zhu, J., Shi, J.: Virtual reality and mixed reality for virtual learning environments. Comput. Graph. **30**(1), 20–28 (2006)
20. Van Raaij, E.M., Schepers, J.J.: The acceptance and use of a virtual learning environment in China. Comput. Educ. **50**(3), 838–852 (2008)
21. Waheed, H., et al.: Balancing sequential data to predict students at-risk using adversarial networks. Comput. Electr. Eng. **93**, 107274 (2021)
22. Waheed, H., Hassan, S.U., Aljohani, N.R., Hardman, J., Alelyani, S., Nawaz, R.: Predicting academic performance of students from vle big data using deep learning models. Comput. Human Behav. **104**, 106189 (2020)
23. Waheed, H., Hassan, S.U., Aljohani, N.R., Wasif, M.: A bibliometric perspective of learning analytics research landscape. Behav. Inf. Technol. **37**(10–11), 941–957 (2018)
24. Xing, W., Chen, X., Stein, J., Marcinkowski, M.: Temporal predication of dropouts in moocs: reaching the low hanging fruit through stacking generalization. Comput. Human Behav. **58**, 119–129 (2016)

Probabilistic Decision Trees for Predicting 12-Month University Students Likely to Experience Suicidal Ideation

Efthyvoulos Drousiotis[1]([✉]), Dan W. Joyce[2], Robert C. Dempsey[3],
Alina Haines[4], Paul G. Spirakis[5], Lei Shi[6], and Simon Maskell[1]

[1] Department of Electrical Engineering and Electronics, University of Liverpool,
Liverpool L69 3GJ, UK
{E.Drousiotis,S.Maskell}@liverpool.ac.uk

[2] Institute of Population Health, University of Liverpool, Liverpool L69 3GJ, UK
D.Joyce@liverpool.ac.uk

[3] Department of Psychology, Manchester Metropolitan University,
Manchester M15 6BH, UK
r.dempsey@mmu.ac.uk

[4] Department of Nursing, Manchester Metropolitan University,
Manchester M15 6BH, UK
a.haines@mmu.ac.uk

[5] Department of Computer Science, University of Liverpool, Liverpool L69 3BX, UK
spirakis@liverpool.ac.uk

[6] School of Computing, Newcastle University, Newcastle NE4 5TG, UK
Lei.Shi@newcastle.ac.uk

Abstract. Environmental stressors combined with a predisposition to experience mental health problems increase the risk for SI (Suicidal Ideation) among college/university students. However, university health and wellbeing services know little about machine learning methods and techniques to identify as early as possible students with higher risk. We developed an algorithm to identify university students with suicidal thoughts and behaviours using features universities already collect. We used data collected in 2020 from the American College Health Association (ACHA), a cross-sectional population-based survey including 50, 307 volunteer students. A state-of-the-art parallel Markov Chain Monte Carlo (MCMC) Decision tree was used to overcome overfitting problems and target classes with fewer representatives efficiently. Two models were fitted to the survey data featuring a range of demographic and clinical risk factors measured on the ACHA survey. The first model included variables universities would typically collect from their students (e.g., key demographics, residential status, and key health conditions). The second model included these same variables plus additional suicide-risk variables which universities would not typically measure as standard

Supplementary Information The online version contains supplementary material available at https://doi.org/10.1007/978-3-031-34111-3_40.

practice (e.g., students' sense of belonging at university). Models' performance was measured using precision, recall, F1 score, and accuracy metrics to identify any potential overfitting of the data efficiently.

Keywords: Bayesian Decision Trees · Suicidal Ideation (SI) · ACHA · Machine Learning

1   Introduction and Related Work

Suicidal thoughts, intent, plans, and attempts are concepts with varying definitions [18], resulting in variability of measurement and consequently difficulty establishing robust conclusions about which populations or individual-level clinical factors merit either screening or, at least, surveillance. Prediction for an individual's absolute risk of dying by suicide is difficult, not least because tools claiming to demonstrate predictive performance have significant caveats – for example, even in robustly developed, validated and calibrated suicide risk prediction tools [16], for thresholds of a 1% risk of suicide they display very low positive predictive value (i.e. they are poor at discriminating those who will commit suicide) but a significantly higher negative predictive value (i.e. the tool can reliably predict those who will *not* commit suicide). This pattern of relatively poor positive predictive performance alongside neglect of *how* these tools could augment human actors' work in helping people at risk of suicide [40] has led to some national guidelines recommending *against* using any structured assessment tools for managing the risk of suicide. For example, in the United Kingdom, the National Institute for Health and Care Excellence guidelines advise against using risk stratification tools [26].

The relationship between Suicidal Ideation (SI) to either attempting or committing suicide is complex. For example, the assumption of a straightforward 'linear progression' from SI to action is not empirically supported. Moreover, several key models of suicide, such as the Interpersonal Theory of Suicide [38], the Integrated Motivational-Volitional model [27], and the Three Step Theory of Suicide [21] separate the development of SI from the progression of ideation to an attempt. Given this complexity, locating individuals who might benefit from enhanced support and early intervention for both mental health problems and features associated with suicide may be logistically and practically more appropriate.

A study of UK university students designed to test the central tenets of the Three Step Theory [11] identified that SI develops in the presence of self-reported psychological pain and hopelessness cognitions. Further, "connectedness" (to others) appears to play a role in preventing the escalation of ideation to action, but also, a lack of social connectedness was independently associated with SI. University or college can be stressful for students, especially for those who are psychologically vulnerable and have poor support. University students are at an elevated risk for SI, planning, and attempts [15] potentially arising due to increased academic pressure, psycho-social stress, heavy workloads, and difficulties adapting to a new environment [5]. Around 16%–25% of students have experienced some form of SI during university, and approximately 40% and 20% of students with SI reported that they have considered or attempted suicide respectively [25].

Early identification of at-risk students is important for effective suicide prevention and allows universities to refer students to appropriate well-being, counseling, and pastoral support. Various influences and predictors on the experience of suicidal ideation amongst university students have been identified in the existing literature. In terms of mental health-related variables, the experience of more severe depressive symptoms, psychosis, and greater perceived stress have been associated with higher suicide risk [1,32], with similar associations between increased mental health symptoms and past 12-month suicidal ideation reported [3,33]. Whilst there have been limited prospective studies, there is evidence that increased suicide risk over 12 months amongst students is associated with the experience of clinically significant mood and other common mental health conditions (e.g. generalised anxiety), stressful life events, childhood adversities, reporting of physical or sexual assault [6]. Various other risk factors for self-harm and suicidality amongst university students have been identified, including sleep difficulties [36], alcohol use problems [9,29], being of a younger age and/or status as an undergraduate student [32], as well as interpersonal difficulties, such as unsupportive family environments [42].

Theoretical models of suicide [21,38] suggest addressing SI as a potentially modifiable factor in preventing suicide. Identifying students with SI is, however, challenging as most of the studies [34] rely on information about an individual's mental health obtained from (e.g.) interactions with skilled pastoral support workers. Most of the previous studies [2,8,10], including those aiming to predict SI among different populations, focus on identifying predictors for SI using posthoc, inferential statistical analyses, which may be helpful to inform predictive models. For example, inferential statistical methods also require a priori models describing the relationships between predictors and outcomes to test a specific hypothesis. As a result, there may be a number of different pathways to suicidality amongst at-risk university students considering the various risk factors that may interact to increase the vulnerability to suicidal thoughts and behaviours (i.e., suicide-related events).

The majority of the literature [5,15,20,22,23,37,41] uses traditional statistical and linear methods to analyse and identify putative factors that may be predictors of SI. Linear models and inferential statistical hypothesis testing often assume linearity of individual predictor's contribution to an outcome and very often, the models assume additivity of risk. Given the complexity of suicide in general, such approaches could hamper the ability to locate variables (or their combinations) that inform decision-making in a meaningful way [19,39]. Melissa et al. [24] conducted the only study that uses a non-linear machine learning (Random Forest) algorithm to identify possible predictors for students with SI considering 70 features. However, identifying factors associated with SI does not necessarily imply that they could help predict future students with SI [7].

The aforementioned studies were mainly conducted as explanatory analyses to help inform universities about the possible factors leading to SI in student populations. In contrast, our study attempts to efficiently and effectively predict students with SI using data universities and colleges possess before a student starts their studies. Universities need understandable algorithms that are easily applied to data they already have, for example, to stratify students at risk of SI and to target resources appropriately to those who might most benefit.

Most of the papers in the literature tend to report analyses conducted on samples that contain relatively small amounts of data, with some large inconsistencies in sample sizes across previous studies. This problem is previously addressed [35], where the median number of participants across studies related to suicidal ideation was 79 and the mean 710. The features sample size in past studies have varied from 1085 to 5572 [15,20,22,24,37,41]. To address this issue of inconsistent and relatively small sample sizes used in past research, we conducted machine learning-based analyses on a sample of 50,307 students from the American College Health Association (ACHA) survey to provide a more robust and reliable understanding of the predictors of suicidal ideation in university students. To achieve this aim, we conducted two separate analyses. Firstly, a machine learning model featuring data that universities are likely to collect as part of their normal operations was fitted to the data (e.g., information about the student's general health). Secondly, we tested a more comprehensive model featuring this information plus a variety of variables from the ACHA survey implicated in suicidality (e.g., social connectedness variables) which universities may not normally collect from their students. We ran these two models to investigate which offers the more robust and accurate predictive model of suicidal ideation in university students and identify possible important vulnerability factors for suicidality in students that universities may need to collect in the future. A scalable and transparent state-of-the-art machine learning algorithm, a parallel MCMC Decision Tree, processed the models.

2   Methods

2.1   Dataset and Data Preparation

The dataset used in this study is provided by ACHA[1](American College Health Association), a nationally recognised research survey that provides precise data about students' health habits, behaviours, and perceptions. The dataset contains information from 2020 of 50,307 students (68% *females*, 31% *males*, < 1% *intersex*) and 694 features including demographics, Likert scale questions, and multiple choice questions (MCQ).

The mean age of the sample was 22.5 years. Most students reported living either on campus or in university housing (39.6%) or off-campus or in non-university housing(46.4%). 12.8% of the students lived in their parents'/guardian' or other family member's house, 0.2% temporarily stayed with a relative, friend, or "couch surfing" until they found housing, < 0.1% did not

---

[1] https://www.acha.org/ACHA/Resources/Survey_Data/ACHA/Resources/ Survey_Data.aspx.

(currently) have a place to live, and 0.9% lived in other types of accommodation. 52% of the students were not in a relationship, 39.3% were in a relationship, and 8.7% were married or partnered. Of the 50,307 participants in the sample, 53.8% never thought about killing themselves, 25.7% had a brief passing thought about suicide/planning suicide, 15.3% had a plan at least once to kill themselves, and 5.2% had attempted to kill themselves. Specifically, 55.7% of girls, 57.8% of boys, and 44.4% of intersex students never thought about killing themselves, 27.3% of girls, 25.9% of boys, and 22.2% of intersex students had a brief passing thought about suicide/planning suicide, 11.1% of girls, 12.9% of boys, and 27.3% of intersex students had a plan at least one to kill themselves, and 5.9% of girls, 3.4% of boys, and 5.6% of intersex students had attempted to kill themselves. The main baseline characteristics did not significantly differ based on gender.

From the 694 available features, we used only the 16 features that universities already had (information asked during their UCAS application) to predict students' SI. For the secondary analysis, we used 182 features implicated in suicide risk which universities did not typically collect from students. Due to the large number of features we used for the secondary model, please find the table containing the features and the associated features' importance on the supplementary material. Our target variable asks the students if they thought about suicide in the past year, meaning that we predict students with suicidal ideation. For this particular question, there are five possible answers, never (1), rarely (2), sometimes (3), often (4), and very often (5). Participants who chose answers 2 to 5 were coded as positive for SI. We avoided any data pre-processing techniques (Oversampling, Undersampling, Principal Component Analysis, etc.), as we wanted our data to be as original as possible and keep the transparent nature of our algorithm, and allow practical conclusions to be drawn based on the raw data as collected on the ACHA survey. Table 1 demonstrates the imbalanced nature of our data, showing the number of students who reported SI compared to those who did not report SI. Specifically, 34,626 students didn't report any SI during the last year, while 15,681 students reported at least one SI during the last year.

Table 1. Percentage of students reporting SI

Number of students	Percentage	SI
34626	68.3%	No (0)
15681	31.17%	Yes (1)

2.2 Markov Chain Monte Carlo Decision Tree

A decision tree typically starts with a root node, which branches into possible outcomes. Each of those outcomes leads to additional decision nodes, which branch off into other possibilities ending up in leaf nodes. This gives it a tree-like shape.

Our model describes the conditional distribution of y given x, where x is a vector of predictors $[x = (x_1, x_2, ..., x_p)]$. The main components of the $tree(T)$

include the depth of the tree, $(d(T))$, the features, $(k(T))$, and the thresholds, $(c(T))$, for each node where $\theta = [k(T), c(T)]$, and the conditional probabilities $p(Y|T, \theta, x)$ for each leaf node, $(L(T))$. If x lies in the region corresponding to the i_{th} terminal node, then $y|x$ has distribution $f(y|\theta_i)$, where f represents a parametric family indexed by θ_i. The model is called a probabilistic classification tree, according to the quantitative response y.

As Decision Trees are identified by (θ, T), a Bayesian analysis of the problem proceeds by specifying a prior probability distribution, $p(\theta, T)$. Because θ indexes the parametric model for each T, it will usually be convenient to use the relationship

$$p(Y_1 :_N, T, \theta | x_1 :_N) = p(Y|T, \theta, x)p(\theta|T)p(T) \tag{1}$$

The Metropolis-Hastings (MH) algorithm for simulating the Markov Chain in Decision Trees (see Eq. 2) is defined as follows. Starting with an initial tree T_0, iteratively simulate the transitions from T_i to $T_i + 1$ by these two steps:

1. Generate a candidate value T' with probability distribution $q(T_i, T')$.
2. Set $T_{i+1} = T'$ with probability

$$a(T_i, T') = \min(1, \frac{\pi(Y_1 :_N, T', \theta'|x_1 :_N)}{\pi(Y_1 :_N, T, \theta|x_1 :_N)} \frac{q(T, \theta|T', \theta')}{q(T', \theta'|T, \theta)}) \tag{2}$$

Otherwise set $T_{i+1} = T_i$.

More information and a detailed explanation of the algorithm can be found here [14]

To evaluate our predictive model's performance, we used the following four metrics.

- Precision: the ratio of the correctly predicted positive observations to the total predicted positive observations.
- Recall: the ratio of correctly predicted positive observations to all observations in the actual positive class.
- F1-score: the weighted average of Precision row and Recall row. Therefore, this score takes both false positives and false negatives into account.
- Accuracy: the most intuitive performance measure and it is simply a ratio of correctly predicted observations to the total observations.

We also performed cross-validation by randomly splitting the initial dataset into 10 folds, where each fold was used as a test, and we repeated this process until all the folds were used as test sets.

The main advantage of the probabilistic machine learning (ML) models over conventional ML is that they are known to generalise better on imbalanced data and are less overfitting prone [12,13], allowing us to avoid data pre-processing techniques. We have further modified the algorithm to produce even more accurate results by adding special weights to the students with SI. Specifically, we instructed our algorithms to classify a student as a 0 (people with no SI) only if it is more than 69% confident. This practice enabled us to further increase our performance metrics (accuracy, F1-score) and fight off overfitting due to the imbalanced nature of the dataset. In general, we believe that applying heavy data pre-processing techniques alters the dataset nature, leading us to solve a different problem, ending up having algorithms working only for the specific dataset and not being able to generalise. Our philosophy is to change and modify the algorithms to fit the problem, not vice versa.

3 Results

3.1 Predicting

For the students with SI using the features universities normally collect (e.g., through university application forms), the model had an out-of-bag error of 29.2% ± 0.9, leading to an accuracy of 70.8% ± 0.9. The predictive (0) values were 0.77, whereas the predictive (1) values were 0.55, meaning that 77% and 55% of predicted cases were actually cases. Table 2 shows the scores analytically for predicting students with SI. Specifically precision score is 65.33% ± 0.7, recall score is 64.16% ± 0.4, and f1-score 64.8% ± 0.4 Analyses of the importance of the variables for the prediction, measured by the times each variable is used on the predictive model, revealed that the following four variables were the most predictive, as shown in Table 3: Depression, Eating Disorder, Approximate Cumulative Average Grade, and Attending Classes, Discussion sections, or Labs.

3.2 Secondary Analysis

For the students with SI using the features universities might not ordinarily collect, the model had an out-of-bag error of 27.1% ± 3.96, leading to an accuracy of 72.9% ± 3.96. The predictive (0) values were 0.83, whereas the predictive (1) values were 0.58, meaning that 83% and 58% of predicted cases were actually cases. Table 2 shows the scores analytically for predicting students with SI. Specifically precision score is 70.30% ± 2.28, recall score is 71.3% ± 2.23, and f1-score 69.8% ± 2.99 Analyses of the importance of the variables for the prediction, measured by the times each variable is used on the predictive model, revealed that the following four variables were the most predictive, as shown in Table 3: Financial Problems, Bullying, Allergies to pets/animals, Gastroesophageal Reflux Disease/Acid Reflux.

Table 2. Metrics for predicting students with SI

	Precision	Recall	F1-score	Accuracy
With Uni Features	65.33 ± 0.74	64.16 ± 0.37	65.83 ± 0.37	70.83 ± 0.89
Without Uni Features	70.30 ± 2.28	71.30 ± 2.23	69.80 ± 2.99	72.9 ± 3.96

Table 3. Features Importance for Variables Universities Collect from Students

Features	Feature Importance(%)
Age	1.6
Anxiety (Generalized Anxiety, Social Anxiety, Panic Disorder	6.8
Approximate Cumulative Average Grade	9.1
Attending Classes, Discussion sections, or Labs	8.0
Bipolar and Related Conditions (Bipolar I, II, Hypomanic Episode)	7.4
Biracial or Multiracial	5.5
Black or African American	4.2
Blind/Low Vision	5.2
Depression(Major Depression, Persistent Depressive	15.0
Diabetes or pre-diabetes/insulin resistance	2.7
Eating Disorder(Anorexia Nervosa, Bulimia Nervosa, Binge - Eating)	10.0
Enrollment Status	3.60
Insomnia	5.4
Middle Eastern/North African or Arab Origin	1.3
Parent or Guardian of a Child	7.6
Sex assigned at birth	5.6

4 Discussion

Predicting which university students are at higher risk of SI and potentially suicidal behaviours is a difficult task. Past studies in this area have been limited by using relatively small and unrepresentative samples of data and relying on researcher-led choices of which data to use in predictive models of suicidal ideation, meaning a lack of consistency and comprehensiveness in previous research [15,22,24]. To address these issues, we applied machine learning approaches to understand the variables associated with suicidal ideation amongst students based on an existing large survey of US students (over 50,000 participants) and the testing of predictive variables that universities routinely and seldom collect from incoming students.

Using a parallel MCMC Decision Tree model for the features universities already have, we found that four main baseline variables predicted SI: Depression, Eating Disorder, Approximate Cumulative Average Grade, and Attending Classes(Discussion sections, Labs) with a significance level of 15%, 10%, 9.1%, 8% accordingly. The model including those variables showed a good predictive performance (accuracy = 70.83 ± 0.89) estimated using cross-validation. In secondary analyses in a wider sample of (number of) features, the main predictive variables differed from the main analyses. Having Financial Problems contributed to a

4.13%, Bullying contributed to a 3.03%, Allergies to pets/animals contributed to a 4.13%, and Gastroesophageal Reflux Disease or acid reflux contributed to a 3.87%. The model, including the dataset with bigger feature space, had an improved predictive accuracy than the one using only the universities' typical features, with a predictive accuracy of 72.9 ± 3.96. We also achieved better results for both test cases (predicting students with SI, secondary analyses) compared to other studies predicting students with SI utilising a machine learning model(Random Forest). Specifically, [24] achieved 0.4 and 0.36 predicted (1) values for girls and boys, respectively, meaning that 40% and 36% of predicted cases were actual cases. In comparison, we achieved 0.55 and 0.58, which leads to a significant increase of 15% for girls and 19% for boys when we use features universities have, while 18% and 22% improvement achieved for our secondary analyses.

Machine learning approaches offer universities potentially powerful means of understanding the risk factors for suicidality amongst their student populations. There may be the potential for universities to use similar models at a local level considering risk factors that may be unique to their campuses, location, and student population. Understanding more local-level risk factors may be important for university health and wellbeing services to better identify those at risk for suicidal ideation and to provide more targeted early intervention support for students at a heightened risk.

There are some strengths and limitations to consider with the present study. As discussed earlier, previous studies of the risk factors associated with suicidal ideation amongst university students have been limited by their analysis of relatively small samples [20,37]. In contrast, our study drew on data from a large national sample of US university students (over 50,000 students) and applied machine learning approaches to develop predictive models of students' suicidal ideation. Based on a prior call [17], the present machine learning study has allowed for the modelling of numerous variables in a predictive model of suicidal ideation. Such models offer a more detailed understanding of university student suicidal ideation and accommodate the modelling of potentially hundreds of predictors and their complex inter-relationships, compared to the dominance of regression-based analyses in the literature, which only accommodate the testing of relatively simplistic models of suicidality [17]. In addition, the use of an existing, large, representative national survey to model potential predictors of suicidality amongst university students reduced potential research ethical issues associated with collecting suicide-related data from at-risk individuals.

There are, however, some limitations to the present study to consider. The study analysed data from an ongoing national US student survey from only one-time point. Given the complex and dynamic nature of suicidality, how these factors identified in the machine learning model influence suicidality over the longer term requires further exploration. It should also be noted that the specific predictors identified here may not be generalisable to students in other countries, where there may be more local and unique pressures on students implicated in suicidal ideation. We also focused on the experience of suicidal ideation as a broad outcome in the machine learning models and did not include detailed assessments of the types of suicidal thoughts students experienced (such as active planning versus more passive ideation), and so care should be taken in assuming that these factors are similarly implicated in suicidal behaviours amongst students. Although, it is important to identify the potential factors implicated in the suicidal ideation-to-enaction process, particularly those associated with earlier suicidal thoughts where targeted interventions may be particularly effective. In addition, the survey data used in the machine learning approach here did not feature many key psychological variables implicated in the suicidality pathways, such as feelings of defeat and entrapment [17,30,31]. The factors in the models also tended to be more risk-focused in nature rather than encapsulate more protective factors against suicidality, and did not explicitly test existing models of suicidality which attempt to outline the ideation-to-enaction pathway [4,27,28]. Integrating factors associated with reduced suicidality, including more factors of a bio-psycho-social basis, may be promising for future machine learning approaches focusing on understanding suicidality in at-risk populations.

5   Conclusion

University students are a high-risk group for suicidal thoughts, feelings, and behaviours, but predicting which specific students are at higher risk is a difficult endeavour. Machine learning-based approaches offer a unique way of understanding suicide risk based on their ability to model a large and complex range of factors at the same time. Still, few machine learning approaches have been used to understand suicide risk in university students. Our study differs from most of the literature, as we discussed in Sect. 1. We trained a state-of-the-art MCMC Decision Tree with a large sample (over 50,000 participants) for the first time. We showed that such a machine learning-based approach could significantly contribute towards identifying and predicting suicidal ideation among university students. Unlike the other studies, we focused on the actual predictive model and how to produce optimal solutions instead of only identifying possible factors leading students to SI. Our approach can potentially help universities quickly identify and provide early interventions targeting students with these suicide-risk factors. Moreover, our model outperforms significantly any other similar implementation by an average of 17%, and 20% when a wider sample of features is used. This study, though, has some limitations. The study focused only on SI and not suicidal behaviours, as we should note that the results may not be generalisable to students in other countries.

References

1. Akram, U.: Prevalence and psychiatric correlates of suicidal ideation in UK university students. J. Affect. Disord. **272**, 191–197 (2020)
2. Mohamad Ashari, Z., Liow, Y.E., Binti Zainudin, N.F.: Psychological risk factors and suicidal ideation among undergraduate students of a Malaysian public university•. Jurnal Kemanusiaan **19**, 33–40 (2022)

3. Bantjes, J.R., Kagee, A., McGowan, T., Steel, H.: Symptoms of posttraumatic stress, depression, and anxiety as predictors of suicidal ideation among South African university students. J. Am. Coll. Health **64**(6), 429–437 (2016)
4. Barzilay, S., Apter, A.: Psychological models of suicide. Arch. Suicide Res. **18**(4), 295–312 (2014)
5. Blasco, M.J., et al.: Predictive models for suicidal thoughts and behaviors among Spanish university students: rationale and methods of the universal (university & mental health) project. BMC Psychiatry **16**(1), 1–13 (2016)
6. Blasco, M.J., et al.: First-onset and persistence of suicidal ideation in university students: a one-year follow-up study. J. Affect. Disord. **256**, 192–204 (2019)
7. Bzdok, D., Varoquaux, G., Steyerberg, E.W.: Prediction, not association, paves the road to precision medicine. JAMA Psychiatry **78**(2), 127–128 (2021)
8. Cong, C.W., Ling, W.S.: The predicting effects of depression and selfesteem on suicidal ideation among adolescents in Kuala Lumpur, Malaysia: Received 2019-10-10; Accepted 2020-01-06; Published 2020-04-17. J. Health Transl. Med. **23**(1), 60–66 (2020)
9. Coryell, W., et al.: Alcohol intake in relation to suicidal ideation and behavior among university students. J. Am. Coll. Health 1–5 (2021)
10. De Choudhury, M., Kiciman, E., Dredze, M., Coppersmith, G., Kumar, M.: Discovering shifts to suicidal ideation from mental health content in social media. In: Proceedings of the 2016 CHI Conference on Human Factors in Computing Systems, pp. 2098–2110 (2016)
11. Dhingra, K., Klonsky, E.D., Tapola, V.: An empirical test of the three-step theory of suicide in UK university students. Suicide Life-Threat. Behav. **49**(2), 478–487 (2019)
12. Drousiotis, E., Pentaliotis, P., Shi, L., Cristea, A.I.: Capturing fairness and uncertainty in student dropout prediction – a comparison study. In: Roll, I., McNamara, D., Sosnovsky, S., Luckin, R., Dimitrova, V. (eds.) AIED 2021. LNCS (LNAI), vol. 12749, pp. 139–144. Springer, Cham (2021). https://doi.org/10.1007/978-3-030-78270-2_25
13. Drousiotis, E., Pentaliotis, P., Shi, L., Cristea, A.I.: Balancing fined-tuned machine learning models between continuous and discrete variables - a comprehensive analysis using educational data. In: Rodrigo, M.M., Matsuda, N., Cristea, A.I., Dimitrova, V. (eds.) Artificial Intelligence in Education. AIED 2022. LNCS, vol. 13355. Springer, Cham (2022). https://doi.org/10.1007/978-3-031-11644-5_21
14. Drousiotis, E., Spirakis, P.G.: Single MCMC chain parallelisation on decision trees. In: Simos, D.E., Rasskazova, V.A., Archetti, F., Kotsireas, I.S., Pardalos, P.M. (eds) Learning and Intelligent Optimization. LION 2022. LNCS, vol. 13621, pp. 191–204. Springer, Cham (2022). https://doi.org/10.1007/978-3-031-24866-5_15
15. Eskin, M., et al.: Suicidal behavior and psychological distress in university students: a 12-nation study. Arch. Suicide Res. **20**(3), 369–388 (2016)
16. Fazel, S., Wolf, A., Larsson, H., Mallett, S., Fanshawe, T.R.: The prediction of suicide in severe mental illness: development and validation of a clinical prediction rule (OxMIS). Transl. Psychiatry **9**(1), 1–10 (2019)
17. Franklin, J.C., et al.: Risk factors for suicidal thoughts and behaviors: a meta-analysis of 50 years of research. Psychol. Bull. **143**(2), 187 (2017)
18. Goodfellow, B., Kolves, K., De Leo, D.: Contemporary nomenclatures of suicidal behaviors: a systematic literature review. Suicide Life-Threat. Behav. **48**(3), 353–366 (2018)
19. Hedegaard, H., Warner, M.: Suicide mortality in the united states, 1999–2019 (2021)

20. Keyes, C.L.M., Eisenberg, D., Perry, G.S., Dube, S.R., Kroenke, K., Dhingra, S.S.: The relationship of level of positive mental health with current mental disorders in predicting suicidal behavior and academic impairment in college students. J. Am. Coll. Health **60**(2), 126–133 (2012)

21. Klonsky, E.D., May, A.M.: The three-step theory (3ST): a new theory of suicide rooted in the "ideation-to-action" framework. Int. J. Cogn. Therapy **8**(2), 114–129 (2015)

22. Knorr, A.C., Ammerman, B.A., Hamilton, A.J., McCloskey, M.S.: Predicting status along the continuum of suicidal thoughts and behavior among those with a history of nonsuicidal self-injury. Psychiatry Res. **273**, 514–522 (2019)

23. Liu, C.H., Stevens, C., Wong, S.H.M., Yasui, M., Chen, J.A.: The prevalence and predictors of mental health diagnoses and suicide among us college students: implications for addressing disparities in service use. Depression Anxiety **36**(1), 8–17 (2019)

24. Macalli, M., et al.: A machine learning approach for predicting suicidal thoughts and behaviours among college students. Sci. Rep. **11**(1), 1–8 (2021)

25. Mortier, P., et al.: The prevalence of suicidal thoughts and behaviours among college students: a meta-analysis. Psychol. Med. **48**(4), 554–565 (2018)

26. NICE. Self-harm: assessment, management and preventing recurrence. https://www.nice.org.uk/guidance/ng225

27. O'Connor, R.C., Kirtley, O.J.: The integrated motivational-volitional model of suicidal behaviour. Philos. Trans. R. Soc. B Biol. Sci. **373**(1754), 20170268 (2018)

28. O'Connor, R.C., Nock, M.K.: The psychology of suicidal behaviour. Lancet Psychiatry **1**(1), 73–85 (2014)

29. O'Neill, S., et al.: Socio-demographic, mental health and childhood adversity risk factors for self-harm and suicidal behaviour in college students in Northern Ireland. J. Affect. Disord. **239**, 58–65 (2018)

30. Owen, R., Dempsey, R., Jones, S., Gooding, P.: Defeat and entrapment in bipolar disorder: exploring the relationship with suicidal ideation from a psychological theoretical perspective. Suicide Life-Threat. Behav. **48**(1), 116–128 (2018)

31. O'Connor, R.C., Portzky, G.: The relationship between entrapment and suicidal behavior through the lens of the integrated motivational-volitional model of suicidal behavior. Curr. Opinion Psychol. **22**, 12–17 (2018)

32. Parker, M., et al.: Prevalence of moderate and acute suicidal ideation among a national sample of tribal college and university students 2014–2015. Arch. Suicide Res. **25**(3), 406–423 (2021)

33. Rahman, Md.E., Islam, Md.S., Mamun, M.A., Moonajilin, Mst.S., Yi, S.: Prevalence and factors associated with suicidal ideation among university students in Bangladesh. Arch. Suicide Res. **26**(2), 975–984 (2022)

34. Ream, G.L.: The interpersonal-psychological theory of suicide in college student suicide screening. Suicide Life-Threat. Behav. **46**(2), 239–247 (2016)

35. Ribeiro, J.D., et al.: Self-injurious thoughts and behaviors as risk factors for future suicide ideation, attempts, and death: a meta-analysis of longitudinal studies. Psychol. Med. **46**(2), 225–236 (2016)

36. Russell, K., Allan, S., Beattie, L., Bohan, J., MacMahon, K., Rasmussen, S.: Sleep problem, suicide and self-harm in university students: a systematic review. Sleep Med. Rev. **44**, 58–69 (2019)

37. Shim, G., Jeong, B.: Predicting suicidal ideation in college students with mental health screening questionnaires. Psychiatry Investig. **15**(11), 1037 (2018)

38. Van Orden, K.A., Witte, T.K., Cukrowicz, K.C., Braithwaite, S.R., Selby, E.A., Joiner Jr., T.E.: The interpersonal theory of suicide. Psychol. Rev. **117**(2), 575 (2010)

39. Walsh, C.G., Ribeiro, J.D., Franklin, J.C.: Predicting risk of suicide attempts over time through machine learning. Clin. Psychol. Sci. **5**(3), 457–469 (2017)

40. Whiting, D., Fazel, S.: How accurate are suicide risk prediction models? Asking the right questions for clinical practice. Evid. Based Ment. Health **22**(3), 125–128 (2019)

41. Wilcox, H.C., Arria, A.M., Caldeira, K.M., Vincent, K.B., Pinchevsky, G.M., O'Grady, K.E.: Prevalence and predictors of persistent suicide ideation, plans, and attempts during college. J. Affect. Disord. **127**(1–3), 287–294 (2010)

42. Zhai, H., et al.: Correlation between family environment and suicidal ideation in university students in China. Int. J. Environ. Res. Public Health **12**(2), 1412–1424 (2015)

CNN - Convolutional Neural Networks
YOLO CNN

3D Attention Based YOLO-SWINF for Real-Time Video Object Detection

Pradeep Moturi🆔, Mukund Khanna🆔, and Kunal Singh$^{(\boxtimes)}$🆔

AI@Scale, Fractal Analytics, Mumbai, India
{pradeep.moturi,mukund.khanna,kunal.singh}@fractal.ai
https://fractal.ai/

Abstract. Video object detection has a lot of applications that require detections in real-time, but these applications are unable to leverage the high accuracy of current SOTA video object detection models due to their high computational requirements. A popular approach to overcome this limitation is to reduce the frame sampling rate, but this comes at the cost of losing important temporal information from these frames. Thus, the most widely used object detection models for real-time applications are image-based single-stage models. Therefore, there is a need for a model that can capture the temporal information from the other frames in a video to boost detection results while still staying real-time. To this end, we propose a YOLOX based video object detection model YOLO-SWINF. Particularly, we introduce a 3D-attention based module that uses a three-dimensional window to capture information across the temporal dimension. We integrate this module with the YOLOX backbone to take advantage of the single-stage nature of YOLOX. We extensively test this module on the ImageNet-VID dataset and show that it has an improvement of 3 AP points over the baseline with just less than 1 ms increase in inference time. Our model is comparable to current real-time SOTA models in accuracy while being the fastest. Our YOLO-SWINF-X model achieves 80.4% AP at 38FPS on NVIDIA 1080Ti GPU.

Keywords: Video object detection · 3D Attention module · Real-time · YOLOX

1 Introduction

One of the main focuses of deep learning and computer vision research is object detection in videos. Most real-world applications of object detection like people tracking, self-driving cars, surveillance etc., require detection models to be run on a set of input frames in the form of videos. These videos often suffer from a degradation in quality due to various reasons like motion blur, camera defocus, and occlusion which significantly increases the difficulty of detection. Another constraint in these applications is that the detections are often needed in real-time. The current state-of-the-art deep learning models deal with these issues by

© IFIP International Federation for Information Processing 2023
Published by Springer Nature Switzerland AG 2023
I. Maglogiannis et al. (Eds.): AIAI 2023, IFIP AICT 675, pp. 491–502, 2023.
https://doi.org/10.1007/978-3-031-34111-3_41

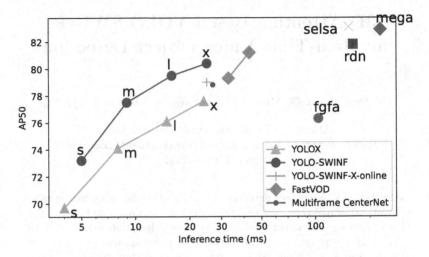

Fig. 1. AP50 vs Inference time in milliseconds with the x axis being in log scale and our YOLO-SWINF models are tested on NVIDIA 1080 Ti GPU while the other models inference times are tested on NVIDIA 2080Ti GPU

combining information from other frames, but these models are computationally intensive meaning they are often not real-time. These problems become even more apparent when these large-scale models need to be deployed on computationally limited platforms. This necessitates a trade-off between model complexity and inference time by using smaller models which are faster but have worse performance. So, this presents an intriguing application-based research challenge of designing object detection models that can provide a better trade-off between detection accuracy and inference time while simultaneously being able to gather information from other frames of the video to solve the issue of video quality degradation.

One simple way of getting detection results in real-time is to use single-stage object detectors like the YOLO [2,4,7,8,14] series models on each frame of the video. These models localise and categorise the objects in an image all at once and are thus able to meet the real-time requirements but fall short of the required standard for accuracy as they do not inculcate results from other frames. Another approach is to use image based two-stage object detectors. These detectors choose region proposals in the image and subsequently do classification on these regions. Two-stage detectors [15] are more accurate than one-stage detectors, but do not get results in real-time because of their two-stage nature. Like single-stage detectors they also do not combine the temporal information from other frames and are susceptible to the same problem. To use two-stage detectors one approach is to skip the processing frames (in other words, by reducing the sampling frequency for processing). Yet doing so also means passing up on potentially crucial information in between frames. And to get detections for the skipped frames, the detected boxes need to be interpolated which further degrades their performance.

As a result, using simple single frame object detectors is not ideal. Hence, a model is needed that can incorporate temporal information, offer greater accuracy than one-stage detectors, and be faster than two-stage detectors. The current state-of-the-art methods for video object detection (VOD), such as MEGA [3], and SELSA [23], which use the temporal information between the frames to identify objects are extremely slow and are not real-time even on most GPUs. They use two-stage detectors as backbone to identify the region proposals in the target frame and the neighbouring frames, and then use a feature aggregation module to combine the features across the temporal dimension. The complexity of the frame aggregation method and the fact that existing VOD detectors are two-stage are the key drawbacks of present VOD technologies, which result in slow inference speed. They can solve the problem of frame aggregation, but it comes at the cost of speed.

Contribution: In this research, we present a 3D attention based temporal fusion block that was incorporated at the end of the backbone of YOLOX [4] models to create light-weight VOD models that can exploit temporal information effectively and under real-time restrictions. Because of its anchor-free, single-stage design, the YOLOX [4] model offers a fair trade-off between detection accuracy and inference speed, which is why we chose it to evaluate our module. As can be observed from Fig. 1. We achieve an AP50 of 80.4% while running at 38 FPS on NVIDIA 1080Ti GPU. Furthermore, our medium model is comparable to baseline YOLOX-X model in performance and can run at over 4× the FPS.

2   Related Work

This section will explore the current approaches in object detection which are related to this work. Video object detection is an extension of image-based detectors to a continuous stream of images; therefore, we also explore single frame object detectors. Single frame object detectors can be broadly classified into two categories- Two stage and One stage detector. As the name suggests, two-stage detectors first identify the key regions in an image which may have an object using a RPN and then extract the features from that region using techniques like ROIpool and ROIalign. The final detections are obtained using a classification and regression head which uses these region features as an input. Some of the well-known two-stage detectors in academia are RCNN [16], Faster RCNN [15] and Mask RCNN [9]. Although these models have good performance in object detection tasks, they fail in real-world scenarios when the frames suffer from degradation which reduces their performance. Thus, these models, are not suited for video object detection. Whereas one stage object detector directly gives the class probability and bounding box coordinates from the single input image, without the intermediate step of extracting region proposals. There are many one-stage object detectors such as the YOLO [2,4,7,14] series, SSD [22],

RetinaNet [20] and FCOS [26]. These detectors are faster than two-stage object detectors since they do the detection in one go. However, these models lack the accuracy provided by two-stage object detectors. Like two-stage detectors these models also heavily depend on the quality of the input frames and are unable to solve issues like motion blue or occlusion reducing their usefulness for video object detection tasks.

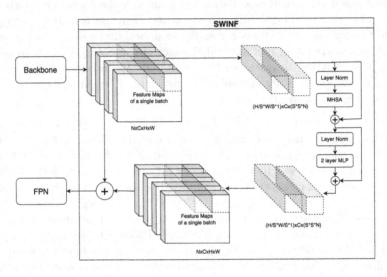

Fig. 2. Architecture diagram of SwinF module where X represents the input image size, the training is done in two phases, during phase 1 the baseline YOLOX model is trained i.e., the backbone, the neck and the head

To overcome this problem of degradation of video frames, temporal data from other frames in the video can be used for more accurate identification of keyframe contamination. As the name implies, VOD approaches use data from nearby frames to identify objects. To extract and aggregate this data to get cues from various frames, there are numerous methods available.

The detectors like DFF [29], FGFA [28], THP [27], and MANet [21] integrate the motion information in the video by explicitly calculating the optical flow of the images and aggregating the features accordingly. One major drawback with this class of detectors is that training a model for flow extraction is expensive and they are inherently slow because the model needs to compute the optical flow of each image to get detections. The accuracy of the detections also depends on the accuracy of the optical flow estimations.

Techniques like REPP [18], Seq-NMS [6], Seq-Box [1] matching are box level post-processing methods that link objects across frames by feature similarity and enhance detections scores for the frames. Other techniques like, TrackNet [10] and Global Correlation Network [11], simultaneously detect a 3D tube enclosing a moving object in a video segment by extending the faster R-CNN framework [15]. Thus, they do detection and tracking invadjust an end-to-end manner.

Most of the existing detectors in this class are based on two-stage detectors which makes them unsuitable for real-time applications or they are post-processing techniques which are used after the detections are already available. RNN-based detectors consist of methods like Mobile-VOD [12] which combine fast single image object detection with LSTM layers to create an inter-weaved recurrent convolutional neural network. ROLO [5] uses a convolutional network as a back-bone to extract bounding boxes from each frame and feed these features into an LSTM network. These methods apply LSTMs as post-processing on top of net-work outputs which effectively makes them two-stage and reduced the inference speed. Lastly, Attention based models utilize attention mechanism to capture temporal dependencies. The models like MEGA [3]- and SELSA [23] focusing on carrying temporal information in form of attention on region proposals. SELSA proposed a long-range feature aggregation approach based on semantic similarity between the region level features. MEGA proposes a long-range memory module which enables the key frame to get access to the information from global and local frames. Although these approaches give a considerable boost to detection accuracy, they are based on two stage detectors and suffer from slow inference speed.

3   Proposed Method

As previously discussed, the major drawback of existing video object detection methods is that they are not real-time due to their two-stage nature while the single-stage detectors lack the detection accuracy. To overcome this limitation, we propose YOLO-SWINF to collate spatial and temporal information from neighbouring frames in a video. We use YOLOX [4] models as our baseline, because they are single stage detectors. A YOLOX model consists of a CSP-Darknet backbone, a PAFPN neck and a decoupled head. The PAFPN neck takes as input three feature maps from the backbone at three different level for feature aggregation and outputs 3 feature maps to the decoupled head. The head then processes these outputs to get detections. Followed by this, object confidence thresholding and Non-Max Suppression (NMS) are applied to obtain final object bounding boxes. We place our Swin [25] based SwinF module at the end of the backbone and just before the PAFPN neck. The overall architecture is depicted in Fig. 2. The input to the YOLOX model is a batch of feature maps with B sets where each set consists of N neighbouring frames randomly sampled from a random video. Thus, the input to the model is of shape (B, N, 3, 576, 576). This tensor is flattened along the first two dimensions to get the input of the backbone as shape (B*N,3, 576, 576), effectively making the batch size as B*N. This tensor is passed through the backbone to get an output of shape (B*N, C, H, W) where C is the number of channels and HxW is the feature map size. The input to the attention module requires each batch to have all the neighbouring frames, thus the input is split back into shape (B, N, C, H, W).

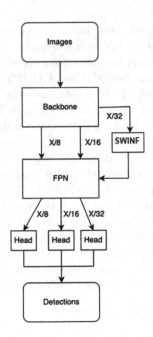

Fig. 3. End to End design of YOLO-SWINF, we place our block at the end of 'Dark5' output of the CSPDarknet platform; our module YOLO-SWINF stants for YOLO SWIN Fusion

The attention module is a SWIN block consisting of a window attention layer with a 3D window of shape (N, S, S) followed by an MLP layer which brings the total number of windows to (H/S * W/S * 1). Each layer is preceded by a layer normalization and followed by a dropout layer. We found that setting the dropout probability to zero gave better results, so dropout is disabled. The input is permuted to channel first dimension because we want the 3D window to traverse along the temporal dimension. This ensure that each window is looking at all the frames when doing attention. The window size in the spatial dimension, S is set to 6 to get a fair-trade off between computational complexity and accuracy. After the attention enhanced feature maps are calculated for all the frames in a batch, a residual connection is used to add the input feature maps to the attention enhanced feature maps. The hypothesis is that in cases when there is too much object movement then the attention feature maps might end up focusing on the wrong object. Thus, we use a residual connection to ensure that some of the previous context is also carried forward.

The output feature maps are again of shape (B, N, C, H, W). But the PAFPN neck requires the input to be 4 dimensional of shape (batch size, feature map size). Thus, the output is again flattened across the first two dimension to get the input to the PAFPN neck as (B*N, C, H, W). These enhanced feature maps are normally passed through the neck and decoupled head, and the detections are obtained just like in a normal YOLOX model. The complete architecture is explained in Fig. 3.

4   Experiments

We initialize our baseline YOLOX models with COCO [19] pre-trained weights provided by YOLOX. We mix the images in the ImageNet-VID [17] dataset with those in the ImageNet-DET [17] dataset belonging to the same class in the training data. We use all the images in the ImageNet-DET dataset and 1/10th of the images in the ImageNet-VID dataset to train the baseline model. The ImageNet-VID dataset consists of 3,862 videos for training and 555 videos for validation. There are 30 classes in the ImageNet-VID dataset, i.e., a subset of the 200 categories of ImageNet-DET. All the base models are trained for 7 epochs with the first epoch being used for warmup as we found that for a small dataset like Imagenet 7 epochs were enough for the model to reach convergenc. SGD optimizer is used with a batch size of 16 on a single A4000 GPU. A cosine learning rate-scheduler is used to alter the learning rate. Mosaic [2] and Mixup [2] augmentations are used for the first 5 epochs with the last two epochs being done without any strong data augmentation. An image size of 576×576 is used with multi-scale training enabled.

Table 1. Comparison with baseline YOLOX model results

Model	AP50	Inference time (ms)
YOLOX-S	69.5	4.56
YOLOX-M	74.1	8.93
YOLOX-L	76.1	15.04
YOLOX-X	77.6	24.69
YOLO-SWINF-S	**73.2**	**5.14**
YOLO-SWINF-M	**77.1**	**9.65**
YOLO-SWINF-L	**79.3**	**16.00**
YOLO-SWINF-X	**80.4**	**25.81**

We add the SwinF module at the end of the backbone and before the PAFPN neck. For training this model we freeze the entire base model and stop gradient computation for the backbone to save memory and training time. Only the attention module is trained using SGD for 7 epochs with the first epoch being used for warmup. Again we found that the model converges before the 7th epoch in each case. No strong data augmentation like Mosaic or Mixup is used and multi-scale training is also disabled because all strong data augmentation was found to negatively affect the accuracy. All perspective and affine transforms are also uniform across a single batch of images to ensure that each window is looking at the same region in an image. To train the SwinF module we found that using just 1/3rd of the ImageNet-VID dataset was enough for the model to converge.

We use an image size of 576 × 576 and a batch size of 4 with each batch consisting of 16 frames randomly sampled from a video. Thus, each batch is selected from one video. To evaluate the performance of the models, we use the standard metrics for object detection on ImageNet-VID validation set. Specifically, we report the AP50 (AP calculated at IoU threshold of 0.5) and inference time of our models to show their efficiency. All models are validated on 1080Ti GPU with FP-16 precision unless otherwise mentioned. A confidence threshold of 0.001 is used with an NMS threshold of 0.5. The results with comparison with baseline are present in Table 1 and comparison with other methods is present in Table 2. Overall our experiments show that our module outperforms the baseline consistently by 3 AP points across small to extra large versions. YOLO-SWINF method is able to provide the best inference efficiency when compared to other SOTA models. Our YOLO-SWINF-S model is also much faster than baseline YOLOX-M model while having similar performance. Similarly our YOLO-SWINF-M model is comparable to YOLOX-X model in terms of accuracy while simultaneously being faster.

Table 2. Comparison with other SOTA methods: A-the inference time was taken from corresponding papers, B-inference time was tested on 2080Ti, our YOLO-SWINF models were tested on 1080 Ti GPU, while models with * were tested in online mode whereas '-' denotes the model is not released and the speed is not reported in original paper. Thus we use a computationally slower GPU to test our inference times compared to other SOTA models

Model	Backbone	AP50	Inference time (ms)
FGFA	R101	76.3	104.2(B)
SELSA	X101	83.1	153.8(B)
RDN	R101	81.8	162.6(B)
RDN	X101	83.2	–
MEGA	R101	82.9	230.4(B)
MEGA	X101	84.1	–
TROIA	X101	84.3	285.7(B)
MAMBA	R101	84.6	110.3(A)
HVR	X101	84.8	–
TransVOD	R101	81.9	–
QueryProp	R50	80.3	21.9(A)
QueryProp	R101	82.3	30.8(A)
FastVOD-NET*	R101	79.3	34.13 (A)
FastVOD-NET*	R101	81.2	43.47 (A)
MultiFrame CenterNET*	R101	78.8	27.8 (A)
YOLO-SWINF-S	**YOLOX**	**73.2**	**5.14**
YOLO-SWINF-M	**YOLOX**	**77.1**	**9.65**
YOLO-SWINF-L	**YOLOX**	**79.3**	**16.00**
YOLO-SWINF-X	**YOLOX**	**80.4**	**25.81**
YOLO-SWINF-X*	**YOLOX**	**79**	**25.81**

5   Ablation Studies

5.1   Frame Sampling Strategy

Frame sampling strategy is important for video object detectors to get a good balance between accuracy and inference time. Two of the most widely used frame sampling strategies are global and local sampling schemes. We also run experiments using these two techniques. In the continuous frame, sampling scheme Fc continuous frames are selected from a video with a fixed frame gap D. In the random sampling scheme, Fg frames are randomly sampled from each video. We conduct experiments with varied frame counts Fg (=2,5,10,16,32) to understand the impact of global sampling. To understand the effect of continuous sampling the frame gap D (=1,3,5,7,10,15) is changed while maintaining a constant frame count Fc (=16) We perform validation experiments with the above-mentioned schemes using the YOLO-SWINF-S model, which was trained using 16 randomly selected frames. The results are shown in Table 3 and Table 4. As can be observed, the performance just using 5 global frames is better than the performance when using 16 local frames irrespective of frame gap. The best results are obtained with 16 randomly sampled frames after which the performance starts to plateau.

Table 3. Number of random frames study: YOLO-SWINF-S model is validated using different number of randomly sampled frames

Number of Frames	AP50
2	70.4
5	72.3
10	72.9
16	73.2
32	73.1

Table 4. Online setting validation study where YOLO-SWINF-S model is validated using 16 continuous frames with different sampling rates

Frame gap	AP50
1	69.7
3	70.6
5	71.6
7	71.2
10	70.9
15	69.4

5.2   Head Dimension

Just like vanilla attention, SwinF also uses multiple heads to run attention in parallel as it allows for attending to parts of the sequence differently (e.g., longer-term dependencies versus shorter-term dependencies) which leads to better feature representation. The processing power of each head depends on the number of channels used to represent each embedding vector. Thus, to decide the best value for the head dimension we run ablation studies with different values of the head dimension. We train YOLO-SWINF-S with three different values of the head dimension. The results are showed in Table 5. As can be observed the best value for hidden dimension is 64 and then the AP50 decreases on further increasing the hidden dimension.

Table 5. Ablation study on head dimension where YOLO-SwinF-S model was trained using different head dimensions

Head dimension	AP50
16	73.1
64	73.2
128	72.8

6   Conclusion

In this paper, we present YOLOX based YOLO-SWINF models for fast and accurate VOD. A SwinF based temporal attention module was introduced to collate temporal information from neighbouring frames in a video and boost detection results for each frame. We position our module directly in front of the YOLOX backbone to ensure optimal detection accuracy. Our module uses a multi-headed attention operation with a sliding 3D window attention as described in SWIN Vision Transformer [25] to combine data from many frames, speeding up inference while also increasing accuracy. We demonstrated that, with only marginal increase in latency, YOLO-SWINF outperforms the baseline YOLOX models. To evaluate the efficacy of our model, we ran multiple experiments and ablation studies. Our YOLO-SWINF-X model achieves a high detection accuracy of 80.4% AP with an inference time of 25.81 ms on NVIDIA 1080Ti GPU while our YOLO-SWINF-S and M models could be the better choice for platforms with limited computation power.

References

1. Belhassen, H., Zhang, H., Fresse, V., Bourennane, E.: Improving video object detection by seq-bbox matching. VISIGRAPP (2019). https://doi.org/10.1109/ISCC53001.2021.9631435

2. Bochkovskiy, A., Wang, C., Liao H.: YOLOv4: optimal speed and accuracy of object detection. ArXiv (2020). arXiv:2004.10934
3. Chen, Y., Cao, Y., Hu, H., Wang, L.: Memory enhanced global-local aggregation for video object detection. In: IEEE/CVF Conference on Computer Vision and Pattern Recognition (CVPR), pp. 10334–10343 (2020). https://doi.org/10.1109/CVPR42600.2020.01035
4. Ge, Z., Liu, S., Wang, F., Li, Z., Sun, J.: YOLOx: exceeding yolo series in 2021. ArXiv (2021). arXiv:2107.08430
5. Guanghan, N., Zhi, Z., Chen, H., Zhihai, H., Xiaobo, R., Haohong, W.: Spatially supervised recurrent convolutional neural networks for visual object tracking. CoRR (2016). https://doi.org/10.1109/ISCAS.2017.8050867
6. Han, W., et al.: Seq-nms for video object detection. ArXiv (2016). https://doi.org/10.48550/arXiv.1602.08465
7. . Jocher, G.: YOLOv5 (2021). https://github.com/ultralytics/yolov5. https://doi.org/10.5281/zenodo.4154370
8. Joseph, R., Santosh, K.D., Ross, B.G., Ali, F.: You only look once: unified, real-time object detection. CoRR (2015). https://doi.org/10.1109/CVPR.2016.91
9. Kaiming, H., Georgia, G., Piotr, D., Ross, B.G.: Mask R-CNN. CoRR (2017). https://doi.org/10.1109/ICCV.2017.322
10. Li, C., Dobler, G., Feng, X., Wang, Y.: Tracknet: simultaneous object detection and tracking and its application in traffic video analysis. ArXiv (2019) https://doi.org/10.48550/arXiv.1902.01466
11. Lin, X., Guo, Y., Wang, J.: Global correlation network: end-to-end joint multi-object detection and tracking. ArXiv (2021). https://doi.org/10.21203/rs.3.rs-1107274/v1
12. Liu, M., Zhu, M.: Mobile video object detection with temporally-aware feature maps. In: IEEE/CVF Conference on Computer Vision and Pattern Recognition, pp. 5686–5695 (2018). https://doi.org/10.1109/CVPR.2018.00596
13. Qi, Q., Wang, X., Hou, T., Yan, Y., Wang, H.: FastVOD-Net: a real-time and high-accuracy video object detector. IEEE Trans. Intell. Transp. Syst. **23**, 20926–20942 (2022). https://doi.org/10.1109/TITS.2022.3176721
14. Redmon, J., Farhadi, A.: YOLOv3: an incremental improvement. ArXiv (2018). https://doi.org/10.1109/ACCESS.2021.3103522
15. Ren, S., He, K., Girshick, R., Sun, J.: Faster r-cnn: towards real-time object detection with region proposal networks. IEEE Trans. Pattern Anal. Mach. Intell. **39**, 1137–1149 (2015). https://doi.org/10.1109/TPAMI.2016.2577031
16. Ross, B.G., Jeff, D., Trevor, D., Jitendra, M.: Rich feature hierarchies for accurate object detection and semantic segmentation. CoRR (2013). https://doi.org/10.1109/CVPR.2014.81
17. Russakovsky, O., et al.: Imagenet large scale visual recognition challenge. Int. J. Comput. Vision **115**, 211–252 (2014). https://doi.org/10.1007/s11263-015-0816-y
18. Sabater, A., Montesano, L., Murillo, A.: Robust and efficient post-processing for video object detection. In: IEEE/RSJ International Conference on Intelligent Robots and Systems (IROS), pp. 10536–10542 (2020). https://doi.org/10.1109/IROS45743.2020.9341600
19. Yi, L.T., et al.: Microsoft COCO: common objects in context. CoRR (2014). https://doi.org/10.1007/978-3-319-10602-1_48
20. TsungYi, L., Priya, G., Ross, B.G., Kaiming, H., Piotr, D.: Focal loss for dense object detection. CoRR (2017). https://doi.org/10.1109/iccv.2017.324

21. Wang, S., Zhou, Y., Yan, J., Deng, Z.: Fully motion-aware network for video object detection. In: Proceedings of the European conference on computer vision (ECCV), pp. 542–557 (2018). https://doi.org/10.1007/978-3-030-01261-8_33

22. Wei, L., et al.: Single shot multibox detector. CoRR (2016). https://doi.org/10.1109/ICMEW.2017.8026312

23. Wu, H., Chen, Y., Wang, N., Zhang, Z.: Sequence level semantics aggregation for video object detection. In: IEEE/CVF International Conference on Computer Vision (ICCV), pp. 9216–9224 (2019) https://doi.org/10.1109/iccv.2019.00931

24. Zhou, Y., Bai, Y., Chen, Y.: Multiframe centernet heatmap ROI aggregation for real-time video object detection. IEEE Access 10, 54870–54877 (2022). https://doi.org/10.1109/ACCESS.2022.3174195

25. Ze, L., et al.: Video swin transformer. CoRR (2021). https://doi.org/10.1109/cvpr52688.2022.00320

26. Zhi, T., Chunhua, S., Hao, C., Tong, H.: Fully convolutional one-stage object detection. CoRR (2016). https://doi.org/10.1109/iccv.2019.00972

27. Zhu, X., Dai, J., Zhu, X., Wei, Y., Yuan, L.: Towards high performance video object detection for mobiles. ArXiv (2018). https://doi.org/10.1109/cvpr.2018.00753

28. Zhu, X., Wang, Y., Dai, J., Wei, Y.: Flow-guided feature aggregation for video object detection. In: IEEE International Conference on Computer Vision (ICVV), pp. 408–417 (2017). https://doi.org/10.1109/iccv.2017.52

29. Zhu, X., Xiong, Y., Dai, J., Yuan, L., Wei, Y.: Deep feature flow for video recognition. In: IEEE Conference on Computer Vision and Pattern Recognition (CVPR), pp. 4141–4150 (2017). https://doi.org/10.1109/cvpr.2017.441

Analysis of Data Augmentation Techniques for Mobile Robots Localization by Means of Convolutional Neural Networks

Orlando José Céspedes[1], Sergio Cebollada[1,2](✉) ⓘ, Juan José Cabrera[1] ⓘ,
Oscar Reinoso[1,2] ⓘ, and Luis Payá[1] ⓘ

[1] Institute for Engineering Research, Miguel Hernández University, Elche, Spain
orlando.cespedes@goumh.es,
{s.cebollada,juan.cabreram,o.reinoso,lpaya}@umh.es
[2] Valencian Graduate School and Research Network for Artificial Intelligence,
Valencia, Spain

Abstract. This work presents an evaluation regarding the use of data augmentation to carry out the rough localization step within a hierarchical localization framework. The method consists of two steps: first, the robot captures an image and it is introduced into a CNN in order to estimate the room where it was captured (rough localization). After that, a holistic descriptor is obtained from the network and it is compared with the descriptors stored in the model. The most similar image provides the position where the robot captured the image (fine localization). Regarding the rough localization, it is essential that the CNN achieves a high accuracy, since an error in this step would imply a considerable localization error. With this aim, several visual effects were separately analyzed in order to know their impact on the CNN when data augmentation is tackled. The results permit designing a data augmentation which is useful for training a CNN that solves the localization problem in real operation conditions, including changes in the lighting conditions.

Keywords: Mobile Robotics · Omnidirectional Vision · Hierarchical Localization · Deep Learning · Data Augmentation

1 Introduction

Artificial intelligence (AI) techniques have been commonly proposed to address computer vision and robotics problems. Among the existing techniques, Convolutional Neural Networks (CNNs) are one of the most popular to address a variety of problems. With the emergence of 360° vision sensors, the use of omnidirectional images has been widely proposed to address localization tasks in mobile robotics. Regarding the methods to extract relevant information from the images, the use of global-appearance descriptors has been extensively evaluated and the results show

Supplementary Information The online version contains supplementary material available at https://doi.org/10.1007/978-3-031-34111-3_42.

this approach as a successful solution. Furthermore, recent works have proposed obtaining such holistic descriptors from intermediate layers of CNNs. For example, Aguilar et al. [1] propose a pedestrian detector for UAVs (Unmanned Aerial Vehicles) based on a combination of Haar-LBP features with Adaboost and cascade classifiers with Meanshift; Wang et al. [11], use an autoencoder for fusion and extraction of multiple visual features from different sensors with the aim of carrying out motion planning based on deep reinforcement learning.

Previous works [4] have proposed hierarchical visual models to carry out the localization task efficiently. This method consists in arranging the visual information hierarchically in different layers of information in such a way that the localization can be solved in two main steps. First, a coarse localization to roughly know in which room or area the robot is and second, a fine localization in this pre-selected area. CNNs have proved to be a successful technique in many practical applications. There are well known architectures which have been used as starting point to address new computer vision tasks. For instance, GoogLeNet was proposed by Szegedy et al. [10]. This network has 22 layers, it is trained for object classification but it uses 12 times fewer parameters than AlexNet. As for the use of CNN to solve localization tasks, Kopitkov and Indelman [5] propose using CNN holistic descriptors to estimate the robot position of learning a generative viewpoint-dependent model of CNN features with a spatially-varying Gaussian distribution. Sarlin et al. [8] carry out a hierarchical modelling using a CNN, which extracts local features and holistic descriptors for 6-DOF localization. The coarse localization is solved by using global retrieval and global descriptors and the fine localization is solved by matching local features.

Regarding the use of CNNs, a complete and varied training is essential, thus, a large training dataset must be available. Since a lack of a large enough dataset is quite common, data augmentation (DA) can be used to increase the training instances to avoid overfitting. As for the DA for a mobile robot localization task, it is essential apply visual effects that may occur in real operation conditions with the aim of making the model robuster against those effects. Considering as many effects as possible would increase the effectiveness of the CNN, but this would imply more processing power and memory. For example, Perez and Wang [7] present a study about the effectiveness of the data augmentation to solve the classification task. Shorten and Khoshgoftaar [9] present a survey about the existing methods for data augmentation and related developments. Nonetheless, the previously proposed data augmentation methods do not exactly analyze the visual phenomena that can occur when the mobile robot moves through the target environment under real-operation conditions. Therefore, the present work performs a data augmentation analysis which focuses on a wide range of those specific visual effects.

In light of the above information, the aim of this work is to analyze the influence of some visual effects in order to carry out a data augmentation for CNN training to address hierarchical localization. This work focuses on the rough localization step, which is solved by using the output layer of the CNN for room retrieval. Hence, the efficiency of each visual effect will be assessed through the ability of the CNN to robustly estimate the room where the image was captured.

To address the proposed evaluation, the unique source of information is the set of images obtained by an omnidirectional vision sensor installed on the mobile robot, which moves in an indoor environment under real operation conditions.

2   Methodology

2.1   CNN Adaption

Building a CNN from scratch to solve a specific task can be tough, since it requires of a deep expertise and also having a proper dataset to address the training. Moreover, as studied in previous works [2], adapting and re-training well-known networks for a different purpose can lead to accurate results. In this sense, the present work proposes departing from the Places CNN [12], which was trained for scene recognition. Places presents an architecture similar to AlexNet [6] and it was trained with around 2.5 million images to classify the candidate image among 205 categories of scenes. Figure 1 shows the architecture for a better comprehension.

Fig. 1. Architecture of the Places CNN [12]. This network was created to address a scene recognition task among 205 types.

This work proposes to train the CNN departing from panoramic images to address a room retrieval in an indoor environment composed of nine different rooms, hence, some layers of the original CNN are replaced. First, the input layer is re-adapted from $227 \times 227 \times 3$ to $128 \times 512 \times 3$. Second, the fully-connected layer fc8, softmax and output layer are replaced to fit them to the new classification task (scene recognition among 9 possible indoor rooms). After the replacement of those layers, the new CNN is trained to solve the rough localization (room retrieval).

2.2   Hierarchical Localization Approach

The aim of this work is to address visual localization by means of a hierarchical approach using deep learning as follows: first, a rough localization step is carried out to retrieve an area of the environment, and second, a fine localization step is tackled in that pre-selected area to refine the position fitting.

The output of the CNN is used to solve the rough localization step. In this sense, to train the CNN, a set of images that cover the target environment is captured, and each image has a label that indicates the room from which it was taken. With this information, the CNN is trained to solve the room retrieval problem. Once the CNN is correctly trained, the hierarchical localization is solved as follows: a test image is introduced into the CNN and the output layer indicates the room where it was captured. Simultaneously, a holistic descriptor is obtained from an intermediate layer of the same CNN and this descriptor is compared with all the descriptors of images in the map. The nearest neighbour is retrieved and, then, the coordinates of the capture point of the retrieved imaged are considered the current position of the robot.

2.3 Data Augmentation Techniques

Training a model means establishing the parameters to address the desired task. Hence, if the model has a wide variety of parameters, the training process needs many examples. Often, the number of instances in the training process is small. In this sense, data augmentation is a good solution, because it is possible to avoid overfitting. This basically consists in creating new instances of 'data' by applying different visual effects. Apart from avoiding overfitting, considering visual effects that may occur in real operation conditions will make the CNN robuster against those effects.

In previous works that train a model for visual localization [3] diverse effects were applied, such as orientation changes, reflections, general changes in illumination, noise, occlusions, etc., and it was proved that the use of this technique improves. These effects are applied over each image in the original dataset either individually or jointly. However, all the generated images are put together in a new augmented training dataset. Therefore, the influence of each kind of effect over the performance of the resulting CNN is not clear. The aim of this work is to apply different data augmentation effects individually, in order to assess their impact in the resulting CNN.

The present work focuses on two kinds of visual effects: changes of illumination conditions and changes of orientation. As for the changes of illumination conditions, we consider the following effects:

- **Spotlights and shadows**: Circular sources of light such as bulbs appear very often in indoor environments. Moreover, the presence of darker areas by object shades is also usual. Hence, it is proposed to increase the pixels values to simulate more light intensity (spotlight) and decreasing to simulate shadows (shadow spotlights). Position, shape of the spotlights and maximum values are randomly selected in order to consider different changes of illumination. Spotlights and shadow spotlights are applied separately for different data augmentation options.
- **General brightness and darkness**: The low intensity values of the original images are increased in order to create new images brighter than the original ones. This effect simulates a higher general level of illumination in the scene (for example, a sunny day). On the contrary, the high intensity values are decreased in order to create new images darker than the original ones. This effect simulates a lower light supply (for example, capturing the images at night). Brightness and darkness are applied separately, but used for the same data augmentation.

- **Contrast**: The contrast of the image plays an important role as it permits differentiating objects in the scene. Moreover, images with low contrast tend to have a smoother appearance with few shadows and reflections.
- **Saturation**: Color saturation refers to the color intensity given by the pixels. The less saturation, the less colorful is the image (even looking a gray-scale image for very low saturation). Such phenomenon may also occur in real environments and it is also considered in the data augmentation.

Concerning the orientation changes, they can happen during imaging capturing when the robot captures images in the same position but with a different orientation. Regarding this data augmentation option, for each original image, new ones are generated by applying a rotation of n, where $n = i \times 10°, i \in [1, 35]$. Hence for each image, 35 additional images are generated.

3 Experiments

This section presents the results obtained through the use of the CNN to carry out the rough localization step. Concerning the training process, it consists in using either the original cloudy dataset (composed of 519 images) or the augmented (cloudy) dataset. Three main experiments are tackled. First, the use of a data augmentation based on orientation changes is evaluated. Second, each illumination effect is considered separately when training the CNN. Finally, a third experiment is developed whose data augmentation consists in applying jointly all the visual effects.

As for the rough localization step, once the model has been trained, the process is as follows: (1) the robot captures a new omnidirectional image from an unknown position within the environment. (2) The image is converted to panoramic. (3) The panoramic image is introduced into the CNN in order to estimate the most likely room where the image was obtained. The images used for training the model are not used to evaluate the localization task and three test datasets with different illumination conditions have been considered with the aim of evaluating the robustness of the CNN. Hence, the datasets implicated in the present work for testing the proposed approach are the following:

- Cloudy dataset, whose illumination is the same as the one used for training the CNNs. This dataset contains 2778 images (different from the images in the training dataset).
- Night dataset, whose images were obtained at night, hence, some areas present a considerable lack of light. This dataset contains 2707 images.
- Sunny dataset, whose images were captured during a sunny day, hence, the illumination is higher in general and the windows are also a source of light. This dataset contains 2807 images.

With the aim of validating the robustness of each resulting CNN, this work proposes the use of the accuracy metric. Moreover, it is also interesting to analyze the confusion matrix obtained for each test.

3.1   Experiment 1: Orientation Changes

As mentioned before, it is very likely that the orientation of the robot is not the same as the one presented during the mapping process, thus, the model should present robustness against changes of orientation. In this experiment, the data augmentation technique consisted in applying 35 different orientation changes over each of the the training images. After that, the CNN is trained and tested using the three test datasets. The results are shown in the Fig. 2 (a).

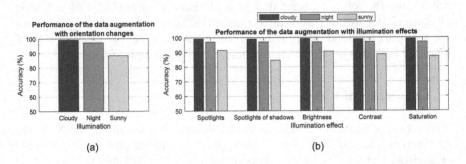

(a)   (b)

Fig. 2. Room retrieval results for DA with (a) orientation changes and (b) with illumination effects. Accuracy of the CNN to estimate the room where the test images were captured. Results presented under cloudy (blue), night (red) and sunny (yellow) illumination conditions. (Color figure online)

Regarding the performance under cloudy conditions (no change in the lighting conditions with respect to the training), the model reaches an accuracy of 99.17% . Nonetheless, the accuracy decreases when illumination changes are presented: 97.27% and 88.31% for night and sunny test datasets respectively. From these results, in case of using only orientation changes in the data augmentation, the conclusion is that the network retrieves the room without problems when there are no illumination changes, but it outputs worse results, specially at the presence of brighter images. Therefore, a profound study about illumination effects will be developed in the following experiment.

3.2   Experiment 2: Illumination Effects

This subsection tests the influence of illumination effects in detail in order to improve the performance of the CNN. Five effects are considered: spotlights, spotlights of shadows, general brightness/darkness, contrast and saturation. Every type of effect is applied individually over the training dataset to obtain each augmented dataset. Different effects are not blended with the aim of knowing the importance of each effect. For each image, five different levels of spotlights/contrast/saturation are applied. Regarding the brightness effect, for each image, three levels of brightness and three levels of darkness are applied.

The results for the different effects under the three illumination conditions are shown in the Fig. 2(b).

Concerning the results under the night illumination conditions, the best accuracy is obtained with the 'spotlights' effect (97.16%) and the worst accuracy with the 'brightness/darkness' effect (96.9%). However, the difference between those results is not significant. As for the performance under the sunny illumination conditions, the accuracy is lower than with the night dataset. However, it is remarkable that the accuracy has improved in comparison with the results obtained with the 'orientation changes'. The best accuracy is obtained with the spotlights effect (91.38%) and the worst case (Saturation, 87.17%) is similar to the accuracy obtained with the 'orientation change' data augmentation.

If the accuracy results for the test datasets are considered in average, (see Table 1) we can see the weight of each visual effect concerning the rough localization.

Table 1. Classification of the illumination effects regarding their average accuracy (considering jointly the cloudy, night and sunny test datasets)

Visual effect	Average accuracy (%)
1. Spotlights	95.90
2. Brightness	95.57
3. Contrast	94.86
4. Saturation	94.48
5. Spotlights shadows	93.54

Finally, Fig. 3 shows the accuracy obtained by using a CNN which was trained without data augmentation and the computing time required to train all the evaluated models. Since the models were trained with different numbers of images, this variable is normalized by dividing the computing time by the total number of images used to train each network.

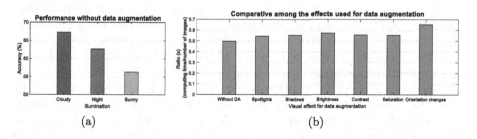

(a)   (b)

Fig. 3. (a) Accuracy of the CNN to estimate the room without applying data augmentation and (b) normalized computing time for training the neural network.

In general, all the evaluated data augmentation techniques lead to a higher accuracy than using the CNN trained only with raw data. Concerning illumination changes, the six proposed methods improve the accuracy. It should be pointed out that the data augmentation technique based in orientation changes provides relatively good results under night and sunny illumination conditions, reaching the best accuracy when evaluating the night dataset. As for the accuracy under sunny illumination conditions (the most challenging ones), 'spotlights' (91.38%) and 'brightness' (90.59%) are the effects that provide more than 90% of accuracy. Regarding the computing time, there are not significant differences between the methods, since the fastest one (without data augmentation) requires 0.5 s per image and the slowest (with orientation changes) needs 0.65 s per image. Moreover, this process is offline, thus computing time is not as crucial as accuracy. As for the computing time with illumination effects, all proposed DA techniques present similar values (around 0.55 s per image).

3.3   Experiment 3: Evaluation of the Data Augmentation Considering All the Effects Jointly

The last evaluation concerning this study consisted in carrying out the training of the CNN by using a data augmentation using jointly all the effects. The aim of this experiment is to analyze whether the mix of effects can lead to a better room retrieval performance. The training of this neural network was similar to the previous ones, but the number of epochs was reduced to 20, because by that epoch, the training and validation accuracy stopped increasing and more epochs would have led to overfitting. The data augmentation consisted in considering a unique augmented dataset that contains the images created for the six previous data augmentation techniques and no images with more than one visual effect were created for this purpose. The results under the three illumination conditions are shown in the Fig. 4. This figure shows a comparison between three CNN models: without data augmentation, with data augmentation based in 'spotlights' effects and with data augmentation based in all the studied effects (spotlights, spotlights of shadow, brightness/darkness, contrast, saturation and orientation changes).

This figure shows that the results for the data augmentation based in all effects present better accuracy than without data augmentation and similar than using only 'spotlights' data augmentation. As for sunny illumination conditions, the accuracy gets worse than using 'spotlights' data augmentation.

Apart from the accuracy, the study of the confusion matrices can lead to more insightful conclusions. Figure 5 shows an example of the confusion matrix obtained under night illumination conditions. These results were obtained by doing room retrieval using CNN with data augmentation applying all effects. This figure shows that the room confusion is only given between next-door rooms. For example, corridor presents more incorrect predictions because it is connected to the most of the places. Figures of confusion matrix without data augmentation and with data augmentation applying all effects under the three illumination conditions can be found in the Electronic Supplementary Material. From these

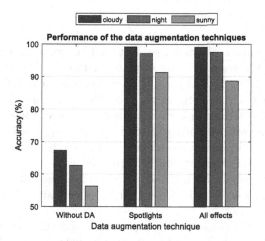

Fig. 4. Accuracy of the CNN for room retrieval under cloudy, night and sunny illumination conditions. The models were trained (left bars) without data augmentation, (center bars) with data augmentation with 'spotlights' effects and (right bars) with all studied effects.

figures, considering sunny illumination as the worst scenario and using data augmentation, the produced errors are relatively low and can be controlled by reinforcing the algorithm as it was proposed in previous works. For instance, using likelihood thresholds to select more than one room as candidate when the first retrieved room is not confident enough [4].

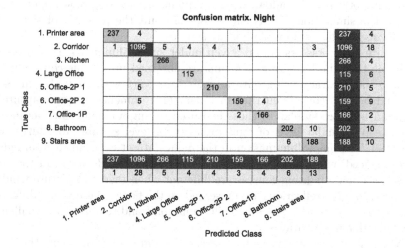

Fig. 5. Confusion matrix under night illumination conditions. CNN trained with data augmentation.

4   Conclusions

In this work, we have evaluated a set of visual effects to carry out a data augmentation for CNN training. The objective of the CNN is to address a room retrieval task, which is used as rough step within a hierarchical localization approach. The evaluated visual effects were considered because they may appear in images when the localization task is addressed. Hence, these effects should be considered by the network during the training process in order to be capable of coping with them. This study has focused on two kinds of visual effects: orientation and illumination changes, which frequently happen when the environment is revisited by the robot. With the aim of analyzing the influence of each effect, they were evaluated separately. After that, all effects are considered jointly in a unique training dataset.

In general, all the considered DA techniques provide benefits for the room retrieval task. The accuracy is substantially higher by using a CNN trained with any data augmentation technique than without it. As for the data augmentation with orientation changes, it shows that the accuracy is improved in general in comparison without performing data augmentation. It should be noted that this technique also improved the results concerning changes of lighting conditions, which may not be expected at the beginning of this study.

Regarding the illumination effects, 'spotlights' was able to successfully simulate the visual effects that are present both under night conditions, whose main light sources are in the upper part of the environment, and sunny conditions, whose lighting sources are located in the upper part of the environment and in the windows/picture windows. 'Spotlights of shades' was the least suitable effect to train the neural network for room retrieval purposes. This may be due to a lower importance of shadows from the point of view of global appearance or because the simulation of this effect does not suit the presence of shadows as properly as spotlights do with lighting sources.

Despite the worse results are given under sunny illumination conditions, it is notable that the best improvements are obtained under this condition if we compare the accuracy using data augmentation and without it. In this sense, it should be also considered that in indoor environments, images captured at night can be more similar to those captured during a cloudy day, because the rooms keep a similar level of light intensity (a level suitable to address work activities). The main illumination in the night dataset is obtained from lighting sources placed on the ceiling, as in the cloudy dataset. However, in the sunny dataset, the main lighting sources are different when there are picture windows. Moreover, lighting reflections are presented on the floor. These visual differences explain the reason why the sunny illumination condition is more challenging regarding global appearance.

When all effects are used to address the data augmentation, the results improve at night and get worse for sunny conditions. This is pointing out that effects, such as the darkness produced by 'brightness/darkness' effect and the orientation changes' effect, allow to improve the accuracy. Concerning the worsening under sunny conditions in comparison with the 'spotlights' data augmentation, this can indicate that the 'spotlights' effect has lost its importance within the training dataset. Hence, to avoid it, a weighting regarding the number of images per effect could be explored.

In future works, we will focus on developing a method to quantify the weight for each visual effect for data augmentation. We will also extend our study to other effects such occlusions produced by furniture changes and the presence of objects in front of the camera. Also, we will study more in detail how to include illumination effects that suit better the night and sunny conditions and we will study other deep learning approaches such as transformers or networks using attention mechanism.

Acknowledgements. This work has been supported by the ValgrAI (Valencian Graduate School and Research Network for Artificial Intelligence) and Generalitat Valenciana. This work is also part of the project PID2020-116418RB-I00 funded by MCIN/AEI/10.13039/501100011033, and of the project PROMETEO/2021/075 funded by Generalitat Valenciana.

References

1. Aguilar, W.G., Luna, M.A., Moya, J.F., Abad, V., Parra, H., Ruiz, H.: Pedestrian detection for UAVs using cascade classifiers with meanshift. In: 2017 IEEE 11th International Conference on Semantic Computing (ICSC), pp. 509–514. IEEE (2017)
2. Ballesta, M., Payá, L., Cebollada, S., Reinoso, O., Murcia, F.: A cnn regression approach to mobile robot localization using omnidirectional images. Appl. Sci. **11**(16), 7521 (2021)
3. Cabrera, J.J., Cebollada, S., Flores, M., Reinoso, Ó., Payá, L.: Training, optimization and validation of a cnn for room retrieval and description of omnidirectional images. SN Comput. Sci. **3**(4), 1–13 (2022)
4. Cebollada, S., Payá, L., Jiang, X., Reinoso, O.: Development and use of a convolutional neural network for hierarchical appearance-based localization. Artif. Intell. Rev. **55**(4), 2847–2874 (2022)
5. Kopitkov, D., Indelman, V.: Bayesian information recovery from CNN for probabilistic inference. In: 2018 IEEE/RSJ International Conference on Intelligent Robots and Systems (IROS), pp. 7795–7802 (2018). https://doi.org/10.1109/IROS. 2018.8594506
6. Krizhevsky, A., Sutskever, I., Hinton, G.E.: Imagenet classification with deep convolutional neural networks. In: Advances in Neural Information Processing Systems, pp. 1097–1105 (2012)
7. Perez, L., Wang, J.: The effectiveness of data augmentation in image classification using deep learning. arXiv preprint arXiv:1712.04621 (2017)
8. Sarlin, P., Cadena, C., Siegwart, R., Dymczyk, M.: From coarse to fine: robust hierarchical localization at large scale. In: 2019 IEEE/CVF Conference on Computer Vision and Pattern Recognition (CVPR), pp. 12708–12717 (2019). https:// doi.org/10.1109/CVPR.2019.01300
9. Shorten, C., Khoshgoftaar, T.M.: A survey on image data augmentation for deep learning. J. Big Data **6**(1), 60 (2019)
10. Szegedy, C., et al.: Going deeper with convolutions. In: Proceedings of the IEEE Conference on Computer Vision and Pattern Recognition, pp. 1–9 (2015)

11. Wang, H., Yang, W., Huang, W., Lin, Z., Tang, Y.: Multi-feature fusion for deep reinforcement learning: sequential control of mobile robots. In: Cheng, L., Leung, A.C.S., Ozawa, S. (eds.) ICONIP 2018. LNCS, vol. 11307, pp. 303–315. Springer, Cham (2018). https://doi.org/10.1007/978-3-030-04239-4_27
12. Zhou, B., Lapedriza, A., Xiao, J., Torralba, A., Oliva, A.: Learning deep features for scene recognition using places database. In: Advances in Neural Information Processing Systems, pp. 487–495 (2014)

Intrusion Detection Using Attention-Based CNN-LSTM Model

Ban Al-Omar$^{(\boxtimes)}$ and Zouheir Trabelsi

United Arab Emirates University, Al-Ain, UAE
{700039223,Trabelsi}@uaeu.ac.ae

Abstract. With the rise of sophisticated cyberattacks and the advent of complex and diverse technological systems, traditional methods of intrusion detection have become insufficient. The inability to prevent intrusions poses a severe threat to the credibility of security services, which may result in the compromise of data confidentiality, integrity, and availability. To address this challenge, research has proposed the use of Artificial Intelligence (AI) and deep learning (DL) models to enhance the effectiveness of intrusion detection. In this study, we present an Intrusion Detection System (IDS) that utilizes attention-based Convolutional Neural Network (CNN) and Long Short-Term Memory (LSTM) models. The attention mechanism of the model allows for the identification of significant features in network traffic data for more precise predictions. Using the benchmark dataset UNSW-NB15, we validate the robustness and effectiveness of our model, achieving a detection rate of over 95%. Our results emphasize the robustness and effectiveness of the proposed system, demonstrating the immense potential of AI and DL models in bolstering intrusion detection.

Keywords: Intrusion Detection · Attention Based · CNN-LSTM

1 Introduction

With the continuous rise of threats and attacks, ensuring the effectiveness of IDS on computer networks has become strenuous. The present-day systems' heterogeneous, dynamic, and complex attributes have intensified the difficulty of addressing multiple forms of attacks. Network intrusion detection can be classified into two modes according to the behaviour of intrusion detection: Anomaly-Based Intrusion Detection Systems and Signature-Based Intrusion Detection Systems (SIDS) [4,27].

The Anomaly-Based approach detects new attacks by establishing a model of normal activities within a system and identify potential attacks from behaviours that deviate from the established normal behaviour pattern. SIDS, on the other hand, uses matching techniques to detect known attacks. The SIDS extracts

Supported by United Arab Emirates University.

packet payloads and whenever a behaviour signature matches one from a previous intrusion existing in the signature database, the behaviour is classified as an intrusion [2,19].

The IDS's effectiveness is evaluated by its ability to accurately detect actual intrusions. In practice, the IDS's efficacy is determined by its capacity to minimize the false-positive rate (FPR) rather than maximizing the true-positive rate (TPR), as described in [2].

The current IDS have many significant limitations. For example, rare normal behaviours are sometimes classified as abnormal behaviours by anomaly detection IDS. At the same time, the diversity in the implementation mechanisms of the operating systems makes building a unified pattern library very difficult, hence, decreasing the efficiency of SIDS [20]. Several ML and DL techniques have been studied for the design of IDS. In particular, these techniques are used as classifiers to classify whether events are benign or attacks. They are used as well to identify the type of attacks. The use of DL outperform the use of traditional IDS due to its capabilities in handling a large amount of data, and building models that can be generalized to be effective in new network environments and new forms of attacks [12,13].

The objective of this paper is to demonstrate the application of AT-CNN-LSTM in intrusion detection. The key contributions of this paper are:

1. Introduction of an efficient and lightweight deep learning model that leverages attention-based CNN-LSTM. LSTM has become popular in intrusion detection due to its ability to effectively model and learn from sequential data. Capturing patterns in sequential data using LSTM networks is crucial in intrusion detection as it enables the detection of complex and sophisticated attacks that occur over time and requires a temporal understanding of the network traffic data. CNN, on the other hand, can learn patterns in the spatial distribution of network traffic, such as spikes or dips in traffic volume, and use these patterns to identify potential attacks. When combined with LSTM networks, CNNs can help to improve the accuracy and reliability of intrusion detection systems [6].
2. The use of the attention mechanism in the proposed model to enhance the ability of the model to focus on relevant features in the input data while ignoring the noise and irrelevant information. This attention mechanism, combined with the ability of the hybrid CNN-LSTM model to handle both spatial and temporal features, leads to a more accurate and efficient intrusion detection system.
3. Validation of the proposed model on the standard UNSW2015-NB15 network security dataset and performance evaluation based on accuracy, precision, recall and F1-score.

The structure of this paper is as follows: Sect. 2, provides an overview of prior research. Section 3 outlines the model design. Model evaluation and discussion are presented in Sect. 4. The paper concludes with the key findings of our work in Sect. 5.

2 Related Works

A considerable amount of research has been published on potential ways to improve intrusion detection using ML and DL. This section highlights research that has employed deep learning in intrusion detection.

A. Aldallal in [1] developed an IDS also using recurrent neural networks based on GRU and improved LSTM to classify the network flows instances as benign or malevolent. The CICIDS 2018 benchmark dataset was used to evaluate the model. The proposed model outperformed the benchmarks by 12.045%.

The authors of [7] assessed the performance of two RNN models, namely LSTM and GRU, for intrusion detection using the NSL-KDD dataset. Their goal was to classify three attack types (DoS, Probe, and R2L) among benign connections. The results showed accuracies of 96% for Probe attacks, 92% for DoS attacks, and 88% for R2L attacks.

The authors of [9] developed a binary classification model using K-means and Random Forest (RF). They utilized CNN and LSTM to classify attacks into different types. The effectiveness of their proposed model was evaluated on two benchmark datasets, achieving an accuracy of 85.24% and 99.91%.

In [11], the authors addressed the class imbalance problem using the Difficult Set Sampling Technique (DSSTE) algorithm. They evaluated their model on NSL-KDD and CSE-CIC-IDS 2018 benchmark datasets, employing classical classification algorithms including RF, SVM, XGBoost, LSTM, AlexNet, and Mini-VGGNet. Experimental results showed that the DSSTE algorithm performed better.

In [13], the authors used a stacked autoencoder network for feature extraction, then support vector machine, random forest, decision trees and Naive Bayes for classification. The dataset UNB ISCX 2012 dataset is used to validate the proposed model and the maximum accuracy obtained is 90.2%.

In [14] the authors used a sequential autoencoder using LSTM to build an IDS model. The autoencoder was used for dimension reduction and feature extraction. The model was verified using the evaluation dataset ISCX IDS 2012.

The authors of [24] introduced an IDS model composed of recurrent neural networks with GRU, MLP, and softmax models, and evaluated their performance on KDD 99 and NSL-KDD datasets. The proposed model achieved an overall prediction rate of 99.42% on KDD 99 and 99.31% on NSL-KDD.

In recent times, the attention mechanism has gained considerable attention as a method for improving the performance of deep learning models. By selectively attending to different parts of the input, the model can better capture the important features that are critical for accurate predictions. The attention mechanism has been successfully applied in various domains such as natural language processing, computer vision, and speech recognition.

A study presented in [10] put forward an air pollution forecasting model that utilized an attention-based LSTM neural network. The model was found to perform better than other methods that were implemented without an attention layer.

The effectiveness of an attention mechanism and autoencoder for intrusion detection was investigated by the authors in [23]. The proposed model was evaluated using a real in-vehicle CAN bus message dataset and was found to outperform traditional machine learning algorithms.

In [25], the authors have used a multilayer attention mechanism intrusion detection model for power information network. The attention layer improved the detection rate by 1.99% compared to the no-attention layer.

3   Methodology

This section explains the steps for building the proposed intrusion detection system, including data preprocessing, CNN, LSTM, Self-Attention mechanism and model selection.

3.1   Data Preprocessing

UNSW-NB15 is one of the largest and most widely used benchmark datasets for evaluating intrusion detection systems [16–18,20]. The dataset contains over two million network connection records and includes a wide range of attack types, including Backdoor, Denial of Service (DoS), Exploits, Fuzzers, Generic, Normal, Reconnaissance, Shellcode, and Worms [21].

Effective ML requires proper data preprocessing which includes extracting numerical and statistical features, reducing sparsity and making the data suitable for machine learning algorithms. In the case of the UNSW-NB15 dataset, missing values were removed, categorical features were converted to numerical values using one-hot encoding and features were normalized using Min-Max scaling. Additionally, Synthetic Minority Over-sampling Technique was applied to address the class imbalance and to ensure that the model gets a more balanced exposure to all classes during training [22,28].

3.2   Convolutional Neural Network (CNN)

CNN is a type of neural network architecture that uses convolutional layers that apply a set of filters to the input in order to extract features at different scales and locations. These features are then pooled and passed through fully connected layers for classification or regression. The following is the equation for CNN Convolutional layer [15,26]:

$$h_{i,j}^l = f\left(\sum_{m=1}^{M}\sum_{n=1}^{N} w_{m,n}^l x_{i+m-1,j+n-1}^{l-1} + b_l\right) \tag{1}$$

where $h_{i,j}^l$ is the activation at position (i,j) in the feature map at layer l, $w_{m,n}^l$ are the learnable convolutional filters, $x_{i+m-1,j+n-1}^{l-1}$ are the activations in the feature map at layer $l-1$, b_l is the bias term, and f is the activation function.

3.3   Long Short-Term Memory (LSTM)

LSTM networks are an advanced type of Recurrent Neural Networks (RNNs) that are specifically designed to avoid the issue of vanishing or exploding gradients that traditional RNNs often face. LSTMs achieve this by providing gates within the basic unit of the network. These gates include the forget gate, input gate, and output gate, which allow the network to capture both long-term and short-term memories across time steps. The LSTM unit contains two memory cells: the memory cell C_t, which aggregates relevant information over time as long-term memory, and the candidate memory cell $\hat{C}_t$. The equations for the forward pass of the LSTM cell at a given time step t are presented in various literature [5,8,26].

$$I_t = \sigma \left(X_t W_{xi} + h_{(t-1)} W_{hi} + b_i \right) \tag{2}$$

$$F_t = \sigma \left(X_t W_{xf} + h_{(t-1)} W_{hf} + b_f \right) \tag{3}$$

$$O_t = \sigma \left(X_t W_{xo} + h_{(t-1)} W_{ho} + b_o \right) \tag{4}$$

$$\widehat{C_t} = \tanh(X_t W_{xc} + h_{(t-1)} W_{hc} + b_c) \tag{5}$$

$$C_t = F_t \odot C_{(t-1)} + I_t \odot \widehat{C_t} \tag{6}$$

$$h_t = O_t \odot \tanh(C_t) \tag{7}$$

$$\widehat{y}_t = f(W_h \, h_t + b_h) \tag{8}$$

The LSTM node at time step t is represented by vector values I_t, F_t, O_t, C_t, h_t, y_t, which correspond to the input gate, forget gate, output gate, cell state, LSTM block output, predicted output, respectively. The weights between the input layer and gates at time step t are W_{xi}, W_{xf}, and W_{xo}. The weights between the hidden recurrent layer and gates are W_{hi}, W_{hf}, and W_{ho}, while the weights between the cell state and gates are W_{ci}, W_{cf}, and W_{co}. The biases of the input gate, forget gate and output gate are b_i, b_f, and b_o, respectively. The output, weights, bias, and activation function of the fully connected networks is represented by $\hat{y}$, W_h, b_h, and f. The activation functions used include the sigmoid function (σ), element-wise multiplication ($\odot$), and hyperbolic tangent function (tanh) [8,26].

3.4   Self-Attention Mechanism

The self-Attention mechanism is a type of attention mechanism that enables a model to focus on different parts of the input sequence and weigh their importance when making predictions [3]. The input sequence to the attention block is transformed into three vectors: the query vector, the key vector, and the value vector. The query vector is used to calculate the similarity between the input sequence and a particular element, the key vector is used to store the representation of the input sequence, and the value vector is used to store the output. The self-attention weight for position i is computed as [15]:

$$\alpha_i = \frac{\exp(g(h_i))}{\sum_{j=1}^{T} \exp(g(h_j))} \tag{9}$$

where h_i is the hidden state of the input sequence at position i, and g is a function that computes the score between the query and the key. In self-attention, the query and key are both the hidden states of the input sequence.

The context vector for position i is then computed as:

$$c_i = \sum_{j=1}^{T} \alpha_j h_j \tag{10}$$

The context vector c_i is then used as input to the feed-forward network.

3.5 Proposed Model

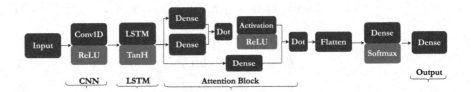

Fig. 1. The structure of the proposed model

The full model architecture is shown in Fig. 1. The model takes as input a sequence of network traffic data represented as a matrix with three dimensions: the number of traffic samples, the number of time steps for each sample and the number of features for each time step. The training set consists of 309,391 traffic samples and the testing set consists of 132,597 traffic samples. The features include information such as protocol type, source and destination IP addresses, source and destination port numbers, Transport layer protocol (TCP, UDP, ICMP), IP protocol version (IPv4 or IPv6), Time-to-live (TTL) value of IP packets, packet length and fragmentation information, flags indicating whether packets are part of an established connection or a new connection, and Quality of Service (QoS) information.

In this model, the input is first passed through a 1D convolutional layer (conv1d) with 32 filters of size 3 and relu activation function, which applies a sliding window over the input sequence to extract local patterns or features. The output from the conv1d layer is then passed through an LSTM layer with 32 hidden units and return_sequences=True argument, which allows the LSTM to output a sequence of hidden states instead of a single final state. The selection of the number of filters in the convolutional layer and the number of hidden units in the LSTM layer was determined through a process of hyperparameter tuning, wherein various configurations were experimented with to find the optimal balance between model expressiveness and generalization performance.

The output is passed through a self-attention mechanism, which allows the model to focus on the most relevant parts of the input sequence for the current time step. The self-attention mechanism consists of three fully connected layers (key, value, and query), which project the LSTM outputs onto lower-dimensional spaces, followed by a dot product between the query and key to compute the attention weights. The attention weights are then normalized using a softmax activation function and applied to the value tensor to obtain the attention output.

The model then outputs a probability distribution over the possible network intrusion classes, represented as a matrix with dimensions of a number of samples and a number of possible network intrusion classes. The training and test sets are labelled with these classes, with the training set having 10 possible classes and the test set having the same 10 possible classes.

4   Results Analysis and Discussion

4.1   Setup Environment

The experimental procedure involved utilizing GPU for training the model on Google Jupyter notebooks. The environment specification comprises the processor type, which is Intel(R) Xeon(R) CPU @ 2.30 GHz, the GPU model, which is Tesla P100-PCIE-16GB, the system RAM, which is 13 GB, and the operating system, which is Linux 5.10.147+. Different batch sizes and epochs were applied during the training process. In order to prevent overfitting and conserve computational resources, an early stopping mechanism was implemented with a patience of 7 and a minimum delta of 0.001. The model is then compiled using the 'Adam' optimizer, binarycrossentropy loss function, and accuracy metric.

4.2   Results

Accuracy, precision, recall, and F1 score are adopted as the performance metrics for assessing the efficacy of the model. The confusion matrix in Fig. 2 is used to evaluate the performance of the classification model. The actual classes of attacks are compared to the predicted attack classes made by the model. The rows in the matrix represent the actual classes, while the columns represent the predicted classes.

The model has an overall accuracy of 92.2%, which means that the model is able to classify 92.2% of the samples correctly. The precision of the model is 95.04%, which means that out of all the samples that the model classified as positive, 95.04% were actually positive. The recall of the model is 90.56%, which means that out of all the positive samples in the dataset, the model was able to correctly identify 90.56% of them. The F1-score is 92.72%. The high

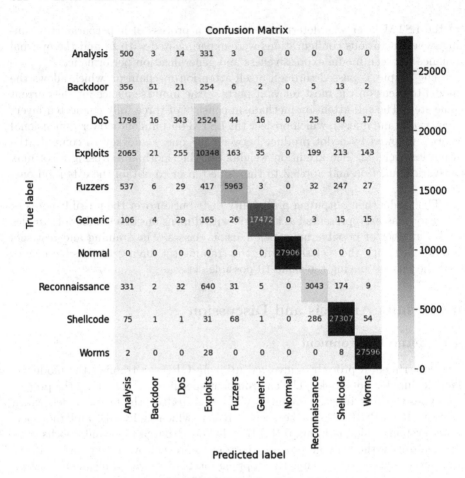

Fig. 2. AT-CNN-LSTM Confusion Matrix

Table 1. Detection Rate of Attacks Categories

Attack Category	Detection Rate
Reconnaissance	87%
Backdoor	83%
DoS	67%
Exploits	71%
Fuzzers	93%
Generic	99%
Normal	100%
Analysis	8%
Shellcode	97%
Worms	99%

accuracy, precision, recall, and F1 score of the model indicates that the model is able to identify and classify network traffic with a high degree of accuracy while minimizing false positives and false negatives for each class. This indicates that the system is effective in detecting a wide range of attacks and thus minimizing the risk of disrupting legitimate network activity.

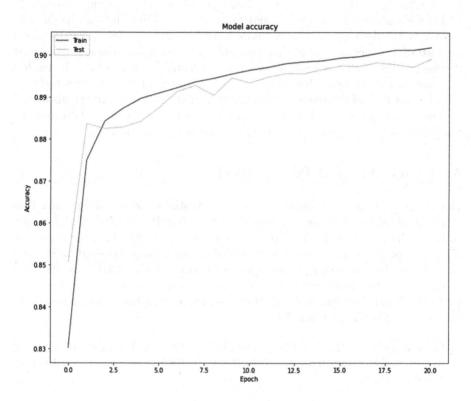

Fig. 3. At-CNN-LSTM: Epochs vs Accuracy

Table 1 shows the detection rates for different categories of attacks. The table shows that the model is capable of accurately detecting a wide range of attacks. The model has a high detection rate for most of the attack categories, including Generic (99%) and Normal (100%). The model has also a high detection rate for Fuzzers (93%) and Worms (99%), which are two types of attacks that involve massive network scans and automated propagation. This indicates that the model is capable of detecting attacks that are carried out at a large scale. The model also has a reasonable detection rate for other types of attacks, such as Reconnaissance (87%), Backdoor (83%), Exploits (71%), and Shellcode (97%). These attacks can be particularly challenging to detect since they often involve sophisticated techniques that can evade traditional security measures. However, the model's high detection rates for these attack categories demonstrate its effectiveness in identifying such threats. The low detection rates for Analysis and

DoS attacks can be attributed to several factors. These attacks are known to involve different techniques that can be difficult to detect, as they may involve small and subtle changes in network traffic that can blend in with normal traffic. This is especially true for DoS attacks, which are designed to overwhelm network resources and can be challenging to distinguish from legitimate traffic. Furthermore, the performance of the model in detecting these attacks is highly dependent on the quality and quantity of training data available. The UNSW-NB15 dataset contains a limited number of examples of Analysis and DoS attacks, which affects the models' ability to learn the characteristics that distinguish these attacks from normal traffic effectively. As a result, the models may not be able to generalize well to new, unseen examples of these attacks.

The accuracy of the model is visualized against the number of epochs in Fig. 3. The two figure show that the accuracy of both the training data and the validation data increases over time until it reaches a plateau at 20.

5 Conclusion and Future Work

In conclusion, this study demonstrates the potential of deep learning models in intrusion detection systems. The proposed Attention Based CNN-LSTM model, utilizing the attention mechanism, shows promising results in detecting intrusions with over 95% precision. The results of the performance evaluation indicate that the model has high precision and recall scores, which further validate the robustness and effectiveness of the proposed system. The findings of this study provide a solid foundation for further research in developing advanced deep-learning models for intrusion detection.

Acknowledgments. This work was supported by the United Arab Emirates (UAE) University UAEU Program for Advanced Research (UPAR) Research Grant Program under Grant 31T122.

References

1. Aldallal, A.: Toward efficient intrusion detection system using hybrid deep learning approach. Symmetry **14**(9), 1916 (2022)
2. Bakhsh, S.T., Alghamdi, S., Alsemmeari, R.A., Hassan, S.R.: An adaptive intrusion detection and prevention system for internet of things. Int. J. Distribut. Sens. Netw. **15**(11) (2021)
3. Cao, K., Zhu, J., Feng, W., Ma, C., Liu, M., Du, T.: Network intrusion detection based on dense dilated convolutions and attention mechanism. In: 2021 International Wireless Communications and Mobile Computing (IWCMC), pp. 463–468 (2021)
4. Deore, B., Bhosale, S.: Hybrid optimization enabled robust CNN-ISTM technique for network intrusion detection. IEEE Access **10**, 65611–65622 (2022)
5. Freire, P.J., Srivallapanondh, S., Napoli, A., Prilepsky, J.E., Turitsyn, S.K.: Computational complexity evaluation of neural network applications in signal processing (2022)

6. Gao, J.: Network intrusion detection method combining CNN and biLSTM in cloud computing environment. Comput. Intell. Neurosci. **2022**, 1–11 (2022)

7. Koniki, R., Ampapurapu, M.D., Kollu, P.K.: An anomaly based network intrusion detection system using LSTM and GRU. In: 2022 International Conference on Electronic Systems and Intelligent Computing (ICESIC), pp. 79–84. IEEE (2022)

8. Li, B., Gao, P., Li, X., Chen, D.: Intelligent attitude control of aircraft based on LSTM. IOP Conf. Ser.: Mater. Sci. Eng. **646**(1), 012013 (2019)

9. Liu, C., Gu, Z., Wang, J.: A hybrid intrusion detection system based on scalable k-means+ random forest and deep learning. IEEE Access **9**, 75729–75740 (2021)

10. Liu, D., Lee, S., Huang, Y., Chiu, C.: Air pollution forecasting based on attention-based LSTM neural network and ensemble learning. Exp. Syst. **37**(3) (2020)

11. Liu, L., Wang, P., Lin, J., Liu, L.: Intrusion detection of imbalanced network traffic based on machine learning and deep learning. IEEE Access **9**, 7550–7563 (2021)

12. Megantara, A.A., Ahmad, T.: A hybrid machine learning method for increasing the performance of network intrusion detection systems. J Big Data **8**(1), 142 (2021)

13. Mighan, S.N., Kahani, M.: A novel scalable intrusion detection system based on deep learning. Int. J. Inf. Secur. **20**(3), 387–403 (2021)

14. Mirza, A.H., Cosan, S.: Computer network intrusion detection using sequential LSTM neural networks autoencoders. In: 2018 26th Signal Processing and Communications Applications Conference (SIU), pp. 1–4. IEEE (2018)

15. Mohanty, S.N., Nalinipriya, G., Jena, O.P., Sarkar, A.: Machine Learning for Healthcare Applications. Wiley-Scrivener, Hoboken (2021)

16. Moustafa, N., Slay, J.: UNSW-nb15: A comprehensive data set for network intrusion detection systems (UNSW-nb15 network data set). In: 2015 Military Communications and Information Systems Conference (MilCIS), pp. 1–6. IEEE (2015)

17. Moustafa, N., Slay, J.: The evaluation of network anomaly detection systems: Statistical analysis of the UNSW-nb15 data set and the comparison with the kdd99 data set. Inf. Secur. J.: Glob. Perspect. **25**(1–3), 18–31 (2016)

18. Moustafa, N., Slay, J., Creech, G.: Novel geometric area analysis technique for anomaly detection using trapezoidal area estimation on large-scale networks. IEEE Trans. Big Data **5**(4), 481–494 (2019)

19. Panagiotou, P., Mengidis, N., Tsikrika, T., Vrochidis, S., Kompatsiaris, I.: Host-based intrusion detection using signature-based and ai-driven anomaly detection methods. Inf. Secur. **50**(1), 37–48 (2021). Copyright - Copyright ProCon Ltd. 2021; Last updated - 2021–11–02

20. Sarhan, M., Layeghy, S., Moustafa, N., Portmann, M.: Netflow datasets for machine learning-based network intrusion detection systems. J. Netw. Comput. Appl. **371**, 117–135 (2021)

21. Saurabh, K., et al.: Lbdmids: LSTM based deep learning model for intrusion detection systems for IOT networks. arXiv preprint arXiv:2206.10975 (2022)

22. Waqar, M., Dawood, H., Dawood, H., Majeed, N., Banjar, A., Alharbey, R.: An efficient smote-based deep learning model for heart attack prediction. Sci. Program. **2021**, 1–12 (2021)

23. Wei, P., Wang, B., Dai, X., Li, L., He, F.: A novel intrusion detection model for the can bus packet of in-vehicle network based on attention mechanism and autoencoder. Digit. Commun. Netw. S2352864822000700 (2022)

24. Xu, C., Shen, J., Du, X., Zhang, F.: An intrusion detection system using a deep neural network with gated recurrent units. IEEE Access **6**, 48697–48707 (2018)

25. Yang, H., Bai, Y., Chen, T., Shi, Y., Yang, R., Ma, H.: Intrusion detection model for power information network based on multi-layer attention mechanism. In: 2022 IEEE 10th Joint International Information Technology and Artificial Intelligence Conference (ITAIC), pp. 825–828 (2022)
26. Zhang, A., Lipton, Z.C., Li, M., Smola, A.J.: Dive into deep learning (2019)
27. Zhang, C., Jia, D., Wang, L., Wang, W., Liu, F., Yang, A.: Comparative research on network intrusion detection methods based on machine learning. Comput. Secur. **121**, 102861 (2022)
28. Zhang, Y., Zhang, H., Zhang, X., Qi, D.: Deep learning intrusion detection model based on optimized imbalanced network data. In: 2018 IEEE 18th International Conference on Communication Technology (ICCT), pp. 1128–1132 (2018)

Real-Time Arabic Digit Spotting with TinyML-Optimized CNNs on Edge Devices

Yasmine Abu Adla[✉], Mazen A. R. Saghir, and Mariette Awad

Department of Electrical and Computer Engineering,
American University of Beirut, Beirut, Lebanon
{yaa41,mazen,ma162}@aub.edu.lb

Abstract. TinyML is a rapidly evolving field at the intersection of machine learning and embedded systems. This paper describes and evaluates a TinyML-optimized convolutional neural network (CNN) for real-time digit spotting in the Arabic language when executed on three different computational platforms. The proposed system is designed to recognize a set of Arabic digits from a continuous audio stream in real-time, enabling the development of intelligent voice-activated applications on edge devices.

Our results show that our TinyML-optimized CNN model can achieve 90%–93% inference accuracy, within 0.06–38 ms, while occupying only 19–139 KB of memory. These results demonstrate the feasibility of deploying a CNN-based Arabic digit spotting system on resource-constrained edge devices. They also provide insights into the trade-offs between performance and resource utilization on different hardware platforms. This work has important implications for the development of intelligent voice-activated applications in the Arabic language on edge devices, which enables new opportunities for real-time speech processing at the edge.

Keywords: TinyML · Convolutional Neural Network · Real-time Digit Spotting · Model Compression · Edge Devices

1 Introduction

Voice assistants like Apple Siri, Google Assistant, and Amazon Alexa are widely used in smart phones and speakers to search for information, play media, and control home appliances [3]. Voice assistants rely on sophisticated machine learning (ML), deep learning, and natural language processing models to process and understand speech. The models are based on deep, complex, neural networks that require large data storage and intensive computations for both training and inference. And because smart phones and speakers have limited resources to store and run these models, speech queries are typically processed in cloud data centers. To operate reliably, these devices therefore require high-bandwidth access to the Internet. However, as more speech-enabled devices come online,

ⓒ IFIP International Federation for Information Processing 2023
Published by Springer Nature Switzerland AG 2023
I. Maglogiannis et al. (Eds.): AIAI 2023, IFIP AICT 675, pp. 527–538, 2023.
https://doi.org/10.1007/978-3-031-34111-3_44

it will become harder to provide the necessary communication, storage, and compute bandwidth to handle the increased speech traffic in cloud data centers. To address this problem, researchers in industry and academia are developing techniques to compress machine learning models so they can run on resource-limited devices deployed closer to their data sources at the edge of the cloud [5]. For example, Google, who developed the popular *TensorFlow* machine learning framework, has also developed *TensorFlow Lite* (TFLite) to compress large machine learning models and deploy them on smart phones and edge devices. More recently, Google introduced *Tensorflow Lite for Microcontrollers* (TFLM) to enable tiny machine learning (TinyML) models to run on inexpensive and resource-constrained microcontrollers. TFLM applies a number of compression techniques to compress TensorFlow Lite models, but little is known about how best to apply these techniques or their actual impact on the size, accuracy, and prediction time of compressed machine learning models.

In natural language processing, keyword spotting from an audio stream is a challenging task in any language. But Arabic presents unique challenges compared to other languages. A major challenge is the variability of Arabic dialects, which can lead to differences in pronunciation that affect the acoustic signal. Arabic has a rich and complex phonetic system, with many phonemes that are not present in other languages. This makes it more difficult to develop a robust acoustic model that can accurately recognize keywords in different dialects and accents. In addition, the presence of diacritical marks in Arabic can further complicate the recognition process, as these marks can change the sound of the letters and affect the acoustic features of the signal. These factors, combined with the scarcity of research in this area, make the development and evaluation of Arabic keyword spotting systems more complex than in other languages. However, addressing these challenges can lead to more accurate and reliable systems that can improve the accessibility and usability of digital tools for Arabic speakers.

In this paper, we use TinyML optimizations to achieve real-time Arabic digit spotting using convolutional neural networks running on edge devices. Our approach is designed to recognize a set of Arabic digits from a continuous audio stream in real-time, enabling the development of intelligent voice-activated applications on edge devices. We trained and optimized our CNN models using Arabic speech datasets and deployed them on three different computational devices: a commercial laptop computer, a Raspberry Pi single-board computer, and an Arduino microcontroller. We compared the execution of our model on these devices under different TinyML optimizations and evaluated its performance in terms of accuracy and latency. Our results demonstrate the viability of deploying a TinyML-optimized CNN-based Arabic digit spotting system on edge devices, which reduces the dependence on cloud deployments. Our approach also provides insights into the trade-offs between performance and resource utilization on different hardware platforms, which can inform the development of future edge devices with optimized performance and power efficiency. The findings of this research have important implications for the development of intelligent voice-activated applications on edge devices, which can enhance the accessibility and convenience of smart systems for a wider range of users.

Our paper is organized into five sections. In Section II we provide an overview of TinyML. Then, in Section III, we present our CNN model, and in Section IV we present the impact of the different compression techniques on the size, accuracy, and prediction time of our model. Finally, in Section V we present our conclusions and describe future work.

2   Overview of TinyML

TinyML is a rapidly evolving field at the intersection of machine learning and embedded systems. It enables the processing of deep learning algorithms of high accuracy on microcontrollers (MCUs) in applications that require low latency or have limited communication bandwidth access. TinyML enables compressed ML models to be deployed on resource-constrained and communication-limited microcontrollers without compromising accuracy [8,14]. This offers several advantages over deploying ML models in the cloud, including:

1. **Lower Latency:** Deploying and running models locally eliminates the overhead of transferring data to, and results from, the cloud. It also eliminates the added latency of queueing and scheduling inference tasks in the cloud. In interactive or safety-critical applications, low-latency inference is a key advantage.
2. **Less Data Exchange:** By running inference locally, only results with high information content need be shared with higher-level functions in the cloud. This greatly reduces the volume of data that needs to be exchanged and saves communication bandwidth.
3. **Lower Cost and Energy Consumption:** Because they can run on inexpensive and low-power microcontrollers, TinyML models are more cost- and energy-efficient than their cloud counterparts. This enables them to run for months, and even years, using small batteries or energy harvesting circuits.
4. **Higher Privacy and Security:** For data-sensitive applications, processing data locally enhances its privacy. It also makes it easier to employ adequate measures to secure the data including running the models offline.

2.1   TinyML Frameworks

Several Integrated Development Environments (IDEs) are available for generating TinyML models. These include Edge Impulse, Microsoft's Embedded Learning Library (ELL), ST Microelectronics' STM32Cube.AI, and ARM's ARM-NN SDK [4,10,15]. These IDEs generate TinyML models developed using common ML frameworks like Keras, ONNX, or TensorFlow into quantized and machine optimized models expressed in a high-level language. IDEs for STM and ARM microcontrollers are designed to generate optimized models for specific microcontroller families, and are therefore unable to support other hardware platforms.

On the other hand, TFLM and Edge Impulse support a wide range of devices, which is why we decided to use these two IDEs to develop and optimize our models and deploy them on different computational devices.

Google TensorFlow Lite for Microcontrollers. Google's TFLM is a platform for generating TinyML models. It consists of a *converter* that transforms Tensorflow Lite models into serialized FlatBuffer models [1]. The FlatBuffers serialization library uses schemas to transform hierarchical data structures into flat binary buffers implemented as C++ arrays. The buffers are smaller than the original data structures, and they can be accessed without the need to parse or unpack data. This makes them especially well suited for use in bare metal embedded systems. TFLM also includes an *interpreter*, which is a lightweight runtime engine that runs the TFLite model on the device and uses code generated from the FlatBuffers schema to access data efficiently. The TFLite interpreter executes a series of pre-compiled operations that make up the TFLite model. Each operation corresponds to a mathematical operation or transformation, such as convolution or activation, that is applied to the model's input data. The interpreter uses optimized algorithms and data structures to perform these operations efficiently on the device. It also abstracts the underlying hardware, making it easy to port a TinyML model to different microcontrollers and apply hardware-independent optimizations to a model.

Edge Impulse. Edge Impulse (EI) is a comprehensive platform for building, testing, and deploying machine learning models on edge devices. It provides a web-based interface that allows users to easily upload and label their own data, train machine learning models, and deploy them to edge devices. Once the models are trained, EI provides optimized libraries for running them on a variety of edge devices, including microcontrollers, embedded processors, and smartphones. The libraries are optimized for memory and processing efficiency, allowing models to run in real-time on resource-constrained devices. One of the key features of EI is its ability to generate optimized C code from machine learning models trained on the platform. This allows users to deploy their models directly to edge devices, without the need for additional libraries or runtime environments. To generate C code from a machine learning model, EI uses a tool called the Enterprise Objects Framework (EON) Compiler. The EON Compiler takes a trained model and generates C code that implements the model's inference algorithm. The generated code is optimized for memory and processing efficiency, and is designed to run on a specific hardware platform.

2.2 Techniques for Model Compression

One of the most challenging aspects of deploying ML algorithms, such as Neural Networks, are satisfying their software and hardware requirements. When running complex ML algorithms on embedded devices, it is necessary to consider the small memory size and limited computational power of MCUs. In fact, the ML model, with all its parameters, weights, and connections, must be small enough to fit on MCUs that have constrained on-chip SRAM memory (192–512 KB) and flash memory (256 KB–2 MB).

To overcome the main challenges and limitations that of running TinyML on embedded platforms, EI and TensorFlow Lite use a variety of techniques to compress machine learning models. Specifically, for speech recognition applications, the optimizations are applied to sequence models such as CNNs, Recurrent Neural Networks (RNNs), or Long Short-Term Memory (LSTM) networks. This section provides an overview of the common techniques used by EI and TFLite for compressing ML models.

Quantization. Quantization is a technique that significantly reduces the memory footprint of a deep neural network without compromising the model's accuracy [11]. It is based on reducing the number of bits used to represent a model's parameters. Quantization usually replaces 32-bit floating-point values produced during training with 16-bit floating-point or 8-bit fixed-point values that are used during inference. In addition to reducing the amount of memory needed to store a model, quantized models can usually run faster because they use simpler integer arithmetic units to operate on data.

There are two main approaches to quantization. In *quantization-aware training* [7], expected quantization errors due to inference are used during training to learn quantized model parameter values. This technique is time consuming, but it reduces the size of a model and enhances its accuracy at the same time [11]. In *post-training quantization*, model parameter values are quantized after a model has been trained. This approach generates quantized models more quickly but generally achieves lower model accuracy. However, in some cases, higher quantization errors can help a model generalize better, which increases model accuracy over new data [11]. In this study, we explore three forms of post-training quantization:

– **Float16 Quantization:** A model's 32-bit floating-point weights and activations are converted to 16-bit, half-precision, IEEE floating-point values [1].

– **Dynamic Range Quantization:** A model's weights are converted from 32-bit floating-point to 8-bit fixed-point, but activations are stored as 32-bit floating point values. During inference, activations are quantized dynamically to 8-bit fixed-point values based on their dynamic ranges. This helps reduce model execution latency [6].

– **Integer Quantization:** A model's weights and activations are converted to the nearest 8-bit fixed-point values. To guide quantization, representative data sets are used to drive the TensorFlow Lite converter and provide information about the dynamic ranges of different model parameters [6].

3   TinyML-Based CNNs for Real-Time Arabic Digit Spotting

Developing a TinyML model begins by developing a regular ML model and optimizing it to meet desired size and performance objectives. In this section we detail the steps we followed to develop a TinyML model for real-time Arabic Keyword spotting. We first describe the dataset used and the steps we followed to pre-process and clean the data. We then explain how we chose our ML model and discuss the experimental methods we followed to conduct our study.

3.1   Dataset

Our dataset consists of isolated single Arabic words spoken in the *Khaleeji* dialect[1] [2]. The words consisted of Arabic digits (0–9) spoken by 50 middle-aged men. Each subject recorded each digit ten times in a noise-free environment. Although this dataset may result in a model biased toward male speakers and the *Khaleeji* dialect, our focus in this study was to evaluate the impact of compression techniques on the size and performance of a suitable TinyML model. An expanded data set that includes samples from mixed-gender speakers in a variety of dialects can reduce or eliminate these biases.

3.2   Data Pre-processing and Cleaning

Before using the dataset to develop and train a suitable ML model, we pre-processed and cleaned the data by extracting its Mel-frequency cepstral coefficients (MFCCs) and normalizing the results, respectively. Extracting MFCCs is a common approach to pre-processing speech samples. The Mel frequency cepstrum is a method for capturing a speech sample's short-term power spectrum. MFCCs provide information about the spectral characteristics of the speech sample, enabling them to be used as input features to an ML model [13].

The MFCC values for a given speech sample are expressed as a matrix with 12 columns corresponding to the calculated cepstral values and a number of rows corresponding to the duration of a sample. Because there are variations in the time is takes to utter different digits, the number of rows for MFCC matrices can vary. To ensure that the ML model will process all speech samples uniformly, we used the maximum number of rows to express all MFCC matrices, and we set to zero any unused rows associated with a speech sample. We also verified that setting unused rows in an MFCC matrix to zero did not change or corrupt the corresponding speech samples when transformed back to the time domain.

3.3   Automatic Speech Recognition Models

For this study, we evaluated the performance of CNNs and LSTM networks for keyword spotting in Arabic speech. While LSTMs have been shown to achieve

---

[1] The dialect spoken in Arab states around the Persian Gulf.

high accuracy on a variety of speech recognition tasks, they generally have a larger memory footprint compared to CNNs. For our dataset, the CNN-based model achieved an accuracy of 93% with a memory footprint of 139 KB, while the LSTM model achieved an accuracy of 95% with a memory footprint of 10,365 KB. Given the comparable accuracy and significantly smaller memory footprint of the CNN-based model, we decided to use it for our system. This decision allowed us to deploy our model on a range of computational devices with varying levels of memory and processing power.

We developed the CNN-based model for Arabic keyword spotting using the Keras Tuner with Bayesian Optimization [9]. We assessed over 20 design iterations using the TensorFlow framework to build the optimal model architecture. Figure 1 shows the final structure of our CNN model. The model consists of two Convolutional Neural Network (CNN) layers with 8 and 16 filters, respectively, and a kernel size of 3. The ReLU activation function is used for both layers, and a dropout rate of 0.25 is applied after each pooling layer to prevent overfitting. The max-pooling layer with a pool size of 2 and stride of 2 is applied after each convolutional layer. The output from the second pooling layer is flattened, and a softmax activation function is applied to the final dense layer with the number of neurons equal to the number of classes (i.e., 10 for digit recognition).

We trained our CNN model on data from 35 speakers (70%), out of which 10% was used for validation, and tested them on the remaining 15 speakers (30%). We also used an Adam optimizer, a categorical cross entropy loss function, and optimized for accuracy. During training we used a batch size of 32 on 100 epochs.

3.4   Choice of Computational Platform

The choice of computational platform plays a significant role in determining the overall performance of an edge AI application. In our study, we evaluated the performance of our spoken digit recognition model on three different platforms: a laptop computer, Raspberry Pi SBC, and Arduino Nano BLE microcontroller. The laptop computer is a powerful device capable of running complex machine learning models with ease, but it requires a significant amount of power and is not suitable for battery-powered applications. The Raspberry Pi is a popular choice for edge AI applications as it offers a balance between performance and power consumption. It has a relatively low cost and can be used for a wide range of applications. The Arduino Nano 33 BLE, on the other hand, is a microcontroller that is suitable for low-power applications. While it may not have the processing power of the Raspberry Pi or the laptop computer, it can still perform basic machine learning tasks well, and is ideal for battery-powered applications.

Table 1 compares the technical specifications of three devices that can be used for model deployment: laptop computer, Raspberry Pi 4 Model B, and Arduino Nano 33 BLE Sense [12].

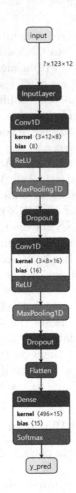

Fig. 1. Our CNN Model

Table 1. Computational Platforms

Platform	Processor	Cores	Frequency	Memory (RAM)	Memory (Flash)	Price
Dell Latitude 5410 Laptop Computer	64-bit Intel Core i5-10210U	4	1.6 GHz	16 GB	1 TB	$1000.00
Raspberry Pi 4 Model B	64-bit ARM Cortex-A72	4	1.4 GHz	2 GB, 4 GB, or 8 GB	32 GB	$30.00
Arduino Nano 33 BLE Sense	32-bit ARM Cortex-M4	1		256 KB	1 MB	$32.00

4   Impact of Model Compression

In our study, we evaluated the performance of the machine learning models on three different computational platforms. For the laptop computer and Raspberry Pi, we used TensorFlow Lite (TFLite) to deploy the models, while for the Arduino microcontroller, we used Edge Impulse's EON compiler. We chose TFLite for the laptop and Raspberry Pi due to its compatibility with a wide range of devices and its support for optimized inference on mobile and embedded devices. On the other hand, we chose EON for the Arduino Nano since it provides a seamless integration of machine learning models with low-powered microcontrollers.

In this section we present the results of applying different compression techniques to our TensorFlow baseline model when converting our model to TFLite or to C code using the EON compiler provided by EI. We then evaluate the performance of the models in terms of accuracy and latency when deploying them on a Laptop, Raspberry Pi, and Arduino Nano MCU.

4.1   Impact on Parameter and Model Size

We measured the memory footprint of the ML models on each platform, including the RAM and flash memory usage. On the Arduino Nano, we measured only the flash and random access memory (RAM) memory usage, while on the Raspberry Pi and laptop, we measured the RAM usage. This information was crucial in selecting the appropriate platform and model compression techniques to ensure that the models can satisfy the memory constraints of each platform while maintaining the desired accuracy.

Our baseline CNN model uses 8,151 parameters and requires 139 KB of storage. On the other hand, all compressed models use 3,597 parameters. This corresponds to a 56% reduction, but it is noteworthy that beyond the optimizations of the TFLite model, the different compression optimizations do not seem to impact the number of model parameters.

Table 2 shows the impact of these optimizations on the number of model parameters and size for the CNN model. In terms of model size, the TFLite model requires 19 KB of storage on both the laptop computer and Raspberry Pi. This corresponds to a 86% size reduction compared to the baseline model and is likely due to the use of FlatBuffers.

Applying integer quantization optimization to the TFLite model further reduces its size to 10 KB. Applying the EON framework on the float32 model gave us a model that required 8.4 KB of RAM usage and 27.8 KB of flash usage. On the other hand, using the EON framework to quantize the model to 8-bit integer format changed the memory footprint to 5.1 KB of RAM and 29.1 KB of flash. It is worth noting that the increase in flash memory usage from 27.8 KB to 29.1 KB when changing from Float32 to Int8 can be attributed to several factors. First, the EON compression algorithm may not perform as well on integer data compared to floating-point data. This is because the compression algorithm is optimized for floating-point numbers and may not be as effective when applied to integer data. Additionally, the overhead of the compression algorithm (such as storing the compression dictionary) may become more significant when the data size is smaller, which can also contribute to the increase in file size.

Table 2. Impact of Compression Optimizations on CNN Model Characteristics

CNN Model Characteristics	TensorFlow Baseline	TensorFlow Compression		EON Compression	
		TFLite	Integer Quantization	Float32	Integer Quantization
Number of Parameters	8,151	3,597			
Size (KB)	139	19	10	RAM: 8.4 - Flash: 27.8	RAM: 5.1 - Flash: 29.1

4.2 Impact on Model Accuracy

The accuracy of the CNN model refers to its ability to correctly classify its speech inputs. Figure 2 shows the accuracy of our spoken Arabic digit recognition models when executed on different computational platforms.

Both the TensorFlow baseline and TFLite models achieve comparable accuracies of 93% and 90%, respectively. This is likely due to the model structure not changing fundamentally beyond the more memory-efficient implementation of the TFLite model. Similarly, applying the quantization optimizations to the float32 model also achieves comparable accuracies of 90%. This again is likely due to quantization not changing model structures fundamentally.

Additionally, we found that our models achieved high accuracy on all platforms, with the highest accuracy achieved on the laptop platform. Specifically, the laptop achieved an accuracy of 93%, the Raspberry Pi achieved an accuracy of 92%, and the Arduino achieved an accuracy of 90%. These results demonstrate the effectiveness of our approach in achieving high accuracy on resource-constrained edge devices. We also note that the differences in accuracy between the three platforms are relatively small, indicating that our models are robust to variations in hardware and can perform well on a range of devices.

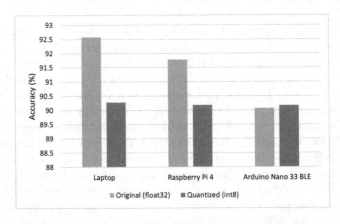

Fig. 2. Accuracy for Different Platforms and Compressions

4.3   Impact on Inference Time

Fast inference is a critical aspect of deep learning models, especially in applications where real-time operation is necessary. Deep learning models have demonstrated remarkable performance in various domains, such as computer vision, speech recognition, and natural language processing. However, the high computational cost associated with these models can pose a challenge in real-world deployment, particularly in edge computing environments. Fast inference is essential for enabling real-time response to input data, which is especially important in time-sensitive applications. In addition, fast inference is essential for enabling the deployment of deep learning models on resource-constrained devices such as smartphones and embedded systems. Therefore, optimizing deep learning models for fast prediction is critical for their successful deployment in real-world applications.

In general, reducing the size of a ML model reduces its inference time. This is due to the corresponding reduction in the number of operations that need to be executed and, in the case of TFLite, faster access to model parameters using efficient data structures like FlatBuffers. We observed this after converting our baseline TensorFlow model to a TFLite model, which reduced inference time from 38 ms to 11 ms and 0.057 ms, when running it on the laptop computer (baseline and TFLite) and the Raspberry Pi (TFLite), respectively. On the other hand, when we applied the TFLite quantization optimizations we observed different results. When deploying the CNN on the laptop computer or the Raspberry Pi, integer quantization achieved an inference time of 0.9 ms and 0.15 ms, respectively.

When running the uncompressed float32 digit spotting model on the Arduino Nano microcontroller, we observed a relatively high latency of 113 ms. This is likely due to the limited computational power and memory resources of the device, which result in longer processing times for the model. However, when we applied the EON integer 8 quantization technique we were able to reduce inference time on the Arduino Nano microcontroller from 113 ms (float32) to 5 ms (int8), respectively. These results demonstrate the viability of using TinyML optimization methods to achieve fast inference times for real-time speech processing applications.

5   Conclusions and Future Work

In this paper we explored the performance, latency and memory footprint of a real-time Arabic digit spotting model on different computational platforms. Our results demonstrate that the choice of platform can have a significant impact on both the latency and accuracy of a model. Specifically, we found that the Arduino Nano microcontroller, while having limited computational power, was still able to run a model with acceptable accuracy and latency. On the other hand, the Raspberry Pi and laptop computer were able to run the model with higher accuracy and lower latency due to their higher computational performance.

Future work in this area could focus on optimizing the ML model for specific platforms, as well as exploring additional compression techniques to further reduce the memory footprint. Given the rapidly evolving field of edge computing, continued research in this area is important to ensure that ML workloads can be effectively deployed on a variety of edge computing devices.

References

1. TensorFlow Lite for Microcontrollers. https://www.tensorflow.org/lite/microcontrollers
2. Alalshekmubarak, A., Smith, L.S.: On Improving the Classification Capability of Reservoir Computing for Arabic Speech Recognition. In: Wermter, S., et al. (eds.) ICANN 2014. LNCS, vol. 8681, pp. 225–232. Springer, Cham (2014). https://doi.org/10.1007/978-3-319-11179-7_29
3. Ammari, T., Kaye, J., Tsai, J.Y., Bentley, F.: Music, search, and IoT: How people (really) use voice assistants. ACM Trans. Comput. Hum. Interact. **26**(3) (2019). https://doi.org/10.1145/3311956
4. ARM: ARM NN SDK. https://www.arm.com/products/silicon-ip-cpu/ethos/arm-nn
5. Cao, K., Liu, Y., Meng, G., Sun, Q.: An overview on edge computing research. IEEE Access **8**, 85714–85728 (2020). https://doi.org/10.1109/ACCESS.2020.2991734
6. Amir, G., et al.: A survey of quantization methods for efficient neural network inference. arXiv preprint arXiv:2103.13630 (2021)
7. Benoit, J., et al.: Quantization and training of neural networks for efficient integer-arithmetic-only inference. In: Proceedings of the IEEE Conference on Computer Vision and Pattern Recognition, pp. 2704–2713 (2018)
8. Reddi, J., et al.: Widening Access to Applied Machine Learning With TinyML. Harvard Data Sci. Rev. **4** (2022)
9. Keras: BayesianOptimization Tuner
10. Microsoft: Embedded Learning Library (2020). https://microsoft.github.io/ELL/
11. Novac, P.-E., et al.: Quantization and deployment of deep neural networks on microcontrollers. Sensors **21**(9), 2984 (2021). https://doi.org/10.3390/s21092984. https://arxiv.org/abs/2105.13331
12. Saha, S.S., Sandha, S.S., Srivastava, M.: Machine learning for microcontroller-class hardware: A review. IEEE Sens. J. **22**(22), 21362–21390 (2022). https://doi.org/10.1109/jsen.2022.3210773
13. Sithara, A., Thomas, A., Mathew, D.: Study of MFCC and IHC feature extraction methods with probabilistic acoustic models for speaker biometric applications. Proc. Comput. Sci. **143**, 267–276 (2018)
14. Soro, S.: TinyML for Ubiquitous Edge AI (2021). arXiv preprint arxiv.org/2102.01255 https://doi.org/10.48550/ARXIV.2102.01255
15. STMicroelectronics: Artificial Intelligence Ecosystem for STM32. https://www.st.com/content/stcom/en/ecosystems/artificial-intelligence-ecosystem-stm32.html

Sleep Disorder Classification Using Convolutional Neural Networks

Chun-Cheng Peng and Chu-Yun Kou[✉]

Department of Information and Communication Engineering, Chaoyang University
of Technology, Taichung, Taiwan (R.O.C.)
goudapeng@cyut.edu.tw, s10930624@o365.cyut.edu.tw

Abstract. Sleep disorders can cause many inconveniences, such as mental fatigue, poor concentration, emotional instability, memory loss, reduced work efficiency, and increased accident rates. Among them, obstructive sleep apnea is a common sleep disorder characterized by repeated apnea and snoring during nighttime, affecting sleep quality, daily life, and work. Therefore, predicting obstructive sleep apnea events can help people better identify and treat sleep disorders and improve quality of life and work efficiency. To enhance the performance of predicting obstructive apnea, we use the MIT-BIH polysomnographic database in this article. We used deep learning methods, specifically transfer learning, with the AlexNet framework to predict the outcome of OSA events. The results show that the best optimization algorithm is SGDM. The accuracy rate is 86.63%, the sensitivity is 92.20%, the precision is 90.55%, and the AUC is 91.95%. This study demonstrates the strong potential of using artificial intelligence techniques, specifically deep learning and transfer learning, to predict OSA events from ECG signals, which could provide valuable information for diagnosing and treating sleep disorders.

Keywords: Sleep Disorder · Classification · Deep Learning · Transfer Learning

1 Introduction

Being a widespread problem that affects the quality of life and productivity of human beings, it is estimated that 50 to 70 million adults in the United States suffer from sleep disturbance [1]. Lack of good sleep can lead to severe health problems. According to the World Health Organization [2], sleep disorders can lead to physical or psychological problems, such as affecting cardiovascular health, inability to concentrate, or emotional instability, increased risk of depression and anxiety, and increased likelihood of developing high blood pressure and diabetes. Therefore, getting enough quality sleep is essential for good health and mental balance.

Fortunately, deep learning in artificial intelligence can provide more precise, effective, and convenient solutions for detecting and recognizing sleep disorders [3, 4]. For example, physiological indicators and sleep data can be integrated with deep-learning

© IFIP International Federation for Information Processing 2023
Published by Springer Nature Switzerland AG 2023
I. Maglogiannis et al. (Eds.): AIAI 2023, IFIP AICT 675, pp. 539–548, 2023.
https://doi.org/10.1007/978-3-031-34111-3_45

training to give patients instant feedback on their sleep qualities. Through intelligent analysis, these data can provide useful suggestions on how to improve sleep.

In general, Obstructive Sleep Apnea (OSA) events are medically detected by standard single polysomnography signals, i.e., electroencephalogram, electrocardiogram (ECG), and respiration. In this study, the frequency-domain signals of ECG data are transformed by continuous wavelets to generate time-domain images classified and predicted by the Convolutional Neural Network (CNN). In addition, the AlexNet is trained to predict the outcome of OSA events. The MIT-BIH polysomnogram is then applied in the evaluation stage, which not only reduces the number of layers of the convolutional neural network but also improves the evaluation index data compared with other papers.

The rest of this paper is organized as follows. After the OSA and the target dataset are defined, the related deep-learning models are reviewed in Sect. 2, while the proposed approach is illustrated in Sect. 3. Followed by experimental results and discussions in Sect. 4, conclusions and future works are drawn in Sect. 5.

2   Related Works

2.1   Obstructive Sleep Apnea and the Target Dataset

Sleep apnea is the repeated collapse of the upper airway (including the nasopharynx, oropharynx, and larynx) during sleep, which blocks the airway and makes breathing difficult [5–7]. In severe cases, the airway is completely blocked, making it impossible to inhale air and hold our breath (asphyxia). At a certain moment, the air cannot enter the lungs smoothly, the body's blood oxygen concentration drops, and the brain is easily awakened due to lack of oxygen, resulting in frequent interruptions of sleep.

According to the studies by the Sleep Center of Stanford University in the United States [7, 8], it is easy to cause airway obstruction due to the collapse of the base of the tongue during sleep. Obstructive sleep apnea occurs in about 4% of men and 2% of women. The most common symptom is snoring, usually very loud, followed by a sudden loud gasp in the middle of the night after a period of silence. In addition, if you feel dry mouth, tired after waking up, or have frequent headaches, daytime lethargy, and irritability, these are also common symptoms of sleep apnea.

The dataset used in this study comes from the MIT-BIH polysomnographic database and uses ECG signals [9]. The recording site was the sleep laboratory of Beth Israel Hospital in Boston, and the subjects were 16 men with an average age of 43 years and a weight of 119 kg. The dataset contains more than 80 h of polysomnographic signals. It labels these signals, including sleep stages (awake, stages 1–4, and rapid eye movement), types of apnea events (obstructive apnea and central apnea), hypopnea, and leg exercises. ECG signal for the MIT-BIH polysomnographic database. Figure 1 illustrates a 30-s signal of normal respiration and a 30-s signal during an OA event.

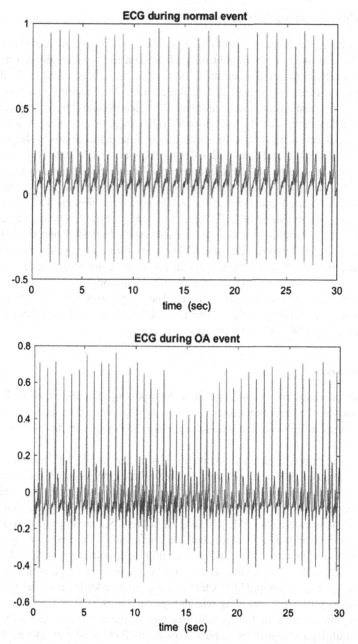

Fig. 1. ECG signal sample. 30 s during normal breathing and OA events, respectively.

2.2 Machine Learning for OSA

Machine learning has become one of the critical auxiliary diagnostic methods in modern medicine. It can use a large amount of medical data to automatically learn and train efficient classification, prediction, and identification models and then assist doctors in diagnosing and treating diseases. For example, in medical imaging, machine learning technology can assist physicians in automatically detecting and classifying diseases such as tumors [10], pneumonia [11], and lymphoma [12], thereby improving the accuracy and efficiency of diseases. In addition, machine learning has applications in sleep disorders, such as recurrence plots and convolutional neural networks (RP-CNN) [13]. RP-CNN is a machine learning method based on recurrent graphs and convolutional neural networks for predicting obstructive sleep apnea events, in that paper, the result obtained was the architecture using Resnet18 and the Adam optimizer, this method first converted physiological signals (such as ECG, EEG, etc.) into a time-frequency representation using multi-channel multi-resolution spectral analysis techniques. Then, these time series were converted into a two-dimensional (2D) pattern formed by cycle graph technology to better capture the dynamic characteristics and complexity of the signal. Finally, the recurrent map is learned and classified using a convolutional neural network to predict sleep apnea events, especially OSA events. The study results stated that sleep apnea events could be effectively predicted using the RP-CNN method with precision, recall, and F1 values of 0.88, 0.87, and 0.87, respectively.

2.3 Optimizers

The optimization algorithm is used to adjust the model's parameters to minimize the cost function's value. The cost function is usually used to evaluate the model's performance, so minimizing the cost function's value can make the model's prediction more accurate [14].

The choice of optimization algorithm usually affects the model's training speed and final performance. Therefore, in order to obtain better performance, it is essential to choose a suitable optimization algorithm. The general applied optimization algorithms for deep learning include Adaptive Moment Estimation (Adam, [15]), Stochastic Gradient Descent Momentum (SGDM, [16]) and Root Mean Square Propagation (RMSprop, [17]). These three optimization algorithms are briefly introduced respectively as follows.

Adam is an optimization algorithm for adaptive moment estimation. It combines adaptive gradient descent and momentum optimization to converge to the global minimum of the cost function quickly. Adam also has some additional advantages, such as adaptive adjustment of the learning rate and resisting noise.

As a stochastic gradient descent with momentum, the momentum term of SGDM can help the optimization algorithm to pass through the local minimum and accelerate the convergence speed. There are also some variants of SGDM, such as Nesterov Accelerated Gradient, which can better solve some problems of the momentum algorithm.

RMSprop is an optimization algorithm for adaptive learning rates. It can adjust the learning rate according to the size of the gradient to adaptively adjust the update speed of different weights. This enables RMSprop to handle parameters efficiently at different scales, leading to better model optimization.

3   Proposed Approach

3.1   Data Preprocessing

In the MIT-BIH polysomnographic database, the signal is marked every 30 s. First of all, we need to cut all the signals every 30 s and mark them, accordingly, perform continuous wavelet transformation (CWT) [18] on the cut signals, and express them in a wavelet magnitude graph. The formula definition is stated as in Eq. (1).

$$F(\tau, s) = \frac{1}{\sqrt{|s|}} \int_{-\infty}^{\infty} f(t) \psi^* \left(\frac{t - \tau}{s} \right) dt, \tag{1}$$

where $F(\tau,s)$ is the converted signal, τ, and s are translation parameters and scaling factors, respectively, and ψ is expressed as a mother wavelet. A 2D CWT mass-quality map with color changes corresponding to the ECG signal was generated by CWT, as displayed in Fig. 2.

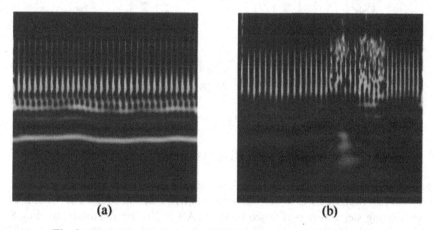

(a)   (b)

Fig. 2.   ECG signal converts 2D CWT. (a) normal event (b) OA events

3.2   Transfer Learning—Alexnet

Transfer Learning is mainly to modify the output layer and hyperparameters of the existing model architecture so that it can be used for new image classification, and migration learning can reduce the time we need to rebuild the CNN model [14].

In the experiment, the well-known Alexnet [19] is applied and adjusted the final classification into 2 classes for the corresponding ECG classification, as exhibited in Fig. 3, where s represents the stride size.

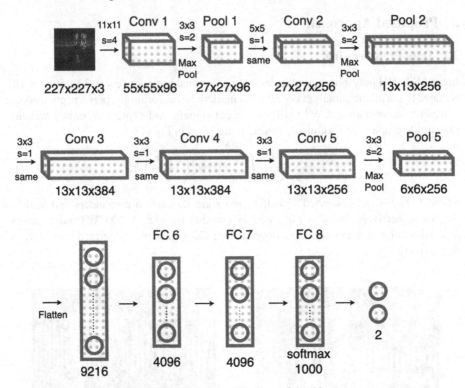

Fig. 3. Constructed architecture of the Alexnet

4 Experimental Results and Discussions

The experiments of this paper are simulated on a Windows platform, with an Intel(R) Core (TW) i9-10900K CPU @ 3.70 GHz and NVIDIA GeForce RTX 2080 SUPER 8G. All processing steps were performed in MATLAB 2020a. By randomly dividing 80% and 20% of the whole dataset for training and testing, i.e., there are 5486 normal and 1702 OA events in the training set and 1371 and 425 normal and OA patterns in the testing set. The Alexnet framework is applied to training by the previously mentioned three different optimization algorithms. Each of these three optimizers performs 10 specific training runs and then averages to find the best algorithm. The training initial learning rate, maximum epoch, and mini-batch size are set to 10^{-4}, 30, and 32, respectively. Other optimizers mainly apply MATLAB preset parameters and only the adjusted parameter values are explained.

In addition, the testing results are evaluated by the five commonly considered performance indicators, namely accuracy, sensitivity, specificity, precision, and AUC [20]. The specific formula are defined as follows:

$$Accuracy = \frac{TP + TN}{TP + TN + FP + FN}, \tag{2}$$

$$Sensitivity = \frac{TP}{TP + FN}, \tag{3}$$

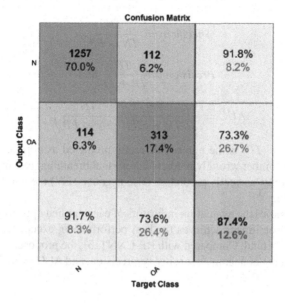

(a) SGDM

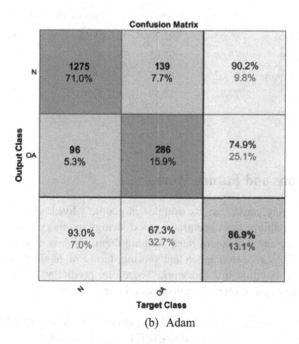

(b) Adam

(c) RMSprop

Fig. 4. Confusion matrices of the test results

$$Specificity = \frac{TN}{TN + FP}, \tag{4}$$

$$Precision = \frac{TP}{TP + FP} \text{ and} \tag{5}$$

$$AUC = \frac{1}{2}\left(\frac{TP}{TP + FN} + \frac{TN}{TN + FP}\right), \tag{6}$$

where true positive (TP) is the number correctly predicted as normal breathing, false positive (FP) the number wrongly predicted as normal breathing, true negative (TN) the number of OA events correctly predicted, false negative (FN) the number of OA event mispredictions (Fig. 4).

Table 1 summaries the evaluation indicators of each applied optimization algorithm, while the SGDM optimizer achieves the best performance, except for about 0.4% of precision lagging behind. Compared with RP-CNN [13], the proposed approach outperforms, in terms of better accuracy, sensitivity, precision, and AUC, with fewer adjustable parameters.

Table 1. Evaluation metrics for predicting ECG signals (in %)

Method	Accuracy	Sensitivity	Specificity	Precision	AUC
Alexnet with SGDM	86.63	92.20	68.68	90.55	91.95
Alexnet with Adam	85.69	92.05	65.18	89.59	89.39
Alexnet with RMSprop	84.67	89.53	69.01	90.92	91.15
ResNet18 with RP-CNN [15]	77.71	77.59	77.36	77.25	77.24

5   Conclusions and Future Works

Sleep disorders may cause various troubles in people's lives, such as mental fatigue during the day, inability to concentrate, mood swings, memory loss, decreased work efficiency and increased accident rates. Among them, OSA is a common sleep disorder characterized by repeated apnea and snoring during night sleep, which may affect sleep quality and daytime life and work. Therefore, predicting OSA events can help people better identify and treat sleep disorders, improving their quality of life and work efficiency.

In this paper, aiming to tackle the OSA classification issue, the MIT-BIH polysomnographic dataset is firstly transformed to 2D CWT maps and then fed into the AlexNet architecture, in order to verify the corresponding recognizing capability of the constructed system. Via the optimization by SGDM, Adam and RMSprop algorithms, experimental evidence shows that the best test accuracy of our proposed approach has reached 86.63%, and with strong potential to be further enhanced.

In the future, hyperparameter optimization schemes, such as Bayesian optimization, and Sparrow Search algorithm will be implemented, in order to advance the system performance for the recognition of sleep disorders.

References

1. How to Diagnose & Treat the 5 Most Common Sleep Disorders. American Association of Sleep Technologists. https://www.aastweb.org/blog/how-to-diagnose-treat-the-5-most-common-sleep-disorders. Accessed 25 Jan 2023
2. Regional Office for Europe, European Centre for Environment and Health Bonn Office, World Health Organization. WHO Technical Meeting on Sleep and Health: Bonn Germany, 14–17 (2004). https://apps.who.int/iris/handle/10665/349782. Accessed 26 Jan 2023
3. Goldstein, C., Berry, R., et al.: Artificial intelligence in sleep medicine: An American Academy of sleep medicine position statement. J. Clin. Sleep Med. **16**(4), 605–607 (2020). https://doi.org/10.5664/jcsm.8288
4. Hepsiba, D., Vijay Anand, L., Princy, J.: Deep learning for sleep disorders: A review. In: Proceedings of 2021 Seventh International Conference on Bio Signals, Images, and Instrumentation (ICBSII) (2021). https://doi.org/10.1109/ICBSII51839.2021.9445159
5. Malhotra, A., White, D.: Obstructive sleep apnea. The Lancet **360**(9328), 237–254 (2002). https://doi.org/10.1016/S0140-6736(02)09464-3
6. Kribbs, B., Pack, I., Kline, R., et al.: Objective measurement of patterns of nasal CPAP use by patients with obstructive sleep apnea. ATS Journals **147**(4), 887–895 (2012). https://doi.org/10.1164/ajrccm/147.4.887
7. Epstein, L., et al.: Adult obstructive sleep apnea task force of the American Academy of sleep medicine. Clinical Guideline for the Evaluation, Management and Long-Term Care of Obstructive Sleep Apnea in Adults. J. Clin. Sleep Med. **5**(3), 263–276 (2000). https://doi.org/10.5664/jcsm.27497
8. Moore, K.: Site-specific versus diffuse treatment presenting severity of obstructive sleep apnea. Sleep Breath. **4**(04), 145–146 (2000). https://doi.org/10.1055/s-2000-19520
9. Ichimaru, Y., Moody, B.: Development of the polysomnographic database on CD-ROM. Psychiat. Clin. Neurosci. **53**(2), 175–177 (1999). https://doi.org/10.1046/j.1440-1819.1999.00527
10. Esteva, A., Kuprel, B., Novoa, A., et al.: Dermatologist-level classification of skin cancer with deep neural networks. Nature **542**(7639), 115–118 (2017). https://doi.org/10.1038/nature21056
11. Rajpurkar, P., et al.: Chexnet: Radiologist-level Pneumonia detection on chest X-rays with deep learning. arXiv preprint arXiv:1711.05225 (2017). https://doi.org/10.48550/arXiv.1711.05225
12. Bejnordi, E., et al.: Diagnostic assessment of deep learning algorithms for detection of lymph node metastases in women with breast cancer. JAMA **318**(22), 2199–2210 (2017). https://doi.org/10.1001/jama.2017.14585
13. Taghizadegan, Y., Dabanloo, N.J., Maghooli, K., Sheikhani, A.: Obstructive sleep apnea event prediction using recurrence plots and convolutional neural networks (RP-CNNs) from polysomnographic signals. Biomed. Signal Process. Control **69**, 102928 (2021). https://doi.org/10.1016/j.bspc.2021.102928
14. Abd Almisreb, A., Jamil, N., Din, M.: Utilizing AlexNet deep transfer learning for ear recognition. In: Proceedings of 2018 Fourth International Conference on Information Retrieval and Knowledge Management (CAMP), pp. 1–5. IEEE (2018). https://doi.org/10.1109/INFRKM.2018.8464769

15. Diederik, K., Jimmy, B.: Adam: A method for stochastic optimization. arXiv preprint. arXiv: 1412.6980 (2014)
16. Rumelhart, E., Hinton, E., Williams, J.: Learning representations by Back-Propagating errors. Nature **323**(6088), 533–536 (1986). https://doi.org/10.1038/323533a0
17. Hinton, G., Srivastava, N., Swersky, K.: Neural networks for machine learning lecture 6a overview of Mini-Batch Gradient Descent. Cited on **14**(8), 2 (2012)
18. Mallat, S.: A Wavelet Tour of Signal Processing. Academic Press (1999)
19. Krizhevsky, A., Sutskever, I., Hinton, E.: ImageNet classification with deep convolutional neural networks. Commun. ACM **60**(6), 84–90 (2017). https://doi.org/10.1145/3065386
20. Sokolova, M., Lapalme, G.: A systematic analysis of performance measures for classification tasks. Inf. Process. Manag. **45**(4), 427–437 (2009). https://doi.org/10.1016/j.ipm.2009.03.002

The Effect of Tensor Rank on CNN's Performance

Eleftheria Vorgiazidou[1] , Konstantinos Delibasis[1(✉)] ,
and Ilias Maglogiannis[2]

[1] Department of Computer Science and Biomedical Informatics,
University of Thessaly, Papasiopoulou Street 2-4, 35131 Lamia, Greece
vorgiazidouele@gmail.com, kdelibasis@gmail.com
[2] Department of Digital Systems, University of Piraeus,
Karaoli and Dimitriou Street 80, 18534 Pireaus, Greece
imaglo@unipi.gr

Abstract. The goal of this work is to combine existing convolutional layers (CLs) to design a computationally efficient Convolutional Neural Network (CNN) for image classification tasks. The current limitations of CNNs in terms of memory requirements and computational cost have driven the demand for a simplification of their architecture. This work investigates the use of two consecutive CLs with 1-D filters to replace one layer of full rank 2-D set of filters. First we provide the mathematical formalism, derive the properties of the equivalent tensor and calculate the rank of tensor's slices in closed form. We apply this architecture with several parameterizations to the well known AlexNet without transfer learning and experiment with three different image classification tasks, which are compared against the original architecture. Results showed that for most parameterizations, the achieved reduction in dimensionality, which yields lower computational complexity and cost, maintains equivalent, or even marginally better classification accuracy.

Keywords: low-rank tensor · tensor decomposition · CNN

1 Introduction and Related Work

CNNs are one of the most important feature learning tools widely used in Computer Vision, Machine Learning and Artificial Intelligence in general. However, CNNs are considered computationally "heavy" systems as they require many arithmetic operations during convolutions and consume a large amount of memory. Concerns about the size and complexity of the models brought a consequent

This research has been co-financed by the European Union and Greek national funds through the Operational Program Competitiveness, Entrepreneurship and Innovation, under the call RESEARCH - CREATE - INNOVATE (project code: DFVA Deep Football Video Analytics T2EKΔK-04581).

I. Maglogiannis et al. (Eds.): AIAI 2023, IFIP AICT 675, pp. 549–560, 2023.
https://doi.org/10.1007/978-3-031-34111-3_46

demand for their simplification. One approach to reducing memory requirements and computational complexity is by compressing and decomposing convolution kernels.

After a thorough literature review, we noticed that few similar CNN architectures have been implemented, aimed to lower the rank of convolutional filters. Mamalet et al. [12] proposed the use of merged layers consisting of horizontal and vertical filters with a stride of 2 and separable filters, which aim to be low-rank from scratch. Rigamonti et al. [14] demonstrated that multiple filters can be replaced by fewer separable ones with rank equal to 1 resulting in negligible loss of accuracy. The same year, Denil et al. [2] represented the learnable weights' vector as a product of two low-rank components with smaller dimensions to reduce parameterization. Therefore, Denton et al. [3] used linear algebra and linear compression techniques, such as Singular Value Decomposition (SVD) [15], to yield low-rank convolution kernels while clustering the filters. Jaderberg et al. [7] proposed two different approximations both optimized based on reconstruction and empirical reconstruction filters' error maximum elimination. In the 1st the 2-D convolution filters are replaced by outer products of 1-D vertical and horizontal filters in the same CL, which is followed by a pointwise CL. In the 2nd approach, each CL is replaced by a sequence of two CLs, using vertical and horizontal kernels respectively, with a different number of filters.

Lebedev et al. [9] used the Canonical Polyadic Decomposition (CPD) [5] method to extract a sum of 4 equivalent rank-1 2-D tensors, which substitute the original convolution kernels consecutively. Tai et al. [16] tried to achieve the decomposition of 4-D tensors into a sequence of two horizontal and vertical low-rank convolution kernels and trained the deep networks with the reduced new parameters using batch normalization. Astrid et al. [1] also implemented the decomposition of kernels derived from fully connected layers using both CPD and SVD approach and developed an algorithm that intelligently chooses the tensor's rank. Phan et al. [13] rejected CPD and proposed an algorithm that uses either a corrected version of CPD or Tensor Kronecker Decomposition (TKD) method. Later, Lee et al. [10] proposed a non-common approach that builds a neural network consisting of 3-D rank-1 filters alternating with 1-D ones, which they were derived by decomposing the former, during the testing phase to speed up the process flow. These methods have been successfully applied to networks such as MobileNet [6], ResNet [4], yielding better results.

For this work, we researched and implemented a neural network architecture that uses, instead of one set of full rank filters, two cascaded 1-D filters. More specifically we investigated the mathematical properties and ability to classify images of a CNN with less memory requirements and computational cost, consisting of separable rank-1 filters. Our initial results of this application show that the equivalent CNN does not reduce the classification accuracy, although it is improved in terms of computational and memory requirements.

2 Methodology

2.1 Investigation of Convolutional Layer Decomposition

In this section, we adopt the method of Jaderberg *et al.* [7] and we decompose the CL with full-rank tensors into 2 CLs: the 1st one contains vertical convolutional kernels while the 2nd one horizontal convolutional kernels. We provide the mathematical formalism and we express the equivalent tensor as a sum of vertical and horizontal convolutions, investigating its mathematical properties. To this end we chose the well known AlexNet architecture [8]. Each filter of the AlexNet's 1st CL of 11×11 dimensions, is obviously a rank-11 matrix. We will show that it can be replaced by a sum of outer products of two separable ones, 11×1 and 1×11 that are rank-1 matrices.

Let an input (I) consisting of three channels I_1, I_2, I_3, ($C = 3$), be forward-passed in the 1st layer of the CNN. In the proposed implementation, the input layer of the neural network is followed by two CLs instead of one, to lower the rank of the equivalent kernels required for the convolution process. This method is applied to all CLs of the neural network. Figure 1 depicts the overview of the proposed workflow.

More specifically, let F, C denote the filter size and the number of image channels respectively. The input is convolved with a number of n_v vertical filters (or kernels), $K_1, K_2, \ldots, K_{n_v}$ of dimension $F \times 1 \times C$, each with $C = 3$ number of channels. Channel c of kernel i is denoted by K_{ic}. The channel i of the output A of the 1st CL is the following:

$$A_i = I_1 * K_{i1} + I_2 * K_{i2} + I_3 * K_{i3} + bk_i = \sum_{c=1}^{C} I_c K_{ic} + bk_i, \qquad (1)$$

where $i \in 1, 2, \ldots, n_v$ and bk_i stands for K_i's bias. This output is convolved with the 2nd CL with n_h horizontal filters of dimension $1 \times F \times n_v$ (the number of channels now is equal to n_v). Therefore, each kernel O has a depth of n_v, with $O_{j,c}$ being the channel c of the jth horizontal kernel, with $j = 1, \ldots n_h$ and $c = 1, \ldots n_v$. Thus, the output B of the 2nd CL is the following:

$$B_j = A_1 * O_{j1} + A_2 * O_{j2} + \ldots + A_{n_v} * O_{jn_v} + bo_j = \sum_{c=1}^{n_v} A_c O_{jc} + bo_j, \qquad (2)$$

where bo_j stands for O_j' bias.

Let us consider the equivalent low-rank tensor T that is convolved with I and generates the same output B, depicted as a workflow in Fig. 2. The dimensions of T are $F \times F \times C \times n_h$, regardless the value of n_v. Further, let us name the slices of T as T_{jc}, with $j = 1, 2, \ldots, n_h$ and $c = 1, 2, \ldots, C$.

Substituting Eq. 1 into 2 respectively results in a different representation of output B, which leads us to postulate a proposition about rank's computation for each T_{jc} slice of the equivalent tensor T.

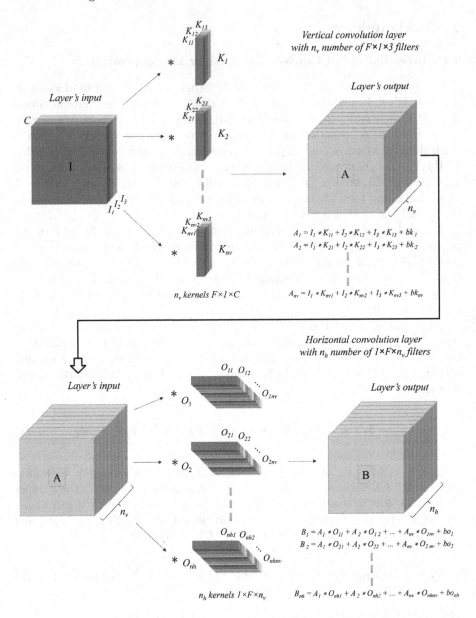

Fig. 1. Low-rank layers architecture.

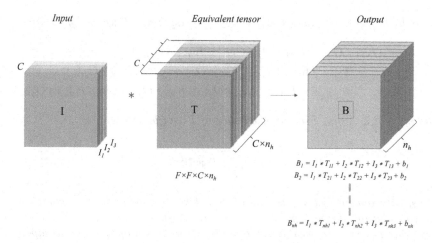

Fig. 2. Procedure of B's generation through an equivalent tensor.

Theorem 1. *The rank of each slice T_{jc} of tensor T is given by :*

$$rank(T_{jc}) = \begin{cases} n_v, & if\, n_v < F \\ F, & if\, n_v \geq F \end{cases} \qquad (3)$$

Proof. Generalizing Eq. 2 for any index $j = 1, 2, \ldots, n_h$ and substituting the expression for the output $A_i, i = 1, \ldots, n_v$ of the vertical layer from Eq. 1 yields the following expression for the output B of the horizontal layer:

$$B_j = (I_1 * K_{11} + I_2 * K_{12} + I_3 * K_{13} + bk_1) * O_{j1}$$
$$+(I_1 * K_{21} + I_2 * K_{22} + I_3 * K_{23} + bk_2) * O_{j2} + \ldots$$
$$+(I_1 * K_{n_v1} + I_2 * K_{n_v2} + I_3 * K_{n_v3} + bk_{n_v}) * O_{jn_v} + b_{o_j}. (4)$$

Considering that the biases b_{o_j} of the 1st CL are equal to 0 and exploiting the distributive property, the Eq. 4, takes the following form:

$$B_j = I_1 * (K_{11} * O_{j1} + K_{21} * O_{j2} + \ldots + K_{n_v1} * O_{jn_v})$$
$$+I_2 * (K_{12} * O_{j1} + K_{22} * O_{j2} + \ldots + K_{n_v2} * O_{jn_v})$$
$$+I_3 * (K_{13} * O_{j1} + K_{23} * O_{j2} + \ldots + K_{n_v3} * O_{jn_v}) + b_{oj}$$
$$= I_1 \sum_{i=1}^{n_v} K_{i1} * O_{ji} + I_2 \sum_{i=1}^{n_v} K_{i2} * O_{ji} + I_3 \sum_{i=1}^{n_v} K_{i3} * O_{ji} + b_{oj}$$
$$= \sum_{c=1}^{C} \sum_{i=1}^{n_v} K_{ic} * O_{ji} + b_{oj}. (5)$$

On the other hand, utilizing the definition of the equivalent tensor T, the output B_j becomes:

$$B_j = I_1 * T_{j1} + I_2 * T_{j2} + I_3 * T_{j3} + b_j = \sum_{c=1}^{C} I_c * T_{jc} + b_j, \qquad (6)$$

where b_j is the same bias as bo_j. Combining Eq. 5 and 6 we easily obtain

$$T_{j1} = (K_{11} * O_{j1} + K_{21} * O_{j2} + \ldots + K_{n_v 1} * O_{jn_v}),$$
$$T_{j2} = (K_{12} * O_{j1} + K_{22} * O_{j2} + \ldots + K_{n_v 2} * O_{jn_v}),$$
$$T_{j3} = (K_{13} * O_{j1} + K_{23} * O_{j2} + \ldots + K_{n_v 3} * O_{jn_v}),\tag{7}$$

where $j \in 1, 2, \ldots n_h$. Finally, each slice of T can be written as:

$$T_{jc} = \sum_{q=1}^{n_v} K_{qc} * O_{jq}.\tag{8}$$

Thus, each tensor slice T_{jc} is sum of rank-1 kernels, as each one's component is the convolution of two separable 1-D filters. Assuming that $n_v < F$ the denoted terms are $F \times F$ kernels with rank equal to n_v, as a sum of n_v rank-1 components, otherwise, if $n_v \geq F$, the kernels are full-rank, with a rank of F, as the rank cannot overcome the kernel's dimension. So, each 2-D slice of T_{jc} is a rank-n_v matrix when $n_v < F$, or a rank-F matrix when $n_v > F$. □

2.2   Network's Architecture and Experimentation

The AlexNet CNN [8] consists of 5 CLs. All five model's untrained CLs are replaced by two successive layers, operating with rank-1 vertical and horizontal filters instead of full-rank ones. The 1st CL needs some additional modification, as it has filters with the largest dimensions, in contrast to the rest of the layers which contain filters of very small sizes. We experimented with the number of vertical kernels $n_v = 1, 2, 3, 4, 5, 8, 11, 20, 40$ and 96 used in this 1st layer, as it defines the rank of the equivalent tensor's slices, as proven in 2.1. The other CLs operated with $n_v = n_h$ kernels.

The proposed model incorporates half the corresponding original stride and padding values in each convolutional vertical and horizontal step, i.e. in the 1st CL of the original architecture, the stride value was 4, whereas each of the 2 CL with the vertical and horizontal kernels where set to stride =2. In case of padding equal to 1, the padding is divided to 1 and 0 in the two successive low-rank layers. The proposed architecture is depicted in Fig. 3, including all applied modifications and details about the stride, padding and size of each layer's output. It should be mentioned that no pretrained weights have been transferred to our implementation of AlexNet, in order to allow the experiments to emphasize on the differences between the architectures.

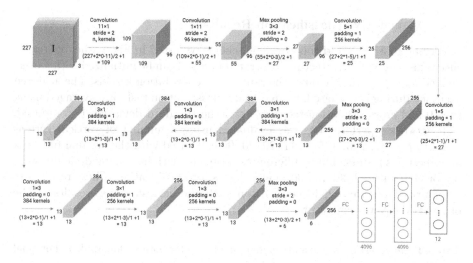

Fig. 3. Proposed AlexNet architecture.

3   Results

3.1   Dataset Description and Preprocessing

The training and evaluation of the proposed model was performed using samples from 12, 20 and 30 different image categories, obtained from the freely available Caltech101 database [11], split into training, validation and test sets as shown on Table 1. An elementary transformation of the data into RGB images of dimension 227×227 is followed, simultaneously implementing data augmentation to the training and validation data, using randomly applied rotation, reflection and shear at both axes.

Table 1. Dataset's composition.

Classes	Training Samples	Validation Samples	Test Samples
12	2842	710	394
20	3207	801	445
30	3639	908	505

3.2   Network's Train Parameters

After experimentation, the mini-batch size was set to 8 images for every gradient update and the learning rate was set to 0.001, constantly. Stochastic gradient descent with momentum was selected as the optimization method and the maximum number of training epochs was set to 30, while the validation patience parameter was set to 10.

3.3   Quantitative Classification Results

According to Sect. 2 and the workflow scheme we listed in Fig. 1, the low tensor slice rank proposed architecture illustrated in Fig. 3 can be initialized with a user-defined n_v value, which defines the rank of the convolution kernels. The achieved accuracy during test phase for three image classification tasks are averaged using the 10-fold cross validation technique and the standard deviation is computed. The network's performance was evaluated using a number of vertical kernels equal to $n_v = 1, 2, 3, 4, 5, 8, 11, 20, 40, 96$ compared with the original full-rank architecture's results. Three different experiments with increasing difficulty were performed, with 12, 20 and 30 image classes for classification. These results are summarized on Table 2, in comparison with the corresponding results of the original AlexNet architecture.

Table 2. Mean test accuracy and standard deviation for both n_v low-rank and original architectures.

Low-rank Architecture	Classes		
n_v	12	20	30
1	82.64 ± 2.71	75.84 ± 3.04	67.81 ± 3.83
2	84.67 ± 3.65	75.79 ± 3.80	65.84 ± 2.67
3	84.11 ± 2.24	76.26 ± 3.24	68.17 ± 4.47
4	83.86 ± 3.71	77.52 ± 2.18	66.08 ± 5.54
5	84.95 ± 1.61	77.70 ± 3.60	66.31 ± 4.28
8	83.93 ± 2.89	76.89 ± 3.40	68.21 ± 3.75
11	84.19 ± 3.44	77.34 ± 4.11	67.24 ± 4.02
20	84.36 ± 2.83	75.25 ± 3.10	69.32 ± 2.23
40	84.80 ± 2.37	77.09 ± 2.06	69.26 ± 3.64
96	85.00 ± 2.56	77.79 ± 2.08	68.17 ± 3.90
Original Architecture	83.86 ± 2.61	76.17 ± 4.34	67.03 ± 3.44

As it can be observed in the results presented on Table 2, the accuracy achieved by the low tensor slice rank architecture shows a slowly increasing trend, for the first increasing values of n_v. In all three experiments, the low rank architecture marginally surpasses the original one in terms of classification accuracy for approximately $n_v \geq 2$. Finally, increasing the number of image classes clearly deteriorates the achieved accuracy, of both the original and the low rank architectures. Although one may have expected that the deep learning architectures would be almost unaffected by modest number of classes, it has to be mentioned that the deep neural networks that are used in this work have been trained from scratch on a rather small number of images. We refrained from using trained networks, since this would hinter the difference in performance of the architectures under comparison.

3.4   Arithmetic Complexity Reduction

Implementing the low-rank modifications, two CLs now operate with 1-D filters in a serial manner, instead of one CL with full rank 2-D filter, which results in reducing the complexity as follows. According to the Fig. 1, the CL operating with vertical separable filters presents $O(n_v CFHW)$ complexity, where H, W describe the height and the width for input I respectively. Similarly, the complexity of the layer operating with horizontal separable filters may be expressed as $O(n_h n_v FH'W')$, where H', W' define the height and the width for the layer's input A. The overall complexity is calculated as

$$O(n_v(C + n_h)F(HW + H'W')).$$

If convolution's stride is set as $s = 1$, then $H = H', W = W'$, otherwise, if $s > 1$, then $H > H', W > W'$. So, for $s = 1$, the complexity appears as $O(n_v CFHW + n_h n_v FHW)$. Executing convolution with full-rank filters would yield a complexity result equal to

$$O(n_h CF^2 HW).$$

The significance of this complexity reduction is demonstrated on Table 3, where the number of required arithmetic operations for both low tensor slice rank modified and original's full-rank layers are provided. So using separable filters reduces the computational cost along every CL as less arithmetic operations are required to perform convolution. More specifically, the differences in complexity are captured through a detailed example for multiple n_v values and AlexNet's specific values $C = 3, n_h = 96, F = 11, H = 227, W = 227, H' = 109, W' = 109$ features.

The results on Table 3 present the rank of each T_{jc} slice of the equivalent tensor utilized, the total low-rank complexity across every n_v model and the difference between the original and the low-rank complexity for the 1st CL of AlexNet, along with the complexity's % reduction rate. The resulting complexity is reduced by 2 orders of magnitude (equivalently 1.7 billion less operations for forward pass through AlexNet) for $n_v = 1$. The $n_v = 96$ is the worst case scenario studied, achieving percentage reduction of 23.83% (equivalently 427,990,464 less operations).

In the same manner, we calculated the complexity for the 4 remaining CLs of AlexNet on Table 4, that are also constructed with a cascade of 2 CLs 1-D filters, but are not depended on the internal value n_v, comparing each with the corresponding original architecture complexity, in terms of their numerical and % percentage difference.

Overall, it is revealed that implementing a low tensor slice rank model would require millions less operations in every single CL, approaching a reduction of 8 hundred million operations in total when n_v is equal to n_h=96 and surprisingly a reduction of 2 billion operations in total when executing a n_v=1 low-rank architecture. It is therefore clear that with such a huge reduction in arithmetic complexity and memory resources used during the convolution, we have created

Table 3. Number of arithmetic operations for different n_v low-rank models for the 1st CL of AlexNet and the corresponding difference from the original layer's complexity.

Low-rank Architecture n_v	Rank of T_{jc} Slice	Complexity	Reduction	% Reduction
1	1	14,246,793	1,781,435,799	99.20
2	2	28,493,586	1,767,189,006	98.41
3	3	42,740,379	1,752,942,213	97.61
4	4	56,987,172	1,738,695,420	96.82
5	5	71,233,965	1,724,448,627	96.03
8	8	113,974,344	1,681,708,248	93.65
11	11	156,714,723	1,638,967,869	91.27
20	11	284,935,860	1,510,746,732	84.13
40	11	569,871,720	1,225,810,872	68.26
96	11	1,367,692,128	427,990,464	23.83
Original Architecture	11	1,795,682,592	0	0

Table 4. Number of arithmetic operations required for the remaining AlexNet's CLs according to both original and low-rank architecture.

CL	Original Complexity	Low-rank Complexity	Reduction	% Reduction
2	447,897,600	294,379,520	153,518,080	34.27
3	149,520,384	124,600,320	24,920,064	16.66
4	224,280,576	149,520,384	74,760,192	33.33
5	149,520,384	83,066,880	66,453,504	44.44

a much "lighter" neural system, that achieves the same or slightly improved classification accuracy.

3.5   Memory Requirement Reduction

Constructing a CNN with smaller filter dimensions in each CL can greatly reduce the number of learnable parameters. The learnable parameters derived from the original structure in total reach a number of 2,332,704, while the low-rank structure is defined by a much smaller n_v-dependent number of parameters equal to 1,650,688+1,089n_v. Table 5 presents these results for different n_v values, along with the absolute % difference from the original values. As it can be observed in Table 5 the difference in the total number of parameters for the low-rank architectures compared with the full-rank ones is quite significant, approaching 30%, which translates to approximately 680,927 for AlexNet. Despite the parameter reduction, the accuracy achieved by the low-rank architecture in every experiment is consistently not worse, or even marginally better than the original architecture.

Table 5. Number of learnable weights for both original AlexNet and low-rank architectures considering all CLs.

Low-rank Architecture n_v	Parameters	Reduction	% Reduction
1	1,651,777	680,927	29.19
2	1,652,866	679,838	29.14
3	1,653,955	678,749	29.09
4	1,655,044	677,660	29.05
5	1,656,133	676,571	29.00
8	1,659,400	673,304	28.86
11	1,662,667	670,037	28.72
20	1,672,468	660,236	28.30
40	1,694,248	638,456	27.36
96	1,755,232	577,472	24.75
Original Architecture	2,332,704	0	0

4   Conclusions

In this work we investigated the mathematical properties of replacing a CL with full rank kernels by a series of two layers, each with 1-D kernels. From the proposed model we conclude that a reduction in the arithmetic complexity, computational cost and memory requirement of the resulting architecture can be achieved, without deteriorating its performance. As the rank of the T_{jc} slice increases from 1 to 96, the difference in the number of arithmetic operations required compared to the original architecture's complexity decreases significantly. These conclusions suggest that the low tensor slice rank model can significantly reduce the complexity of the overall CLs by at least 747,642,304 operations with a maximum reduction of 2,101,087,639 operations. About memory requirements, the low tensor slice rank architecture reduces the number of parameters in the CLs compared to the original AlexNet architecture over half a million, at a percentage of 25–30%.

In further work we will study the mathematical properties of more low-rank neural architectures. We will also expand the datasets and the repetitions of the experimentation to establish statistical significance. Finally, we will investigate the applicability of this approach to deep learning architectures for object detection in video, which is a task that would greatly benefit from reduced arithmetic operations. Such an appropriate dataset is already available to our team in the DFVA Deep Football Video Analytics, as described in the Acknowledgments.

Acknowledgements. This research has been co-financed by the European Union and Greek national funds through the Operational Program Competitiveness, Entrepreneurship and Innovation, under the call RESEARCH - CREATE - INNO-VATE (project code: DFVA Deep Football Video Analytics T2EKΔK-04581).

References

1. Astrid, M., Lee, S.I.: Deep compression of convolutional neural networks with low-rank approximation. ETRI J. **40**(4), 421–434 (2018)
2. Denil, M., Shakibi, B., Dinh, L., Ranzato, M., De Freitas, N.: Predicting parameters in deep learning. Adv. Neural Inf. Process. Syst. **26** (2013)
3. Denton, E.L., Zaremba, W., Bruna, J., LeCun, Y., Fergus, R.: Exploiting linear structure within convolutional networks for efficient evaluation. Adv. Neural Inf. Process. Syst. **27** (2014)
4. He, K., Zhang, X., Ren, S., Sun, J.: Deep residual learning for image recognition. In: Proceedings of the IEEE Conference on Computer Vision and Pattern Recognition, pp. 770–778 (2016)
5. Hitchcock, F.L.: The expression of a tensor or a polyadic as a sum of products. J. Math. Phys. **6**(1–4), 164–189 (1927)
6. Howard, A.G., et al.: Mobilenets: Efficient convolutional neural networks for mobile vision applications. arXiv preprint arXiv:1704.04861 (2017)
7. Jaderberg, M., Vedaldi, A., Zisserman, A.: Speeding up convolutional neural networks with low rank expansions. arXiv preprint arXiv:1405.3866 (2014)
8. Krizhevsky, A., Sutskever, I., Hinton, G.E.: Imagenet classification with deep convolutional neural networks. Commun. ACM **60**(6), 84–90 (2017)
9. Lebedev, V., Ganin, Y., Rakhuba, M., Oseledets, I., Lempitsky, V.: Speeding-up convolutional neural networks using fine-tuned cp-decomposition. arXiv preprint arXiv:1412.6553 (2014)
10. Lee, S., Kim, H., Jeong, B., Yoon, J.: A training method for low rank convolutional neural networks based on alternating tensor compose-decompose method. Appl. Sci. **11**(2), 643 (2021)
11. Li, F., Andreetto, M., Ranzato, M., Perona, P.: Caltech101. Computational Vision Group, California Institute of Technology (2003)
12. Mamalet, F., Garcia, C.: Simplifying ConvNets for fast learning. In: Villa, A.E.P., Duch, W., Érdi, P., Masulli, F., Palm, G. (eds.) ICANN 2012. LNCS, vol. 7553, pp. 58–65. Springer, Heidelberg (2012). https://doi.org/10.1007/978-3-642-33266-1_8
13. Phan, A.-H., et al.: Stable low-rank tensor decomposition for compression of convolutional neural network. In: Vedaldi, A., Bischof, H., Brox, T., Frahm, J.-M. (eds.) ECCV 2020. LNCS, vol. 12374, pp. 522–539. Springer, Cham (2020). https://doi.org/10.1007/978-3-030-58526-6_31
14. Rigamonti, R., Sironi, A., Lepetit, V., Fua, P.: Learning separable filters. In: Proceedings of the IEEE Conference on Computer Vision and Pattern Recognition, pp. 2754–2761 (2013)
15. Stewart, G.W.: On the early history of the singular value decomposition. SIAM Rev. **35**(4), 551–566 (1993)
16. Tai, C., et al.: Convolutional neural networks with low-rank regularization. arXiv preprint arXiv:1511.06067 (2015)

Tracking-by-Self Detection: A Self-supervised Framework for Multiple Animal Tracking

C. B. Dev Narayan[1], Fayaz Rahman[1], Mohib Ullah[2(✉)], Faouzi Alaya Cheikh[2],
Ali Shariq Imran[2], Christopher Coello[3], Øyvind Nordbø[3],
G. Santhosh Kumar[1], and Madhu S. Nair[1]

[1] Artificial Intelligence and Computer Vision Lab, Department of Computer Science,
Cochin University of Science and Technology, Kochi 682022, India
[2] Norwegian University of Science and Technology, 2815 Gjøvik, Norway
mohib.ullah@ntnu.no
[3] Norsvin SA, Storhamargata 44, 2317 Hamar, Norway

Abstract. Animal tracking is a crucial aspect of animal phenotyping, and industries are using computer vision-based methods to enhance their products. In this paper, we adopt the tracking-by-detection approach and propose a self-supervised framework for multiple animal tracking. Self-supervised learning techniques have recently been employed to train models using unlabeled data and have demonstrated improved accuracy on benchmark datasets. Our proposed framework utilizes an Efficient-Det detector that was pre-trained with self-supervised learning using a modified Barlow twins method. The detected animals are associated with tracks using our proposed variant of Deepsort, which utilizes appearance information to improve the detection-to-track association. We trained and tested the framework on a customized dataset from a Norwegian pig farm, which consisted of four test and four train sequences, as well as a detection dataset containing 1674 labelled frames and 3000 unlabeled images for self-supervised learning. To evaluate the performance of our framework, we used standard tracking metrics such as $HOTA$ (Higher order tracking accuracy), $MOTA$ (Multiple object tracking accuracy), and $IDF1$ (Identification metrics). The implementation of our framework is publicly available at https://github.com/DeVcB13d/Animal_tracking_with_ssl.

Keywords: Tracking · self-supervised detection · self-supervised learning · deepsort · convolutional neural networks

1 Introduction

The ability to track animals is crucial for both animal science research and breeding programs. Breeding companies can utilize computer vision-based solutions to monitor animals and develop new traits that can improve breeding programs while also adhering to animal welfare regulations [1]. The study of live animal

© IFIP International Federation for Information Processing 2023
Published by Springer Nature Switzerland AG 2023
I. Maglogiannis et al. (Eds.): AIAI 2023, IFIP AICT 675, pp. 561–572, 2023.
https://doi.org/10.1007/978-3-031-34111-3_47

behaviour has become an important research field where animals' movements (motion), posture, gestures, facial expressions, and other factors are observed and analyzed [2,3]. Animal behaviour research has its roots in biology, physiology, and animal welfare, all of which can benefit from computer vision algorithms [4]. For example, through animal tracking, we can obtain valuable information that can be used to improve breeding programs [5].

2   Related Work

With advances in technology, animal tracking has become critical in animal husbandry. In addition to high-resolution video frames, on-animal sensors like ear tags can also be used to identify and monitor animals [6]. Compared to manual monitoring, computer vision provides a non-invasive and sustainable solution for tracking animals [7]. Recent developments in object detection [8] and segmentation [9] have made tracking-by-detection the leading approach in multiple objects tracking [10–14]. Object detectors are used to identify objects in a frame, and then these detections are associated with a track, contributing to improved tracking accuracy [15]. Self-supervised [16] and Semi-supervised [17] frameworks, which leverage unlabeled data for better model generalization and performance, have recently gained attention over fully supervised learning. Many object detectors use semi-supervised learning to improve their accuracy, such as [18–20]. We developed a self-supervised framework for animal tracking inspired by self-learning. Our framework uses a modified version of Barlow twins [21] to pre-train the EfficientDet-D0 detector on unlabeled data for improved detection results. The detections are then associated with tracks using the Deepsort framework [22].

In a nutshell, the key contributions of our work are:

- We propose a self-supervised learning framework for multiple animal tracking, with the help of an object detector trained by application of a modified Barlow twins method for improvement in multiple object tracking.
- We manually annotated a total of 8 videos for testing and training our framework.

The rest of the paper is organized in the following order. We describe the proposed model in Sect. 3. The dataset details, performance metrics and implementation details are given in Sect. 4. Section 5 lists the quantitative and qualitative results. The discussion and final remarks are given in Sect. 6 that concludes the paper.

3   Methodology

3.1   Self-supervised Object Detector

In this framework, we use EfficientDet-D0 for the detection of animals in a video frame [23,24]. The detector network comprises an Image-Net pre-trained EfficientNet-B0 as its backbone network [25]. The network uses a feature pyramid network, namely, BiFPN [23], to extract features, which is fed into a class

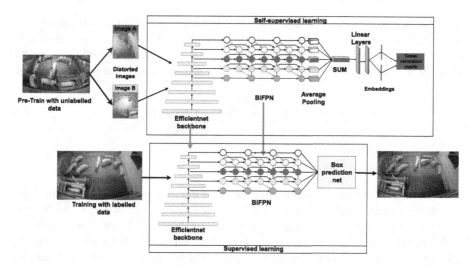

Fig. 1. Self-detection training architecture: Pre-training with our modified Barlow Twins method is depicted at the top. The resulting detector model, then trained with labelled data, is depicted at the bottom. The weights from the BiFPN and Efficient-Net backbone after the self-supervised learning task are used for the supervised learning task.

and box prediction network for predicting boxes and their corresponding confidence scores. The final boxes are filtered by application of Soft-NMS (Soft - Non-maximum Suppression) [26]. Here, contrary to direct training using labelled data as in a fully supervised learning paradigm, we pre-train the object detection model on unlabelled data using a modified Barlow twins strategy [21] where we apply the method on a condensed representation of the output of the Feature Pyramid Network instead of the detector's backbone. This method aims to learn embeddings invariant to distortions applied to the sample. In other words, it aims to find a representation that conserves information about the sample while being least informative about the specific distortions applied on the frames. The proposed self-detection-based training architecture is depicted in Fig. 1. For pre-training, the representations from the BiFPN(bi-directional feature pyramid network) are each passed through an average pooling layer and the layers are summed and passed through 2 linear layers to obtain the final embeddings, which are used to compute a cross-correlation matrix. During pre-training using unlabelled data, a distorted version of the input image is passed through the network to produce an embedding for each distorted image. The weights learned in the pre-training phase are then transferred for the task of supervised learning, shown at the bottom.

Loss Function. The loss function used in pre-training calculates the cross-correlation matrix between the embeddings from the network for each of the different distortions, given by (Eq. 1)

$$L_{bt} = \sum_i \left(1 - C_{ii}\right)^2 + \lambda \sum_i \sum_{j \neq i} C_{ij}^2 \tag{1}$$

Here, λ is a constant used to trade off the importance of the two loss terms, and C is the cross-correlation matrix with its dimensions the same as that of the output of the projection layer. The cross-correlation matrix between embeddings A and B, where b indexes samples and i,j indexes the embeddings given by z is given by (Eq. 2)

$$C_{ij} = \frac{\sum_b z_{b,i}^A z_{b,j}^B}{\sqrt{\sum_b (z_{b,i}^A)^2}\sqrt{\sum_b (z_{b,j}^B)^2}} \tag{2}$$

3.2   Modelling of Tracks

The detections from two consecutive frames are modelled as a motion model using the Bayesian filter [27], which is used to predict the new location of the bounding box in the next arriving frame and associate them to a track. Each track ($\mathbf{x}$) is described by an 8-D state space model, which represents the current position, orientation, size, and velocities (or changes in these parameters) of the bounding box over time (Eq. 3).

$$\mathbf{x} = [u, v, \gamma, h, \dot{u}, \dot{v}, \dot{\gamma}, \dot{h}] \tag{3}$$

where (u, v) represent the center of bounding box, γ the aspect ratio, and h the height respectively. And $(\dot{u}, \dot{v}, \dot{\gamma}, \dot{h})$ represent their respective velocities in terms of image coordinates. When detection is associated with a target track, the detected bounding box is used to update its target state where the velocity components are solved optimally via the Bayesian framework [27]. If a box is not detected, its new coordinates are updated simply by means of a linear velocity model [10].

3.3   Deep Appearance Descriptor

We use a convolutional neural network(CNN) trained on a re-identification(Re-ID) dataset to be able to distinguish between individual animals. The CNN architecture is based on [22]. It is a wide residual network with two convolution layers followed by six residual blocks. The global feature map of dimensionality 128 is computed in a dense layer, followed by final batch normalization and l_2 normalization. The appearance descriptor is obtained by passing the area cropped under each detected bounding box through the above CNN to obtain their embeddings which are used as appearance descriptors (r_j). The appearance descriptors are used to measure the smallest cosine distance between the descriptors of the jth detection and ith track stored in an array R as shown in (Eq. 4)

$$d^{(2)}(i, j) = min\{1 - r_j^T r_k^{(i)} | r_k^{(i)} \in R_{(i)}\} \tag{4}$$

3.4   Association of Detections

For associating the state predictions in (Eq. 3) from the Bayesian filter described in Sect. 3.2 with the new detections from the detector, a cost matrix C (Eq. 6) is created between the state predictions and detections as a weighted sum of Mahalanobis distance of the boxes (Eq. 5) and cosine distance of the object appearance descriptors (Eq. 4) which is obtained by passing the cropped part of the frame under the detected bounding box through the CNN described in Sect. 3.3. The squared Mahalanobis distance is given by (Eq. 5)

$$d^{(1)}(i,j) = (d_j - y_i)^T S_i^{-1}(d_j - y_i) \tag{5}$$

Here, the projection of the track of the i-th object into the measurement space is denoted as (y_i, S_i) and the j-th bounding box detection is denoted as d_j. The cost matrix C is calculated as a weighted sum of the squared Mahalanobis distance and the cosine distance shown in (Eq. 6).

$$C_{(i,j)} = \lambda d^{(1)}(i,j) + (1 - \lambda)d^{(2)}(i,j) \tag{6}$$

Here λ is a hyperparameter to trade off the importance between both measurements. The cost matrix is used to solve a linear assignment problem to assign tracks to the newly arrived detections. The overall architecture of our proposed model for tracking is illustrated in Fig. 2.

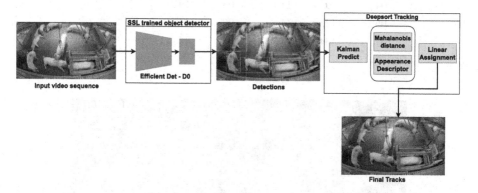

Fig. 2. Tracking architecture: The proposed self-supervised tracking architecture.

4   Experiments

4.1   Dataset Description

MOT Dataset. The data was collected at Norsvin SA's testing facility in Hamar. The animals were housed in groups of eleven or twelve animals of similar sizes in each pen during the growth period from 30–120 kgs. Videos were recorded 24/7 using LOREX (4K Ultra HD IP NVR) and ELOTEC (4MP Bullet, IP67) cameras with a resolution of 1920 × 1080 under different lighting conditions. A selection of 8 different video sequences was split into 4 test and four train video samples (50–50 split). The split was done in accordance with the standard MOT20 benchmark [28]. The videos were manually annotated using CVAT [29], and a sample annotation is shown in Fig. 3. Information on the videos used for tracking is provided in

Table 1. The tracking annotation strictly followed the MOT16 and MOT20 [28,30] format, with each annotation file being a CSV file containing details of a single bounding box per line, following the specified format given by 7.

$$(Frame, ID, x, y, w, h, Confidence, Type, Visibility) \qquad (7)$$

where x and y are the top-left coordinates of the bounding box, w and h are the height and width of the bounding box, ID is an unique number given to the object, $confidence$ is the confidence score of the detected box, $Type$ is the object class, and $Visibility$ its visibility of the object respectively.

Table 1. Details of test and train sequences. Each of the videos has a resolution of 1920×1080 and a frame rate of 20 FPS

Training set			Test set		
Video	Frames	Animals	Video	Frames	Animals
02	3269	11	01	1994	11
04	590	11	03	1919	10
05	4426	11	06	4429	11
07	4464	9	08	4436	11

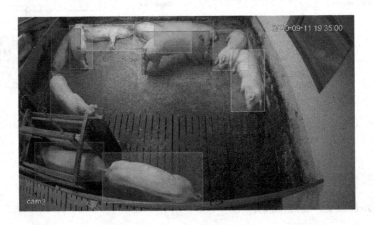

Fig. 3. Sample tracking annotation

4.2 Detection Dataset

For the creation of a detection dataset, frames were extracted from a set of videos, different from those used in the MOT dataset, and manually annotated by the Darwin V7 labs [31], and COCO annotator [32]. These annotations contain bounding boxes, segmentation masks, and key points for each animal instance in the frame. The dataset used in this work contains 1674 images as training data with their ground truths. The ground truths are bounding boxes stored in JSON files created through manual animal boundary tracing by experts using COCO API. The dataset was split into 1339 training data points and 335 testing data points in an 80–20 split.

4.3   Evaluation Metrics

We evaluate our model using the metrics: Multiple Object Tracking Accuracy (MOTA), Identification Metrics (IDF1), and Higher Order Tracking Accuracy (HOTA).

ID Switches and Track Fragmentation: Identity Switches (IDSW) occurs when two different objects gets their identities exchanged due to close contact or occlusion. Track fragmentation (FRAG) is the number of times an object trajectory gets fragmented or interrupted during tracking.

Multiple Object Tracking Accuracy: In MOTA matching is done at a detection level between *gtDets* (Ground Truth Detection) and *prDets* (Prediction Detections) [33] . The detections are matched if the bounding boxes have an IoU threshold of $\alpha > 0.5$. Matched detections are considered True Positives (TP) and unmatched False Positives (FP).

$$MOTA = 1 - \frac{|FN| + |FP| + |IDSW|}{|gtDet|} \tag{8}$$

Identification Metrics: The identification metrics does mapping across trajectories in comparison to MOTA that does mapping across detections. IDTPs (identity true positives) are matches over overlapping trajectories, IDFPs (identity false positives) are the remaining gtDets and prDets that are not matched. [34]

$$IDF1 = \frac{|IDTP|}{|IDTP| + 0.5|IDFN| + 0.5|IDFP|} \tag{9}$$

Higher Order Tracking Accuracy: In HOTA, TP, FN and FP are determined at a detection level [34]. To measure associations the metrics TPA(c) (True Positive Association of a TP 'c') which is the set of TPs that have the same gtID and prID as c. The $HOTA_\alpha$ for an association-IoU threshold of α is given by (Eq. 10)

$$HOTA_\alpha = \sqrt{\frac{\sum_{c \in \{TP\}} A(c)}{|TP| + |FN| + |FP|}} \tag{10}$$

where, the Jaccard index $A(c)$ is given by (Eq. 11)

$$A(c) = \frac{|TPA(c)|}{|TPA(c)| + |FNA(c)| + |FPA(c)|} \tag{11}$$

4.4   Implementation Details

We conducted all of our experiments using the open-source library PyTorch [35] and OpenCV for processing the videos [36]. The experiments were performed on a machine with 16GB NVIDIA GeForce RTX3080 Laptop GPU. As a pre-processing step, the frames are resized to 500×500 and normalized to the range $[0, 1]$ using the mean and standard deviation of Imagenet [37], with mean of $[0.485, 0.456, 0.406]$ and standard deviation of $[0.229, 0.224, 0.225]$.

4.5   Training of Self-supervised Object Detector

For pre-training using Barlow Twins, we used the augmentations in Bootstrap Your Own Latent(BYOL) approach [38]. Further implementation details of training of the object detector is given in Table 2. The hyperparameters used were adapted from existing literature.

Table 2. Implementation details of pre-training and training of object detector

Hyperparameter	Pre-Training	Training
Batch size	16	24
Learning rate	$1e-4$	$3e-3$
Epochs	50	24
Optimizer	AdamW	AdamW

4.6   Training of Deep Association Model

A re-identification(Re-ID) dataset was constructed from the annotated training videos consisting of 43 unique animals each with 4257 train and 1032 test images. The hyperparameters used are given in Table 3. The hyperparameters used were adapted from existing literature. The deep association model was able to achieve a final classification accuracy of 92%.

Table 3. Implementation details of training the deep association model

Hyperparameter	Value
Batch size	64
Learning rate	0.1
Epochs	54
Optimizer	SGD

5   Results

The evaluation results of our detection model, is given in Table 4. We evaluate the tracking model on our dataset (Table 1) and the results for each videos are given in Table 5. We compared our framework with popular methods such as Simple Online and Realtime Tracking (SORT) [12] and ByteTrack [14] of which the results are depicted in Table 6. The qualitative results of our model is given in Fig. 4. It can be seen from the comparatively higher values of MOTA and HOTA that the method is able to improve the matching of detections and the value of IDF1 indicates the improved mapping of the object tracks. Also, the method is able to reduce ID switches and track fragmentation. From the results, it is apparent that the proposed method gives improved results proving that our model is on par with the reference and common architectures, whilst having fewer parameters making it suitable for online tracking applications.

Table 4. Detection results on validation split of our detection dataset.

IoU Threshold	Area	mAP
0.5 : 0.95	all	0.599
0.5	all	0.952
0.75	all	0.707

Table 5. Quanitative results of our proposed model on the test set of the tracking dataset.

VIDEO	HOTA(%)	MOTA(%)	IDF1(%)	IDSW	FRAG
02	62.40	82.48	80.90	73	221
04	62.92	78.49	80.51	16	22
05	62.62	84.46	72.42	50	90
07	78.44	84.74	91.30	26	2
Overall	67.86	84.74	80.94	165	335

Table 6. Comparison of our proposed framework with other tracking methods.

Method	HOTA(%)	MOTA(%)	IDF1(%)	IDSW	FRAG
SORT [12]	30.71	75.7	53.40	11684	216
DEEPSORT [22]	64.15	84.17	74.04	491	431
BYTETRACK [14]	50.27	36.89	54.41	71	270
Proposed	67.86	84.74	80.94	165	335

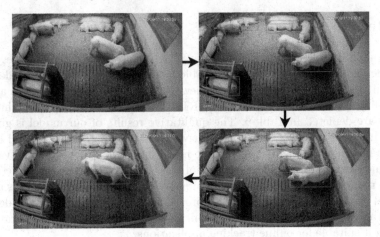

Fig. 4. Qualitative results of tracking of multiple animals across frames

5.1 Discussion

The potential reasons for the high accuracy and efficiency can be summarized in the following:

- The object detector, which has been trained using self-learning techniques, demonstrates high efficiency and accuracy in detecting objects.
- The framework employs an object detector with 3.8 million compact parameters and a deep appearance descriptor with 2.8 million parameters, enabling efficient online tracking capabilities.
- Leveraging the ReID (Re-Identification) dataset for training the deep appearance descriptor results in improved accuracy in associating objects in our framework.

6 Conclusion

We propose a framework for tracking by means of self-learning, wherein we pretrain base object detectors with a modified Barlow Twins by using unlabeled data. A custom-built dataset is used to train and evaluate the model. We are able to achieve improved tracking results with our proposed framework while being highly efficient in terms of the number of parameters.

Acknowledgment. We would like to thank Norsvin SA for sharing data and the Research Council of Norway for funding this study, within the BIONÆR program, project numbers 282252 and 321409. In special, we would also like to thank Rune Sagevik, Norsvin SA for the image acquisition.

References

1. Herlin, A., Brunberg, E., Hultgren, J., Högberg, N., Rydberg, A., Skarin, A.: Animal welfare implications of digital tools for monitoring and management of cattle and sheep on pasture. Animals **11**(3), 829 (2021)

2. Afridi, H., Ullah, M., Nordbø, Ø., Alaya Cheikh, F., Guro Larsgard, A.: Optimized deep-learning-based method for cattle udder traits classification. Mathematics **10**(17), 3097 (2022)

3. Pham-Duc, T., et al.: Improvement on mechanics attention deep learning model for classification ear-tag of swine. In; 2022 9th NAFOSTED Conference on Information and Computer Science (NICS), pp. 345–350. IEEE (2022)

4. Xue, X., Henderson, T.C.: Video-based animal behavior analysis from multiple cameras. In: 2006 IEEE International Conference on Multisensor Fusion and Integration for Intelligent Systems, pp. 335–340 (2006)

5. Okinda, C., et al.: A review on computer vision systems in monitoring of poultry: A welfare perspective. Artif. Intell. Agricult. **4**, 184–208 (2020)

6. Kays, R., Crofoot, M.C., Jetz, W., Wikelski, M.: Terrestrial animal tracking as an eye on life and planet. Science, **348**(6240):aaa2478 (2015)

7. Kresovic, M., Nguyen, T., Ullah, M., Afridi, H., Alaya Cheikh, F.: Pigpose: A real-time framework for farm animal pose estimation and tracking. In: Artificial Intelligence Applications and Innovations: 18th IFIP WG 12.5 International Conference, AIAI 2022, Hersonissos, Crete, June 17–20, 2022, Proceedings, Part I, pp. 204–215. Springer (2022). https://doi.org/10.1007/978-3-031-08333-4_17

8. Daud Khan, S., et al.: An efficient deep learning framework for face mask detection in complex scenes. In: Artificial Intelligence Applications and Innovations, pp. 159–169. Springer (2022). https://doi.org/10.1007/978-3-031-08333-4_13

9. Mamadou, K., Ullah, M., Nordbø, Ø., Alaya Cheikh, F.: Multi-encoder convolution block attention model for binary segmentation. In: 2022 International Conference on Frontiers of Information Technology (FIT), pp. 183–188. IEEE (2022)

10. Wojke, N., Bewley, A., Paulus, D.: Simple online and realtime tracking with a deep association metric. In: 2017 IEEE International Conference on Image Processing (ICIP), pp. 3645–3649. IEEE (2017)

11. Ullah, M., Alaya Cheikh, F.: A directed sparse graphical model for multi-target tracking. In: Proceedings of the IEEE Conference on Computer Vision and Pattern Recognition Workshops, pp. 1816–1823 (2018)

12. Bewley, A., Ge, Z., Ott, L., Ramos, F., Upcroft, B.: Simple online and realtime tracking. In: 2016 IEEE International Conference on Image Processing (ICIP), pp. 3464–3468. IEEE (2016)

13. Ullah, M., Alaya Cheikh, F.: Deep feature based end-to-end transportation network for multi-target tracking. In: 2018 25th IEEE International Conference on Image Processing (ICIP), pp. 3738–3742. IEEE (2018)

14. Zhang, Y., et al.: Bytetrack: Multi-object tracking by associating every detection box. In: Computer Vision-ECCV 2022: 17th European Conference, Tel Aviv, Israel, October 23–27, 2022, Proceedings, Part XXII, pp. 1–21. Springer (2022). https://doi.org/10.1007/978-3-031-20047-2_1

15. Quddus Khan, A., Khan, S., Ullah, M., Alaya Cheikh, F.: A bottom-up approach for pig skeleton extraction using RGB data. In: International Conference on Image and Signal Processing, pp. 54–61. Springer (2020). https://doi.org/10.1007/978-3-030-51935-3_6

16. Jia, Y., et al.: Selfee, self-supervised features extraction of animal behaviors. Elife **11**, e76218 (2022)

17. Ullah, M., Shagdar, Z., Ullah, H., Alaya Cheikh, F.: Semi-supervised principal neighbourhood aggregation model for SAR image classification. In: 2022 16th International Conference on Signal-Image Technology & Internet-Based Systems (SITIS), pp. 211–217. IEEE (2022)

18. Chen, B., Li, P., Chen, X., Wang, B., Zhang, L., Hua, X.-S.: Dense learning based semi-supervised object detection. In: Proceedings of the IEEE/CVF Conference on Computer Vision and Pattern Recognition, pp. 4815–4824 (2022)

19. Tang, P., Ramaiah, C., Wang, Y., Xu, R., Xiong, C.: Proposal learning for semi-supervised object detection. In: Proceedings of the IEEE/CVF Winter Conference on Applications of Computer Vision (WACV), pp. 2291–2301 (2021)

20. Xu, M., et al.: End-to-end semi-supervised object detection with soft teacher. In: Proceedings of the IEEE/CVF International Conference on Computer Vision (ICCV), pp. 3060–3069 (2021)

21. Zbontar, J., Jing, L., Misra, I., LeCun, Y., Deny, S.: Barlow twins: Self-supervised learning via redundancy reduction. In: International Conference on Machine Learning, pp. 12310–12320. PMLR (2021)

22. Wojke, N., Bewley, A.: Deep cosine metric learning for person re-identification. In: 2018 IEEE Winter Conference on Applications of Computer Vision (WACV), pp. 748–756. IEEE (2018)

23. Tan, M., Pang, R., Le, Q.V.: Efficientdet: Scalable and efficient object detection. In: Proceedings of the IEEE/CVF Conference on Computer Vision and Pattern Recognition, pp. 10781–10790 (2020)

24. Ullah, E., Ullah, M., Sajjad, M., Alaya Cheikh, F.: Deep learning based wheat ears count in robot images for wheat phenotyping. Electron. Imag. **34**, 1–6 (2022)

25. Tan, M., Le, Q.V.: Efficientnet: Rethinking model scaling for convolutional neural networks. arXiv preprint arXiv:1905.11946 (2019)

26. Bodla, N., Singh, B., Chellappa, R., Davis, L.S.: Soft-NMS-improving object detection with one line of code. In: Proceedings of the IEEE International Conference on Computer Vision, pp. 5561–5569 (2017)

27. Kalman, R.E. A new approach to linear filtering and prediction problems (1960)

28. Dendorfer, P., et al.: Mot20: A benchmark for multi object tracking in crowded scenes. arXiv preprint arXiv:2003.09003 (2020)

29. CVAT.ai Corporation. Computer Vision Annotation Tool (CVAT) 9 (2022)

30. Milan, A., et al.: Mot16: A benchmark for multi-object tracking. arXiv preprint arXiv:1603.00831 (2016)

31. Darwin V7 Labs. https://darwin.v7labs.com/

32. Brooks, J.: COCO Annotator. https://github.com/jsbroks/coco-annotator/ (2019)

33. Bernardin, K., Stiefelhagen, R.: Evaluating multiple object tracking performance: The clear mot metrics. EURASIP J. Image Video Process. 1–10, 2008 (2008)

34. Luiten, J., et al.: Hota: A higher order metric for evaluating multi-object tracking. Int. J. Comput. Vis. **129**(2), 548–578 (2021)

35. Paszke, et al.: Pytorch: An imperative style, high-performance deep learning library. In: Advances in Neural Information Processing Systems, vol. 32, pp. 8024–8035. Curran Associates Inc. (2019)

36. Bradski, G.: The OpenCV Library. Dr. Dobb's Journal of Software Tools (2000)

37. Deng, J., Dong, W., Socher, R., Li, L.-J., Li, K., Li, F.-F.: Imagenet: A large-scale hierarchical image database. In: 2009 IEEE Conference on Computer Vision and Pattern Recognition, pp. 248–255 (2009)

38. Tan, M., Le, Q.V.: Efficientnet: Rethinking model scaling for convolutional neural networks. arXiv preprint arxiv:1905.11946 (2019)

Doctoral Track

AI Approach to LALD Rare Disease

Àlex Padrós Zamora[1,2]([✉]) [iD], Antoni Morell Perez[1] [iD], Jose Lopez Vicario[1] [iD],
Francesc Cayuela Solano[2] [iD], María del Carmen Barbero Freixas[2] [iD],
and Ramón Vilanova Arbos[1] [iD]

[1] Department of Telecommunications and Systems Engineering,
School of Engineering, Universitat Autonoma de Barcelona,
Bellaterra 08193, Barcelona, Spain
alex.padros@autonoma.cat,
{Antoni.Morell,Jose.Vicario,Ramon.Vilanova}@uab.cat
[2] BDCare Research S.L., UAB Research Park,
Eureka Building, 08193 Bellaterra, Barcelona, Spain

Abstract. This PhD thesis aims to present an Artificial Intelligence
solution based on Deep Learning for the diagnosis of a rare disease known
as "Lysosomal Acid Lipase Deficiency" (LALD) using health data such
as blood tests, medical history or images of the rear of the eye. Since we
are dealing with health data, some special data pre-processing steps as
well as data anonymization need to be applied. LALD is a rare disease,
which implies that the volume of data is small and many techniques for
unbalanced data cases are applied. That is, data augmentation solutions,
transfer learning or generative approaches, such as SMOTE or Generative Adversarial Networks.

Keywords: Rare disease · Artificial Intelligence · Deep Learning ·
LALD

1 PhD Topics and Objectives

As of today, there are over 10.900 documented rare diseases that affect 6–8%
of the total population sometime in their life, but its treatment and diagnostic
constitute a significant medical and health challenge. This project raises the
development of a toolkit aimed to help in the early diagnosis of rare diseases.
It aims to be a crossed-solution for many different rare diseases, but we will
start with LALD (Lysosomal Acid Lipase Deficiency). The reason why we have
chosen this disease is because the BDCare Research team currently has a high
knowledge of it and they are part of the group of experts. The value of this
proposal is based on combining Artificial Intelligence (AI) technologies such as
Deep Learning (DL) algorithms, which will work with a volume of data quite
lower than usual (scarce data) for these kind of techniques for contributing to
improve this under-diagnosis. The low prevalence of rare diseases is a differential
fact that influences and adds value and innovation to the proposal, unlike the rest
of technological products and AI systems for health, which work with massive

© IFIP International Federation for Information Processing 2023
Published by Springer Nature Switzerland AG 2023
I. Maglogiannis et al. (Eds.): AIAI 2023, IFIP AICT 675, pp. 575–580, 2023.
https://doi.org/10.1007/978-3-031-34111-3

volumes of data. The objective is to implement this tool in such a way that it automatically analyzes data for the pre-diagnosis.

LALD is a genetic disease that presents a recessive automatic transition pattern, potentially mortal and under-diagnosed. It is a hereditary, progressive and rare disorder. It affects to the capacity of the body to produce an enzyme called "lysosomal acid lipase", which is necessary for the fat or cholesterol breakdown. Nowadays, the challenges in the diagnosis of LALD lie in the fact that it is off the diagnostic radar of the vast majority of medical society due to its low prevalence (between 1:40.000 and 1:300.000) and that LALD signs and symptoms are not specific of the disease, they usually imitate other genetic and metabolic affections, which leads to a late diagnosis. This leads to think that there might be a certain percentage of under-diagnosed patients.

In this project, we will use data from different clinical analysis, such as blood tests, medical history or fundus images, that we are obtaining from different hospitals for predicting possible affected patients, which will be subsequently diagnosed by a physician. The objective is that the algorithms we will develop will be of supervised classification with three possible outputs: affected, carrier, and not related to the disease, as an enhancement to the current screening algorithm which only detects whether a patient is affected or not. Deep Learning is the principal field that we will work with, but other parts such as data preprocessing will consume a huge part our time. We will also generate synthetic data for enlarging our datasets and enrich our models.

A fundamental aspect of this project is security, given that we will be working with personal and health data, which are catalogued by GDPR (General Data Protection Regulation) with the highest level of security. Data must be encrypted and anonymized properly.

2   Literature Review

Currently, the diagnosis is made by the evaluation of LALD activity in the dry drop test and/or with the presence of a mutation in the LIPA gene, by means of a genetic study, and only when there is high clinical suspicion [2]. None of the approaches use AI techniques.

There has been a lot of research in the field of DL for health due to its ability to process and analyze vast amounts of complex data with remarkable accuracy. Until 2021, the number of publications in DL for any disease was over 160.000, but only 332 was devoted to rare diseases [8]. The majority of these 332 papers used image data for their purposes, so Convolutional Neural Networks (CNNs) have been the predominant architectures.

Since we are dealing with rare diseases, we will have a huge problem to take care of in our classification: unbalanced data. Models that are trained with this type of datasets are easily biased towards the majority class. To tackle these problems, various strategies can be employed [5], such as adjusting the cost function with cost-sensitive learning, balancing the class distribution through oversampling or undersampling with resampling, improving performance by leveraging pre-trained models with transfer learning, combining multiple models with ensemble methods, and generating synthetic samples for the minority class using techniques like SMOTE [3], which is a commonly used approach.

When data comes from images, there are many ways of generating new examples from existing ones. The most common way is by data augmentation, although Neural Networks are also used to create synthetic samples. A popular approach is using Generative Adversarial Networks (GANs) [6], which consist of two neural networks: a generator and a discriminator. The goal of a GAN is to generate realistic and complex synthetic data that is similar to the training data. Even though, they are unstable and slow to train. Also, Diffusion Models [7] have gained popularity; they simulate a stochastic process in which the image evolves over time by slowly diffusing random perturbations. The model is trained to predict the future distribution of an image given its past observations.

3   Methodology

3.1   Problem Description

The main objective of this work is to develop a solution based on Neural Networks that give as output a classification into three classes: affected, carrier and not affected, as an improvement of the current screening algorithm that only detects possible affected or unaffected people. The first two classes are the ones which are minority, compared to the third. Data arrives in many different formats, such as fundus images or blood tests/medical history with many categorical, numerical and demographic variables. This data needs to be standardized in such a way that is adequate for training our classifiers, as we present in the following subsections.

The idea is to train three type of Neural Networks: one type considering non-image data such as blood tests and medical history, another type taking as input fundus images with CNNs, and the last one merging both. Different metrics will be applied to validate the predictive power of our models: precision, recall, F1-score, Cohen's Kappa score, Matthew's correlation coefficient and cross-entropy loss are the most common ones for multi-class classification and are adequate for unbalanced problems.

3.2   Data Pre-processing

One crucial step for being able to train our models is to fill the missing values of our datasets. Our data mainly comes from blood tests, which are a laboratory analysis performed on a blood sample that is usually extracted from a vein. They group multiple tests for specific blood components, such as glucose or cholesterol. Each of these tests have an associated reference range, a range or the interval of values that is deemed normal for a physiological measurement in healthy people. Thanks to these reference ranges, we can fill in a numerical missing value by taking the midpoint value of the reference interval for each blood component variable. After that, since we can have blood tests from different sources, we need to ensure that our numerical values have all the same units. For this reason, we apply a step where we multiply each variable for its corresponding factor that sends them to the international system unit value. Also, blood test values can vary depending on the source because of noise, requiring a specific correction factor for each. If the missing value is from categorical type, we fill it using k-nearest neighbors imputation. That is, finding the k-nearest neighbors of the missing value and then using the mode of the neighbors to impute the missing value. These kind of variables must be one-hot encoded later in order to convert them to numerical type. After that, the dataset is normalized by means of the min-max normalization technique.

3.3 Balancing the Dataset

We are facing an unbalanced problem due to the scarcity of positive cases in LALD diagnosis. To prevent model bias and overfitting, we balance the dataset using SMOTETomek [1], an extension of SMOTE. SMOTETomek combines synthetic sample generation with Tomek Link removal to balance the dataset. Let x and y be two samples that belong to different classes. The tuple (x, y) is called a Tomek Link if, given a distance $d(x, y)$, there does not exist another sample z such that $d(x, z) < d(x, y)$ or $d(y, z) < d(x, y)$. The full process works as follows:

1. Randomly select a sample x from the minority class and get its k nearest neighbors.
2. Let $\lambda_1, \ldots, \lambda_k \in [0, 1]$ be random numbers and $x_1, \ldots, x_k$ the k nearest neighbors of x. Generate synthetic samples as follows:

$$\tilde{x}_i = x + \lambda_i (x_i - x) \tag{1}$$

   for $i = 1, \ldots, k$.
3. Iterate steps 1 and 2 until the desired minority class proportion is achieved.
4. Select a random sample from the majority class. If its nearest neighbor belongs to the minority class (i.e. a Tomek Link), remove the Tomek Link. Repeat this step for all samples from the majority class.

This method is interesting because when we over-sample the minority class, we increase the likelihood of occurring overfitting. Tomek Link removal cleans ambiguous samples across classes.

3.4 Anonymize Data

When dealing with health data, some of the variables contain demographic information (e.g. ZIP code, date of birth, gender ...). Removing the full identifiers of the patients, such as names or addresses, is not enough to guarantee full anonymity in our data [12], a previous step of data anonymization needs to be applied. One common way of doing so is looking for k-anonymity, a property for dataset tables that was firstly introduced by Sweeney and Samarati [11], which states that a dataset is said to be k-anonymous if every combination of values for demographic columns in the dataset appears at least for k different records.

Converting a dataset to k-anonymous is not an easy task, and there is currently a lot of research in this area. In fact, the problem of finding an optimal strategy for k-anonymity is NP-hard for $k > 2$ [10]. An algorithm for achieving k-anonymity is Mondrian, a top-down greedy data anonymization algorithm for relational datasets, proposed by Kristen LeFevre [9].

3.5 Generate Synthetic Data with Generative Adversarial Networks

Another type of data that we use for training our ML models are fundus images, i.e. the rear of an eye. Again, the number of available images is scarce, so we need to create artificial images for augmenting our dataset. We can do this by using GANs [6]. These kind on neural networks take as input random noise and then they learn complex transformations for sampling an image from the training distribution, i.e. an artificial image that is similar to our dataset ones. GANs play a two-player game for training the neural network: a discriminator network, which tries to distinguish between real and fake images, and a generator network, which generates real-looking images and tries to fool the discriminator. They train jointly in a minimax game, which has as objective function:

$$\min_{\theta_g} \max_{\theta_d} \mathbb{E}_{x \sim p_{\text{data}}} \left[\log \left(D_{\theta_d}(x) \right) \right] + \mathbb{E}_{z \sim p(z)} \left[\log \left(1 - D_{\theta_d} \left(G_{\theta_g}(z) \right) \right) \right]. \quad (2)$$

Here, x has been sampled from the training distribution and z has been sampled from a simple distribution, such as random noise. Discriminator θ_d wants to maximize objective such that $D_{\theta_d}(x)$ is close to 1 (real image) and $D_{\theta_d} \left(G_{\theta_g}(z) \right)$ is close to 0 (fake image). $G_{\theta_g}(z)$ denotes a generated image, where generator θ_g wants to minimize objective such that $D_{\theta_d} \left(G_{\theta_g}(z) \right)$ is close to 1.

GANs are adequate for our case because there exist architectures that are specialized for generating fundus images as Yu Chen et al. present in [4].

3.6 Training Phase

In the training phase, both original and synthetically generated samples shall be taken as data. A procedure based on Transfer Learning will be applied too, where we will rely on pre-trained models in other types of scenarios with larger and balanced datasets, such as the ones in [13] for the fundus images. A fine-tuning process will be carried out to adapt it to the LALD case.

4 Expected Results

The objective of the models is to provide the doctors at each center with a list of potential LALD patients, based on the routinely data obtained from blood tests and fundus images. However, it is up to the medical staff to decide whether further testing is necessary, such as a dry drop test, a genetic test or any other test that may be stipulated for the diagnosis of LALD. Although the objective of the thesis is to obtain good results in the classification of the diagnosis, techniques that facilitate the interpretation of the model obtained and the weight of the different variables in the result will also be explored (white box ML or explainable models). This last point intends to provide additional knowledge of the possible key factors of the disease.

Acknowledgements. This work was economically supported by BDCare Research and Agencia de Gestió d'Ajuts Universitaris i de Recerca through the DI grant 2022 DI 033.

References

1. Batista, G., Bazzan, A., Monard, M.C.: Balancing training data for automated annotation of keywords: a case study. Proc. Workshop Bioinf. 10–18 (2003)
2. Camarena, C., et al.: Update on lysosomal acid lipase deficiency: Diagnosis, treatment and patient management. Medicina Clinica (English Edition) 148 (2017). https://doi.org/10.1016/j.medcle.2017.04.021
3. Chawla, N.V., Bowyer, K.W., Hall, L.O., Kegelmeyer, W.P.: SMOTE: Synthetic minority over-sampling technique. J. Art. Intel. Res. **16**, 321–357 (2002).https://doi.org/10.1613/jair.953
4. Chen, Y., Long, J., Guo, J., Yi, Y.: RF-GANs: a method to synthesize retinal fundus images based on generative adversarial network. Intell. Neurosci. **2021**, 1–17 (2021). https://doi.org/10.1155/2021/3812865
5. Fernández, A., García, S., Galar, M., Prati, R.C., Krawczyk, B., Herrera, F.: Learning from imbalanced data sets, vol. 10. Springer (2018). https://doi.org/10.1007/978-3-319-98074-4
6. Goodfellow, I.J., Pouget-Abadie, J., Mirza, M., Xu, B., Warde-Farley, D., Ozair, S., et al.: Generative adversarial networks (2014). 10.48550/ARXIV.1406.2661
7. Ho, J., Jain, A., Abbeel, P.: Denoising diffusion probabilistic models. CoRR abs/2006.11239 (2020)
8. Lee, J., et al.: Deep learning for rare disease: A scoping review. Journal of Biomed. Inf. 135 (2022). https://doi.org/10.1016/j.jbi.2022.104227
9. LeFevre, K., DeWitt, D., Ramakrishnan, R.: Mondrian multidimensional k-anonymity. In: 22nd International Conference on Data Engineering (ICDE'06). pp. 25–25 (2006). https://doi.org/10.1109/ICDE.2006.101
10. Meyerson, A., Williams, R.: On the complexity of optimal k-anonymity. In: Proceedings of the Twenty-Third ACM SIGMOD-SIGACT-SIGART Symposium on Principles of Database Systems. pp. 223–228. PODS '04, Association for Computing Machinery, New York, NY, USA (2004). https://doi.org/10.1145/1055558.1055591
11. Samarati, P., Sweeney, L.: Protecting privacy when disclosing information: k-anonymity and its enforcement through generalization and suppression (1998). https://doi.org/10.1184/R1/6625469.v1
12. Sweeney, L.: Simple demographics often identify people uniquely. Health **671** (2000). https://doi.org/10.1184/R1/6625769.v1
13. Voets, M., Mollersen, K., Bongo, L.A.: Reproduction study using public data of: development and validation of a deep learning algorithm for detection of diabetic retinopathy in retinal fundus photographs. PLOS ONE **14**(6), 1–11 (2019). https://doi.org/10.1371/journal.pone.0217541

Author Index

Printed in the United States
by Baker & Taylor Publisher Services